The Lost Manuscript of Frédéric Cailliaud

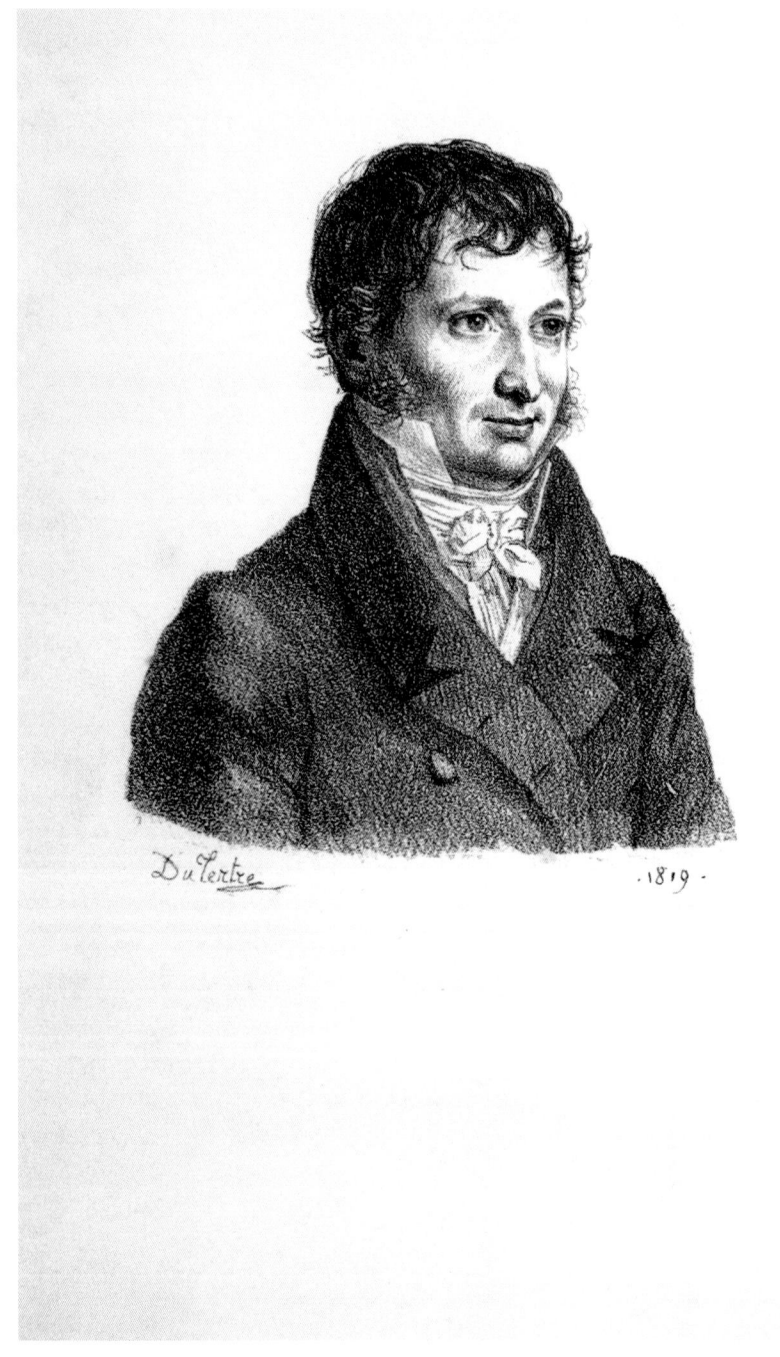

1 Portrait of Frédéric Cailliaud, drawn by André Dutertre. *Courtesy of W. Benson Harer, Jr. Photographed by Gustavo Camps.*

The Lost Manuscript of Frédéric Cailliaud

Arts and Crafts of the Ancient Egyptians,
Nubians, and Ethiopians

—

Translated and edited by
Andrew Bednarski

with contributions by
Philippe Mainterot

The American University in Cairo Press
Cairo • New York

This publication was made possible by the generous support of the American Research Center in Egypt and Dr. W. Benson Harer.

First published in 2014 by
The American University in Cairo Press
113 Sharia Kasr el Aini, Cairo, Egypt
420 Fifth Avenue, New York, NY 10018
www.aucpress.com

Exclusive distribution outside Egypt and North America by I.B.Tauris & Co Ltd., 6 Salem Road, London, W2 4BU

Dar el Kutub No. 22887/12
ISBN 978 977 416 616 7

Dar el Kutub Cataloging-in-Publication Data

Bednarski, Andrew
        The Lost Manuscript of Frédéric Cailliaud: Arts and Crafts of the Ancient Egyptians, Nubians, and Ethiopians / Andrew Bednarski.—Cairo: The American University in Cairo Press, 2014.
        p.   cm.
        ISBN 978 977 416 616 7
        1. Art—Ancient Egypt
        2. Egypt—Antiquities
        3. Handcraft—Egypt
        709.32

1 2 3 4 5   18 17 16 15 14

Designed by Andrea El-Akshar
Printed in China

To my father,

Edward John Bednarski (1947–2006),

who encouraged me in my own adventures.

You are missed.

Contents

The original French text of Cailliaud's manuscript can be found at www.aucpress.com/t-Cailliaud.aspx.

LIST OF ILLUSTRATIONS

Cailliaud's Plates

Plate 1 photographed by Owen Murray. All other plates courtesy of W. Benson Harer, Jr., photographed by Gustavo Camps.

FOREWORD

W. Benson Harer, Jr.

ooks may well be the most important invention in human history. They provide a simple method to accurately transfer information from one person to another and from one generation to another.

Bibliophiles collect books for a wide variety of reasons. I am an obstetrician/gynecologist with a passion for Egyptology. I collect books on that subject mainly for information since I have not had access to a good library. My wife is a passionate collector of eighteenth- and nineteenth-century children's literature. In 2005, I joined her to prowl through a London book fair with little expectation of finding anything of interest to me. Nevertheless, I inquired regularly if the dealers had anything about Egypt.

Then temptation appeared. A British dealer showed me a beautiful collection of plates published in the 1830s that I had never heard about, although I had heard about the artist/author, Frédéric Cailliaud. I admired it, but, despite its beauty and rarity, would not want to bust my budget for a book of illustrations, regardless of their beauty. However, I became intrigued when told that this was the intended second volume of a work that never had the first volume published. While this information was not exactly true, the wealth of textual material that accompanied the plates I had seen remained an original, unpublished manuscript! Still it would be an expensive departure from my usual collection, so I quickly passed on it.

As I wandered through the stalls finding nothing, my thoughts kept returning to Cailliaud's unfulfilled work. I recalled the comment of James Branch Cabell, "The least satisfying of all memories are those of temptations successfully resisted." Furthermore, this was an opportunity unlikely to be either repeated or matched.

Meanwhile, my wife, Pamela, was having much more success. Perhaps to justify her own lack of restraint, she encouraged me to consider it further. We agreed that Samuel Johnson was right when he said, "It is better to live rich than to die rich." And so I returned to open the negotiations which ultimately placed this work in our hands.

Part of the pleasure of owning anything of merit is to share it with others. It would be difficult to do so with this material on a one-to-one basis, but we thought that perhaps we could fulfill Cailliaud's original intent and have the work published. Fortunately, Dr. Gerry Scott looked at it and shared our vision. He has shepherded the work through to publication. We enlisted May Trad from the Egyptian Museum to go through the laborious process of transcribing a large portion of the manuscript from its archaic French into correct, modern vernacular. Then Dr. Andrew Bednarski took the manuscript in the next, logical direction. He painstakingly revised May Trad's transcription so that it accurately reflected the French written by Cailliaud, thereby creating a critical edition of the manuscript. Dr. Bednarski translated into English as much of the manuscript as deemed within the remit of a publication project, and then supplemented those translations with footnotes for the convenience of the modern reader. The resulting publication of this work has enlarged the vision Cailliaud put forth in his manuscript. The result is to vastly expand the audience to appreciate Cailliaud's pioneering labors from the early days of Egyptology. Enjoy!

PROJECT OVERVIEW

Gerry D. Scott III

I t is both exciting and rewarding to rediscover something that has been lost to both history and scholarship. In the case of the archaeology of ancient human cultures, such discoveries bring back to our knowledge, imagination, and research the human experience of our predecessors. The rediscovery of an early piece of scholarship about such past cultures is perhaps just as exciting and rewarding. That is precisely the case with the present work.

Frédéric Cailliaud was among the first generation of scholars who founded the discipline of Egyptology through their investigation, recording, and commentary on Egypt's ancient remains. He produced two landmark Egyptological publications fairly early in his career, but intended to publish a third in which he would share his thoughts about the daily life of the ancient Egyptians through an examination of their arts and crafts as they were depicted in the remaining monuments. Toward this end, Cailliaud did publish an extremely limited edition of the plates with which he intended to illustrate his study. However, he never brought the text volume to fruition, and it was lost to scholarship.

Recently, Dr. W. Benson Harer, Jr., a member of the American Research Center in Egypt (ARCE) as well as a former member of its governing board, acquired a manuscript which contained this missing text, in several distinct parts, as well as initial drawings of the plates and other interesting material. Thanks to the contributions of several scholars and the leadership of Andrew Bednarski, an ARCE member and staff member, it has been possible at last to produce a close approximation of the work Cailliaud planned and worked toward, but never published.

It is entirely fitting that ARCE join with the American University in Cairo Press (AUCP) to bring this work to publication, as ARCE and AUCP have jointly produced several volumes in recent years presenting ARCE's contributions to documenting and preserving Egypt's invaluable cultural heritage. In bringing Cailliaud's text to publication for the first time, together with his rare plates, it is now possible to present a work which is at once a piece of historical literature within the fields of Egyptology and nineteenth-century science and a research tool for contemporary scholarship. In addition, the present volume contains several drafts of Cailliaud's plates that clearly show his working method, two entirely new plates, and a contemporary commentary on his work.

We are grateful to those who have made the publication of the lost manuscript of Cailliaud's *Arts and Crafts of the Ancient Egyptians, Nubians, and Ethiopians* possible. We hope that it will prove a useful addition to the literature for those who are interested in such fields as Egyptology, classical studies, the history of science, and an earlier age of exploration and inquiry.

Acknowledgments

W. Benson Harer, Jr.—whose forethought and perseverance brought this into being.

Gerry D. Scott III—whose interest and insight made the project possible.

May Trad—for her exacting work constructing an initial hard-copy transcription of Cailliaud's chapters.

Julie Patenaude—for proofreading and transcribing May's text into soft copies and for her diligent work proofreading my translations.

Aurélie Cuenod—for proofreading both the text's reworked transcriptions and the translations.

Philippe Mainterot—for reviewing this text, and for his unwavering support, enthusiasm, and friendship.

Many thanks also to Meghan Strong, Mennat-Allah el-Dory, Steven Bednarski, W. Raymond Johnson, JJ Shirly, and Johanna Baboukis and the rest of the AUCP staff.

Note on
Contributors

Andrew Bednarski is a historian and Egyptologist who earned his PhD from the University of Cambridge. He works for the American Research Center in Egypt as the assistant to the director for special projects and as the APS project Egyptologist.

Philippe Mainterot is a historian and Egyptologist who earned his PhD from the Université de Poitiers. He works for the Université de Poitiers as Enseignant-chercheur.

Gerry D. Scott III is the director of the American Research Center in Egypt. He earned his PhD in Egyptology from Yale University.

W. Benson Harer, Jr., holds an MD from the University of Pennsylvania. He is adjunct professor, retired, with the Department of Art, California State University, San Bernardino.

Pierre Watelet is the director of the Muséum d'histoire naturelle de Nantes.

Prologue

Pierre Watelet

I
n 1823, at thirty-six years of age, this intrepid traveler, a pioneer of Egyptology, returned to France. There he became one of the most celebrated men of his time, and was awarded the cross of the Legion of Honor upon the recommendation of François-René de Chateaubriand. At the height of his fame, however, he chose a modest post in his hometown of Nantes: that of assistant curator of the natural history museum. He eventually became its director in 1836.

For forty-six years, Frédéric Cailliaud proudly flew the flag of natural science. He did so partly through his talent for observation and drawing, already put to good use during his Egyptian travels, and partly through his wide network. He acquired, thus, a new reputation as a European specialist of shellfish. He studied perforations in rocks, made by Pholadidae, and those in wooden ships' hulls, made by teredo, in an effort to understand the chemical or mechanical means of this phenomenon. He was also interested in the ability of sea urchins to bore into the rock of small cavities, and he published widely while maintaining correspondence with both French and international scholars. He skillfully perfected the art of longitudinally sawing shells in order "to show the interior, generally unknown to this day," which earned him a bronze medal at the Paris World Fair of 1867. Over the course of fifteen years he traveled through all of the districts of the Loire-Inférieure and, with his knowledge of rocks and minerals, created a new geological map of the region in 1861.

The enrichment of the museum's collections was one of his main preoccupations. He never ceased to demand a more spacious building, and one better suited to the collection's preservation. Ultimately, he saw his wish fulfilled, but the work only began in 1868 and Cailliaud passed away on 1 May 1869, a few months after the laying of the first stone. Today, the marble bust of Frédéric Cailliaud occupies a place of honor in the entrance to the museum that preserves some of the souvenirs from his Egyptian campaigns: travel accounts; correspondence; emeralds from the legendary mines of Mount Zubara; some shells from the dunes of Gebel Zeit, which borders the Red Sea; and a mummy brought from Thebes, given in 1819 and stripped of its bandages. The most remarkable items, though, are a Sudanese scepter made of amebesh[1] wood that was offered by the king of Argo, Tandal Muhammad Idriss, to Cailliaud in 1821,[2] and sixty-five illustrated plates from his *Arts and Crafts*, wonderfully preserved, accompanied by a manuscript for his *Research on the Arts and Crafts, and the Manners of Civic and Domestic Life, of the Ancient Peoples of Egypt, Nubia, and Ethiopia*. This manuscript is an older version than that published here by the American Research Center in Egypt.

While Frédéric Cailliaud devoted the greater part of his life to Nantes and to his museum, it was Egypt that made him famous. We are indebted to Andrew Bednarski and Philippe Mainterot to have greatly contributed to the rediscovery of his enormous work.

---

1 *Terminalia psidiifolia*. See Frédéric Cailliaud, *Voyage à Méroé, au Fleuve Blanc, au-delà de Fazoql, dans le midi du royaume de Sennar, à Syouah et dans cinq autres oasis*, vol. 4 (Paris: Imprimerie royale, 1826–27), 382–83.
2 See Michel Chauvet, *Frédéric Cailliaud, les aventures d'un naturaliste en Égypte et au Soudan 1815–1822* (Saint-Sébastien-sur-Loire: ACL, 1989), 349–52.

CONTEXT

THE LIFE, TRAVELS, AND WORKS OF FRÉDÉRIC CAILLIAUD

Philippe Mainterot

F ew people today know much about the life and work of the French explorer Frédéric Cailliaud (1787–1869), but he was a giant in his time. Shortly after Napoleon Bonaparte's failed 1798 invasion opened Egypt to European inquiry, Cailliaud traveled through unknown, alien lands, recording all that he saw. Between 1815 and 1822, he was one of the first Europeans to explore the deserts on either side of the Nile, and he ventured through Sudan to the present-day frontiers of Ethiopia, frequently putting himself in mortal danger. Along with providing important historical information and stories of daring, Cailliaud's work also allows us to reconstruct an important period in the formation of nineteenth-century European knowledge on ancient Egypt, the very period in which the discipline of Egyptology was born. When discussing the history of Egyptology, he should, in fact, be regarded as one of the pioneers of this new science, at the forefront with his illustrious contemporary Jean-François Champollion (1790–1832), whose efforts at deciphering hieroglyphs owe much to Cailliaud. He was, after all, one of the first Europeans to visit, and bring back accurate drawings of, most of the famous archaeological sites in Egypt and Sudan. In addition, Cailliaud assembled the best collection of Egyptian and Sudanese objects that France would see until the late 1800s. The recent rediscovery of Cailliaud's unpublished manuscript, "Arts and Crafts of the Ancient Egyptians, Nubians, and Ethiopians," which forms the basis for this book, allows us, for the first time, to highlight an integral part of Cailliaud's work, undertaken between 1830 and 1869. This unfinished magnum opus, meant to synthesize Cailliaud's work on Nile civilizations, only confirms his première position among the pioneers of Egyptology.

Cailliaud was born in Nantes on 9 June 1787. The city of Nantes is located on the Loire river, fifty kilometers (thirty-two miles) from the Atlantic coast. During the eighteenth century, prior to the abolition of slavery, Nantes and its port were the slave-trade capital of France, which made it one of the richest cities in the country. Cailliaud was the third child of Jean Cailliaud and Marie-Rosalie

3

Monniers. His father was a master locksmith and, from 1789 onward, a municipal councilor. Jean Cailliaud wanted his son to follow him in his career, but the young man preferred the art of jewelry making, much like his brother, Jean-René. His training as a jeweler inspired him to take drawing lessons and he proved to be a gifted student. In 1809, Cailliaud left Nantes in the direction of Paris where, while working as a jeweler, he took courses in mineralogy and natural history at the Muséum national. At the end of two years of study, he undertook a trip across Europe to complete his training. In May 1811 he visited Belgium, then Amsterdam, where he frequented the workshops of precious-stone cutters. His European trek continued to Rome, where he arrived on 30 October 1813. From there he visited Campania, where he undertook numerous mineralogical studies of Mount Vesuvius over the course of nearly nine months. After a stay in Sicily, which lasted the first six months of 1814, during which time he built up his mineralogical collection from Mount Etna, Cailliaud made preparations to leave for the Orient. The mounting political tensions in Italy after the fall of Napoleon's empire gave him ample reason to do so. With the withdrawal of the French military from Italy, and the departure of the then-resident French citizenry, Cailliaud needed to flee the region. He bought a boat and hired a crew to take him to Greece. There he made the acquaintance of Théodore Lascaris (d. 1817), who hired him to continue his travels in Anatolia.[1] Moving as far as Constantinople,[2] and upon the recommendation of Lascaris, Cailliaud put his jeweler's talents at the service of the Ottoman ruler Sultan Mahmud II. He was employed by the sultan in Topkapi Palace, enriching with precious stones the sheaths of swords destined to be gifts to foreign guests. Having saved some money through this employment, Cailliaud decided to continue his Mediterranean journey as he wanted to visit new countries and continue his mineralogical studies. This desire, naturally, led him to Egypt, as the country's monuments had begun to appear in print in such works as Dominique Vivant Denon's[3] 1802 *Travels in Upper and Lower Egypt*, and, above all, in the first volumes of the *Description de l'Égypte*,[4] available in 1810.

When Cailliaud landed in Egypt in 1815,[5] he made the acquaintance of the French vice-consul, Bernardino Drovetti (1776–1852),[6] in Alexandria. Having been in this position since 1802, Drovetti enjoyed considerable influence with the Egyptian government, despite having had his position revoked following the First Restoration of 1814.[7] During his years in office, and with the consent of the Egyptian government, Drovetti had established a scholarly group to research pharaonic antiquities. For the first few months of his stay in Egypt, Drovetti viewed Cailliaud as a potential competitor in his search for antiquities. He soon granted him his protection, however, and offered him a position on an expedition he was organizing to Egypt's southern limit. Between January and June 1816, the two men, accompanied by Drovetti's dragoman,[8] ascended the Nile to Wadi Halfa, close to the Second Cataract. This trip was not only Cailliaud's first opportunity to familiarize himself with how Egyptians throughout the country lived, it also allowed him to behold, firsthand and in situ, the remains of pharaonic civilization. The group visited the ancient sites of Abydos, Dendara, Luxor, the Theban necropolis, Kom Ombo, Elephantine, and Philae.[9] At Abu Simbel, they tried unsuccessfully to free the great temple of Ramesses II from the sand.

Upon their return, Drovetti was interested in Cailliaud's talents and decided to present him to the viceroy of Egypt, Muhammad Ali (1769–1849). Drovetti praised Cailliaud's qualities as a designer, as a goldsmith, and for his knowledge of stones, to the ruler. As a result of Drovetti's good relations with Muhammad Ali, and from the confidence he clearly placed in Cailliaud, the viceroy

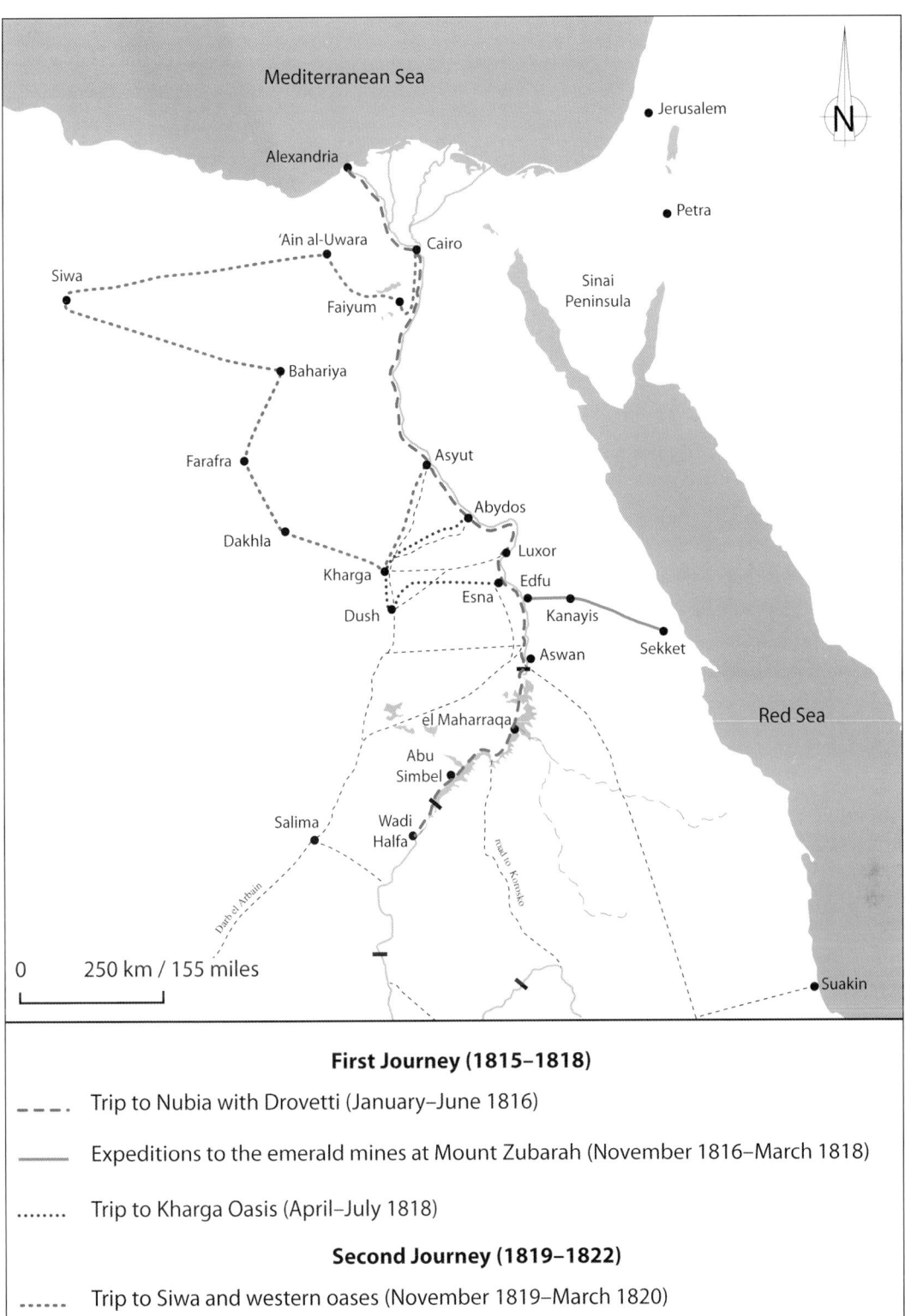

Mediterranean Sea

Jerusalem

Alexandria

'Ain al-Uwara   Cairo

Siwa

Faiyum

Petra

Sinai
Peninsula

Bahariya

Farafra

Asyut

Abydos

Dakhla

Luxor

Kharga

Edfu

Dush

Esna

Kanayis

Aswan

Sekket

Red Sea

el Maharraqa

Abu
Simbel

Salima

Wadi
Halfa

Darb el Arbain

road to Korosko

0   250 km / 155 miles

Suakin

First Journey (1815–1818)

‒ ‒ ‒ ·   Trip to Nubia with Drovetti (January–June 1816)

───   Expeditions to the emerald mines at Mount Zubarah (November 1816–March 1818)

....   Trip to Kharga Oasis (April–July 1818)

Second Journey (1819–1822)

......   Trip to Siwa and western oases (November 1819–March 1820)

2 Map of Frédéric Cailliaud's first journey through Egypt and his trip to Siwa. *Courtesy of Philippe Mainterot.*

appointed him to the position of government mineralogist. He then charged Cailliaud with finding lost emerald mines in Upper Egypt, supposedly located between the Nile and the Red Sea, whose exploitation had ceased during the ancient reign of Ptolemy VI. Accompanied by a team of workmen and granted firmans,[10] Cailliaud ascended the Nile once more to Philae. Interested in the site's ancient temple, Cailliaud copied Greek inscriptions engraved on the base of an obelisk prior to its removal by Giovanni Belzoni years later.[11] The party then turned north, reached Edfu,[12] and crossed the desert to the east. After walking for several days, Cailliaud discovered the cave temple of Seti I in Kanayis[13] before finding the ancient emerald mines of Mount Zubara. Cailliaud then organized three expeditions to reopen the mines between November 1816 and March 1818. These proved disappointing, however, as only a small number of precious stones were recovered. Only 4.5 kilograms (ten pounds) of emeralds were actually extracted from Mount Zubara and brought back to Muhammad Ali—enough to prove Cailliaud's abilities to the ruler, but not enough to warrant further exploitation of the mines.

Between each mission on the Red Sea shore, Cailliaud made numerous trips to the Theban necropolis to search for antiquities, amassing in the span of two years a rich collection. Working alone, or buying antiquities with his own funds, Cailliaud could not compete with other Europeans who had personal fortunes at their disposal, such as William John Bankes (1786–1855),[14] Lord Belmore (1774–1841),[15] and the Comte de Forbin (1777–1841).[16] With regard to the discovery of antiquities in general, competition between the French and English was at that time growing, particularly in the Luxor area. Both sides accused the other of looting or deliberately overpricing objects discovered by the inhabitants of the local village of Qurna. This conflict was occasionally fueled by the local peasants, who tended to sell their finds according to the nationality of the buyer or to the highest bidder. Cailliaud lived there, in the ancient tombs of the Theban necropolis, like the people of Qurna, and spent much time making sketches of tomb scenes and carefully copying hieroglyphic inscriptions. The attention to detail in Cailliaud's drawings and his skills as a copyist proved invaluable when he published his work, the accuracy of which was quickly recognized by the scientific world. In fact, when he made his copies, he had no knowledge of hieroglyphs.[17] He copied numerous inscriptions without understanding their meaning, simply drawing them with extreme diligence. According to Cailliaud, the paintings adorning the walls of these tombs had suffered little from the effects of either climate or vandalism. As a result of his work, Cailliaud's drawings allow us to reconstruct the decoration of certain tombs that have been damaged since his time in Egypt. An example of just such a damaged tomb is that of Ramesses III,[18] while the tomb of Neferhotep,[19] a topic to which we will return shortly, provides a good example of how Cailliaud's work can be used to study a tomb now lost to us.

During each of his stays in Thebes, Cailliaud noted the presence of large numbers of foreign travelers who paid high wages to Egyptian workers to excavate. Most of these Europeans were simply hoping to find treasure and fights broke out regularly between rival groups. Excavating tombs was much more lucrative for the inhabitants of Luxor's west bank than agricultural work which, over time, they began to abandon. To capitalize on this scramble for antiquities, they plundered graves with the consent of local authorities and to the great delight of Europeans. Among these travelers was the British consul general, Henry Salt (1780–1827).[20] Trained as a painter and writer, he was appointed consul general in Egypt in 1815. He collected antiquities during his tenure, and a good portion of his collection was acquired first by the Egyptian Department of the British Museum and then by the Louvre. Salt explored much of the Theban region, and was helped in his collecting efforts by several agents, including the famous Paduan, Giovanni Belzoni (1778–1823), Giovanni d'Athanasi (1798–1854), and Giambattista Caviglia (1770–1845).

Cailliaud met Salt for the first time in the Valley of the Kings. After this initial meeting, Salt suggested that, together, they visit the tomb of Seti I,[21] which had recently been opened by Belzoni in 1817. Cailliaud compiled an amazing description of this tomb, citing the famous alabaster sarcophagus, and paying tribute to Belzoni for his wonderful discovery. Paradoxically, relations between Cailliaud and the Paduan excavator were far from cordial throughout Cailliaud's first trip to Egypt. Indeed, in October 1816, during preparations for the transportation of Young Memnon[22] toward the Nile, Cailliaud, accompanied by Jean-Jacques Rifaud (1786–1852), a French agent of Drovetti, counseled Belzoni against removing the bust, judging the operation to be too risky. In response, Belzoni wrote: "I will not waste my time in describing the remarks made by the two French agents of Mr. D[rovetti], on seeing the head: suffice it to say, they positively declared, in spite of the evident mark it bore on its breast, that the French army did not take it away because they thought it not worth the taking!"[23] In his travel account, Belzoni repeatedly criticized Cailliaud, accusing him of wanting to harm him at all cost.[24] Another episode in the stormy relationship between the two men took place at Philae. During a trip there in September 1815, Belzoni took possession, on behalf of Salt, of several blocks decorated with reliefs. Upon his return in May 1817, much to his surprise, he found the blocks to have been mutilated. Nearby, a charcoal inscription had been scrawled in French, stating, "failed operation." Belzoni had no doubt who was responsible. Only three of Drovetti's agents had passed by Philae in October 1816: Cailliaud, Rifaud, and Joseph Rosignana. Belzoni believed the culprit to have been Cailliaud as he always carried a small hammer with him with which to break rock samples.[25] His guilt was never proven, however, and Cailliaud made no mention of such an incident in his journal. It is, however, possible that he did commit this travesty as, over the course of his travels in Egypt, Cailliaud detached numerous painted reliefs from the walls of many tombs.[26] It is also clear that Cailliaud liked to toy with other Europeans, as Salt learned the hard way. Cailliaud sent Salt an Arab bearing a modern pipe, the kind that was in use at that time in Ethiopia, on which he had engraved hieroglyphs. To further deceive the learned Salt, Cailliaud smeared bitumen inside it to hide the smell of tobacco and further pass it off as an antiquity. Astounded by such a find, the consul general quickly bought it for a hefty price and planned to write a scientific paper on this new curiosity. Cailliaud was greatly amused to have fooled a scholar as brilliant as Salt, and the story of the charade quickly spread among travelers of the period.[27]

With the mining expeditions at Mount Zubara completed, Cailliaud decided to undertake a new journey, this time to Kharga Oasis. Located west of Thebes, Kharga had hitherto been little explored by Europeans. As with other travelers in Egypt at this time, such as Belzoni, Cailliaud wanted to be the first to discover pharaonic ruins and leave his mark on archaeological history. A successful trip to unknown lands seemed a perfect means by which to achieve this. Accompanied by six members of the Ababda tribe[28] lent to him by Muhammad Ali, Cailliaud left Esna[29] for the Western Desert. After six days of travel, Cailliaud became the first European to discover the temple of Dush,[30] in the southernmost part of the oasis. He explored the site and drew numerous views of monuments. The travelers resumed their journey to Kharga proper, arriving there after a four-day trek. Cailliaud visited Hibis Temple,[31] largely built by Darius I, and made drawings. After a rapid exploration of the oasis, Cailliaud and his escort returned to the shores of the Nile. The traveler immediately moved in the direction of Cairo and informed the viceroy of his desire to return to France to present his discoveries to the scholars of his day, promising to return at a later date. Armed with recommendations from Salt for the French scientific authorities, Cailliaud left Egypt with his notes and collections for Marseille, where he arrived on 28 November 1818. He was then thirty-one years old, having left his family nine years earlier.

News of Cailliaud's discoveries in Egypt rapidly spread all the way to Paris. Interested in the new material he had collected, the scholar Edmé-François Jomard (1777–1862), charged with publishing the *Description de l'Égypte*, decided to place the young Cailliaud under his protection. As a titular member of the Académie des inscriptions et belles-lettres, he had learned of Cailliaud's work through a series of articles published in scientific journals and through presentations at meetings of the Institut de France between 1818 and 1819. Cailliaud arrived in Paris in February 1819. The Commission d'Égypte, the body responsible for the publication of the *Description*, saw in Cailliaud's explorations the continuation of work undertaken by the French scholars who had accompanied Bonaparte's 1798 expedition to Egypt. On the commission's recommendation, the French government acquired the portfolio of drawings and antiquities brought back by the traveler. The Bibliothèque royale was specifically chosen by the government to house his antiquities collection.[32] Jomard was also charged with publishing Cailliaud's notes. Satisfied with the results of his first trip to Egypt, the government decided to send Cailliaud once more to the banks of the Nile, this time on an official, government mission. His objective was to continue the exploration of Egypt and its monuments in areas where Napoleon's scholars had been unable to penetrate, specifically into the oases west of the Nile and into Sudan, the land of ancient Nubia, south of the temple of Philae. In these places, he was charged with surveying monuments, collecting pharaonic antiquities, and mapping the terrain through which he passed. To help him in these tasks, the government gave him financial credit, materials, and a midshipman named Pierre-Constant Letorzec (1798–1857),[33] who was responsible for conducting the astronomical observations needed for mapping.

The two men arrived in Alexandria on 1 October 1819 and went to Cairo to meet with Muhammad Ali. The viceroy conferred on them firmans to move freely about and to excavate on Egyptian land. Very quickly, Cailliaud set up their first exploratory mission: the Oasis of Siwa, on the edge of the Western Desert. It was there that Alexander the Great had been acknowledged as the descendant of the God Amun by the oasis's oracle in 332 BC.[34] Due to its extreme distance from the shores of the Nile, Siwa had previously only been visited by a small host of European explorers. A handful of them had succeeded in reaching the oasis's ruins and returned with their accounts. Others had been turned away or murdered by the local population. Cailliaud's planned trip to Siwa could have been a disaster; in addition to crossing the desert, he had to meet the local peoples, who were not subject to the authority of the viceroy, and who might view him as an enemy. Accompanied by an interpreter and two servants, Cailliaud and Letorzec ascended the Nile to Faiyum[35] before heading into the Western Desert. After eighteen days of travel on their dromedaries, they arrived at the gates of Siwa on 9 December 1819. Unfortunately, the sheikh of the village saw the arrival of these strangers as a bad omen, and it was only after several days of discussions that Cailliaud was allowed to study the ruins of the temple of Umm al-Ibeida.[36]

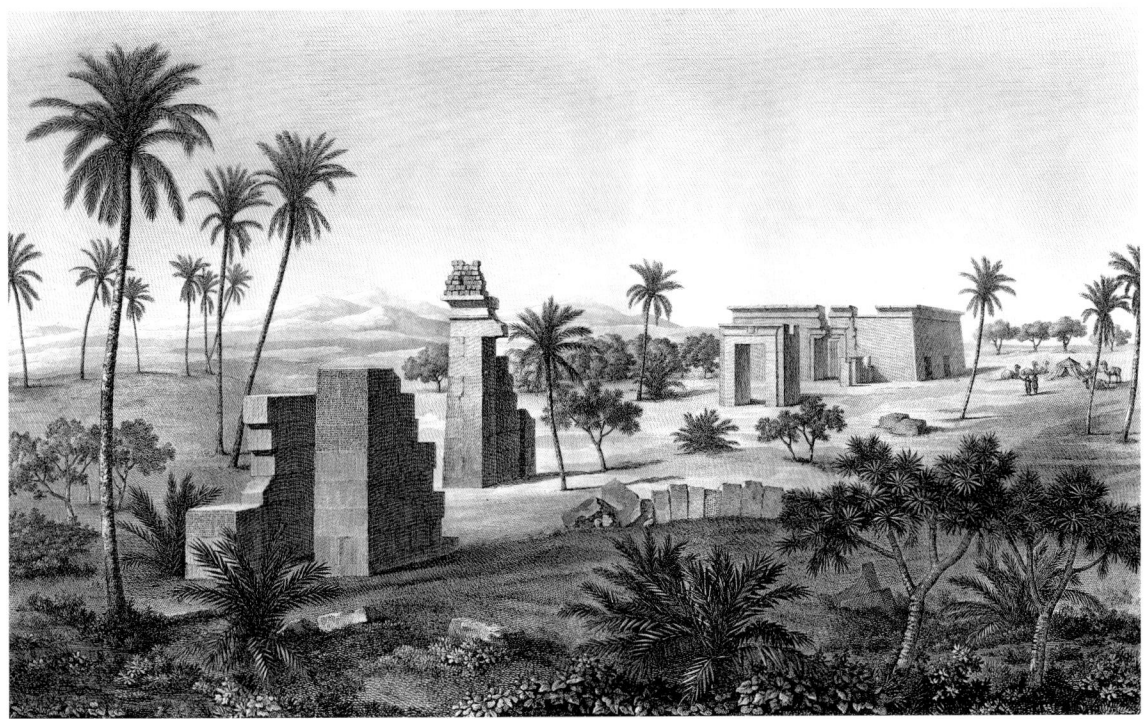

3 *Travels in the Oasis of Thebes*, plate XVIII. A general view of the temple of Kharga. *Courtesy of the Musée Dobrée, Nantes.*

Following their instructions received in France, Cailliaud and Letorzec traversed the Western Desert in a southerly direction to return to the Nile. In so doing, they successively crossed the oases of Bahariya, Farafra, Dakhla, and Kharga, making notes on each of their monuments to complete the work started by Cailliaud on his previous trip. As a result, they crossed close to 1,800 kilometers (about 1,100 miles) of the Western Desert in the span of three months. This trip exhausted them, but they were satisfied to have gathered accounts of the peoples from these different, little-known lands.

Prior to returning to Cairo at the end of March 1820, Cailliaud learned that Muhammad Ali was mounting a military expedition to Sudan. This was entrusted to his third son, Isma'il Pasha. The purpose of the expedition was not only to pacify these lands in order to exploit their mining potential, the historical precedent for which was established in the pharaonic period, but also to capture new slaves.[37] Hoping to profit from this opportunity to explore new lands, Cailliaud had Drovetti present him to the prince, who accorded him his protection and invited him to participate in the expedition. In addition, Muhammad Ali entrusted Cailliaud with a mission to prospect in the area of Fazoql,[38] in order to exploit its supposed gold mines. The first part of this long journey was to be made by water, and the requisitioning of all means of transportation for the military expedition meant Cailliaud had to buy his own boat.

Sailing south, Cailliaud and Letorzec stopped in Luxor, where they hoped to amass a new collection of antiquities. They set themselves up in the very heart of the Theban necropolis and built a house of earthen bricks between the funerary temple of Seti I in Qurna and that of Queen Hatshepsut in Deir al-Bahari. This home was destined to hold Cailliaud's collections. The scarcity of wood planks in the region forced him to use pieces of painted sarcophagi for the roof. Having abandoned the tombs to house and protect his discoveries, Cailliaud made a lasting impression on the locals by building this unique residence. As on his previous trip, Cailliaud began excavating and buying antiquities from the inhabitants of the necropolis. From this, he amassed not only funerary objects, such as sarcophagi, canopic vases,[39] stelae,[40] amulets, and *shabtis*,[41] but also objects from the daily lives of the ancient Egyptians, such as cosmetic items, jewelry, clothing, and tools. The presence of these everyday objects, mixed in with funerary material, made Cailliaud's second collection atypical when compared to those of other contemporaneous European travelers. Such travelers were typically more concerned with the aesthetic value or the marketability of their acquisitions rather than their historical or ethnographic worth. Cailliaud also acquired complete funerary assemblages, such as that of Padimenipet.[42] This material came from a mass Ramesside grave that had been reused in the Roman period for the family of Soter, archon[43] of Thebes during the reign of Emperor Trajan. All the funerary equipment from this tomb was divided and sold to Europeans who found themselves in the necropolis. Alongside the acquisition of antiquities, Cailliaud began to apply his drawing skills to reproduce a large number of murals and reliefs from the tombs.

Cailliaud rejoined Isma'il Pasha's camp on 24 August 1820 in Aswan so as to prepare for the expedition's departure. A conspiracy to discredit him with the Pasha, however, was soon hatched. Several Italian travelers,[44] among them Domenico Frediani (1783–1823), succeeded in persuading the prince to exclude Cailliaud from the voyage, thinking that by doing so they would be the first to identify previously unknown ruins, such as the famed city of Meroe.[45] In ancient times, Meroe had, for several centuries, been the capital of the kingdom of Kush. Prior to 1822, the legendary city of Meroe, known from ancient Greek and Roman sources, had yet to be relocated. Cailliaud hoped to use the opportunity presented by the military venture to identify it before other European travelers. The pretext offered to the French traveler as to why he could not participate was that the environment would be too dangerous for him to undertake his research properly; it would be better for him to wait for the territories to be conquered before prospecting for the mines. They also claimed that his firmans did not apply to the lands the expedition would cross and that he should, therefore, return to Cairo in order to clarify the situation directly with the viceroy and obtain the necessary permits. This race against time required Cailliaud to return as quickly as possible to Alexandria, so as to limit the head start of his competitors into Nubia. Fortunately, he was able to plead his case before Muhammad Ali, who confirmed his position as government mineralogist, the position he had held during his first voyage to Egypt, and gave him all the necessary supporting documents.

Wanting to rejoin Isma'il Pasha's army, which was further upstream, south of Aswan, quickly, Cailliaud and Letorzec crossed Lower Nubia. They visited its temples and made several stops at sites they deemed of great archaeological interest. They were able, as a result, to survey as the Commission d'Égypte had urged. They worked at Semna and Kumma,[46] on the island of Sai,[47] in the temples of Sedeinga[48] and Soleb,[49] in the ruins of Sesebi,[50] around the city of Kerma,[51] and, finally, on the island of Argo.[52] These misadventures, caused by Isma'il Pasha's entourage, who forced him to return to Cairo and lose his place at the head of the expedition, ultimately allowed Cailliaud to study the monuments at greater length. Once the army had passed through an area, the conquered lands proved to be much calmer than before. Also, had Cailliaud been among the Egyptian troops, he would not have been able to explore the ruins in such a methodical way as he

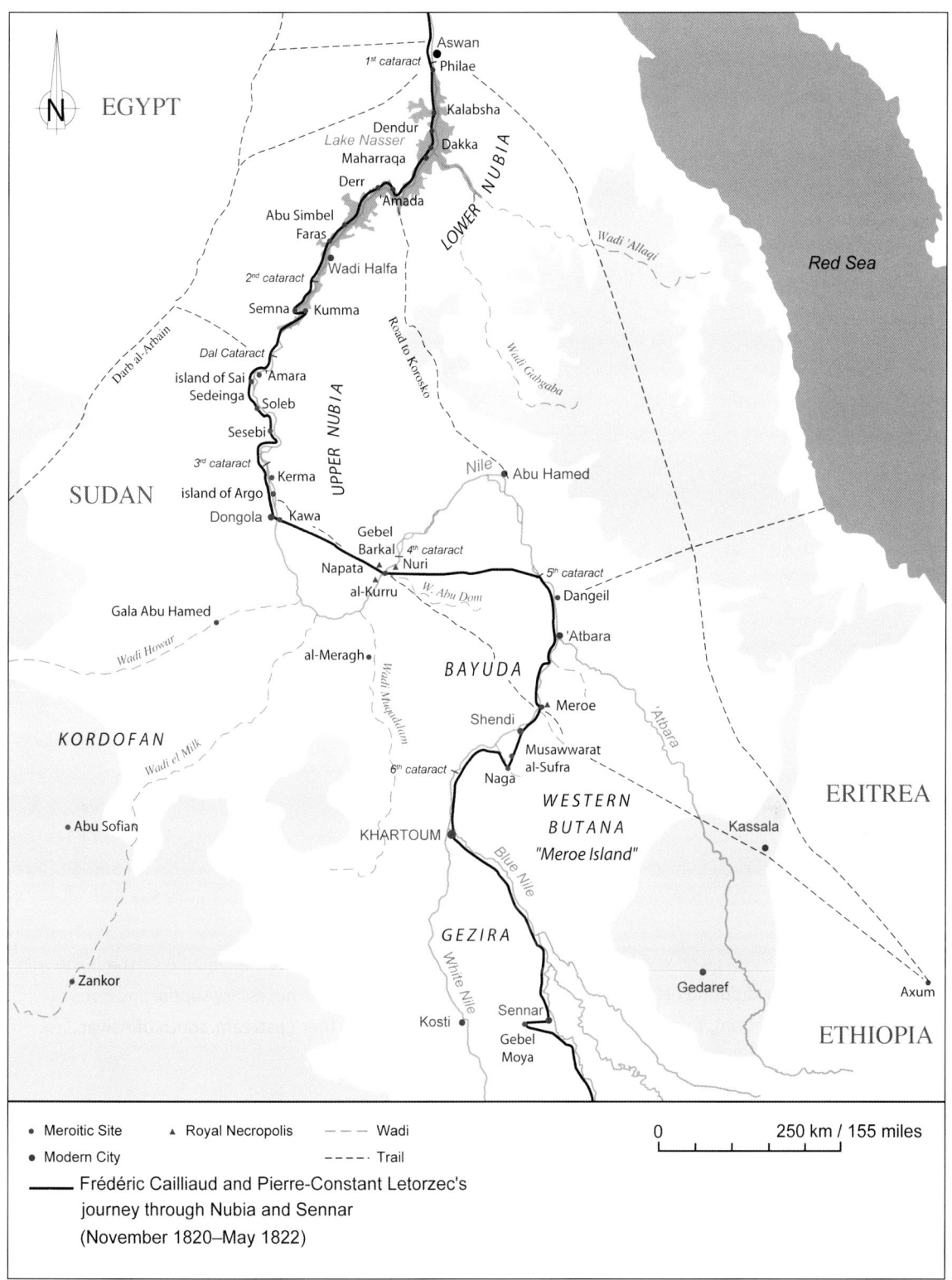

The map contains the following labels:

EGYPT

N

Aswan
1st cataract
Philae
Kalabsha
Dendur
Lake Nasser
Dakka
Maharraqa
Derr
Amada
Abu Simbel
Faras
Wadi 'Allaqi
Red Sea
Wadi Halfa
2nd cataract
LOWER NUBIA
Semna
Kumma
Road to Korosko
Wadi Gabgaba
Darb al-Arbain
Dal Cataract
island of Sai
Amara
Sedeinga
Soleb
UPPER NUBIA
Sesebi
3rd cataract
Kerma
Nile
Abu Hamed
island of Argo
Dongola
Kawa
SUDAN
Gebel
Barkal
4th cataract
Napata
Nuri
al-Kurru
5th cataract
W. Abu Dom
Dangeil
Gala Abu Hamed
'Atbara
Wadi Howar
al-Meragh
BAYUDA
Wadi Muqaddam
Meroe
KORDOFAN
Shendi
Wadi el Milk
Musawwarat
al-Sufra
6th cataract
Naga
'Atbara
WESTERN
BUTANA
Kassala
"Meroe Island"
ERITREA
Abu Sofian
KHARTOUM
Blue Nile
GEZIRA
Zankor
White Nile
Gedaref
Axum
Kosti
Sennar
ETHIOPIA
Gebel
Moya

Legend:
• Meroitic Site   ▲ Royal Necropolis   — — — Wadi
• Modern City   - - - - Trail
0   250 km / 155 miles

—— Frédéric Cailliaud and Pierre-Constant Letorzec's
journey through Nubia and Sennar
(November 1820–May 1822)

4 Map of Frédéric Cailliaud's journey to Nubia with Pierre-Constant Letorzec. *Courtesy of Philippe Mainterot.*

did. On 9 February 1821, at Gebel Barkal,[53] they finally caught up with Isma'il Pasha's army, which comprised impressive numbers: about four thousand men, 1,800 cavalry, two thousand servants, three hundred dromedaries, and twenty-four pieces of artillery. To his amazement, Cailliaud was warmly welcomed by the Italians who accompanied the prince. In his absence, they had been able to visit the temples of Lower Nubia and reached Gebel Barkal before him. They were certain that there they had discovered Meroe, the ancient capital of the kingdom of Kush, and that they would, as a result, be immortalized. Cailliaud expressed doubt over their identification of Gebel Barkal as the site of Meroe, as it was too far north according to the location of the city given by the ancient authors Herodotus and Strabo.[54]

From the Fourth Cataract, the Nile runs northeast. To save time, the army decided to head southeast and cut across the Bayuda Desert. Long marches at night followed in succession so as to avoid the heat. As ancient monuments were scarce in this part of Nubia, Cailliaud undertook some mineralogical investigations, taking notes on the flora and fauna of the countryside they crossed. The army rejoined the Nile at al-Baqir. Shortly thereafter, the threat of enemy cavalry appeared in the region of Shendi (which Cailliaud spells 'Chendy' and 'Chandy'). All men were expected to be ready to fight, and that included the European travelers! Despite this threat, the route to Berber (spelled 'Barbar' by Cailliaud) was unencumbered. Arriving at this village, Cailliaud met with the locals and recorded his observations of their lifestyle and homes. He met several faqirs, educated men, who gave him much information on the peoples he had encountered. Cailliaud made them write the names of the villages he had seen in Arabic to avoid the sorts of misunderstanding and mis-communication typical of early nineteenth-century travel accounts. All of this was done to map the unknown lands through which he traveled, as the Commission d'Égypte had hoped.

On 19 March 1821, when Cailliaud was invited to the tent of Isma'il Pasha, the conversation turned to the potential gold mines and diamonds that they hoped to find. Cailliaud received per-mission from the prince to take the road to Shendi ahead of the Egyptian army, to prospect. He offered him the protection of several soldiers and, finally, added that Cailliaud might indulge in all the scientific work that interested him. Isma'il Pasha also suggested that, for their security, Cailliaud and his companion adopt aliases. Frédéric Cailliaud thus became Murad Effendi and Pierre-Constant Letorzec Abdallah al-Faqir. To further effect these personas, both men dressed like Turks, with shaven heads and long beards. This adaptation to their environment was reminiscent of earlier travelers, such as John Lewis Burckhardt (1784–1817), who, under the identity of Sheikh Ibrahim, preceded the two Frenchmen on the road to the kingdom of Sennar[55] in 1813. Their local guide confided to them that, in the area, there were large numbers of stones placed by the ancients, one atop the other, in the shape of stairs. Cailliaud, enthused by his guide's words, wanted to reach the site of such monuments as quickly as possible. The small group set off at dawn on 25 April 1821, and saw the first ruins of Meroe's necropolis pyramids shortly thereafter. These ruins, found near the eighteenth parallel, related much better to the location of Meroe cited by ancient Greek and Roman authors than those of Gebel Barkal. This discovery allowed Cailliaud to respond to his Italian competitors and argue that Gebel Barkal could not have been the capital of the kingdom of Kush. The true discovery of Meroe thus belongs exclusively to Cailliaud, accompanied by Letorzec. For fifteen days, the two men surveyed the ruins; they drew the monuments, drew plans for the town and the cemetery, and copied all the reliefs that adorned the pylons beside the pyramids.

Despite this important discovery, Cailliaud was not able to stay in the immediate vicinity of the ruins of Meroe. He had to complete the mission that had been entrusted to him by Muhammad Ali: to find the gold mines of Nubia. After prospecting, he and his group rejoined Isma'il Pasha's troops at Shendi. From that moment on, ambushes, pillaging, violent skirmishes, and outright battles with the locals were the French travelers' daily lot. Several local rebels who had killed Egyptian soldiers were taken prisoner. After a summary trial, Cailliaud recorded what he witnessed, horrified by the ordeal: rebels were impaled and their bodies left exposed for two days as a reminder of what would befall those who resisted the army.[56] On 27 May 1821, the army arrived in Omdurman, the meeting point of the Blue and White Niles, opposite the present-day city of Khartoum and the center of the kingdom of Sennar. Cailliaud stayed there for five months while the army tried to conquer the region. During this time, he studied the manners and customs of the inhabitants, their agriculture, their commerce, their politics, their religion, and the architecture of Omdurman. Through this contact with the natives, Cailliaud established a lexicon of the names of the different provinces he had crossed, a list of the names of cities in those provinces, and their spelling in Arabic, all the way from Siwa Oasis to Singa. After the expedition arrived in Fazoql, Cailliaud received an order to prospect in the surrounding mountains to search for traces of gold. On 19 January 1822, at Mount Tumat, Cailliaud found excavations, marked by vulture feathers, that had previously been exploited by local miners. These holes in the ground descended into a gallery six meters deep, but Cailliaud soon realized that the precious metal they contained could not be extracted in the quantities expected by Isma'il Pasha. Instead, assisted by about thirty men who had been placed at his disposal, Cailliaud prospected along the nearby waterways. Unfortunately, only a few grams of ore were extracted from these gold-bearing sands after seventeen days of work. Cailliaud and Letorzec's mission ended south of the kingdom of Sennar, close to the present-day border with Ethiopia. As a result of all of their traveling, they were able to establish a new map of the lands of ancient Nubia from Aswan to the tenth latitude north, and subsequently fulfill part of the mission that had been entrusted to them by the Commission d'Égypte.

As the Sudanese gold mines could not be exploited intensively, Isma'il Pasha decided that Cailliaud should return to Egypt to deliver the 200 kilograms (441 pounds) of gold sand that had been harvested and to plead with the viceroy to order the army's return. This order likely saved Cailliaud and Letorzec's lives. After stabilizing the army's positions in the region of Sennar, Isma'il Pasha moved his troops toward Egypt. Near Shendi, he and his entourage met for a banquet to celebrate the impending return to their country. A former king of the region named Nimir, however, had his men surround the square in which the banquet was held and set fire to Isma'il's tents. The fire spread quickly, leaving the occupants no chance of escape. All were burned alive.

Having avoided this fate, Cailliaud and Letorzec descended the Nile toward Egypt, stopping at different archaeological sites that they had not visited when traveling with the army as a result of its rapid pace south. They arrived at the site of Naga[57] on 14 March 1822 and found another French traveler there, Linant de Bellefonds (1799–1883), who decided to accompany them. They studied the monuments of Naga before exploring the ruins of Musawwarat al-Sufra[58] and then returning to Meroe to finish the drawings Cailliaud had started a year earlier. They also stopped at Gebel Barkal to study the sanctuary of Amun at the foot of the mountain. After their long journey in Sudan, Cailliaud and Letorzec returned to Egypt at the start of June 1822.

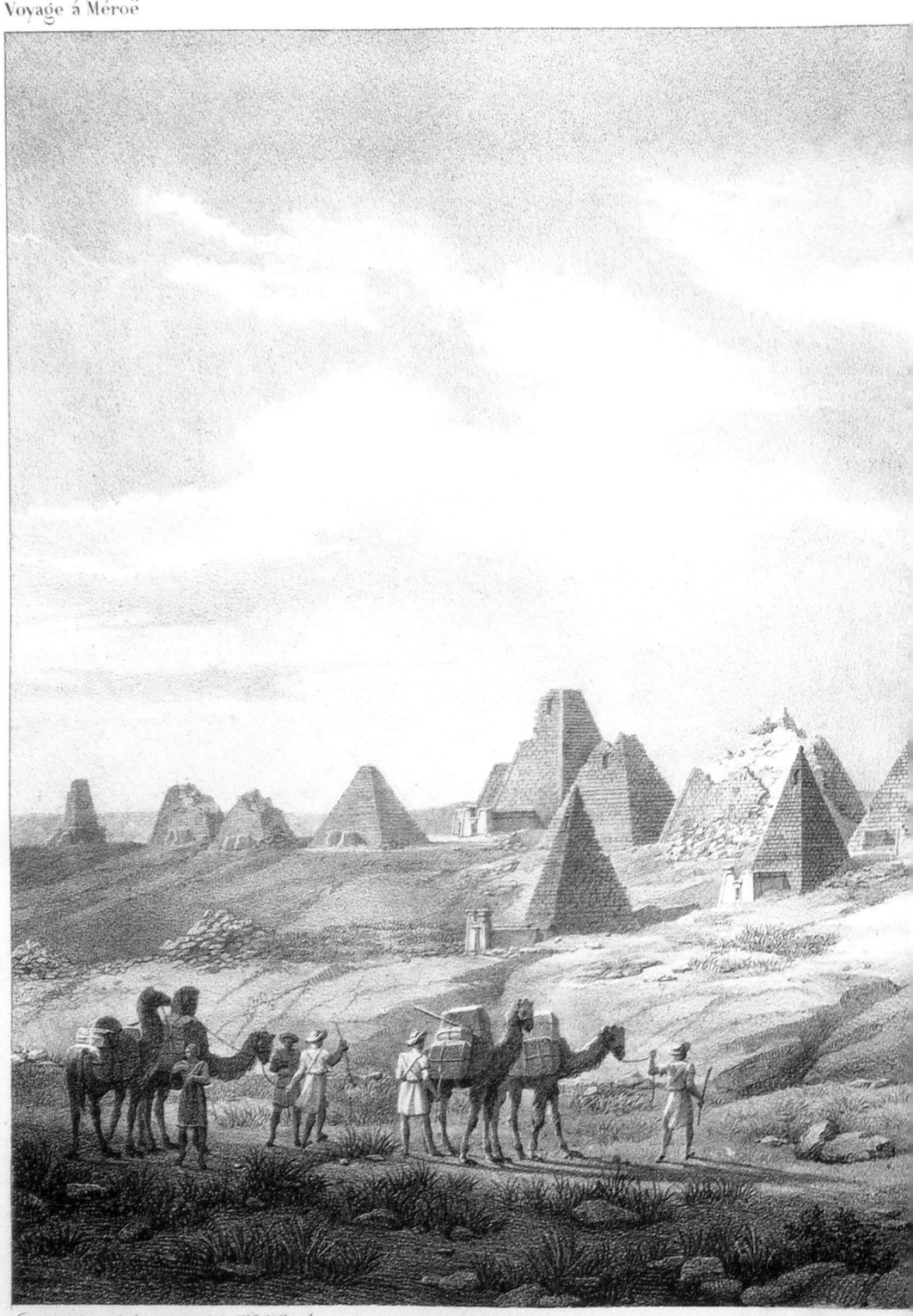

Derry, d'apres le dessin original de M.r Cailliaud.

VUE GÉNÉRALE DES PYRAMIDES

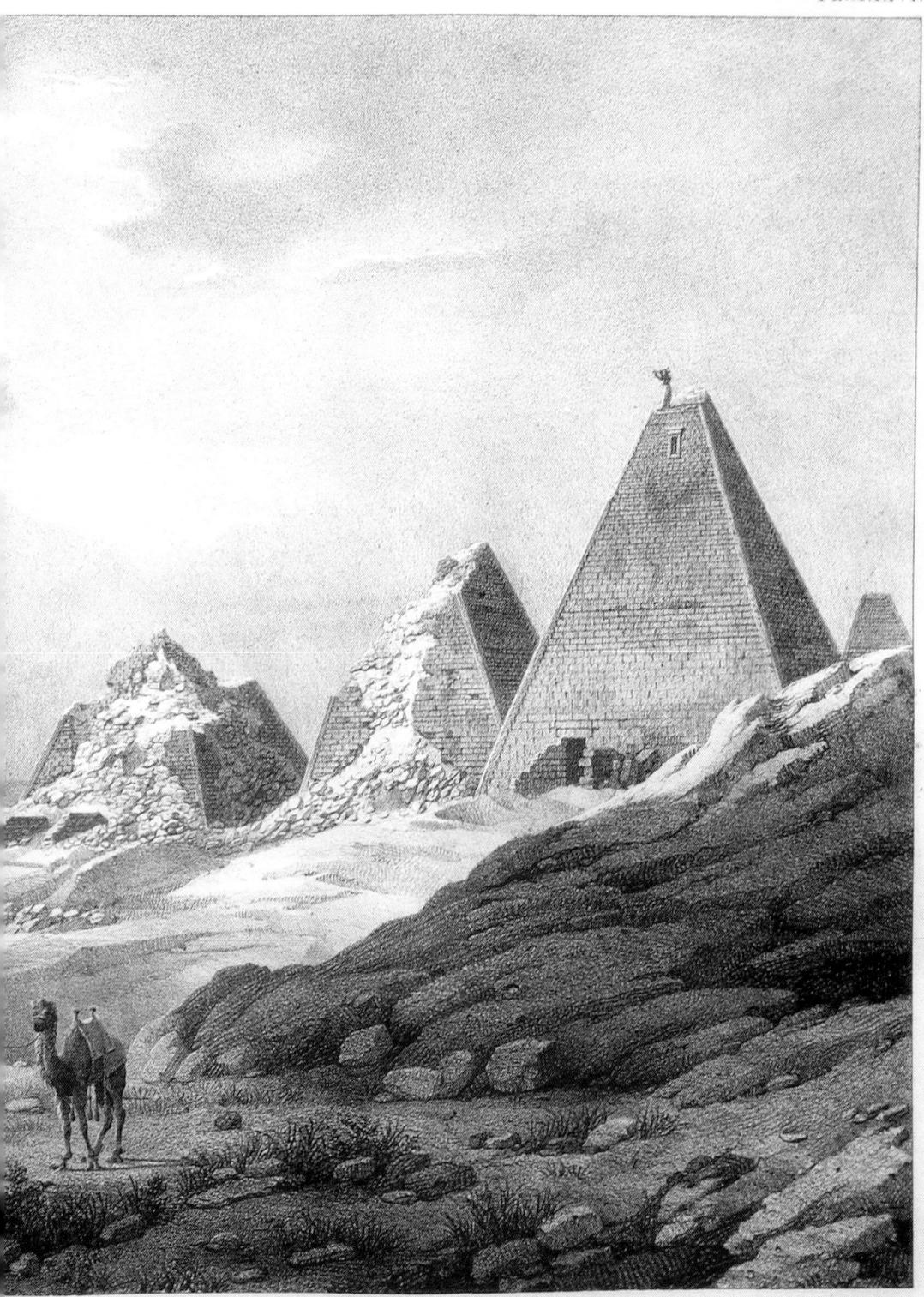

Imp. Lith. de C. Constans.

LIÉUE DU NIL, PRISE DU NORD-EST.

5 *Voyage à Méroé*, vol. 1, plate XXXVI. A view of Sudanese pyramids.
Courtesy of the Muséum d'histoire naturelle, Nantes.

After such a perilous trip, it appears that Cailliaud wanted a bit of rest. Before heading toward Cairo, however, a stop in Luxor seemed as necessary for his health as for that of his traveling companion. It also allowed him time to prepare for the shipment of the collection of antiquities he had amassed to France and to acquire new pieces.

To this end, Cailliaud put himself to work in the Theban necropolis. The diversity and number of pharaonic monuments present in the area formed a variety of subjects of study that can still be seen in his drawings. Along with his work as a copyist in the tombs, Cailliaud adopted methods similar to those of contemporary antiquaries and other tomb robbers. Such activities are particularly evident in the case of a tomb discovered in 1822. Earlier that summer, shortly before Cailliaud's return to Luxor, one of Salt's agents, Giovanni d'Athanasi, discovered a tomb in the north end of Dra Abu al-Naga. One can imagine that news of the discovery of a tomb in the Theban necropolis spread like wildfire. Such gossip not only publicized the success of an excavation, it also claimed ownership of a tomb and its contents for the explorer who found it. As a result, word-of-mouth accreditation cut short any debate over a discovery's scientific and commercial exploitation. Despite the discovery of this tomb by the British consul general's workmen, Cailliaud mentioned in his account that he entered the tomb to draw its painted murals.

> A small tomb, whose entry had just been discovered, offered me various curious subjects painted as frescos and with fine preservation. I noted scenes of hunting, fishing, grape harvesting, and groups of musicians. I drew a portion of it, always striving to copy complete scenes. A large clump of lotus stems, from a very exact drawing, juts from the water: it is covered with geese and other waterfowl.... On another wall of this tomb, we find the same large figure that I have already mentioned; his outfit makes him easily recognizable. … Here he is hunting for wild beasts. He has his bow pulled back and will let fly an arrow: in the hand which holds this, he also holds the quiver from which he took the arrow.[59]

The tomb, whose exact location is now lost, belonged to Neferhotep, chief of royal granaries during the reigns of Thutmose III and Amenhotep II.[60] Prior to its rediscovery by d'Athanasi, it had been visited by the savants of Napoleon's Egyptian expedition before 1801. D'Athanasi recounted his memories of Cailliaud a few years later and accused him of vandalizing the monument. He states:

> Not satisfied with having copied to his heart's content whatever caught his fancy, he [Cailliaud] sent a messenger to Luxor, on the opposite bank of the river, to procure some iron tools, with which he forthwith set to work, detaching the crust of the wall into pieces which he began sending to his house. My Arabs, who were working in the excavations not far from the spot, having recognized the embellishments of the tomb, forced them away from the men who were carrying them off; and one of them without loss of time, hurried to the tomb and demanded of M. Cailliaud from whom he had obtained permission to take away the embellishments in this manner. On this enquiry, M. Cailliaud seized a piece of iron and threw it at the head of my Arab who had come to warn him of his error; but the latter without being disconcerted, answered his attack in the same fashion, snatching

from him at the same time all his implements, as well as the designs he had just been detaching from their places, and which he brought to me.[61]

Cailliaud did, in fact, cut out a painted limestone block depicting a papyrus thicket, which formed part of a larger scene of fowling in the marshes (fig. 6). This block joined Cailliaud's collection.[62] While the act of theft was far from laudable, it is understandable given how common such behavior was at the beginning of the nineteenth century. Cailliaud would have seen similar portions of painted wall scenes, taken directly from tombs, in Drovetti's collections, as well as in the collections of British excavators, such as Salt.

In the summer of 1822, Cailliaud went to Abydos. There, he copied the Abydos Kings' List, carved in a room of the temple of Ramesses II (fig. 7). This relief had been discovered in 1818 by William John Bankes, and contains the names of Ramesses II's predecessors who ruled Egypt. Bankes never published his discovery, which allowed Cailliaud to be the first to disseminate a copy of the important record. This Kings' List was later detached from the temple and taken by Jean-François Mimaut, the French consul, to Alexandria, and was then bought upon his death in 1837 by the British Museum, where it currently resides.

While he was in Abydos, a letter from Letorzec informed Cailliaud that some of their belongings and money necessary for the purchase of further collections had been stolen from their house in Luxor. He immediately returned to Luxor, but found neither his money nor the guilty party. Deciding not to secure other funds, which would have required a lengthy wait, Cailliaud instead resigned himself to selling his camels to fund their collecting. While preparing their return to Cairo, he and Letorzec resumed their excavations in the Theban necropolis and drawing activities in the tombs. For more than a month, Cailliaud relentlessly copied reliefs and paintings in the necropolis,

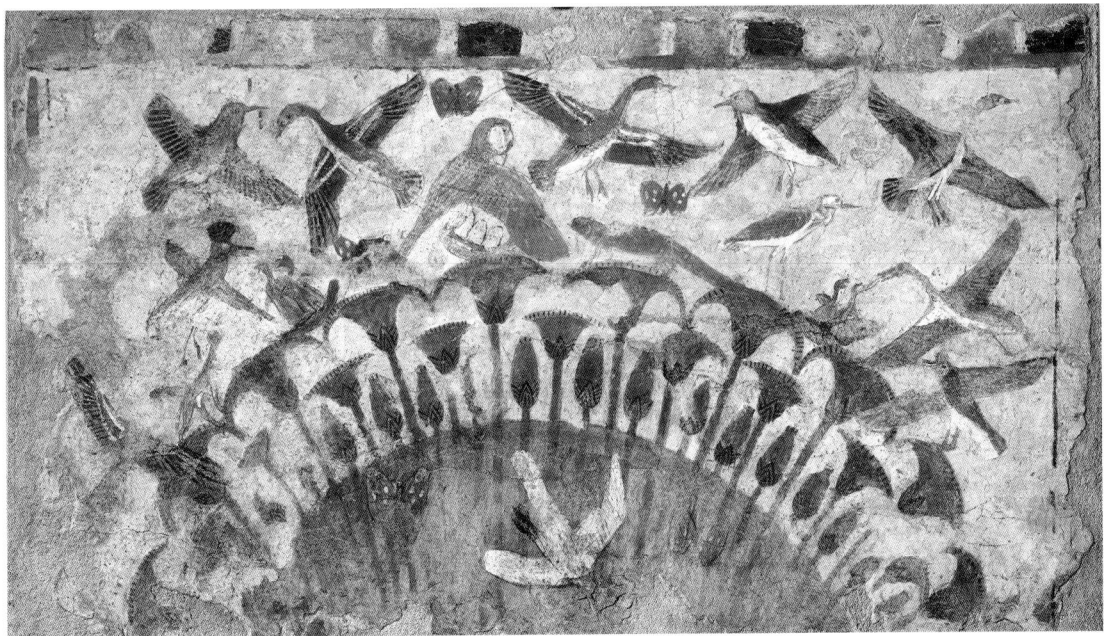

6 Painted block from the tomb of Neferhotep, Louvre Museum E 13101. *Courtesy of the Louvre Museum, Paris.*

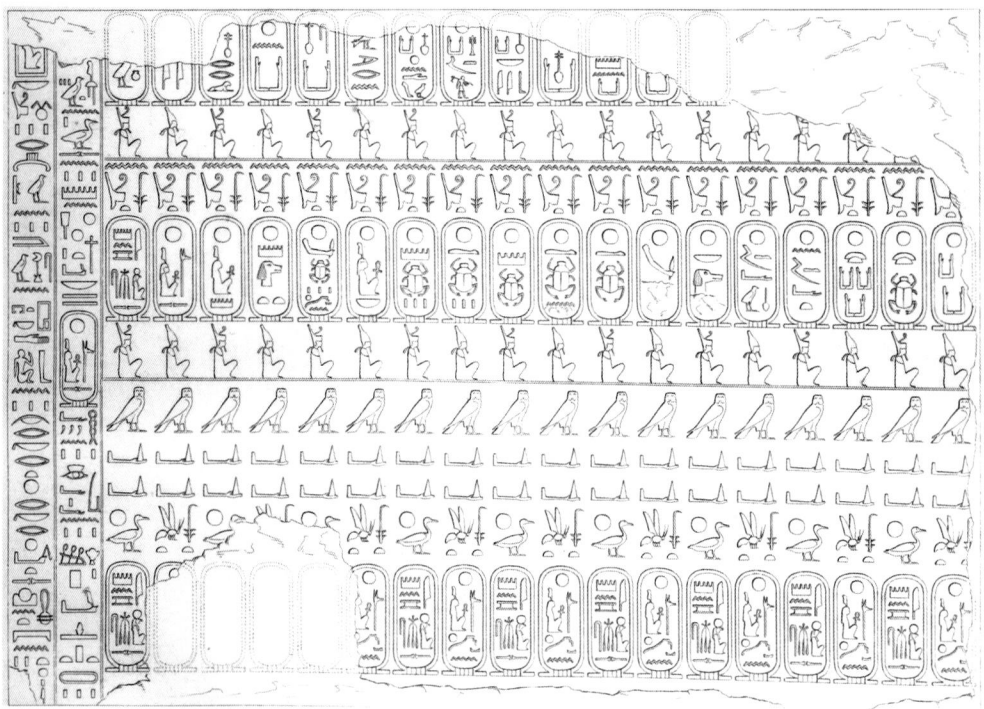

7 Abydos Kings' List, as drawn by Frédéric Cailliaud. *Voyage à Méroé*, vol. 2, plate LXXII. *Courtesy of the Muséum d'histoire naturelle, Nantes.*

as well as some in al-Kab, about 161 kilometers (100 miles) south. When it finally came time to leave Luxor, a whole day had to be devoted to loading collections and personal effects onto a boat. Cailliaud makes it clear that during this season the village of Qurna was "about a quarter of a league,"[63] or about one kilometer, from the river. It is easy to imagine the difficulty that Cailliaud would have had organizing the loading of his material, which had to be done with very basic means of transportation or by carrying it on one's back. Knowing the sheer volume of Cailliaud's second collection, we can also appreciate how hard the packing must have been. The boat reached Cairo the morning of 27 September 1822. The next day, Cailliaud and Letorzec went to the site of Saqqara,[64] where the step pyramid of the pharaoh Djoser had been opened the year before by Baron von Minutoli (1772–1846). Cailliaud cleared the entrance to the monument, which had been blocked with sand, before he entered it. Lost in the maze of underground tunnels, Cailliaud and Letorzec admired, by the glow of their torches, the extraordinary faience-tiled walls of this labyrinth. For three days, Cailliaud mapped the unknown underground complex of Djoser's pyramid, hoping to eventually publish their work. Cailliaud decided, at that point, to return to France and publish his findings on Meroe before another traveler had the chance. For the journey back to France, Cailliaud and Letorzec found a Genoese brig in Alexandria bound for Marseille. After saying their farewells to Drovetti, they boarded the ship, which weighed anchor on 30 October 1822.

From the moment Cailliaud arrived in France, he devoted himself to organizing his studies and to publishing his work. His efforts would not only augment nineteenth-century knowledge of antiquity, they would help to create a new scientific discipline: Egyptology. His contribution to this new discipline is largely epitomized by the novel nature of his discoveries, as well as by the quality of his work as a draftsman. On this topic, it is sufficient simply to admire the delicacy of his drawings and the precision of his topographical plans, all done with the rudimentary means at his disposal. The period in which Cailliaud undertook his travels and published his findings saw French scientific interest in ancient Egypt develop rapidly, largely as a result of the publication of the Napoleonic *Description de l'Égypte* from 1810 onward. Cailliaud met with Jomard, the editor of the *Description*, upon his return to France, and he offered Cailliaud numerous opportunities to advance his publication efforts. This pivotal figure in the history of French science in the first half of the nineteenth century enabled Cailliaud to make his discoveries known. Jomard's formatting of Cailliaud's journal from his first trip to Egypt gave birth to *Travels in the Oasis of Thebes*.[65] From a technical standpoint, Jomard did everything possible to make the work a reference guide to pharaonic antiquities in keeping with the *Description de l'Égypte*. His perfectionist ideals, however, continually delayed the book's publication and nearly cost Cailliaud credit for his discoveries in light of the work done by other travelers, such as Belzoni. The multiple publication delays also did a disservice to the final work, and these delays were heavily criticized.[66] (See "The Harer Papers," below.) In fact, the second part of *Travels in the Oasis of Thebes*, dedicated to Cailliaud's collections, did not appear until 1862, shortly before Jomard's death. By then Cailliaud was seventy-five years old, and the objects he had brought back to France in 1819 and 1822 had long since been forgotten. It was likely for this reason, to avoid the previously encountered problems of producing such a complex work, that Cailliaud himself undertook the editing and publication of his second journey, entitled *Travels to Meroe and the White Nile*.[67] Jomard's complete absence from the production of this work is a clear sign of Cailliaud's scientific independence from his former patron. It should be remembered, however, that it was Jomard's intervention and his connection to the highest echelons of French government that had resulted in Cailliaud being sent to Egypt on behalf of Louis XVIII's government and sponsored by the Académie des inscriptions et belles-lettres. In spite of the criticisms leveled at his first travel account, both *Travels in the Oasis of Thebes* and *Travels to Meroe* remain important works in the history of ancient Egypt's rediscovery.[68] They are part of a small corpus of travelers' accounts that record the state of pharaonic monuments in the first quarter of the nineteenth century.

It appears that Cailliaud was diverted away from Jomard's influence upon returning from his second trip to Egypt, much to the benefit of the Champollion brothers.[69] It is important to highlight the work that Cailliaud did in Egypt with regard to Jean-François Champollion's own scientific efforts. Champollion's hieroglyphic system, for example, was partially validated by using Cailliaud's accurate copy of the inscription on the pedestal of the obelisk from Philae. This system was first, and most famously, put to use by deciphering the cartouches on the Rosetta Stone. Champollion cited Cailliaud's copy of the obelisk inscription when he presented his "Lettre à Monsieur Dacier," a document considered to be the birth certificate of Egyptology, before the Académie des inscriptions et belles-lettres on 27 September 1822. Similarly, Cailliaud's copy of the Abydos Kings' List allowed Champollion to establish a chronology for the rulers of Egypt. Between 1822 and 1832, a collaboration between Cailliaud and the decipherer of Egyptian hieroglyphs gradually came into being. It began with the insertion of Champollion's treatise on the funerary equipment of Padimenipet in Cailliaud's *Travels to Meroe*, continued through a list of tips given by Cailliaud to the Champollion brothers prior to the younger's Franco-Tuscan expedition of 1828–29, and is evident in the publication of Cailliaud's *Research on the Arts and Crafts*, which uses a number of plates made from work done during the Franco-Tuscan expedition.

Cailliaud's contribution to the birth and development of Egyptology was not limited to his close collaboration with the Champollion brothers. Indeed, the collections brought back to France through his efforts provided new material for understanding pharaonic civilization. In addition to the funerary equipment from Padimenipet, certain items from Cailliaud's collection, in particular the epigraphic documents, were examined by Théodule Devéria (1831–71) and François Chabas (1817–82). Both were Egyptologists and epigraphers who eventually published the ostraca[70] collected by Cailliaud. Similarly, Cailliaud's accounts of his travels, his plans, his drawings, and his map of Egypt and Nubia proved to be valuable records, not only for his contemporaries, but for modern-day Egyptologists. His findings were used, for example, in the compilation of the very first travel guides to Egypt,[71] and still serve as historical eyewitness accounts for a number of archaeological sites in Egypt and Sudan.

The objects that Cailliaud brought back also found a place in his scientific work. As a whole, these artifacts are considered to be one of the most important collections of Egyptian antiquities brought to France in the first half of the nineteenth century. Along with their scientific worth, they also contributed to the development of French museum heritage. Some of these objects are today recognized as masterpieces of pharaonic art and form the cornerstones of several museums. With few exceptions, however, modern-day information on these antiquities has been unavailable, a result of their turbulent museological histories and uncertain provenances. Until recently, it seemed an impossible task to reconstruct from where these objects came and how they got to their current museums. Research was, nonetheless, undertaken to trace the paths these objects followed after their arrival in France in Cailliaud's luggage, up to their present-day locations. After an exhaustive museological investigation, 335 objects brought from Egypt by Cailliaud, and distributed among French museums, were identified.[72] The task of identifying them was complicated by a lack of descriptions of antiquities in Cailliaud's own inventories, and by a lengthy period of dispersal, which spanned nearly a century and a half. It should be noted that the antiquities identified were those depicted in Cailliaud's own books or those that had benefited from more advanced descriptions in inventories and archives. Even though the group of objects identified is only a portion of the one thousand objects brought back by Cailliaud, the results obtained from this study form an important step forward in our understanding of his work, particularly when one considers the difficulties in gathering information on this collection.

The majority of Cailliaud's antiquities are now kept in three institutions: the Musée Dobrée in Nantes, with 126 objects; France's Bibliothèque nationale, with seventy-four objects, and the Louvre's Department of Egyptian Antiquities, with sixty-three objects. The respective origins for these holdings stem from Cailliaud's 1869 bequest to the archaeological museum of his hometown and the purchase of part of his collection by the Bibliothèque royale between 1819 and 1824, part of which was housed in the Louvre in 1907. The recent study of Cailliaud's collection not only allows us to reconstruct the museological history of these objects, it also provides us with important information on the locations of the objects' discovery. This information, in turn, allows us to clarify certain historical points regarding excavations in the Theban necropolis between 1815 and 1822: firstly, through the provenance of objects brought to light; and secondly, through the drawings of tomb-wall scenes copied by

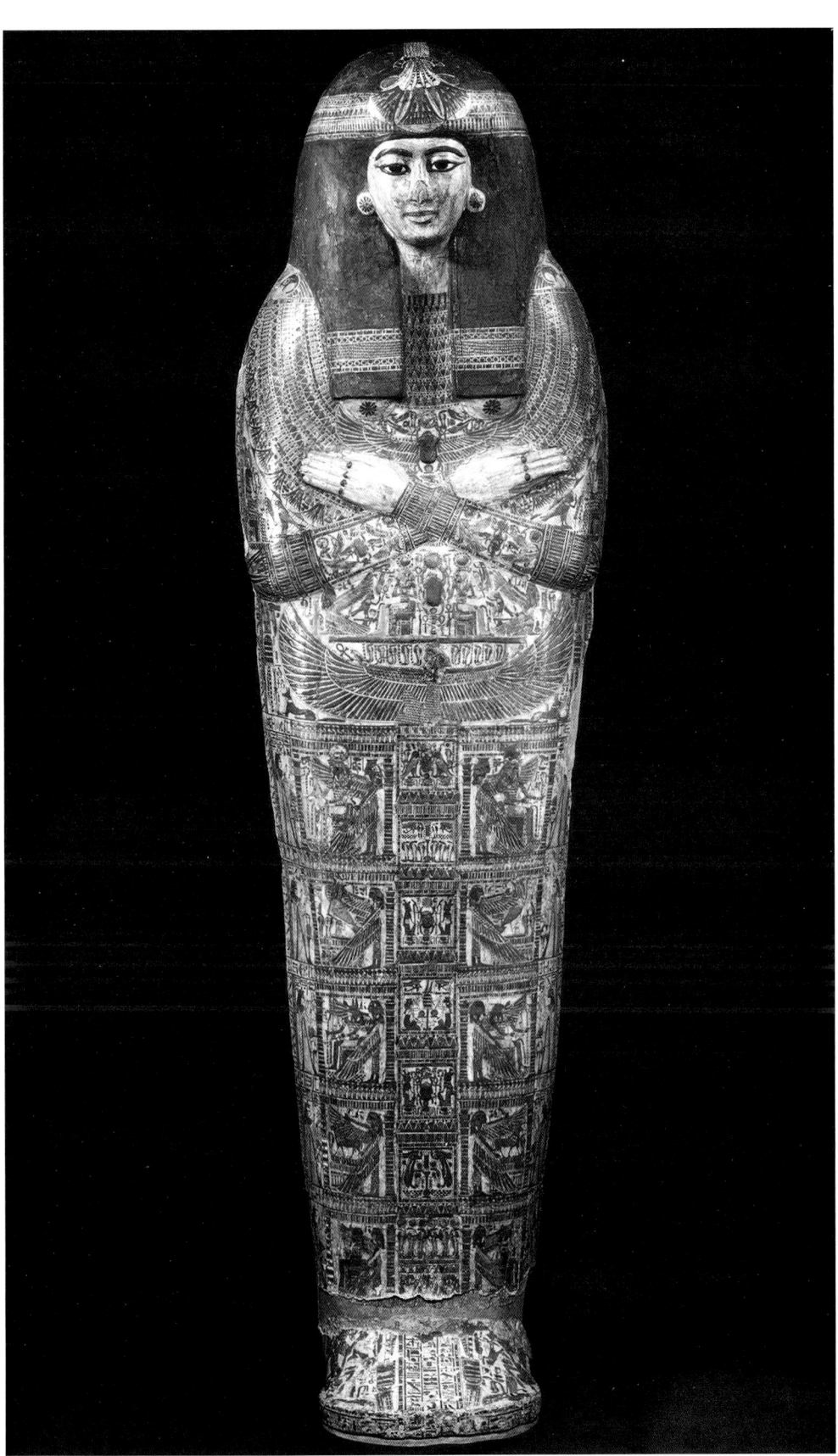

8 Inner coffin of
Tanethereret, Louvre
Museum E 13034.
*Courtesy of the
Louvre Museum,
Paris. Photographed
by G. Poncet.*

Cailliaud and reproduced in his *Arts and Crafts* and, now, in this book. One example of such a clarification concerns the unprovenanced sarcophagus and mummy cover of the singer of Amun-Re, Tanethereret (fig. 8).[73] We are now able to attribute this object to the Cailliaud collection from a vignette depicted in this book's plate 23, and which adorns the outer surface of the coffin.

This recent research into Cailliaud's work also allows us to develop a framework of sponsors, institutions, and other figures who contributed to the construction of antiquarian knowledge. This framework, in turn, can be used to assess European motives and actions in Egypt in the first half of the nineteenth century. French government interest in Egypt during this period was largely manifested through a policy that funded and protected travelers and scientists under the reigns of Louis XVIII and Charles X. This was assisted by a second policy of acquiring works of art and archaeological objects to further knowledge and move learning out of the realm of the theoretical. This policy enabled objects that represented such knowledge to be tangibly materialized in French society—that is to say, objects that were used in the construction of French museum heritage. The government's interest in the history of Mediterranean civilizations was also manifested in the works and patronage of leading scientific institutions, such as the Académie des inscriptions et belles-lettres, which, in turn, supported travelers like Cailliaud. This institution should be considered one of the crucibles of Egyptology as a result of the historical and philological debates that it held in the first two decades of the nineteenth century. A poignant example of such debates is Champollion's presentation of his hieroglyphic system in 1822.

While similar to cabinets of curiosities,[74] Cailliaud's collection differs in his concern that his objects be useful to contemporary scientists. Even so, his collection was not appreciated for its true value. It was largely composed of small objects and, as a result, could not compete for attention with the large antiquities and more extensive collections amassed by wealthy Europeans, such as the British consul Henry Salt or the French consul Bernardino Drovetti. Unlike the Cailliaud material, the objects collected in Egypt by Salt and Drovetti, which had no unifying scientific imperative behind them, were quickly sold to European museums. Many of the objects from these collections are now considered masterpieces of the British Museum, the Turin Museum, and the Louvre. In addition, having been deposited in the Bibliothèque royale, now the Bibliothèque nationale, the Cailliaud collection could not hope to attract much attention after the opening of the Louvre's Egyptian Museum in 1826, which was partly formed from Salt's and Drovetti's collections. Cailliaud's collection was, as a result, relegated to the background before gradually being forgotten. During its time, however, it was the most important collection by a French traveler between Napoleon's Egyptian expedition of 1798 and the antiquities amassed during August Mariette's excavation of Memphis' Serapeum in 1852. The collection is noteworthy not only for its historical interest, but also for the quality and variety of its objects, which give it enormous anthropological value.

Upon his arrival in France, Cailliaud returned to his hometown and rose to the position of assistant curator in Nantes' Muséum d'histoire naturelle in 1826. His role as mineralogist for Muhammad Ali and his discovery of the emerald mines of Mount Zubara gave him standing in the scientific world and were instrumental in his disciplinary conversion. He became director in 1836 and then devoted himself to his two new areas of focus: mineralogy and conchology, in which he was one of Europe's leading specialists right up until his death in 1869.

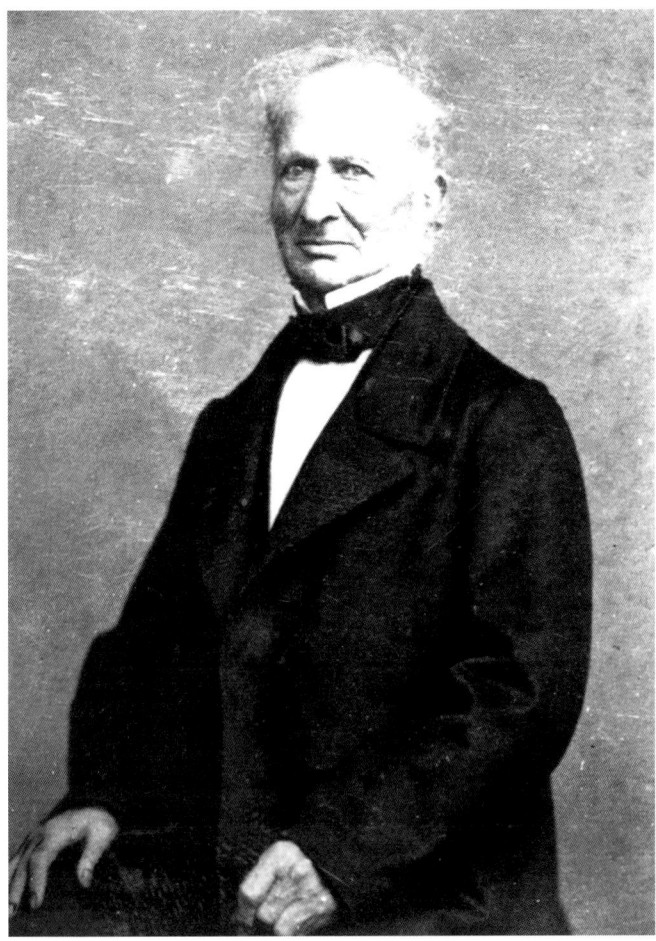

9 Photograph of Frédéric Cailliaud, 1860s. *Courtesy of the Muséum d'histoire naturelle, Nantes.*

By 1822, Cailliaud had begun planning a book on the arts and crafts of the ancient Egyptians, using the material he had collected and the drawings he had made in the temples and tombs during his two trips to Egypt. To realize his project, he eventually solicited the help of the Champollion brothers, the younger of whom returned to France in 1830 after his Franco-Tuscan expedition to Egypt. Unfortunately, as discussed below, Cailliaud's publication project was continually disrupted and was only ever partially completed.

A link between Cailliaud and the Champollion brothers may have been created by Jomard, who presented pieces from Cailliaud's first collection to the elder Champollion in May 1820. This association was likely strengthened by the brothers' repeated praise for the publication of Cailliaud's work. At the same time, the documentation Cailliaud provided for the decipherment and elaboration of the hieroglyphic writing system cemented this link and reinforced Cailliaud's contributions to the nascent field of Egyptology. It comes as no surprise, therefore, that while preparing his ultimate work dedicated to Egypt, his *Arts and Crafts*, Cailliaud solicited the help of Jean-François Champollion to obtain copies of wall scenes made during his Franco-Tuscan expedition. As a result, we find about twenty images in *Arts and Crafts* that were directly taken from the plates of *Monuments of Egypt and Nubia*, the brainchild of the younger Champollion and Ippolito Rosellini.[75] These images had been initially sent to Cailliaud by Jean-François Champollion himself, then by Jacques-Joseph Champollion-Figeac upon the death of his brother in 1832. It is for this reason that one can see under several of the images in *Arts and Crafts* the following phrase: "Sent by Mr. Champollion the younger."

A careful study of these plates and a comparison with those of *Monuments of Egypt and Nubia* allows us to identify the original artists of the images that the Champollion brothers sent to Cailliaud. They included works by Alessandro Ricci (d. 1834), Nestor l'Hôte (1804–42), Salvatore Cherubini (1797–1869), Giuseppe Angelelli (1803–44), Ippolito Rosellini (1800–43), and Pierre Lehoux (1813–83). Cailliaud also collaborated with Champollion-Figeac in 1839, giving him permission to reproduce several plates, most notably those from the tomb of Neferhotep, from *Travels to Meroe* in his work *Ancient Egypt*.[76]

Cailliaud's *Arts and Crafts* was destined for chaos. An article by Champollion-Figeac appeared in the *Bulletin Férussac* in 1832, announcing its imminent production and the form it was supposed to take. In the article, Champollion commented on Cailliaud's historical and scientific observations. The technique of using tracings with annotations for coloring still visible on the original drawings allowed for very precise reproductions. As Champollion's article announced, the individual collections of plates would appear between 1831 and 1836. The work comprised a total of eighty-nine plates, of which ten were printed in a double-size format. Unfortunately, only one hundred copies of these illustrations were printed, and, of these, about half were destroyed when the building in which they were being stored collapsed. As a result, *Arts and Crafts* is nowadays a rare work to find in public libraries or private collections. Cailliaud's friend, Baron Girardot (1815–83),[77] kept the collection of copper plates used to engrave *Arts and Crafts* upon Cailliaud's death, but these have yet to be recovered. The text meant to accompany the plates was reworked many times by Cailliaud in the last years of his life. Among the Cailliaud archives in Nantes' Muséum d'histoire naturelle is one of the handwritten versions of this work, entitled *Research on the Arts and Crafts, and the Manners of Civic and Domestic Life, of the Ancient Peoples of Egypt, Nubia, and Ethiopia*.[78] This version was originally divided into nine books, the second of which has disappeared. A detailed study of this collection of books makes it clear that it was a French adaptation of John Gardner Wilkinson's *Manners and Customs of the Ancient Egyptians*.[79] This first project was aborted in favor of subsequent versions, one of which is based largely on Cailliaud's own research and reflections. It is this later version that forms the core of the work now published in this volume.

Correspondence between Cailliaud and François Chabas, kept in the Institut de France, tells us something of this final project. In 1866, while he was curator at Nantes' Muséum d'histoire naturelle, Cailliaud worked on editing a new version of text for his *Arts and Crafts* and a new explanation of his plates. As he was unable to decipher hieroglyphs, Cailliaud turned to Chabas, one of the period's specialists, giving him his work on Egyptian tombs and sending him his tracings. Cailliaud asked him to decipher the name of the owner of the tomb that contained the four gold vases that he had copied in Thebes during his travels and that were reproduced in his *Arts and Crafts*, on plates 24 and 24a. This tomb owner's name is read as Imiseba, owner of tomb 65 in Sheikh Abd al-Qurna.[80] It is also to Chabas that we owe the reading of the name of Tanethereret, in plate 23, the translation of the captions for the carpenters in plate 5, and the translation for the captions from the tomb of Nedjemger, plate 65 figure 1, in the Theban necropolis.[81]

Cailliaud, who saw the progress being made in the new science of Egyptology, appears to have admired Chabas's work.[82] It is interesting to note that Cailliaud never referred to himself as an Egyptologist. His interest in natural history and mineralogy, already evident in his youth, was developed in Egypt and ultimately captured his attention, never to let him go after his return to France. His ignorance of the hieroglyphic writing system, unlike other contemporary travelers such as Wilkinson, only further distanced him from Egyptology. Cailliaud remained, nevertheless, in direct contact with the world of Egyptology through his correspondence and through his subsequent friendship with the Champollion brothers and Chabas. These people eventually paid homage to him as a pioneer in the study of Egyptian civilization. At the end of his life, Cailliaud handed on to his son the task of publishing his final Egyptological work, but he never managed to fulfill his father's wishes.[83] At long last this book remedies this error, bringing to light the lost masterpiece of an important traveler, scientist, and historian.

1   Anatolia is both a historical and a geographic term that refers to the westernmost portion of Asia. It encompasses the majority of Turkey and is demarcated by the Black Sea to the north, the Aegean Sea to the west, the Mediterranean Sea to the south, and the Armenian highlands to the east.

2   Constantinople was the capital of the Ottoman Empire and is today called Istanbul.

3   Dominique Vivant, Baron Denon (1747–1825) was a French artist, writer, diplomat, and antiquarian. He was appointed as the first director of the Louvre by Napoleon after the Egyptian campaign of 1798–1801.

4   The *Description de l'Égypte* was a multi-volume publication, the first part of which appeared in 1810 and the last part of which appeared in 1829. The work offered a comprehensive, scientific description of ancient and modern Egypt, including its natural history. It is the collaborative work of about 160 civilian scholars and scientists who accompanied Napoleon's expedition to Egypt between 1798 and 1801.

5   Cailliaud's travels in Egypt have been reconstructed using journals he made during his journeys, now kept in Nantes' Natural History Museum: Frédéric Cailliaud, "Journal du premier voyage en Nubie de Frédéric Cailliaud avec le chevalier Drovetti en 1816"; Frédéric Cailliaud, "Journal du voyage au désert en Egypte supérieure (1816–1818)"; Frédéric Cailliaud, "Journal du second voyage en Egypte à Méroé et au fleuve blanc (octobre 1819—avril 1822)." For further bibliographic information on Cailliaud's work and travels see: Philippe Mainterot, *Aux origines de l'égyptologie. Voyages et collections de Frédéric Cailliaud (1787–1869)* (Rennes: Presses Universitaires de Rennes, 2011); Michel Chauvet, *Frédéric Cailliaud, les aventures d'un naturaliste en Égypte et au Soudan 1815–1822* (Saint-Sébastien-sur-Loire: ACL, 1989).

6   See Ronald T. Ridley, *Napoleon's Proconsul in Egypt: The Life and Times of Bernardino Drovetti* (London: Rubicon Press, 1998).

7   When Louis XVIII was restored to the French throne after the defeat of Napoleon Bonaparte.

8   A title given to translators and interpreters, from the Arabic *targama*.

9   These archaeological sites are located in Middle and Upper Egypt. Abydos, Dendara, Kom Ombo, and Philae are famous for their temples. Luxor is the modern name for ancient Thebes, and is famous for its temples and necropolis on the west bank of the Nile. During his first journey to the necropolis, Cailliaud visited some royal and private tombs with Drovetti, where he found a Late Period sarcophagus. This object was the first important piece of his antiquities collection. Elephantine is an island settlement site located beside the modern city of Aswan.

10 Official permissions to carry out a task. The word is derived from a Persian word used to designate an order or decree from a pasha of the Ottoman Empire.

11 The obelisk of Ptolemy VIII, now in the park of Kingston Lacy House in Great Britain. See Thomas H.G. James, *Egyptian Antiquities at Kingston Lacy, Dorset: The Collection of William John Bankes* (San Francisco: KMT Communications, 1993–94).

12 The temple of Edfu is located on the west bank of the Nile. In the Greek and Roman periods it was known as Apollonopolis Magna. It is the second-largest standing temple in Egypt, after Karnak, and one of the best preserved. The temple is dedicated to the falcon god Horus and was built in the Ptolemaic period between 237 and 57 BC.

13 Kanayis is a rock-cut temple built under the reign of Seti I, on the ancient road linking the Nile Valley to the gold mines in the Eastern Desert. It is also known as Redesiya or Wadi Abbad Temple.

14 A British traveler and collector who visited Egypt, Nubia, and Syria between 1815 and 1819. He assembled a large collection of Egyptian antiquities now kept at Kingston Lacy House in Dorset.

15 Somerset Lowry-Corry, second Earl of Belmore, traveled extensively in Egypt between 1816 and 1818. He excavated in the west of Thebes and ascended the Nile as far as the Second Cataract. He also traveled through Syria and Palestine. He amassed a considerable collection of antiquities that he brought to England and prepared for publication. He later brought a second large collection of antiquities, intended for Henry Salt, to England. The majority of Belmore's objects were purchased by the British Museum in 1843.

16 Comte Auguste de Forbin was a painter, art writer, and traveler who became the general director of museums at the Louvre and Musée de Luxembourg. He visited Egypt between 1812 and 1818, and again in 1828, to acquire antiquities for the Louvre.

17 Champollion's official results on the decipherment of hieroglyphs were presented at the Académie des inscriptions et belles-lettres on 14 September 1822, in the famous document entitled "Lettre à Monsieur Dacier relative à l'alphabet des hieroglyphes phonétiques." The principles on which this system was based, however, were debated well into the later half of the century.

18 Numbered KV 11. The initials KV stand for Kings' Valley. Bertha Porter and Rosalind L.B. Moss, *Topographical Bibliography of Ancient Egyptian Hieroglyphic Texts, Reliefs, and Paintings. I. The Theban Necropolis. Part 2. Royal Tombs and Smaller Cemeteries* (Oxford: Clarendon Press, 1973), 518.

19 Numbered A5 in Bertha Porter and Rosalind L.B. Moss, *Topographical Bibliography of Ancient Egyptian Hieroglyphic Texts, Reliefs, and Paintings. I. The Theban Necropolis. Part 1. Private Tombs* (Oxford: Clarendon Press, 1960), 448.

20 See Deborah Manley and Peta Rée, *Henry Salt: Artist, Traveller, Diplomat, Egyptologist* (London: Libri Publications Ltd., 2002).

21 Numbered KV 17. See Porter and Moss, *Topographical Bibliography I.2*, 535.

22 'Young Memnon' was the name given to the bust section of a colossal statue of Ramesses II from his funerary temple, known colloquially as the Ramesseum, on Luxor's west bank. It was cut from a single block of bichromal granite. Ramesses is shown wearing the traditional cloth headdress of a pharaoh, surmounted by a cobra diadem. Belzoni transported the 7,500-kilogram (16,535-pound) bust from the Ramesseum to Thebes after seventeen days of work, with the help of 130 people. He sent it to Cairo by boat, then to the British Museum, where it is now kept under the acquisition number EA 19.

23 Giovanni Belzoni, *Narrative of the Operations and Recent Discoveries in Egypt and Nubia* (London: John Murray, 1820), 110. See also Jean-Jacques Fiechter, *La moisson des dieux* (Paris: Julliard, 1994), 63.

24 For example: "Mr. Caliud [sic] meditated more mischief before his departure." Belzoni, *Narrative of the Operations,* 248.

25 "Mr Jaques [sic] [Rifaud], who had parted from the others and was alone, came to us and, by way of exculpating himself, said that Caliud [sic] was the man who mutilated the figure with his little hammer, which he always carried with him to break stones." Belzoni, *Narrative of the Operations*, 248.

26 Examples include a relief from the Theban tomb of Niay (TT 286), a scribe of the table, kept in the Louvre (E 13108). Porter and Moss, *Topographical Bibliography I.2*, 819.

27 "He introduced the little story of the pipe made by Caliud [sic] and sold as an antique to Mr. Salt, laughed much, and wondered how a person so full of knowledge could suffer himself to be so easily deceived by a Frenchman. I told him that anyone might well be deceived, as we bought many things from the peasants, good and bad together in lots, without even looking to see what they were, till they were brought home." Belzoni, *Narrative of the Operations*, 287. See also Louis de Forbin, *Voyage dans le Levant en 1817 et 1818* (Paris: Delaunay, 1819), 268–69.

28 The Ababda, or Ababdeh, are a nomadic people. They live in the region between the Red Sea and the Nile, in the area of Aswan.

29 An ancient temple site, known as Latopolis from the Greek period onward, located on the west bank of the Nile, some 55 kilometers (34.2 miles) south of Luxor.

30 The temple of Dush was probably erected under the reign of the Roman emperor Domitian, enlarged by Trajan, who added a courtyard, and then partly decorated and further enlarged by Hadrian. A monumental stone gateway fronts the temple and contains a dedicatory inscription by Trajan dated to AD 116, as well as graffiti by Cailliaud and other nineteenth-century travelers.

31 Located in Kharga Oasis, Hibis Temple was built from local limestone for the god Amun. It is the largest temple dating to the Persian periods in Egypt.

32 Before the creation of the Louvre's Department of Egyptian Antiquities in 1826, all archaeological objects acquired by the government were kept in the Cabinet du roi, formerly the Cabinet des médailles, within the Bibliothèque royale, now called the Bibliothèque nationale de France.

33 Pierre-Constant Letorzec served in the French navy until 1819, when he accompanied Cailliaud on his second journey to Egypt. On his return to France, he became a captain in the French merchant marine. He died in Nantes.

34 See Ahmed Fakhry, *Siwa Oasis* (Cairo: American University in Cairo Press, 2005).

35 The Faiyum Oasis is a depression and drainage basin for the Nile, located about 130 kilometers (81 miles) south of Cairo.

36 A temple of Jupiter-Amun built by King Nectanebo II. Only part of the façade remains, as much of the rest was destroyed during an earthquake in 1811.

37 Muhammad Ali's desire for captured slaves was in keeping with the economic and domestic life of Cairo at this time. Egypt supported a thriving slave trade in the early nineteenth century, with slaves forming an integral part of society. While slaves were brought from many parts of the Mediterranean, to be sold or used, a large number were brought over long distances overland from other African nations. For further information on this topic from a contemporaneous source, see Edward William Lane, *An Account of the Manners and Customs of the Modern Egyptians: Written in Egypt during the Years 1833, –34, and –35, Partly from Notes Made during a Former Visit to That Country in the Years 1825, –26, –27, and –28* (London: Charles Knight and Co., 1836).

38 An area south of Khartoum in Sudan.

39 Canopic jars were used by the ancient Egyptians during the mummification process to store and preserve the viscera of the deceased. There were four jars, each meant to maintain specific organs. Each jar was associated with one of the Four Sons of Horus: the intestines with Qebesenuef, a falcon-headed god; the stomach with Duamutef, a jackal-headed god; the lungs with Hapi, a baboon-headed god; and the liver with Imseti, a human-headed god.

40 In ancient Egypt, stelae were inscribed slabs of stone or wood, usually with a rounded top. They were placed in temples, with a dedicatory or documentary inscription, or in tombs, with an inscription naming the deceased and invoking offerings meant to sustain them in the afterlife.

41 A *shabti*, also spelled as *shawabti* or *ushabti*, was a statuette intended to work on behalf of a dead person when the person was called upon to do manual labor in the afterlife. They are usually in mummy form, inscribed with the deceased person's name and spell number six from the *Book of the Dead*, which magically activated them.

42 An assemblage kept in the Louvre's Department of Egyptian Antiquities, comprising the mummy and its sarcophagus (E 13016 and E 13048), the funerary shroud (E 13382), a beaded mesh covering (E 13218), and the funerary crown (E 13417).

43 Magistrate charged with the administration of a city.

44 In addition to this small band of Europeans was an American, George Bethune English, a former U.S. artillery officer from Cambridge, Massachusetts. He entered the service of the Egyptian army prior to the expedition south and published an account of his travels in 1822. See George Bethune English, *A Narrative of the Expedition to Dongola and Senaar* (London: John Murray, 1822).

45 Ancient Meroe gave its name to the Island of Meroe, the modern region of Butana, which is an area bounded by the Nile from the Atbarah river to Khartoum, the Atbarah, and the Blue Nile. For further information on Meroe, see Michel Baud, ed., *Méroé, un empire sur le Nil* (Paris: Louvre, 2010). Regarding the plot against him, Cailliaud writes: "The night of the 30th, a Piedmontese doctor, in the service of Isma'il Pasha, came to notify me that they sought for me to lose favor with the prince . . . they succeeded, thus, in persuading the prince, and he decided that I would not follow the expedition. The purpose of my detractors was to make this journey themselves, or to bring enough delays so that they could arrive before me at the theater of antiquities." Frédéric Cailliaud, *Voyage à Méroé, au Fleuve Blanc, au-delà de Fazoql, dans le midi du royaume de Sennar, à Syouah et dans cinq autres oasis* (Paris: Imprimerie royale, 1826–27), 278.

46 Semna and Kumma were two parts of a series of fortresses established during the Twelfth Dynasty in the region of the Second Cataract, in Lower Nubia. Semna was a fortified town established in the reign of Senusret I on the west bank of the Nile. Kumma was built on the opposite shore.

47 Sai is located between the Second and Third Cataracts of the Nile. One of the largest islands in the Nubian Nile, it measures 12 kilometers (7.5 miles) north to south, and 5.5 kilometers (3.4 miles) east to west. It marked one of the southernmost boundaries of pharaonic Egyptian expansion.

48 A temple of the Eighteenth Dynasty, dedicated to Queen Tiyi, wife of Amenhotep III.

49 A temple dedicated to the god Amun and built for the jubilee festival of Amenhotep III.

50 A temple built under the reign of Amenhotep IV/Akhenaten inside a fortress and dedicated to the sun god, Aten.

51 Kerma, now called Dokki Gel, was the capital city of the kingdom of Kerma. It is an archaeological site dating back five thousand years. Kerma marks the settlement site of one of the earliest African civilizations, which, by 1600 BC, commanded an empire that rivaled Egypt and that stretched from the First to the Fourth Cataract.

52 A temple, dedicated to the god Amun, was built on the island during the Twenty-fifth Dynasty. Cailliaud discovered two colossi near this temple.

53 Gebel Barkal is a small mountain located about 400 kilometers (249 miles) north of Khartoum on the shores of the Nile. Its rocky peak would have appeared, to the eyes of the ancient Egyptians, as a manifestation of the god Amun. From certain angles, an outcropping looks like a cobra wearing either a solar disc or the White Crown of Egypt, which were only worn by gods and royalty. The ruins around Gebel Barkal include thirteen temples and three palaces.

54 Philippe Mainterot, "Les Éthiopiens et leur cité fabuleuse dans les récits classiques," in *Méroé, un empire sur le Nil*, ed. Michel Baud (Paris: Louvre, 2010).

55 The kingdom of Sennar, known in Sudanese tradition as the Blue Sultanate, is an English term referring to a geographic and administrative unit in the north of Sudan named Funj, after an ethnic group, or Sennar after its capital. The capital ruled a substantial area of northeast Africa between 1504 and 1821. For further information on Sennar, see John L. Burckhardt, *Travels in Nubia* (London: John Murray, 1819).

56 Cailliaud, *Voyage à Méroé*, vol. 2, 241–42.

57 Naga was a town located on the east bank of the Nile. It now contains the remains of an enormous palace, a temple dedicated to the lion god Apedemak, and a kiosk clearly showing Greek, Roman, and Egyptian stylistic influences.

58 Musawwarat al-Sufra, located some 150 kilometers (93 miles) northeast of Khartoum, is a large site with ruins dating to the time of the kingdom of Kush. The main structure of the site is known as the Great Enclosure. It consists of three main temples, courtyards, passages, and ramps.

59 Cailliaud, *Voyage à Méroé*, vol. 3, 292–96. The scenes to which he refers were later published in Frédéric Cailliaud, *Recherches sur les arts et métiers, les usages de la vie civile et domestique des anciens peuples de l'Égypte, de la Nubie et de l'Éthiopie* (Paris: Debure frères, 1831–37), plates 35 and 37. These plates can be found in this work, under the same plate numbers.

60 See Lise Manniche, *Lost Tombs: A Study of Certain Eighteenth Dynasty Monuments in the Theban Necropolis* (London: KPI, 1988), 43–47; Porter and Moss, *Topographical Bibliography I.1*, 448.

61 Giovanni d'Athanasi, *A Brief Account of the Researches and Discoveries in Upper Egypt* (London: John Hearne, 1836), 106–107.

62 Now kept in the Louvre's Department of Egyptian Antiquities, under accession number E 13101.

63 Cailliaud, *Voyage à Méroé*, vol. 3, 316.

64 Saqqara is a vast, ancient burial ground that serviced the capital city of Memphis. It is located 31 kilometers (19 miles) south of Cairo. The site contains several pyramids, including the famous Step Pyramid of Djoser, and an enormous number of elite burials from nearly every period of ancient Egyptian history. It is one of the most important burial sites for the study of ancient Egypt.

65 See Edmé-François Jomard, *Voyage à l'Oasis de Thèbes et dans les déserts situés à l'orient et à l'occident de la Thébaïde* (Paris: Imprimerie royale, 1821–62); Edmé-François Jomard, *Travels in the Oasis of Thebes, and in the Deserts Situated East and West of the Thebaid: in the years 1815, 16, 17, and 18 by M. Frederic Cailliaud* (London: Sir Richard Phillips and Co., 1822).

66 Jomard's fixation with the highest level of technical perfection, as he demanded with the *Description de l'Égypte,* delayed publication and gave reason for Cailliaud and Jomard's critics to question the work's luxurious publication format. Désiré Raoul-Rochette, for example, stated: "With provision of care and embellishments to this publication, the editor, very innocently, contributed to delays and, consequently, reduced interest." Désiré Raoul-Rochette, "Analyse critique du *Voyage à l'Oasis de Thèbes*," *Journal des Savants* (1822): 361.

67 Cailliaud, *Voyage à Méroé*.

68 On *Travels in the Oasis of Thebes*, Conrad Malte-Brun gives a positive review, stating: "M. Jomard could give to *Travels in the Oasis* the same degree of perfection, with the cooperation of skilful artists whose talent, for twelve years, he encountered in the work of the national book [the *Description de l'Égypte*]. . . . Art competed with science to make this book worthy of the protection of the Government and the suffrage of an informed public." Conrad Malte-Brun, "Analyse critique du *Voyage à l'Oasis de Thèbes*," *Nouvelles Annales des Voyages*, first series, vol. 15 (1822): 101. On *Travels to Meroe*, Malte-Brun similarly states: "Fame has long kept alive the travels of Mr. Cailliaud. We regretted, however, not seeing the account appear, and certain precedents caused us to fear that this publication would be diluted into countless quartos or folios. The two present volumes have dispelled our fears. We find in them an interesting account, simple and clear, free from extraneous discussions, and aimed at the casual observer. They are bereft of false or uncertain erudition, animated by colorful, local truth, and by a sincere, personal, emotional tone that so-called science would ban from this genre of work." Conrad Malte-Brun, "Analyse critique du *Voyage à l'Oasis de Thèbes*," *Nouvelles Annales des Voyages*, second series, vol. 1 (1826): 81.

69 Jean-François Champollion (1790–1832), the decipherer of hieroglyphic, and Jacques-Joseph Champollion-Figeac (1778–1867). Jacques-Joseph was twelve years his brother's elder and passed on a taste for antiquarianism to his younger sibling. Although a great scholar, he remained in the shadows to better showcase his younger brother. After his brother's premature death, Jacques-Joseph published Jean-François' unfinished work, to which he had contributed. The brothers had a rocky relationship with Edmé-François Jomard.

70 Fragments of stone or pottery with writing on them. The ancient Egyptians used such fragments to record a wide variety of things, including letters, lists, and sums. See Charles-Théodule Devéria, "L'Ostracon de la collection Cailliaud," in *Mémoires et Fragments*, ed. Gaston Maspéro (Paris: E. Leroux, 1896–97); François Chabas, "Sur un ostracon de la collection Cailliaud," *ZÄS* 5 (1867).

71 See John Gardner Wilkinson, *Modern Egypt and Thebes* (London: John Murray, 1843); Karl Baedeker, *Egypt, Handbook for Travellers* (Leipzig: K. Baedeker, 1892); Ernest A. Wallis Budge, *Cook's Handbook for Egypt and the Sudan* (London: Thomas Cook and Son, 1906).

72 Mainterot, *Aux origines de l'égyptologie*.

73 Now held in the Louvre (E 13034).

74 Cabinets of curiosities were encyclopedic collections of objects compiled between the sixteenth and eighteenth centuries in Europe. They often included types of objects whose categorical boundaries had yet to be defined. In modern terminology, they could include objects representative of natural history, geology, ethnography, religious or historical relics, works of art, and antiquities. These cabinets were the precursors of modern museums.

75 Jean-François Champollion, *Monuments de l'Égypte et de la Nubie* (Paris: Firmin Didot, 1835–45).

76 Jean-Jacques Champollion-Figeac, *Égypte ancienne* (Paris: Firmin Didot, 1839).

77 Auguste Théodore de Girardot was general secretary of the Loire-Inférieure's prefecture, an administrative unit of the French government now called the Loire-Atlantique, which included Nantes, in 1854. He wrote two biographies of Cailliaud, one in 1859 and the other in 1875.

78 *Recherches sur les arts et métiers, les usages de la vie civile et domestique des anciens peuples de l'Égypte, de la Nubie et de l'Éthiopie* (Paris: Debure frères, 1831–37). It comprises 361 pages and measures approximately 16.5 x 21.5 centimeters (6.5 x 8.5 inches).

79 John Gardner Wilkinson, *Manners and Customs of the Ancient Egyptians. Including their Private Life, Government, Laws, Arts, Manufactures, Religion, and Early History; derived from a comparison of the paintings, sculptures, and monuments still existing, with the accounts of ancient authors* (London: John Murray, 1837–41). Wilkinson (1797–1875) was an English traveler, writer, and pioneer Egyptologist. His *Manners and Customs* was published in three volumes in 1837, subsequently illustrated by Joseph Bonomi (1796–1878), and added to with a second series in 1841. This work stood as the best general treatment of ancient Egyptian history and culture through the second half of the nineteenth century. Acclaim for his work won Wilkinson a knighthood in 1839. He is now recognized as the founder of Egyptology in Great Britain.

80 Porter and Moss, *Topographical Bibliography I.1*, 129.

81 Theban Tomb 138. See Porter and Moss, *Topographical Bibliography I.1*, 251; and the Theban Mapping Project's bibliography for Tomb 138, http://www.tmpbibliography.com/resources/bibliography_5nv_tombs_of_the_nobles_tt138_nedjemger.html.

82 "I published my Egyptian trials long before the many discoveries on the explanation of hieroglyphic." "Lettre de Frédéric Cailliaud à François Chabas," 12 July 1863 (Paris: Bibliothèque de l'Institut de France).

83 Auguste de Girardot, *Frédéric Cailliaud de Nantes, voyageur, antiquaire, naturaliste* (Paris: A. Labitte, 1875), 39.

THE HARER PAPERS

Andrew Bednarski

F rédéric Cailliaud's two Egyptological works, *Travels in the Oasis of Thebes* and *Travels to Meroe*, were groundbreaking. They chronicled his explorations east, west, north, and south, offering detailed accounts of the places he visited, the monuments he examined, and the people he observed. As a result, they provided a wealth of antiquarian, ethnographic, and geographic information on parts of the world little known to Europeans. The first chapter of this study addressed the impact that Cailliaud's work had upon scholarship and general knowledge. It gives concrete examples of how his work helped change the western understanding of ancient Egypt, and how his contributions were received by French scholars. Beyond these examples, though, it is difficult for us, in our twenty-first-century interconnected world of specialist and mass tourism, to appreciate how his work was perceived by a wider nineteenth-century French public. It is hard for us, now, to imagine not being able to visit or find information on even the most remote parts of the planet. The historical equivalent of what Cailliaud did in today's world would, perhaps, be a visit to known but unexplored portions of the moon: entirely possible, given the available technology, but almost inconceivable to the average person, and largely the stuff of heroes and national projects.

Travel accounts by scientific explorers were nothing new in the early nineteenth century, nor were large-format publications on Egypt. Cailliaud's *Travels to Meroe*, however, stands apart from the bulk of such literature by its sheer size, broad scope, and a particular focus on the geology of Egypt and Sudan. By the 1830s, Cailliaud had published his work on Meroe and was waiting for his former patron, Edmé-François Jomard, to complete the editorial work on the second volume of his *Travels in the Oasis of Thebes*. During this time, Cailliaud turned his attention to a different kind of Egyptological publication: something other than an account of his wanderings, something meant to synthesize his experiences. This project changed considerably over the years, with Cailliaud adding to it and reworking it at different points in his life. He called it *Research on the Arts and*

Crafts, and the Manners of Civic and Domestic Life, of the Ancient Peoples of Egypt, Nubia, and Ethiopia, Followed by Details on the Customs of the Modern Peoples of these Countries.[1] As stated in the first chapter of the present work, the visual corpus for this project was ready for publication before the accompanying text. The idea of publishing different portions of a large-scale project at different times, sometimes with great delay between the various sections, was by no means unusual in the early nineteenth century. Delays with such projects were common. As a result, the publication of the images for Cailliaud's *Arts and Crafts*, long before the completion of a final textual draft, would not have been cause for initial concern.

Outside of France, the appearance of these plates, even devoid of commentary, created something of a sensation in English literary and antiquarian circles, as can be seen in the nineteenth-century periodical *The Athenaeum*.[2] In 1837, the year in which the final portion of Cailliaud's plates appeared, the journal carried a long article on ancient Egyptian civilization.[3] The article, divided into three parts, cited biblical passages, classical authors, and the works of nineteenth-century scholars in a discussion on a dizzying number of topics, including ceramics, hunting, fowling, animal husbandry, farming, irrigation, viniculture, fishing, boat building, leatherworking, cordage, shoes, weaving, clothing, glassblowing, woodworking, statuary, economics, games, and musicians and musical instruments. Throughout the article, and for each of the topics just mentioned, images from Cailliaud's plates were used to illustrate the discussion. These images were the result of woodcuts, based upon and reduced in scale from Cailliaud's plates. While *The Athenaeum* produced woodcuts to illustrate other articles in 1837, the thirty-six devoted to recreating images from Cailliaud's plates are a disproportionately higher number than those found in any other article of that year. As a result, it seems fair to say that the money and time invested in reproducing these images, and the fact that they form the basis for the entire broad-ranging article, indicate that both the journal and the reviewer thought very highly of Cailliaud's work. The review also makes it clear that not only were the images informative for the study of ancient Egypt, they were also considered to be a new source of information for general historical inquiry. *The Athenaeum*'s favorable use and assessment of Cailliaud's plates was very quickly translated into French and published in the Nantes journal *Le Breton* between 29 September and 4 November 1837.[4]

Such a positive reception of Cailliaud's work in a British periodical is especially noteworthy when we consider what was written about him at other times. In 1821, for example, *The New Monthly Magazine and Universal Register* reported that Cailliaud's discovery of the emerald mines of Mount Zubara was purely the result of lucky chance.[5] The same article was also dismissive of Cailliaud's description of the site, claiming that Giovanni Belzoni, who had visited it after the Frenchman, would likely give a better account of it. The article reported on Cailliaud setting out for Siwa Oasis and ending up exploring Saqqara. The importance of such a trip to the oasis, however, was dismissed by the author, who claimed that the same journey had already been undertaken by Belzoni.[6] The following month saw *The New Monthly* report positively on Cailliaud's forthcoming publication describing the mines at Mount Zubara and Egyptian antiquities, but couched its report in the context of previous British-based exploration, such as that undertaken by Belzoni and Henry Salt: "The discoveries of Messrs. Burkhardt, Belzoni, Bankes, Salt, &c. have brought our countrymen acquainted with many, or most, of these particulars: nevertheless, we shall await the appearance of M. Cailliaud's volumes with impatience."[7] As if damning through faint praise was not damaging enough, Cailliaud's professional relations were soon called into question by the important *Quarterly Review*.[8] An article in this journal mentioned an attempt on Belzoni's life and accused two of Drovetti's agents as the culprits. What was the reason for the attack? The author claimed it was because Belzoni had contradicted Cailliaud's assertion that Cailliaud had located the ancient site of Berenice.[9]

More vicious criticism of Cailliaud circulated in British periodical literature in the early 1820s. An article in the *Literary Gazette and Journal of Belles Lettres*,[10] for example, goes so far as to criticize both the accuracy of Cailliaud's drawings and, echoing the French criticisms mentioned in chapter 1, the publication format chosen for *Travels in the Oasis of Thebes*. The article, which compares the works of contemporaneous travelers, states:

> M. Letronne mentions the differences between Sir A[rchibald] Edmonstone's drawings
> of the temple at El-Khargeh [Kharga], and those of M. Cailliaud. 'Sir A. Edmonstone (says
> he) assures us that the two large views in M. Cailliaud's travels (pl. 18, 19) give but a very
> imperfect idea of it; this in fact results from a comparison of these plates with the two pretty
> vignettes which accompany his narrative'. To this passage M. L. adds the following note.
> 'Let us here call to mind, for the sake of the sciences and of M. Cailliaud, how much all well-
> informed persons have regretted, that it was determined at all events to make of the shape-
> less sketches *(informes croquis)* brought back by this traveller, large views, engraved by the
> same artists to whom we are indebted for the fine plates in the Description of Egypt'.[11]

The *Quarterly Review* continued this line of criticism with a scathing review of Jomard and Cailliaud's *Travels in the Oasis of Thebes*. To set the stage for its biting remarks, the article gives a rather modest description of Cailliaud as a jeweler from Nantes who was employed by Muhammad Ali to find precious stones in Egypt. With regard to his work, the reviewer states his expectations: "Judging from that portion of the work which appears to be his own, we should set him down as a plain, matter-of-fact man, from whom we may hereafter expect a simple, unadorned narrative of occurrences, and a description of those regions of Africa on the confines of Abyssinia, from which he has not yet returned."[12] The article then proceeds to belittle the work of the French scholars who accompanied Napoleon Bonaparte into Egypt, and the mammoth publication of their findings in the form of the *Description de l'Égypte*. The author claims that, since the time of Napoleon's invasion, it had become common practice for any French traveler to Egypt to submit their findings, however insignificant, to Jomard, the editor of the *Description*, for publication. Cailliaud's contributions to Jomard's *Travels in the Oasis of Thebes* are unceremoniously lumped into this assessment.

> It is a sort of monopoly, to which a Frenchman, so far from resisting, appears most willingly
> to submit; and consigns, without hesitation, whatever remarks he may have collected, to
> the managers of the 'Grand Livre' [the *Description de l'Égypte*], of whom M. Jomard ranks
> in the first class: by him the manuscripts are rédigés [drawn up], and the charts and
> sketches dressés [built up] to correspond with the anterior labours of the savans [the
> scholars who accompanied Napoleon's expedition]; so that it is not always easy to separate
> the observations of the original writer from those of M. Jomard. The travels of MM. Cailli-
> aud and Drovetti, now before us, have undergone this operation, and, scanty as they are,

have been so rédigés et dressés as to render them in their new shape fit companions to that elephantine work, the 'Description de l'Egypte';—a work which M. Jomard modestly assures us, 'has accustomed its readers to that scrupulous fidelity, to that precision and that delicacy of execution, without which, at the present day, no work of the kind could obtain their support!' We have had occasion to notice the 'scrupulous fidelity' which characterizes it; and we shall presently exhibit a few more instances of its pretensions to 'extraordinary precision.' In the meantime, we would just hint to M. Jomard that magnitude is not accuracy, and that in proportion as he increases the size of mere sketches, whether geographical or pictorial, he aggravates their defects.[13]

Although he apparently enjoyed Cailliaud's account in *Travels*, the reviewer specifically mentioned Belzoni's assessment that the mines at Mount Zubara held nothing of any real interest.[14] He then, again, criticized Jomard for attempting to produce the work on the same scale as the *Description*: "Such is the outline of the meagre materials which (with views, and ground-plans, and geographical illustrations, furnished by M. Jomard) have been recorded on paper of a size which no one can approach with comfort, in order, as we have said, to assimilate it with the 'Grand Livre d'Egypte.'"[15] Like *The Literary Gazette* article cited above, the review compared Jomard and Cailliaud's work to Edmonstone's, praising the latter's superiority and claiming that it "conveys more intelligible and accurate information, than the elaborate and pompous volume of the French travellers."[16] Clearly, not everybody appreciated Cailliaud's efforts. I will return to the topic of Cailliaud's work and its relationship with English-language scholarship shortly.

After the publication and distribution of the surviving copies of Cailliaud's plates, his close friend, Baron de Girardot, urged him to finish the intended accompanying text. Cailliaud took this prompting to heart and began reworking his ideas, but passed away before he was able to complete things.[17] As we saw in chapter 1, upon Cailliaud's death in 1869, the uncompleted text for this final Egyptological effort passed into the hands of his son, Auguste Damase.[18] Michel Chauvet states in his biography of Cailliaud that his son did not have the time needed to make sense of this material and rework it for publication.[19] At that point, the manuscript's movement proves difficult to track. Library plates within the collection of material attribute it as once belonging to Charles Thorel, and then Paul Lagrave.[20] Both men were book collectors with an interest in Egyptology. The material reenters the historical record after surfacing in the southern United States, where it formed part of a collection that belonged to "the descendants of a 'Doctor' [*sic*] from the South who had a large library of travel & exploration material, not restricted to Egyptology."[21] Presumably, after the doctor's demise sometime around 2002, the majority of his collection was donated to his local library. The remainder of the items, and possibly those items not considered desirable, were consigned to auction at Christie's in New York. They were, in turn, purchased for an undisclosed amount in December 2002 by two professional booksellers working for their respective companies: Christine Thomson, working for Bernard J. Shapero Rare Books, and Rupert Halliwell of Sims Reed Ltd.[22] Thomson appears to have brought the collection back to Cailliaud's hometown of Nantes sometime in 2004, where it was combined with the remainder of his archival material in the city's Muséum d'histoire naturelle. There, Thomson turned her thoughts toward producing an English translation of the material, but eventually decided against it, given the amount of time needed to work through the papers.[23] In 2005, the decision was made to sell the material once again. Thomson offered the papers to Nantes' Muséum d'histoire naturelle, but it found itself unable to raise the funds necessary to make the material a permanent addition to its archives.[24] As a result, Sims Reed Ltd. decided to exhibit it that same year, along with about one hundred other items, at the International Antiquarian Book Fair at London's Olympia exhibition venue. There it was purchased by a long-time member of the American Research Center in Egypt, Dr. W. Benson Harer Jr. It was Dr. Harer who brought the papers to the attention of ARCE's director, Dr. Gerry D. Scott III, who, in turn, initiated a project to edit, translate, and publish them.

What are these neglected and long-lost papers? The material in question includes eight booklets of text, two drafts of chapters for a work, a mass of written material clearly meant to be reworked into another form, a series of images, and a jumble of notes. All of this material appears to represent Cailliaud's effort to produce a single, broad-ranging work on ancient and modern Egypt. In total, the handwritten material comes to about 1,100 pages, of which the booklets form about seven hundred pages and the two chapter drafts, undefined material, and notes form the remaining four hundred or so pages.

Let us start first with a brief description of the booklets. Seven of these, which measure approximately 16.5 x 22 centimeters (6.5 x 8.7 inches), present a sometimes flowing, sometimes fragmented narrative on ancient Egyptian civilization. They are extremely easy for a reader to navigate, as the topics covered on every page are written at the top of that page. These subject headings demonstrate the ambitions of the author, as they indicate the broad number of topics covered within. Appendix 2, at the end of this book, offers a summary of these headings. The pages are numbered in red pencil, although these were, perhaps, added at a later date. Written in the same hand as the two chapter drafts of text, these booklets are organized with the following titles: Volume 1, second series, first book; Volume 1, second series, second book; Volume 2, second series; Volume 3, first book; Volume 3, second book; Volume 3, third book; Volume 3. A clue to what these booklets are, and how they relate to the rest of the Harer Papers, is offered by the use of the subtitle "second series." In the archives of Nantes' Muséum d'histoire naturelle are eight surviving booklets from what was originally a series of nine.[25] These booklets, written by Cailliaud, cover subjects similar to those found in the Harer Papers' booklets. These booklets are also structured like the Harer Papers' booklets, with subject headings written at the top of every page. Also, like the Harer Papers' booklets, the Nantes booklets rely heavily on classical sources, with Cailliaud's personal observations interspersed throughout.[26] It is for these reasons that Dr. Philippe Mainterot, who catalogued the Nantes archives, believes they predate the booklets in the Harer Papers.[27] Cailliaud's system for producing a work seems to have involved laboriously writing his ideas out in multiple drafts. With every draft his ideas became better structured, and, as we will see with the other material in the Harer Papers, as Cailliaud's thinking matured, his reliance on classical and biblical texts diminished. It would appear, therefore, that the Nantes museum has the earliest surviving version of Cailliaud's effort to produce a synthetic work on ancient and modern Egypt. The later, and presumably more developed, surviving version of this effort takes the form of the series of booklets within the Harer Papers.

In addition to this series, the Harer Papers contain an eighth booklet, measuring approximately 20.5 x 26.5 centimeters (8.1 x 10.4 inches) and comprising twelve pages. Unlike the series of other booklets contained in the papers, which at first glance make no mention of Cailliaud's images, this booklet is solely devoted to portions of Cailliaud's published plates. Entitled *Notes on the Egyptian Antiquity Plates of Mr. Caillaud* [sic],[28] the booklet offers short explanations on some of the scenes in some of the published plates.[29] How does this booklet relate to the rest of the papers? It apparently had little initially to do with Cailliaud's work itself, as on page 12 we find a sentence that begins with "These drawings of Caillaud [sic]." This sentence and the initial title of the booklet make it likely that it was written by someone other than Cailliaud, quite possibly after his death.

The next section of the Harer Papers takes the form of drafts of chapters in various stages of completion. It is these chapters that are reproduced in the following section of the present book. As the chapters rely far less on classical sources and far more on contemporaneous scholarship and his own observations, it is reasonable to conclude that these chapters were Cailliaud's attempt to rework many of the ideas he committed to his series of booklets. Twenty such chapters were obviously intended, but only eighteen have been edited and reproduced in the following section, as the text for chapter 19 has disappeared from the collection and chapter 20 was not worked into a usable state, nor does it refer to any of the accompanying plates, unlike the other chapters. In total, there are two drafts of each chapter, an earlier and a later draft, with the exception of chapters 6.1, 6.2, 6.3, 9, 11, 15, and 18. Only a single draft of each of these has survived.

The chapter drafts are written on paper of different sizes, sometimes roughly A4 sized, sometimes roughly A3, with lines that run both vertically and horizontally. Curiously, many of the pages seem to be covered in a lightly sparkling substance that, when the paper is touched, ceases to catch the light in the same way. While the text of the chapters is written in black ink, references to corresponding plates are underlined in red ink. The two drafts of the manuscript are easy to differentiate by the chapters' title pages; usually the backs of pages with the heading "Prefecture of the Loire-Inférieure."[30]

The earlier drafts of each chapter generally have title pages stating the name of the project, Cailliaud's name, the subject covered in the chapter, and then one of the following: "second manuscript"; "copied author's manuscript"; "author's manuscript"; "of the author"; and "Cailliaud's manuscript." In contrast, the title pages for the later drafts usually state Cailliaud's name, the name of the project, the subject of the chapter,[31] then: "2nd copy"; "2nd copy of the author's manuscript"; "2nd copy of his manuscript"; and, for chapter 16, "copy of his manuscript." For these later drafts, though, it is important to note that the "2nd" in "2nd copy" and "2nd copy of author's manuscript" is written and underlined in red, and was very likely added later. With this fact in mind, the lack of a "second" in front of chapter 16's "copy of his manuscript" seems less suspicious. Not every draft of every chapter, however, has a title page that conforms to these parameters. The title page for chapter 6, for example, states "not copied manuscript." As only one draft of this chapter exists in the Harer Papers, it seems safe to assume, therefore, that this chapter was never copied into a later form. Like chapter 6, chapter 9 is only contained in a single draft and has a title page that states only the subject of the chapter. The title page of the second draft of chapter 17 states only the chapter number, the chapter's topic, and a page range. Chapter 18 is contained in a single draft with a title page bearing only the number 18 on it. In contrast, no text has survived at all for chapter 19; all we have left is a surviving title page stating the intended topic: "The Army, Expedition, and Enrollment." Chapter 20 is another single-draft chapter, albeit an extremely fragmentary one, which has its contents crudely listed with the number 20 on its title page. At what point in the papers' history were these title pages created and modified? We simply do not know. As the reader will see in the following section, the lengths of the chapters differ greatly depending on the subject matter. The shortest is chapter 11, with the original French text on cordage amounting approximately to a mere 350 words. Chapter 14, "On the Extraction and Use of Metals," is by far the longest at approximately eight thousand words. While the discrepancy between the lengths of chapters might be due to the incomplete nature of the work, the primacy of chapter 14 is most likely the direct result of Cailliaud's specialization in mineralogy, a focus also reflected in his *Travels to Meroe*.

In addition to these drafts of chapters, the Harer Papers contain several texts in far less completed stages of production. Given the cursory state of chapter 20, I have included this chapter in this category. The topics of these chapters-to-be are just as varied as those presented in the more developed drafts, and can be roughly divided into the following categories: sacred music, priests, oracles, and musical instruments; sculpture; war and conquest; navigation; commerce and produce for export; chronology; the priest; temples; religious administration; oracles; quarries and quarrying; quarrying of granite; a description of the cataracts by Edmé-François Jomard, Cailliaud's one-time patron; and explanations of images not published in Cailliaud's original plates. Of these tentative chapters, only Jomard's description of the cataracts makes any valid reference to Cailliaud's published plates. When the intended topics of these early chapters are combined with the more developed chapters, we can appreciate just what an impressive breadth of knowledge Cailliaud was trying to convey.

The style of the actual chapters can be slightly daunting for anyone not acquainted with nineteenth-century writing. I promise readers, though, that if they can persevere beyond the opening sentence, they will be rewarded, as Cailliaud's language generally descends from its initial lofty prose. The style of Cailliaud's introduction, however, is not out of place for a work of its kind. He starts by making his goal, to explore the history of human development, explicit: "In search of sating its primary needs in the immense richness of nature, human intelligence could not have foreseen the varying knowledge at which it would arrive, and the development of today's industry, well perfected as it is." If we compare this opening sentence with that of John Gardner Wilkinson's contemporaneous *Manners and Customs of the Ancient Egyptians*, we can see similarities in both goal and style: "In order to form an accurate opinion of the manners of an ancient people, it is of paramount importance to inquire into their origin and history, and to trace the progress of those steps which gradually led to their improvement and civilization."[32] This similarity between Cailliaud's and Wilkinson's texts is the result of more than coincidence. According to Mainterot, the draft of Cailliaud's work in the Muséum d'histoire naturelle is largely a translation of portions of Wilkinson's work.[33] If the chronology of the manuscript put forward here, from booklets in Nantes, to booklets in the Harer Papers, to chapters in the Harer Papers, is valid, then what we can observe is the transformation of Cailliaud's work from simple translations to a broad-ranging, thematic encyclopedia. An investigation into the changing form and content of Cailliaud's work within these different versions, however, is not within the scope of this book.

What is within the scope of this project is an examination of the two later chapter drafts within the Harer Papers, and their relationship to Cailliaud's visual corpus. These chapter drafts appear to comprise Cailliaud's final effort to provide his published plates with a written account. The drafts and the wealth of information they contain were made possible by the sheer amount of data Cailliaud had recorded: from his notes and journals, to his extensive published travel account south, to the lengthy earlier booklets found in Nantes and the Harer Papers. Cailliaud's own words perhaps best explain his attention to detail and his desire to record, as mentioned in a discussion on the pyramids of Meroe:

> Without a doubt, some readers will find that I enter into very minute detail on that which I have seen, on that which I have observed: but they would do well to reflect that these details will not be lacking in interest to the eyes of travelers who go in droves to visit Egypt; it is very likely that, after a while, there will not be found a single person who had more time than me to explore the lands through which I traveled.[34]

Cailliaud's tendency to record as much as possible and rehash his ideas in multiple drafts left him with large amounts of written material with which to work. Yet the text of the later chapter drafts was not the result of him simply repeating old ideas. His descriptions of a gold cup in both *Travels to Meroe* and *Arts and Crafts*, for example, are similar, but different enough to support the assertion that while he reworked his material, he also updated and reconsidered his ideas.[35] The same can be said about his observations of wooden locks in Sudan,[36] his assessment of how the ancient Egyptians mourned their dead,[37] how modern craftsmen along the Nile used their feet as skillfully as their hands while working,[38] and, most noticeably, in his descriptions of the fowling scene from the tomb of Neferhotep.[39]

While the chapter drafts appear to embody the last surviving version of Cailliaud's thoughts on his plates, they remain, regrettably, incomplete. The degree of incompleteness and how far along a chapter was in the editorial process differs from chapter to chapter. As mentioned above in the description of the title pages, most chapters had an earlier and a later draft. The following section of this book is composed of the latest version of each chapter, with occasional commentary on aspects of the earlier version when available. My goal has not been to complete the later drafts, but, instead, to present them in the state in which they were left. As a result, readers of the French transcription will note that, occasionally, Cailliaud's grammar, punctuation, and spelling are incorrect. Also, for ancient Egyptian words, Cailliaud's spelling was frequently inconsistent. On this last point, such variations might have been the result of chapter drafts being written at different points in time. I have tried to avoid correcting errors as much as possible without ruining the flow of how the text scans. I have, however, made several exceptions to this rule. Just as Cailliaud was inconsistent in his use of punctuation, he was also inconsistent with starting the first word of a new sentence with a capital letter. For the ease of readership, after the clear use of a period, I have changed the first lower-case letter of a word found at the beginning of a sentence to an upper-case letter. I have also added periods before the clear use of capital letters to begin new sentences on new lines. In other instances of capitalization, however, I have let Cailliaud's text continue to tantalize. He repeatedly capitalizes certain nouns, such as the names of animals in chapter 1. This use of capitalization, and his consistent use of semicolons in the French text, occasionally gives the reader the feeling that Cailliaud is scientifically enumerating what he observed. Was this his intention? Another correction that I have permitted myself relates to Cailliaud's consistent omission of accents on French words that begin with "e." Rather than continually present words such as "Égypte," "Égyptien,"

"égyptien," and "Éthiopie" without their accents, which looks strange to a modern reader, or present these words without their accents and with an editor's note after each instance, I have chosen to present them with their accents. For other words with accents, I have given Cailliaud the benefit of the doubt: I have transcribed words with their correct accents, provided Cailliaud made an effort to put some sort of mark above that letter. I have also moved the location of parentheses to the correct side of commas when a clause and parenthetical reference coincide. Presumably, many of these problems would have been corrected at a later date, prior to publication.

Another aspect of the incomplete nature of the chapter drafts is the fact that not all of the plates published by Cailliaud are referenced.[40] The majority of those that are not, however, clearly coincide with those subjects visible in the chapters-to-be. The subjects depicted in the numerous unpublished images within the Harer Papers also reflect, either intentionally or accidentally, the subjects of these intended chapters. One example of a body of text meant to be reworked into a chapter and referring to a plate is found in Jomard's section on the Nile cataracts. The text in this section specifically references Cailliaud's plate 14 when discussing how Egyptian quarrymen navigated large stones. While the chapter drafts provide us with a wealth of information, it is clear that much work still needed to be done at the time of Cailliaud's death.

The chapter drafts reproduced in the following section are the result of a very long process. Cailliaud first recorded information included in his chapter drafts while he was a young man in Egypt. The majority of his work was later reformatted into his two famous publications. Some of this information was then combined with inspiration from Wilkinson's *Manners and Customs*, which led to the creation of the booklets in Nantes and then, presumably, the Harer Papers. Finally, we have the chapter drafts. How much information, aside from possibly chapter 19, has been lost since the time of Cailliaud's death is impossible to say. Nonetheless, the totality of the information available to scholars in the form of Cailliaud's published and unpublished material presents future researchers with a staggering amount of information with which to reconstruct Cailliaud's thoughts and work. The opportunity that the Nantes archives and Harer Papers afford for investigations into the development of a nineteenth-century scientific text is, as a result, truly remarkable.

An analysis of the earlier and later chapter drafts demonstrates how fruitful future inquiry such as this can prove to researchers who want to understand Cailliaud's scholarship and the editorial processes of his time. Tantalizing glimpses into how Cailliaud strove to represent himself in his work, for example, are quickly visible when we compare these two drafts. Throughout the drafts, Cailliaud repeatedly changes references to some of his accomplishments. In the earlier draft of chapter 1, for example, Cailliaud describes the fowling scene of Neferhotep's tomb, stating, "It is in a tomb at Qurna, in the territory of Thebes, that I copied these most curious scenes."[41] In the later draft of the chapter, however, Cailliaud crossed out "I," substituting it for "we."[42] Such a deliberate change is surprising as Cailliaud's original account of his work in the tomb, recorded in his *Travels to Meroe*, accords all of the credit to him.[43] Similar changes are rife throughout the chapters,[44] even though, at other times, Cailliaud readily employs the personal pronoun "I." Nowhere is this editing more glaring, however, than in chapter 16, in a passage discussing the murder of Isma'il Pasha and his entourage:

> We were fortunate enough to be able to draw these remarkable subjects from the 23rd
> to the 25th of March 1822, a period which preceded the return of the Turkish army that

we left in Ethiopia. Well we returned alone to Egypt, as, upon the return of his expedition, Prince Isma'il, his doctor, and several of his people were massacred and burned. A deplorable fate that we, undoubtedly, would have shared.[45]

The first sentence of this passage originally read "I was excited . . . to take these remarkable subjects from the 23rd to the 25th of March 1822, before the return of the Turkish army that I left in Ethiopia. Well I returned alone to Egypt . . . . A deplorable fate that I, undoubtedly, would have shared."[46] The original passage, coupled with its changes, is striking. Unlike the previous corrections in his chapter drafts, Cailliaud is not talking about work, such as copying a tomb scene, that might be attributed to him alone. Cailliaud's traveling companion, Letorzec, was with him throughout the Nubian campaign and left Sudan with him for Egypt, albeit in an enfeebled state. There is no way that, historically, Cailliaud can be considered to have "returned alone to Egypt." What prompts a person to take sole credit for work earlier in life, and then develop a more inclusive vocabulary when recounting the same incident later in life? What prompts someone to systematically correct the recounting of several accomplishments in this way? Are we seeing the corrections of an older man, secure in his station and the acceptance of all he has done, now willing to include the work of others in his historical record?

The chapter drafts are filled with other examples of Cailliaud changing his mind while writing. Chapters 4, 5, 6.2, and the rough drafts of certain plates all make references to images from a tomb in Beni Hasan, supposedly owned by a man named Rotei.[47] In chapter 12, however, Cailliaud states: "These subjects come from a tomb in Beni Hasan, where there was inhumed an important individual from the Old Kingdom, named Kheli, and not Rotei as we had firstly written."[48]

In chapter 14, we also find Cailliaud referring to the "rich baris of Amun-Ra,"[49] but it is only in chapter 15 that he explains the meaning of the word 'baris' to the reader.[50] Also in chapter 14, while discussing a pyramid in Meroe, Cailliaud relates how the military leader of his expedition, Prince Isma'il, expressly forbade him from excavating, as he did not want his army to be seen as impious by the locals. "In any case," writes Cailliaud, "we would not have destroyed one of the most beautiful monuments of ancient Meroe."[51] Yet, in chapter 2, Cailliaud laments the fact that the he had been unable to dig into the pyramid, stating: "We regretted not being able to penetrate the tombs of Meroe and Napata."[52] Lastly, Cailliaud alternates between an imperial system of measurement and the metric system. The two drafts contain frequent corrections of units from imperial to metric, but we also find instances where use of the imperial system was left uncorrected. Chapter 14, in fact, contains both units in different descriptions.[53]

These and other changes give the reader the feeling that s/he is witnessing a work in progress, something developing before one's eyes. When, then, were the chapter drafts written and reworked? At what point in his life did Cailliaud begin the chapter drafts, when did he rework them, and when was the last time he touched them? Unfortunately, the Harer Collection offers few answers to these questions. During his time in Egypt, Cailliaud was undoubtedly inspired to create a work that dealt with aspects of everyday life in ancient Egypt, using tomb scenes to illustrate his thoughts. In a passage in *Travels in the Oasis of Thebes* he states how instructive these images were for understanding ancient Egyptian history, customs, and arts.[54] The fact that he recorded scenes focused less on divine themes and more on themes of, albeit stylized, hunting, fowling, and production further supports the notion that he wanted to produce a work of this sort. This collection of scenes was later augmented by similar images given to him by the Champollion brothers for the express purpose of publication. Cailliaud's images were then published between 1831 and 1837, a period which coincided with two important publications by Wilkinson. In 1835, Wilkinson published his *Topography of Thebes, and General View of Egypt*.[55] The work provided one of the best scholarly accounts of Egypt, both ancient and modern, available at the time of its publication. Despite its title, the work addressed more than Egypt's topography, as it contained sections on the daily life of the ancient Egyptians, with one chapter in particular entitled "The Manners and Customs of the Ancient Egyptians." It was this material that formed the basis for Wilkinson's later *Manners and Customs of the Ancient Egyptians*.[56] By the time *Topography* appeared in 1835, in fact, it contained an announcement for *Manners and Customs*,[57] which was published two years later. We know that Wilkinson's efforts at describing the everyday life of the Egyptians inspired Cailliaud's booklets in Nantes, the first evidence we have of him writing a work of this sort. It appears that these booklets led to those contained in the Harer Papers and they in turn led to the chapter drafts. Such a chronology brings us to the late 1830s as the earliest formal starting point for the creation of Cailliaud's chapter drafts, the final form his work would take. As one can see in the following section, the chapter drafts cite information from numerous publications from the mid-1830s right up to 1865. Also, as stated in chapter 1, we know that Cailliaud corresponded with François Chabas in 1866 in an attempt to finish his work. These letters deal almost exclusively with Cailliaud's efforts to prepare both an explanation of and text for his *Arts and Crafts*.[58] As you will see in the following section, Cailliaud gives full credit to Chabas for the translations that he used. While this timeline does not tell us exactly when Cailliaud started and stopped his work, it is clear that he diligently incorporated a fair amount of contemporaneous scholarship from the 1830s through to the 1860s, and that he worked on his material almost up to his death in 1869.

A curious element to the chapter drafts is the fact that two distinct hands are clearly visible throughout. The changes in hand sometimes occur between chapters or between an earlier and later draft of a chapter. Sometimes the hand changes in mid-chapter[59] and, occasionally, even in mid-sentence.[60] Sometimes a portion of text is written in one hand, while the corrections made to that text are done in another.[61] Mainterot believes both of the hands visible in the chapter drafts belonged to Cailliaud, and claims to have seen multiple instances of such changes throughout Cailliaud's written work in the Nantes archives.[62] Why he changed hands and at what point he did so might help future research to establish a system of progression for the creation of these drafts.

This chapter has highlighted some of the challenges of publishing the Harer Papers and the chapter drafts contained within it: how best to represent the differences between the earlier and later drafts; the incomplete nature of the work; the questions surrounding the dates on which it was worked; and, therefore, the context in which it was written and the sources of information available to Cailliaud. Yet another issue should be made explicit in any attempt to publish the material. The information contained in the Harer Papers has been reworked many times, and thus gives us insight into the editorial process through which it went in the nineteenth century. By taking a portion of the papers and printing it in a comprehensible format, I have added to the editorial process and possibly moved a step further away from some of Cailliaud's intentions: by inserting text, by deleting sections of text, through the process of translation, by adding footnotes, by adding commentaries, and by framing information in a specific layout within a book very much of the twenty-first century. While I hope that I am completing one of Cailliaud's goals by publishing the work, this final product is perhaps different from what he would have produced.

Aside from publishing a text to accompany and explain his plates, Cailliaud's academic goal is clear from the opening page of his work. His words make explicit that he wanted to chart the "progress of industry," the development of mankind's use of its environment thousands of years before defining moments in western civilization. What were such moments to Cailliaud? The chapter drafts tell us that they included the Trojan War, Greek and Roman civilization, and the birth of Christ. From this perspective, we can view Cailliaud as very much a product of his time, a scholar deeply affected by the Enlightenment and an expanding European worldview. The early to mid-nineteenth century, after all, still bore witness to European colonial ambitions. It was also the period in which the sciences, as we recognize them today, began to formalize. Further still, the early 1800s was a time in which the authority of the Bible was brought under scrutiny, and mankind's place in world history was reassessed. During this period, previously unknown sources of historical information were revealed to European audiences, and the tools with which to find and make sense of them—archaeology, philology, and comparative studies—developed rapidly. As a result, Cailliaud's interest in and focus on Egypt was not unusual. By the time of his travels, Egypt was already considered one of the oldest civilizations in history and a source of new information that might change European understanding of human development. Cailliaud's methodology for exploring what he perceived to be the earliest sources of information on civilization was to combine examinations of tomb scenes with archaeological exploration and observations of the modern Egyptians.

During the period in which Cailliaud wrote his chapter drafts, similar methodologies could be found in the works of other writers. I have already mentioned Wilkinson's works, which were the product of twelve years of living among local populations, learning Arabic, and exploring and recording the monuments of Egypt. It is clear that Cailliaud drew inspiration from Wilkinson, whom he met in Egypt while studying monuments at Akhmim.[63] Cailliaud's later chapter drafts contain several references to Wilkinson's work: chapter 5 paraphrased information on hops and the papyrus plant from his writings, and chapter 7 cited him on the topic of pyramid construction. The earlier draft of chapter 5, though, gives further insight into what Cailliaud thought of Wilkinson. In this draft he deferred to Wilkinson on the topic of Nile alluvium and then mentioned the role he intended him to play in his work: "A most distinguished archaeologist savant, through his important publications on Egypt, Mr. Wilkinson will often be our guide and our interpreter in this work."[64] This and a second reference, referring to wine residue samples examined by Wilkinson,[65] were omitted from the chapter's later draft. Another scholar who combined extensive travels through Egypt with investigations into monuments, and a narrative involving both ancient and modern peoples, was Edward William Lane.[66] His recently published *Description of Egypt*, for example, was meant to be a treatise on ancient Egyptian civilization. Its narrative described monuments throughout the country and originally contained studies of Egypt's modern inhabitants. It was this latter material that Lane used to build his famous *An Account of the Manners and Customs of the Modern Egyptians*.[67]

Cailliaud kept his goal of understanding the development of mankind's technological and social developments at the forefront of his mind while writing. His chapters on woodworking, glassmaking, and metalworking make explicit both his opinion of and the means by which he evaluated Egyptian material. In this we can once again view Cailliaud as a product of both his time and his culture, as his yardstick for evaluating such things is decidedly European. In chapters 9, 12, and 14 of the following section, he discusses production techniques used by the ancients, commenting that similar techniques were still used in France. In chapter 10 he compares a certain style of Egyptian basket to one still found in France during his lifetime. A rather charming passage in chapter 5 goes so far as to compare the Egyptian practice of carrying items on a pole with those of Dutch milkmaids. Such comparisons would only have made his description of aspects of ancient Egyptian civilization more comprehensible to nineteenth-century readers. Cailliaud's expected Eurocentric approach is particularly evident in chapters 12 and 14, where he praises the good "taste" of the ancient Egyptians, claiming that their furniture and jewelry could rival the elegance of such items found in Europe during his lifetime.

The publication of the Harer Papers combines, for the first time, Cailliaud's sensational visual corpus, documenting the world of the ancient and nineteenth-century Nile, with his never-before-seen text. The result is much more than a traveler's account of Egypt and Sudan in the nineteenth century. Cailliaud's lavishly illustrated study of Nile civilization was produced on the heels of Napoleon's invasion of Egypt, amid the colonial scramble for influence abroad, at a time when European scientific inquiry was developing new intellectual tools with which to question the origins and place of mankind in the world, and by a man who rose to become a central figure in French scholarship. Cailliaud's *Arts and Crafts* presents a unique glimpse into cutting-edge early-nineteenth-century scientific and colonial exploration by one of Europe's top minds. The result offers an exciting snapshot: a broad-ranging work in progress, frozen in mid-effort. It is a pleasure to be able to take Cailliaud's work from obscurity and present it as a new source for professional, amateur, ancient, and modern historians alike.

Cailliaud's original French text can be accessed via the URL and the QR code at the end of the table of contents, p. viii.

---

1   *Recherches sur les arts et métiers, les usages de la vie civile et domestique des anciens peuples de l'Égypte, de la Nubie et de l'Éthiopie, suivies de détails sur les mœurs des peuples modernes de ces contrées.*

2   Launched in 1828 by James Silk Buckingham, *The Athenaeum* attempted to provide a moral work for readers that would fight against materialism. It became an important vehicle for the spread of culture in the Victorian era. The editors' views on literature and art were romantic, and the literary opinions expressed were usually liberal and mild. Its overall tone was enthusiastic and youthful, with a hint of optimistic reform. It was particularly interested in the popularization of science. By the 1830s, it had a well-established connection to French literature, having introduced a series of foreign correspondence in the 1820s. See Leslie A. Marchand, *The Athenaeum: A Mirror of Victorian Culture* (New York: Octagon Books, 1971), 2–24.

3   "Reviews. Egyptian Antiquities. *Recherches sur les Arts &c. des anciens peuples de l'Egypte, &c.* Par M. F. Cailliaud. Paris, Dubure; London, Dulau & Co.," *The Athenaeum. Journal of English and Foreign Literature, Science, and the Fine Arts*, no. 507 (Saturday 15 July 1837): 513–16; "Egyptian Antiquities. [Second Notice.]," *The Athenaeum*, no. 508 (Saturday 22 July 1837): 533–37; "Egyptian Antiquities. [Third Notice.]," *The Athenaeum*, no. 509 (Saturday 29 July 1837): 550–53.

4   Auguste de Girardot, *Frédéric Cailliaud de Nantes, voyageur, antiquaire, naturaliste* (Paris: A. Labitte, 1875), 40.

5   Created by Henry Colburn in 1814, *The New Monthly* was meant neither as a political weapon nor as an aid to the arts. Instead, it served as a corrective to Bonapartist sympathies. The journal was not intended to be bound

to any political party, but, instead, to act as a record and chronicle of the times. It was meant to be acceptable to philosophers and scholars, to businessmen, and to men of leisure. As such, it regularly mentioned foreign works on a variety of subjects. See Ruth Hiller, Linda Dobbins, and Linda Jones, "The New Monthly Magazine, 1821–1854: Introduction," in *The Wellesley Index to Victorian Periodicals 1824–1900*, vol. 3, ed. Walter E. Houghton (Toronto: University of Toronto Press, 1979).

6   "Foreign Varieties. France," *The New Monthly Magazine and Universal Register*, vol. 13, part 1 (1 April 1820): 480–81.

7   "Foreign Varieties. France," *The New Monthly Magazine*, vol. 13, part 1 (1 May 1820): 589.

8   Founded in 1809 to combat the Tory *Edinburgh Review*, it offered its many readers solid articles and essays describing as many works of current literature as possible. It presented these pieces, encompassing all areas of knowledge, in a non-specialist, almost encyclopedic format. Unlike other British magazines of this period, the *Quarterly* was a sound, scholarly work, making it all the more damning for an academic to receive a poor review in it. Its editorials were generally conservative, but this conservatism could be broad and its criticisms of literature and art are the stuff of a great periodical. It regularly ran articles on foreign, particularly French, works. See Esther Houghton, Priscilla Ross, and Mary Wallace, "The Quarterly Review, 1824–1900," in *The Wellesley Index to Victorian Periodicals*, ed. Walter E. Houghton (Toronto: University of Toronto Press, 1966); Joanne Shattock, *Politics and Reviewers: The* Edinburgh *and the* Quarterly *in the Early Victorian Age* (London: Leicester University Press, 1989), 3–13.

9   Berenice was an ancient city on the Red Sea. For the *Quarterly Review* article, see: "Art. III—*Voyage dans le Levant en 1817 et 1818*. Tome I. Large folio. Par le Comte de Forbin. Paris," *Quarterly Review*, vol. 23 (May and July 1820): 94.

10 Founded by Henry Colburn in 1817, it provided extracts from expensive books and periodicals at a price that was affordable to working- and middle-class groups. Its topicality grabbed readers' attention, providing a sense of immediacy that monthly and quarterly periodicals could not match, as it consistently reviewed new works as soon as they were published. For its first fifteen years, it wielded greater authority for a larger number of readers than the more respectable journals; a favorable review often ensured good sales, while a negative review typically hurt a work's profit margins. It targeted the less rigorous tastes of the novel-reading populace, providing lengthy sections on books that often spanned several issues, but it did not limit itself to literary news and reviews. Its articles are usually labeled condemnatory or appreciative, rather than analytical. Its genius was that it gave less wealthy readers an immediate and extensive familiarity with the latest literature, including French works. See Jonathan Topham, "Thomas Byerley, John Limbird, and the Production of Cheap Periodicals in Regency Britain," *Book History 8* (2005); Jonathan Topham, "'The Mirror of Literature, Amusement and Instruction' and Cheap Miscellanies in Early Nineteenth-century Britain," in *Science in the Nineteenth-Century Periodical: Reading the Magazine of Nature*, ed. Geoffrey Cantor et al. (Cambridge: Cambridge University Press, 2004); Alvin Sullivan, *British Literary Magazines, the Romantic Age, 1789–1836* (Westport: Greenwood Press, 1983), 242–44.

11 "Arts and Sciences. Egypt: The Oases," *The Literary Gazette and Journal of the Belles Lettres*, no. 343 (Saturday 16 August 1823): 522.

12 "Art. III—1. Voyage à l'Oasis de Thèbes et dans les Déserts situés à l'Orient et à l'Occident de la Thébaïde, faits pendant les Années 1815, 1816, 1817 et 1818. Par M. Frédéric Cailliaud; et le Voyage à l'Oasis du Dakel; par M. Le Chevalier Drovetti, Consul-Général de France en Egypte; rédigé et publié par M. Jomard, &c. Fol. Paris," *Quarterly Review* 28 (October 1822–January 1823): 60.

13 "Art. III—1. Voyage à l'Oasis de Thèbes," 62–63.

14 "Art. III—1. Voyage à l'Oasis de Thèbes," 63–66.

15 "Art. III—1. Voyage à l'Oasis de Thèbes," 67.

16 "Art. III—1. Voyage à l'Oasis de Thèbes," 67.

17 de Girardot, *Frédéric Cailliaud de Nantes*, 39.

18 Cailliaud's final message to his son made him the executor of his manuscripts on his trips to Egypt. See Michel Chauvet, *Frédéric Cailliaud, les aventures d'un naturaliste en Égypte et au Soudan 1815–1822* (Saint-Sébastien-sur-Loire: ACL, 1989), 340; and de Girardot, *Frédéric Cailliaud de Nantes*, 39.

19 Chauvet, *Frédéric Cailliaud, les aventures d'un naturaliste en Égypte et au Soudan 1815–1822*, 340.

20 The reference to Lagrave may be to a successful French architect who was born in 1864 and died in 1933.

21 Personal correspondence with Rupert Halliwell, 24 June 2009.

22 Personal correspondence with Rupert Halliwell, 10 January 2011.

23 Personal correspondence with Christine Thomson, 26 February 2008.

24 Personal correspondence with Béatrice David of the Nantes Muséum d'histoire naturelle, January or February 2008.

25 Boîte 3, no. 28.

26 Chauvet, *Frédéric Cailliaud*, 340.

27 Personal correspondence with Philippe Mainterot, 22 June 2009.

28 *Notes sur les planches d'antiquités égyptiennes de Mr. Caillaud* [sic].

29 More specifically, aspects of the following plates are described: 1, 2, 5a, 9, 9a [mislabeled as 9], 11, 12, 13, 15a, 16, 17, 17a, 20, 21a [mislabeled as 21], 21b, 22, 23, 29b, 31, 33a, 35, 37, 37a, 38, 40, 63, and 65.

30 This department, now called Prefecture of the Loire-Atlantique, is an administrative unit of the French government.

31 The chapter titles sometimes follow a Latin tradition for titles by using the following formula: on + [chapter subject]. For example: chapter 11, "Du cordier / On Cordage."

32 John Gardner Wilkinson, *Manners and Customs of the Ancient Egyptians. Including their Private Life, Government, Laws, Arts, Manufactures, Religion, and Early History; derived from a comparison of the paintings, sculptures, and monuments still existing, with the accounts of ancient authors*, vol. 1 (London: John Murray, 1837–41), v.

33 Philippe Mainterot, *Aux origines de l'égyptologie. Voyages et collections de Frédéric Cailliaud (1787–1869)* (Rennes: Presses Universitaires de Rennes, 2011), 211.

34 Frédéric Cailliaud, *Voyage à Méroé, au Fleuve Blanc, au-delà de Fazoql, dans le midi du royaume de Sennar, à Syouah et dans cinq autres oasis,* vol. 2 (Paris: Imprimerie royale, 1826–27), 175.

35 Compare Cailliaud, *Voyage à Méroé*, vol. 3, 330, with what is written in *Arts and Crafts*, chapter 2.14.

36 Compare Cailliaud, *Voyage à Méroé*, vol. 2, 101, with *Arts and Crafts*, chapter 12.

37 Compare Cailliaud, *Voyage à Méroé*, vol. 2, 282, with *Arts and Crafts*, chapter 17.

38 Compare Cailliaud, *Voyage à Méroé*, vol. 2, 292, with *Arts and Crafts*, chapter 12.

39 Compare Cailliaud, *Voyage à Méroé*, vol. 3, 292–93, with *Arts and Crafts*, chapter 1.

40 The following plates are not referenced by the later chapter drafts: 7, 11, 12, 13, 14, 17, 17a, 18, 19, 25a, 29a, 39, 40, 40a, 41a, 42, 43a, 43b, 58, 66.

41 Harer Papers: earlier draft of chapter 1, page 4, note 5.

42 Harer Papers: later draft of chapter 1, page 4.

43 Cailliaud, *Voyage à Méroé*, vol. 3, 292–93.

44 See Harer Papers: later draft of chapter 2, page 5, note 1; later draft of chapter 4, page 3; later draft of chapter 10, pages 1 and 4; later draft of chapter 12, page 3; and later draft of chapter 14, page 1.

45 Harer Papers: later draft of chapter 16, page 4.

46 Harer Papers: later draft of chapter 16, page 4.

47 Harer Papers: later draft of chapter 4, page 6; later draft of chapter 5, page 9; only draft of chapter 6.2, page 1.

48 Harer Papers: later draft of chapter 12, page 14.

49 Harer Papers: later draft of chapter 14, page 10.

50 Harer Papers: later draft of chapter 15, page 7.

51 Harer Papers: later draft of chapter 15, page 19.

52 Harer Papers: later draft of chapter 2, page 5.

53 See Harer Papers: later draft of chapter 14, page 29, for inches cited in a discussion of bronze discs; later draft of chapter 14, pages 5, 23, 31, 36, and 37, for the use of centimeters.

54 Edmé-François Jomard, *Voyage a l'Oasis de Thèbes et dans les déserts situés à l'orient et à l'occident de la Thébaïde*, vol. 1 (Paris: Imprimerie royale, 1821–62), 81–82.

55 John Gardner Wilkinson, *Topography of Thebes, and General View of Egypt. Being a Short Account of the Principal Objects Worthy of Notice in the Valley of the Nile, to the Second Cataract and Wadee Samneh, with the Fyoom, Oases, and Eastern Desert, from Sooez to Berenice; with Remarks on the Manners and Customs of the Ancient Egyptians and the Productions of the Country, &c. &c.* (London: John Murray, 1835).

56 Jason Thompson, *Sir Gardner Wilkinson and His Circle* (Austin TX: University of Texas Press, 1992), 133.

57 Thompson, *Sir Gardner Wilkinson*, 141.

58 Michel Dewachter, "Introduction. Un pionnier de l'égyptologie: Mourad Effendi, alias Frédéric Cailliaud," in *Frédéric Cailliaud. Les aventures d'un naturaliste en Égypte et au Soudan*, by Michel Chauvet (Saint-Sébastien: ACL–Crocus, 1989), 40.

59 For example, Harer Papers: earlier draft of chapter 1, page 7.

60 For example, Harer Papers: later draft of chapter 5, page 15.

61 For example, Harer Papers: later draft of chapter 8, pages 3–4.

62 Mainterot has noted that such changes in hand are particularly evident in Cailliaud's notebooks, stored in the archives of the Muséum d'histoire naturelle in Nantes.

63 Cailliaud, *Voyage à Méroé*, vol. 3, 305.

64 Harer Papers: earlier draft of chapter 5, page 9.

65 Harer Papers: earlier draft of chapter 5, page 10.

66 Edward William Lane (1801–76) was an important Arabist and student of the Near East. His *An Account of the Manners and Customs of the Modern Egyptians: Written in Egypt during the Years 1833, –34, and –35, Partly from Notes Made during a Former Visit to That Country in the Years 1825, –26, –27, and –28* (London: Charles Knight and Co., 1836) was twinned with Wilkinson's *Manners and Customs of the Ancient Egyptians* to form an authoritative study of Egypt in the mid-1800s. See Jason Thompson, *Edward William Lane, 1801–1876: The Life of the Pioneering Egyptologist and Orientalist* (London: Haus Publishing, 2010), 398.

67 Edward William Lane, *Description of Egypt. Notes and views in Egypt and Nubia, made during the years 1825, –26, –27, –28: Chiefly consisting of a series of descriptions and delineations of the monuments, scenery, &c. of those countries; The views, with few exceptions, made with the camera-lucida*, ed. Jason Thompson (Cairo: American University in Cairo Press, 2000), xviii–xxi.

The Arts and Crafts of the Ancient Egyptians, Nubians, and Ethiopians

CHAPTER 1

FOWLING[1]

I n search of sating its primary needs in the immense richness of nature, human intelligence could not have foreseen the varying knowledge at which it would arrive, and the development of today's industry, well perfected as it is.

Animals alone might attend to the base necessities of man by offering him drink, food, and durable clothing. How many peoples still know of nothing else? Even those who were in direct communication with a great nation such as Egypt 4,000 years ago have still changed nothing in this primitive custom. The hide of a sheep, worn around the hips, is still the only piece of clothing for the Blacks[2] of the great region of Bertat, located to the east of Fazoql.[3]

We will try to follow the progress of industry by starting with the simplest of works which must have satisfied the basic needs of man. Hunting was the first of his pursuits. We will start with that of birds before proceeding to the many, formidable quadrupeds. Of all the species for fowling, that of wild geese and ducks was, without exception, the most productive and the most common among the ancient Egyptians. The sculptures of temples and the paintings of tombs show us these scenes in the greatest detail. We cannot doubt that

---

1 This page begins with two notes by Cailliaud, one after the other: "It might be necessary to omit the preamble (1st page) if this chapter is not the first"; "Consider whether or not we should leave the section on the artificial incubation of eggs. This is well known today and it is not found represented in the plates—at least I have not seen it."

2 The French word used by Cailliaud translates directly to 'Negro.'

3 A region between the Blue Nile and Sobat river, along the border of present-day Sudan and Ethiopia. It was here that Cailliaud and his expedition searched for gold deposits.

the number of these aquatic birds was much greater than remains today. Reeds, and more especially *Cyperus*,[4] used by the Egyptians in various works and in the creation of paper, were common in the Nile Valley, in lakes, in the marshes of Lower Egypt, and in particular areas of habitation, and offered easy shelter for these birds. The intelligent hunter was almost always certain of encountering his prey there. Such a hunt is thus generally represented to us amid these plants.

To better move about the marshes, often shallow and choked with numerous plants, the Egyptians used small papyrus barques of an extremely light construction (Herodotus).[5]

According to Plutarch, one had nothing to fear of crocodiles when using these boats.[6] This presumption might naturally be explained by the use of the boats in waters rarely frequented by this animal.

The Egyptians do not appear to have adopted the bow for such hunting, perhaps as a result of the uncertain target offered by a bird?

The first hunters must have thrown rocks to gain their prey. This primitive method is found in Egyptian paintings (pl. 35, fig. 1). Here we see the hunter on a light barque approaching a papyrus forest covered with birds. In his left hand he holds a heron by its feet, whose cries must have attracted the game.

With the right hand, the hunter throws at the geese, aiming for their neck, with a slightly curved piece of wood.[7] This instrument, 50 centimeters long, was specially made for this purpose. It was flat and rounded. Its size and curvature is close to that of the back leg of a gazelle. Many of these instruments were found in the tombs of Thebes and are exhibited in the museums of Paris, Turin, and Berlin.

This simple process leads us to think that it must have been easy to approach these birds in order to surprise them and to hit them as they rose from their lairs. This hunt is found faithfully represented by the rich, colored details in the tombs of the ancient Theban necropolis. We have reproduced them here. Tall stalks of *Cyperus papyrus* are flush with geese and other birds. A group flutters about the tops of the plants, having created their nests and laid their eggs. Many of these birds brood, others give food to their young, already hatched. Chameleons and an ichneumon come to eat the eggs, but the mothers are attentive and one of them, opening a large beak, rushes upon one of the reptiles.

The hunter, named Neferhotep, appears to be of a high social status. He is standing on a barque, surrounded by his wife and their children. He throws the above-mentioned projectile at the geese and two are caught. Domestic servants already have others in their

---

4 *Cyperus papyrus.*
5 See Herodotus, *The Histories, Revised* (London: Penguin Group, 2003), 2.96.4; Robert B. Strassler, *The Landmark Herodotus: The Histories* (New York: Pantheon Books, 2007), 156.
6 See John Gwyn Griffiths, ed., *Plutarch's De Iside et Osiride* (Cambridge: University of Wales Press, 1970), 18.358. Plutarch claims crocodiles do not harm these boats because they are associated with Isis, whom they either fear or revere.
7 The ubiquitous throw-stick.

hands. It is in a tomb at Qurna,[8] in the territory of Thebes, that we copied these most curious scenes, combining those of fishing and grape harvesting. They were the subject of a painting that adorned one of the halls of the Egyptian Museum in the Louvre.[9]

But hunting by net was the most common method, preferred for the numerous plants in which hunters could hide. Large, long nets were stretched out and, once they were sufficiently full of prey, an attentive observer, hidden in the papyrus, would appear slowly, raising a finger to his mouth to indicate silence (Plutarch),[10] or with upraised arms. He would give the signal and suddenly the nets would be pulled closed and the cord rolled, little by little, on a stake of wood, affixed to the ground. It took no less than nine men to accomplish this work, as we can see in plate 36. Hunting was so important for the Egyptians that they placed representations of it in their temples, amid the most venerated objects, and they associated it with their kings and gods. Ramesses III (Sesostris),[11] with Horus and Chnuphis[12] on either side of him, holds the net with both hands. Thoth, raising a sash, gives the awaited signal in the presence of the goddess Neith.[13]

The numerous scenes of private life which we still encounter in the tombs of Beni Hasan and Thebes show us hunters with their various traps covered with nets which close in two parts (pl. 37A, fig. 2).

Their most abundant and most productive hunt was that of geese, ducks, quail, partridge, bustard, gutta, and various small species.

The warm climate of Egypt does not allow for the preservation of fresh meats. We see that, upon returning from the hunt, the geese destined to be consumed first were immediately

---

8 The tomb of Neferhotep is labeled as A5 in Bertha Porter and Rosalind L.B. Moss, *Topographical Bibliography of Ancient Egyptian Hieroglyphic Texts, Reliefs, and Paintings. I. The Theban Necropolis. Part 1. Private Tombs* (Oxford: Clarendon Press, 1960), 448. Its location in the Theban hills is now unknown. It was built during Egypt's mid-Eighteenth Dynasty, sometime around the reigns of Thutmose III and Amenhotep II, somewhere in the vicinity of modern-day Dra Abu al-Naga. For more information on its possible location, see Friederike Kampp, *Die Thebanische Nekropole 2. Teil* (Mainz: Philipp von Zabern, 1996), 616. The Harer Papers contain a possible plan of the tomb, with a vague description of that tomb's location. This plan is presented in part 3 of this book, "The Visual Corpus and Cailliaud."

9 See Ludwig Keimer, "Sur un monument égyptien du Musée du Louvre. Contribution à l'histoire de l'égyptologie," *Revue d'Egyptologie* 4 (1940).

10 Cailliaud's note only refers to the use of a finger to the mouth to indicate silence. See Griffiths, *Iside et Osiride*, 68.

11 Cailliaud lists two different kings in this sentence: Ramesses III and, in parentheses, the all-conquering pharaoh Sesostris, a variation of the name Senusret, mentioned in the works of Herodotus and Diodorus. He has confused Ramesses III for Herodotus' and Diodorus' version of Sesostris. The king in the scene is, in fact, Ramesses II.

12 Chnuphis is the god Khnum.

13 Actually the goddess Seshat, not Neith. For the description of this scene Cailliaud writes: "Palace of Menephtha [Merenptah] I in Karnak, *Antiquités de l'Égypte et de la Nubie*, vol. 3, pl. 287." He is referring to Jean-François Champollion, *Monuments de l'Égypte et de la Nubie*, vol. 3 (Paris: Firmin Didot, 1845), pl. CCLXXXVII. The scene appears on the southeast wall of Karnak's Hypostyle Hall and is one of three registers depicting the Valley Festival. The king is shown with Horus and Khnum, all of whom pull a net with birds in it. Thoth stands in front of the other figures, a piece of cloth stretched between his hands, while Seshat stands behind him. See Bertha Porter and Rosalind L.B. Moss, *Topographical Bibliography of Ancient Egyptian Texts, Reliefs, and Paintings. II. Theban Temples* (Oxford: Clarendon Press, 1972), 47.

deplumed and gutted. The carcass was conserved with salt in large earthen vases, sometimes similar to amphora destined for wine, and thereafter sealed with clay.

Once servants had arranged in proper order the vases of preserves, the surviving geese, and other meat from the hunt, a scribe took an exact account, wrote it down, and communicated it to the steward of the house (pl. 35 and pl. 36).

Great care was taken in the collection of eggs, especially those of geese and chickens, so that they might be incubated. Also, these animals had become very common on private estates. These eggs, instead of being abandoned to natural incubation, were submitted to an artificial process by which they were made to hatch, a thousand young at a time. This industry, still so important in Egypt, goes back to extreme antiquity. It was, without doubt, inspired by the observations of the manner in which the ostrich and the crocodile make their eggs hatch in the sand, in the heat of the sun. This must have led them to create heated incubators for this purpose. According to Diodorus,[14] the Egyptians shrouded this industry in mystery, of which a few authors have spoken incorrectly by stating that eggs were placed in dung.

The Emperor Hadrian, in his letter to Servianus,[15] states when speaking of Egyptians: "They hatch their chickens in a manner that I would be ashamed to recount to you."

Aristotle, the most ancient of authors who has spoken on this subject, said "that the eggs were hatched with the warmth of dung."[16] This expression might change the opinion first set forth, as (according to Mr. Rozière[17] in his *Description de l'Égypte*) dung, or the excrement of animals, mixed with chopped straw, was burnt in Egypt. This custom existed in ancient times as it does today. This dung, when burning, gives a gentle warmth like that of the peat of Brittany, and lends itself perfectly to the hatching of eggs.[18]

Pliny's assertion helps to explain this operation. "The eggs," he states, "were placed on straw in an incubator in which the temperature was maintained with the aid of an even fire. They were kept there until the moment the chickens hatched. Throughout this whole

---

14 Diodorus Siculus, *The Library of History*, 1.74. See Diodorus Siculus, *Library of History: Loeb Classical Library*, translated by Charles Henry Oldfather (Cambridge MA: Harvard University Press, 1933–67), http://penelope.uchicago.edu/Thayer/E/Roman/Texts/Diodorus_Siculus/1D*.html#ref5.

15 This quotation comes from the *Augustan History*, a work produced by Isaac Casaubon in 1603. The text is a compilation of late Roman, Latin biographies. Despite being treated with skepticism, the work was considered an authentic, historical source by scholars for three hundred years. The quotation used by Cailliaud is from a letter, likely fraudulent due to several historical inaccuracies within it, by Hadrian to his brother-in-law, Servianus, while the emperor was in Egypt.

16 Aristotle, *The History of Animals*, 6.2.3. See Aristotle, *The History of Animals*, translated by D'Arcy Wentworth Thompson (London: John Bell, 1907), http://classics.mit.edu/Aristotle/history_anim.6.vi.html.

17 François-Michel de Rozière (1775–1842), author of an article on the artificial incubation of chickens in Egypt. See François-Michel de Rozière and Pierre Charles Rouyer, "L'art de faire éclore les poulets en Égypte par le moyen des fours," in *Description de l'Égypte ou Recueil des observations et des recherches qui ont été faites en Égypte pendant l'expédition de l'armée française*, vol. 1, ed. Edmé-François Jomard (Paris: Imprimerie impériale, 1809).

18 Cailliaud writes: "In Arabic this mixture is called 'Galleh.' In the villages women make it into a mortar which they apply in handfuls to the exterior walls of their houses. The unfired earth of these walls and the action of the sun promptly absorbs the humidity and the odor of this combustible, which is sold in the hundreds and is generally used in ovens and in kitchens."

period a workman occupied himself, day and night, turning the eggs" (Pliny, *Natural History*, book X, 55).

The Egyptians did not have knowledge of the thermometer, which is vital to this operation. It is to much practice that they owe the success of their industry, which is perpetuated from father to son.

In Upper Egypt, the ovens are filled at the start of February. In the Delta, this work is done a bit later. In order to hatch eggs, 21 days with an average temperature of 32° Réamur[19] are required. One can perform three or four operations per year. For 100 eggs, one ordinarily returned to the owner 50 chicks, 25 or 30 might still remain for the salary of the establishment, and about a third do not survive. In 24 hours, one might see appear up to 60,000 chicks.[20]

We count approximately 200 ovens in Egypt which can annually hatch 24 million chicks. One ordinarily sells 100 of these chicks at the rate of three francs of our money, but it also happens that they do not bother to count them and that they sell them by the measure, like bushels of grain.

Besides, birds are of a very modest price in Upper Egypt. In 1822, for one chicken, I paid 25 centimes; in 1816, only 15 centimes.

Artificial incubation has always been practiced in China. The Romans also adopted its use, probably in imitation of the Egyptians. Pliny recounts that Roman women sometimes had the patience to hatch an egg by carrying it continually in their bosom, and that they could draw a prediction from it on the sex of the child with whom they were pregnant.[21]

---

19 This scale is also known as the octogesimal division, and dates to the 1730s. Named after René Antoine Ferchault de Réamur, this scale posits the freezing point for water at 0 and its boiling point at 80. Thus, 32° Réamur is 25.6° C or 89.6° F.

20 Cailliaud writes: "These details are largely taken from the *Description de l'Égypte*, by Mr. Rozière." See de Rozière and Rouyer, "L'art de faire éclore."

21 Pliny, *Natural History*, 10.76. See Pliny the Elder, *Natural History*, translated by John Bostock (London: Taylor and Francis, 1855), http://www.perseus.tufts.edu/hopper.

CHAPTER 2

HUNTING

On this subject the details of tomb paintings must often compensate for the silence of ancient authors. This activity, one of the first and most useful for primitive peoples, was a resource for the working classes and a pleasure for the rich during the time of the pharaohs. The number of hunters was such that Plato speaks of them as a caste among the ancient Egyptians.[22]

We understand that, in this burning heat, hunting would have been impossible if it had meant undertaking the physical exercise which accompanies this pleasure in our temperate climate. Some of the paintings show important people in their chariots, armed with their arrows, chasing animals in the open desert. If they had had the habit of riding on horses, we would have had them represented on these animals in their hunting parties, passing over obstacles and following difficult routes along which their chariots could neither travel nor surmount. Dogs preceded the hunters and sometimes a lion was trained to fulfill the same duty (according to Diodorus).[23] In Beni Hasan, a hunter is represented with his lion. It has just pulled down an antelope (ibex) that it pins to the ground, one paw on its throat.[24]

---

22 Cailliaud might be referring to a passage from Plato's *Timaeus*. See Plato, *Timaeus*, translated by Benjamin Jowett, The Internet Classics Archive, http://classics.mit.edu//Plato/timaeus.html.

23 Cailliaud might be referring to Diodorus, 1.48. See Diodorus Siculus, *Library of History*, http://penelope. uchicago.edu/Thayer/E/Roman/Texts/Diodorus_Siculus/1C*.html

24 It is uncertain to which tomb in Beni Hasan Cailliaud refers. We know from the accompanying plates that Cailliaud copied scenes from a number of tombs in Beni Hasan. For a full list of these plates, see Appendix 1 at the end of this book. Tombs 15 (Bakt III) and 17 (Khety) had well-intact hunting scenes when they

Pairs of dogs were driven on leashes by servants fitted with all the necessary paraphernalia: arrows, cases for holding bows, bowstrings, pieces of skin which served to protect a portion of the left arm from the friction of the bowstring, and baskets of provisions. Water held in skins clearly announces a journey into the desert. They are carried by two people with the help of a long stick on the shoulder, along with the antelopes and other materials. The enormous limestone and sandstone plateau of the Libyan Desert must have been, by its very nature, less favorable to hunting than the eastern desert between the Nile and the Red Sea, cut by numerous valleys, hemmed in by sheer mountains and dry riverbeds. The hunters would flush out animals from afar while nets and enclosures would stop them. The dogs, the traps, and the hunters' arrows easily made numerous victims.

In the desert, water regularly attracts animals morning and night. Hunters posted among the reeds awaited their prey with traps and nooses.

They kept confined in vast spaces, as is still done nowadays, numerous animals held in reserve: ostriches and wild cats. Ancient paintings show these pens (pl. 37) in which are massed oxen, wild calf, various sorts of antelope, wild cat, hyena, oryx, and gazelle, separated from the hunter by roped enclosures. The skill of the artist renders the natural mannerisms of these animals: some bound, others run rapidly, an ostrich is taken in a noose; some are pierced with arrows, others are taken down by greyhounds, while a favorite dog remains next to the hunter. A servant, the porter of a bow case, leads a greyhound while others collect arrows and take animals away.

This subject is taken from the tomb of Neferhotep.[25]

Hunting was lucrative for those who made a living from traps, lacings, and dogs, and the destruction of harmful animals was rewarded. All of these hunts are still practiced in Upper and Lower Ethiopia: an ostrich, when chased to extremes, can still be caught by means of a lasso.

---

were recorded in the late 1800s, and might match Cailliaud's description. See Percy E. Newberry, *Beni Hasan. Part II* (London: Egypt Exploration Fund, 1893), pl. IV, XIII; Bertha Porter and Rosalind L.B. Moss, *Topographical Bibliography of Ancient Egyptian Hieroglyphic Texts, Reliefs, and Paintings. IV. Lower and Middle Egypt* (Oxford: Clarendon Press, 1934), 151–59. Tomb 2 (Amenemhat) also depicts a hunting scene, with a lion pawing an antelope. See Newberry, *Beni Hasan. Part I*, pl. XIII; Porter and Moss, *Topographical Bibliography IV*, 141–44. This tomb was accessible from at least the time of the Napoleonic scholars' journey and was copied by Wilkinson. In addition, Tomb 14 (Khnumhotep) had a badly degraded hunting scene at the time of recording, in the late 1800s, which might have included a lion pinning an antelope to the ground. See Newberry, *Beni Hasan. Part I*, pl. XLVI; Porter and Moss, *Topographical Bibliography IV*, 149–51. For more recent works on these tombs see Naguib Kanawati and Alexandra Woods, *Beni Hassan: Art and Daily Life in an Egyptian Province* (Cairo: Supreme Council of Antiquities, 2010).

25 The tomb of Neferhotep is labeled as A5 in Porter and Moss, *Topographical Bibliography I.1*, 448. Its location in the Theban hills is now unknown. It was built during Egypt's mid-Eighteenth Dynasty, sometime around the reigns of Thutmose III and Amenhotep II, somewhere in the vicinity of modern-day Dra Abu al-Naga. For more information on its possible location, see Kampp, *Die Thebanische Nekropole*, 616. The Harer Papers contain a possible plan of the tomb, with a vague description of that tomb's location. This plan is presented in the chapter of this book titled "The Visual Corpus and Cailliaud."

The people of Sennar, of Meroe, and of Napata, in Upper and Lower Ethiopia,[26] had even more resources for hunting than the Egyptians. They had animals which the arid sands of Egypt could not feed.[27]

We shall say a few words on the return of the hunt described above and in the same painting. We can note the spirit of order which is revealed in all the private life scenes of these people.

Here an intendant carries in his hand the *Pat*,[28] an insignia of his rank. The yield from the hunt is presented to him: the surviving antelopes, oryx, and gazelles; a wild calf is carried on a bar by two men; an ostrich is held by the neck, the feathers and eggs of another are carefully brought back.

It is in the tombs of Beni Hasan that we still find most of the colored representations of quadrupeds.

---

26 All of these locations are in modern-day Sudan. Sennar is approximately 250 kilometers (160 miles) south of Khartoum, on the Blue Nile. Meroe is midway between the Fifth and Sixth Cataracts and Napata is located above the Fourth Cataract.

27 Cailliaud writes: "We regretted not being able to penetrate the tombs of Meroe and Napata where we might have found, as in those of Egypt, scenes of private life for these ancient peoples. We said, in the *Travels to Meroe*, that at the time of my discovery of these monuments in April 1821, Isma'il, son of Muhammad Ali, fearing to pass before the eyes of the natives for authorizing the violation of the tombs, expressly forbade us from any attempt to penetrate them." The phrase "fearing to pass before the eyes of the natives" is a literal translation from the French and means that Isma'il feared to be judged by the natives.

28 Actually the *aba*-scepter: a scepter denoting authority, typically carried by Egyptian officials in two-dimensional representations. It is represented by sign S42 in Gardiner's sign list. See Alan Gardiner, *Egyptian Grammar, Being an Introduction to the Study of Hieroglyphs* (Oxford: Oxford University Press, 1950), 509.

CHAPTER 3

FISHING

The burning climate of Egypt made seeking the pleasure of fishing preferable to all others, and by men of all ages eager for the freshness of water. It is a subject that we frequently find represented in the sculptures of temples and in the paintings of tombs.

We will cite here an example that we took from a tomb in the Theban necropolis (pl. 35). We see a marsh covered with numerous aquatic plants: papyrus, byblus, lotus, etc. It is inhabited by numerous fish. The hunters and the fishermen are mounted on light boats. The person to whom this sepulchral chamber belongs is Neferhotep.[29] His tall stature, his manner of dress, and his bracelets indicate a person of high rank.

He is standing in the middle of the boat, his body slender, his arms extended. He strikes with a long harpoon and catches a bolti,[30] the largest fish in the marsh.

A woman adorned with lotuses places her arm on her husband as if to secure his unsteady pose on this frail vessel. A young, kneeling girl takes from the water a stalk of papyrus from which she plucks a flower. Opposite her a young boy holds in his hands a small harpoon to imitate his father.

---

29 The tomb of Neferhotep is labeled as A5 in Porter and Moss, *Topographical Bibliography I. 1*, 448. Its location in the Theban hills is now unknown. It was built during Egypt's mid-Eighteenth Dynasty, sometime around the reigns of Thutmose III and Amenhotep II, somewhere in the vicinity of modern-day Dra Abu al-Naga. The Harer Papers contain a possible plan of the tomb with vague directions to its location. This plan is presented in the chapter of this book titled "The Visual Corpus and Cailliaud." For more information on its possible location, see Kampp, *Die Thebanische Nekropole*, 616.

30 Nile tilapia. See Douglas Brewer and Renée Friedman, *Fish and Fishing in Ancient Egypt* (Cairo: American University in Cairo Press, 1989), 77. This fish is represented by sign K1 in Gardiner's sign list. See Gardiner, *Egyptian Grammar*, 476. Cailliaud uses the Egyptian Arabic names, insofar as he understood them, for the fish cited in this chapter.

These boats, with their slender and light form, appear to be held together by cross-pieces. Their extremities end in the shape of papyrus flowers and are fashioned with stalks by means of a tar plaster, as the ancient authors describe them.

The Nile did not always suffice for rich people. They had in their parks ponds fed by the periodic inundation of the river. They fished and conserved fish from these, as did the Romans after them.

After fishing by harpoon we will cite that of fishing by line and tow-line, observed in the paintings of a tomb[31] in Beni Hasan (the ancient Heptanomide).[32]

Plate 37A, fig. 1. It depicts a marsh, or rather a canal. Two men, modestly dressed, stand by a river. One takes from the river, with effort, a large fish caught on a line. The other, kneeling, fishes with a tow-line and draws his prey: the schilbe fish.[33]

The periodic flooding of the Nile spread its waters in the interior of the valleys by conduits dug by the hands of men. It filled the lakes and brought quantities of fish. Strabo and Herodotus mention the two movements of the water: the flooding and the water's retreat.[34] The waters of Lake Moeris[35] yielded to the state a talent[35] a day, 4,825 francs, during one of these periods, and 20 mina,[36] 1,600 francs, during the other.

A painting from a tomb at al-Kab,[37] ancient Elethyia (pl. 36),[38] represents large-scale, commercial fishing by means of a net that we call 'seine.'[39]

A long row of posts with large heads sunk in a line form, along with the net, a dam that stops the fish. They also serve as an embankment to the fishermen, so that they might stand above the water and ease their work. Seven men pull up their net. Another, who is partly missing due to damage to the painting, appears to give the signal with two rods. Two men transport the fish in baskets suspended from their shoulders so as to deliver them for preparation. The person charged with this work has one knee on the ground, armed with a sharp tool in the shape of a small axe blade. He slits the fish, takes off the head, guts it, opens it,

31 Tomb 3. The owner of this tomb is alternately referred to in literature as either Khnumhotep III or Khnumhotep II. For references to the cited scene in the tomb of Khnumhotep III, see Newberry, *Beni Hasan. Part I*, 41–72, pl. XXIX; Porter and Moss, *Topographical Bibliography IV*, 144–49. For a more recent work on this tomb, in which the owner is cited as Khnumhotep II, see Kanawati and Woods, *Beni Hassan*, 33–38.
32 This is an ancient Greek name for the area of Beni Hasan.
33 Either the *Schilbe mystus* or *Schilbe uranoscopus*. See Brewer and Friedman, *Fish and Fishing*, 64.
34 For Herodotus, see Herodotus, *The Histories*, 2.93; Strassler, *The Landmark Herodotus*, 155. For Strabo, see Strabo, *The Geography of Strabo: Loeb Classical Library*, translated by Horace L. Jones (Cambridge MA: Harvard University Press, 1917–32), Book 17.
35 In the Greek world, the talent was the primary unit of weight and a unit of currency for large sums of money. It was also used in Rome and the Middle East. See Kenneth W. Harl, *Roman Economy, 300 B.C. to A.D. 700* (Baltimore MD: Johns Hopkins University Press, 1996), 482.
36 Another denomination of money used in ancient cultures such as Greece. See Harl, *Roman Economy*, 482.
37 Tomb 3, Paheri. See: Bertha Porter and Rosalind L.B. Moss, *Topographical Bibliography of Ancient Egyptian Hieroglyphic Texts, Reliefs, and Paintings. V. Upper Egypt: Sites* (Oxford: Clarendon Press, 1937), 179; Joseph J. Tylor and Francis Ll. Griffith, *The Tomb of Paheri at El Kab* (London: Egypt Exploration Fund, 1894).
38 A version of the ancient Greek name for the area of al-Kab: Eileithyiaspolis.
39 Cailliaud writes: "The Berlin Museum possesses a net analogous to this one. Its cords are made of flax with small knots, trimmed with weights, with pieces of floating wood, and with a gourd. It was found well-folded under the head of a male mummy, probably a fisherman, its owner, in a tomb in the Theban necropolis."

lays it out, salts it, and exposes it to sun so as to dry it. Other fishermen repair the net. The hairstyle of many of these men has a particular look: it appears wet, which would indicate that they are divers. These men ordinarily have long beards. Once again we see the supervisor, leaning on a long staff.[40]

We encounter short letters on papyrus, rolled and sealed with virgin wax and with clay: the accounts of taxes, of vested interests, etc., written on pieces of pottery, on small planks, on linen, on fragments of limestone, and all concealed in small baskets, and more generally in small funerary coffers placed in the tombs.

We are obliged to a savant Egyptologist, Mr. Devéria,[41] for the translation of one of these curious texts called ostracon[42] which we found in a tomb of the ancient Theban necropolis. It is a receipt of rent or tax. It bears seven lines of hieratic writing presenting the paleographic characters from the time of the 19th Dynasty, and written in black ink by an experienced hand on a fragment of limestone of approximately 14 centimeters squared. Mr. Devéria transcribes this inscription backward, that is to say from left to right, he regrets not finding indication of the reign.

"Year six, month of Payni, day 22, the fishermen came to the scribe Neferhotepu. Seti's fish, 90, Bakueren's fish, 840. Day 27, fish yield of User-Nakht,[43] 830. Butuger's[44] yield, fish, 75. Tax 10 from the nets, the fishermen gave me (?) a gold (?) drachma."[45]

It is a question of a genuine tithe or tax of a tenth, etc.[46] We see here that these four towns[47] produced 1,830 fish, for which a gold drachma was given for the tithe of fillets.

Mr. Devéria adds: "This ostracon teaches us, moreover, that fishing was already an important [source of] exploitation in a time not too distant from the one in which Moses lived, and that during this distant period, the state taxed the right to fish at a high enough rate that it could produce an important revenue."[48]

---

40 Cailliaud writes: "Fresh fish were also conserved in floating reservoirs."

41 Charles Théodule Devéria (1831–71). See Morris L. Bierbrier, ed., *Who Was Who in Egyptology* (London: Egypt Exploration Society, 1995), 124.

42 An ostracon is a fragment of stone or pottery that was used as a surface on which to write. Cailliaud writes: "Extract from volume XXV of the 'Mémoires de la société des antiquaires de France.'" He is referring to a letter from Devéria to himself, read at the Society of French Antiquarians on 1 June and 6 July 1859. The letter, which includes a transcription of the ostracon's hieroglyphic text, was published by Devéria in 1859. See Charles Théodule Devéria, "Lettre à M. Cailliaud sur un ostracon égyptien," *Mémoires de la Société des Antiquaires de France*, vol. 25 (3rd series, vol. 5, 15 June). The letter was republished in 1896, and is cited in Louis-A. Christophe, "Le ravitaillement en poissons des artisans de la nécropole thébaine à la fin du règne de Ramsès III," *Bulletin de l'Institut français d'archéologie orientale* 65 (1967).

43 Read as Userhat-nakht. See Christophe, "Le ravitaillement," 186.

44 Read as Butef-gereg. See Christophe, "Le ravitaillement," 182.

45 Cailliaud was right to indicate Devéria's uncertainty on the reading of this portion of the ostracon. The drachma was not used during the New Kingdom, when this ostracon was written, a period in which Egypt had neither coinage nor the concept of money. At this time, the Egyptian economy used the *deben* as a value of commodity. For more information on the *deben* and the cost of fish during the Ramesside period, see Jac. J. Janssen, *Commodity Prices from the Ramessid Period* (Leiden: Brill, 1975).

46 For information on how the Egyptians organized fishing, see Christophe, "Le ravitaillement," 1967.

47 Cailliaud mistakes the proper names listed on the ostracon for place names. They are, in fact, the names of the fishermen who caught the fish. See Devéria, "Lettre à M. Cailliaud."

48 Cailliaud is quoting from the letter written by Devéria to himself, and read at the Society of Antiquaries. See Devéria, "Lettre à M. Cailliaud," 142.

The Greeks, like the Egyptians, held a strong monopoly on fishing, and we find in Egypt Greek ostraca that treat this subject.

The most prized fish were firstly: the bolti, the most sought-after of all those of the Nile; the schall;[49] the bynni;[50] the isher;[51] the bayad;[52] the schibla;[53] the garmoot.[54] We know that in the territory of the great Thebaid, the law forbade the eating of sacred fish like the oxyrhynchus,[55] the lepidotus,[56] the phagrus,[57] etc.

49 *Synodontis.* See Brewer and Friedman, *Fish and Fishing*, 67.
50 Probably *Barbus bynni.* See Brewer and Friedman, *Fish and Fishing*, 59.
51 Probably *Lates niloticus.* See Brewer and Friedman, *Fish and Fishing*, 74.
52 Either the *Bagras docmac* or *Bagras bayad.* See Brewer and Friedman, *Fish and Fishing*, 66.
53 Possibly another spelling of *schilbe.* See Brewer and Friedman, *Fish and Fishing*, 64.
54 This may refer either to the *Clarias* or *Heterobranchus* genera. Two species of *Clarias* inhabit the Nile (*Clarias lazera* and *Clarias anguillaris*), as do two species of *Heterobranchus* (*Heterobranchus bidorsalis* and *Heterobranchus longifilis*). The two genera are often confused by local Egyptian fishermen. See Brewer and Friedman, *Fish and Fishing*, 60–63.
55 Possibly of the *Mormyrus* family. See Brewer and Friedman, *Fish and Fishing*, 18. The oxyrhynchus fish is represented as sign K4 in Gardiner's sign list. See Gardiner, *Egyptian Grammar*, 477.
56 The Greek name means 'scaly.' For this reason Brewer and Friedman suggest it might be the carp-like *Barbus.* See Brewer and Friedman, *Fish and Fishing*, 18.
57 *Hyperopisus bebe.* See Brewer and Friedman, *Fish and Fishing*, 53.

CHAPTER 4

HERDSMEN AND ANIMALS

The shepherds, herdsmen, and guardians of flocks in general were regarded by the Egyptians as an ignoble, dirty, repugnant class, with uncultivated beards. The job of pig-keepers was dishonorable to the point where entrance to temples was forbidden to them, as states Herodotus.[58] We see them represented in a ridiculous manner in certain paintings in the tombs of Memphis, at Beni Hasan, and at Qurna.

Did the invasion of the pastoral kings and the devastation committed by them inspire in the Egyptians this profound disgust for herdsmen? Joseph warned his brothers of this repulsion upon their arrival.

The occupation of shepherds was forcefully perpetuated from father to son. As well, they had much experience in the art of raising, improving, and multiplying the different races of animals delivered into their care. Diodorus talks of their knowledge, of this hereditary experience, and of their skill which they circulated with success among other nations.[59] We can imagine for ourselves the nature of their lives by their current successors: to guard and to drive beasts, to separate them when fighting with the knock of a stick, to manage reproduction, to draw milk. All of these topics are frequently represented in the tombs. Diodorus tells us that the wool was sheared and that the mothers bore two litters per year.[60]

---

58 Herodotus, *The Histories, Revised* (London: Penguin Group, 2003), 2.47; Strassler, *The Landmark Herodotus*, 138.
59 Diodorus Siculus, *The Library of History*, 1.74. See Diodorus Siculus, *Library of History*, http://penelope. uchicago.edu/Thayer/E/Roman/Texts/Diodorus_Siculus/1D*.html#ref5.
60 Diodorus, *Library of History*, 1.87. See Diodorus Siculus, *Library of History*, http://penelope.uchicago. edu/Thayer/E/Roman/Texts/Diodorus_Siculus/1D*.html

We have dealt with hunting among the ancient Egyptians and of their parks, in which they brought together wild and domesticated animals, and in which they might also have easily studied their manners and customs. They learned to tame those that were responsive: the cat, the dog, the gazelle, which became the favorite creature of women and the plaything of children, antelopes and jackals, represented in the monuments beside their masters.

Numerous birds were equally accustomed to live with people: the ibis and the bustard, taken from Ethiopia, geese, ducks, storks, and cranes. The war which the ibis wages against nefarious reptiles caused it to be venerated.

Ethiopia provided, still, the taming of monkeys, giraffes, lions, and elephants. This last creature is represented in the sculptures of a temple on the Isle of Meroe: it is mounted by a guide.[61] The lion is often represented at the feet of monarchs as well as in the decoration of their war chariots as a symbol of power. Champollion records that the kings made them follow them into battle. "The Pharaoh Sesostris[62] is in his triumphal chariot, his lion follows him freely" (low relief, colored, from the large temple of Abu Simbel, *Monuments of Egypt and Nubia*, vol. I, pl. XV).[63]

Ramesses Meiamun[64] in his chariot marches at the head of his army against the Asiatic people. A free lion walks close to him: sculpture of the palace of Ramesses IV[65] in Medinet Habu, territory of Thebes (*Monuments of Egypt and Nubia*, vol. III, pl. CCXVIII).[66]

Ramesses II is seated in his naos. At his feet is a sleeping lion. Sculptures from Beit al-Wali in Nubia (same work, vol. I, pl. LXII).[67] We saw in a temple in Meroe, a king and a queen sculpted with lions at their feet (*Travels to Meroe and to the White Nile*, vol. II, pl. XIV and XVI).

We often find pharaohs shown with dogs close to them. They are shown lying down or excited, or in battle, throwing themselves at the enemy.

During the assault on an Asiatic citadel the pharaoh drives his chariot preceded by a dog who throws himself on the enemy (*Travels to Meroe*, vol. II, pl. LXXIII). These sculptural details are often very difficult to recognize and the artist who made the design of this scene in Champollion's *Monuments of Egypt* drew this dog as a horse. The savant, consul, and English antiquarian Salt,[68] who drew this object like me, was of my opinion in this regard.

---

61 The structure of the sentence leaves some uncertainty as to what exactly is being mounted: is a guide mounted atop the elephant, or was the island or temple climbed by means of a guide?

62 This is a reference to Ramesses II. Cailliaud has confused him with the all-conquering pharaoh Sesostris (a variation of Senusret), mentioned in the works of Herodotus and Diodorus.

63 Jean-François Champollion, *Monuments de l'Égypte et de la Nubie*, vol. 1 (Paris: Firmin Didot, 1835), pl. XV.

64 This is a reference to Ramesses III. Cailliaud has conflated Ramesses II and Ramesses III, possibly because of the similarities in their names. By the time of the New Kingdom, Egyptian kings had several names. Ramesses II's birth name was Ramesses Meryamun, and his throne name Usermaatra Setepenra. Ramesses III's birth name was Ramesses Heqaiunu, and his throne name Usermaatra Meryamun. See Peter Clayton, *Chronicle of the Pharaohs* (London: Thames and Hudson, 1994).

65 This should read Ramesses III.

66 Champollion, *Monuments de l'Égypte*, vol. 3, pl. CCXVIII. Cailliaud's description does not match the actual publication, as no clear lion is visible in the scene.

67 Champollion, *Monuments de l'Égypte*, vol. 1, pl. LXII.

68 Henry Salt (1780–1827), British diplomat and collector. See Bierbrier, ed., *Who Was Who*, 370.

In another low relief, Ramesses II, standing, menaces with his well-shaped dog, a kneeling, begging enemy, whom he holds by his hair. A dog of the jackal race throws himself on the conquered person.

The ancient Egyptians amused themselves by recounting all the care they gave to their animals. The veterinary art appears here to have been divided into diverse specialties. We see them represented (pl. 21A) in a painting of the tomb of New.[69]

We see here goats being treated. One of them, lying on the ground, is attached to a post by means of a cord so that the veterinarian might operate. He pulls the jaws open to inspect the mouth. A vase placed underneath must contain the remedy. The hieroglyphic inscription which accompanies this subject expounds the quality of the "goat doctor."

Further on, we see oxen equally ill. One of them forcefully sticks out his tongue, colored green to indicate the sickness. The veterinarian introduces into its mouth medication, contained in a vase placed close to him. The inscription states, "The ox doctor." It is Champollion the younger who gave me these translations.

We find still other animals cared for by their special doctors. These paintings are contemporary with the XVIII dynasty.

Plate 21B, figs. 1 and 2, represent shepherds driving geese, swans, or cranes. He takes them at will by means of a long stick ending in a crook which seizes them by the neck. The bird's attempts to free itself only tighten the noose further. This painting is found in the tomb of a military chief named Rotei in Beni Hasan.[70]

The flocks were represented in the tombs so as to recall the opulence of the deceased. In that of Neferhotep,[71] the goats and rams are accompanied by the number two thousand.

An analogous subject is seen in a tomb close to the pyramids of Memphis.[72] The master, standing, is leaning on a long cane, a dog of the jackal race is close to him, as well as a small servant supplied with a double fan. A person of condition to judge him by his clothes, covered with a scarf, receives from his shepherds the count of his livestock: 760 donkeys, 834 oxen, 974 rams, and 2,234 goats (pl. 38). Here we have only represented the donkeys and goats. I gave the complete subject in the *Travels to Meroe*, vol. II, pl. LXXIII.

---

69 Actually Tomb 3 in Beni Hasan, which possibly dates to the Twelfth Dynasty. The owner of this tomb is alternately referred to in literature as either Khnumhotep III or Khnumhotep II. For references to the cited scene in the tomb of Khnumhotep III, see Porter and Moss, *Topographical Bibliography IV*, 144–49; Newberry, *Beni Hasan. Part I*, 41–72, pl. XXX. For a more recent work on this tomb, in which the owner is cited as Khnumhotep II, see Kanawati and Woods, *Beni Hassan*, 33–37, 39.

70 Tomb 17: the owner's name is Khety, not Rotei, and the tomb dates to the Eleventh Dynasty. See Porter and Moss, *Topographical Bibliography IV*, 154–59; Newberry, *Beni Hasan. Part I*, 51–62; Kanawati and Woods, *Beni Hassan*, 49–57.

71 Cailliaud is referring to Tomb 3, referenced alternately in the literature as belonging to either Khnumhotep II or Khnumhotep III, in Beni Hasan.

72 The Fifth Dynasty, or perhaps later, tomb of Rakhaefankh, numbered G 7948 in Giza. See Bertha Porter and Rosalind L.B Moss, *Topographical Bibliography of Ancient Egyptian Hieroglyphic Texts, Reliefs, and Paintings. III. Memphis. Part I* (Oxford: Clarendon Press, 1974), 208; George A. Reisner, *A History of the Giza Necropolis* (Cambridge MA: Harvard University Press, 1942), 238, 315; the bibliography on Boston's Museum of Fine Arts' Giza Archives, http://www.gizapyramids.org/code/emuseum.asp

Amid the numerous tombs carved into the limestone hillside of Beni Hasan al-Gadim, the ancient Heptanomide,[73] we cited the most remarkable, those of Neferhotep[74] and Menisthph,[75] chiefs of a very large family. The Neferhotep from the large necropolis in Thebes, in whose tomb we have seen the taste for hunting and fishing, was perhaps the brother of [the one in] Beni Hasan. The tomb of this last person represents numerous scenes of daily life, gymnastic exercises, military actions of archery, the use of the ram guided by an individual placed under a portable shelter in the form of a cone,[76] the yield of eggplants, vegetables from the country, figs, navigation, hunting and its many quadrupeds and in birds, each bearing its name in hieroglyphs. The preservation of these paintings and the accurateness of the design still allows for the identification of each species of butterfly, of grasshopper, of dragonfly, of a succession of numerous birds, of fish, of quadrupeds. In short, it is a natural history collection of ancient Egypt. Champollion said that Neferhotep was perhaps the Cuvier[77] of Egypt before the siege of Troy. We can add that he was the chief administrator of the western lands of the Heptanomide. In these paintings prisoners, recognized as Greeks,[78] are presented to him by his son, who gives him a note on papyrus bearing the number of 37 prisoners, and the date, important for history, of year 6 of the reign of King Osortasen[79] of the XVI Dynasty, ten centuries before the Trojan War.[80]

---

73 An ancient Greek name for the area of Beni Hasan.

74 Cailliaud is referring to Tomb 3 in Beni Hasan. The owner of this tomb is alternately referred to in the literature as Khnumhotep II or Khnumhotep III. See Porter and Moss, *Topographical Bibliography IV*, 144–49; Newberry, *Beni Hasan. Part I*, 41–72, pl. XXII–XXXVIII; Kanawati and Woods, *Beni Hassan*, 33–40.

75 This appears to be another nineteenth-century name for Khety, owner of Tomb 17. See Porter and Moss, *Topographical Bibliography IV*, 154–59; Newberry, *Beni Hasan. Part I*, 51–62; Kanawati and Woods, *Beni Hassan*, 49–57.

76 In this description Cailliaud appears to be combining elements from Tomb 3, that of Khnumhotep, with elements from Tomb 17, that of Khety, as no siege engines are depicted in the tomb of Khnumhotep. See Newberry, *Beni Hasan. Parts I and II*.

77 This is a reference to George Cuvier, an important nineteenth-century naturalist, zoologist, and contemporary of Cailliaud.

78 These foreigners are neither prisoners nor Greek. They are identified simply as Aamu, or Asiatic people.

79 A variant reading of Usertesen, which is an incorrect reading of the name Senusret, a name held by several Middle Kingdom pharaohs.

80 Cailliaud leaves a question mark beside this sentence, perhaps indicating his uncertainty about the date. He was right to be cautious, as the tomb possibly dates to Egypt's Twelfth Dynasty, and possibly to the reign of Senusret II. See Newberry, *Beni Hasan Part I*, 41.

CHAPTER 5

AGRICULTURE, FLAX, IRRIGATION, VINES, GARDENING, TREES

What admiration must have struck the first men who saw the shoots and growth of crops from seeds left on the fertile ground, and the multitude of vegetables, so varied, that was often indispensable for their existence? The different appearances and their diverse proportions still strike our imagination: from the fragile body of the ear, to the monstrous baobab with a trunk of 25 meters in circumference.[81] This enormous vegetable continues to be worshiped by the idolatrous people of the northern confines of Ethiopia.

AGRICULTURE

The Egyptians, more than any other people in antiquity, knew to give thanks to the god of this sublime phenomenon from the production of nature. They wrote in all their temples proof of their veneration for agriculture. It is thus that the image of a crude instrument, the hoe, used to dig up the earth by the humble laborer, was often placed on the chest of their greatest gods, like in the hands of their kings where this pick takes the place of the scepter of our monarchs.[82]

---

81 Cailliaud writes: "It often attains this size in Senegal: we measured 20 meters for the circumference in upper Ethiopia, where the ancients knew of it, where it is still common. The Blacks call it Ufa. Its northern limit is Astaboras, isle of Meroe, where it is very rare."

82 Cailliaud writes: "The King Moeris, wearing the headdress of Osiris, cuts into the earth with a hoe at the feet of the god Amun-Re, generator, from the temple of Moeris in Medinet-Habu (Thebes) (Champollion, vol. II, pl. CXCV, fig. 1)." See Jean-François Champollion, *Monuments de l'Égypte et de la Nubie*, vol. 2 (Paris: Firmin Didot, 1845), pl. CXCV. Cailliaud is referring to a scene on the exterior of the sanctuary of the Eighteenth Dynasty Small Temple of Medinet Habu. See Porter and Moss, *Topographical Bibliography II*, 468. In this scene, Pharaoh Thutmose III is depicted cutting the ground with a hoe as part of a foundation ceremony for the temple. Cailliaud has confused Thutmose III with a King Moeris, mentioned in Herodotus and equated by Strassler with the Twelfth Dynasty King Amenemhat III. See Herodotus, *The Histories*, 2.101; Strassler, *The Landmark Herodotus*, 160.

The image of this instrument of labor followed them into the sanctuary of the dead. It is often found reproduced on the chests of idols who carry on their backs a sack of seeds, and with which they surrounded the dead as if to protect them.[83] The first fruits and crops were offered to the gods in recognition of the overflowing fecundity of the Nile.

Their gratitude for the benefits of the earth is substantiated still by the sculptures in temples where the monarch himself holds the golden, sacred sickle with which he cuts the ears of a sheaf of wheat to make an offering to the gods, consecrating thus the first fruits of abundance allocated by them. We also saw it was an honor to carry, instead of a scepter, the simple pastoral stick of the attendant of the fields.[84]

A law among the modern Ethiopians of Sennar requires that a king cultivate and seed a field by his own hands. This work, we are told, makes him worthy of the surname of the man of the fields as a title in addition to his royalty—we were no less surprised to find numerous such customs from ancient Egypt.[85]

We find the various branches of agriculture represented in the tombs. We will review the preparation of the earth with different models of plow and the hoe, the various harvests, the cultivation of vines, grape harvesting, the harvest of flax, of papyrus, etc.

Plate 30, taken from a tomb in al-Kab,[86] ancient Elethyia,[87] shows us four men placed along two rows, in which two of the men are only slightly shown in profile. They pick at the earth by means of hoes. These are large picks, formed from pieces of wood in which the gap is maintained by a cord and undoubtedly trimmed on the ends with iron or bronze. We note that this part, entering into the earth, is not of the same length as our picks. On the Egyptian hoe it is longer than the haft, which avoids the need for the workmen to bend over like ours.

These laborers are barely clothed, as are those still along the banks of the Nile, from the Barabras[88] in Nubia to the Fazoql.

---

83 Cailliaud is referring to funerary figurines, known as *shabti*, *shawabti*, or *ushabti*. They were created to work on behalf of a dead person when he or she was called upon to do manual labor in the afterlife. They are usually in mummy form, inscribed with the deceased person's name and spell number six from the Book of the Dead, which magically activated them. See Harry M. Stewart, *Egyptian Shabtis* (Princes Risborough: Shire Publications Ltd., 1995).

84 Cailliaud writes: "In a solemn ceremony with the queen, and in the presence of nine of his ancestors represented as figures with their royal cartouches, King Ramesses-Meiamun makes libations and other offerings to the god Amun. With a golden sickle he cuts the ears of a sheaf of wheat which is presented to him by a priest. Low-relief from the palace of Ramesses IV in Medinet Habu (Champollion, vol. III, pl. CCXIV) [see Champollion, *Monuments de l'Égypte* vol. 3, pl. CCXIV; University of Chicago Oriental Institute Publications, *Medinet Habu—Volume IV. Plates 193–249. Festival Scenes of Ramses III* (Chicago: University of Chicago Press, 1940), pl. 196 [A, B], 197–208; Porter and Moss, *Topographical Bibliography II*, 500]. Another pharaoh, Ramesses the Great, by way of offering with the sacred sickle likewise cuts the ears of a sheaf of wheat (sculpture from the large temple of Qurna, Champollion, vol. II, pl. CL)." See: Champollion, *Monuments de l'Égypte* vol. 3, pl. CL; Oriental Institute, *Medinet Habu IV*, pl. 213–14; Porter and Moss, *Topographical Bibliography II*, 434.

85 Cailliaud writes: "*Travels to Meroe and to the White Nile*, 1826."

86 Tomb 3, that of Paheri. See Porter and Moss, *Topographical Bibliography V*, 177; Tylor and Griffith, *The Tomb of Paheri*.

87 A version of the ancient Greek name for the area of al-Kab: Eileithyiaspolis.

88 A name given both generally to the Nubian peoples of Sudan and southern Egypt, and to a group of people living along the Nile between Wadi Halfa and Aswan.

These four pickers undoubtedly prepare the earth for the passage of the plow, pulled by four men.

In a second scene, placed under this one, two plows are pulled by oxen hitched together by their horns, and spurred into action by a double whip. The cultivators push on the plowshare to drive it through the earth. Then come two people who sow, holding a basket of seeds in one hand while they scatter seeds from a great height with the other.

We see in the first figure of plate 31 a plow like the preceding ones, but lighter and pulled by a mule. There again the driver pushes forcefully on the plowshare. The following plow, figure 2, is harnessed to two oxen. It has two arms on which the driver leans so as to push with all his body weight. These last harnesses are pulled with yokes. These paintings come from a tomb of the Theban necropolis.[89]

The most minute inspection in which we have indulged in these representations of labor among the Egyptians taught us that they started by picking the earth in order to place seed. They then, in succession, used the hand plow, next one pulled by mules, and then oxen hitched together by the horns or by a yoke. We see them represented in the monuments of the XVIII Dynasty (3,000 years before J[esus] C[hrist]).

In the tomb of Paphe,[90] in al-Kab (Elethyia),[91] we find represented a large field of wheat (pl. 32), which occupies ten harvesters. They hold in one hand fistfuls of stalks of wheat below the ears, and with the other they will saw with a serrated sickle.[92] They are dressed in kilts, like all workers. The artist shows us here that the poor might drink cool beverages like the rich by means of vases in porous clay exposed to air, where, as we see in one painting, a fan is waved to cool the drink.

Two different heights of wheat indicate two qualities.

After cutting the wheat, which we have just seen, comes the transport of ears and its treading (pl. 33).[93] An individual, his arm raised, shows the ear in one hand. He appears to indicate the maturity and the abundance of the yield. The ears are kept in a large basket carried on a bar, on the shoulders, by two men who run rather than walk to transport them to the place where they are trodden. Two other porters return, one with a basket, the other a stick.

The threshing is done by five oxen, which a man spurs into motion with a whip. A young boy gathers the ears by means of a broom. Herodotus says that the Egyptians used

---

89 The tomb of Ramesses III, KV 11. See Porter and Moss, *Topographical Bibliography I.2*, 521; Nicholas Reeves and Richard H. Wilkinson, *The Complete Valley of the Kings: Tombs and Treasures of Egypt's Greatest Pharaohs* (London: Thames and Hudson, 2006), 159–61; the Theban Mapping Project's bibliography for KV 11, http://www.tmpbibliography.com/resources/bibliography_2kv_valley_of_kings_kv11_ramesses_iii.html

90 Tomb 3, that of Paheri. See Porter and Moss, *Topographical Bibliography V*, 179; Tylor and Griffith, *The Tomb of Paheri*.

91 A version of the ancient Greek name for the area of al-Kab: Eileithyiaspolis.

92 Cailliaud writes: "This custom, lost in Egypt, where they cut it on the ground, is still practiced in Ethiopia. In keeping with this ancient method the stems of wheat, of dura, etc., remain in the ground and conserve their freshness. They only cut it as needed as food for beasts."

93 Cailliaud is again referring to the tomb of Paheri. See Porter and Moss, *Topographical Bibliography V*, 177; Tylor and Griffith, *The Tomb of Paheri*.

pigs in the stomping of the crop to separate the grains from the straw and also to plow seeds.[94] But the ancient monuments represent nothing similar. We know that these animals were renowned to be ignoble, disgusting, and unfit to be shown. Such was also perhaps the case with the camel which, having come from Asia from a slightly distant period, could have been shown on the monuments where we did not find them.[95] There are still oxen that do the stomping of wheat in Egypt, as in the most distant antiquity.

We are led to believe that the plow was invented along the banks of the Nile. No other people have thus enjoyed as much as them in the benefit of this instrument. No other people have venerated it as much.

We will end with the last duties of the wheat harvest. The scene begins, as always, from right to left (from al-Kab, pl. 33).[96] Two men, standing, are occupied with sifting grain. Each of them is supplied with the half-shell of a gourd. They fill them with grain while holding one half-shell on top of the other, then raising them as high as possible. They open them up slightly, little by little, so as to make the wheat fall at the mercy of the wind, which separates the chaff. Another young man sifts. A fourth sweeps together, with a broom, the grain which might be lost. Two large batches of wheat are sifted, and four men transport it into the magazine. Again, here, the artist shows two men in front of two others. He does this by showing a small part of the second group's profile, indicating two men hidden behind the first two. The inside of the magazine shows us mounds of wheat and a measurer who empties his container. A porter who has just emptied his sacks returns to fill them. Let us not forget the scribe who, seated high atop a pile of wheat so as to see and record everything, writes a report which is dictated to him.

The Egyptians conserved their grain by means of earthen silos covered by a dome so as to facilitate the drainage of rain. The tomb of Rotei,[97] in Beni Hasan al-Gadim (Heptano-mide)[98] gives us an example (pl. 34A, fig. 3). Nineteen domed silos, placed side by side, are closed by a door, while an opening serves as ventilation. Stairs, undoubtedly portable, led to the top of these domes from where one threw the grain to fill the silo. The wheat was measured: a man was responsible for doing this. He would climb the stairs. The scribe takes note of the number of measures—above we see a cross section of the floor for trampling the grain with its raised circular border so that nothing might be lost.

Other examples of these silos are shown to us with two levels.

---

94 Cailliaud writes: "Herodotus, book II, chapter XIV." See Herodotus, *The Histories*, 2.14.2; Strassler, *The Landmark Herodotus*, 123.

95 The oldest domesticated camel remains in Egypt are dated to the first millennium BC. The earliest possible date given for these remains is the late ninth century BC. For further information on the dating of these remains and the camel in general, see Peter Rowley-Conwy, "The Camel in the Nile Valley: New Radio-carbon Accelerator Dates from Qasr Ibrim," in *Journal of Egyptian Archaeology* 74 (1988): 245–48; Ian L. Mason, "Camels," in *Evolution of Domesticated Animals*, ed. Ian. L. Mason (London: Longman, 1984), 106–15.

96 Cailliaud is again referring to the tomb of Paheri. See note 93 above.

97 Tomb 17: the owner's name is Khety, not Rotei. See Porter and Moss, *Topographical Bibliography IV*, 156; Newberry, *Beni Hasan. Part I*, 51–62; Kanawati and Woods, *Beni Hassan*, 49–57.

98 An ancient Greek name for the area of Beni Hasan.

FLAX

We found crops of flax in the principal cave of al-Kab (Elethyia),[99] the tomb of Paphe according to Champollion (pl. 32).[100] Here women are teamed up in the work of men. One of them uproots the flax by the handful. Another brings to the workers a vase in each hand and a basket of provisions. Here also is shown the same careful spirit; two young girls, hunched over, collect the seeds of flax strewn on the ground. The harvest of sheaves is bound and transported for cleaning. The individual charged with this work is placed in the shadow of a tree. He holds in his hand a fistful of flax which he passes through a comb to detach the grain. A sheaf is at his feet.

IRRIGATION

We know that since antiquity Egypt was the granary of abundance of the neighboring countries.[101] Various plants produced three or four yields per year. Today the wheat sown in November is harvested at the end of April. One hundred days suffices for the harvest of barley, one hundred and twenty for broad beans. Flax sown mid-November is harvested at the end of February.

The silt from the river has always been a powerful fertilizer in Egypt. Wide-ranging irrigation in the Nile Valley was spread with much art, the fruit of great experience in the examination of the periodic flooding of the river. The fertile water was distributed over the lands by means of canals and locks around villages and up to the edges of the desert. The distribution of water was, therefore, in Egypt, a most-studied science[102] dating from the most distant antiquity.[103] Each year brought new improvements.

The Nileometric scales,[104] which gauged the various heights of the river, were observed daily: they announced increases. The rising of the water was felt at the start of June at the Nilometer of Elephantine, and fifteen days later in the waters of Memphis. The inundation spread until August, according to Pliny.[105] The insufficient floods of 9 to 12 cubits resulted in a missed harvest. Those of 14 to 15 cubits were the most favorable. In surpassing 16 cubits, they caused damage. These floods are still about the same in our day.

In the years of drought, the people's spirit was pierced by the punishment that was inflicted by the gods. It bore witness to a real joy and a profound acknowledgment of the

---

99 A version of the ancient Greek name for the area of al-Kab: Eileithyiaspolis.

100 Tomb 3, that of Paheri. See note 90 above.

101 Cailliaud writes: "Genesis: chapter XII, verse 2; chapter XLII, verse 2." Cailliaud appears to be citing scriptural passages such as Genesis chapter 41, verse 57: "*Moreover, all the world came to Joseph in Egypt to buy grain, because the famine became severe throughout the world*" (New Revised Standard Version).

102 In fact, pharaonic irrigation was fairly basic. See Karl W. Butzer, *Early Hydraulic Civilization in Egypt* (Chicago: University of Chicago Press, 1976). It should be noted that the Nile no longer floods naturally, as a result of the damming of the river at Aswan in the twentieth century.

103 Cailliaud writes: "Strabo, book 17." See, for example, Strabo, *The Geography*, 17.3, 17.30, 17.37, and 17.48.

104 He is referring here to Nilometers. See Veronica Seton-Williams and Peter Stocks, *Blue Guide. Egypt* (London: A&C Black, 1993), 220, 635.

105 Cailliaud writes: "Pliny, book 18." See Pliny the Elder, *Natural History*.

protector gods when the rising of the water was complete. Solemn holidays were celebrated in all of Egypt.[106]

The inundation often overwhelmed the surface of lands and required multiple surveys to understand the limits of each property.[107]

We see plate 34A. A laborer holds his plow and takes large steps to show that he measures the land in strides.[108]

When the waters receded they were retained, if needed, by dikes and small locks which held the irrigation the whole time it was required. The powerful action of the sun absorbed the water. After tilling with the plow and making small, shallow furrows, one seeded and harrowed by means of faggots of dry wood pulled by oxen. Finally, one trampled the ground with numerous groups of pigs, sheep, goats, and donkeys.[109]

We see in the paintings of tombs a light barque, bearing on the canals a surveyor who inspects the state of sites—always the spirit of order, of foresight, and of economy.

VINES AND GRAPE HARVESTS

According to the ancient authors, the vine was cultivated in Egypt at the edge of the desert because one found its terrain sandy and rocky, as well as having a light soil. Various wines were renowned. The most valued was that of Mareotis[110] because of the nature of the soil, which was not covered by the alluvium of the Nile. Athenaeus says that the grapes of Mareotis were most remarkable for their sweetness.[111] It was a white wine, which did not go to the head and which had the advantage of being preserved for a long time. He adds that the Teniotic, another wine, from the site of Tenia, also in Egypt, was superior still to the preceding one in its aromatic perfume. But Herodotus gives, still, superiority to that of Anthylla.[112]

Different wines were considered to have medicinal properties. Those of Coptos and Alexandria were offered to the gods in libations. These offerings were, however, prohibited in the temple of Heliopolis.[113] The use of wine was generally very moderate. It was forbidden during the time of abstinence and during solemn purifications.

---

106 Cailliaud writes: "Diodorus 2. c.1.36." See Diodorus Siculus, *Library of History*, http://penelope.uchicago.edu/Thayer/E/Roman/Texts/Diodorus_Siculus/1B*.html

107 Cailliaud writes: "Strabo, 17. Diodorus, 1." See Strabo, *The Geography*, 17; Diodorus, *Library of History*, 1.81, http://penelope.uchicago.edu/Thayer/E/Roman/Texts/Diodorus_Siculus/1D*.html

108 This scene is from Tomb 2, that of Amenemhat, in Beni Hasan. See Porter and Moss, *Topographical Bibliography IV*, 142; Newberry, *Beni Hasan. Part I*.

109 Cailliaud writes: "Herodotus, II, chapter 14." See Herodotus, *The Histories*, 2.14.2; Strassler, *The Landmark Herodotus*, 123.

110 Cailliaud writes: "Strabo, book 17." He is referring both to the area around Lake Mariut and to Strabo 17.14. See Strabo, *The Geography*.

111 An author from the Greek colony of Naukratis, a city in Egypt's Nile Delta. His one surviving work is called the *Deipnosophistai*, or "Scholars at Dinner."

112 Cailliaud writes simply: "Book II." Mainterot claims to have found a corresponding passage in the Nantes archives, and believes this is a reference to Herodotus, *The Histories*, 2.97.

113 Cailliaud writes: "Herodotus, II, 63." The citation does refer to a passage mentioning Heliopolis, but does not correspond to a mentioned prohibition on wine. See Herodotus, *The Histories*, 2.63; Strassler, *The Landmark Herodotus*, 145. For discussions on the place of wine in Egyptian society, including intoxication, see Hilary Wilson, *Egyptian Food and Drink* (London: Shire Publications, 2008); Helmut Brunner, "Trunkenheit," in *Lexicon der Ägyptologie*, vol. 6, edited by Wolfgang Helck and Eberhard Otto (Wiesbaden: Otto Harrassowitz, 1985).

The Egyptians originally had the custom of putting wines in flasks of skin, a custom followed still in several countries and which gives it a certain tar flavor. Later, they placed it in amphorae.

We will pass to a review of scenes of grape harvesting that we took from the tombs of the Theban necropolis (pl. 34).[114] A canopy, supported by two columns imitating the stem and the flower of a papyrus plant, surround the subject. The wine press appears to be made of a limestone block perfectly fashioned with an entablature, surmounted by a roll and with a cornice, as used in temple pylons. However, we note here that the style is not pyramidal. The wine press is overloaded with black grapes, which were trampled by seven individuals. All of them hold in one hand ropes which hang from the ceiling. We might easily imitate this custom which must have facilitated this kind of work in giving to the workmen a pressure point and more balance. The wine leaves the press by two openings. One appears to give clear wine, the other, from an upper level, rejects the bulk of the harvest in a particular basin. The profile of the figures of the people is recognized here as a mulatto race, originally from the Blacks whom we found in the south of Ethiopia and from the Sennarians living between the White and Blue Nile. We will cite another subject of painted grape harvesting, like the preceding one, in a tomb in the territory of Thebes (pl. 35).[115] The lower frieze, figure 2, shows us several vine stocks in arbors arranged in a bower. A man and woman are occupied with gathering the grapes with which they fill a basket. Another person waters the vines with one of the vases which he carries on his shoulder with the help of a balancing pole for this use. Close to this is the wine press, where an individual empties a basket of grapes. Two date palms receive at the top of their trunks a crossbeam from which hang four ropes, the ends of which are held by four grape-pickers who trample the grapes. Here again, as in the preceding scene, the white-colored wine press appears to be carved from a block of stone. The wine, which is red, is discharged into a basin.

Above, the upper frieze shows us in two lines the amphorae which must have contained the wine. Two individuals appear to stopper them. Baskets of choice grapes and a bundle of grape clusters are conserved. Above this, still, an offering of the first fruits of the harvest is addressed to a uraeus.[116] To the left, a standing scribe, holding his palette and his reed pen, writes the number of items.

---

114 Cailliaud is referring to scenes copied from Theban Tomb number 49, that of Neferhotep. See Porter and Moss, *Topographical Bibliography I.1*, 93; Nina de Garis Davies, *The Tomb of Nefer-hotep at Thebes*, vol. 2 (New York: Metropolitan Museum of Art, 1933), pl. i, iii, iv, vi, xli–xlix, lx; the bibliography on Theban Tomb 49 listed on the Theban Mapping Project, http://www.tmpbibliography.com/resources/bibliography_5nv_ tombs_of_the_nobles_tt49_neferhotep.html

115 Cailliaud is citing images from a tomb built for a different Neferhotep from the one mentioned previously. This tomb is labeled A5 in Porter and Moss, *Topographical Bibliography I.1*, 448. Its location in the Theban hills is now unknown. It was built during Egypt's mid-Eighteenth Dynasty, sometime around the reigns of Tuthmosis III and Amenhotep II, somewhere in the vicinity of modern-day Dra Abu al-Naga. For more information on its possible location, see Kampp, *Die Thebanische Nekropole*, 616. The Harer Collection contains a possible plan of the tomb, with a vague description of that tomb's location. This plan is presented in the chapter of this book titled "The Visual Corpus and Cailliaud."

116 This is likely a depiction of the goddess Renenutet. She is typically depicted in cobra form and is commonly found in wine or harvest scenes, as one of her roles was protector of the harvest. See Richard H. Wilkinson, *The Complete Gods and Goddesses of Ancient Egypt* (London: Thames and Hudson, 2003), 225–26.

The lower frieze, to the left, returns to the grape harvest. Men bring to a depot, which is in front, baskets of choice grapes, a bundle of grape clusters, and lotus flowers. In front of them, lying on the ground with joined hands, are guilty men to whom will be administered a beating as punishment. Immediately after that, we see a depot consisting of wine in amphorae, of choice baskets of grapes put in reserve, and of lotus flowers. The whole is presented to a scribe who must register all produce.[117] According to Herodotus,[118] the ancient Egyptians made use of date palm wine for the preparations used in embalming. According to Pliny,[119] date palm wine was common and widespread. He cites the method of making it, which consisted of fermenting in certain proportions of water the fruit of the palm tree, chosen very ripe, crushed, and then pressed.

The current inhabitants of Egypt proceed differently. They make incisions in the highest reach of the date palm's trunk. A vase immediately attached under the cut receives the liquid which flows from the sap. Newly extracted, it has the appearance of new, light wine, but after an intentional fermentation it acquires intoxicating properties.

This practice is rare today due to the damage that results in the palm tree which, generally, does not survive this operation. We have seen this process practiced instead in the oases where these date trees are abundant.

The ancient Egyptians used dates, grape clusters, figs, and some other fruits which, when submitted to fermentation, produced different beverages with their own particular names (Pliny 14, 16).[120]

The hop was unknown, says Mr. Wilkinson,[121] but barley combined with different plants and roots was used for the production of a particularly esteemed beer in Egypt.

According to Strabo,[122] the papyrus plant of the ancients was known under the different names of Cyperus, Papyrus, Byblus, and Hierticus. It grows still, today, in small numbers in the marshes of the Delta, in the area around Rosetta, around Damietta, and in the Faiyum, where it acquires a height of about one and a half meters.

We know all the importance attached anciently to the use of *Cyperus papyrus*, especially for the manufacture of paper, which gave it the value of a state monopoly.[123] According to Mr. Wilkinson, this plant sometimes achieved up to two meters in height. It was used for different things. The stems served in the fabrication of paper and in the manufacture of small, light boats. Also made from it were numerous baskets, quality mats for which the custom is widespread in Egypt, sandals, and other domestic objects. In the tufts of straw we found

---

117 Cailliaud writes: "The portion of the frieze above this last subject belongs to the fishing and to the hunting of geese on papyri which we see in the above frieze (fig. 1)."
118 Cailliaud writes: "II, 86." See: Herodotus, *The Histories*, 2.86; Strassler, *The Landmark Herodotus*, 152.
119 Cailliaud writes: "14, 16." See Pliny, *Natural History*, 14 and 16.
120 Pliny, *Natural History*, 14 and 16.
121 This is a reference to the famous British Egyptologist John Gardner Wilkinson (1797–1875).
122 Cailliaud writes: "Book 17, p. 550–1." See Strabo, *The Geography*, 17.15. *Cyperus*, however, is not mentioned in Strabo's passage.
123 Cailliaud writes: "It is more widespread today in Sicily, in the small river of Syracuse, where we picked it and saw it used as a curiosity, in imitation of the ancient Egyptians, to make paper."

a food of which the cultivators made more general use, with dura or sorghum, which replaces wheat in Upper Egypt above Thebes.

These abundant grass crops, at a price much lower than wheat, extend from Egypt into Nubia and in Ethiopia. Plate 31, figure 4, right-hand frieze. We will consider this culture as belonging to dura-sorghum, named above. Two cultivators, scythe in hand, get ready to cut the head. The crop is shown at the edge of water, indicated by undulating lines. This scene was painted in the tomb of Pharaoh Ramesses IV, the younger (Meiamun),[124] first king of the XIX Dynasty, in Biban al-Maluk, Theban territory (after Champollion).

We know that the Lotus was the flower of predilection for the ancient Egyptians. They used it as decoration in their celebrations. Throughout their various offerings and libations women adorned their brows with it, and the gods themselves were decorated with it. The stalks of this *Nymphaea* were also used practically: the basket maker used it to advantage. Plate 31, figure 4, frieze to the left, shows us a field of these *Nymphaea*, represented in water. It is recognizable by its calyx.

The artist was pleased to represent, with a regular symmetry between blooming flowers, shorter stalks showing buds. Two cultivators get ready to uproot these plants. This scene follows the last one, garnered[125] from the same tomb, that of Ramesses IV.[126]

Figure 3 shows us three men walking, carrying on their shoulder, with the help of a stick, lotuses. This subject is from a tomb in Beni Hasan al-Gadim.[127]

GARDENING

Gardening and other cultivations were watered by the hands of men. When necessary, one had recourse to a pail and pendulum (called a *shaduf*),[128] with the pail made of skin, which was plunged into the river or in the reservoirs. A painting in the tomb[129] of the Theban necropolis gives us this image along with that of the date palm, *doum* (pl. 33A, fig. 1).[130]

The weight of the pendulum raises the pail. When it is full the worker tips it into a ditch, which is divided and which branches along the surface of the earth, sometimes to a significant distance. This custom is still used in Egypt and the upper regions of Nubia. The ancients

---

124 Actually the tomb of Ramesses III, KV 11, in the Valley of the Kings. See Porter and Moss, *Topographical Bibliography I.2*, 521; the Theban Mapping Project's bibliography for KV 11, http://www.tmpbibliography. com/resources/bibliography_2kv_valley_of_kings_kv11_ramesses_iii.html. Cailliaud has conflated Ramesses II and Ramesses III; see note 64 above. See Clayton, *Chronicle of the Pharaohs*.

125 The verb used, 'recueillir,' is actually 'to gather, to pick, or to harvest,' possibly resulting in an unintended pun.

126 Actually the tomb of Ramesses III, KV 11, in the Valley of the Kings. See note 124 above.

127 This scene does not, in fact, come from a tomb in Beni Hasan, but rather from an unidentified tomb in Zawyat al-Mayyitin, in the modern-day Minya governorate.

128 This tool is still found in Egypt. It is composed of an upright frame that supports a counterbalanced pole with a pail.

129 Theban Tomb 49, that of Neferhotep. See Porter and Moss, *Topographical Bibliography I.1*, 93; Nina Davies, *The Tomb of Nefer-hotep*, pl. i, iii, iv, vi, xli–xlix, lx; the bibliography on Theban Tomb 49 listed on the Theban Mapping Project, http://www.tmpbibliography.com/resources/bibliography_5nv_tombs_of_the_nobles_ tt49_neferhotep.html

130 The *Hyphaene thebaica* or gingerbread tree.

do not appear to have made use of the crenulated wheel, turned by a carousel, a much-preferred system for certain localities than the *shaduf*, and widespread in Egypt.

In the gardens, one was obliged to transport water with the help of a balancing rod on the shoulder.

This subject is shown to us in the tomb, already cited, of Neferhotep in Beni Hasan al-Gadim (pl. 33A, figs. 2, 3).[131]

This painting shows us a basin from which two cultivators draw water, one after the other, to water a neighboring field of watermelons. The vases which they use have exactly the same form as those still used in Egypt by women, who carry them on the head. The practice of transporting things by means of a balancing pole was not preserved in Egypt, but we have noted it in Sennar, Fazoql, and in all of Ethiopia.

The same tomb of Neferhotep,[132] so greatly exploited and so rich in varied and most curious subjects, shows us, in the following tableau, harvests of fruits.[133] *Bamia*,[134] still widespread in Egypt, is collected. It is a long, green fruit that one eats boiled. Three people equipped with baskets are occupied with gathering it. Another transports it with the help of a balancing pole. This practice is convenient and advantageous, and we are surprised that it did not spread more.[135]

The sycomore was always appreciated for the quality of its wood, and especially by the ancient Egyptians. They used it, along with acacia wood, for making sarcophagi. Still today, this wood is sought and is insufficient for the needs of industry. The inexhaustible Nevotph preserved for us the image of the sycomore fig (pl. 34A, fig. 2)[136] and the harvest of its fruit, little valued today. As baskets are filled, three baboons (cynocephalus),[137] perched in the tree, eat figs at their leisure. We note that the people who gather this fruit do not stop them because these animals, as we know, enjoyed a certain consideration among the ancients, undoubtedly because of their intelligence.

Plate 34A, figure 1. We have noted that this custom is much appreciated in Amsterdam, principally during the period where ice overruns the canals which, as we know, become in this circumstance the roads for the country. The milkmaid on her skates has a balancing pole on her shoulders from which her containers or her baskets of vegetables are suspended.

---

131 Cailliaud is referring to Tomb 3 in Beni Hasan. The owner of this tomb is alternately referred to as Khnumhotep II or Khnumhotep III in literature. For references to the cited scene in the tomb of Khnumhotep III, see Porter and Moss, *Topographical Bibliography IV*, 145; Newberry, *Beni Hasan. Part I*, pl. XXIX. For a more recent reference to the scene, in which the owner is cited as Khnumhotep II, see Kanawati and Woods, *Beni Hassan*, 36, 38.

132 Cailliaud is referring to Tomb 3 in Beni Hasan. The owner of this tomb is alternately referred to as either Khnumhotep II or Khnumhotep III. See Porter and Moss, *Topographical Bibliography IV*, 144–49; Newberry, *Beni Hasan. Part I*, 41–72, pl. XXIV–XXXVIII; Kanawati and Woods, *Beni Hassan*, 33–40.

133 Cailliaud writes: "Plate 34A, figure 1."

134 Okra.

135 A note in the right-hand margin states: "For this note see the end of the article." He is referring to the last paragraph in this section on gardening.

136 From Tomb 3 in Beni Hasan, the owner of which is alternately referred to in the literature as Khnumhotep II or Khnumhotep III. SSee note 131 above.

137 This word means, literally, 'dog-faced.' Cailliaud uses it in reference to the appearance of baboons in Egypt.

They follow each movement of the courageous Dutchwoman, who, sometimes on one foot, sometimes on the other, indulges in the full dash of her skates. For foreigners (and we remember) this fact is one of the curiosities of this country.

FRUIT TREES

In ancient times, as in our day, the most remarkable tree in Egypt was the palm tree. Its fruits are very abundant. The ancients already used the woody parts. We find in the tombs small brooms, made from parts of branches, baskets woven from leaves, sandals, rope made from the filaments, and dates sometimes pressed as preserve. Pliny recounts these facts and says that the lifespan of the palm tree was between 60 and 70 years.[138]

One dried a portion of the dates; others, fresh, were pressed into paste in baskets. We observed that this custom was practiced in the oases to facilitate the export of fruits by caravans. We found the inhabitants of these desert regions very experienced in extracting the *eau de vie* from dates while saying "Muhammad, close your eyes."[139] The fruit trees known by the ancients were only small in number. Pliny cites the sycomore, peach, fig, almond, olive, the *nebq*, the *Persea*, and the Palm of Christ tree from which they extracted oil.[140] The ancient Egyptians loved to have rare trees and plants in their gardens and in their parks. They were brought from far-off countries as tribute. The paintings and sculptures represent foreigners leading their animals to be offered as presents to the king, as well as flowers and shrubs.

---

138 Cailliaud writes: "Book 13, 4." Pliny, *Natural History*, 13.4.
139 It is unknown why this would be said while tapping a palm tree.
140 The castor oil plant.

ON THE EXTRACTION OF ESSENCES AND OTHER LIQUIDS

W̲e saw the laborer class, in all its simplicity, enaged in working the fields.[142] Here, two women have just harvested a flower which they have in their basket. They show specimens which appear to us to have much in common with the flowers of the orange tree. Figure 7:[143] A third woman sniffs at its scent, which proves that it is an odiferous flower and, as a result, likely to be used. Figure 8:[144] Two other women, very much occupied with their work, press into a sack the produce saturated with this flower, which is collected in a vase.

The force majeure that these women deliver so easily with the help of two long levers becomes here a simple and strong motor which our industry has yet to put into action.[145] It would be easy and advantageous for us to imitate this custom for work of this type.

These women are foreign to Egypt.[146] Their big lips and the yellow color of their skin make us consider them as originally from the black race. Their tunic is held by a shoulder strap and they wear necklaces.

---

141 The cover page for chapter 6 lists three unrelated subjects. I have separated these into subsections of the same chapter to maintain both the spirit of the cover page and the format of a thematic encyclopedia.

142 Cailliaud writes: "Pl. 15A, fig. 9."

143 Cailliaud is still referring to pl. 15A.

144 Cailliaud is referring again to pl. 15A.

145 The first sentence of this paragraph is deleted: "Here is a lesson to be learned; easy for us to imitate in our interiors for work of this type."

146 For discussions on ethnic groups in ancient Egypt, see Theodore Celenko, *Egypt in Africa* (Indianapolis: Indianapolis Museum of Art, 1996); Barry J. Kemp, "Imperialism in New Kingdom Egypt (c. 1575–1087 B.C.)," in *Imperialism in the Ancient World*, edited by Peter D.A. Garnsey and Charles Richard Whittaker (Cambridge UK: Cambridge University Press, 1978); Donald B. Redford, *Egypt, Canaan, and Israel in Ancient Times* (Princeton: Princeton University Press, 1993).

We must note another press in a sack;[147] this one is fixed in a solidly built frame. The sack is, for more resistance, covered with a strong net with a large mesh and is, at its ends, passed through solid rings. One of them is fixed in one of the posts of the apparatus. The other is mobile and rotates at will through a lever moved by three standing men who turn it by the strength of their arms. The liquid falls in abundance into a vase. A fourth individual, pressing one hand on the sack, appears to observe the correct execution of the work. This subject is thus painted in the tomb of Menopth in Beni Hasan al-Gadim.[148]

A third press, more analogous to the first,[149] shows us once more the frequent custom of the ancients of using levers in their fruit presses. Their sacks were tightly bound, undoubtedly to resist such a strong force. Here we see the efforts undertaken by five men to turn the sack in order to extend it (it seems to us). Two men mounted on the backs of two others pull on levers. A fifth one, in a horizontal pose, has the sack as a pressure point. He pushes feet and hands against the levers so as to move them aside, thus joining his efforts to those of his companions to twist the bag as much as possible. The exaggeration of this last pose seems to us the contrivance of the Egyptian artist. The liquor, tinted blue, falls abundantly into a vase indicated as granite. The men wear nothing but the kilt, with these last ones having the head covered with a skullcap. This subject comes from a tomb in the area around Memphis.[150]

---

147 Cailliaud writes: "Plate 5A, fig. 5."
148 Tomb 15: the tomb owner's name is Bakt III, not Menopth, as spelled by Cailliaud, or Menothph, as spelled in Champollion, *Monuments de l'Égypte*, vol. 3, pl. CCCLXXXIX. See Newberry, *Beni Hasan. Part II*, pl. VI; Kanawati and Woods, *Beni Hassan*, 46.
149 Cailliaud writes: "Plate 6, fig. 2."
150 The tomb of Iymery in Giza. See Porter and Moss, *Topographical Bibliography III.1*, 173, and the bibliography on Boston's Museum of Fine Arts' Giza Archives, http://www.gizapyramids.org/code/emuseum.asp

ON GAMES

B all games were undoubtedly the recreation of children, but women indulged in it with much energy and a remarkable perseverance. They added varied poses so as to lend more attraction to this very simple game. The decorations of most ancient tombs show several subjects of this genre. Plate 41 is taken from the tomb of the chief Rotei in Beni Hasan.[152]

Figure 1. Three women throw their balls with both hands. No sooner is one received than the other is sent back. The movements follow each other and the balls crisscross rapidly. One of them, demonstrating more dexterity than the others, crosses her arms on her chest and, in this position, appears to catch and return balls.

Figure 2. Two women, head and body bent behind them, remain supported by their arms which press against the ground. They thus execute a pose of extreme flexibility which is still practiced by jugglers of our day.

Figure 3. The same ball game is repeated in a different position. Two full-length women, placed a certain distance apart from each other, their bodies tilted horizontally, their arms pressed against their knees as a means of support, carry on their backs two of their companions. These last women throw and catch balls. Another woman of the group holds herself on one leg only, the other crossed, and her arms immobile. This pose, along with that of the two people supporting the women players, is undoubtedly inflicted upon them for their lack of skill in the game.

---

151 The cover page for chapter 6 lists three unrelated subjects. I have separated these into subsections of the same chapter to maintain both the spirit of the cover page and the format of a thematic encyclopedia.

152 Tomb 17: the owner's name is Khety, not Rotei. See Newberry, *Beni Hasan. Part II*, pl. XIII; Kanawati and Woods, *Beni Hassan*, 41.

Figures 4 and 5. Two women here execute a tour de force as they grapple. It looks as if the one on top has to throw her companion over her shoulder so that she lands on her feet. Several people hold themselves here on one leg, the arms perfectly immobilized. This leg, thus crossed, is, in hieroglyphs, the sign of the dance which these women had to be trained in doing.

They wear tight-fitting clothing, probably knitted to obtain the necessary elasticity. It is held up by straps on the shoulders. Their particular hairstyle presents two long, hanging tresses. Their throats are adorned with necklaces and they have bracelets at the bottom of their legs and arms. These uniform fittings give the women a certain appearance which was suitable for their reception in certain fashionable houses where they were in demand.[153]

The outfits of these women and the exercises in which they partake clearly show us nomads who are earning their keep. Their clothing, along with the yellow color of their skin, indicates foreigners, probably from Ethiopia.[154]

Among the Egyptians we do not have a single representation of the practice that the Romans had in this game, of hitting the ball against the ground.

These balls, found in the tombs of the necropolis of Thebes, are of 6–7 centimeters in diameter. They are stuffed with husks of wheat, sometimes rolled bran or rush, and covered by pieces of leather or hide.

A game, that of a child, still widely in use today in Italy, is *mora*. Despite all its simplicity, which involves raising as many fingers as indicated by him who commands the game, the Italians put a keen interest into it (pl. 38, fig. 3A. Subject comes from the Theban necropolis).[155]

The game of hot cockles is still played among the men (pl. 37A, fig. 5). Three people are playing: one kneeling, his face against the ground, guesses which of the two others hit him. We note here that the players have closed fists: this could be to punch the waiting player's back, or, instead, their hands conceal pawns, of which he must guess the number in order to be freed.

The game of even or odds was still very much played, as we see represented (pl. 37A, fig. 7).[156] For objects to hide, they made use of a small porcelain shell, called money of guinea,[157] and sometimes natural knucklebones or other imitation objects made from fragments of bone and hippopotamus ivory. We note that the players are generally seated on the ground on one of their heels. This pose is also adopted for the occupation of more serious genres. He who has not guessed correctly appears to receive a two-fingered slap on the cheek, administered by the other player. A tour de force is shown by a man standing on his head with his arms crossed over the chest (fig. 3).

---

153 For further information on dancers in ancient Egypt, see: Dimitri Meeks, "Dance," in *The Oxford Encyclopedia of Ancient Egypt*, vol. 1, edited by Donald Redford (Oxford UK: Oxford University Press, 2001); Irena Lexova, *Ancient Egyptian Dances* (Mineola NY: Dover Publications, 1999).

154 For discussions on ethnic groups in ancient Egypt, see Celenko, *Egypt in Africa*; Kemp, "Imperialism in New Kingdom Egypt"; Redford, *Egypt, Canaan, and Israel in Ancient Times*.

155 It is unknown from which tomb this scene was copied.

156 Also known as 'pair ou non' or 'even or not,' this game requires a player to guess whether the number of objects hidden in the hand is even or odd.

157 This was the name used for such a shell in Cailliaud's lifetime.

Many games cannot be recognized: Figure 4, that of straws; Figure 6, that of the hoop.

A game of skill consisted of throwing long spikes in the shape of straight spearheads at logs of squared-off wood laid on the ground. This type of pointed form had to strike closest to the fixed marks on the block.

The above-cited subjects come from the inexhaustible tomb in this genre, that of chief Rotei in Beni Hasan al-Gadim.[158]

The game of knucklebones, along with that of dice, must have also been known by the Egyptians, but perhaps not in extreme antiquity. We know that the Greeks and Romans frequently made use of them. A painting from Herculaneum shows us the daughters of Niobe[159] playing knucklebones in the company of their mother and Latona.[160]

The upper class, even the kings and their entourage, generally loved hunting and fishing. These exercises refreshed them from their serious occupations. As we have said, however, they must have pursued them in a measured way, as the burning climate of Egypt sometimes rendered these amusements tedious. As replacements for them, they gave themselves to peaceful recreations in the home. We have cited Ramesses IV Meiamun[161] playing chess[162] with the queen and one of his daughters.[163]

The inexhaustible resources of tombs and temples, where the perseverance of this great people pleased them to depict their entire history and all the scenes of their past life in sculptures or paintings, show us their taste for the game of chess or draughts.[164] In the rich tomb of the chief Rotei in Beni Hasan (pl. 41A, figs. 3, 4),[165] two individuals, skullcaps on their heads, with only the kilt for clothing, are in front of a table, half crouching on the ground on one of their heels. They seem greatly at ease and begin a game of chess. All the pawns appear still to be in their original places. It is the repetition of preceding figures, with the small difference that with figures 1 and 2 the pawns are scattered here and there to indicate that the game has begun.

We found in the tombs pawns for this game. They are small cones in wood, in ceramic that is glazed black for some and others blue, and in limestone, while others, more carefully done, were in alabaster. The Drovetti collection in Turin possessed a certain number, along with a wooden tray with a squared edge covered in numerous squares for these different games.

---

158 Tomb 17, that of Khety. See Newberry, *Beni Hasan. Part II*, pl. XVI; Kanawati and Woods, *Beni Hassan*, 54.

159 A figure in Greek mythology who is punished by the gods for her hubris. Upon the urging of the goddess Leto, Apollo and Artemis slay Niobe's children with arrows. After her husband kills himself, Niobe is unable to move from grief and turns to stone.

160 Latona is the Latin version of Leto, the goddess who brings about the death of Niobe's family.

161 This is a reference to Ramesses III. Cailliaud has conflated Ramesses II and Ramesses III; see note 64 above. See Clayton, *Chronicle of the Pharaohs*.

162 Ancient Egyptians did not play chess. They did, however, have a number of board games, such as *senet*. See Irving Finkel, ed., *Ancient Board Games in Perspective* (London: British Museum Press, 1998).

163 Cailliaud is referring to a scene in Medinet Habu, the mortuary temple of Ramesses III, which he also cites in chapter 15.

164 See Finkel, ed., *Ancient Board Games*.

165 Tomb 17, that of Khety. See note 158 above.

CHAPTER 6.3 [166]

TRANSPORT OF STATUES

Plate 43. Transport of a colossal statue, a most curious subject, coming from a tomb in Beni Hasan.[167] This statue is in limestone; its height must be around eight meters. It is placed on a sled to which it is firmly attached by means of double ropes, then secured by ends of wood in a tourniquet, like the custom used to hold our saws. To protect the colossus from damage that might befall it from immediate contact with the ropes, they carefully introduced cushions of hide under the cables.

86 men placed in four rows pull on ropes attached to the front of the sled. Not all are Egyptians. Those wearing long clothes are foreigners, almost always compelled to hard labor. A man standing on the base of the statue pours water or fat, probably to make the sled slide better on the planks which cover the ground. Four men carry, by means of a balancing pole, vases of liquid similar to this last one for the same purpose. Three other individuals bear on their shoulders a piece of wood ending in the teeth of a saw. 15 men follow the procession to lend a hand in case it is needed. Three among them have in hand a stick as a symbol of authority. On the knees of the statue is a full-length man, clapping his hands one against the other to mark the cadence of the song of the workmen and, by this method, to obtain simultaneous pulling.

---

166 The cover page for chapter 6 lists three unrelated subjects. I have separated these into subsections of the same chapter to maintain both the spirit of the cover page and the format of a thematic encyclopedia.

167 The tomb, number 2, dedicated to Djehutyhotep II, is located, more precisely, in Deir al-Bersha. See Percy E. Newberry, *El Bersheh. Part I* (London: The Egypt Exploration Fund, 1895), pl. XV; Porter and Moss, *Topographical Bibliography IV*, 179–81; the listed bibliography on the website of the Belgian Mission to Deir al-Bersha, http://www.dayralbarsha.com/node/12

This custom is still generally followed for communal work in Egypt. Another individual appears to hold a percussion instrument which he beats to repeat and to send further the signal of the last-mentioned person.

We note at the head of the procession 60 men of the upper class, divided into 10 squads walking in time, starting, like us, with the left foot. They hold in their right hand a stick, of the light quarterstaff kind, and in the left hand the palm of victory.[168] This scene of transportation, which we attribute to the most ancient reign of Osertasen II,[169] is thus conducted with a certain solemnity.

---

168 Cailliaud has recorded the figures at the top of the scene holding both sticks and palm fronds. Unlike the previously mentioned thin sticks, these appear more like clubs. Newberry's definitive recording of the scene, however, only shows the figures holding fronds, and suggests that Cailliaud confused the shapes of the items being held. Additionally, Cailliaud's use of the term 'palm of victory' is overly dramatic. These groups of men are coming to greet the arrival of the statue. As the inscription in the tomb over their heads tells us, the place from which they come is celebrating the creation of the colossus. The palm fronds presumably form part of this celebration. See Newberry, *El Bersheh. Part I*, 21–22.

169 The tomb dates to the mid-Twelfth Dynasty reigns of Senusret II and III.

CHAPTER 7

MANUFACTURE AND
USE OF UNFIRED BRICKS[170]

ne of the first needs of man was to shelter himself against the inclemency of the seasons, in caves, under huts made of branches, etc. Then, depending on the country, he used stone and shaped clay. The industry of bricks baked by a hot sun must have begun early in Egypt where trees are rare and the nights cold.[171]

The paintings from a tomb of the Theban necropolis will give us the details for this sort of manufacture (pl. 9A).[172]

Here, Jews are distinguished from Egyptians by their physiognomy.[173] Several of them wear a small beard, but their yellow color above all marks them out. We know that this class of laborers was used in the Orient for the most difficult sorts of work. Here, they draw

---

170 For more information on mud-brick architecture, see Barry Kemp, "Soil (including Mud-brick Architecture)," in *Ancient Egyptian Materials and Technology*, edited by Ian Shaw and Paul T. Nicholson (Cambridge UK: Cambridge University Press, 2000).

171 Cailliaud writes: "The meteorological observations of Mr. Letorzec, our travel companion, recount for us the rapid transition from hot days to frozen nights. In the Libyan desert, close to the oasis of Siwa under the 24th degree latitude north, in 1819, the 27th December, from eight to nine o'clock in the morning, the centigrade thermometer was 0.0 degrees. From six to seven o'clock in the evening it recorded 13.2. In the morning of the 28th it was at 1.2. In the evening it reached 12.5. On the 31st, in the morning, it recorded 1.1 and in the evening 15.2. The strongest heat of the month was on the 11th with 24.7. The following month, on the morning of the 15th, it was 6.1. From midday to 1 o'clock it was 27.9. The highest temperature was on the 24th, when it was 35.5."

172 Theban Tomb 100, that of Rekhmire. See Porter and Moss, *Topographical Bibliography I.1* (Oxford UK: Clarendon Press, 1960), 211; Norman de Garis Davies, *The Tomb of Rekh-mi-Re' at Thebes*, vol. 2 (New York: Arno Press, 1973), pl. lii–lv, lviii–lxii, lxiii; the Theban Mapping Project's bibliography for Tomb 100, http://www.tmpbibliography.com/resources/bibliography_5nv_tombs_of_the_nobles_tt100_rekhmire.html

173 There is no reason to believe the people depicted in this plate are Jewish or from anywhere other than Egypt. They are represented with all of the characteristics used to depict Egyptians.

water from a basin. One of them has plunged in up to his elbows. Another picks at a mound of clay. The legs of the workmen, which are covered in it, show us that they trampled and kneaded this earth with their feet. Next, they give it to two molders. Sometimes bricks received stamps of the names of kings while in the mold. We found those of Ramesses II in Thebes. In the lower frieze, two workmen transport things on their shoulders, one of them a block of clay, the other a vase of water, while a third transports unfired bricks. Another transports things by means of a balancing pole. At the head of the group, a supervisor, rod in hand, appears to give orders. A large heap of clay is prepared. An aide carries each brick to the workman, who uses them in the construction of two walls: one horizontal, the other sloping like a ramp for climbing. Their color clearly shows us that they are of unfired brick. It is made of clay dried in the sun. Above, we see piles of baked bricks. Two workmen transport them on ropes with the help of their balancing pole. We see from one of them that they loaded them themselves while the supervisor crouches, his rod in hand.

Very large bricks were used in the construction of ramparts and enclosure walls. They were often 0.36 m long and 0.20 m wide. The use of these unfired bricks was always an immense advantage for Egypt and Nubia with the exception of certain deluxe houses where they perhaps used baked bricks. Private houses and public buildings were generally erected in clay simply dried in the sun. This easy and inexpensive construction occupied a considerable number of hands. The works of this genre, which endured more than 33 centuries, are still considerable in many parts of Egypt, Nubia, and Ethiopia. We will cite the temples of Mount Barkal in Ethiopia and the wall or rampart bordering the desert from Aswan to Philae. Its thickness is 1.90 m, its height close to 4 m, its extent was about 6 km. The enclosure wall of Ombos was about 750 m around. We have found similar works in the oases of the desert of Syria, as well as an enclosure of 828 m which surrounded the temples and various constructions of al-Musawwarat on the island of Meroe.[174]

The numerous pyramids, also of unfired brick, erected in the territory of Memphis (Saqqara), as well as the tombs of the necropolis of Thebes, still show us their use in the construction of vaults, the knowledge of which was known more than 3,880 years ago.[175] Only the Egyptian temples were built in stone.

---

174 Cailliaud writes: "Travels to Meroe, vol. III, p. 140."
175 Cailliaud writes: "According to the research of Wilkinson."

CHAPTER 8

THE POTTER'S ART[176]

T he work of the potter belongs to the most distant period of art in Egypt, despite the citation of Pliny, who mistakenly says that it was imported from Athens.[177] The proof of our assertion is found in the ancient representations of works of this art in the tombs of Egypt, which existed before the arrival of Joseph in this country and which greatly preceded the foundation of Athens. Strabo says that the art of throwing pottery was well known by Homer nine or ten centuries before Jesus Christ.[178]

We will review the painted representations which remain of this art, and which are still provided by the famous tomb of Menothph in Beni Hasan al-Gadim.[179]

In the upper frieze, two men knead clay with their feet. Their stance is assured, symmetrical, and uniform, indicating a studied method that is followed and well-timed movements, like those of smiths striking iron on an anvil.

The hieroglyphic inscription . . . .[180]

A third workman handles molds and touches up the clay.

---

176 For more information on Egyptian pottery, see Janine Bourriau, Paul T. Nicholson, and Pamela J. Rose, "Pottery," in *Ancient Egyptian Materials and Technology*, edited by Ian Shaw and Paul T. Nicholson (Cambridge UK: Cambridge University Press, 2000).

177 Cailliaud writes: "Book 7, p. 56." See Pliny the Elder, *Natural History*.

178 Cailliaud writes "Seneca, Epistle 90." See Lucius Annaeus Seneca, *Moral Epistles: The Loeb Classical Library*, vol. 2, translated by Richard M. Gummere (Cambridge MA: Harvard University Press, 1917–25), http://www.stoics.com/seneca_epistles_book_2.html#%E2%80%98XC1

179 Cailliaud writes: "Pl. 16." The tomb to which he refers is number 15 in Beni Hasan, that of Bakt III, not Menothph, as spelled by Cailliaud here and by Champollion. See Champollion, *Monuments de l'Égypte*, vol. 3 (Paris: Firmin Didot, 1835–45), pl. CCCLXXXIX; Newberry, *Beni Hasan. Part II*, pl. VII.

180 Cailliaud does not include the inscription to which he refers.

The inscription above . . . .[181]

The next person presents clay transformed into a cone so that it might be placed on the neighboring, vacant wheel. He holds the wheel that will receive it with his hand.

The following turner has his left leg down in a hole at the base of the wheel where his foot puts it in motion. With his two hands, the worker will build up the small mass of clay that must complete his work. The following two workmen also only show one leg, like the first, but here it's the left leg, as the other turns the wheel. By means of thumb and fingers the workmen fashion the clay at will. On completing their vases, which receive the final touches,[182] they are often obliged to bathe their hands in vases of water which we see around them.

The lower frieze shows us two workmen who have pulled their legs up on the ground. With their hand, they stop their wheels to remove the completed work. These are still conical vases, similar to the preceding ones: they are much used today in Egypt for tasks around the house.

The following person presents a vase. Two hieroglyphic signs . . . .[183]

The next workman has a knee on the ground and holds a kind of plate. The three signs above . . . .[184]

The first oven is heated to bake the pottery. The hieroglyphic signs . . . .[185]

One removes from a second oven the pottery, in various forms, that is baked. These are primarily bowls. The inscription . . . .[186]

Finally, a man transports them by means of a balancing pole.

Various models of large pottery are scattered about this plate. Some have necks, others have a shrunken spout like a teapot. The former are still widespread in Egypt.

We were surprised to find in the Theban necropolis four vases which must predate knowledge of the wheel in this country.[187] They have the height and are of the genre of a bottle. The opening of the neck is, however, wider. The bottom is not flat, but is, on the contrary, conical like many ancient vases destined to be placed in holes in racks, in keeping with an ancient custom from Egypt.[188] They are made from two molded pieces in two equal parts, dividing the vase longitudinally along its axis: these two pieces are then brought

---

181 Cailliaud does not include the inscription to which he refers.

182 The French expression used is *un coup de pouce*, an idiom which means 'a push in the right direction,' but literally translates to 'a press of the thumb.' Cailliaud is possibly using it as a pun, because, in order to move a piece of pottery along in its production, one needs to shape it with the press of one's thumbs.

183 Cailliaud does not include the inscription to which he refers.

184 Cailliaud does not include the signs to which he refers.

185 Cailliaud does not include the signs to which he refers.

186 Cailliaud does not include the inscription to which he refers.

187 Cailliaud is referring to a method of pottery making that does not rely on centrifugal force to shape clay. His assumption that the pots in question must have been made before the Egyptians knew how to apply centrifugal force in pottery, however, is wrong. Both hand-building and centrifugal force techniques were used by Egyptian Predynastic potters. These two processes continued to be used throughout Egyptian history. One of the earliest depictions of an actual wheel being used in the production of ancient Egyptian pottery comes from the Fifth Dynasty tomb of Ti in Saqqara. See Dorothea Arnold and Janine Bourriau, eds., *An Introduction to Ancient Egyptian Pottery* (Mainz: Philipp von Zabern, 1993); Bourriau, Nicholson, and Rose, "Pottery."

188 Cailliaud writes: "Pl. 32."

together and joined one against the other. Despite this particularity they are well rounded, all the while showing their method of manufacture which predates the potter's wheel. These vases are fitted with small handles. They are well glazed in blue enamel on which festoons and lotus flowers are drawn in black.[189]

Another vase, analogous to the preceding one, also has the shape of a bottle, but with a cylindrical neck and a flat bottom, called 'Gullah' or 'Bardak.' This vase is common and replaced the ancient conical-bottomed vase. They are made in Qena and in Coptos, in Upper Egypt. They are of porous earth and, when exposed to a current of air, they have the property of cooling water. This is a great joy in Egypt's climate.[190]

The Leiden Museum possesses about 40 terra cotta plates showing on their interiors gods drawn in black and white lines: the sacred barques of Re and Osiris, images of Isis, of Nephthys, of Thoth, of Mui, of Atmu, of Tefne,[191] and of Horus, who guides the rudder. On this curious collection of plates used in sacred tasks, all these divinities are shown accompanied by hieroglyphic, funerary legends.

Vases are divided into three series. One comprises pottery destined for domestic life. It was generally in terra cotta to withstand the effect of the fire.

The second is composed of vases destined for sacred use. They are distinguished by their form and inscriptions.

The third series contains vases that served funerary uses. They were in pottery, in faience, or in stone, as well as semicircles upon which to rest the head during sleep, and the scribal palette.

Numerous objects of this genre, common in the main museums, tell us that their manufacture must have occupied a large number of workmen.

Among the fine vases and those choice pieces of the ancients, we must note one of flattened form, like a gourd or a circular drum, with a diameter of twelve centimeters. This vase was made on a wheel, in two rounded pieces, with the pieces brought together and joined one against the other. The adjoined neck resembles the calyx of a lotus. The handles are represented by two cynocephalus monkeys; a garland of flowers and hieroglyphs decorate the body of the vase, which is in glazed faience of a pretty green color. The Louvre

---

189 Cailliaud writes: "These four vases belong to the collection which we brought back, and which is annexed to the new Antiquities Gallery in Paris, Imperial Library." Two of these vases are possibly in the Bibiliothèque nationale's Cabinet des médailles, without inventory numbers. See Philippe Mainterot, "Une contribution à la naissance de l'égyptologie: voyages et collections du Nantais Frédéric Cailliaud (1787–1869). Catalogue des objets" (PhD thesis, Université de Poitiers, 2008), fiches 183 and 184; Georges Legrain, "Inventaire méthodique de la collection d'antiquités égyptiennes conservée au Cabinet des Antiques et Médailles" (Paris: Bibliothèque nationale, Rés. ms. 47007 PAR BN Fo, 1894–96), 849. A third vase might be E.13216-CM.201 in the Louvre. See Mainterot, *Une contribution*, fiche 182; Laurianne Martinez-Sève et al., *Faïences de l'Antiquité: de l'Égypte à l'Iran* (Paris: Louvre, 2005), 16–17. For an explanation of what became of the objects Cailliaud brought back from Egypt, see Philippe Mainterot, *Aux origines de l'égyptologie: Voyages et collections de Frédéric Cailliaud (1787–1869)* (Rennes: Presses Universitaires de Rennes, 2011), 251–86.

190 Cailliaud writes: "In Edfu, or Upper Egypt, the Copts occupy themselves especially with pottery: it is a hereditary industry preserved among them. They still hold to various, ancient forms from antiquity. The earth that they use is a fine clay mixed with Nile silt and ash, which takes a pretty red color in the fire."

191 These last three names are likely incorrect versions of Mut, Atum, and Tefnut.

contains many of these vases, all similar even in their hieroglyphs. Mr. de Rougé writes that their inscriptions bear a wish for a happy year. We collected in the tombs of Qurna in Thebes a vase that is the same as those in the Louvre in form and decoration. It appears to have served as a present for the New Year.[192]

Alabaster was ordinarily chosen for vases called canopic, of which the lids represented the heads of the four funerary genies of the Amenti:[193] Qebesenuef (head of a falcon), Duamutef (head of a jackal), Hapi (head of a cynocephalus),[194] and Imseti (human head).[195] These four genies, sons of Osiris,[196] shown embalming their father, had the great reputation of assisting the deceased. This custom required four vases for a deceased person. In each of these vases the entrails and the viscera taken from the body were embalmed separately. Each part was consecrated in a special manner to the titular genie of one of the four sons of Osiris.[197] This custom required many of these vases to be manufactured. They are also common in museums.[198]

We find them from the greatest antiquity, before knowledge of the wheel, but there are also many that are thrown. There also exist vases of this same form, in limestone. These were more widespread, probably because they were cheaper.

Alabaster was much used because this stone is easy to work. The Egyptians used it for numerous objects of all genres, large and small, from the sarcophagi of kings to the smallest kohl pot. Museums possess many of them in their rich collections. There are basins, plates, cups, glasses, chalices, and other objects of numerous, varied, and elegant forms for which the models were often taken from nature, among animals. This is why the lion, the gazelle, the cynocephalus, the porcupine, the swan, the ibis, fish sometimes whole, are shown and arranged so that the body of the animal formed the body of the vase. There are also figures of Isis, of Typhon,[199] and other genies.

Serpentine, steatite, and other talcose rocks, as well as proper limestone, must have been used, because of their hardness, in the same manner as alabaster and worked by the same artists.

What is more surprising are vases in hard stone. These could not be worked with a tool on the wheel, like the preceding ones. Here the blow of a hammer, properly

---

192 Cailliaud writes: "It is shown in the second book of our *Travels in the Oasis of Thebes*, 2 etc., pl. 38, fig. 1 to 4. Recorded in-folio with twenty-five antiquities plates, inscriptions, and papyrus manuscripts." This object is in the Bibliothèque nationale's Cabinet des médailles, without an inventory number. Mainterot ascribes its location to al-Kab, rather than Qurna as stated by Cailliaud, and dates it to around the time of the Twenty-sixth Dynasty (664–525 BC). See Mainterot, "Une contribution", fiche 23; Martinez-Sève et al., *Faïences de l'Antiquité*, 147–49.

193 A nineteenth-century version of the ancient Egyptian word *Imentet*, meaning 'the west,' or 'the land of the dead.'

194 Cailliaud is again using this word, which literally means 'dog-faced,' to describe the features of baboons in Egypt.

195 These are the four sons of Horus, believed to protect the viscera of embalmed mummies.

196 Actually Horus.

197 Actually Horus.

198 Cailliaud writes: "Those of Paris, of London, of Turin, of Berlin, and of Leiden possess more than 300 of them. They are interesting for the titles and the inscriptions in favor of the deceased, addressed to the funerary genies, to Isis, to Nephthis, to Neith, etc."

199 An ancient Greek name for Seth.

delivered, first broke the rock into small fragments to approximate, as much as possible, the desired form. Next came the barley grain as hammer and pointed punch must have picked the stone and removed at will the desired parts, but only grain by grain and after much time. It required even more barley to make the pick marks of the tools disappear with emery, to soften and polish the surfaces. With these last two methods the wheel was surely used.[200]

Various kinds of porphyry, granite, basalt, diorite, feldspar, even lapis lazuli were worked with success and with much art by the ancients, who even achieved very thin and light objects.

These vases in hard stones were more generally employed for sacred use and as funerary objects.

We know that the famous Murrhine vases[201] that the Romans received from various lands in the Orient came partly from Egypt. We know two types: the most admired were those from Persia. According to Pliny,[202] it was around the end of the Roman Republic that Murrhine vases became known in Rome. The first six were taken from the treasure of Mithridates. They were judged worthy of being consecrated to the gods. They were placed in the temple of Jupiter in the Capitol. After the fall of Cleopatra, Augustus removed from Alexandria a Murrhine vase considered to be one of the most precious objects of his triumph. Pliny adds "that Emperor Nero wanted still to surpass the luxury that was already scandalous among the Romans, and that he paid more than a million of our money for a Murrhine cup."[203] Petronius, Nero's favorite, also bought a Murrhine vase at a very high price. He broke it before his death, and believed it would be revenge against the emperor who would have inherited it.

Modern people were, for a long time, mistaken about the nature of these once very precious vases which later became common. This about-face was not surprising as soon as we recognized that these vases were made with lime fluorite, called fluorspar.[204]

England still produces, in our day, pieces from which we might make pretty Murrhine vases, if only we could find saps who would pay dearly for them.

The Egyptians, who were long experienced in the manufacture of glass and enamels, imitated Murrhine vases in Thebes and in Coptos. Although these vases were made with false substances, they acquired a certain fashion and were sent abroad.

---

200 For information on how stone vessels were actually worked and polished, see Barbara G. Aston and James A. Harrell, "Stone," in *Ancient Egyptian Materials and Technology*, edited by Ian Shaw and Paul T. Nicholson (Cambridge UK: Cambridge University Press, 2000), in particular 64–65.

201 Pliny describes these vases as coming from Parthia. They were much admired by ancient peoples because of their reflective nature and brilliant sheen. Such vases were a luxury item in ancient Rome. See Pliny, *Natural History*, 37.8.

202 Cailliaud writes: "Natural History, Book XXXVII, chapter 2." See Pliny, *Natural History*, 37, http://www.perseus.tufts.edu/hopper/text?doc=Perseus%3Atext%3A1999.02.0137%3Abook%3D37%3Achapter%3D2

203 See Pliny, *Natural History*, 37, http://www.perseus.tufts.edu/hopper/text?doc=Plin.+Nat.+37&fromdoc=Perseus%3Atext%3A1999.02.0137

204 Cailliaud writes: "Mr. Rozière, from the French expedition to Egypt, appears to be one of the first who recognized the material of these famous vases."

CHAPTER 9

TANNERS, LEATHERWORKERS[205]

T he wild animal, having become the prey of the primitive hunter, gave him, in addition to food, durable clothing. Its pelt was his only protection. This idea was suggested by our encounter, in Upper Ethiopia under the 10th degree of latitude north, with Black tribes and others who still only wear as clothing the hide of a goat, or that of a sheep, attached by means of a belt.[206]

The preparation of skins had acquired great perfection among the Egyptians, judging by the numerous uses they made of them, and by the objects that we find despite their easy destruction.

The ancient authors tell us that the bulk of leatherworkers occupied a quarter separated from the Libyan section of Thebes.[207] In all periods the neighborhood of the leather finishers was unpleasant and one knew to isolate them because of the miasma that these preparations spread.

If we rigorously assess them from the perspective of the paintings and sculptures that the monuments show, we will recognize firstly that the working classes were without shoes.

---

205 For more information on tanning and leatherworking, see Carol Van Driel-Murray, "Leatherwork and Skin Products," in *Ancient Egyptian Materials and Technology*, edited by Ian Shaw and Paul T. Nicholson (Cambridge UK: Cambridge University Press, 2000).

206 Cailliaud writes: "Text, pl. 6, fig. 1." He is not referring to the plates in this book, as the figures in plate 6 are not wearing animal skins around their waists. Cailliaud's reference is not to his *Travels in the Oasis of Thebes* or *Travels to Meroe*, either.

207 Such a quarter could only have come into existence in the late Ramesside–Third Intermediate Period, when a strong Libyan presence appeared in Thebes. See M. Anthony Leahy, *Libya and Egypt c. 1300–750 BC* (London: School of Oriental and African Studies, Centre of Near and Middle Eastern Studies, 1990).

This was frequently the case for high functionaries and others; even kings are presented with bare feet as well as arms. Little clothing over the rest of the body was used because of the high temperature of the climate.

Sandals were preferred over all other shoes. They were used here considerably. Their strong soles ordinarily comprised three thicknesses of leather, joined and sewn with a thin strap of leather[208] in what is called *points piqués*.[209] Two straps, one fitted under the heel held the top of the foot, the other, added to the first, extended to the middle of the sole up to the tip of the foot. It crossed [the foot] and served to hold the big toe. Sometimes another strap was passed behind the heel. People of the upper class wore sandals that were much longer than their feet, with curved tips.[210] These tips protected the foot against shocks from irregular terrain and against certain encumbrances. The paintings from tombs show us kings wearing these sandals and thus their use goes back to the most ancient antiquity in Egypt. In our day, they are still in use in Ethiopia and we have seen them on the feet of the kings[211] of Sennar, of Fazoql, and south of these regions. Ethiopia has preserved ancient customs which have been lost in Egypt.[212] Other sandals are to a greater or lesser degree garnished on the tops of the feet with ribbons, bows, and with large leather straps with stamped designs or with appliqué work. They come from the sculptures of the pylon of the temple to the west of Naga, close to Meroe in Ethiopia. These sandals do not exceed the length of the foot,[213] their luxury consisted of more or less rich attachments. Those of plate 21, figure 12, are worn by a queen holding in one hand, and by the hair, a group of 31 captives from Asia and Ethiopia. They are kneeling, one hand on the chest, the other arm raised in supplication. The heroine raises above them a blade with which she threatens to strike them. This queen, thus dressed in symbols of power, is not found on any monuments of Egypt. She recalls here the authority of women in Ethiopia at the time of Queen Candace during the last dynasty of the Ethiopian kings.

Other sandals from the same site are notable for a great variety of attachments that give a cachet of elegance.[214] They are cut for each foot. The introduction of the big toe in the loop necessarily requires them to be worn on the correct side.

Certain leather shoes had upper portions in which the edge, positioned on the sole, was sewn on the outside. It received for support a leather strap that encircled the shoe. The soles were . . . and the whole was crossed by a strong stitching in straps of leather and in *points piqués*.[215]

---

208 Cailliaud writes: "Replaced today by the shoemaker's thread: the waxed string of cobblers."
209 A type of stitching.
210 Cailliaud writes: "Pl. 21, fig. 4."
211 The word used here is "Melikes," a French version of the Arabic word for 'king.'
212 Cailliaud writes: "Text, pl. 5, fig. 2, those of women, pl. 3, fig. 2, pl. 4, fig. 1." This reference does not match the plates in this work, nor the plates in Cailliaud's two main publications.
213 Cailliaud writes: "Pl. 21, fig. 12."
214 Cailliaud writes: "Same plate, figs. 6 to 11."
215 The French text does not present a complete sentence. The existing phrase clearly indicates that Cailliaud intended to insert something further.

These exterior stitchings have a certain commonality with those of the shoes of Provence. This primitive shoe, so imperfect beside our own, sufficed, however, the inhabitants of countries in which rain is rare.

Let us note here that the cut of the soles for each foot was not limited to sandals which required only the measure of the attachment of a strap fixing the big toe. Shoes with upper parts are equally cut for the right and left feet. This custom was, therefore, generally widespread among the Egyptians. It dates to less than a century in France.

The museums of Paris possess 20 pairs of sandals and shoes in leather, well conserved, and of a good selection. Those of London and Turin are equally supplied.

The Egyptians possessed the art of tanning hides.[216] Reds and greens were used most. We find shoes and slippers more or less decorated with rosettes and other designs, sometimes gilded. Leaves of papyrus were introduced between two pieces of fine hide, others are of shagreen hide.[217] Ankle boots were less widespread. We brought back a pair for children. One of the feet of the mummy was still in one, and they were in a heavy leather,[218] red and green, with decorated appliqué-work rosettes. The soles are fine and are here, again, cut for each foot. They come from the Theban necropolis.

Often the bodies of harps were covered with green, heavy leather and shagreen hides. The museums of Paris and Turin possess examples where there are cases for bows as well as large frills of various designs, sometimes gilded, which one wore around the neck as decoration. We will cite more, especially a genre of small wraps, found on the mummies of priests for whom these decorations were particularly intended. They are in heavy, red and yellow leather, bearing figures with legends and hieroglyphic cartouches, struck like a dry stamp, forming reliefs on the hide (the ancients had only to put black in these engraved molds and they would be imprinted). The legend of the first prophet, the great priest of Amun, Penotjem,[219] or Penonm, after Ramesses IX Maeamun,[220] of the 20th Dynasty, is an example. He seized royal status and encircled his name in the cartouche reserved for pharaohs of this period, which dates to over 33 centuries from our day.[221]

Strips of hide were used for numerous objects. After having been soaked they were greatly extended in a work of ordinary attachments. But they greatly contracted in drying and acquired thus a strong resistance. In order to obtain the longest ligatures possible, they were cut into large, circular pieces. The tool was in bronze or iron, in a semicircle and very

---

216 The verb used here is *maroquiner*, referring to the kinds of leather for which Morocco was famous in the nineteenth century.

217 A type of roughened, untanned leather, often dyed green.

218 The adjective "Moroccan" is used.

219 Cailliaud is referring to Pinedjem I who, during the reign of Smendes in the Twenty-first Dynasty, declared himself pharaoh of Upper Egypt. See Aidan Dodson and Dyan Hilton, *The Complete Royal Families of Ancient Egypt* (London: Thames and Hudson, 2004), 200–209.

220 Cailliaud mistakenly writes that Pinedjem gained power after Ramesses IX. See previous note.

221 Cailliaud writes: "The first of these objects was brought back at the time of our first voyage of 1815 to 1818 and are shown in *Travels in the Oasis of Thebes*, pl. 44, figs. 1, 2, Paris collection, Imperial Library." For an explanation of what became of the objects Cailliaud brought back from Egypt, see Mainterot, *Aux origines de l'égyptologie*, 251–86.

similar to that still in use for the same purpose among the workmen of Egypt.[222] This tool, with a semicircular blade, still appeared on the banners and coats of arms of the corporation of cobblers in almost all of France in the 13th century.

Straps of hide were used to fasten beds, chairs, and stools of all types. We will cite in the article on woodworking a fact that proves to us that ligatures of hide also served in the construction of certain doors. In the greatest antiquity of the ages, when metals were little known, they undoubtedly served in the manufacture of many other objects.

Various scenes in the tombs show us leather craftsmen, as they were in their boutiques 33 centuries ago, exhibiting their merchandise to passers-by.[223] One of them raises a skin, completely tanned. Another cuts leather. The next one exhibits the soles of sandals. The leather currier works a hide on a three-footed support. The other workshop,[224] like the preceding one, is composed of four individuals. It designs more especially fabric for sandals. The workmen have before them their trestle and a small number of tools at their disposal: a semicircular knife; an awl; a hammer. One of them pierces a sandal with a punch. Above are the straps, all prepared to be affixed. Pieces of hide are to be curried; one is in the hands of a workman who, standing, works it on a sort of block to soften it. The next one, with the awl, pierces a strap, another pulls it with the strength of his teeth[225] and passes it through the upper part of the sole. We also note the display of several rough sandals, and beside them the remains of a piece of leather.

Leather was, above all, greatly used for the harnesses of horses, chariots, for the covers of couches, armchairs, chairs, and stools. It covered, with more or less luxury, the furniture of both the rich and the worker.

Fine hides were used only rarely for the bandages of certain mummies. Balls for games were also in fine hide. One stuffed them with husks of barley and cut straw.

The ancient Egyptians also prepared many hides for the manufacture of flasks which had to contain water and wine during the frequent trips which they made into the desert and to the oases, which became important population centers. They purposefully preserved in these skins, which lent to the beverage a taste which many people sought.[226]

---

222 Cailliaud: "Pl. 18A, fig. 1, pl. 20, fig 2."
223 Cailliaud writes: "Pl. 20."
224 Cailliaud writes: "Pl. 20A."
225 Cailliaud writes: "Frequently still in Egypt, the teeth, the feet, and even the toes, principally among the turners, are put to work in the arts and stand in for tools. In their practice there is an amazing dexterity: they complete thus beautiful works in gold embroidery and others on tanned, heavy [the adjective used is "Moroccan"] leather."
226 Cailliaud writes: "Still now, certain wines from the Isle of Cyprus are still more valued for the taste of hide that they acquire in these skins."

CHAPTER 10

ON BASKETRY[227]
(PLATES 30, 32, 33, 35, 36)[228]

B asketry is one of the most ancient industries. Before using animal hide for shoes, palm leaves must have been plaited to make sandals. The need to hold and transport seeds and the produce necessary for life must have inspired early on the thought of forming baskets with the stalks and leaves of plants. The most ancient paintings and sculptures of Egypt show us a large number of these baskets used in various works of agriculture, of grape harvesting, and fishing (pl. 30–32, 33, 35, 36). We can be convinced of the progress of this art among the ancients by the numerous objects of this type found in their tombs.

Our research in the necropolis of Thebes permitted us to gather many of these small straw baskets in various colors and of extremely careful workmanship. They are deposited in the Imperial Library.[229]

Wicker, rare in all periods in Egypt, was advantageously replaced by the palm tree. This precious tree served a great many industries in Egypt and in Nubia. Dates were a considerable produce. A portion of them were dried, and fermented liquor was made from the rest. Its wood is fibrous and not appropriate for the construction of furniture, but its trunk was used for small joists in the roofing of less important constructions. The ribs of branches, beaten at their ends by a hammer, formed brooms with their denuded filaments. One also

---

227 For more information on basketry, see Willemina Z. Wendrich, "Basketry," in *Ancient Egyptian Materials and Technology*, edited by Ian Shaw and Paul T. Nicholson (Cambridge UK: Cambridge University Press, 2000).
228 These plate numbers are written in the margin.
229 Now the Bibliothèque nationale de France, in Paris. For an explanation of what became of the objects Cailliaud brought back from Egypt, see Mainterot, *Aux origines de l'égyptologie*, 251–86.

used the branches to make cages and boxes. Ropes are still made with the filaments and, with the leaves, mats which are still widely used and upon which the Arabs sleep. They are still used in the manufacture of large baskets called 'coufes' and other smaller ones, greatly used for all manner of things. The date palm is effectively for Egypt one of the great blessings of Providence.

Judging by the paintings, they had flat baskets similar to those which we knew in France under the name of *cabas* (pl. 36).[230] We find them in an oval form, and oblong and square. The most common, however, are round. They are fitted with grooves under the cover which press-fits into the basket. Sometimes, to make the smaller of these baskets, one dyed the leaves or straw red, which, when mixed with others of natural colors, would make a richly ornamented fabric. We find them from the size of a small apple, like a sweetmeat box, up to dimensions of 20 and 30 centimeters. Those of tightly woven workmanship could hold water. The use of all these baskets must have been very widespread due to their low price. Women made them. They were consecrated to the cult of the tombs, placed around sarcophagi, and filled with bread, dried fruits, barley, wheat, and often false hair, the strands frizzed and curled, as souvenirs of people beloved by the deceased.

Large, supple baskets of a material similar to those of matting replaced our cloth sacks in industry. They are still very much in use in all of Africa (pl. 3).

We must add to the industry of basketry among the ancients the tops of various stools, fastened with rushes or braided leaves making elegant openwork of a remarkable regularity. We brought back some in our collection, today in the Imperial Library. There is another, similar, one in the Drovetti collection in Turin.

The sandals of which I have spoken above amaze still more: we do not find the slightest thread. The palm tree leaf was woven with art and then cut in narrow strips. It formed a seam and maintained the edges with perfect regularity. One of these is found in our collection located on Richelieu Street.[231] We find there braiding of different sorts. Despite the solidity of the work, these shoes must not have lasted long.

It is believed, and in every likelihood, that their use was reserved for priests who wore them in the temples.

In many provinces of Nubia and Ethiopia these sandals are still known, but little used. The work is extremely crude.

The basket maker covered light earthen vases in sparterie material,[232] in the shape of bottles and other shapes: sieves for flour, etc. We see one of these sieves and a large vase covered in sparterie in the Louvre.

---

230 A flat, two-handled basket.
231 A street in the heart of Paris. Cailliaud's material no longer resides there. For an explanation of what became of the objects Cailliaud brought back from Egypt, see Mainterot, *Aux origines de l'égyptologie*, 251–86. The sandals, depicted in the atlas of Cailliaud's *Voyage à l'Oasis de Thèbes,* were moved from the Louvre to the Musée Dobrée, where they reside under accession number D 961.2.115-116-117. See Jomard, *Voyage à l'Oasis de Thèbes et dans les déserts situés à l'orient et à l'occident de la Thébaïde* (Paris: Imprimerie royale, 1821–62), vol. 1, pl. XLII; Mainterot, *Aux origines de l'égyptologie*, 278.
232 A term generally referring to dense vegetable fiber that has been worked.

Egyptian women, and above all the Nubian women of the area of Aswan, still make baskets similar to those of the ancients. Those for which the material is tightly woven are used to draw water from skins. They have the advantage of not breaking like the crude, terra cotta vases. Also they are preferred in trips across the desert.

The basket makers of Sennar and Chandy are far superior to those of Egypt.

The pretty mats of the country of [sic][233] are equally preferred.

The inhabitants of the ancient Oasis of Amun, today Siwa, located in the Libyan Desert, make small baskets from rice straw of a quality that is still superior to those of Egypt.

---

233 Cailliaud has left a blank space in this sentence. He presumably intended to fill in this space with the name of the country to which he was referring at a later date.

CHAPTER 11

ON CORDAGE

The necessity of cords of all thicknesses, up to the most resistant cables, is demonstrated to us by their various applications in the subjects of art that decorate the tombs, where they are shown to be indispensable. We will note here that the Egyptians must have, more perhaps than all the other people of antiquity, made use of them for the transportation of their monoliths and for most of the enormous materials which they employed in the construction of their buildings.

We only encountered a representation of this industry once in the tombs of Thebes (pl. 18A).[234] Two workmen are occupied in twisting a cable. One of them (fig. 2) sits on a stool and tightly holds the end between his two hands. The other (fig. 3) wears around his hips a belt which supports a sort of strong pair of tongs which, in turn, supports the opposite end of the cable. The upper part of these tongs is fitted with a transverse piece which served, undoubtedly, as a lever and which the workman probably turned with his two hands in the process of twisting the cable. This individual seems to gain backward leverage using all the weight of his body. Several of these finished cables are shown extended to their utmost length on the ground. Others are folded in two strong rolls, fitted with their fastenings.

In their navigation, the Egyptians must have greatly used all types of ropes. We see these shown in paintings. In the transportation of a colossal statue (pl. 43),[235] we note large cables.

234 Theban Tomb 100, that of Rekhmire. See Porter and Moss, *Topographical Bibliography I.1*, 211; Norman Davies, *The Tomb of Rekh-mi-Re'*, vol. 2, pl. lii–lv, lviii–lxii, lxiii; the Theban Mapping Project's bibliography for Tomb 100, http://www.tmpbibliography.com/resources/bibliography_5nv_tombs_of_the_nobles_tt100_rekhmire.html
235 From the tomb of Djehutyhotep II in Deir al-Bersha. See Percy E. Newberry, *El Bersheh. Part I* (London: The Egypt Exploration Fund, 1895), pl. XV; Porter and Moss, *Topographical Bibliography IV*, 180; the listed bibliography on the website of the Belgian Mission to Deir al-Bersha.

During the demolition of a pyramid's summit in Meroe we found filaments of a palm tree cable which served to raise the material. We possess pieces of cords in hemp, in flax, in leaves and filaments of palm tree. We found these last ones in a tomb in ancient Memphis, close to Saqqara. They were used over the bandages, to tie down the mummies of the Apis bull.

The Egyptians did not make use of chains in their works, as we would have found such remains or such representations.[236]

---

236 Cailliaud wrote the following note at this point in the manuscript: "chapter on jewelry."

CHAPTER 12

WOODWORKER[237]

The most memorable and the most common objects that the ancient Egyptians left us of their woodworking are, indisputably, their sarcophagi. These became a particular art for the numerous workmen who were occupied with it: woodworkers, sculptors, and painters. Their religious ideas required that these coffins should have, in part, the shape of the body which they contained. The top represented in low relief the figure, the arms crossed, and the feet. The sides indicated foremost the head and then the elbows. The body was designed to shrink imperceptibly toward the thighs, vaguely indicated, and the fleshy part of the legs. This rough outline of the human body perfectly frames a mummy wrapped in its first bandages, and demanded very difficult work. The ancients must have had silhouettes as models, adopted for the cut and the softened shapes which these sarcophagi represent. Breasts painted on the cases or a projecting beard distinguished the sexes. As art we observe a rabbet,[238] as much on top as underneath, practiced all around, and which follows the various curves of the coffin, affecting, as we have seen, the human shapes. The lid had tenons permanently fixed in mortises which enter into other, similar ones, used in the underneath of the sarcophagus: each one was pegged.

We note that the difficulty of always finding wood strong enough to cut these contours required them often to make these cases from numerous pieces, adjusted and glued together with much art. They appear not to have known our use of tongue-and-groove planks. They

---

237 For more information on woodworking, see Geoffrey Killen, "Wood [Technology]," in *Ancient Egyptian Materials and Technology*, edited by Ian Shaw and Paul T. Nicholson (Cambridge UK: Cambridge University Press, 2000).

238 A broad groove cut into the surface of the case.

were joined, one against the other, with wooden pegs and dowels. The short wood used for these sarcophagi was equally linked end to end by dowels or bevels, doubled up on top of each other, pegged and sometimes glued with a strong adhesive made from the nerves of meat. In breaking these cases we sometimes ascertained the gelatinous fibers of nerves. Out of a large amount of debris we have never encountered a single metal nail in any wooden sarcophagus, box, or ordinary piece of woodworking, common or deluxe. All the pieces are combined and consolidated with pegs and dowels.

In our home in Qurna, more than a cartload of debris from mummy cases was burnt, not without regret for destroying among them the beautiful remains of paintings that perhaps 3000 years had conserved.[239]

These sarcophagi must have passed through the hands of three different artists before being completed. Firstly, one filled with clay many of the holes which occurred in the various pieces of wood, made one after another. Next, a white plaster received the paintings. The care taken in the manufacture of many of these coffins was extreme.

The stretchers, the various boxes, the headrests, the scribal palettes, and other numerous objects of this genre are more or less roughly made, and sometimes well produced.

As we have said: nails of any sort of metal were never used. The different parts were consolidated with pegs, tenons, and mortises. The planks were equally consolidated with dowels and were never tongue-and-groove. What are most remarkable are the dovetails, which are very well fitted.

After the sarcophagi, the chairs, and the sofas, which we will cite further on, we found few remarkable things in woodwork. The better part of their practical furniture was boxes for which we see various representations in the paintings of tombs (pl. 9, figs. 3 and 5). The first one is still used daily in market boutiques in greater Cairo. The borders which encircle them would indicate that they are made of panels, but we were not able to confirm this. The better part of those which we quite frequently find in tombs consists of small boxes consecrated for holding idols and other numerous funerary objects. The lids are affixed with pegs. Others, of the pyramidal style, represent the pylons of a temple. The museums of Paris, Turin, and Leiden possess many. These objects, purely funerary, are mostly roughly made. The better-made ones, while always held together by wooden pegs, have as their lids sliding covers with rotating buttons to make them move. They appear to have served daily uses. Others have the lid affixed by one single peg on which it turns.

The day-to-day woodwork objects used inside and outside of homes are the many stands for the placement of vases on the ground. This refreshed the water through filtration.[240]

The tombs and sanctuaries were violated and the great rarity of wood led to the destruction of these objects.

---

239 This was a common practice among travelers to Luxor in the early nineteenth century, as there was an abundance of ancient wooden remains, and a scarcity of other sources of fuel for heat and cooking.

240 Cailliaud writes: "Pl. 9, figs. 1 and 9. Pl. 21B, fig. 3." Regarding plate 9, the vase stand to which this passage refers is actually between figure numbers 8 and 9.

The entrances to the caves where the mummies were placed were walled, but these sites were ordinarily preceded by a small sanctuary composed of one or several rooms where the family came to pray for the dead. These sanctuaries were closed by doors.[241]

We found a false-door frame surmounted by painted cornices and sculpted with hieroglyphic inscriptions which decorated the posts. The Turin Museum, in the Drovetti collection, possesses a nice example of this work, as well as a litter of about five meters in length, to be carried by four people on the shoulder.

The form of these door decorations is so well designed and carved of such an admirable manner in the construction of their temples, erected in sandstone and granite, that their representations in woodwork no longer amaze us.

Pieces of wood from beds were found and differ little from ours, with tenons and mortises to dismantle them at will. Their means of joining planks in the bottom of their sarcophagi with dowels was the same as that adopted in the construction of their doors, of which we found remains. They must have combined them with crossbeams that were equally pegged. As for ironwork, most of the time there was none.[242] The doors were then secured along their length by a post placed on the opposite edge to that of the lock, and longer than the door. One end of this pin rested below in a stone hole. The other, toward the top, rotated in another hole used in a lock plate; the door rotated on its pivots. It was thus that this lock, composed of a number of pieces, did not receive one piece of metal. Today still, in Nubia and Ethiopia, where iron is rare, we find in the villages doors without the least bit of iron and thus built in the same manner as many of those of the ancients. Although composed of a multitude of pieces, they have no peg, tenon, or mortise. All the pieces, as well as the lock, are held fast by means of ligatures in straps of hide.

We noted, thus, several in Barbar, made of more than 20 small planks, thin and narrower than the small staves of casks. The straps of hide, as we said earlier, used wet, contracted in drying and gave a strong consistency to this piece of work. They were easy, nevertheless, to destroy, as a knife suffices to cut some attachments and to enter silently into the house. One knows beforehand that there is nothing to steal. If one finds money, it is buried, and we must give them credit, as their excessive trust is rarely betrayed. It suffices to show that there is no one in their house by the act of closing their door, so that their home might be respected.

The wood from the country suitable for these sorts of works was small in number: the sycomore, the tamarisk, and various acacias. But Egypt received as tribute from Asia, and more especially from Ethiopia which was better supplied with wood, numerous foreign woods, often transported on the upper parts of the river: ebony, guaiacum, ironwood, wood

---

241 Cailliaud appears to be referring to structures built in the courtyards of rock-cut tombs.

242 Iron ores were plentiful in ancient Egypt and often used in pigments and jewelry. Iron was not used as a metal for much of the dynastic period, however, as the technology involved with smelting was beyond the capabilities of the Egyptians. Iron objects appear in Egypt with increasing frequency from the late New Kingdom onward and were produced on a large scale by the end of the Third Intermediate Period. See Jack Ogden, "Metals," in *Ancient Egyptian Materials and Technology*, edited by Ian Shaw and Paul T. Nicholson (Cambridge UK: Cambridge University Press, 2000).

from Meroe, and others difficult to recognize. The Egyptians so well appreciated these products used particularly in their luxury furniture that they, like us, made representations of them in paintings.

The art of making locks belonged to craftsmen in wood who alone produced them. Mr. Drovetti found pieces of these ancient locks. We found for ourselves part of one in the opening of a tomb in Qurna and a bronze key.

The cabinetmakers were not lax in giving to their furniture the most distinguished forms. In this art, chairs and sofas are worthy of note: the feet like the claws of a lion, reversed backs contoured in volutes, tightly stuffed and covered in rich material; they would rival in taste and elegance those of our era.

A small room in the tomb of Pharaoh Ramesses IV Meiamun in Biban al-Maluk[243] (territory of Thebes) gives the richest representations (pl. 28). On the lower sides of a seat are captive peoples from Asia and Africa, represented marching, tied two-by-two by the neck, the arms equally bound. The arms of the sofa are designed in the shape of a lion; the sovereign reclines allegorically on a symbol of his power and shows, under him, the image of his conquests. These representations are found still under the feet of certain mummies of heroes who, undoubtedly, are noteworthy for their brilliant exploits.

A simple seat, without back, is formed like a lion in its entirety (pl. 26).[244]

A chair bears the cartouches of this pharaoh and the sacred vulture, a symbol of protection, envelops them with its outstretched wings (pl. 27).

One of these seats (pl. 29) appears to be suspended on springs. Two captives are shown with one knee on the ground; they have their arms and necks bound with cords of which the ends are shaped like lotus flowers. The fabrics are rich and still of good taste.

They had reclining beds no less elegant than their chairs. Judging by the pegged assembly we recognize that, like our own, they could be deconstructed. Their stools are no less remarkable (pl. 25). One of them bears the image of two prisoners, here lying with their bows. A light chair with the claws of a lion must be reinforced with ligatures of hide. On the bed we note the wooden semicircle anciently used in Egypt for resting the head upon during sleep. All of these paintings, which we copied at the sites and then scaled down for the drawings, belong to the cited tomb of Ramesses IV.[245]

We found in the tombs of Qurna chairs similar to the last ones in red polished wood, known from Meroe. They were reinforced in openwork with small, twisted pieces of fabric.

243 Cailliaud is actually referring to the tomb of Ramesses III, KV 11, in the Valley of the Kings. See Porter and Moss, *Topographical Bibliography I.2*, 522; Reeves and Wilkinson, *The Complete Valley of the Kings*, 159–61; the Theban Mapping Project's bibliography for KV 11, http://www.tmpbibliography.com/resources/bibliography_2kv_valley_of_kings_kv11_ramesses_iii.html. Cailliaud has conflated Ramesses II and Ramesses III; see note 64 above. See Clayton, *Chronicle of the Pharaohs*.

244 More specifically plate 26, figure 1.

245 Actually the tomb of Ramesses III, KV 11, in the Valley of the Kings. See Porter and Moss, *Topographical Bibliography I.2*, 518–27; Reeves and Wilkinson, *The Complete Valley of the Kings*, 159–61; the Theban Mapping Project's bibliography for KV 11, http://www.tmpbibliography.com/resources/bibliography_2kv_valley_of_kings_kv11_ramesses_iii.html. Cailliaud has conflated Ramesses II and Ramesses III; see note 64 above. See Clayton, *Chronicle of the Pharaohs*.

Sometimes the backs are decorated in inlay work of ebony and the ivory of hippopotami. Both large and small stools are shaped like the first ones described above, as well as the tables covered by inlay work. All the parts were adjusted and joined one to the other by tenon and mortise, glued and pegged just as we practice today.

Among the objects deposited in the Louvre we note small boxes or cassettes for perfume in attractive, hard, polished wood and encrusted with ivory. Small baskets must have frequently taken the place of our numerous small boxes. They made the boxes, however, of very small shapes from a piece of hard, carved wood, as well as types of double cases. The covers were adapted at their ends with a peg, with its head in the shape of a nail on which the cover rotated. This genre of double case was for the toilet of women: it contained red henna[246] for nails and the plumbago or lead sulphide, in powder, with which they drew black around their eyes.

A remarkable piece from the table maker's art is a fragment of a sarcophagus in ironwood covered in encrustations of ivory and various woods from Ethiopia, forming light designs of broken, undulating lines, and moldings executed with great perfection.

The numerous palettes of scribes must have, firstly, belonged to the plane of the cabinetmaker, and were then completed by the sculptor. The Louvre possesses some very nice ones in the sought-after wood of Ethiopia, such as ebony, ironwood, that which is said to be from Meroe, and other hard woods difficult to recognize and which take a nice polish.

The Drovetti collection in Turin shows us six of these palettes, of which one has 11 compartments for the various colors. Another very narrow one has a long, extremely rare, embossment in iron, perhaps on which to engrave the hieroglyphs.

Another small[247] object of daily use is the cited wooden crescent, placed under the head as a pillow. For a long time we misunderstood the use of this object for which representations in small amulets, often in hematite, are found in the tombs. These objects were ordinarily in three pieces, sometimes in two; the crescent alone was attached by tenons. We find them decorated with encrustations in ivory, perfectly cut and smoothed in all its parts with a great regularity of design.

Having many times encountered these crescent-shaped 'feet'[248] placed under the head of mummies who did not receive cases, we might surmise that this custom was reserved for them. In 1821, during our voyage to Meroe, we found this same crescent in daily use among these people, who claimed not to be comfortable in sleep unless they had this wood placed under their head. Used to sleeping roughly on the ground or on frames with straps of hide on which they put, at the most, a sheep's hide, they must have easily become accustomed to the wooden pillow which, in taking the shape of the head, was made more bearable by their heavy hair. But the pleasure that they find, and it is real, is

---

246 This word is not found in the later chapter draft of the Harer Papers. It is inserted from the earlier draft of the manuscript into a blank space left in the later draft.

247 This word is not found in the later chapter draft of the Harer Papers. It is inserted from the earlier draft of the manuscript into a blank space left in the later draft.

248 This is a direct translation of the French, referring to ancient Egyptian headrests.

to let the air circulate around their head and refresh them during their sleep. This means a lot in such a climate.

The wood known from Meroe is still used in Chendy and in Sennar where it is still admired. Wooden beds, small stools, admired saddles for dromedaries, crescent-shaped 'feet' for sleeping, and other small works are made from it.

The rarity of metal would have destroyed, little by little, all that which was found as an ancient tool. Museums are also always poor in this genre of antique. We must, therefore, often use the representations that the ancients made in paintings in their tombs, along with the numerous amulets, of which there are so many, and an infinite number of objects represented in relief, consecrated to their cult and for uses in the arts.

They knew the level with triangular string, very similar to that which we use. The set square, large and small hand axes, always with bronze blades firmly attached with hide ligatures on a curved shaft, were much like our Celtic axes. But what amazes is the use of the bow for drilling. This practice is very similar to that which is still in use in Egypt. Several plates already cited from this work show these tools in the hands of workmen.

The Drovetti collection in Turin possesses one of these drills in forged bronze, with a length of 7 centimeters, in a ferrule[249] with a length of 22 centimeters. Its upper end turns in a knot, the blunt bit worn by use. Most curious is its spade drill bit, like those of our day.

Hammers, very similar to those which we use in caulking boats, chisels, and mortising chisels on handles are noted in several plates of this work. We see the handles of chisels tapered down in the middle. Their bulge at the end makes them easier to use than our own as they were not susceptible to slipping from the hand, so that it is not necessary to press them, as when pulling mortising chisels from the mortise (pl. 1 and 2).

Certain blades for a plane and pieces of a saw were found. Indeed, if we attentively note the numerous fragments from their sarcophagi, we can see the sawing of planks lengthwise and we can better recognize it in the cut of upright wood forming the bottom of certain sarcophagi, where sometimes the plane did not remove the line of the defective saw of the long sawyer. We find these still, perfectly portrayed in paintings.

Plate 5A, figure 1. We observe a plank held vertically with the help of two posts fixed into the ground. The long sawyer, standing, braced his legs, his body leaning forward. With two hands he pushes the saw across this plank which he starts to saw along its length. The hieroglyphic legend bears the caption "to saw."[250]

Figures 2 and 3. Two woodworkers, half crouching, fashion two shovel handles, with the help of a kind of adze. Here, the artist has certainly not drawn the subject accurately in the action of work. Figure 2 must have naturally held his shovel handle above the point where he strikes with his sharp tool, so as not to cut his wrist. The following figure, equally flawed, cannot take such momentum on his adze to come to strike conveniently a thin and unsupported piece of wood. The artist only wanted to indicate the genre of the work.

---

249 A short, metal sleeve used to strengthen a tool handle, located at the end holding the tool.
250 The French actually translates to "bears the noun 'to saw.'" Cailliaud writes: "Mr. Chabas' translation."

In the legend, which is greatly confused (says Mr. Chabas), we make out the Egyptian name for woodworker, *netjera*, as in Arabic.[251]

These subjects come from a tomb in Beni Hasan, where there was inhumed an important individual from the Old Kingdom, named Kheli,[252] and not Rotei as we had first written. [253]

We must note other workmen in the same genre of work (pl. 15A, first register).

Six woodworkers *(retjera)*,[254] crouching on the ground, make bows and spears. The type of adze of which they make use was rarely found in the tombs. The handle is in wood, the sharp edge in bronze is supported along the length in the angular portion of the shaft; it is firmly attached with strips of hide.

Here again, for the position of the hands, the artist was no more precise than in the previous subject.

"This profession (says Mr. Chabas) is mentioned in one of the hieratic papyri of the British Museum, as requiring these title holders to make frequent trips to place their works."

If in the numerous plates of this work we note all that show workmen working, we will be amazed at the little service given by the small number of tools at their disposal. But it is the same case in Egypt today.

Nothing is more amazing than to see the works that come out of the hands, and we might say the feet, of a woodworker or an Arab turner, working on the ground without a workbench, and with such a small number of instruments so poorly maintained. The turner, above all, is worthy of remark as his wheel is placed on the floor. With one hand he moves the bow, with the other he holds the tool that he fixes on the stand by means of a foot, and with the other foot he maintains the solidity of the wheel. In many countries the Arabs work as much with their feet as with their hands, and with much agility.

---

251 Actually *nagar*, also pronounced 'najar,' and written نجّار.
252 Cailliaud is referring to Tomb 17, that of Khety, in Beni Hasan. See Porter and Moss, *Topographical Bibliography IV*, 156; Newberry, *Beni Hasan. Part I*, 51–62; Kanawati and Woods, *Beni Hassan*, 49–57.
253 This name is found on the rough and earlier drafts of this plate.
254 It is uncertain why Cailliaud spells this word differently at this point, as opposed to how he spelled it earlier in the chapter. The word for carpenter/woodworker in Arabic is نجّار, pronounced 'nagar' or 'najar.'

CHAPTER 13

GLASSMAKING[255]

T he Egyptians knew the art of glassmaking from the most distant antiquity. Mr. de Rougé wrote on this subject: "The first creation decorated in undulations of various colors must be claimed for Egypt, even though we find similar ones in Greek and Roman tombs."[256] Indeed, we find in the monuments, sculpted or painted, a multitude of models of these pretty vases along with amulets and symbols in the most varied colors.

These small objects are made in imitation of certain agates—onyx, lined and undulating with various colors throughout. Blue, yellow, and white are generally used and arranged in transverse or oblique lines. Small, circular, flat gourds with two handles are also made. On a Prussian blue background are drawn lines in festoons of yellow and white enameled glass.[257] The Turin Museum is well supplied with these most curious objects. There is also an extraordinary piece: the head of a ram in a mixture of yellow glass, the eyes, the horns, and the ears are in white enamel.

---

255 For more information on Egyptian glass, see Paul T. Nicholson and Julian Henderson, "Glass," in *Ancient Egyptian Materials and Technology*, edited by Ian Shaw and Paul T. Nicholson (Cambridge UK: Cambridge University Press, 2000).

256 Cailliaud makes reference to a citation here but omits the actual citation. The same reference in the earlier draft of the manuscript contains the following citation: "Summary notice on the Egyptian monuments of the Louvre Museum, 1865."

257 Cailliaud's understanding of ancient Egyptian glazing, faience, and glass production was imperfect. For more information on Egyptian glass, glazed ceramics, and faience, see Paul T. Nicholson and Edward Peltenburg, "Egyptian Faience," in *Ancient Egyptian Materials and Technology*, edited by Ian Shaw and Paul T. Nicholson (Cambridge UK: Cambridge University Press, 2000).

We know two different preparations for these lined pieces of glass of various colors. In one, the design traverses the whole thickness of the glass. They are, thus, similar on both sides. In the other, they only penetrate a quarter of the thickness of the glass, like the vases in the shape of a drum that we cited. The colored surface was applied as a mixture of enamel by brush and then passed under the enameler's lamp to blend it and encrust the surface of the vase. The designs thus made inevitably had some irregularities on their surface which required, undoubtedly, the work of the emery polisher to complete them.

Opaque or diaphanous glass, imitating emerald, and stones of other colors, were used as beads or as pendants to make necklaces. We find them also in stars, in small flowers, and in blue, red, white, yellow, green, and turquoise rosettes. They served to create the eye of natural grandeur[258] which was used for amulets, and the combined two fingers, a sign indicating the middle. The museums of Paris, London, and Turin possess many objects of this genre.

White glass is found very rarely. The Turin Museum possesses a large, round basin of close to a meter in circumference, found intact in a sparterie[259] basket that served as a case, and a glass[260] of which the border is blue, and wherein is seen the figure of Osiris.

We encountered in the Oasis of Thebes,[261] in the Libyan Desert, two remains of painting and gilding on white glass. One fragment, with a length of 0.11 m, of a circular tray, must have had a diameter of 0.29 m.[262] On it we see a funerary scene, undoubtedly incomplete. Two mummies are separated by figures of the gods, Chnuphis[263] at the head, then a mummy of a woman, yellow, with a symbol of the solar disc atop the head and the uraeus which often hangs on the heads of kings as a symbol of protection. The third figure could be a young king, yellow, without beard, holding in one hand the divine scepter with the head of Cucupha,[264] in the other the symbol of divine life. The background of this design is of a pretty red. Next comes a second mummy with the head of the leontocephalus (head of a lion) god, then the god Ptah,[265] very much erased, holding in two hands a uraeus, and finally a human head, fingers on the mouth.[266] The border is gilded.

The other part of the tray, also in white glass, and badly damaged, must have been circular, judging by the only remains of the shapeless border which it presents. It is decorated with small squares in pretty red, with yellow circles in the center, and separated by large, yellow points. These vases, probably consecrated to the cult, must have been the first to have been found.[267]

---

258 It is presumed that Cailliaud is referring to the *wadjet*-eye, also known as the Eye of Ra, or Eye of Horus, which often took the form of an amulet.

259 A term generally referring to dense vegetable fiber that has been worked. In this case, the plant fiber has been worked into the shape of a basket.

260 Meaning a drinking glass, not a piece of glass.

261 Kharga Oasis.

262 Cailliaud's unit of measurement is not clear.

263 A version of the god Khnum's name.

264 A nineteenth-century term referring to a mythical animal with long ears, found on the scepters of kings. Cailliaud is likely referring to the scepter with the head of the god Seth atop it.

265 Presumably Cailliaud is referring to this god, although he spells the name Phtha.

266 Cailliaud's account undoubtedly describes a scene of mummiform gods, and perhaps a king.

267 Cailliaud writes: "Antiquities collection in the Imperial Library." This is now the Bibliothèque nationale in Paris.

ENAMEL[268]

To the art of glassmaking is linked that of mosaics in cloisonné,[269] practiced by the Egyptians. They combined enamel strands in bundles of various colors and various sizes, so as to form flowers, rosettes, squares, and other designs. The whole was passed under the enameler's lamp to be combined in such a way as to create a prism with which one encircled black enamel of a certain thickness. The prism was cut in slices and used in finery, in necklaces, in encrustations on various furnishings, etc.

We found in Tuna (Upper Egypt) several examples of this genre of work. One was designed with a rosette in blue, white, and red on a black background; another in blue glass with blue and red lotus flowers; a third one with a blue background, with small, very well-drawn rosettes in yellow; and a final one in white glass with a starry design.[270]

Actual compositions of enamel mixtures are often found. They had them in blue, white, black, red, crimson, green, turquoise, and in mixed colors. They made figures of gods and animals, of cynocephalus monkeys in adoration, of jackals, of uraei, etc. Many of these symbolic representations were molded as by impression on one face only, the other remained without impression.

They made many enamel beads, not rounded, but in the shape of little wheels, along with tubes 2 centimeters long. Our observations on a great many of these, for which some were half completed and the others uncompleted, led us to recognize the manufacturing process. A chuck of metal, in bronze, or rather in iron, received first of all a light, muddy plaster, resistant to the fusion of enamel. Then it was thoroughly covered by several layers of enamel forming the bulk of the beads or tubes which they wanted to obtain. Finally, it was passed under the enameler's lamp. One thus obtained a tube of enamel that remained on its chuck without adhering to it, because of the muddy plaster. The third and final stage comprised cutting the tube into pieces. This work was done in contact with a tool analogous to a rake, the sharp teeth of which pushed against the molten tube. The teeth functioned like saws, working one or two circuits. It only remained to remove each bead or small tube from on top of the chuck.

These enamels were used in finery, in necklaces, and in long strands. With the small ones, similar to beads, works analogous to those in beads in use in our day were made. Symbolic figures and hieroglyphs were drawn on them.

The prettiest of the funerary works of this genre found on some mummies is a long network made of tubes and other beads of enamel of various colors. It is framed by a border

---

268 For more information on this subject, see Nicholson and Peltenburg, "Egyptian Faience."

269 The French term used is *émaux soudés*, which literally means linked, or soldered, enamel.

270 Cailliaud writes: "Collection annexed to the Antiquities Cabinet in the Imperial Library. The Greeks and the Romans greatly practiced this art of glassmaking in mosaic, along with the fabrication of vases formed of undulations in various colours. The museums of Rome and of Naples possess numerous examples." The Imperial Library's collections became part of Paris' Bibliothèque nationale, which subsequently transferred portions of its collection to other institutions. The piece in question, published in the atlas of Cailliaud's *Voyage à l'Oasis*, now resides in the Bibliothèque nationale's department of Monnaies, médailles et antiques. See Jomard, *Voyage à l'Oasis de Thèbes*, vol. 2, pl. XLIV; Mainterot, *Aux origines de l'égyptologie*, 266–67.

and the upper part is a tableau of symbolic figures, all designed with these enamel beads (wheel-shaped), of varied colors and threaded on a string of perfectly preserved linen.[271]

The symbolic figures are known: in the center, the scarab, symbol of the god Khepri, the creator-sun.

To the right and to the left are two figures of the talisman called Djed,[272] a symbol of stability and permanence.

On either end are two jackals, crouching on naoi, symbols of the god Ap-Heru[273] who opens and closes the roads to heaven.[274]

The undulations of the lower frieze are representations of water.

Let us now note the workman who is shown to us in plate 6B, figure 4.[275] Seated on a concave, wooden stool,[276] he holds on his knees a bowl filled with enamel tubes. He threads them with care to create a necklace. In front of him a large basket is filled with these same tubes. On top of it can be seen a completed necklace.

In front, another workman seated on a stool puts in motion a large bow to work three drills, piercing three holes at a time—something that is no longer practiced. The color of these tools leads one to assume that they are in bronze. We tried this manner of work and succeeded, but we had to first pierce holes of 3 to 4 millimeters to assist the drills. Holding by hand their upper part, the distance between the holes is lessened, it might be at most about 1 centimeter, the hand being able only to maintain the upper distance of the drills without having to press down. It is only their weight that makes them bite into the object to be pierced. Egyptian painting shows us that these instruments are bigger in their upper part, in the shape of a club. It is this size that determines the distance between the holes, the drills having to turn perpendicularly.

But, without holding the drills by hand, which practice appears to us the snobbery of the workmen, it would be much easier and simpler to maintain them with a piece of pierced metal. We could turn them much more easily and we could have, if need be, the advantage of pressing down.

The small details into which we have entered, the examination of numerous manufactured objects which we found ourselves or saw in museums, and the numerous painted and sculpted representations, have proven to us that this art was very advanced in extreme antiquity.

---

271 Cailliaud writes: "Pl. 22. Two were brought by us to the collection annexed to the Antiques Cabinet in Paris." This bead netting, originally published in the atlas of Cailliaud's *Voyage à l'Oasis*, is now kept in the Louvre, under the accession number E 13218. See Jomard, *Voyage à l'Oasis de Thèbes*, vol. 2, pl. XLV; Mainterot, *Aux origines de l'égyptologie*, 271, pl. XIII.

272 Written as "tat" by Cailliaud.

273 Cailliaud is likely referring to Wepwawet, the jackal god whose name means 'Opener of the Ways,' which describes his role of leading the dead into the afterlife.

274 Cailliaud writes: "Mr. Chabas' observations."

275 From Theban Tomb 100, that of Rekhmire. See Porter and Moss, *Topographical Bibliography I.1*, 211; Norman Davies, *The Tomb of Rekh-mi-Re'*, vol. 2, pl. lii–lv, lviii–lxii, lxiii; the Theban Mapping Project's bibliography for Tomb 100, http://www.tmpbibliography.com/resources/bibliography_5nv_tombs_of_the_nobles_tt100_rekhmire.html

276 Cailliaud inserts a reference number here, but omits the actual reference. The reference can be found, however, in the earlier draft of the manuscript: "This shape of seat, with a concave top, is very useful and calls to mind our dromedary saddles, where one is seated as in a small fishing boat, with legs crossed on the neck of the animal."

To the technical details that we have just given, we will add the examination of certain ancient paintings related to the enameler. Plate 10, figure 2[277] shows an enameler seated on a stool similar to the last one cited. He is placed in front of the hearth of an ardent flame, blowpipe at the mouth, tongs in hand, and the blue enamel substance is at his feet. Our enamelers use bellows, moved by the feet, to have both hands free for the manipulation of tools and enamels, whereas the workman with whom we are occupied blows into the blowpipe. Behind him is the stump of a tree, probably hollowed out so as to support a cover with handles. On top is found a shelf which must have had two circular openings to receive two basins in blue enamel, undoubtedly as samples. We see also the rod with an affixed hand, a censer used to offer perfume.

In the numerous representations of painted vases which we see in the tombs, we can only recognize those of which the originals were in glass. The custom must have, however, become widespread.

Plate 10, figure 1[278] shows us six workmen crouching, one knee on the ground, surrounding a furnace in which they had already blown vases, pointed at their ends, and from which they take vitrified matter at the end of long, carved tubes or rods of glass.

Plate 6B, figure 3[279] represents two glassblowers seated on the ground, blowing in their pipes, garnished on the other end with vitreous matter, bright red, in fusion, which they maintain in an ardent brazier. Nothing accompanies these. The indispensable details in such works could not themselves be conveniently represented through drawings without perspective, but, such as they are, they show us the Egyptians possessing all the instruments and tools necessary for the practice of arts that are already well advanced.

---

277 From Theban tomb 100, that of Rekhmire. See: Porter and Moss, *Topographical Bibliography I.1*, 211; Norman Davies, *The Tomb of Rekh-mi-Re'*, vol. 2, pl. lii–lv, lviii–lxii, lxiii; the Theban Mapping Project's bibliography for Tomb 100, http://www.tmpbibliography.com/resources/bibliography_5nv_tombs_of_the_nobles_tt100_rekhmire.html

278 From Theban Tomb 36, that of Ibi. See Porter and Moss, *Topographical Bibliography I.1*, 65; Norman de Garis Davies, *The Rock Tombs of Deir el Gebrawi. Part I. Tomb of Aba and Smaller Tombs of the Southern Group* (London: Egypt Exploration Fund, 1902), pl. xxiv–xxv; the Theban Mapping Project's bibliography for Tomb 36, http://www.tmpbibliography.com/resources/bibliography_5nv_tombs_of_the_nobles_tt36_ibi.html

279 From tomb number 17, that of Khety, in Beni Hasan. See Porter and Moss, *Topographical Bibliography IV*, 156; Newberry, *Beni Hasan. Part I*, pl. XIV; Kanawati and Woods, *Beni Hassan*, 54.

CHAPTER 14

USE OF METALS[280]

ON GOLD AND OTHER METALS

All must recognize that the ancient Egyptians drew a large portion of their gold from lands located to the south of Sennar, from the gold-bearing sands of Qamamyl in the kingdom of Bertat, under the 10th degree, ½ latitude north. These sands are considered in the country as the most productive. We visited them on 19 January 1822.[281]

We followed Isma'il Pasha with his army. He stopped at this site so that we might research the gold deposits after which he had lusted for so long. He gave us as a guide a Black,[282] an interpreter, and an escort in order to search for the precious metal. Over the course of several days we visited the shafts exploited by the Blacks[283] of the country. The alluvial bed, in sandy clay, more or less ferruginous, is of five to six meters thick, down to granite and gneiss. Our Black[284] assured us that after heavy rainfall they sometimes find, on the surface of the ground, pieces of gold the size of the end of a finger. In one day we found the value of 12 grains of gold. Much time was needed to arrive at an exact understanding of the yield of these gold-bearing sands. The army was increasingly weakened, it was anxious to retrace its steps, and yet we still had to go forward.

The country of Kordofan, in the west, also possesses gold-bearing sands. The last conquests of Muhammad Ali Pasha in this region made known the degree of their importance.

---

280 For more information on this subject, see Jack Ogden, "Metals."
281 Cailliaud writes: "*Travels to Meroe*, vol. III, pages 3, 9, 13, 16."
282 A direct translation of the French word is 'Negro.'
283 Cailliaud uses the French word for 'Blacks,' not the word for 'Negro.'
284 A direct translation of the French word is 'Negro.'

It is believed that gold was the first metal known and used among the ancient Egyptians.[285] Its discovery must have been favored by its color in its natural state, and the conformation of the soil. The rains which last during five or six months of the year furrow the hillside terrain and valleys with a multitude of torrents in which nature conducts a grand washing-out and often abandons on the surface of the soil more or less considerable nuggets of gold. The color attracts the attention of the people of the country. These nuggets must have been forged in their natural state without being melted, and crudely shaped by friction with quartzite pebbles.

The ancients exploited first the gold-bearing sands, then the gold mines, with their veins, close to the Red Sea, in the desert inhabited by the Bisharin Arabs,[286] in the ancient Troglodytic,[287] toward the 21st degree of latitude, at the site called Salaka-Panchrysos.[288] We only imperfectly understand these mines. These sorts of exploitations are still difficult for us despite the use of powder.[289] They must have been much more difficult for the ancients who were deprived of this advantageous means. They made large fires next to the areas of rocks from which they wanted to extract, and the heat split the rocks:[290] a feeble means which must have only worked the surface, but nonetheless enabled their exploitation.[291]

In certain periods, gold was brought in quantities to Egypt by the different tributary people of Africa and Asia. The paintings in the tombs of Thebes[292] show these people in various, and very characterized, types, arriving charged with their tribute where attention is drawn to gold in powder or in ingots, in sealed sacks, or fashioned in rings and as chains filling baskets. The humble attitude of these foreigners in the presence of the pharaohs expresses well enough their submission. One of these sculpted scenes in Beit al-Wali, in Nubia,[293] dates back to the reign of Ramesses II, in the XVIth century[294] before the Christian era.

---

285 See Ogden, "Metals," particularly 161–66.

286 A group of people living in the Atbai, in the Sudanese Nubian Desert. The Atbai is located between the Nile and the Red Sea, south of Ababda and north of Amarar.

287 A place populated by troglodytes, an ancient people who lived in a number of locations, according to classical authors such as Strabo, Diodorus Siculus, and Pliny. All references claim they lived in the desert, along the African Red Sea coast.

288 Cailliaud is referring to the ancient city of Berenice Panchrysos, identified as half a degree from Alaki or Salaka by the geographical author Jean Baptiste Bourguignon d'Anville. See Jomard, *Travels in the Oasis of Thebes, and in the Deserts Situated East and West of the Thebaid: in the years 1815, 16, 17, and 18 by M. Frederic Cailliaud*, vol. 1 (London: Sir Richard Phillips and Co., 1822), 12.

289 Cailliaud is referring to gunpowder.

290 For information on how the ancient Egyptians mined gold, see Ogden, "Metals," in particular 161–62.

291 Cailliaud writes: "Several times we have had occasion to make this remark on the emerald quarries, located close to the Red Sea *(Travels to the Oasis of Thebes and in the deserts in the west and in the east of the Thebaid, years 1815–1818)*." See Jomard, *Travels in the Oasis of Thebes.*

292 Cailliaud is referring to such tombs as Theban Tomb 100, that of Rekhmire, which he visited and from which he recorded numerous scenes. See Norman de Garis Davies, *The Tomb of Rekh-mi-re*, vols. 1 and 2 (New York: Metropolitan Museum of Art, 1943), 19, pl. XVII.

293 Cailliaud is most likely referring to scenes 6–7, as cited in Bertha Porter and Rosalind L.B. Moss, *Topographical Bibliography of Ancient Egyptian Hieroglyphic Texts, Reliefs, and Paintings. VII. Nubia, the Deserts, and Outside Egypt* (Oxford UK: Oxford University Press, 1995), 23. Among other images, this scene depicts Ramesses II in a kiosk, receiving two registers of Nubians delivering tribute.

294 Actually, the thirteenth century BC.

The principal properties of gold, later recognized by the Egyptians, did not keep them from appreciating this metal as commercially valuable. Considered as unalterable at least in its metallic brilliance, gold must have been quickly used in a solid state for the creation of small idols which represented the principal gods of the Egyptians. We find them sometimes in tombs. Gold was also used for different objects of ornamentation and finery, such as necklaces, earrings, chains, bracelets, rings, and seals of various shapes and styles. The Drovetti collection in Turin possesses some, and the Egyptian Museum in Paris is rich in them. We note large, chain bracelets to be worn along the length of the arm. Many are covered in compositions of enamel[295] for which each piece was cut, encrusted in soldered works, one upon the other, to form various designs. A portion of these objects, found in 1822 in the excavations which Mr. Drovetti undertook in the ruins of Memphis, had been placed in a tomb, but not in their original place, as this tomb had already been excavated. This discovery and many other less important ones in Upper Egypt prove readily enough that if thousands of tombs were violated, it was not through a sentiment of opposition toward the religious idols of these people, but very much through cupidity, so as to remove the objects of value locked away in these tombs. The opening of the pyramids in Memphis, for example, can confirm this thinking. It is said several years' worth of Egypt's revenue was paid to do this work. It is unlikely that one would had given such considerable sums to open all the pyramids, if, upon opening the first, one had found only embalmed bodies surrounded by stone or wood statues.

In the Egyptian Museum in Paris, we note various pairs of bracelets for a man and for a woman. Several are covered in enamels of different colors, cut and encrusted to form charming designs in flowers. The elegant women of our day would not disdain to adorn themselves with them. We also see in the Egyptian Museum a gold cup, very remarkable in its work. It is very similar to those which are used by the Turks for their sorbet. It bears engraved hieroglyphic characters and others raised in rounded embossment in the interior.

Amid the rich objects found in the ruins of Memphis, we must cite: a mummy mask created from a stamped sheet of gold; forged planks, of the size and shape of the sole of a shoe, which must have been placed under the feet of a mummy; fingerstalls, 4 centimeters long, on which were indicated, with engraving, the shape of nails. These tubes were found placed on the fingers of some rich mummies. They are made of ferrules[296] with the ends soldered.

But the most precious pieces for history are the mounted rings[297] in the shape of rotating seals. These are scarabs or other forms of amulets in solid gold and rock crystal, in lapis lazuli, in amethyst, all engraved with hieroglyphic characters in which are found royal names. One of these rings (pl. 29B, fig. 14), in rock crystal, bears, with the Apis Bull, the name of King Thutmose III, of the XVIIIth dynasty, called Moeris by Herodotus.[298]

---

295 Gold enameling appears to have been very rare in ancient Egypt. See Ogden, "Metals," 166.
296 A ring or cap of metal used to protect, strengthen, or hold something together.
297 All of the rings described here have been identified by Mainterot. See Mainterot, *Aux origines de l'égyptologie*, 136 and note 313.
298 Herodotus mentions King Moeris while discussing the rulers of Egypt. Strassler equates him not with Thutmose III of the Eighteenth Dynasty, but with Amenemhat III of the Twelfth Dynasty. See Herodotus, *The Histories*, 2.101; Strassler, *The Landmark Herodotus*, 160.

Another ring, also able to rotate (pl 29B, fig. 12) to serve as a seal, in solid gold, bears the name Amenophis I.[299]

These seals must have belonged to these pharaohs, and all of these gold objects found together allow the conjecture to be made that Memphis was the location of their sepulchers.[300] These royal cartouches determine the era in which these gold objects were created. The first of these princes ruled 1,736 years, and the other 1,723 years, before the Christian era.[301]

Amid the objects of decoration and of finery deposited in the Egyptian Museum in Paris, we can still cite many things which show us to what point the ancients had brought their industry in the use of gold.

Let us continue the inspection of rings. We see some which are formed of gold serpents, encircling the finger several times. The eyes of the reptile are in enamel, the head and tail are engraved. Other extremely light rings, and of delicate work, are encrusted with enamel.

The earrings are no less remarkable; there are those which end with the head of a bull, lion, and gazelle. It is to be noted that these earrings are hollowed out, made of stamped plaques, and that the solid body is always without cracks. One part is decorated by a small gold strand, die-drawn and passed around the circle which is embellished with cannetille[302] and gold-stamped with knurls, very delicately worked. Others represent serpents crudely engraved. All of this jewelry, without always being as perfect as our own, shows us that the Egyptians were advanced in the art of their manufacture and proves their good taste as a whole.

We note two rich necklaces, one bearing in medallion the eye, a symbol of Osiris,[303] engraved on a gold plaque. The other is distinguished by a multitude of small libation vases forming pendants, similar to those which we find in carnelian. A long chain bracelet is quite remarkable because this work, composed of a multitude of rings, all soldered and intertwined, is the same as that which is still made in our day.

Another is a very beautiful collar *en esclavage*[304] in three rows. The first row represents olives, the second is a mixture of libation vases, small latus fish, lizards, and lotus flowers. The last row is in agate beads from which is hung the image of the head of a symbolic ram, engraved, on a gold plaque.

Another chain bracelet, of a work still finer than the first, supports a plaque depicting on both sides a sparrow hawk seen from the side, and formed by a multitude of gold, soldered beads; workmanship still in use in our day and known under the name of *bijoux à*

---

299 The cartouche bears the name Aakheperrura, the name of Amenhotep II (1427–1400 BC), not Amenhotep I. Amenhotep and Amenophis are variant spellings of the same name.

300 Thutmose III's tomb, KV 34, and Amenhotep II's tomb, KV 35, are both, in fact, in Luxor in the Valley of the Kings. See Porter and Moss, *Topographical Bibliography I.2*, 551–56; the Theban Mapping Project's bibliography for KV 34, http://www.tmpbibliography.com/resources/bibliography_2kv_valley_of_kings_kv34_thutmosis_iii.html; the Theban Mapping Project's bibliography for KV 35, http://www.tmpbibliography.com/resources/bibliography_2kv_valley_of_kings_kv35_amenhotep_ii.html

301 Thutmose III reigned from 1479 to 1425 BC, while Amenhotep II reigned from 1427 to 1400 BC.

302 A filigree ornamentation comprised of coiled wires and popular in the early to mid-1800s.

303 Most likely the Eye of Horus.

304 This style of bracelet or necklace comprises plaques connected together with multiple chains.

grains. Representations of a small porcelain shell, called the money of guinea,[305] were stamped in small plaques of gold and worn like necklaces.

We still find an infinity of separate plaques, often representing the eye, a symbol of Osiris,[306] and other religious subjects, such as scarabs, sparrow hawks, Apis bulls, etc., always engraved on very thin plaques and sometimes raised in round embossment. We also found large funerary scarabs in basalt, a very hard volcanic rock, covered in gold plaques on which were engraved hieroglyphs, solid gold knots, and shells containing gold powder prepared for painting by brush.[307]

One remarkable object is the embossed head of an Apis bull: the ears, the eyes, the mouth, along with the marking on the front, are outlined by numerous, small, soldered gold beads. This object and others analogous to it are colored to cover the soldering.[308]

An amulet, remarkable for its lightness, represents the winged soul. It is encrusted with enamel of various colors.

A cup,[309] hammered with plaques of gold and embossed, has the bottom decorated with bynni fish[310] playing among lotus flowers. Its circumference bears an inscription, also engraved in hieroglyphs, in which Champollion recognized the titles and the name of a royal scribe named Thoth, among whose titles are also listed that of Steward of Tin, Gold, and Silver, under the reign of King Thutmose III (the Moeris[311] of the Greeks).

This object, precious as a piece of work, is made even more so by its inscriptions which reveal to us that the Egyptians knew tin,[312] and recalls for us a famous period, that of the reign of one of the greatest pharaohs of the XVIII Dynasty.[313]

Champollion[314] gives a long description of a rich tomb in the necropolis of Thebes, that of Timasiu,[315] Priest of Osiris, Head of Scribes for the Divine Door of Diospolis (Thebes),

---

305　This was the name used for such a shell in Cailliaud's lifetime.

306　Most likely the Eye of Horus.

307　Cailliaud is referring to a gilded scarab now kept in the Musée Dobrée with accession number 56.2730. See Mainterot, *Aux origines de l'égyptologie*, 297–98, pl. XXVII. The scarab and gold are authentic, but the inscription was likely carved by Cailliaud.

308　Cailliaud writes: "This head is part of our collection in the Cabinet of the Imperial Library." The Imperial Library is now the Bibliothèque nationale de France, in Paris. For an explanation of what became of the objects Cailliaud brought back from Egypt, see Mainterot, *Aux origines de l'égyptologie*, 251–86.

309　Cailliaud is refering to the cup of General Djehuty, kept in the Louvre under accession number N 713. See Frédéric Cailliaud, *Voyage à Méroé, au Fleuve Blanc, au-delà de Fazoql, dans le midi du royaume de Sennar, à Syouah et dans cinq autres oasis* (Paris: Imprimerie royale, 1826–27), 330; Mainterot, *Aux origines de l'égyptologie*, 136.

310　Probably *Barbus bynni*. See Brewer and Friedman, *Fish and Fishing*, 59.

311　Strassler equates Herodotus' Moeris with Amenemhat III of the Twelfth Dynasty. See Herodotus, *The Histories*, 2.101; Strassler, *The Landmark Herodotus*, 160.

312　Tin objects are extremely rare in ancient Egypt until the Roman Period. See Ogden, "Metals."

313　Cailliaud is incorrect in his belief that Moeris was Thutmose III of the Eighteenth Dynasty. Strassler equates him with Amenemhat III of the Twelfth Dynasty. See Herodotus, *The Histories*, 2.101; Strassler, *The Landmark Herodotus*, 160.

314　Champollion, *Monuments de l'Égypte et de la Nubie. Notices descriptives*, vols. 1–2 (Paris: Firmin Didot, 1844), 558–69.

315　Theban Tomb 65 was originally made for Nebamun but usurped by Imiseba. See Porter and Moss, *Topographical Bibliography I.1*, 129–32; the Theban Mapping Project's bibliography for Tomb 65, http://www.tmp bibliography.com/resources/bibliography_5nv_tombs_of_the_nobles_tt65_nebamun_usurped_by_imiseba.html

Residence of Amun. In the temple of Karnak he is called High Priest, Head of the Altar of Amun. This tomb contains numerous paintings of scenes of adoration, offerings, and other religious ceremonies in which figure a group of priests in procession, bearing the rich *baris*[316] of Amun-Ra. The goddess Hathor leads in a grand costume with a skintight tunic, blue background, and enveloped in an ample tulle or lace robe. High priests, heads shaven, are dressed in the skins of a panther, and others in the *calasiris*.[317] The reigning pharaoh, Ramesses IX, called Maiamun[318] of the Twentieth Dynasty, is helmeted. He wears a large muslin tunic, striped or embossed. Twelve cartouches representing pharaohs whom the deceased associated with the cult are conveyed by him to the naos of Amun. We will cite Ramesses III, IV, V, VI, Amenophis II, Thutmose I and III, etc.

We note adorations to Amun-Ra and Ra in which the deceased justifies his life.

But what occupies us here in these paintings are 26 or 28 vases in gold and one in silver.[319] We drew several richly decorated ones and those of the best taste.[320] The body of one of them is covered in flutes in relief and with the heads of antelopes with necklaces around their necks. The long horns of these animals form the handles and flowering stalks of lotuses are introduced into them. The artist depicted on the flowers a couple of birds with their young. An enameled border in blue adds to the elegance of this object. It is exhibited on a stand in an assemblage of woodwork of which the cornice and the pyramidal style are of the Egyptian type.

Plate 24A, figure 1. This vase could be one of the most elegant *porte-montre*[321] of our era.[322] A ribbed frieze decorates its edge and the lotus decorates its body and the shape of the foot. The stalks of this plant form the handles. Two full-length figures are attached to the decoration and support the cup. These people are of pure, Black race,[323] stemming from ancient relations with the African lands much more remote than those which we visited under the 10th degree of latitude. Of Black race, they wear rings in their ears, bracelets on their wrists and on their upper arms. Their shoes are laced on their feet, they have belts made of stalks of papyrus or lotus. They have freedom of movement as servants rather than as slaves.

The represented object (fig. 2) could have links with the vases called canopic, but it is, above all, characterized by two horse heads, richly harnessed, forming the handles, and surmounted by plumes. Fluted friezes and other designs decorate the neck and the flowers of lotuses and papyri decorate the body.

---

316 Cailliaud uses this word to describe the sacred barque of Amun. This word was associated with Egyptian boats and is mentioned in the writings of Herodotus. See Herodotus, *The Histories*, 2.96.4–5; Strassler, *The Landmark Herodotus*, 156.

317 A tunic with fringes at the legs, mentioned by Herodotus. See Herodotus, *The Histories*, 2.81; Strassler, *The Landmark Herodotus*, 151.

318 Ramesses IX, whose throne name was Neferkara Setepenra, reigned from 1126 to 1108 BC.

319 Cailliaud is presumably surmising their material based on the vases' colors.

320 Cailliaud writes: "Pl. 24, fig. 1."

321 Well-known, sculpted pieces in nineteenth-century France. They were often designed to hold clocks.

322 Cailliaud here writes: "(2)." No accompanying footnote is provided for this reference.

323 A direct translation of the French word is 'Negro.'

All the designs that these vases present must have been worked in *repoussé*[324] with a chisel.

Champollion figures in his other magnificent work another gold vase from this tomb.[325] It is simpler in its chiseling than the preceding ones, in the shape of Canopus. The cover represents the head of the Amun ram. It bears on its body the spout of a teapot and the names of Pharaoh Amenophis I.

These imitations, of the best taste, preceded by 1,000 years the pretty productions of Greek art, as Champollion stated, and he noted that they belong to the XVII century before the Christian era.[326]

When we consider, in detail in all their parts, the numerous objects in gold of the ancient Egyptians that we have cited, we must be amazed to recognize here that the better part of our processes were known to them.[327] There is one, among others, which will perhaps surprise even more: it is that the Egyptians might have beaten gold in sheets.[328] We found two possible examples of this work in parchment booklets.

We possess a quantity of objects gilded[329] by means of a mordant on white plaster, a process which is still used today.

In this genre we find mummy masks, figures of idols in wood, principally those of Osiris Serapis, the judge of the underworld, sparrow hawks, an infinite number of small amulets in wood and in wax, and mummies entirely gilded on their skin. On these there is no plaster: bitumen alone apparently fixed the gold to the skin.

Thus, without pushing back this developed industry among the Egyptians to another period than that which is given to us by the discovery of the jewelry of Thutmose III, of the XVIII Dynasty, it follows that 1,736 years before the Christian era, or more than 3,600 years from our day, the Egyptians beat gold into sheets. They used it to gild wood and metals. They pulled it into strands and knew how to solder it, to pour it into molds, to stamp it, to chisel it, to engrave it, to set it, to impress it with knurls, to color it to mask soldering, to cover it with enamel and encrustations in stone, carnelian, lapis lazuli, and in various compositions, and, finally, to fashion it in the manner and in the genre of beads which we were still making only a few years ago. The Egyptians also made chain bracelets.

---

324 Not to be confused with *repoussage*. This technique involves working on the back of a material to produce a pattern or image on the opposite side. For information on gold working, see Ogden, "Metals," 165–66.

325 See Champollion, *Monuments de l'Égypte*, vol. 2, pl. CLVI.

326 Also from the tomb of Imiseba, mentioned above.

327 For a more accurate assessment of ancient Egyptian knowledge on the manufacture of gold objects see Ogden, "Metals," 161–66.

328 For information on the use of sheet gold, see Ogden, "Metals," 165.

329 For information on gilding in ancient Egypt, see the following entries in *Ancient Egyptian Materials and Technology*, edited by Ian Shaw and Paul T. Nicholson (Cambridge UK: Cambridge University Press, 2000): Aston, Harrell, and Shaw, "Stone," 22; Lorna Lee and Stephen Quirke, "Painting Materials," 116; Ogden, "Metals," 159, 164; van Driel-Murray, "Leatherwork and Skin Products," 307; Rowena Gale, Peter Gasson, Nigel Hepper, and Geoffrey Killen, "Wood," 334, 344, 367; Richard Newman and Margaret Serpico, "Adhesives and Binders," 480.

When we saw the foreign collections of Rome, of Naples, and those of the Campana Museum, we were surprised by the conformity which existed between the jewelry of this last epoch and those of the ancient Egyptians. We found in these museums the same shapes of jewelry: the representations of serpents for ear loops, finger rings, bracelets, and frequently small stamped plaques embossed by chisel and worn as necklaces. One of the most remarkable pieces of the collection of Rome is a large collar (pectoral), covering the chest, decorated with designs chiseled in imitation of those of the Egyptians, along with large and small round circles also in gold, to be worn on the neck, on the lower legs, and as bracelets. Scarabs, massive rings with mounted stone settings, jewelry in cannetille[330] form, filigree, and others that are beaded are also present. The last genre was very common among the Etruscans, as it was among the Egyptians.[331]

The fashion of wearing, as decoration for the head, bands of stamped gold leaves was more common among the Etruscans than among the Egyptians, who wore the lotus flower and the papyrus. If the Etruscans perpetuated among themselves the taste for decorating their finery with the representation of reptiles and those of scarabs, it was to imitate the jewelry of the Egyptians and not, as we might believe, for religious veneration. The practiced eye of an artist used to judging the works of this genre will notice, in comparing attentively the different modes of creating these numerous objects, that the Etruscans had copied the Egyptians,[332] but had gained nothing on their predecessors who, in this case as in many others, served as the model for them.

The first important discovery of gold objects made in Meroe, in a pyramid, is that which we will now cite: in November 1830, Mr. Joseph Ferlini, of Bologna, along with Mr. Stefani, an Albanian, came to establish themselves in Meroe and to attempt excavations there without success.[333] They used firstly 100 men, then 350, they say, in an attempt to demolish several pyramids.[334] They were Blacks[335] whom they paid 20 centimes a day. They cleared a staircase which led them into two vaults under a pyramid. They found only human bones piled up, the remains of a saddle of a horse and those of a saddle of a camel, kinds of small bells in metal on which were engraved birds and gods.

A second pyramid was excavated in the same manner. Ferlini states that they found there cadavers. Unfortunately he does not explain himself either on the style of the engravings of the bells or on the cadavers: were they mummies?

Here I textually transcribe the account of the author.

---

330 A filigree ornamentation composed of coiled wires and popular in the early to mid-1800s.

331 Cailliaud is likely referring to granulation, the decoration of an object through the soldering of small balls, or grains, of metal. For the use of granulation in Etruscan jewelry, see Trustees of the British Museum, *Jewellery through 7000 Years* (London: British Museum Publications, 1976), 82. For its use in Egyptian jewelry, see Ogden, "Metals," 165.

332 It seems more likely that technical knowledge of creating jewelry came from the Etruscans, rather than directly from the Egyptians. See Trustees of the British Museum, *Jewellery*, 82.

333 Cailliaud writes: "Account of Mr. Joseph Ferlini, published in Rome by Salvineci, 1838."

334 Cailliaud writes: "The better part of these pyramids offered us degraded remains in front of their sanctuaries, from which we concluded that they generally had been dug. *Travels to Meroe*, vol. 2, page 167."

335 A direct translation of the French word is 'Negro.'

Afflicted by the uselessness of my research in the small pyramids, I decided to make a last attempt on one of the big ones, located on the verge of the hill, and specifically on the one which I had noted as nearly intact. This pyramid was that which Mr. Cailliaud of Nantes had given the description and drawing in his 'Travels to the White and Blue Rivers' (vol. II, p. 157, fig. F).

Having climbed to the top of the pyramid with four workmen to lay hand to the work, I recognized that the demolition could be done very easily as the monument was falling down due to its antiquity . . . we threw stones from the steps . . . no longer able to remain in the intense heat of the sun, for which the burning rays gave up to 48° Réamur,[336] I went to rest myself with Mr. Stefani in the shade of a neighboring pyramid. All of a sudden, I was called by my faithful servant. I ran with my friend to the top of the monument . . . and already I felt my heart open to sweet hope . . . I see my servant, lying on his stomach, seeking to cover with his body the opening which had been discovered. The Blacks, spurred on by cupidity, wanted to chase away my servant with all their strength and plunge their greedy hands to the bottom of the hole. We made good countenance and, weapons in hand, we forced them to descend. We called other, trusted servants and we continued the dig in our presence.

The opening made us glimpse a void which contained objects which we could not distinguish. This cell was formed of large stones crudely assembled. We removed the largest ones that covered it and we recognized a cell having the shape of a long square, made of large superimposed stones, which formed four lateral walls of 6 to 7 feet by 4 in height. The first thing that caught our eye was a large body covered with a cotton fabric of a dazzling whiteness which, when hardly touched, crumbled to dust. It was a kind of table or altar supported by four cylindrical feet and surrounded by a balustrade of wooden bars, alternately large and small. These bars were sculpted and represented symbolic figures. It is under this table (undoubtedly a mausoleum) that was found a bronze vase which contained the precious objects in bronze, enveloped in linen.

They continued the demolition of the same pyramid under the cell. Ferlini states that they found only straw from the desert, braided in the manner of cords, and pieces of wood that had the shape of mallets.[337] Lower, about halfway up the height of the monument, they found a niche formed by three stone blocks in which was found two bronze vases of the most elegant shape, containing a blackish, pulverized substance.

---

336 This scale is also known as the octogesimal division, and dates to the 1730s. Named after René Antoine Ferchault de Réamur, this scale posits the freezing point for water at 0 and its boiling point at 80. Thus, 48° Réamur is 60° C or 140° F.

337 Cailliaud writes: "We recognized the usefulness of these cords, which in the construction of the monument must have served to raise stones. And the mallets must have been used with the chisel to adjust the cuts of these same stones between them, to then put them in place."

These vases appear to us to belong to the Asiatic art of this period, which primarily shows us bearded figures on one of the two, as we see in the tombs of Thebes, where the chiefs of these lands came to pay tribute or offerings of alliance to the sovereigns of Egypt.

The gold objects gathered by Mr. Ferlini are very numerous. He enumerates 10 bracelets in gold with various incrustations in enamel, six to eight necklaces, and 220 other objects: amulets, rings, rotating seals, and other statuettes also in gold. He had 40 ounces of this metal.

In April 1821, Mr. Letorzec and I were climbing this pyramid separated by 2 or 3 meters of stones and debris from the treasure that Mr. Ferlini was to discover. Prince Isma'il expressly forbade us from all excavations, not wanting to be treated, he said, as impious by the natives in violating the sepulchers. In any case, we would not have destroyed one of the most beautiful monuments of ancient Meroe.[338]

ON SILVER[339]

Silver was rarer than gold among the ancient Egyptians,[340] if we judge by the small number of objects that we find made of this metal. Moreover, silver was worked and used like gold in ornaments of finery and in other objects for the cult. It is the figurines that we find most often. In the Drovetti collection in Turin, we note three in silver of the goddess Isis that are magnificent. The evil genie Typhon[341] is represented in solid silver. The largest figurines are made of stamped plaques in two parts and then welded. The museum of London possesses a pretty figure of Amun-Ra and a plaque representing the four genies of the Amenti[342] embossed by chisel. That of Leiden, a head of a sparrow hawk, was similarly formed by chisel.

Among the objects of this genre, we see in the museum of Paris a bronze rod plated in silver, forming a large circle as a necklace in which were passed silver bells, along with amulets in wood and carnelian. We also find necklaces made of small silver plaques representing the symbolic eye mixed together with gilded, silver beads. Others are composed of a multitude of small, silver rings threaded on tresses of hair. We also see necklaces in silver in the genre of those which we have described in gold. They are formed of small plaques representing in embossment the upper part of the porcelain cowry shell.[343] Finally, a last one, very remarkable, in large, silver, faceted beads. We also note a case and solid rings. On one of these rings is the symbolic head of Hathor, engraved on a square plaque, on the other are religious inscriptions and the name of Thutmose III, already cited.

Silver was often used in encrustations in bronze, as ornamentation in the vulture wings of certain gods.[344] We find earrings and necklaces in plaques representing gods and the winged globe embossed or engraved. But, in general, silver objects are much less important

---

338 Cailliaud writes: "*Travels to Meroe*, vol. 1, pl. XLI—pl. XXXV—vol. 2, p. 147."
339 A note here states: "on the number of discoveries." For more information on this subject, see Ogden, "Metals."
340 On the availability of silver in ancient Egypt, see Ogden, "Metals," 170–71.
341 An ancient Greek name for Seth.
342 A nineteenth-century version of the ancient Egyptian word *Imentet*, meaning 'the west,' or 'land of the dead.'
343 *Cypraea moneta*: the shell of a gastropod mollusk which was used for decoration and as a form of common currency in Bengal, in the center of Africa, and in Asia.
344 Gods such as Mut and Nekhbet were represented by vultures.

in volume than those in gold, and of an inferior workmanship. They are also rarer, owing, perhaps, to oxidation which might have destroyed a large number. We do not doubt that the ancient Egyptians used this metal on a large scale in the creation of vases. The monuments of Thebes show shapes of the greatest elegance and the hieroglyphic inscriptions positively distinguish those which are in silver. We have shown one here (pl. 24, fig. 2),[345] coming from the tombs of Qurna. Its shape is very slender, it is covered in lotus leaves arranged in symmetry. The stalks and the flowers of papyrus form the handles, two serpents which appear to exit the vase and one head of Typhon,[346] surmounted with plumes, form the cover. The Egyptians made much use of chasing. The eyes, the eyebrows of Typhon, and other blue points of flowers are made of many encrusted parts of enamel. The regularity of its shapes might denote careful work, and its assemblage is not lacking in elegance.

Champollion says that this work belongs to the XV century before the Christian era,[347] a period that preceded by a thousand years the pretty works of Greek art.

We are uncertain on the localities that might have provided silver to the Egyptians.[348] In the ancient accounts, however, that we have on the mines of the Troglodytic it is said that they gave gold and silver. What we know of the economic regime and of the system of concentration of the Egyptians leads one to believe that they had generally, among themselves or in their surrounding area, metals and other products that they knew how to use.

Various subjects represented in the tombs of the necropolis of Thebes show us foreigners from the interior of Africa and from Asia bringing to the sovereigns of Egypt baskets of silver as ingots and as chains. We see, in meals, vases in the shape of cups and others for which the hieroglyphic inscriptions designate metal and silver. Gold vases appear to have been reserved for religious ceremonies.

ON BRONZE[349]

Of all the metals, the most abundantly widespread in the arts was, without exception, bronze, which was used with profusion in the creation of idols, weapons, instruments of labor, and numerous tools serving the arts. Sacred vases, mirrors, spoons for incense, and funerary or hypocephalic plaques[350] were often made in bronze, along with an infinite number of small instruments, such as knives, tongs, depilatories, spatulas, various small needles, and sharp lancets of appropriate shape and size for surgery, for embalmings, and for many other uses. The Drovetti collection in Turin possesses a good number of these last, very curious, instruments.

---

345 The referenced image is clearly colored gold, presumably to represent the material from which it was made, despite Cailliaud's text claiming it is made of silver.

346 An ancient Greek name for Seth.

347 The vase appears to be a compilation of images found in Theban Tomb 65, the tomb of Imiseba, which dates to the reign of Ramesses IX (1126–1108 BC).

348 See Ogden, "Metals," 170–71.

349 For more information on this subject, see Ogden, "Metals."

350 Hypocephali are small, round objects often made of linen and stucco. They were also made from bronze, gold, papyrus, clay, or wood. From the Late Period onward, they were placed under the deceased's head as a magical means of protection. See Geraldine Pinch, *Magic in Ancient Egypt* (Austin TX: University of Texas Press, 1995), 157.

Bronze became common and was of a faster and easier manufacture than iron. It was sometimes used in the construction of certain buildings in pieces of 20 to 25 centimeters, made into dovetails, and cut between each course of stone of a size to maintain their join. These were much more common in wood, ordinarily in sycomore.

In temples, in public buildings, and in many particular houses, pivot holes and pivots on which rolled doors were made from it. The museum of London possesses a well-conserved one.

It was also used for implements of husbandry, most particularly for plows. Its weight was necessary to make this instrument enter the ground, and its hardness to preserve the end of the plowshare. The Louvre possesses a pointed mass that had been thus used. Hoes or hand picks were also embellished. The museum of Leiden possesses a complete one bearing the cartouche of Thutmose IV of the XVIII Dynasty, instruments of music such as sistra, cymbals, trumpets, and other percussion instruments, two very remarkable helmets, and sharp tools like axes, coins, chisels, mortising chisels, gougers, drills, and others generally used in the arts. We note that often these tools were fitted on handles. They greatly resemble our own and were used by all workmen who worked wood.

As we have not found, or have found very few, iron instruments, we are able to suppose that the ancients had discovered a process to render bronze harder, and into a state for tackling granite rocks.[351]

Might time have destroyed this hardness? The preservation of these instruments does not permit one to suppose this. The forged tools were extremely worn down, with thin blades. Bronze, thus worked, acquired a remarkable elasticity. Its dirty white color comes close to that of alloyed gold in strong proportion with silver. The polish is nice, the sound is silvery.

We find very rarely objects in copper. This metal was almost always mixed with an alloy to give it stiffness.

During the period of Berenice, wife of Ptolemy III, who ruled from year 246 up to year 221 before the arrival of Jesus Christ, bronze was still greatly used in the absence of iron or steel, which was even rarer. We are amazed to find from this reign a bronze stamp for stamping a coin[352] with the head of Queen Berenice, her head veiled. On the reverse, a horn of abundance[353] decorated with the diadem. As this coin was in fine gold, consequently very malleable, the hardness of the bronze was sufficient for stamping. We note that this stamp sufficed. It bears traces of the use that was made in the pushing back of its edges, produced by the great blow that it received.[354]

---

351 For the art of metal forging and for the use of iron in ancient Egypt, see Shaw and Nicholson, eds., *Ancient Egyptian Materials and Technology* (Cambridge UK: Cambridge University Press, 2000).

352 Cailliaud uses the French word *médaille*, which can be translated either as 'coin' or 'medallion.'

353 Cornucopia.

354 Cailliaud writes: "It is on the island of Elephantine that we found this portion of a stamp bearing the head of Berenice. The other part, showing on the reverse the horn of abundance, was collected slightly before our arrival at the same site, by Mr. Dr. Burcart, German. He brought it, it is said, to the Vienna museum. Our own is in Paris, in the rue Richelieu collection. Enthusiasts of medals need not fear counterfeiting." Cailliaud is referring to Johann Ludwig Burckhardt (1784–1817), a pioneering Swiss, not German, scholar.

Among the important objects found in bronze and deposited today in the Louvre, we note, for their composition, several cups of a particular alloy which, when struck, gives a pure and prolonged sound of a most remarkable timbre. One bears a hieroglyphic inscription.

The serpent reproduced everywhere on ornaments, in friezes above doors of temples, is noted to be in bronze. In the collections of the Louvre and London, votive objects are often covered with encrustations in lapis lazuli and the eyes in red jasper.

Among the statuettes, we note the figure of Panthe.[355] It is bearded, the eyes are encrusted in gold, and various symbols which characterize the principal divinities of Egypt must be noted. Panthe is the image of the great god Pan, considered to be the universe personified.

Another bronze represents Amun-Ra, the king of the gods, the Egyptian Jupiter, supreme master of the three zones of the universe. On his headdress are placed long palm leaves. He tramples on bows, the symbol of the barbarian people of Libya.

A second bronze of the same god is even more worthy of mention than the preceding one. In the right hand he holds the handled cross, a symbol of divine life; in the other, the scepter of benevolence, a symbol of moderation. His belt bears the hieroglyphic inscription of Amun-Ra, lord of the three zones of the universe. It is encrusted in gold along with the eyes and necklace.

But one of the richest bronzes due to all its details and ornaments, encrusted in silver, is a statue of Hathor, the celestial Egyptian Venus, wife of the god Ptah.[356] Her long hair, mixed with uraei serpents, is covered by a vulture, crowned with 12 other uraei which support two long palm leaves joined to the sun's disc and to two uraei worn on the *pschent*.[357] The sacred sparrow hawk of the sun covers the back part of the body of the goddess and envelops her with its protective wings. On the base is the name Hathor. These bronzes, which we see are most remarkable, were sometimes enriched still further with encrustations in hard stones such as lapis lazuli, jasper, carnelian, compositions of turquoise, and others.

Among the large number of bronzes in the Louvre, we will cite the *amchir*, or censer. There is one representing an extended hand that stems from a lotus flower and supports a cup in which perfumes were burnt. The end of the handle offers a head of a sparrow hawk.

We note several mirrors of polished metal, of which the handles are in wood, in ivory, or in metal. One of them is particularly worthy of mention because of its handle, also in metal, representing the goddess Hathor, her head surmounted by a lotus flower, and holding in the left hand a dove.

Already several analyses of this metal have been made by Mr. Vanquelin. We will cite these in 100 parts.

Copper	85
Tin	14
Iron	1
	100

---

355 The god Bes.
356 Spelled 'Phtha' by Cailliaud.
357 The double crown.

The analyses of two mirrors, of a hand axe, and of a chisel gave the same alloy results.[358]

Among the best preserved objects, we see several sacred vases or large, handled pails meant to transport sacred water in religious ceremonies. Hieroglyphic tableaux, here, are ordinarily chased and engraved. One of them represents the priest-scribe named Chapokhonsis, son of Psammeticus. He receives the sepulchral honors that are given to him by his son Petesis, Priest of Amun. He offers incense, makes a libation, and says a prayer.

Among the funerary objects, we find bronze used in hypocephali,[359] or discs made of plaques of this metal, seven to eight inches in diameter. They are covered in sacred characters and symbolic figures, engraved with a burin,[360] most often chased. We find them placed under the heads of mummies.

We said that bronze was used in the creation of weapons. One of the most precious objects found in this genre is a dagger with two edges, of which the ivory handle is richly encrusted with gold. The paintings and the sculptures of Egypt do not represent anything similar. The shape of this weapon makes us think that it is foreign. It is from extreme antiquity.[361]

In the Egyptian collection of Leiden, there are numerous curious bronzes, among other things a handsome saber with two edges (false Egyptian style). In the London Museum is a well-preserved battleaxe.

We also find in bronze, arrowheads of a triangular shape, many objects of finery such as rings, bracelets, ornaments for necklaces, and others.

Bronze must have also been much used in the construction of chariots, if we judge by the lightness of their design. Nothing has yet been found in this genre.

If so many objects, amazing in their preservation and interesting for the history of art, were preserved, we owe it to the religious ideas of the Egyptians who enshrined everything in the tombs.

Copper was alloyed with tin to be beaten into plaques,[362] die-drawn, and appropriated for an infinity of objects which could not be made in copper because it is too soft. This metal was worked like gold or silver.

We also find, among the ancient Egyptians, copper beaten into very thin sheets and gilded, which we call today clinquant.[363] All of this demonstrates to us that they did not lack knowledge of combining metals. The composition of bells was known to them.

For the use of different colors in the art of painting, and in that of enamels, we know that copper carbonate[364] combined with chemical processes was successfully used.

---

358 Cailliaud writes: "These last objects are part of the collection formed by Mr. Passalacqua. We know that the Greeks and the Romans made much use of these metal mirrors. In this they undoubtedly copied the Egyptians, as they had done in so many other situations." Cailliaud is referring to Giuseppe Passalacqua, who worked as an explorer and collector in Egypt, and died in 1865.

359 See note 350 above.

360 A type of chisel.

361 Cailliaud writes: "This object, found by Mr. Passalacqua, is part of his rich Egyptian collection, acquired for the Berlin Museum."

362 For metalworking in general, and the use of copper in ancient Egypt, see Ogden, "Metals," in particular 149–61.

363 Imitation gold leaf, or tinsel.

364 For information on the existence and use of copper carbonate in ancient Egypt, see Lee and Quirke, "Painting Materials," 111; Ogden, "Metals," 151, 165.

The state of oxidation of Egyptian bronzes, and the little experience of the observers, made us believe that all their vases were cast. It is, in effect, that way for the greater number, such as very heavy cups, small, handled pails, etc., but not for all. We noted with amazement that the ancient Egyptians knew how to swage[365] metals by raising the edges of a large sheet of metal with a thickness of more or less two millimeters. They transformed it into a vase, a process that exemplified the towns of the Middle Ages and which must be marveled at to find used in an antiquity that goes back more than 30 centuries.

The largest of these known sacred vases are preserved in the Louvre. They are 27 centimeters high. The very thick edges are artistically added with strong soldering. The handles, without being die-drawn, are forged and rounded by hand. The thickness of the vases is 1.5 millimeters. The hieroglyphic inscriptions which cover them are chiseled and not engraved. The metal had to be very malleable to support this genre of work. The Louvre and the Drovetti collection possess several objects of the same genre.

The copper mines found a few years ago close to the Suez isthmus were exploited in very ancient times. Egyptian ruins in the area indicate that it was inhabited.

We have very rarely found objects in tin,[366] but this metal is often used in their alloys, principally for bronze.

In our excursions to the desert of the emerald mines, we found in the ravines, which conveyed products of all sorts, crystals of tin oxide[367] with titanium iron.[368] It is thus very probable that the Egyptians quarried this metal like lead sulphate, found in veins in the same part of the desert.

THE DIFFERENT CATEGORIES

The various categories of objects in which we observed the use of bronze demonstrate to us that the Egyptians knew various modes of manufacture appropriate to each, owing to their use. Weapons, along with all the sharp tools that they made in bronze, were required, according to a desired alloy, to be strongly forged so as to render them malleable and able to be recast. This genre of objects required these preparations as much for the elasticity it gave as for the conservation of the objects' sharpness. Even the axles of chariots had to be forged.

Another series of objects required another preparation for metal: some implements of husbandry, the pivot holes and the pivots for doors, mirrors, large pails with handles, cymbals and sistra,[369] and probably some solid pieces for chariots.

They knew how to smelt bronze, as is proven by the infinite number of statues of all dimensions and the tall statues of more than a meter.[370] These last ones, molded,

---

365 The act of swaging involves turning up the edges of a piece of metal.
366 For the occurrence and use of tin in ancient Egypt, see the following entries in *Ancient Egyptian Materials and Technology*, ed. Shaw and Nicholson: Lee and Quirke, "Painting Materials," 109, 111; Ogden, "Metals," 149, 151, 152, 153, 154, 157, 158, 160, 162, 163, 171; Nicholson and Peltenburg, "Egyptian Faience," 177, 185; Nicholson and Henderson, "Glass," 198, 208.
367 For the occurrence of tin oxide in ancient Egypt, see Nicholson and Henderson, "Glass," 208, 219.
368 For the occurrence of titanium, and iron-titanium, see Lee and Quirke, "Painting Materials," 111, 115.
369 Cailliaud writes: "These last two forged objects could not be sonorous."
370 For information on Egyptian smelting and the smelting of bronze and copper, see Ogden, "Metals," 150, 151, 155, 157, 161, 166–67, 168, 170.

hollow, and of a great lightness, indicate an extensive knowledge of the processes of the art of smelting.

Let us observe the founder and the curious glassblower of which he makes use (pl. 6A, fig. 2). The forge is in use, filled with wood carbon. It is composed of a deep hearth in which, probably, a crucible was placed, which cannot be seen and which contained the metal. A workman maneuvers with two hands a long, metal bar to stir up the flame, which is fed by four blowers, each with their pipe. Their system is powered by two men mounted each on two of these bellows, holding in each hand a tow line attached to their upper portion. The workman in turn raises the bellows with this cord and lowers it through the weight of his body.[371] He is carried then on the other bellow and through this continual swaying he raises and depresses, turn by turn, these two instruments. The second workman behaves in the same manner. This custom is preserved in Egypt, but we only saw two bellows per forge.

In plate 6B, figure 1, the forge is at rest. There are only two bellows visible, but we see the pipes of four. Two workmen take from the forge the crucible containing the molten material. In figure 2, they pour the material into numerous casts in the shape of funnels, which easily receive the metal and lead it into molds placed to this effect in the mass, or in the earth, or in the sand, to mold according to the will of the founders.

The iron objects found up until the present in the tombs prove well enough that the Egyptians knew this metal. However, the use of bronze in the creation of sharp tools as well as in construction makes one suppose that iron was rare.[372] This line of thinking is tempered by considering the easy destruction of this metal, and we are less amazed that the ancients left many more objects in bronze than in iron. Also, melted bronze was cast in molds and it became very easy to divide into an infinite number of amulets and other objects of adoration.

Perhaps the most important of all the iron objects that enrich collections is in the Louvre. It is a saber. Its double-edged blade with a rib in the center, and the shape of its handle, similar to representations that we see in the sculptures, can leave no doubt of its great antiquity.

In the rich collection of Drovetti in Turin, we find many remarkable objects in iron, among them a very curved sickle, a large knife, the ends of chains, three small hand saws of which one has its mount tightened by hide ligaments to a tourniquet made like ours, spatulas and different surgical instruments of which one, very thin and sharp, is decorated with a bird, and the heads of arrows with barbs pointing backward to hold them in the wound.

In the rich Drovetti collection we also count about fifteen bracelets in thin, round, iron wire. Some of them are decorated with the head of a serpent. One opened these bracelets

---

371 Cailliaud originally referred to the pumping of the bellows as a dance before changing the sentence to its present form.

372 In fact, Egypt has an abundant supply of iron ore (Ogden, "Metals," 166). "The availability of iron on anything but a fortuitous or sporadic scale had to await the development of iron smelting. The relatively late adoption of this technology owes more to the complexities of the processes than to a lack of supplies" (Ogden, "Metals," 167).

to pass them onto the arm, and then one closed them. We find more generally these objects in iron. They were preserved from oxidation by the asphalt which covered the mummies.[373] The metal's lack of worth staved off the tomb robbers from seizing these bracelets, as they did objects in gold, in silver, and other metals which could serve their needs.

We will cite several small circles from which are hung various amulets also in iron, small figurines, representations of spears, of the heads of arrows, and of knives of rough workmanship.

In the Drovetti collection, along with that of London, we see still a certain number of rings in iron with stones in carnelian, lapis lazuli, and jasper. Many are engraved.[374]

The Egyptian collection of Leiden possesses a portion of the small objects cited above and, in addition, two pretty keys of 8 to 10 centimeters, having their ring, and, at the end of the stem, the key bit formed in one by three points and in the other by four. In the ancient system this key bit internally raised the same number of points which comprised the locking mechanism. Then the bolt was pulled back by hand and the lock opened. This model of key is still used in all of Egypt and Nubia.

Let us not forget that in the Drovetti collection there are many small keys in iron and in bronze that are set to be worn on the finger like rings. Each of these small keys is, at most, two centimeters long. The stem is bent at a right angle close to the ring which is rounded. The key bit consists (following the ancient custom) of two or three small points, as we said previously. The stem of the key is found thus flattened on the finger which is itself passed through the ring. In keeping with the custom of the ancient Egyptians, we might say that, day and night, the key to the treasure was in the hand of its owner.

The ancients, who knew iron, must have known the means of converting it to steel.[375] This probability is founded on so many reasons that it is almost a certainty.

When we consider the cut of granite for colossal statues, for obelisks 20 meters in length, we easily see that these are not large fetishes made using flint axes by tribes who did not know steel. These monuments bear with them all the characteristics of meditated work, executed with extreme care. Steel alone could have dressed the surfaces of these obelisks in granite and could have permitted that they be covered with sacred characters of an admirable purity. With knurls and emery, by strength of arm, they removed the cuts of picks and chisels from the stone and thus smoothed the granite.

Still harder stones were also well cut. Such are the colossi known as Memnon in Thebes, a quartzite pudding stone,[376] and two immense hieroglyphic tableaux of the same

---

373 Cailliaud's use of the word 'asphalt' is different from how the word is used today. He is referring to naturally occurring, solid bitumen that is found in certain areas, such as the borders of lakes. See Margaret Serpico, "Resins, Amber and Bitumen," in *Ancient Egyptian Materials and Technology*, edited by Ian Shaw and Paul T. Nicholson (Cambridge UK: Cambridge University Press, 2000), 454–56, 466, 468.

374 Cailliaud writes: "The Greeks and the Romans also had the custom of these iron rings. This fashion was undoubtedly transmitted to them by the Egyptians."

375 For the existence of iron and steel, and for a commentary on its relatively late adoption, in ancient Egypt, see Ogden, "Metals," 166–68.

376 Actually quartzite sandstone.

nature which are beside them. The hardness of this rock, partly marked with iron oxide, is reduced to powder. It would serve as emery to wear down granite.[377]

There are still many other rocks of an amazing hardness, and we can say that the cut of stones in Egyptian monuments helps to prove that only the use of iron could have facilitated their execution.[378] Without being able to assign the localities which provided iron to the ancient Egyptians,[379] the accounts of authors are in accordance in saying that they drew it from Ethiopia.[380] We know that for some years traces of this mineral were found in Egypt at several points in the desert that separates the Nile from the Red Sea, close to the copper mines and under the latitudes of Minya and of Quseir. The rarity of combustibles in this area prevented the pasha from undertaking the exploration of these mines.

Close to the Red Sea, some distance from the emerald mines, there is a very exploitable lead mine: it must have been known in ancient times, if we judge by the ruins of buildings which are around there and by the ancient traces of exploitation which we noted.[381]

Amid the objects that the ancients left us, we rarely find any in lead. Some funerary plaques, the winged globe, and other symbolic figures embossed, and engraved, are made of this metal which, like iron, owes its preservation to its custom of being placed on mummies of which the bitumen wrappings preserved it from any oxidation.

In summary, the Egyptians used hard and, above all, strongly recast bronze in the cutting of their talcose and steatite rocks, and in the cutting of their white limestone statuary extracted from the hillside of the necropolis of Thebes. This alloy could still be used in large nooks to break blocks of granite, but it could only very weakly work on sandstone, and not at all on granite, feldspar, basalt, and quartzite pudding-stone rocks, such as those in the Memnonium in the necropolis of Thebes. Bronze points would have been promptly blunted. Iron converted into steel could alone work these rocks.[382] If we

---

377 Cailliaud writes: "The travelers who wanted to leave their names on the sites which they visited went to much effort to inscribe on these colossi of the Valley of Qurna. The best iron only very weakly works the stone."

378 While Egypt has an abundant supply of iron ore, it was only adopted for large-scale, systematic use at a relatively late date (Ogden, "Metals," 167). The roughing out of pieces of stone would primarily have been done using stone tools, with finer bronze or copper tools used as the work progressed (Aston, Harrell, and Shaw, "Stone," 66).

379 Egypt has an abundance of iron ore throughout the country, including such locales as Wadi al-Dabba in the Eastern Desert and Bahariya Oasis in the Western Desert. Meteoric iron would also have been available for exploitation. See Ogden, "Metals," 166–67.

380 Cailliaud writes: "We think that it is from Dalhalte, under the 9th degree of latitude north, three days' march south of Singa, where, in January 1822, Isma'il Pasha set the limit of his conquests. Dalhalte is located three days from Fadassy, in the south and inhabited by the Gallahs who undertake much exploitation of iron mineral there. We find there forges where weapons, sabers, spears, and maces, which are sent from this part of Africa, are made."

381 Cailliaud writes: "This mine is a vein of lead sulfide and carbonate. Mohammed Ali Pasha undertook the exploitation a few years ago, but the shortage of combustible material made him abandon it, as with several other mines of this desert."

382 Cailliaud is mistaken. For the existence of iron and steel, and for a commentary on its relatively late adoption, in ancient Egypt, see Ogden, "Metals," 166–68.

have not found these instruments, this is undoubtedly due to the destructive elements to which iron was exposed. Mr. Place and Mr. Thomas encountered a considerable quantity in the shape of picks in the ruins of Nineveh and they deposited samples in the Museum of Antiques in the Louvre.[383]

Strong tools in bronze, and the very numerous weapons which were certainly, generally, in bronze, are very rarely encountered. Objects were certainly removed in the plundering of tombs for the value of the metal. Let us not be amazed that iron itself, which time could have been able to save, should disappear by the same motive.

---

383 Victor Place and Felix Thomas, who dug at Nineveh in the 1850s.

CHAPTER 15

CLOTHING

The dress of kings and that of priests was particularly distinct, foremost because of their high nobility and according to the rites by which they carried out their various functions.

Here we show King Horus in a large outfit,[384] a sort of apron affixed to the belt and a long tunic with wide, short sleeves over it. This clothing is the richest of those worn by royalty. The steady and regular lines which present themselves on these materials, of such a great thinness judging by the transparency, lead us to recognize certain behavior resulting from starch. We will cite in support of this fact certain Egyptian statues (from the museums of the Louvre and Turin) in diorite and limestone which show us the surface of their clothing covered in fine regular grooves. This leads us to think that these tunics must have been goffered[385] and starched, like certain pieces of lingerie of our day.

The belt, inlaid with various colors, supports the uraeus, a symbol of royalty. Above his arms and at his wrists are bracelets, ordinarily in gold encrusted with enamel.[386] His head is covered by a *tosch*,[387] a royal military headdress decorated with a plate and the

---

384 Cailliaud writes: "Plate 46." The cartouches on the plate bear the name of King Horemheb of the Eighteenth Dynasty.
385 A manner of pressing pleats into fabric.
386 The enameling of gold appears to have been rare in ancient Egypt. See Ogden, "Metals," 166.
387 The king is shown wearing the Blue Crown, known as *khepresh* in ancient Egyptian. The word *tosch* is not used today. See Gardiner, *Egyptian Grammar*, 504.

asp or uraeus, which we know must indicate kingship.[388] These are in gold. The king holds the *pedum*[389] and the flail.[390]

Their footwear was sandals with long points, the custom of which we cited, preserved among the Meliks[391] of Upper Ethiopia.

We note that amid the pompous display of a sovereign's great luxury, rather than a sumptuous headdress, here, again, appears the helmet of war, as a distinction of the warrior character that is often shown in the scenes of the pharaohs.

In the sculptures of Gebel Silsila,[392] this King Horus[393] is grandly borne as the triumphant victor in memory of his brilliant conquests in Asia and in Africa.

We present a second set of clothes, shown here, for the king.[394] He is the most illustrious of pharaohs, in military costume, holding his fighting bow and wearing the *schenti* (the short tunic).[395] Over the long tunic, with short but wide sleeves, the upper part of the body is wrapped in colored and elegant material. The collar is the customary one. Here the war helmet is simple, but the belt in inlaid colors still bears on the front of the body the symbols of royalty.[396] The footwear is always the same, but for minor details.

It is King Ramesses III, Sesostris the Great,[397] thus shown with his likeness judging by his other representations. He bears resemblance to the shaded figure in the large temple of Abu Simbel,[398] a very rare fact in Egyptian paintings. This beautiful, most remarkable monument, carved into the mountain of sandstone, is a result of the glorious reign of this monarch as well as being the most important temples of Egypt. With a hand he points to African prisoners stemming from his conquests, and whom he presents to the three gods of this site.

The sculptures and the paintings show the pharaoh illustrated in the greatest warlike feats. His armed escort has a strong infantry, his numerous war chariots are mounted by the most intrepid and are harnessed to rich steeds, richly caparisoned, that the hero drives into

---

388 Ancient Egyptian gods and goddesses are also shown wearing uraei.
389 Cailliaud is referring to the crook held in the same hand as the flail.
390 Cailliaud writes: "Scepter with crook, or pedum, named 'ofe,' a symbol of moderation and the idea of punishment and correction. The flail expressed the idea of animation. These are the attributes of power in the hands of the gods and the kings. Champollion the Younger, Grammar, p. 302, 323, 324." See Jean-François Champollion, *Grammaire égyptienne* (Paris: Firmin Didot, 1836), 302, 323, 324. The crook, known as *heka* in ancient Egyptian, was a symbol of government, as the corresponding hieroglyph was used in words associated with ruling. The flail, known as *nekhakha*, may have derived from a fly whisk or from a tool used by goat herders. See Gardiner, *Egyptian Grammar*, 508, 510.
391 Cailliaud is using a version of the Arabic word for 'king.'
392 Gebel Silsila was a quarry site used primarily during the Pharaonic, Greek, and Roman periods. Is is located about 65 kilometers (40 miles) north of Aswan.
393 Actually King Horemheb, of the Eighteenth Dynasty.
394 Cailliaud writes: "Pl. 46A."
395 A term commonly used to refer to an ancient Egyptian kilt, not tunic.
396 Cailliaud is referring to the uraei at the bottom of the kilt.
397 Actually Ramesses II. Cailliaud has confused him with the all-conquering Pharaoh Sesostris, a variation of Senusret, mentioned in the works of Herodotus and Diodorus.
398 Cailliaud is probably referring to the perceived use of shadowing, something upon which he comments later in this chapter.

combat. These give a fair idea of the great power, as with the advancement of art, among this people from the XVI century before J[esus] C[hrist].[399]

In certain circumstances, where the king had to wear priestly clothes to be initiated into various ceremonies and sacred orders of the priesthood, he wore the skin of a leopard. In this case his costume only differed from that of the high priests by the ornament worn suspended at the belt with the frieze of a uraeus, a royal symbol, and by his headdress which, on certain occasions, indicated by its varied shape diverse powers. The most particular and widespread was the *pschent*, divided into three. The part at the bottom[400] was the symbol of domination over the lower regions, the part on top of the same[401] was domination over the upper region. The complete *pschent* was thus the great crown of powers united over upper and lower regions, Upper and Lower Egypt.[402] Sometimes the *pschent* was worn even into combat, where we encounter, although rarely, the king with a short wig. The general custom was to have the head and the beard shaved for kings and priests.

The divine headdress with uraeus and ostrich feathers was reserved for the ceremonies of temples and others (that we will not undertake to cite), in various forms, often overloaded with different symbols.

Kings are frequently represented with the simplest clothing: in a *schenti*,[403] the halftunic, which goes down to the belt, and even with the kilt. It is remarkable and noteworthy that we recognize these items in their private family life, as a sign of their filial love.

In the small palace of Ramesses IV Meiamun, leader of the XIX Dynasty in Thebes, the king receives tribute from his children. One of them raises above him the palm of victory.[404] In another tableau his daughters make offerings to him of flowers and of fruits.[405] Elsewhere the king shows them signs of strong affection. They are at his side and the vulture, a symbol of victory, hangs over the head of the pharaoh. Several of his daughters are still close to him.

---

399 Cailliaud writes: "For these representations, see Champollion the Younger, vol. 1, pl. X to XXXV. An inscription at Abu Simbel bears a date of 35 years for the reign of Sesostris, another temple at Derr in Nubia lets us know the names and the titles of 16 of his children, of which 7 were boys and 9 girls (Champollion the Younger)." See Champollion, *Monuments de l'Égypte*, vol. 1, pl. XV. In fact, Ramesses II reigned for over sixty years, from 1279 to 1213 BC. He likely had more than one hundred children by his principal wives and consorts, and much information on them can be gleaned from his various monuments.

400 Cailliaud is referring to the Red Crown, also known as the Crown of Lower Egypt, or *deshret* in ancient Egyptian. See Gardiner, *Egyptian Grammar*, 504.

401 Cailliaud writes: "Pl. 29B, fig. 3, here on the head of the sparrow hawk." He is referring to the White Crown, also known as the Crown of Upper Egypt, or *hedjet* in ancient Egyptian. See Gardiner, *Egyptian Grammar*, 504.

402 Cailliaud writes: "Pl. 63, second frieze, fig. 5. Here attached to a subject from Ethiopia." He is referring to the Double Crown, a combination of the Red and White crowns, called *skhemty* in ancient Egyptian. See Gardiner, *Egyptian Grammar*, 504.

403 A term commonly used to refer to an ancient Egyptian kilt, not tunic.

404 Cailliaud is referring to Medinet Habu, the mortuary temple of Ramesses III, and a scene from Room III, on the first story of the Gateway Tower. See University of Chicago Oriental Institute Publications, *Medinet Habu—Volume VIII. Plates 591–660. The Eastern High Gate* (Chicago: University of Chicago Press, 1970), pl. 650; Porter and Moss, *Topographical Bibliography II*, 486.

405 Cailliaud is referring to a scene from Room X, on the second story of the Gateway Tower. See Oriental Institute, *Medinet Habu VIII*, pl. 648; Porter and Moss, *Topographical Bibliography II*, 487.

He takes their arms and passes his hand under their chin.[406] In other scenes he plays chess[407] with the queen[408] and with one of his daughters. Another of his cherished creatures is at his side. He hugs her with one arm which he wraps around her neck.[409]

These family scenes occupy 10 successive tableaux.[410] Such was this in the antiquity of the pharaohs: the testimony publicly given to his family by a great king, animated by a loving character. It pleased him to reproduce in sculpture, in rock, these scenes of filial tenderness, like the most important scenes of his history, in conquest which would immortalize him.

The clothing of the priests of the upper order is characterized by the skin of a leopard thrown on the shoulder and the covering of part of the body with the white cloth apron. They are often represented thus, barefoot. In the temples they more generally made use of sandals in palm leaves or papyrus.[411] This one marches at the head of a funerary convoy with the *amchir*.[412] He burns incense in divine honor, spreads the sacred waters of libation, makes offerings to the altars of the gods, and supervises the sacrifices. He himself works in the sacred ceremony anointing the body of the king at his coronation.

In other cases, for the priests, the leopard skin was replaced by the *calasiris*: loose-fitting cloth clothing without sleeves, closed at the neck, open at the sides and descending down to the feet. The priests playing the harp are represented thus.[413] This one on the ground, seated on his heels, sings while he plays, his instrument is decorated with marquetry of various colors. The subject comes from a tomb[414] in the Theban necropolis.

Another priest in *calasiris*[415] plays the harp. This one is standing. The instrument has very rich marquetry and again represents the head of a king with the uraeus on the forehead and the headdress partly falling on the chest, common in colossal statues. It is here surmounted by the great crown or the *pschent*,[416] which we have cited as a symbol of power over the lower and upper regions. The figure wears a fake beard as consecration to the gods. We

---

406 Cailliaud is referring to scenes from Rooms VIII, XI, and XII, on the second story of the Gateway Tower. See Oriental Institute, *Medinet Habu VIII*, pl. 639, 646, 651–54; Porter and Moss, *Topographical Bibliography II*, 487.

407 Ancient Egyptians did not play chess. They did, however, have a number of board games, such as *senet*. See Finkel, *Ancient Board Games*.

408 Cailliaud has mistaken one of the princesses for a queen. See Room XIII in Porter and Moss, *Topographical Bibliography II*, 487.

409 Cailliaud is referring to scenes from Room XII, on the second story of the Gateway Tower. See Oriental Institute, *Medinet Habu VIII*, pl. 639–41; Porter and Moss, *Topographical Bibliography II*, 487.

410 Cailliaud writes: "Reproduced by Champollion." See Champollion, *Monuments de l'Égypte*, vols. 2 and 3, pl. CXCIX [1, 2, 4], CC [1–4], CCI [1, 3]. While Cailliaud's description does not include Champollion's scene 2 from his plate CCI, given the subject matter, he is likely counting it as one of the "10 successive tableaux." This scene comes from Room XIII, on the second story of the Gateway Tower. See Oriental Institute, *Medinet Habu VIII*, pl. 630–32; Porter and Moss, *Topographical Bibliography II*, 488.

411 Cailliaud writes: "Pl. 47."

412 A censer.

413 Cailliaud writes: "Pl. 47."

414 The tomb of Ramesses III, KV 11. See Appendix 1 for more information on plate 47.

415 Cailliaud writes: "Pl. 45."

416 The Double Crown.

copied this painting in the tomb of Ramesses IV Meiamun, first king of the XIX Dynasty,[417] in the Valley of the Kings.

Here is shown another priest,[418] bare arms raised in the sign of invocation, the head encircled by a band, the neck decorated with a large necklace, his clothing is the customary white apron. Here he bears a fringe with the band of the upper order.

There was even simpler clothing for priests often charged with the transport of the *baris*,[419] sacred barques. The head was shaven, the body and arms were bare except for a long, white robe, cinched by a belt and full toward the bottom where the ends fell from a long belt. One or two straps, passed over the shoulder, support this robe, producing the effect of the indispensable crinoline of our day. These priestly clothes were starched; we could scarcely believe it.

Other, more formal, priestly clothes only differed from the last by wide, short sleeves, which were part of the tunic.

We see in temple and tomb scenes the return of war expeditions. These are of numerous reunions in which the king, richly wrapped, is carried in his naos by military officers, followed by fan bearers. Priests of the first order invested with the leopard skin burn incense and pour libations. Other, numerous priests charged with the transport of the *baris* (sacred barques) are here in all their splendor. The royal scribes proclaim the great deeds of the king. The chiefs of the army raise the symbol of victory. All are in a pompous procession which displays the greatest magnificence. They pressed themselves into the temples with the people who had to draw from here happy examples, because one justly celebrated the panegyric, or accounts of actions of grace: imbued as they were by recognition, as much for the fate of the arms which had crowned their success, as for the blessings received, and the dangers from which they had escaped. These rendered accounts, in similar circumstances, were always celebrated with pomp in the most brilliant manner.

Such feats, here, express righteous sentiments; proof of a greatly advanced civilization among this people more than 15 centuries before J.[esus] C.[hrist].

We give a costume of a prince,[420] son of Ramesses IV[421] (Meiamun), taken from his palace of Medinet Habu where are shown 10 images of his sons with their rank in the army.[422] He wears the apron of fine material, as if goffered, wrapped around the hips, attached by a long and elegant belt of which the ends fall very low on the clothing; the body is wrapped by a rich fabric in various colors. Bracelets are worn on the tops of the arm as well as on the

---

417 Actually the tomb of Ramesses III, KV 11. Ramesses III reigned as the second king of the Twentieth Dynasty.

418 Cailliaud writes: "Pl. 48."

419 Cailliaud again uses the word *baris* in describing the sacred barque of a god. This word was associated with Egyptian boats and is mentioned in the writings of Herodotus. See Herodotus, *The Histories*, 2.96.4–5; Strassler, *The Landmark Herodotus*, 156.

420 Cailliaud writes: "Pl. 50."

421 Actually Ramesses III.

422 Cailliaud writes: "According to Champollion." He is referring to a scene from the second court's portico. See University of Chicago Oriental Institute Publications, *Medinet Habu—Volume V. Plates 250–362. The Temple Proper. Part 1* (Chicago: University of Chicago Press, 1957), pl. 250, 299, 301–302; Porter and Moss, *Topographical Bibliography II*, 502.

wrists, and a large necklace at the neck. We note that his sandals don't have long points like those of the king. Another special distinction here characterizes the rank of the prince: it is a tuft of hair wrapped in fabric and kept on the side of the shaven head. It descends onto the shoulder. This symbol, which we also see on the heads of statues of Harpocrates, was rigorously observed among the Egyptian princes.[423] This one bears the scepter with an ostrich plume as a characteristic of his rank. The Egyptian artist showed some shadows on the flesh, which is very rarely encountered in Egyptian painting.

We will continue with royalty through the clothing of a queen in her grand finery.[424] First clothed in the tight-fitting tunic, here red, outlining the shape of the body (a costume typical of divinities), the waist of the queen is encircled by a long, rich belt knotted in the front. Its long ends are fringed, covered in fine embroidery, falling below the knees. This first piece of clothing is covered by the long tunic pressing against the body below the breasts. It is light, of great fineness, of a checked material,[425] and toward the bottom decorations of fringes are spaced by embroidery. Two long bands of the same material, equally embroidered and decorated by fringes, fall very low on her back. She wears as jewelry bracelets and necklaces with a gold chain. The queen has the headdress of Hathor with the feathers of a vulture, the royal uraeus decorates her forehead surmounted by the globe with a uraeus and the plumes, a second attribute of the same goddess. An imitation of long hair, decorated with a frieze of uraei, descends down past the shoulders of the queen. In one hand she holds the sistrum with the head of Hathor and the ears of a cow. It is decorated with a lotus and with garlands of papyrus. In the other hand she holds a symbol ordinarily held by princesses and representing a royal bust.

The artist bore little attention to indicate, or not to indicate, shoes, even on the feet of kings. How did his royal dignity not require rigorous measures in this respect? It is believed that this subject must have been taken in great indifference. Here is a queen that we see shown with bare feet.

We will end the category of royalty with the clothes of a princess, a daughter of Ramesses IV Meiamun,[426] taken from his palace, Medinet Habu.[427] The first, tight-fitting layer of clothing, already observed, is concealed by a long tunic with short, wide sleeves, covering only the upper part of the arms, falling from the shoulders to the feet. These materials, fine and transparent, are here again shown as goffered. A long belt, knotted at the waist, falls to below the clothing. The long tuft of hair enveloped by material and decoration was [made?[428]] from her hairdo as a princely insignia. On her head are feathers and the lotus flower. In one hand she holds the sistrum. In the other, the adornment attributed to her rank. She has sandals.

---

423 This characteristic hairstyle of children, now referred to as the sidelock of youth, was used more generally to represent childhood.
424 Cailliaud writes: "Pl. 45A."
425 Cailliaud writes: "The artist abstained from showing the checks on the whole extent of the upper tunic, out of fear of detracting from the glimpse of clothing underneath."
426 Actually Ramesses III.
427 Cailliaud writes: "Pl. 49."
428 The word in the French text could not be read properly.

The costumes of military chiefs, covering more of the person, had more in common with those of women in many of our countries.[429] A length covers the body, with wide and short sleeves. The white cloth garment fastened to the belt formed a petticoat and was covered by an apron. This person is shown in a tomb[430] in Qurna. With one hand he appears to petition a king (who is not shown here). With the other he carries the symbol of victory. The Egyptian artist in this painting took pains to indicate in white the nails of the feet and of the hands, which is not normally done.

The ceremonial clothing for military officers was distinct from that of civil officers. The first wore tunics that were very long in fine, rayed material, along with short, wide sleeves. Underneath was the small apron, secured by a belt, descending to the knees, in equally white material but without rays or the waistline of the tunic. What stood out regarding the clothing for the second group, along with the royal scribes and others of the lower classes, was that the tunics were more or less long, fastened at the belt, and often without sleeves as well as being covered by the customary apron. The whole thing had great similarities with the simplest clothing of priests already cited.

Beyond the priestly class and kings having shaved heads, generally one retained a large hairstyle, like the custom that is still preserved in Nubia and the upper lands.

People of rank,[431] whom we note in their houses where they indulge in the arts of pleasure, are like so many others: generally wearing little over the indispensable kilt which is attached to the belt. Above it is a short apron affixed to the hips. In other cases it is a long tunic. These last ones are in very fine materials judging by their transparency. The hair is ordinarily heavy and well cared for. Although represented with bare feet, their adornment with bracelets and collars indicates well enough a higher class.

The women were no more covered than the men,[432] in long tunics open at the sides and without sleeves, but of a fineness such that the whole person was visible under the transparent material. Necklaces, bracelets, and rings on the fingers were not lacking among the rich. Luxury was more specially noted in the hairstyles of long hair, often in braids in weaves descending to the elbow, the head encircled with a band and the lotus flower on the forehead, which were more generally the distinction born by women of high rank. She is of this group, meant to play the mandolin with all the luxury that it displays. We are undoubtedly amazed to see that she is also represented without shoes. It is, however, not probable that rich women had the custom of walking barefoot.

Another item of clothing for cared-for women[433] repeatedly shown is the light tunic with large sleeves, covering only the upper arms. This woman, whose coloring indicates a

---

429 Cailliaud writes: "Pl. 54."
430 The tomb of Neferhotep, Theban Tomb 50. See: Porter and Moss, *Topographical Bibliography I.1*, 95; Robert Hari, *La tombe thébaine du père divin Neferhotep (TT 50)* (Geneva: Editions de belles-lettres, 1985); the Theban Mapping Project's bibliography for Tomb 50, http://www.tmpbibliography.com/resources/bibliog raphy_5nv_tombs_of_the_nobles_tt50_neferhotep.html
431 Cailliaud writes: "Pl. 35, 36, 37."
432 Cailliaud writes: "Pl. 55."
433 Cailliaud writes: "Pl. 60."

foreign union,[434] is seated on her heels, a custom often followed in private homes. She has in her hand a lotus flower. The bud of this flower is on her forehead which, with her long hair, once again shows us a person of high class.

We see that Egyptian women were in the habit of wearing straps on the shoulders to hold up their tunics under their breasts.[435] This is just such a case: her blue clothing with the black, hanging belt, the bare upper part of the body and arms; like the preceding one, she is of a foreign coloring to Egypt. She makes an offering of pomegranates and lotus flowers. A simple rose-colored band on the forehead, the necklace, the extravagant bracelets on the arms and the lower portion of the legs, denote once more a woman of the upper class.

One figure is to be cited here[436] who in the simplicity of her clothing is, however, distinguished from working women by virtue of her long and puffy tunic, the lightness of its material, and her long hair. The bare feet no longer occupy us in this circumstance, because we note them thus even in royalty.

To close this category on Egyptian women, we will cite two figures taken in facsimile, life-size, coming, like the preceding women, from the Theban necropolis.[437] In their hair-styles are bands of various colors and the lotus flower.

We saw the working class, most especially the men, with great freedom of movement concerning their clothes. They had nothing but the indispensable *sebu*: a piece of cloth rolled into a belt affecting more or less the shape of a short apron to just above the knee.[438]

Others had still less:[439] a simple roll of cloth passed between the legs from the back to the front and attached to a leather belt, a custom preserved in Lower Nubia among the Barabras,[440] in Ethiopia, as well as among the cultivators of Upper Egypt occupied with *shaduf* work.

Other workmen, more or less required to work partly kneeling, seated on the ground on their heels, made use of a sort of short underpants.[441]

We have cited the kilt as belonging to the upper class. It offers more protection by virtue of its appendage, here worn by a scribe tracing the inscription which must be engraved on the back of a colossal statue.[442]

---

434 Cailliaud is here implying a woman of mixed race. There is nothing in the woman's depiction to indicate that she was anything other than Egyptian.

435 Cailliaud writes: "Pl. 56."

436 Cailliaud writes: "Pl. 59."

437 Cailliaud writes: "Pl. 61 and 62." Both plates—which depict men, not women—are based on scenes from Theban Tomb 50, that of Neferhotep. See Porter and Moss, *Topographical Bibliography I.1*, 95; Hari, *La tombe thébaine*; the Theban Mapping Project's bibliography for Tomb 50, http://www.tmpbibliography.com/resources/bibliography_5nv_tombs_of_the_nobles_tt50_neferhotep.html

438 Cailliaud writes: "Pl. 5A, figs. 4, 5 and on many other plates."

439 Cailliaud writes: "Pl. 16, figs. 1, 2, 3."

440 Cailliaud writes: "Pl. 1, fig. 2 in the text." Cailliaud is using a name given both to the Nubian peoples of Sudan and southern Egypt, and to a group of people living along the Nile between Wadi Halfa and Aswan.

441 Cailliaud writes: "Pl. 1 and 2, pl. 10, fig. 1."

442 Cailliaud writes: "Pl. 15A, fig. 2." This plate does not depict a scribe working on the back of a colossal statue. Cailliaud meant to refer to plate 15, figure 2.

We took from the paintings of the Theban tombs an item of clothing that was not wide-spread and which in antiquity must have been brought from Ethiopia.[443] It comprises a piece of cloth, more or less long, which is used for all clothing. The men of Chendy (ancient region of Meroe) often contented themselves with a small piece wrapped around their thighs. The women, along with those of Sennar, by using more, covered more or less of the body according to the changes in temperature.[444]

---

443 Cailliaud writes: "Pl. 51, 52, 53."
444 Cailliaud writes: "Pl. 3, 4, 5, fig. 1 in the text." These references do not appear to correspond correctly to the plates. A note, written in pencil, at the bottom of the page, states: "Here the art of preparing the hair."

CHAPTER 16

THE ART OF PREPARING HAIR[445]

T he different hairstyles among the ancients varied according to the ranks of the people. In the working class, women and men were always bare-headed and provided with heavy hair which protected them against the burning rays of the sun.[446] Their hair was braided and divided into numerous small tresses that descended to the chin and then wound up in many folds according to their length. This hairstyle is seen in a great many funerary statuettes and in the paintings of tombs. We see many of them in plates 1[447] and 2.[448]

In plate 64, in the two last friezes, we see people from the upper class occupied with their toilette. They are coiffed differently from the common people. They are all kneeling on one leg, on cushions. Crouching on their heels, they receive care from their servants who bring cups of water and perfume, placing collars on them, etc. They hold in their hand the flower and the bud of the lotus while they listen to musicians. They are all men served by male servants.

---

445 A note in the margin states: "To be placed after clothing."

446 Cailliaud is claiming that the lower classes wore their own hair long.

447 Philippe Mainterot believes this plate may be based on imagery in Theban Tomb 36, that of Ibi. Further research is needed either to confirm or to refute this belief. Plate 2, however, is based on images from the tomb of Ibi. See Porter and Moss, *Topographical Bibliography I.1*, 65; Norman de Garis Davies, *The Rock Tombs of Deir el Gebrawi. Part I*, pl. xxiv–xxv; the Theban Mapping Project's bibliography for Tomb 36, http://www.tmpbibliography.com/resources/bibliography_5nv_tombs_of_the_nobles_tt36_ibi.html

448 Cailliaud writes: "This custom is still generally preserved in Nubia, as well as many other ancient customs that are no longer found in Egypt. The women of Chendy and of Sennar go to lengths to divide their hair into an infinite multitude of small, extremely fine tresses. To prepare it thus, it was said to us on site, requires up to five days of work. Then the hair is thoroughly soaked with fat. In the hairstyles of Chaykyes and in those of the women of Fazoql the tresses are layered (plate III, IV, from the text of our *Travels to Meroe*). These plates must be placed in [the text?] of Arts and Crafts." The final sentence is a note in the margin.

In the sculptures we note military chiefs wearing long tresses, but men generally wore short hair and the priests had shaved heads. Kings wore little hair because of their helmets. Still today, the Meliques or Malecks,[449] the principal chiefs of Ethiopia, have short hair and cover their heads in dignity.

The women of a more distinguished class wore their hair long, hanging in numerous tresses on the back, on the shoulders, and on the chest. They compensated for what might have been lacking by means of artificial hair. They placed in it lotus flowers and ribbons (pl. 65, fig. 1[450] and pl. 56[451]).

Long wigs with pendulous tresses were often used, especially for mourners (pl. 57[452] and 65, fig. 4[453]). We possess one in our collection:[454] the material is made of hair, plaited in small braids.

We see in the first two rows in plate 64 the toilette of women. They are crouched on cushions. Female servants bring them cups of water or beverages, small pots of perfume, and necklaces. One of them washes the arms of her mistress. Their light tunics are held up by a strap. Some of them make music, for only women enter into this service.

One is amazed to find in the tombs this braided hair, and others also of artificial hair, curled or in flat plaits of a width of four fingers, ending in points the length of the hand. The two pendulous parts fall in locks of smooth and curly hair. It is thus with one of the most curious wigs that we possess, which we found in a tomb in Elethyia.[455] One finds the hair turned on a chuck in the shape of a corkscrew and teased in a manner that was still in fashion a few years ago.

We often found these very curious remains wrapped in linen, placed in baskets or in chests, sometimes closed with a seal in virgin wax or in clay. Often this hair was placed beside the deceased as a souvenir of people who were most dear to him.

The hairstyles and the dress of the ancient Ethiopians present notable differences from those of Egypt. In the sculptures of a temple on the Isle of Meroe (pl. 63)[456] the artist treated with much artistry the rigorous symmetry of hairstyles, sometimes smooth, sometimes

---

449 Cailliaud is again using a version of the Arabic word for 'king.'

450 Based on images from Theban Tomb 138, that of Nedjemger. See Porter and Moss, *Topographical Bibliography I.1*, 252; Erika Feucht, *Die Gräber des Nedjemger (TT 138) und des Hori (TT 259)* (Mainz: Philipp von Zabern, 2006); the Theban Mapping Project's bibliography for Tomb 138, http://www.tmpbibliography. com/resources/bibliography_5nv_tombs_of_the_nobles_tt138_nedjemger.html

451 From the tomb of Ramesses III, KV 11. See Porter and Moss, *Topographical Bibliography I.2*, 520; Reeves and Wilkinson, *The Complete Valley of the Kings*, 159–61; the Theban Mapping Project's bibliography for KV 11, http://www.tmpbibliography.com/resources/bibliography_2kv_valley_of_kings_ kv11_ramesses_iii.html

452 It is not known from which tomb this image was taken.

453 This scene was taken from Theban Tomb 255, that of Roy. See Porter and Moss, *Topographical Bibliography I.2*, 339; Marcelle Baud and Etienne Drioton, *Tombes thébaines: Nécropole de Dirâ' Abû 'n-Nága, Le tombeau de Roy* (Cairo: MIFAO, 1935); the Theban Mapping Project's bibliography for Tomb 255, http://www.tmp bibliography.com/resources/bibliography_5nv_tombs_of_the_nobles_tt255_roy.html

454 For information on what became of Cailliaud's collection, see Mainterot, *Aux origines de l'égyptologie*, 251–302.

455 A version of the ancient Greek name for the area of al-Kab: Eileithyiaspolis.

456 This image comes from the Lion Temple of Apedemak in modern-day Sudan, which is approximately 170 kilometers (106 miles) northeast of Khartoum. See Porter and Moss, *Topographical Bibliography VII*, 269.

plaited or braided. We note a royal family preceded by the goddess Anukis, with the head of a lion, by Phre-Sun with the head of a sparrow hawk, by Anubis with the head of a ram, by Amun with a human head.[457] A queen presents a group of prisoners, tied together, to a king dressed in a long tunic. All the people have rich outfits and wear bracelets. A kind of short cape, worn as a stole on the shoulder, wraps a part of the body, and is made of long, pendulous tufts. It is attached by long cords from which tassels fall on the tunic. This outfit, which appears royal, is not seen in the monuments of Egypt. The figure of a woman holding prisoners appears to indicate a power that women did not have in Egypt.[458]

The queens have very long nails. This custom is still observed in Egypt by women of distinction: they are colored red with henna. In the numerous figures of this monument we do not see the long beard, as in Egyptian sculptures.

We were fortunate enough to be able to draw these remarkable subjects from 23 to 25 March 1822, a period which preceded the return of the Turkish army that we left in Ethiopia. It is well that we returned alone to Egypt, as, upon the return of his expedition, Prince Isma'il, his doctor, and several of his people were massacred and burned. A deplorable fate that we, undoubtedly, would have shared.[459]

---

457 The upper register of this scene is from Naga and depicts the king, queen, and a prince before the gods Apedemak, Ra-Horakhti, Amun, Aqedis or possibly Khonsu, and Amun of Pnubs. See Porter and Moss, *Topographical Bibliography VII*, 269.

458 The lower register of this scene is also from Naga and depicts the king, queen, and a prince standing before Isis, who holds prisoners. The goddesses Mut, the Goddess of the West, Hathor, and Satis stand behind Isis. See Porter and Moss, *Topographical Bibliography VII*, 269. While queens, as a rule, did not have the same power, or iconography, as kings, a handful of notable exceptions did exist. Hatshepsut, a queen who declared herself king and had herself represented in ways normally reserved for male monarchs, is perhaps the best example.

459 Cailliaud writes: "*Travels to Meroe and the White River*, vol. III, pages 124, 336."

CHAPTER 17

ON THE EMBALMMENT OF THE ANCIENT EGYPTIANS[460]

The art of embalming bodies was known among various peoples, principally from Africa and Asia, since the earliest periods of the world. It was, however, the Egyptians who first perfected it,[461] as is easy to recognize by the numerous mummies that they left for our admiration. This religious duty was a sacred obligation in which they indulged with as much passion as respect for their ancestors. Ancient authors report that in the case of a family debt, the sacred pawning of a body became like a mortgage, as it is in our day with a rich homestead.[462]

The bodies were placed in their tombs, which were the result of an often long and expensive execution. Certain families, for a certain period of time, kept in their house the body of the father and, to perpetuate his memory during the dining hours, he was stood at the place at the table that he occupied during his life.[463] It was as if he were presiding

---

460 For more information on ancient Egyptian embalming, see Rosalie A. David, "Mummification," in *Ancient Egyptian Materials and Technology*, edited by Ian Shaw and Paul T. Nicholson (Cambridge UK: Cambridge University Press, 2000), 372–89.

461 Diodorus Siculus, *The Library of History*, 1.34.1. See Diodorus Siculus, *The Library of History*, 1.69–98, http://penelope.uchicago.edu/Thayer/E/Roman/Texts/Diodorus_Siculus/1D*. html#ref5

462 This appears to have been an accepted notion in the early nineteenth century, as Wilkinson has a similar passage in his work, citing Herodotus as an authority. See John Gardner Wilkinson, *The Manners and Customs of the Ancient Egyptians. Including their Private Life, Government, Laws, Arts, Manufactures, Religion, and Early History; derived from a comparison of the paintings, sculptures, and monuments still existing, with the accounts of ancient authors*, vol. 2 (London: John Murray, 1837–41), 51; Herodotus, *The Histories*, 2.136; Strassler, *The Landmark Herodotus*, 179. See also Siculus, *The Library of History*, 1.93; Diodorus Siculus, *Library of History*, http://penelope.uchicago.edu/Thayer/E/Roman/Texts/Diodorus_Siculus/1D*.html#ref5

463 This idea, rooted in the writings of classical authors, appears to have been perpetuated throughout the nineteenth century, as attested in a later edition of Wilkinson's work. See John Gardner Wilkinson, *The Manners*

still before his family, who addressed him with numerous wishes and prayers for his happy sojourn in heaven.

The basis for the most durable embalming among the Egyptians was asphalt,[464] bitumen, and resinous substances. These were introduced into bodies through an opening made earlier by a sharp stone said to come from Ethiopia,[465] on the left side, above the hips, and from which the intestines were removed. These were embalmed in the four vases, called Canopic, under the safekeeping of the four genies of the Amenti:[466] Kebsnir, Tioumant, Châpi, Amset.[467] The brain tissue was pulled out through the nostrils with a bronze hook (which one still finds in tombs). The brain removed, the interior of the skull was washed with palm wine. Then, through the nostrils, bitumen was injected. After having drained the liquid and obtained the desiccation of the body, aromatic substances, resinous substances, asphalt,[468] and bitumen were introduced. These must have attached themselves to the flesh by means of heat which might have been introduced on the spot. The bodies, after having been provided for, might either have been set out in drying ovens at a desired temperature, or they might have been soaked in liquid 'mater.' We know that this substance, called mummy's balm, is sought for use in painting.

A large number, approximately 15 to 20, of linen bandages, rather than cotton, of several meters in length, were fastened one to the other. They encircled first each limb separately and then put them together on the body. The whole thing then received a general wrapping: the arms were crossed over the chest or extended by the side of the body.

We will now discuss certain figures coming from the Theban necropolis.[469]

Plate 8, figures 1 and 2. The workmen, probably embalmers, are occupied with placing the final bandages on two mummies. Close to them is noted an instrument unknown to us and a kind of boiler which might indicate that fire was necessary. The first of these mummies is a man, recognizable by his beard, the second a woman.

Figure 3. Another mummy of a woman, with a lotus flower on its head, is elevated on two supports (replacing our trestles) like the previous ones. A scribe presents himself; his palette in one hand, the other hand raised. He appears to be making comments to the two

---

and Customs of the Ancient Egyptians, vol. 3, edited by Samuel Birch (London: John Murray, 1878), 432. On this topic Wilkinson cites the third book of Silius Italicus's poem. See Silius Italicus, *Punica*, translated by J.D. Duff (London: William Heinemann Ltd., 1961).

464 Cailliaud's use of the word 'asphalt' is different from how the word is used today. He is referring to naturally occurring, solid bitumen that is found in certain areas, such as the borders of lakes. See Serpico, "Resins, Amber and Bitumen," 454–56, 466, 468.

465 Cailliaud is referring to the fact that the blade was supposedly made of obsidian, which he believes came from Ethiopia.

466 A nineteenth-century version of the ancient Egyptian word *Imentet*, meaning 'the west,' or 'land of the dead.'

467 Nineteenth-century spellings of the names of the Four Sons of Horus. Their names, and the organs they protected, were: Qebesenuef, who protected the intestines; Duamutef, who protected the stomach; Hapi, who protected the lungs; and Imseti, who protected the liver. See Wilkinson, *The Complete Gods and Goddesses*, 88–89.

468 Cailliaud is referring to naturally occurring, solid bitumen. See note 464 above.

469 All of the figures mentioned in plate 8 come from Theban Tomb 41, that of Amenemipet. See Porter and Moss, *Topographical Bibliography I.1*, 81; Jan Assmann, *Das Grab des Amenemope TT 41* (Mainz: Philipp von Zabern, 1991); the Theban Mapping Project's bibliography for Tomb 41, http://www.tmpbibliography. com/resources/bibliography_5nv_tombs_of_the_nobles_tt41_amenemope_called_ipy.html

workmen occupied with the positioning of the bandages. Two small pieces of furniture, like stools, are close to them.

Figure 4. Another mummy of a woman has received all its bandages. A very attentive painter applies paint to the mask from numerous containers, to show various colors. Another workman strikes a chisel or an awl to make a hole. Another, crouching, appears to mix mortar. Clay was used to mask and fill the faults of the mummy cases.

Figure 5. A workman, crouching, appears to polish a plaque with both hands on a single stone. Before him is a cartonnage bust, placed on mummies and repeated from the preceding figures. Another worker appears to be responsible for softening the plaster on a similar bust through friction. A third one, with one arm, draws liquid from a large jar. He is seated on a stool the form of which we have often remarked upon. We note the markedly concave top, like the saddle of a dromedary, the comfort of which we have been able to assess ourselves.

Figure 6 and the last. Shows us two workmen occupied in the same art, supplied with bows and drills, and piercing holes. One works on an eye to be placed on a mummy case. The second uses two drills at a time, something we have not yet practiced in our arts. We note two vases which must have contained liquid necessary for this work. A final bust for a man indicates once more the same subject of work as in all the cited figures.

Other less expensive forms of embalming were used by poor families. Most importantly, they were deprived of canopic vases. The cleaned and embalmed intestines were placed back in the body with representations, often in wax, of the four genies so that the deceased might participate in their grace. Sometimes the hole in the body was covered by a plaque of lead, bearing the Eye of Osiris.[470] These injected bodies were laid out for 70 days in natron, the salt penetrating the flesh. Only a small number were both injected and salted.

The warm climate of Egypt and its great dryness, along with the constantly elevated temperature of its tombs, must have greatly contributed to the conservation of this last class of bodies. It would not have been so in the climate of our lands. We have made observations on several mummies that we brought back to Nantes: one of these, prepared with saline, was affected by the humidity, which penetrated the substance and quickly caused its complete disintegration, a body which the climate of Egypt had conserved for perhaps two to three thousand years. The flesh, deprived of salt, became at that point the prey of numerous, large worms which left only a skeleton under the cloth bandages.

One frequently encounters mummies with their hair, their eyebrows, and their teeth. Sometimes they are only gilded on the face, or only the hands and feet. There have been those found with gilt over the whole of the body.

In their bandages, one often finds on the stomach the scarab, its wings outstretched, small, ceramic, and glazed, and faience idols, others in bronze, or in painted or gilded wood. Gold ones are not common, and silver ones are even rarer. Under the bandages of certain mummies, one finds, on the stomach, some manuscript pages or rolls of papyrus placed between the thighs.[471]

---

470 Most likely the Eye of Horus.
471 Cailliaud writes: "Finding ourselves in 1816 in the ruins of the Theban necropolis with consul Drovetti, we collected a large, wooden statuette with a height of 60 centimeters, representing Osiris. It was fixed to its base

They represent the transmigration of the soul at its return to the divine, judgment scenes, etc., in which good or bad actions are weighed under the eyes of Osiris, the god of the Amenti,[472] who declares judgment. The souls of the guilty take the form of a trout, a wolf, or other animals known to be impure, to be thus returned to earth.[473]

We will now cite a scene related to the above subject: plate 65, figure 3.[474] Anubis presides over the revivification of the mummy of a man. He appears to have his arms extended to affect kindness in his favor; the soul in the form of a bird with a human head has descended on the body.[475] It places under the nostrils of the mummy the symbol for respiration. This scene is represented in a naos surmounted by various symbols, the eye of Osiris, and two squatting jackals that are the loyal guardians of funerary sites. The bed on which the mummy lies is noted for the artistically rendered head, tail, and claws of a lion.

In order to give a proper idea of the richness of a large number of mummy cases, we feature, to scale, a scene of paintings which cover them. In certain deluxe embalmings of this genre, a first, interior cover is brought for the mummy, which is then posited in a second, and even (albeit rarely) a third case. All three are covered with the subjects of paintings analogous to those with which we are concerned.

Plate 23. Osiris or Phra (no legend provided) sits, holding in one hand the sign of divine life (the handled cross)[476] and the flagrum (whisk),[477] the symbol of stimulation. In the other he holds the *Pat*[478] (the crook), a symbol of power and temperance. His head is surmounted by the solar disc and traversed by the sacred asp.[479] Behind the god, and enveloping him by her outspread wings, is the goddess Nephthis, who holds the plume, a symbol of justice and truth.[480]

These figures are placed within a rich naos supported by the signs of measurement and stability (*Tat*).[481] A frieze of uraei surmounted with discs crowns the naos. The Osirian (the

---

with a dowel which we had the curiosity to remove. The idol separated thus from its base and, to our great surprise, we found in the body itself a magnificent roll of papyrus, measuring 3 meters 50 centimeters in length. The thickness of the bottom of the legs of the statuette had caught our attention. We might believe this beautiful funerary ritual was thus hidden, forever and a day, in the body of the great god Osiris. We give notice to the directors of the Egyptian Museum who might not have known this."

472 A nineteenth-century version of the ancient Egyptian word *Imentet*, meaning 'the west,' or 'land of the dead.'

473 What exactly the ancient Egyptians believed happened to a soul after death was unknown at the time of Cailliaud's writing. This notion, that impure souls were sent back to earth to inhabit the bodies of taboo animals, comes from classical texts. Wilkinson discusses this subject more fully and cites relevant classical authors. See Wilkinson, *Manners and Customs*, 439–46.

474 This scene comes from Theban Tomb 106, that of Paser. See Porter and Moss, *Topographical Bibliography I.1*, 223; the Theban Mapping Project's bibliography for Tomb 106, http://www.tmpbibliography.com/resources/bibliography_5nv_tombs_of_the_nobles_tt106_paser.html

475 Cailliaud is referring to the *ba*-bird. The *ba* was similar to the Christian religious notion of the soul and embodied many elements of what would be considered a person's personality in modern, western society. See James P. Allen, *Middle Egyptian. An Introduction to the Language and Culture of Hieroglyphs* (Cambridge UK: Cambridge University Press, 2001), 79–81.

476 Cailliaud is referring to the ankh.

477 Cailliaud is referring to the flail, a symbol of kingship.

478 A nineteenth-century term for the crook, known as *heka* in ancient Egyptian and a symbol of government.

479 A uraeus.

480 Cailliaud is referring to the feather of Maat, a symbol of cosmic order, justice, and truth.

481 Cailliaud is referring to *djed* pillars, indeed symbols of stability.

deceased) presents herself in front: mistress of the house, named Tentenahu[482] justified. She makes an offering of flowers and fruits to the god. She holds a sistrum, her hands and arms raised in the act of adoration.

We read, from the uraeus frieze, the following legend, which relates to the god in the naos.

That he agrees to arrive in peace and leave justified.
(lateral column to the right)
Many oxen, many birds, much bread, much incense, much fresh water.[483]

These dedications, with some variations, and others that are analogous, are often repeated on coffins and on their interiors.

We have seen that other mummies were covered over their bandages by cartonnage. This was formed on the mummy with a mask that was often gilded. This cartonnage consists of multiple layers of cloth glued one on top of the other, sometimes with layers of papyrus. The exterior surface is always plastered with white to receive paintings of diverse subjects appropriate to the funerary rites. Some of these wrappings had open-work motifs, were gilded, and were of great richness. They were enclosed in one and sometimes two wooden cases equally covered in paintings analogous to the previous figures.

ON GRIEF FOR THE DECEASED
When someone dies[484] all the women of the family leave the body in its house, cover their faces and heads with mud, and, running through the streets, strike their naked breasts while screaming lamentations. Their friends and family join them in the same demonstration of sorrow.

We will now cite a funerary procession: plate 65, figure 4.[485] The paintings will give us an exact idea of these ancient ceremonies celebrated with as much splendor as veneration. Four oxen pull on a sled a funerary barque with a rich mausoleum decorated with flowers. Within it, lying on a funerary bed, is the mummy of a man. A driver raises a stick to the oxen and drives them. A person precedes it, making signs of grief. One of the servants carries a handled pail containing the sacred water, and in the other hand a tool to draw from this vase which is dedicated to the funerary ceremony. Afterward the high priest

---

482 The deceased's name is Tanethereret. She was a chantress of Amun-Ra during Egypt's Twenty-first Dynasty. The image is taken from her sarcophagus, now kept in the Egyptian Antiquities Department of the Louvre under the accession numbers E 13027, E 13034, and E 13035. For further information on this object, see Mainterot, *Aux origines de l'égyptologie*; Andrzej Niwinski, *The 21st Dynasty Coffins from Thebes: Chronological and Typological Studies. Theben V* (Mainz: Philipp von Zabern, 1988), pl. III, no. 328, 163–64; Porter and Moss, *Topographical Bibliography I.2*, 831; Legrain, "Inventaire méthodique de la collection d'antiquités égyptiennes," vol. 1; Eugène Ledrain, *Monuments égyptiens de la Bibliothèque Nationale* (Paris: F. Vieweg, 1881), pl. LXVIII, no. 54–55.

483 Cailliaud writes: "We are obliged to Mr. Chabas for these translations." For further information on this object's scenes and texts, refer to the sources cited in the previous note.

484 Cailliaud writes: "Herodotus, II, 85." See Herodotus, *The Histories*, 2.85; Strassler, *The Landmark Herodotus*, 152.

485 This scene was taken from Theban Tomb 255, that of Roy. See Porter and Moss, *Topographical Bibliography I.2*, 339; Baud and Drioton, *Tombes thébaines*; the Theban Mapping Project's bibliography for Tomb 255, http://www.tmpbibliography.com/resources/bibliography_5nv_tombs_of_the_nobles_tt255_roy.html

'Sam,'[486] with shaved head, dressed in the skin of a leopard, makes libations of sacred water and burns incense in the *amchir*[487] in honor of the deceased. On the barque, two young girls raise their arms in a sign of grief: they appear to be his children. The widow (we assume), one hand on the head as a sign of mourning, walks closest to the bier with her parents. Then comes a succession of professional mourners,[488] then four priests bearing the funerary chest containing the four canopic vases which hold the intestines of the deceased. On the lid is the jackal of Anubis, the loyal guardian. A weeping woman is kneeling close to these sacred remains. A group of women in civil dress complete the cortege.

We note the grief of all these people by the signs of mourning and sorrow which they affect by raising their arms and holding their hands to their heads. The professional mourners are distinguished by the length of their dresses and that of their hair. The artist wanted, with a glance of the eye, to indicate the tears that they shed.

The offerings made to the gods and divinities are shown by figures from funerary sites. Plate 65, figure 1.

Two people are seated before the celestial tree, the divine sycomore, 'Noohi,' a symbol of the goddess Nou.[489] The goddess shows herself in the tree, from which she presents to her worshipers figs along with water, cut pomegranates, pieces of red meat: divine dishes consecrated to funerary ceremonies.

The hieroglyphic legend makes known that the person had the title "Agent of Khenti,"[490] that is to say, of inside of a building of Ramesses II at Thebes. Close to him is his sister,[491] "beloved, the lady. . ."; their names are erased (translation by Mr. Chabas).

The people are in civil dress, with petticoats and loose-fitting sleeves, with large necklaces, flowers in hand, their feet resting on cushions. Their seats, with the clawed feet of a lion and with inverted backrests, are light and elegant. They show themselves supplied with provisions of figs from the sycomore and other things piled up under the seat of the great lady, who wears long hair held back with bands and ribbons of various colors. This is part of the decoration from a tomb in the Qurna necropolis of Thebes,[492] in which, amid various offerings, one still notices the fire made to the god Phra.[493]

---

486 *Sem*: a class of priest.

487 A censer.

488 Cailliaud writes: "A custom preserved in areas, even in Ethiopia, in Sennar, where it was told to us that the best mourners distinguish themselves so that they might be better paid."

489 The sky-goddess Nut: the sycomore was seen as a manifestation of her. Nut was believed to play a role in the rebirth of Osiris, and, therefore, all those who would be reborn.

490 The deceased's actual title is 'Overseer of the garden in the mortuary temple of Ramesses II in the estate of Amun.' See Porter and Moss, *Topographical Bibliography I.1*, 251; Feucht, *Die Gräber des Nedjemger*; the Theban Mapping Project's bibliography for Tomb 138, http://www.tmpbibliography.com/resources/bibliography_5nv_tombs_of_the_nobles_tt138_nedjemger.html

491 Actually the deceased's wife. During the mid-Eighteenth Dynasty the ancient Egyptian word for 'sister' began to be replaced by the word for 'wife,' which has historically resulted in some confusion among translators. See Jaroslav Černy, "Consanguineous Marriages in Pharaonic Egypt," in *Journal of Egyptian Archaeology* 40 (1954): 23–29.

492 Theban Tomb 138, that of Nedjemger. See Porter and Moss, *Topographical Bibliography I.1*, 251; Feucht, *Die Gräber des Nedjemger*; the Theban Mapping Project's bibliography for tomb 138, http://www.tmpbibliography.com/resources/bibliography_5nv_tombs_of_the_nobles_tt138_nedjemger.html

493 Cailliaud is referring to the god Ra.

We have cited the vows of a widow, imploring the god Osiris to accord to him many oxen, many geese, much bread, and much fresh water.

In relation to this subject we will show Plate 65 figure 2,[494] a table covered with food, as an offering in this genre. In construction it bears along its edges a molding, rounded like on our pedestal tables with marble tops. It is supported in the center on a sort of stool on which is placed a vase in another smaller vase. This vase receives the transudation of the first and cools the water. From the comestibles with which the table is charged, one identifies an entire leg of beef with its foot, so that it might be better recognized, along with the bones which are found in various pieces of meat, likewise of the color red, a bird, two big pieces of prepared fowl, a long vase which appears to be capped by its goblet, lotus buds, etc. These representations of thanksgiving, frequent and widespread, speak in favor of the ancients.

Numerous funerary objects were conserved in the tombs, often to represent those which had been used by the deceased in the arts which they practiced while on earth. The rulers deposited their jewels there.

We have cited elsewhere the deposition of actual wigs, of various hairstyles, of woven hair, and others of particular curls, left as souvenirs of cherished people.

Numerous idols of all sorts surrounded the dead, in thanksgiving, as an act of supplication to the divinities.[495] These were in painted wood, in terra cotta,[496] and in glazed faience.[497] These last ones more generally, of 10 to 15 centimeters, were enameled[498] in the color green with hieroglyphic legends crudely engraved. Others, less common, are in handsome blue enamel,[499] while the hair and the legends are drawn in black enamel. Those in white enamel[500] are much less common, and the hieroglyphs of these last ones are drawn in violet enamel.

Rather generally, all these figurines, their arms crossed on their chests, carry in each hand the image of the hoe, an instrument of labor, and on their backs the basket containing seed. These revered attributes, this homage to agriculture, were perpetuated with the greatest veneration up until the entombment of the deceased. These statuettes, common in great number, were always of the same type in sarcophagi, for the muted forms of the human body, from which one did not deviate, were rigorously prescribed through sacerdotal laws.

---

494   It is not known from which tomb this scene was copied.

495   Cailliaud is describing funerary statuettes known as *shabti*s. These magical figures were meant to take the place of the deceased for work in the afterlife.

496   The author means ceramic.

497   While *shabti*s were made from practically all materials known to the Egyptians, wood, stone, and faience were particularly favored. See various entries in Shaw and Nicholson, eds., *Ancient Egyptian Materials and Technology*; Jean-Luc Bovot, *Chaouabtis. Des travailleurs pharaoniques pour l'éternité* (Paris: Réunion des Musées Nationaux, 2003), 32.

498   Cailliaud is referring to Egyptian faience, not enamel.

499   Cailliaud is, again, referring to Egyptian faience, not enamel.

500   Cailliaud is once more referring to Egyptian faience, not enamel, which created colors within a blue-green spectrum. The white figures with violet inscriptions to which he refers may have been objects whose faience had degraded to the point of losing their color.

CHAPTER 18

CARPENTERS[501]

PLATE 1[502]

Three carpenters are occupied with carving mortises in a long piece of wood. Two of their mallets are similar to those which we use to build and caulk our ships. The third one is a short mass of a single piece. The handles of the chisels are preferable to our own. Thin in the middle, they are held naturally in the hand of the workman, who raises them without any effort.

The red color of the metal of these chisels does not adequately indicate its nature. We will return to this subject. The red and yellow colors of the mallets indicate various qualities of hard wood used in their construction. Many found in the tombs were of a kind of iron-wood. These workmen are all seated on small cushions. They are wearing simple cloth underpants, rare enough among the ancient Egyptians, who more especially wore the kilt, as we will see in the following plates.

PLATE 4[503]

Painting taken from Qurna[504]

This light barque has its ends elegantly turned up, ending in papyrus flowers and mounted

---

501 For more information on this subject, see Killen, "Wood [Technology]." This chapter was originally entitled "Carpenters of Boats" before being changed by Cailliaud.

502 Philippe Mainterot believes this scene may be based on imagery in Theban Tomb 36, that of Ibi. Further research is required either to confirm or to refute this belief.

503 The imagery in this plate is copied from Theban Tomb 50, that of Neferhotep. See Porter and Moss, *Topographical Bibliography I.1*, 96; Robert Hari, *La tombe thébaine*; the Theban Mapping Project's bibliography for Tomb 50, http://www.tmpbibliography.com/resources/bibliography_5nv_tombs_of_the_nobles_tt50_neferhotep.html

504 Cailliaud means the images were copied from a tomb in Qurna, not physically removed.

by standards. The oars placed at the rear are themselves decorated with lotus flowers, and end, along with their supports, in the heads of sacred sparrow hawks. The sail is richly divided into squares with the colors green, red, and white. On the front is shown the jackal, a symbol of Anubis, guardian of divine things. It is evidently one of the boats consecrated to the various rites of the sepulcher to transport the deceased to the necropolis.

PLATE 3[505]

Low relief sculpted in a tomb of ancient Elethyia[506]

This plate is the only one in this work which was colored according to other, analogous, better-preserved paintings in the tombs of Qurna. Two barques sail on the river by means of roughly twelve rowers. One of them is sailing and must climb back up the current while the other, without masting, goes downriver. The rudder resembles that of our large river landing crafts. Large chambers, very tall for the convenience of travelers, occupy the major portion of it. At the end, close to the prow, we note proper wooden grills to facilitate the transport of animals.

Under these barques are others arranged for the transportation of wheat and other cereals, which are loaded and held on the boards by straw mats kept in the shape of walls at the back of the boat. One of them, still tied to the shore, receives its charge. Three porters, undoubtedly bearing baskets of wheat, climb the plank which leads to the boat. A fourth has just emptied his *couffe*.[507] The artist took pains to show on the plank small rails, added on to assure the porters' footing.

PLATE 2[508]

Workmen have already prepared the exterior of a barque from a single piece of yellow wood, which we believe to have been acacia-sant.[509] One of them appears to carve it with blows from an axe. Three others, equipped with chisels and mortising chisels, make the mortises which will receive pieces of rope. Their mallets, in different wood, are in the shape of clubs, and their blue-colored tools would have been in iron. The hieroglyphic characters give the title "making barques." The workmen are dressed like the preceding ones.

This painting, the preceding one, and many of those that follow were copied in the same tomb in Qurna, the ancient necropolis of Thebes.

---

505 This scene is based on imagery from Tomb 3 in Beni Hasan, that of Paheri. See Porter and Moss, *Topographical Bibliography V*, 179; Tylor and Griffith, *The Tomb of Paheri*.

506 A version of the ancient Greek name for the area of al-Kab: Eileithyiaspolis.

507 Cailliaud writes: "Straw baskets greatly used in Egypt."

508 Copied from Theban Tomb 36, that of Ibi. See Porter and Moss, *Topographical Bibliography I.1*, 65; Norman de Garis Davies, *The Rock Tombs of Deir el Gebrawi. Part I*, pl. xxiv–xxv; the Theban Mapping Project's bibliography for Tomb 36, http://www.tmpbibliography.com/resources/bibliography_5nv_tombs_of_the_nobles_tt36_ibi.html

509 *Acacia nilotica*, or the sant tree.

THE PLATES

The Visual Corpus
and Cailliaud

Andrew Bednarski,
with contributions by Gerry D. Scott III

Cailliaud as a copyist

As mentioned in chapters 1 and 2, Frédéric Cailliaud was by no means the first, or last, westerner to travel to Egypt and record its famous tomb and temple scenes. European travelers interested in recording Egyptian monuments could be found as early as the 1600s.[1] By the early 1700s, travel to Egypt had increased, partly as a result of a large diffusion of publications about the country.[2] One such important work was written by Richard Pococke (1704–65) and entitled *A Description of the East and Some Other Countries*.[3] Pococke's work provided readers with impressive, folio-sized images of the land of the Nile. The majority of these scenes were large overviews of structures and terrain, such as his perspective drawing of the Valley of the Kings,[4] or architectural sections of ancient structures, such as a plan of a tomb in the Valley (figs. 10 and 11).[5] Among these images, however, was a reproduction of a wall scene of the Ramesseum: Ramesses the Great's mortuary temple (fig. 12).[6]

Such reproduced images from the walls of tombs and temples would only increase by the early 1800s. Napoleon's 1798 invasion of Egypt gave his contingent of European scholars unprecedented access to many of the country's monuments. One of these learned men, Dominique Vivant Denon (1741–1825), returned to France after the failed military campaign and published his account of the expedition in both French and English in 1802. This work, entitled *Travels in Upper and Lower Egypt*, included approximately three hundred images that were later incorporated into the French government's *Description de l'Égypte*. Denon's work appeared a solid eight years before the first volume of the *Description*, and it provided Europeans with many images of Egypt's temples and tombs.[7] From 1810 onward, Denon's visual feast was followed by the *Description*'s extensive imagery.

The success and broad distribution of these publications made Egyptian imagery, including temple and tomb scenes, widely available to European audiences. These works, in turn, prompted

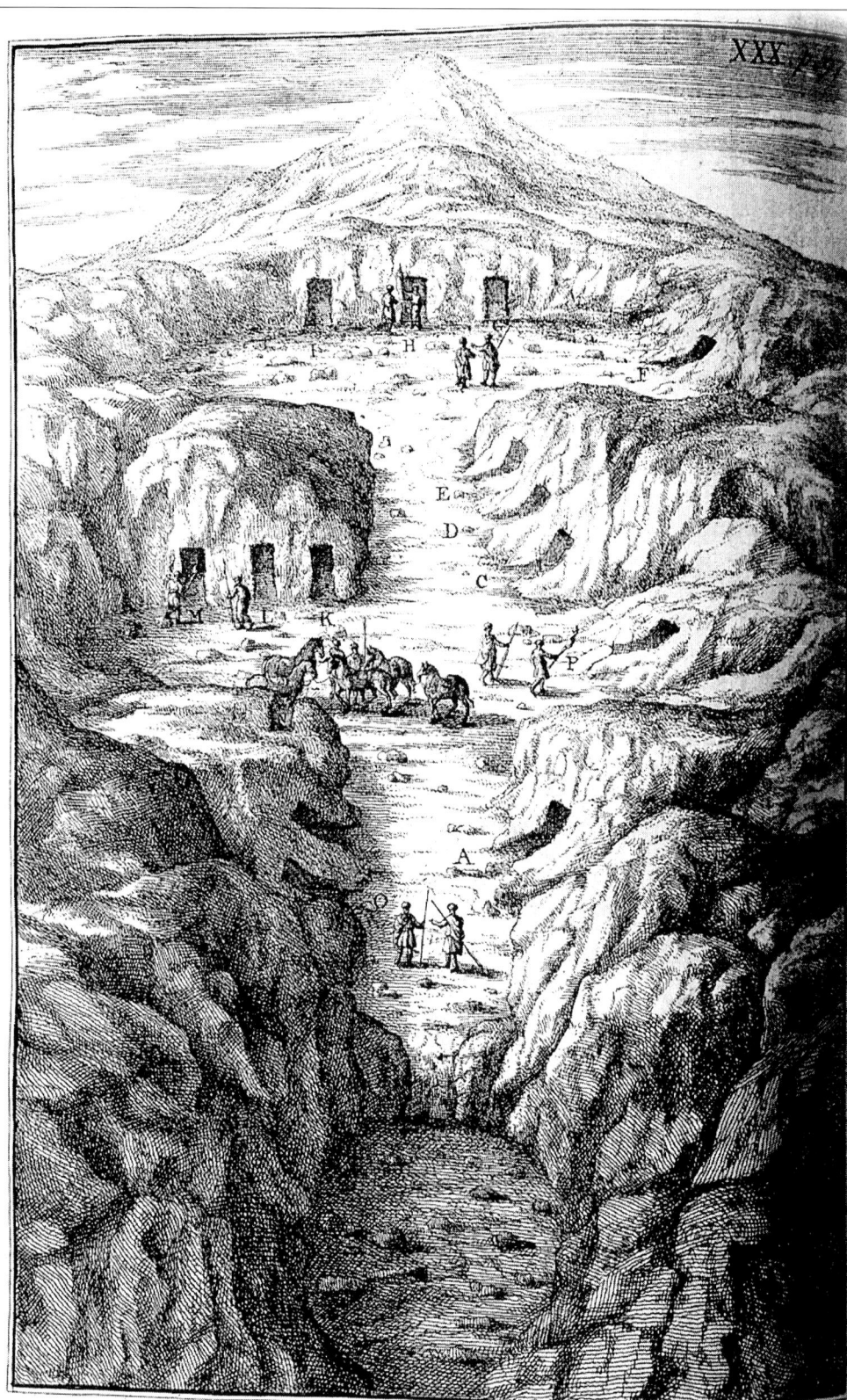

The Sepulchres of the Kings of Thebes.
To the Honourable William Herbert.

10 Richard Pococke's plate XXX, "The Sepulchres of the Kings of Thebes." From *A Description of the East and Some Other Countries*. London: J. & R. Knapton, 1743. *Photographed by Owen Murray.*

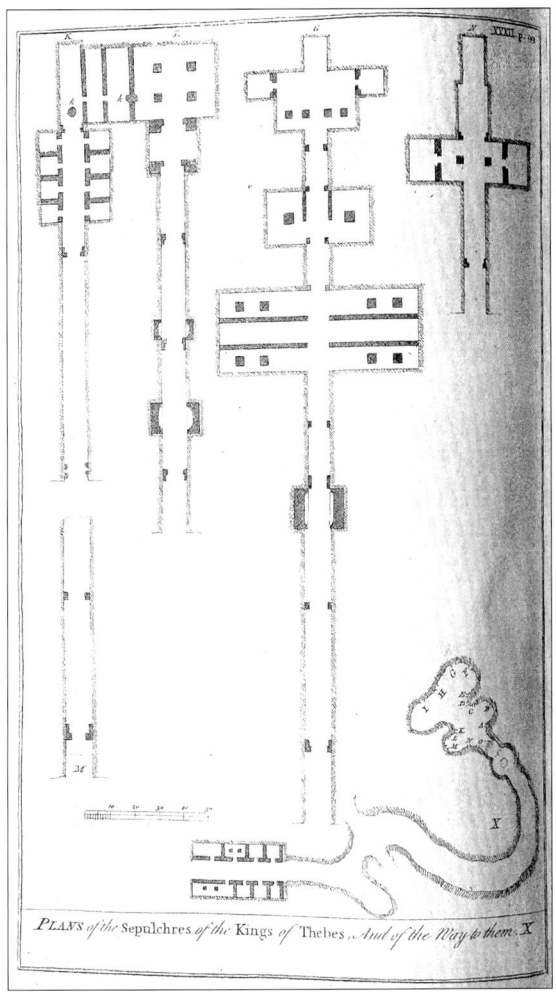

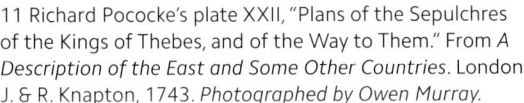

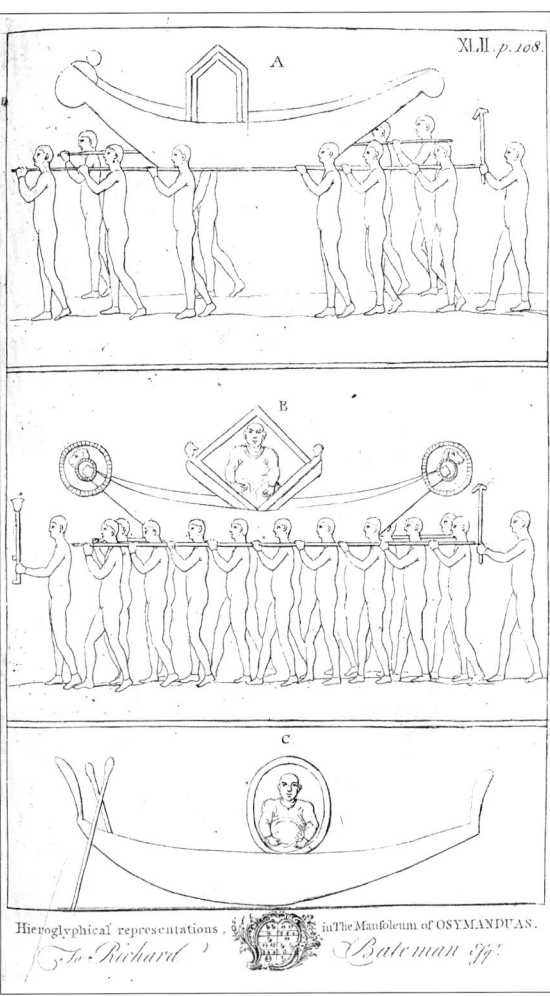

11 Richard Pococke's plate XXII, "Plans of the Sepulchres of the Kings of Thebes, and of the Way to Them." From *A Description of the East and Some Other Countries*. London: J. & R. Knapton, 1743. *Photographed by Owen Murray.*

12 Richard Pococke's plate XLII, "Hieroglyphical Representations in the Mausoleum of Osymandias." From *A Description of the East and Some Other Countries*. London: J. & R. Knapton, 1743. *Photographed by Owen Murray.*

further interest and further exploration in the early nineteenth century. A great many European copyists traveled to Egypt during this period, undoubtedly inspired by images they had seen in books, including, among others, the Scottish and English antiquarians Robert Hay (1799–1853)[8] and John Gardner Wilkinson (1797–1875),[9] the Tuscan Ippolito Rosellini (1800–43),[10] who accompanied Jean-François Champollion's expedition to Egypt, and the Frenchmen Émile Prisse d'Avennes (1807–79)[11] and Frédéric Cailliaud. Earlier work done in Egypt established traditions on which Cailliaud and his contemporaries built their images. Before discussing this point further, however, it is helpful to first compare the images in Cailliaud's corpus with images created by some of his peers. We do not need to look far to do so. As stated in the chapter titled "The Life, Travels, and Works of Frédéric Cailliaud," the Champollion brothers sent a number of images to Cailliaud to help him in his work. Appendix 1 of this book also makes explicit which images, as far as we know, were done by Cailliaud, and which were done by artists employed by the Champollion brothers,

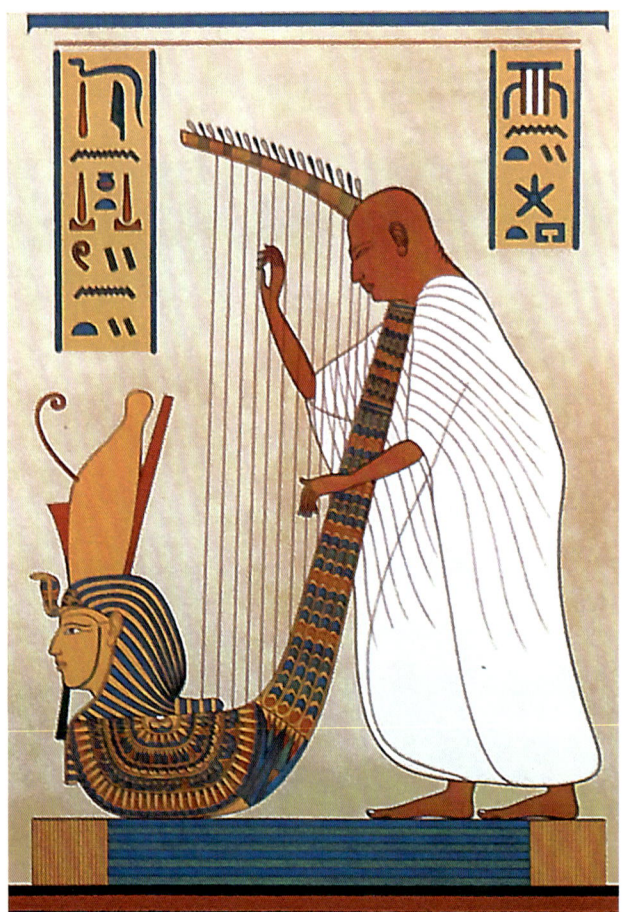

13 Prisse d'Avennes, "Harpers of Ramesses III." From *Atlas of Egyptian Art*, 132. Cairo: American University in Cairo Press, 2007. *Photographed by Owen Murray.*

such as Rosellini. Two things are immediately noticeable when we survey both Appendix 1 and the plates in Cailliaud's work. The first is that Cailliaud was directly responsible for the lion's share of the images he published. The second is that all of the images in his corpus, whether done by him or not, are strikingly uniform. Effort was clearly made for the images in Cailliaud's plates to have a coherent style.

Michel Dewachter has commented on the similarity of the style, if not the proportions, of Cailliaud's images with those of Prisse d'Avennes.[12] In fact, Dewachter goes beyond comparing both men's images, commenting on how both were good artists and draftsmen, both were honored upon their return to France, and both took a long time to edit and produce their works.[13] Similarities are clearly evident between both men's work, as we can see when we compare Prisse d'Avennes' depiction of a blind harper (fig. 13) with the same image drawn by Cailliaud (pl. 45). The general flow of the harper's garment is the same, both artists treat the delicate depictions of the harper's fingers in the same way, and the proportions of the face on the base of the harp are very similar.

These similarities, however, may likely be a result of the scene's relatively simple subject matter and composition, rather than the artists' styles. Certainly, when we compare a scene of brickmaking and bricklaying copied by both Cailliaud and Prisse d'Avennes, we see a great difference both in their interpretation of the composition and in the style of their execution. Cailliaud's interpretation of the scene (pl. 9A), for example, has resulted in much thinner and much more elongated figures than those we find in Prisse's image (fig. 14). The two artists also differ in their approach to stylistic and compositional details, as seen in their depictions of the brick ramp and wall, and the hieroglyphic text. Differences also exist in the placement of particular figures, such as the overseer holding a short staff.

Images from Robert Hay's collection provide other points for contemporaneous comparison. Hay arrived in Egypt two years after Cailliaud left to resume his life in France. Over the course of nine years, Hay commissioned a number of artists, including Joseph Bonomi (1796–1878),[14] Frederick Catherwood (1799–1854),[15] and James Burton (1788–1862),[16] to record images for him, which he collected in large portfolios. While his scholarly ambitions were great, he regrettably never managed to organize the enormous amount of material he collected to a point where it could be published.[17] A rapid survey of Hay's portfolios in the British Library suggests an interest

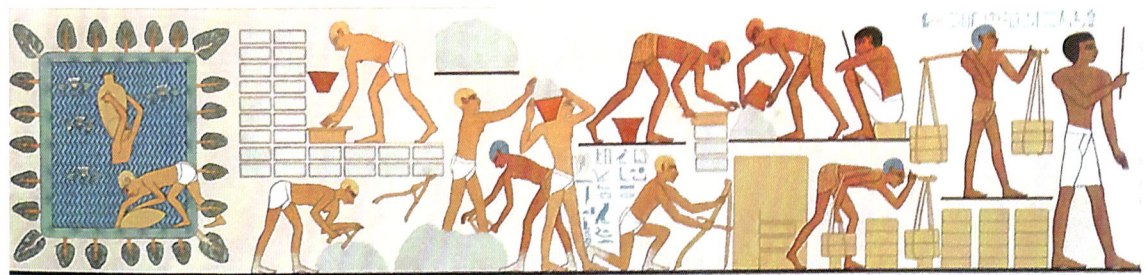

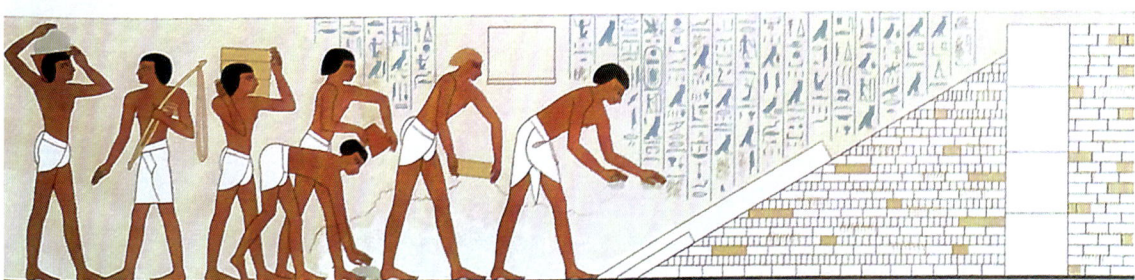

14 Prisse d'Avennes, "Captives Constructing a Temple of Amun." From *Atlas of Egyptian Art*, p. 121. Cairo: American University in Cairo Press, 2007. *Photographed by Owen Murray.*

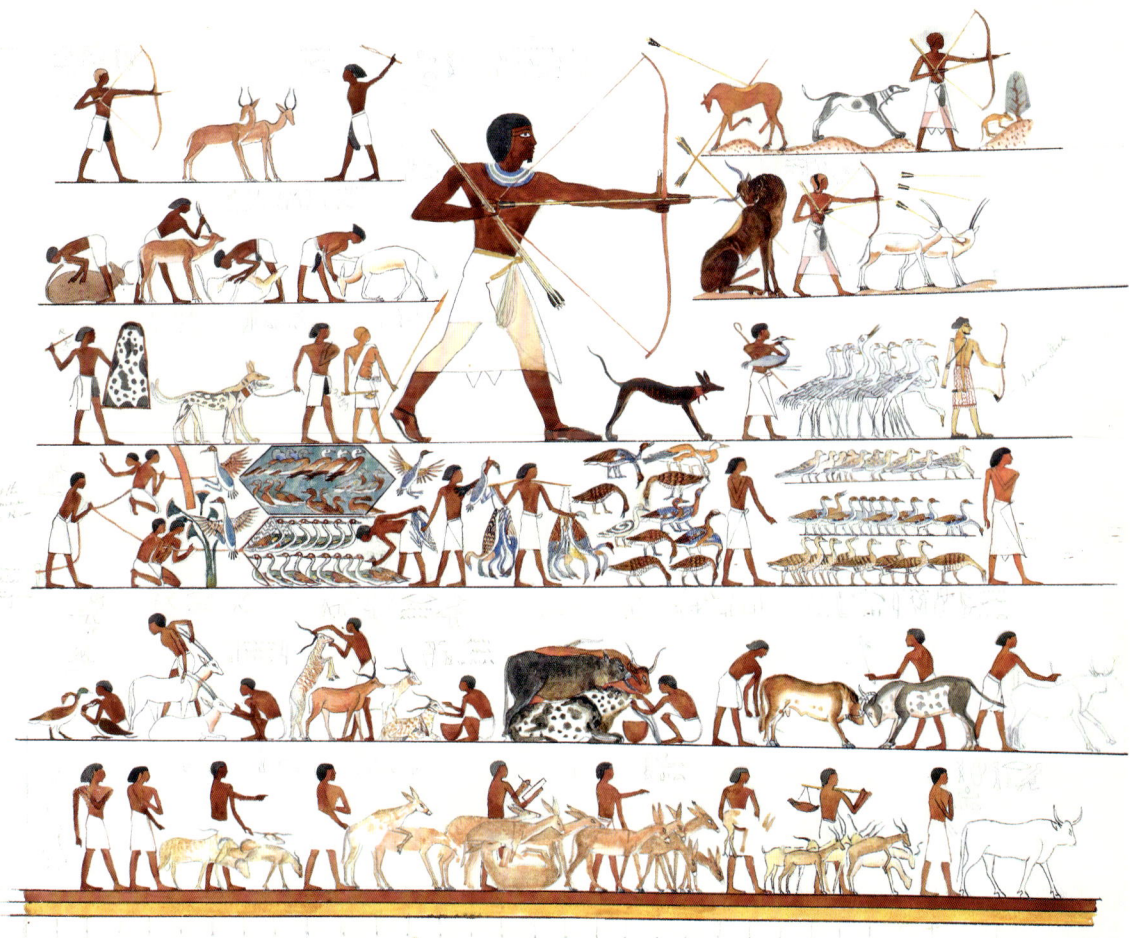

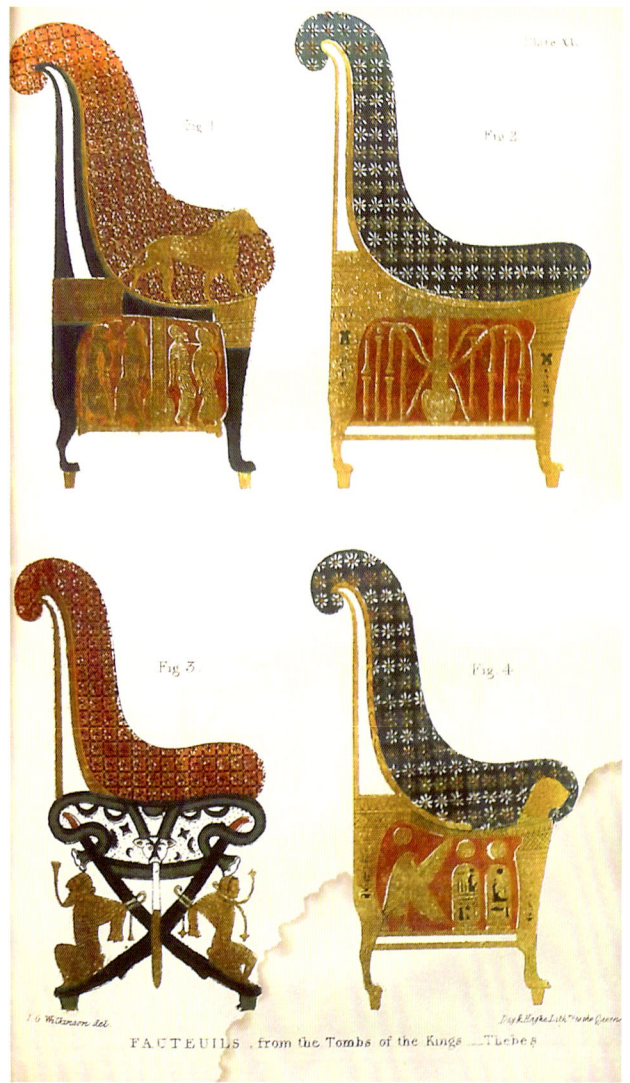

16 John Gardner Wilkinson's plate XI, "Fauteuils, from the Tombs of the Kings—Thebes." From *Manners and Customs of the Ancient Egyptians*. London: John Murray, 1837–41. *Photographed by Owen Murray.*

in reproducing large contexts, sometimes whole scenes from a tomb wall. This focus on larger scenes is evident in an image from Tomb 3, that of Khnumhotep, in Beni Hasan (fig. 15). The artist of the scene recorded many of the different activities depicted on the corresponding portion of wall, thereby retaining the context in which each activity was originally conceived.

Not surprisingly, such a broad focus can result in the loss of detail, as can be seen in the figures' faces. Some of Cailliaud's plates strive to reproduce similarly large contexts, such as his plates 35 and 36, which record images from the tomb of Neferhotep.[18] The majority of his plates, however, reproduce small sections of larger scenes, often compiling them with others into vignettes. A good example of this focus, different from what we observe in the Hay image, is plate 21A.

Using this image we can identify Cailliaud's figures 1 and 2 within the Hay scene. Cailliaud chose these images from all the others in that much larger context for a reason, and, with the help of his accompanying text, we know for the first time why he did so. Cailliaud's fourth chapter briefly discusses ancient Egyptian veterinary practices, and this section clearly demonstrates his desire for an image to illustrate this discussion. This practice of selecting small sections of larger scenes from a variety of tombs to exemplify a point was used repeatedly by Cailliaud. In so doing, Cailliaud often conceptually removed images from their original contexts, reassembled them into vignettes, and, inadvertently, created completely new contexts for the images he selected. Plate 65, illustrated in this book's chapter of plates, is perhaps the best example of this methodology. Each scene within the plate comes from a different tomb in Luxor. Put together, they illustrate points Cailliaud wanted to make both in his chapter on Egyptian embalming and, rather unexpectedly, that on hairstyles.

Cailliaud was not the first European to assemble images from multiple Egyptian monuments onto a page. Both Denon's *Travels* and the Napoleonic *Description* used this practice to collect disparate visual information under specific themes.[19] Nor was Cailliaud alone in his creation of vignettes during the early 1800s. John Gardner Wilkinson assembled images from multiple tombs to illustrate the points he made in his own work, as we can see from his plate depicting chairs (fig. 16).[20] Cailliaud would not be the last of the early nineteenth-century copyists to practice this method of compilation, as we can see from yet another plate of chairs, this one done by Prisse d'Avennes (fig. 17). The original representations of these chairs come from the tomb of Ramesses III in the Valley of the Kings. Cailliaud, Wilkinson, and Prisse d'Avennes grouped them together in their respective studies of domestic objects.

In addition to understanding why Cailliaud selected the images that he did, and why he arranged them as he did, it is important to understand the accuracy of his copies. A first glance at his plates tells us that Cailliaud's interest was not in creating perfect facsimiles of what he saw in the tombs. Even though there are differences between the images he published and what was on the actual walls, Cailliaud's work should not be disregarded as a tool for historical research. While the plates, as a whole, are not completely accurate, many of them are quite close. We can understand the issue of accuracy in Cailliaud's plates better when

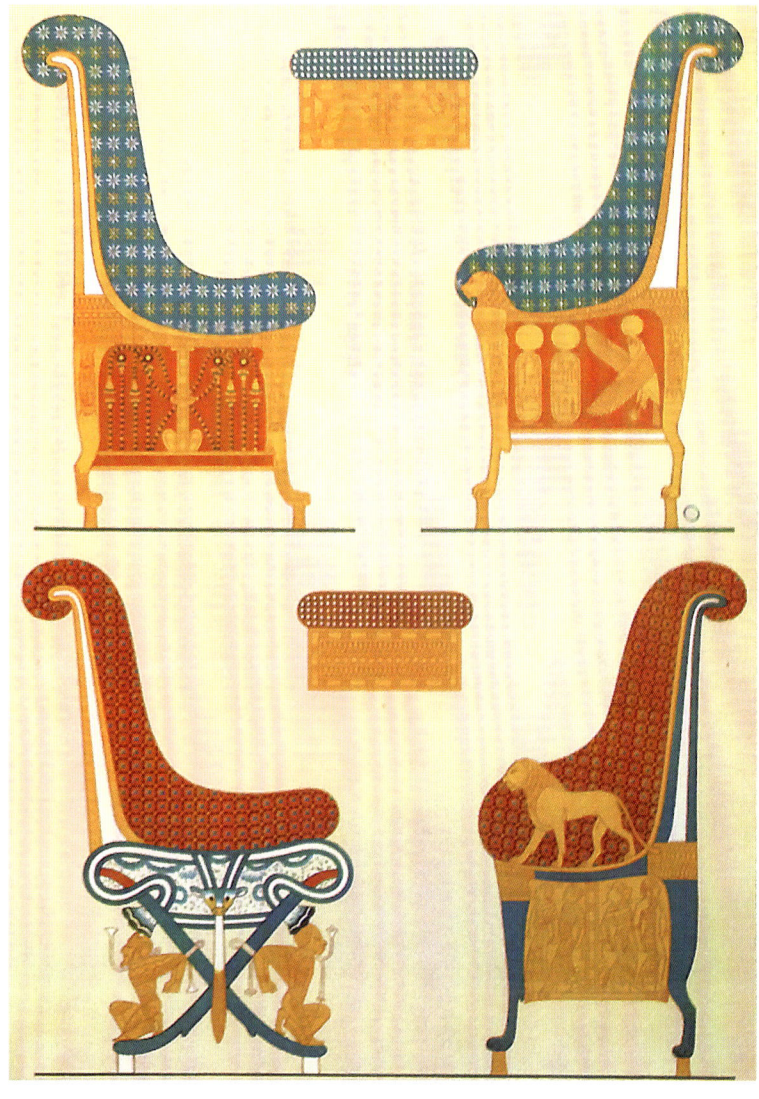

17 Prisse d'Avennes, "Thrones of Ramesses III." From *Atlas of Egyptian Art*, p. 149. Cairo: American University in Cairo Press, 2007. *Photographed by Owen Murray*.

we compare his plate 66, drawn by him, with a photo of the actual wall from which it was taken.

This plate, based on images from the Theban tomb of Rekhmire (fig. 18),[21] depicts a scene of foreign tribute. When we compare the two images, we see several discrepancies. To begin with, we see that, while Cailliaud's proportions for the animals and figures are not accurate depictions of the originals on the tomb wall, they are not far off. Secondly, we can see that the figure leading the elephant in Cailliaud's plate is not actually in front of the giraffe, as depicted on the wall. The elephant and giraffe, in fact, are on two different register lines. In addition, on the wall, the man originally depicted as leading the elephant has been lost altogether. This figure was most likely already lost when Cailliaud recorded the scene, as Wilkinson's own depiction of the wall indicates damage in that area.[22] In addition to rearranging the figures

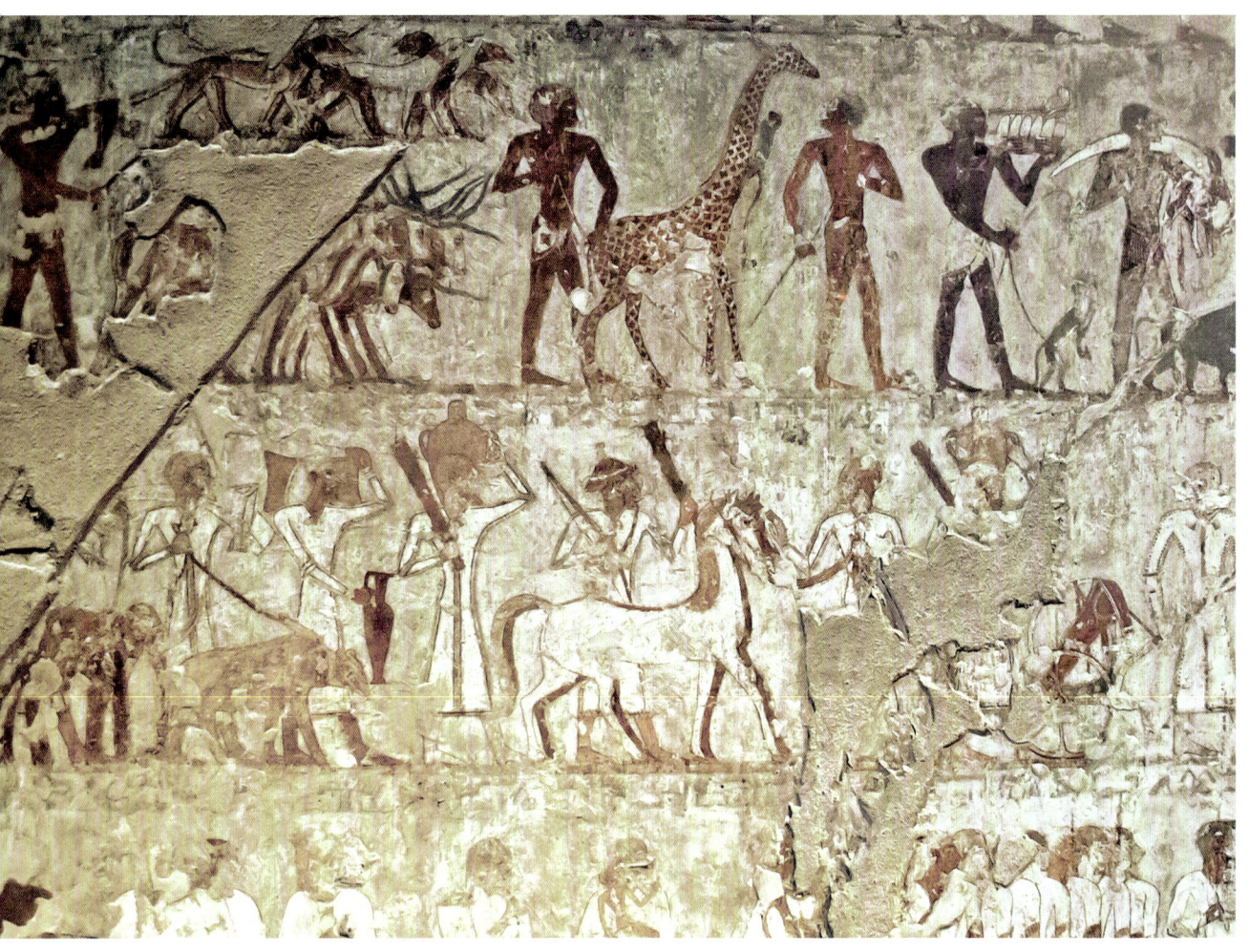

18 Scenes of foreign tribute in the tomb of Rekhmire, Metropolitan Museum of Art 31.6.40 and 31.6.43. *Courtesy of Andrew Bednarski.*

from separate registers, it appears that Cailliaud selected the figure in the hat from further along the wall and inserted him into the space left empty by the absent figure of the man leading the elephant.

Another element affecting the accuracy of an image, and its use in recording the physical state of a monument, is the recording of damage. The inclusion or omission of damage to a scene can drastically affect a viewer's interpretation of that scene. If, for example, the faces within a scene have been destroyed, the viewer is deprived of the figures' original expressions and features. Such loss may prompt him or her to imagine the missing elements or to contemplate possible reasons for the damage. Wilkinson's published image of the scene of foreign tribute from the tomb of Rekhmire recorded damage to the area around the elephant and to the elephant's face, also evident in the photograph. Cailliaud's image, on the other hand, has both the area around the elephant, and the face of the elephant, completed, presumably to make the scene more visually coherent for the viewer.

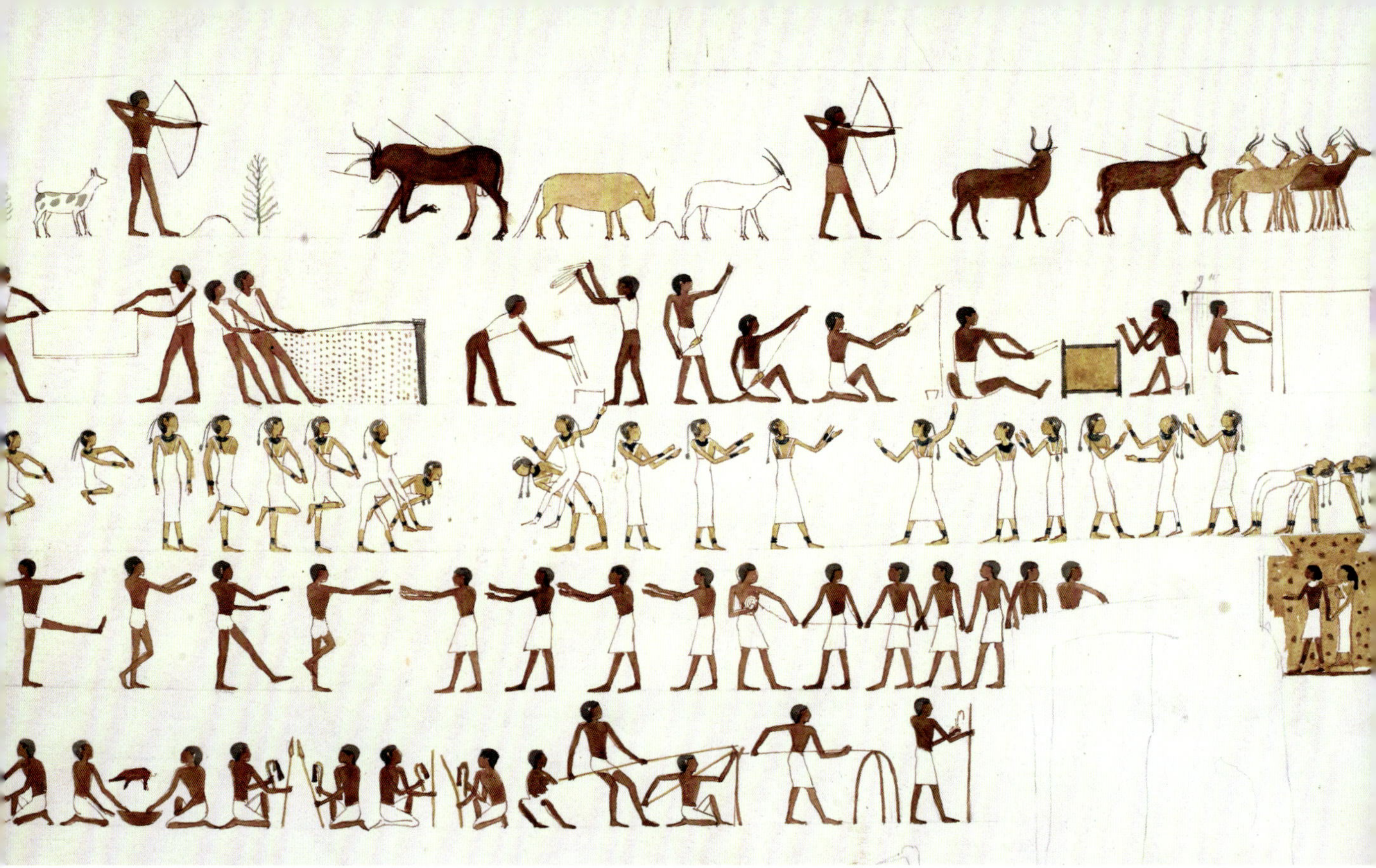

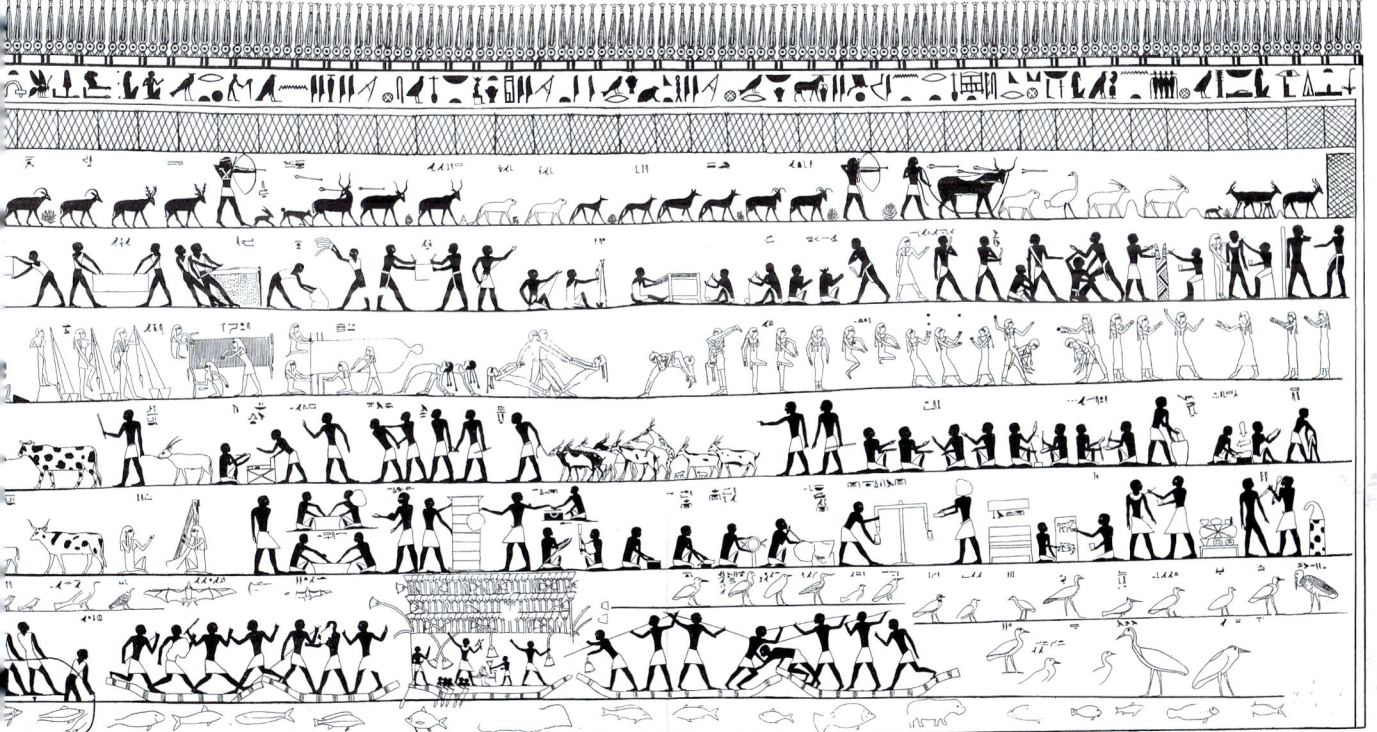

19 Scene of hunting, production, gaming, and dancing from the tomb of Khety, British Library Add.29813.47.
© The British Library Board. All rights reserved, 2014.

20 Percy E. Newberry's plate IV, entitled "Main Chamber, North Wall." From *Beni Hasan. Part II.* London: Egypt
Exploration Fund, 1893. *Photographed by Owen Murray.*

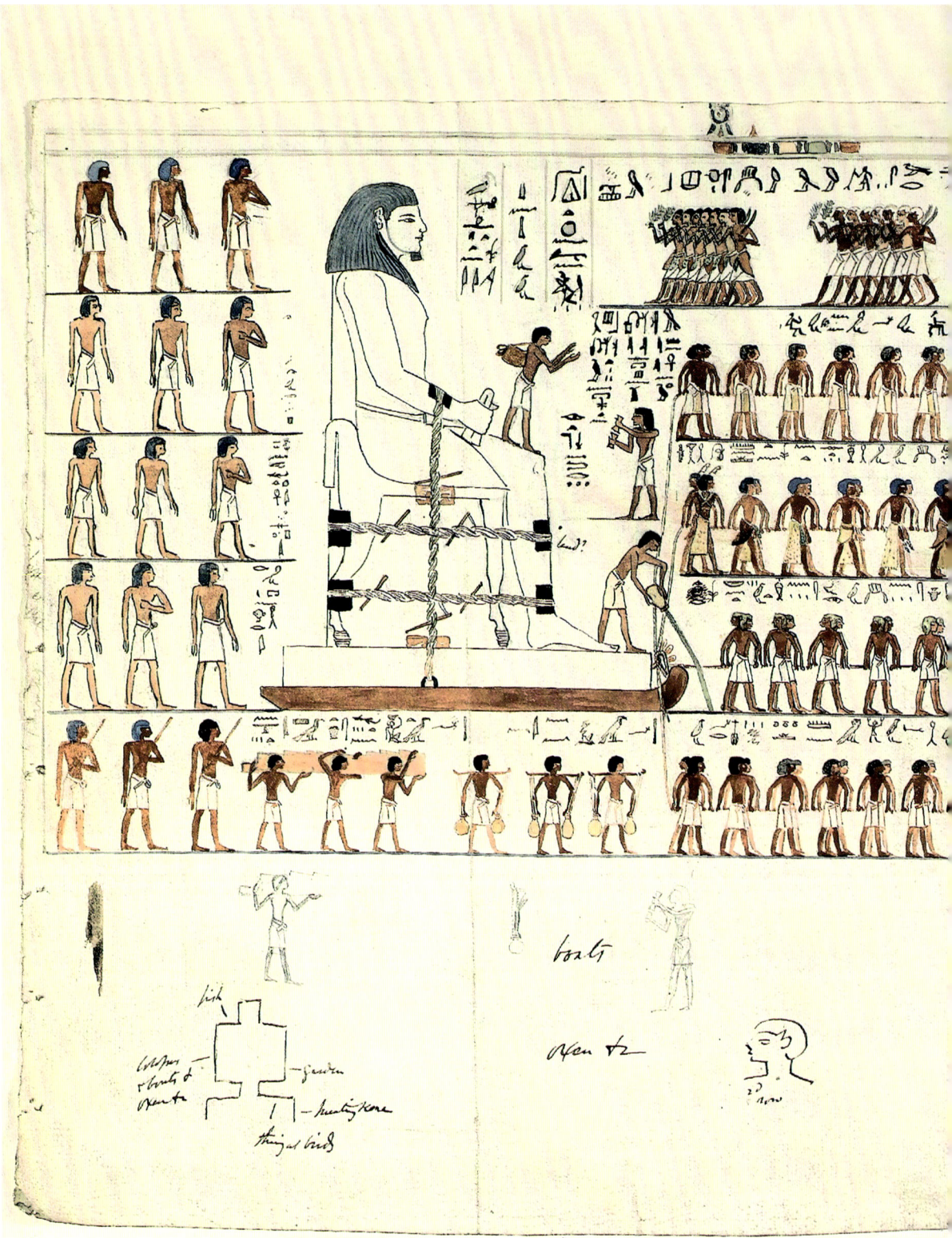

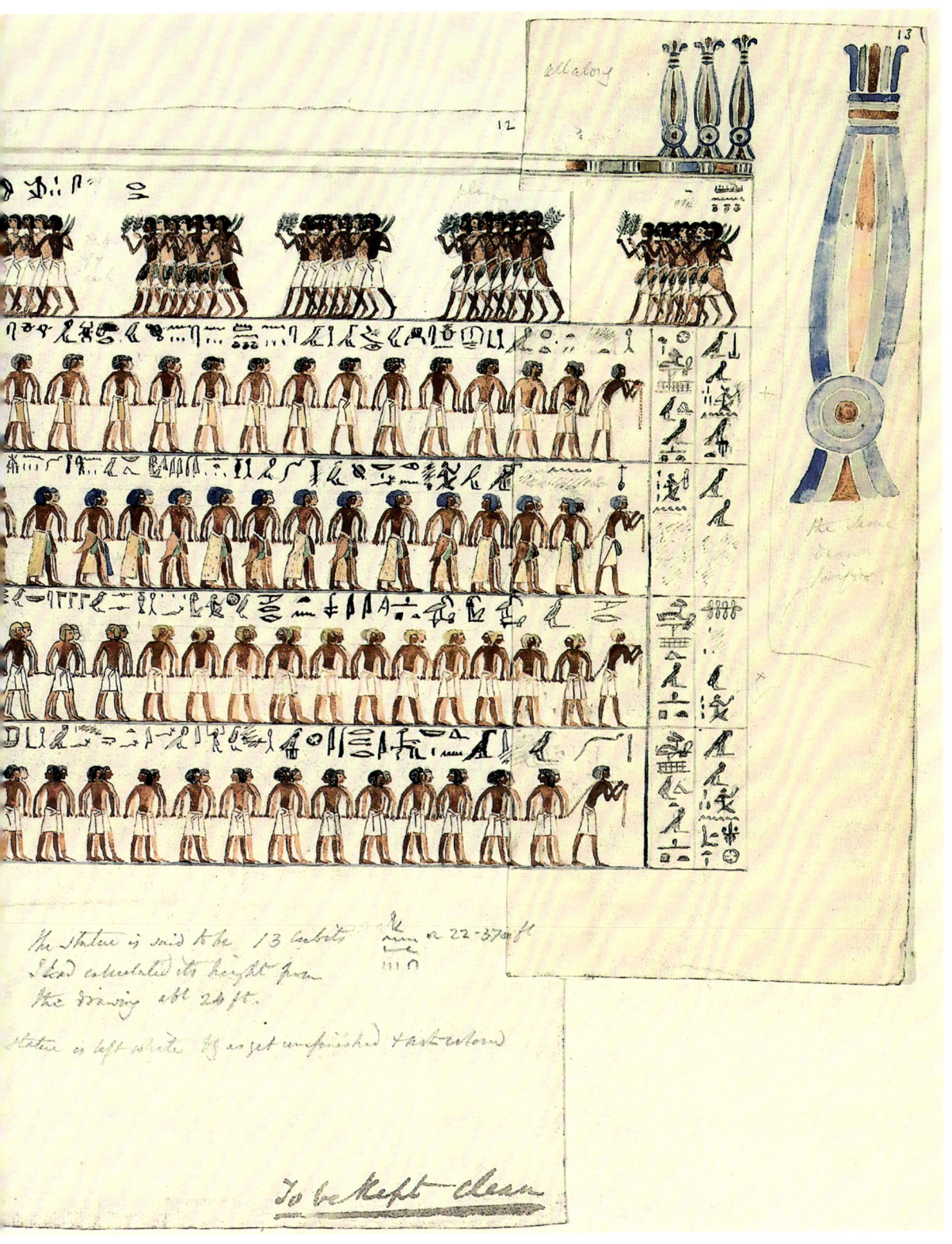

The statue is said to be 13 cubits a 22-37 ½ ft
I had calculated its height from
the drawing abt 24 ft.

Statue is left white bf as yet unfinished + ast colord

To be kept clean

21 "Mode of transporting a colossus from the quarries," Bodleian Library MS.Wilkinson. dep.a.17.12-13. *By kind permission of the National Trust (Gardner-Wilkinson Collection/Bodleian Library).*

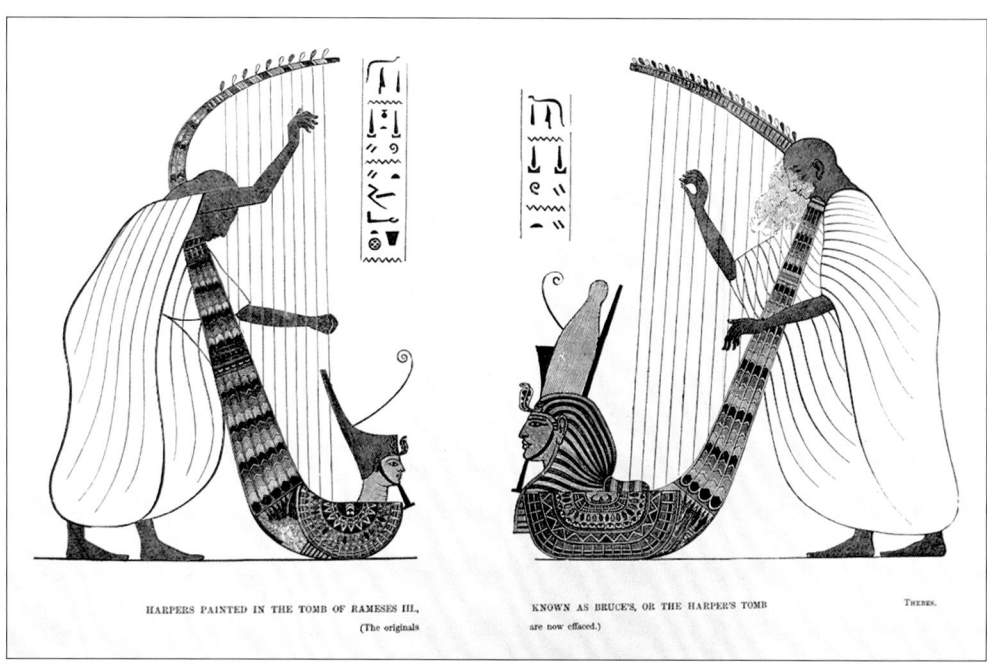

22 John Gardner Wilkinson's plate XIII, "Bruce's Harper." From *Manners and Customs of the Ancient Egyptians.* London: John Murray, 1837–41. *Photographed by Owen Murray.*

The adjustment of figures, their rearrangement in compositions, and the removal of a larger context, are evident in other plates in Cailliaud's corpus. As they continue to do today, the tombs in Beni Hasan provided early nineteenth-century copyists with a wealth of images related to the lives and activities of non-royal ancient peoples. The tomb of Khety,[23] for example, contains a scene of women, sometimes mounted on each other's backs, playing ball games. Cailliaud used imagery from this scene, sent to him by the Champollion brothers, in his plate 41. A brief comparison of this plate with both a depiction in Hay's collection (fig. 19) and an early twentieth-century line drawing, done by Percy Newberry on behalf of the Egypt Exploration Society (fig. 20), sheds further light on how Cailliaud conceived his images.[24]

While far from pretty, Newberry's image is an accurate copy of the scene's composition. By comparing these representations, we can see that Cailliaud's plate again eschewed a larger context, unlike the Hay image, and that once again figures have been moved around to suit a specific composition. These same issues appear in plate 43, based on imagery from further afield, from the tomb of Djehutyhotep in Deir al-Bersha. Wilkinson was also interested in this scene and acquired an image of it, done by William John Bankes, which was then reworked for inclusion in various editions of his *Manners and Customs of the Ancient Egyptians* (fig. 21).[25] When we compare the preliminary version used by Wilkinson with the one contained in the Cailliaud plates, two differences are apparent. Bankes' version went to extraordinary pains to reproduce the scene's larger context, an element largely maintained in the re-uses of the image under Wilkinson's name. Cailliaud's image, however, once again targeted only what was important to Cailliaud, namely the movement of the statue. Secondly, while the figures in Cailliaud's scene have not been moved around, they have certainly been reduced in number, thereby truncating the whole image.

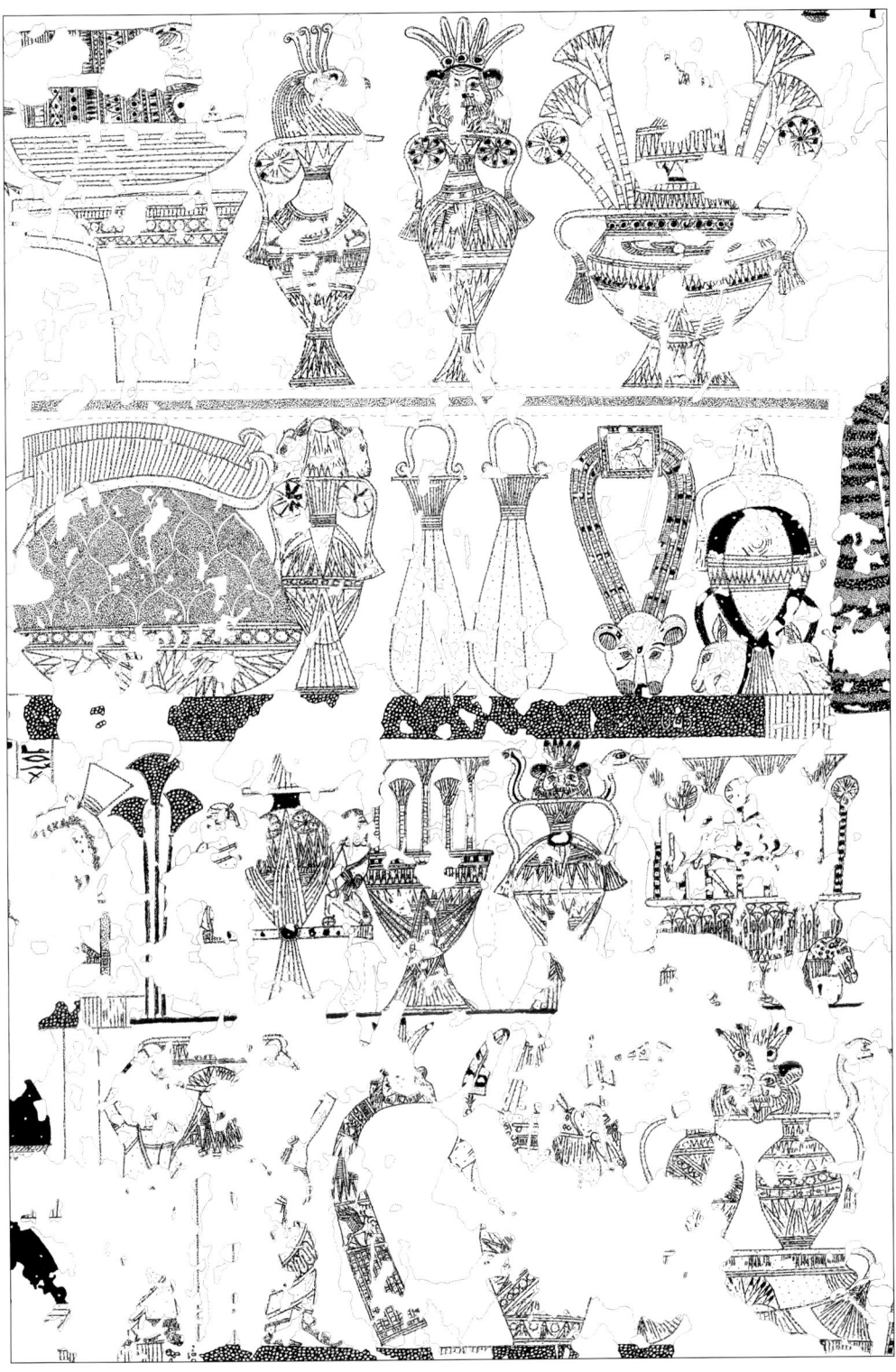

23 Facsimile drawing of the southern front wall of Theban Tomb 65. *Courtesy of Tamás A. Bács. Drawn by Krystián Vértes.*

This truncation of figures or scenes is evident elsewhere in Cailliaud's corpus. The Cailliaud plates also tend to use simple, standardized elements that were easily repeated. In addition to truncation, Cailliaud's scene of the colossus's movement contains a sense of easy reproduction, evident in the figures pulling the statue, compared to the version used by Wilkinson. Rather than employ shading, many of Cailliaud's plates also show a preference for blocks of color that can be easily repeated, allowing for an easy, visual understanding of a scene. Both truncation and the use of color blocks are visible when we compare Cailliaud's depiction of the harper (pl. 45) with Wilkinson's (fig. 22).[26]

In this comparison, it should be noted that Cailliaud, like Prisse d'Avennes, did not depict the harper's near hand resting on strings, as did Wilkinson. Cailliaud has also filled in the damaged face, unlike Wilkinson. The standardization of figures and use of block coloring as a means of recording images was not unique to Cailliaud, as we can see with some of the images already presented. The scene with the ball players that exists in Hay's collection, for example, uses both of these elements, as does Prisse d'Avennes' scene of brickmakers.

Cailliaud clearly took liberties with the composition of his vignettes and the proportions of the figures therein. At other times, however, he simply made mistakes. His plate 24 is a good example of such an error. Part of this plate depicts a gold vase with floral, faunal, and divine motifs. The vase was copied from Theban Tomb 65, that of Imiseba.[27] If we compare the image in the Cailliaud manuscript with a facsimile drawing of the wall from which it came (fig. 23), we immediately get a different appreciation for Cailliaud's work. In this facsimile, we can see that Cailliaud combined elements from the Bes-headed vase with rosettes at the top of the scene with the Bes-headed vase on the second register from the bottom of the scene, the one with the ducks' heads protruding outward. In this scene, Cailliaud probably mistook the ducks for serpents.

It is important to understand the accuracy, composition, and variations that went into Cailliaud's corpus of images, as his plates remain a valuable source of information for scenes that have been lost to us. As mentioned throughout this book, the tomb of Neferhotep,[28] labeled as tomb A5 in Porter and Moss' *Topographical Bibliography*, is just such a lost tomb. Cailliaud's recording of it remains one of the few sources of information on the tomb's decoration. Cailliaud's imagery is similarly important to the study of other monuments, such as the Theban tomb of Imiseba. Cailliaud's plate 24A, for example, records two vessels that once existed on the tomb's walls: one with Nubian figures supporting a cup and another with horses' heads. Scant remains of each of these vessels can be seen in the bottom register of figure 23, a facsimile drawing of the wall from which they were copied. Only fragments of these images now remain in the tomb, making Cailliaud's plate an important source of documentary information. Cailliaud's goal while assembling his images was not to create, or compile, facsimiles. Instead, he strove to use imagery to illustrate points that he made in his chapters. If figures needed to be moved around, changed, or visually completed, so be it.

THE PROCESS AND OTHER ASPECTS OF CAILLIAUD'S VISUAL RECORDS

The abundance of material in the Harer Papers gives us insight into how Cailliaud built his visual corpus. In addition to the published plates, the papers contain studies and preliminary drawings for many of the scenes, sometimes with annotations. In the composite image that forms figure 24, for example, we can see several versions of plate 45A; the final version can be seen in the "Plates" section.

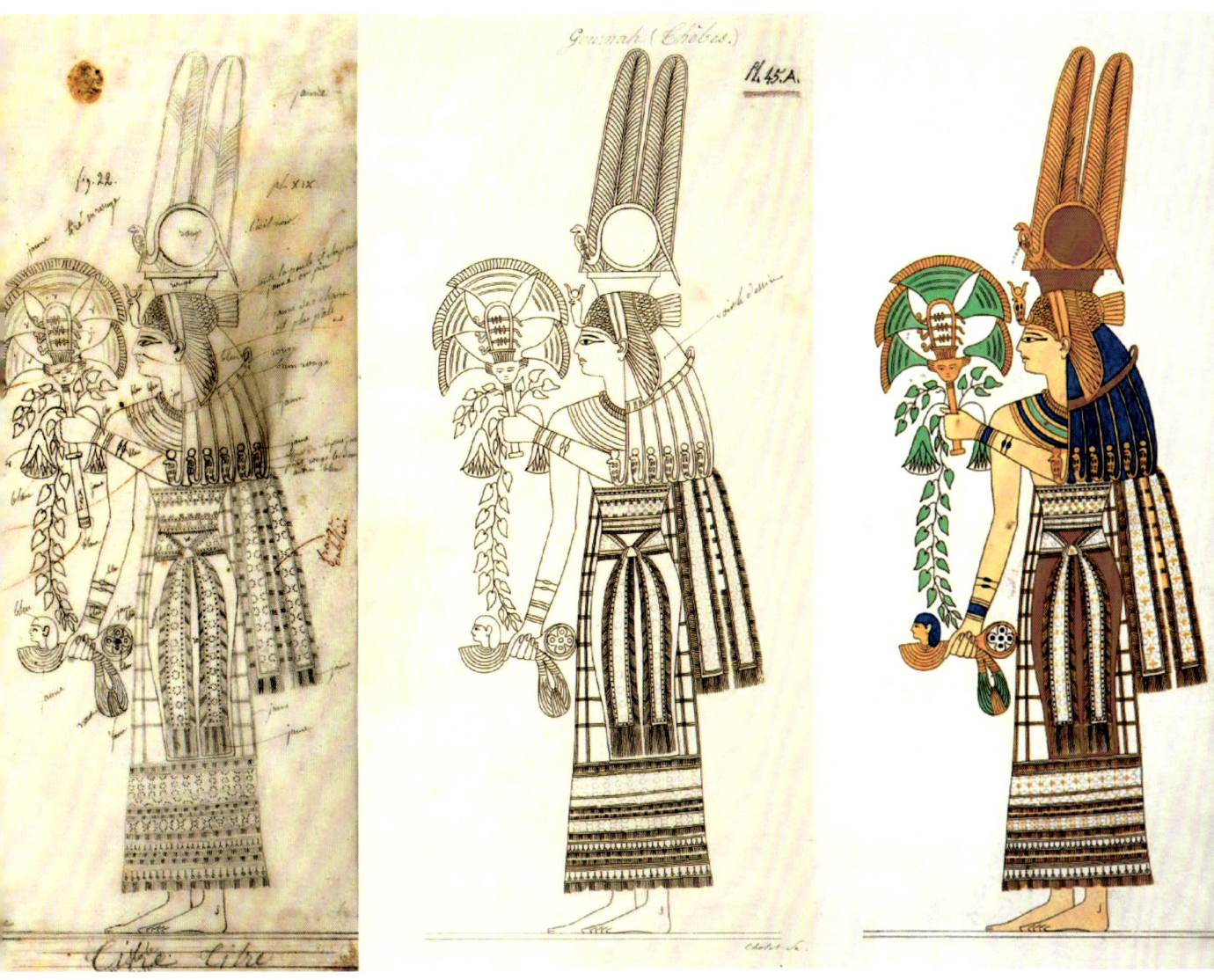

24 Preliminary drafts of Frédéric Cailliaud's plate 45A. *Courtesy of W. Benson Harer, Jr. Photographed by Gustavo Camps.* The image on the right is nearly identical to the final plate.

The draft on the left is filled with annotations, such as "the whole bird and serpent yellow gold; the yellow for the flesh is paler; forgot the fringe; see the model for the small stars on the belt." The draft in the middle comprises the same figure with the mentioned stars on the belt, while the draft on the right is the final scene. A similar process is evident in a preliminary work for plate 5A, showing sawyers, carpenters, and wine pressing (fig. 25). The earliest draft contains annotations regarding colors required for the scene. A further draft has color added to the images, along with the names of the tombs from which the images were taken.

A particularly striking example of an early drawing that was later recomposed into a portion of a larger scene relates to plate 65 (fig. 26). The rightmost image on the upper register of this plate depicts a body, being tended by Anubis, while a portion of the deceased's spirit descends in

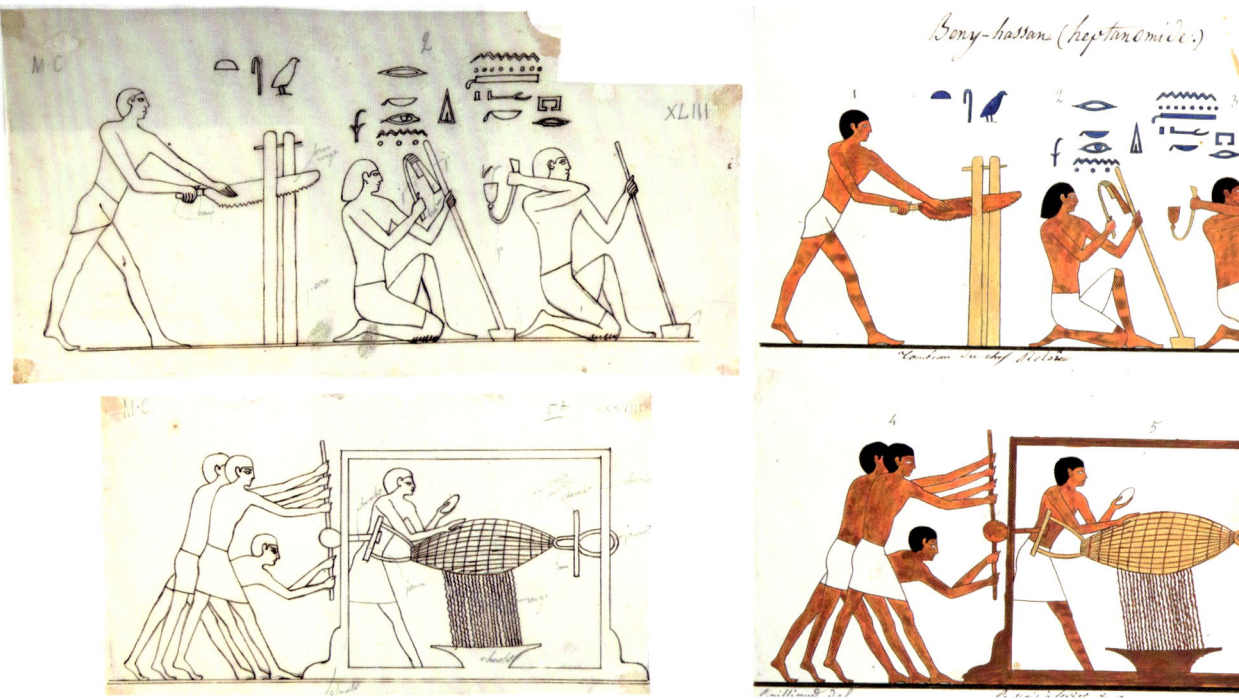

the form of a bird. When we compare this scene to its corresponding preliminary drawing in the Harer Papers, we can see that, as opposed to information being added to the final plate, much has been deleted. The scene has undergone a dramatic visual streamlining. This scene was eventually incorporated into the compilation that is plate 65, published fully in this book's chapter of plates. When we look at the final scale of the scene within this plate, we can appreciate why Cailliaud removed the visual information that he did; the reduction of the scene would have obscured the text to illegibility so, presumably, it was jettisoned. What we see from this rapid survey of Cailliaud's preliminary work is that he built his visual corpus in much the same way that he built his textual corpus: through successive copies in which information was changed, added, or removed, until the desired goal was achieved.

Surprisingly, the Harer Papers also contain two plates that were never included in the original publication. They are presented here, with the incorrect plate numbers of 49 and 50 printed on them respectively (figs. 27 and 28). Both have the same, simple captions of "Qurna, Thebes" and "Painting from a tomb." Cailliaud's name is signed as the artist at the bottom left-hand corner of each, while the engravings can be attributed to a Mr. Smith, responsible for several other plates in the original publication. While the incorrectly numbered plate 49 appears solely in an unfinished state, the erroneously labeled plate 50 takes both an uncolored and a partially colored form. The presence of these two plates, and the wealth of preliminary work in the Harer Papers, give a clue to the papers' movements after Cailliaud's death. In an explanation of the numbering system used for Cailliaud's plates, Baron de Girardot states: "I have, in addition, two plates numbered 49 and 50, which did not form part of the work delivered to subscribers."[29] Girardot continues to enumerate all of the visual material that he possessed, including ninety-four proofs done in black and red, a portion of

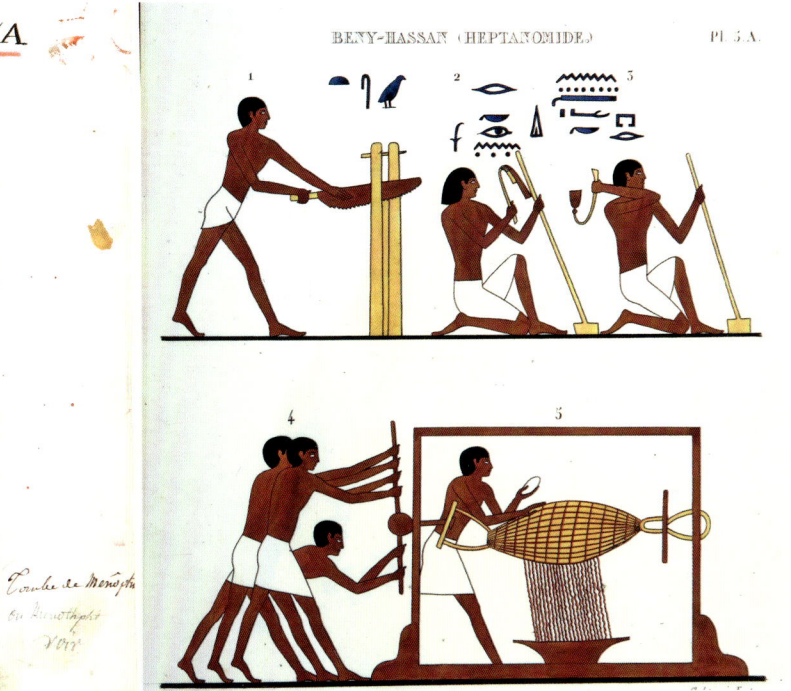

Left: 25 Preliminary drafts of Frédéric Cailliaud's plate 5A and the final plate. *Courtesy of W. Benson Harer, Jr. Photographed by Gustavo Camps.* The image on the right is a smaller version of the final plate.

Below: 26 Preliminary draft and a portion of the final image for Frédéric Cailliaud's plate 65. *Courtesy of W. Benson Harer, Jr. Photographed by Gustavo Camps.* The image on the right is a portion of the final plate.

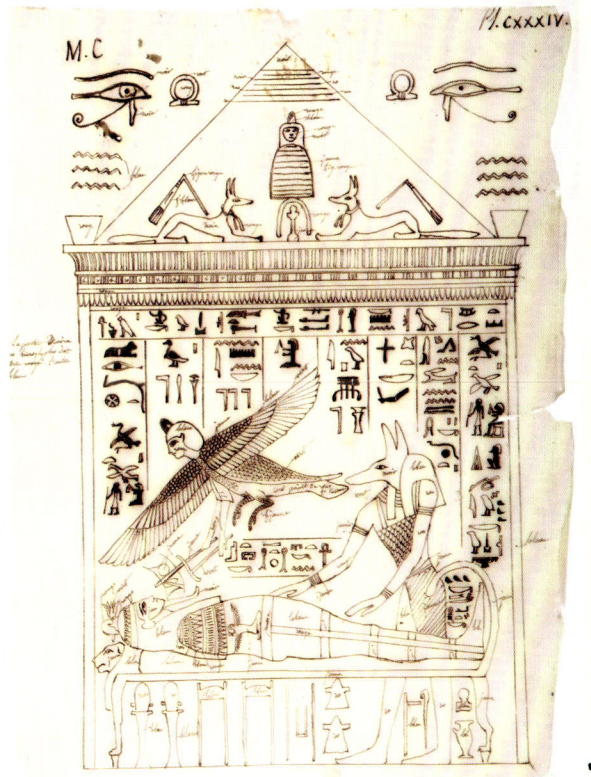

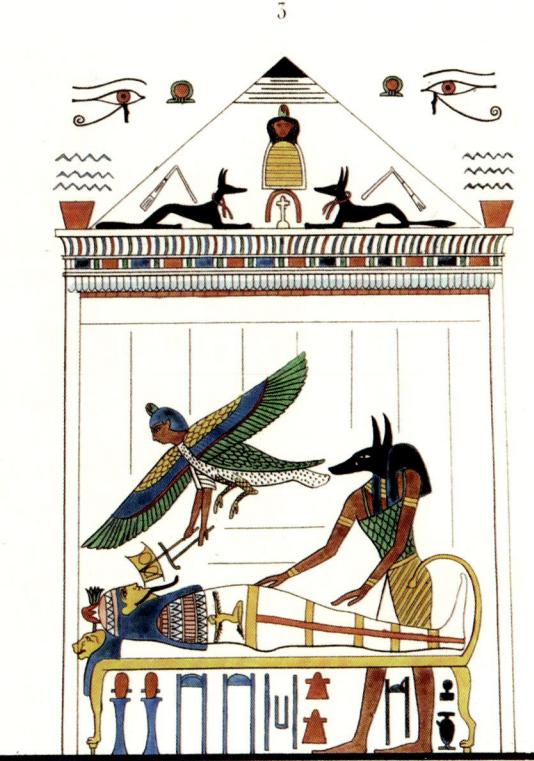

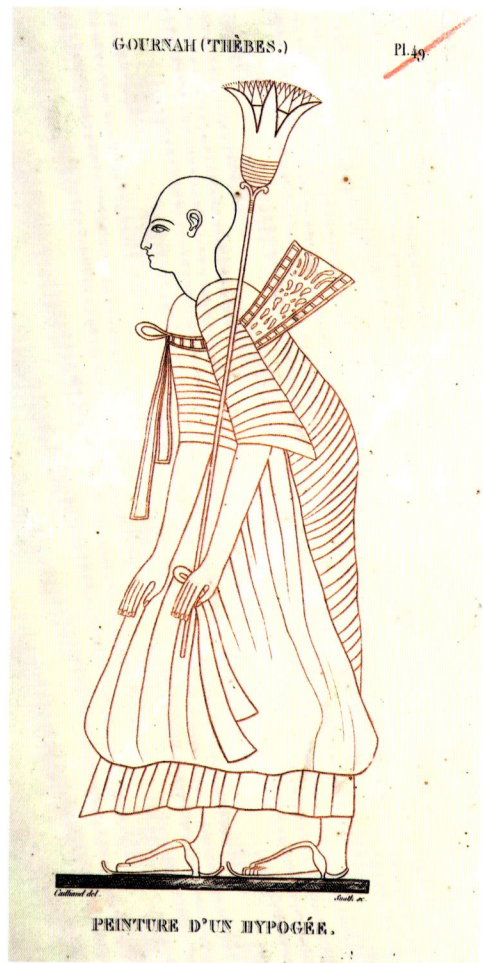

27 One of two unpublished plates in the Harer Papers: incorrectly numbered 49. *Courtesy of W. Benson Harer, Jr. Photographed by Gustavo Camps.*

28 One of two unpublished plates in the Harer Papers: incorrectly numbered 50. *Courtesy of W. Benson Harer, Jr. Photographed by Gustavo Camps.*

the original artwork for Cailliaud's plates, including 250 drawings, most done in Egypt, and several meters of tracings.[30] It seems likely, therefore, that the visual material from Girardot was eventually combined with the textual material from Cailliaud's son to form the present Harer Papers.

Lastly, the Harer Papers' rich visual material contains scenes unrelated to Cailliaud's published plates, and possibly of a more intimate nature. There are drawings of historical interest, such as an image from Tomb 3 in Beni Hasan of a group of Asiatics named the Aamu who came to pay homage to the deceased Khnumhotep (fig. 30). There is even an image of an emerald, a reflection of Cailliaud's first love, mineralogy (fig. 31). This image is an appropriate reminder of the impetus for Cailliaud's original trip to Egypt: his desire to build a personal mineralogical collection by traveling the Mediterranean. It also offers an appropriate bridge to his later career and life. Within the Harer Papers is a scene of a woman clothed in a modest, traditional flowing garment, carrying a jug on her head, a sight Cailliaud would have encountered time and again as he journeyed around the country, and one that can still be seen in Egypt today (fig. 32).

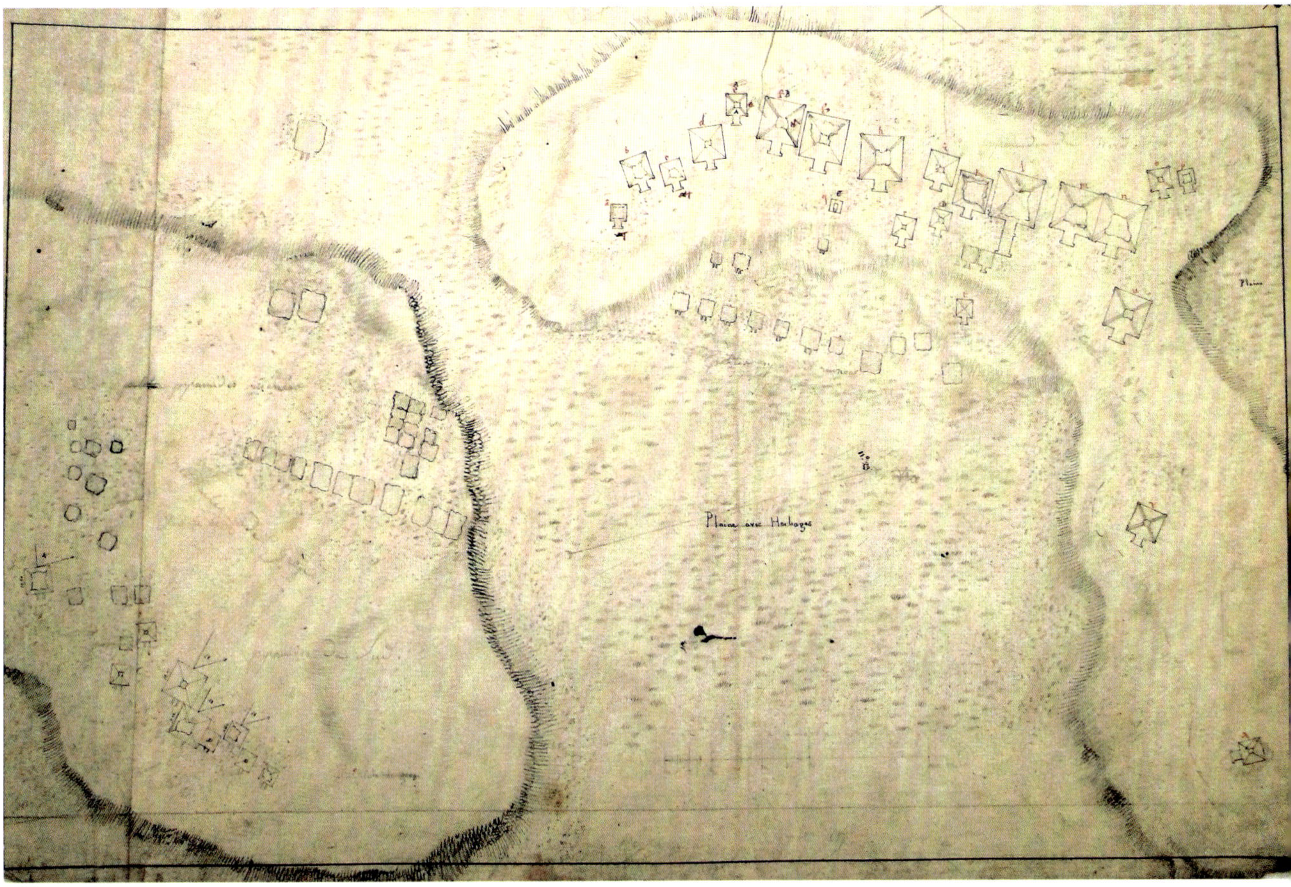

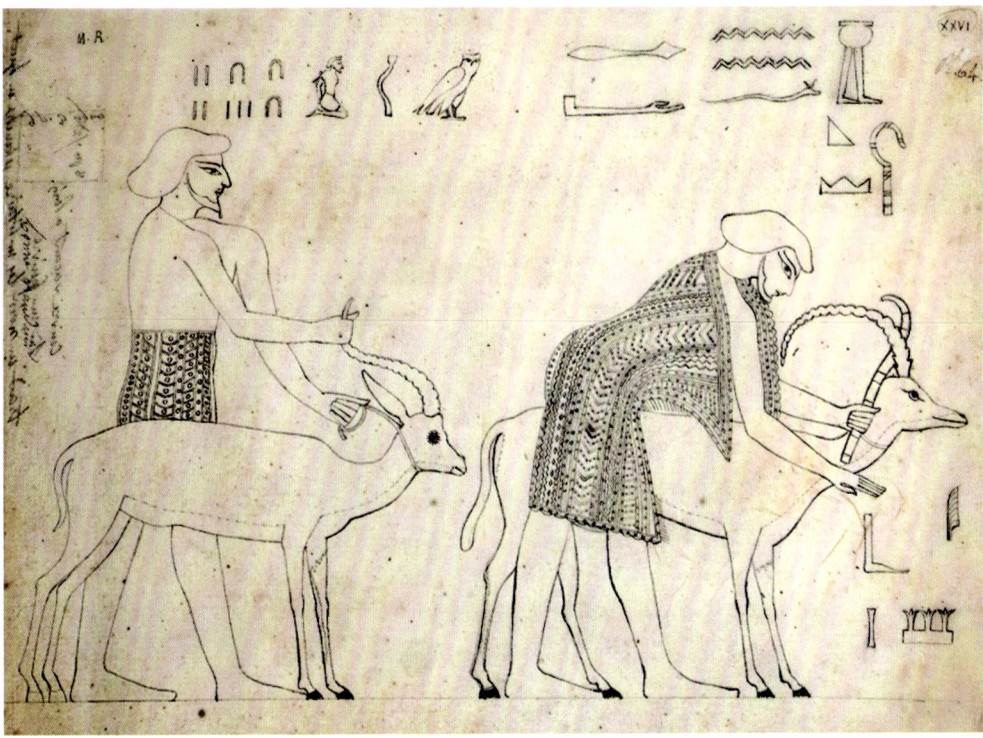

29 An example of one of Frédéric Cailliaud's preparatory drawings of monuments and their surrounding terrain. This is a preliminary plan of his plate 30, published in his *Voyage à Meroe. Courtesy of Philippe Mainterot.*

30 The Aamu, from the tomb of Khnumhotep. *Courtesy of W. Benson Harer, Jr. Photographed by Gustavo Camps.*

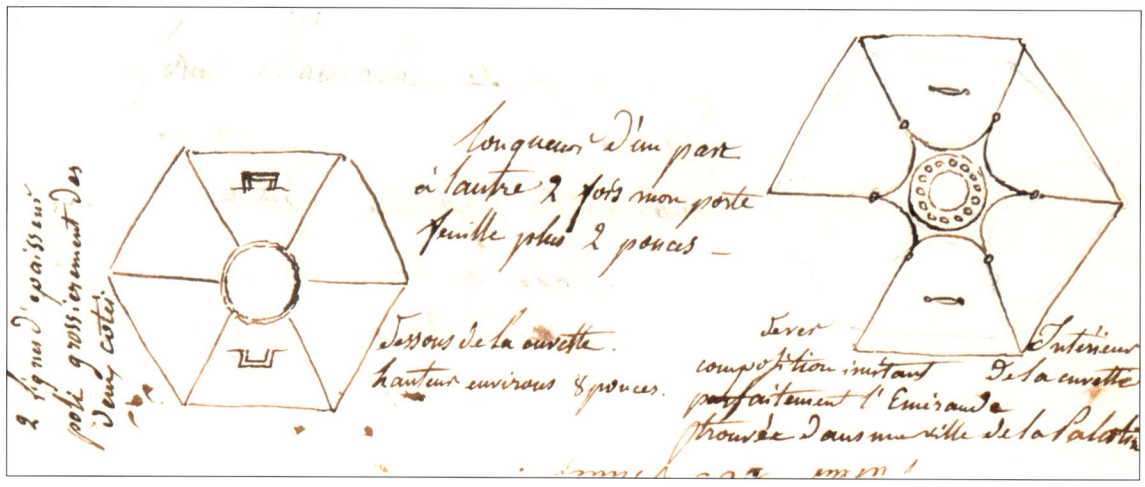

31 A sketch of an emerald. *Courtesy of W. Benson Harer, Jr. Photographed by Gustavo Camps.*

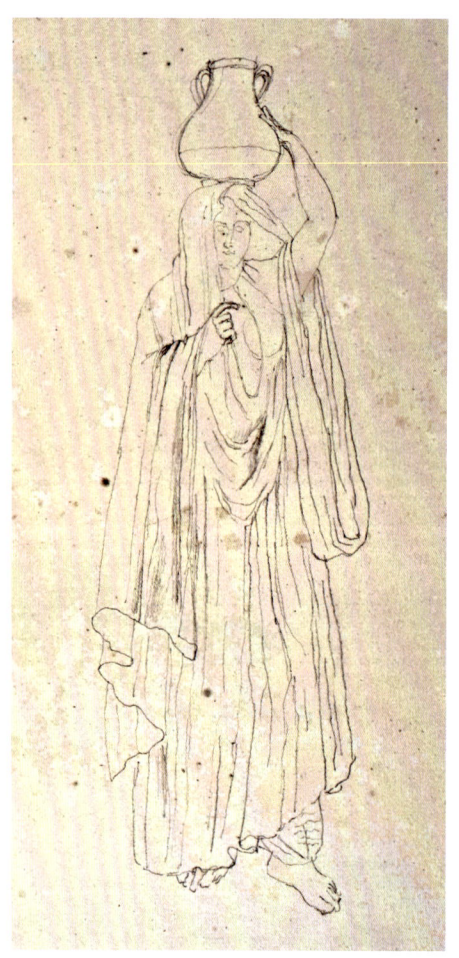

32 A woman carrying a jug. *Courtesy of W. Benson Harer, Jr. Photographed by Gustavo Camps.*

Finally, the Harer Papers contain a page with drawings of two intriguing, crude tomb plans (fig. 33). Both tombs are represented with a top view, a cross section, and measurements. The tomb at the top of the page has the following caption: "1st tomb, 300 feet to the north of the Memnonia.[31] Mountain of Qurna." The second tomb's caption reads: "2nd tomb, at the northern extremity of the mountain of Qurna, containing the subjects of hunting and fishing." The only hunting and fishing scenes published by Cailliaud came from the lost tomb of Neferhotep. As a result, it seems reasonable to assume that this is a plan of that tomb. Both Manniche and Kampp hypothesize the location of Neferhotep's tomb in Dra Abu al-Naga.[32] An educated guess of this sort fits with the brief description listed under Cailliaud's second plan, as Dra Abu al-Naga lies at the northernmost end of the area's necropolis. A review of Kampp's map of the region, entitled "Plan VII" and depicting the general shape of the area's tombs, suggests a number of possible structures that might match Cailliaud's measurements. It would be very rewarding to physically compare the shape and measurements listed on Cailliaud's plan with the tombs in this area.

If this book has proven that the textual material in the Harer Papers is worthy of continued investigation, it is my hope that this chapter has demonstrated the same for Cailliaud's surviving visual corpus. It is also my hope that this chapter constitutes a first step in placing Cailliaud within the history of European copyists in Egypt. While neither his research nor the final publication of his plates focused on a single monument, Cailliaud's work quickly became, and remains, a primary source for people interested in

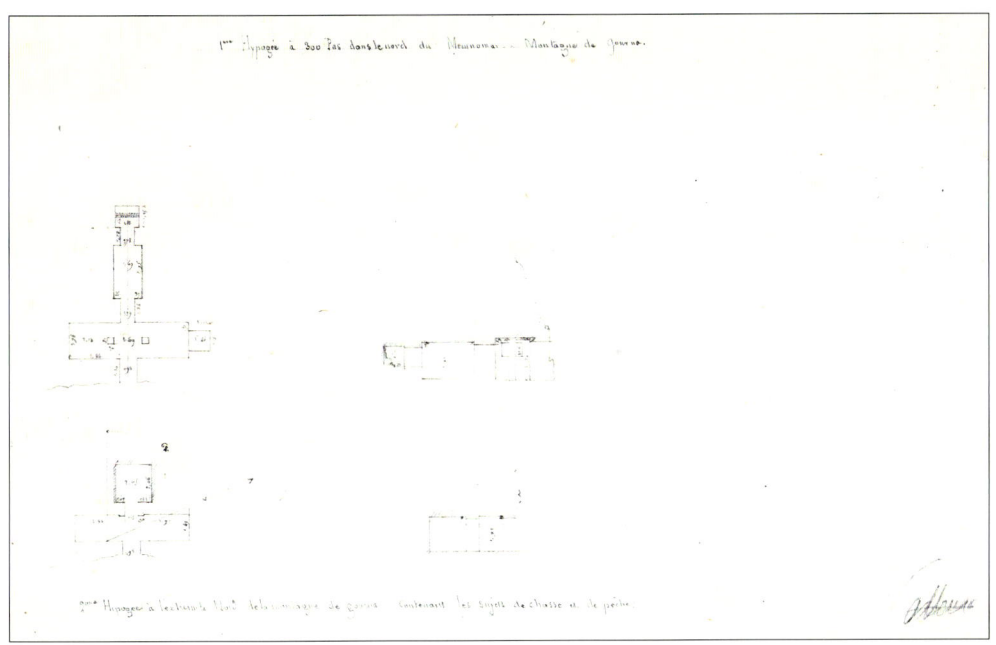

33 Tomb plans, one of which likely refers to the lost tomb of Neferhotep. *Courtesy of W. Benson Harer, Jr. Photographed by Gustavo Camps.*

specific scenes and monuments. At the time of Cailliaud's initial research there were neither specialists in nor people working toward the goal of describing and publishing a single monument. Instead, scholars such as Cailliaud and Wilkinson concentrated on recording images to support broad-sweeping accounts of Egyptian civilization. Their goal appears to have been to amass visual data that would complement words that created a context in which to understand ancient Egypt. This desire to flesh out a context through large-scale publication projects with strong visual corpuses directly stemmed from earlier efforts, such as Pococke's *A Description of the East*, Denon's *Travels*, and the Napoleonic *Description*. While the study of Egyptian monuments narrowed after Cailliaud's time, the desire to record and disseminate temple and tomb scenes in lavish detail continued well beyond the nineteenth century and remains an ongoing focus of historical inquiry into Egypt. Cailliaud's work can, in fact, be viewed as helping to cement the tradition within Egyptology of expensive large-format reproductions of tomb and temple scenes. The most obvious examples of present-day publications of this sort are those produced by the University of Chicago's Oriental Institute. Cailliaud's work was a pioneering effort in the history of nineteenth-century European science. It is remarkable that, nearly two hundred years later, both his textual material and visual corpus remain relevant and continue to provide exciting avenues for research.

---

1 For more information on early European travelers during this time, see "Johann Michael Wansleben," in *Who Was Who in Egyptology*, edited by Morris L. Bierbrier (London: Egypt Exploration Society, 1995), 432–33; "Paul Lucas," *Who Was Who*, 264; and most importantly "Claude Sicard," *Who Was Who*, 390.
2 Jean Leclant, "L'égyptologie avant l'expédition d'Égypte," in *L'expédition d'Égypte, une entreprise des Lumières 1798–1801*, edited by Patrice Bret (Paris: Technique et Documentation, 1999), 125.

3 Richard Pococke visited Egypt between 1737 and 1739 and published an account of his travels between 1743 and 1745. See Bierbrier, *Who Was Who*, 338.

4 Richard Pococke, *A Description of the East and Some Other Countries* (London: J. & R. Knapton, 1743), pl. XXX.

5 Pococke, *A Description*, pl. XXXII.

6 Pococke, *A Description*, pl. XLII.

7 Denon's publication was immensely successful and a multitude of editions have been created since its first appearance. For a full reprint of the French text, see Dominique Vivant Denon, *Voyage dans la Basse et la Haute Égypte pendant les campagnes du général Bonaparte* (Paris: P. Didot l'aîné, 1802). For a more recent, popular, abridged version in English, see Terence M. Russell, *The Discovery of Egypt: Vivant Denon's Travels with Napoleon's Army* (Stroud: Sutton Publishing Limited, 2005).

8 Hay was a traveler, antiquarian, and collector. See Bierbrier, *Who Was Who*, 194.

9 Wilkinson was a traveler and the founder of Egyptology in Great Britain. See Bierbrier, *Who Was Who*, 443–45; Jason Thompson, *Sir Gardner Wilkinson and His Circle* (Austin TX: University of Texas Press, 1992).

10 Rosellini was the founder of Egyptology in Italy. See Marilina Betrò, ed., *Ippolito Rosellini and the Dawn of Egyptology*, translated by Anna Maria Bellizio (Cairo: Agenzia Italiana, 2010); Bierbrier, *Who Was Who*, 362–63.

11 Prisse d'Avennes was an important figure in early French Egyptology. See Bierbrier, *Who Was Who*, 343–44.

12 Michel Dewachter, "Introduction, Un pionnier de l'égyptologie: Mourad Effendi, alias Frédéric Cailliaud (1787–1869)," in Michel Chauvet, *Frédéric Cailliaud. Les aventures d'un naturaliste en Égypte et au Soudan* (Saint-Sébastien: ACL–Crocus, 1989), 14.

13 Dewachter, "Introduction," 14.

14 Bonomi was a British sculptor, draftsman, and traveler. See Bierbrier, *Who Was Who*, 53–54.

15 Catherwood was a British traveler and artist. See Bierbrier, *Who Was Who*, 86.

16 Burton was a British Egyptologist and traveler. See Bierbrier, *Who Was Who*, 76–77.

17 Jason Thompson, *Edward William Lane, 1801–1876: The Life of the Pioneering Egyptologist and Orientalist* (London: Haus Publishing, 2010), 235–50.

18 The tomb of Neferhotep is labeled as A5 in Bertha Porter and Rosalind L.B. Moss, *Topographical Bibliography of Ancient Egyptian Hieroglyphic Texts, Reliefs, and Paintings. I. The Theban Necropolis. Part 1. Private Tombs* (Oxford UK: Clarendon Press, 1960), 448. Its location in the Theban hills is now unknown. It was built during Egypt's mid-Eighteenth Dynasty, sometime around the reigns of Thutmose III and Amenhotep II, somewhere in the vicinity of modern-day Dra Abu al-Naga. For more information on its possible location, see Friederike Kampp, *Die Thebanische Nekropole. 2. Teil* (Mainz: Philipp von Zabern, 1996), 616.

19 See Denon, *Voyage*, pl. LV; Jomard, ed., *Description de l'Égypte, ou recueil des observations et des recherches qui on été faites en Égypte pendant l'expédition de l'armée française*, vol. 2 (Paris: Imprimerie impériale, 1812), pl. 45.

20 John Gardner Wilkinson, *Manners and Customs of the Ancient Egyptians. Including their Private Life, Government, Laws, Arts, Manufactures, Religion, and Early History; derived from a comparison of the paintings, sculptures, and monuments still existing, with the accounts of ancient authors*, vol. 2 (London: John Murray, 1837–41), pl. XI.

21 Theban Tomb 100, that of Rekhmire. See Porter and Moss, *Topographical Bibliography I.1*, 207; Norman de Garis Davies, *The Tomb of Rekh-mi-Re' at Thebes* (New York: Metropolitan Museum of Art, 1943; Arno Press, 1973); the Theban Mapping Project's bibliography for Tomb 100, http://www.tmpbibliography.com/resources/bibliography_5nv_tombs_of_the_nobles_tt100_rekhmire.html

22 Wilkinson, *Manners and Customs*, vol. 1, pl. IV.

23 Cailliaud inscribed his name in this tomb, writing "CA[…]D 1820." See Michel Chauvet, *Frédéric Cailliaud, les aventures d'un naturaliste en Égypte et au Soudan 1815–1822* (Saint-Sébastien-sur-Loire: ACL, 1989), 128. For information on the tomb, see Bertha Porter and Rosalind L.B. Moss, *Topographical Bibliography of Ancient Egyptian Hieroglyphic Texts, Reliefs, and Paintings. IV. Lower and Middle Egypt* (Oxford UK: Clarendon Press, 1934), 154–59; Percy E. Newberry, *Beni Hasan. Part II* (London: The Egypt Exploration Fund, 1895), 51–62; Naguib Kanawati and Alexandra Woods, *Beni Hassan: Art and Daily Life in an Egyptian Province* (Cairo: Supreme Council of Antiquities, 2010), 49–57.

24 Newberry, *Beni Hasan. Part II*, pl. IV.

25 See Wilkinson, *Manners and Customs*, vol. 3, 328; John Gardner Wilkinson, *The Manners and Customs of the Ancient Egyptians*, vol. 2, edited by Samuel Birch (London: John Murray, 1878), 305.

26 Wilkinson, *Manners and Customs*, vol. 2, pl. XIII.

27 Theban Tomb 65. See Porter and Moss, *Topographical Bibliography I.1*, 129; the Theban Mapping Project's bibliography for Tomb 65, http://www.tmpbibliography.com/resources/bibliography_5nv_tombs_of_the_nobles_tt65_nebamun_usurped_by_imiseba.html

28 Porter and Moss, *Topographical Bibliography I.1*, 448.

29 Auguste de Girardot, *Frédéric Cailliaud de Nantes, voyageur, antiquaire, naturaliste* (Paris: A. Labitte, 1875), 39.

30 Girardot, *Frédéric Cailliaud de Nantes*, 39–40, 45.

31 An older name for the mortuary temple of Ramesses II.

32 See Lise Manniche, *Lost Tombs: A Study of Certain Eighteenth Dynasty Monuments in the Theban Necropolis* (London: KPI, 1988), 47; Kampp, *Die Thebanische Nekropole*, 616.

PLATES 1–66

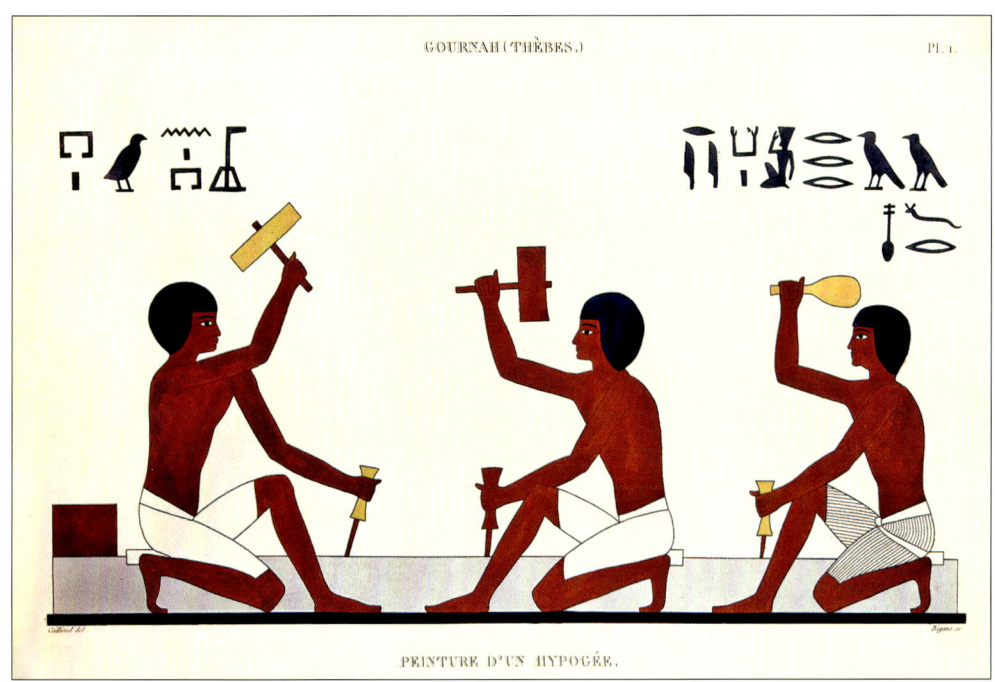

Plate 1.
Woodworkers.

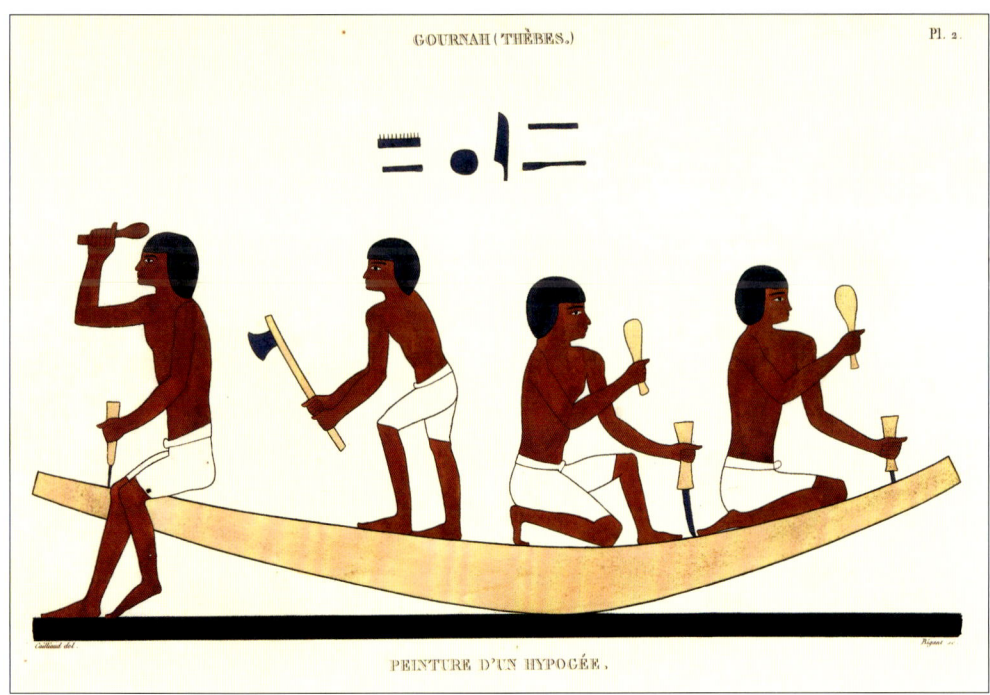

Plate 2.
Boat building.

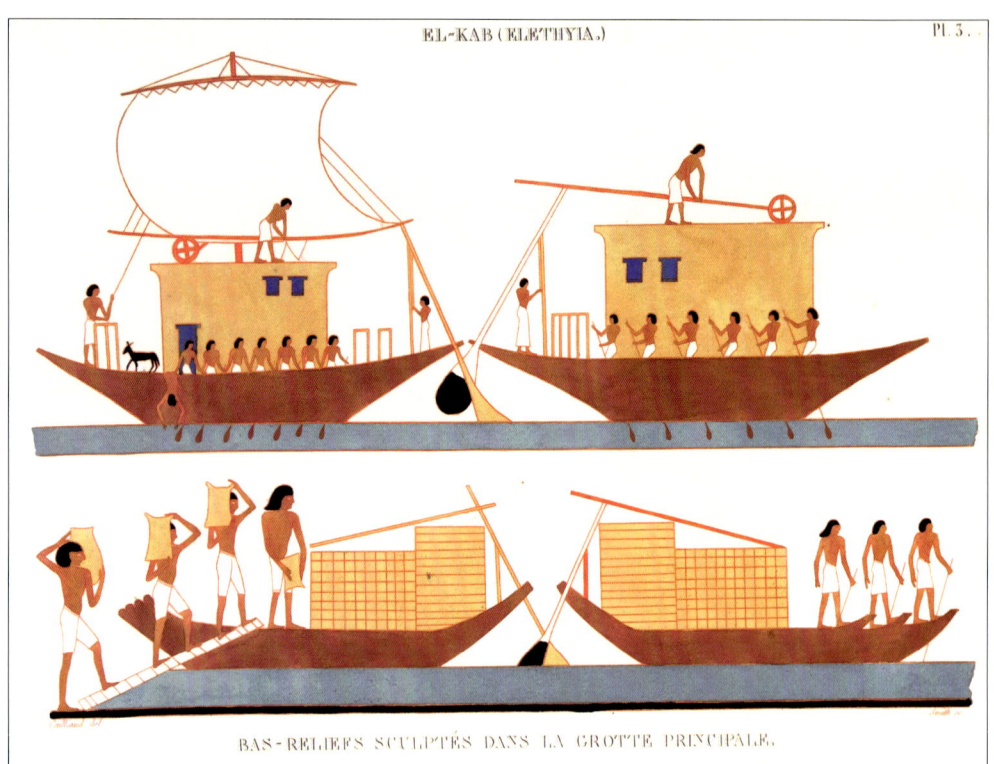

Plate 3. Boats.
Transportation of
Goods. Rudders.

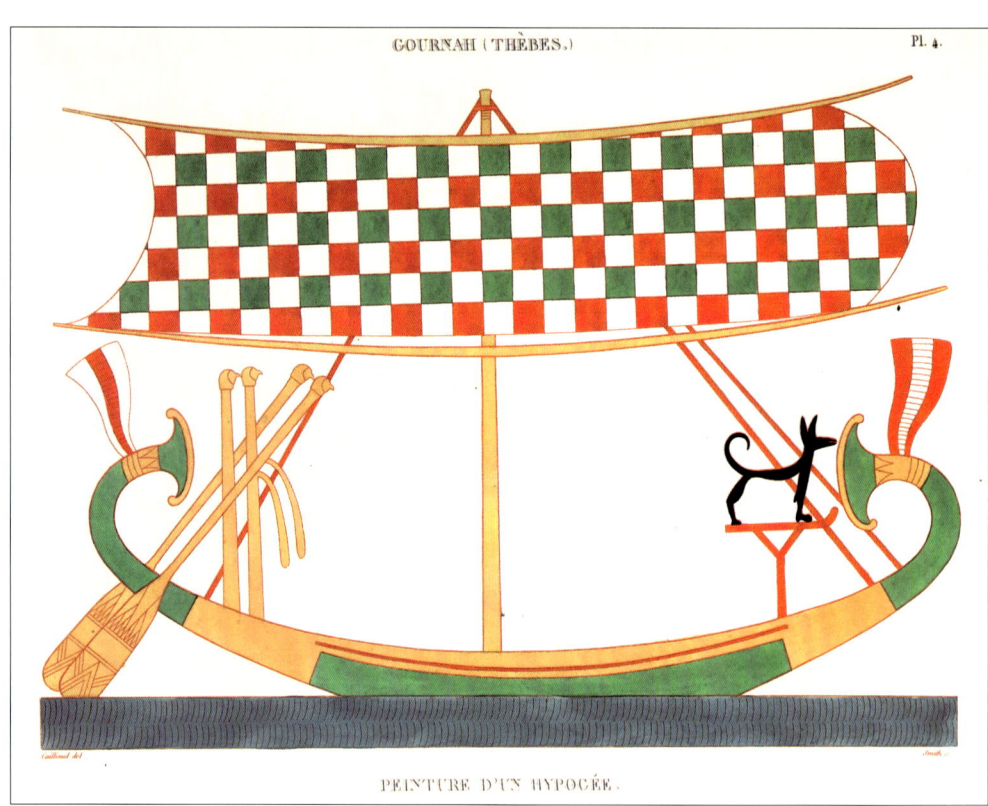

Plate 4.
Funerary barque.

174

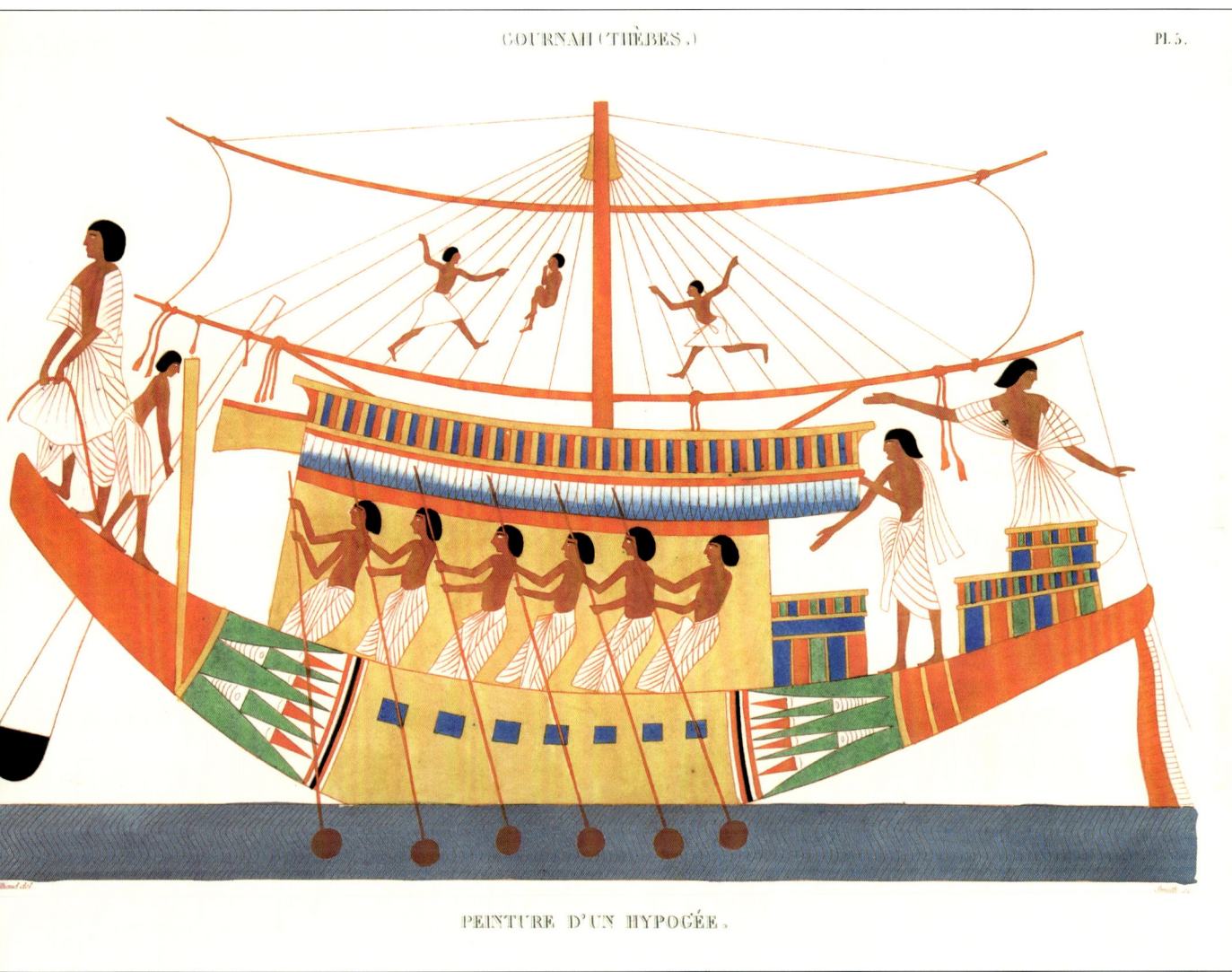

Plate 5. Boat with rowers.

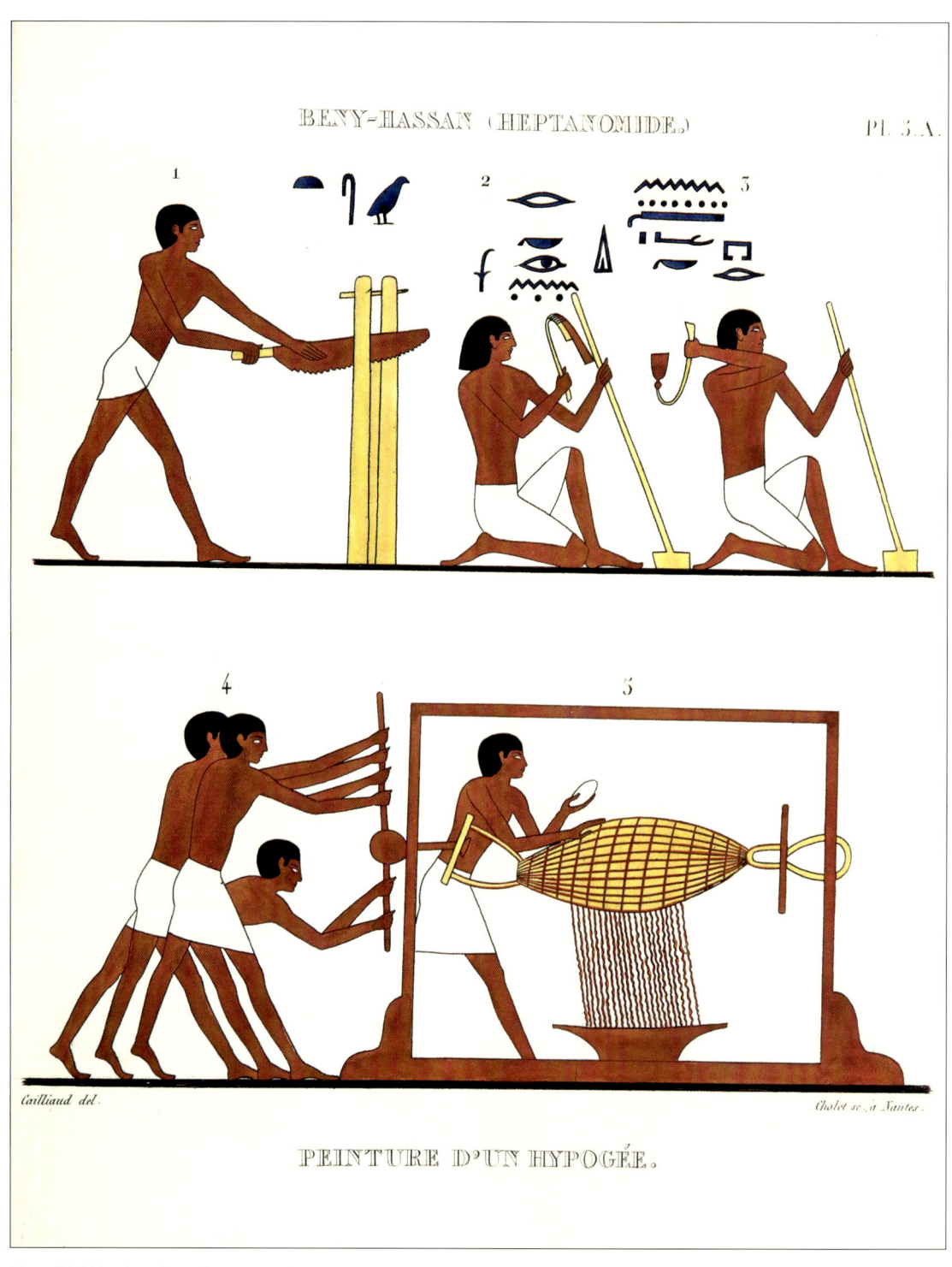

Cailliaud del.

Cholet sc., à Nantes.

PEINTURE D'UN HYPOGÉE.

Plate 5A. Woodworkers. Grape pressing.
Opposite: Plate 6. Chair building. Grape pressing.

1.

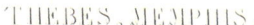

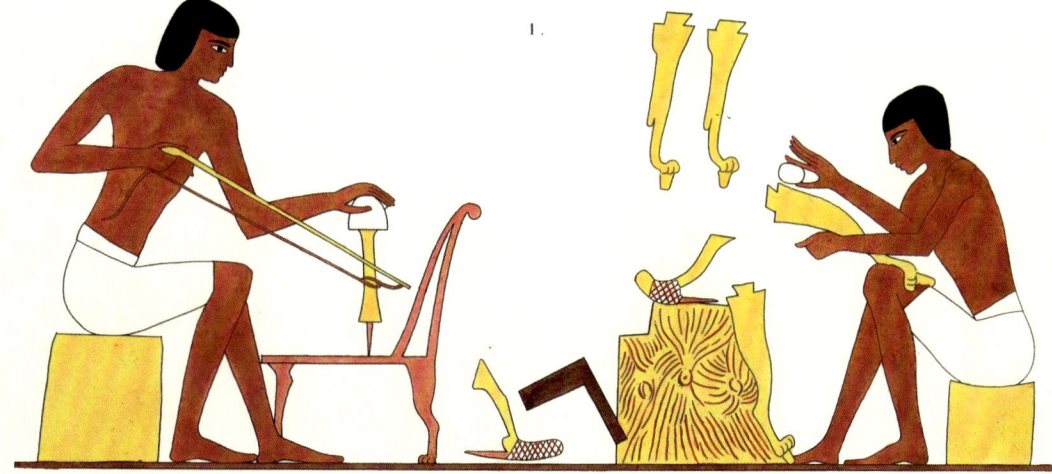

2.

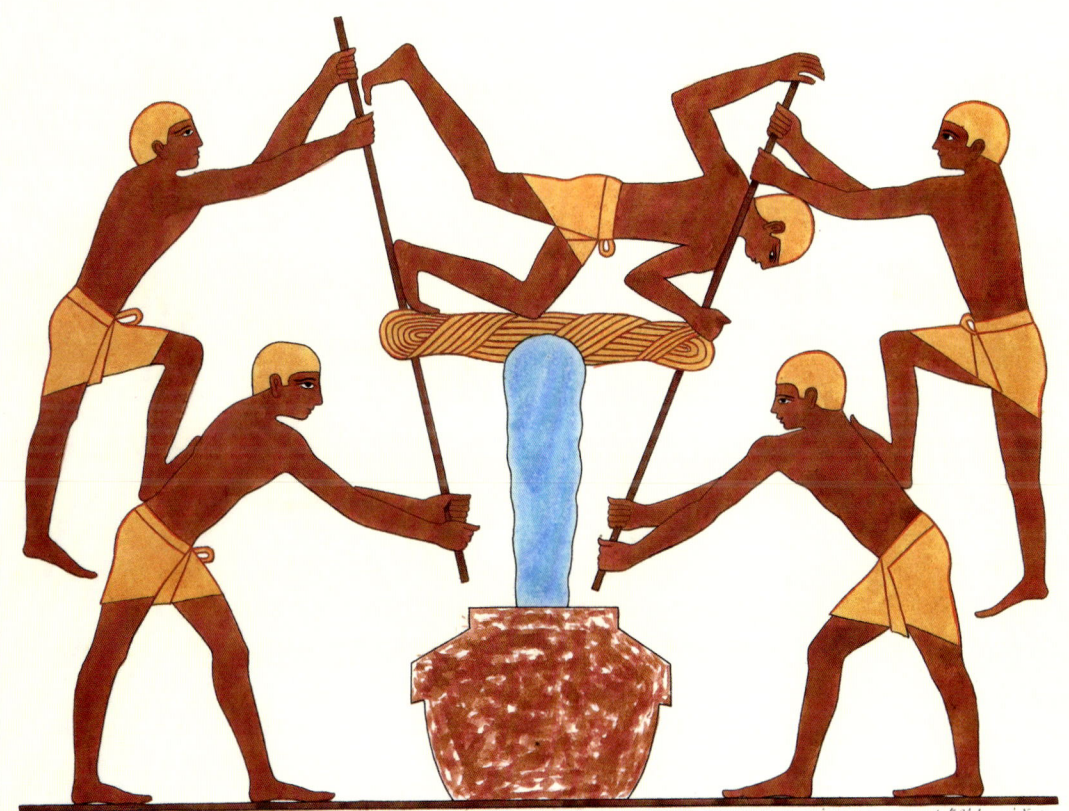

SCULPTURE ET PEINTURE DES HYPOGÉES.

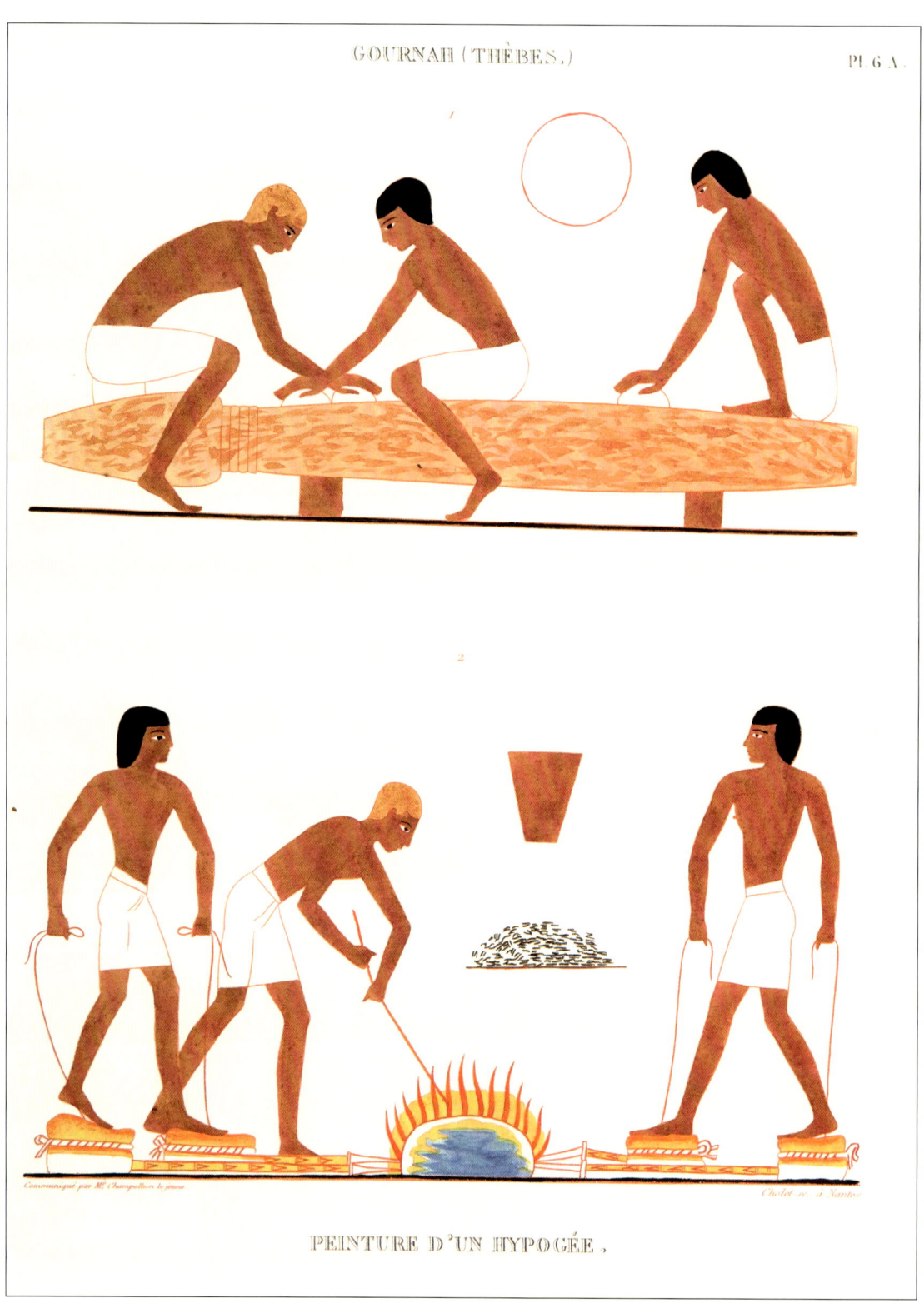

PEINTURE D'UN HYPOGÉE.

Plate 6A. Polishing a column. Metal or glass manufacture.

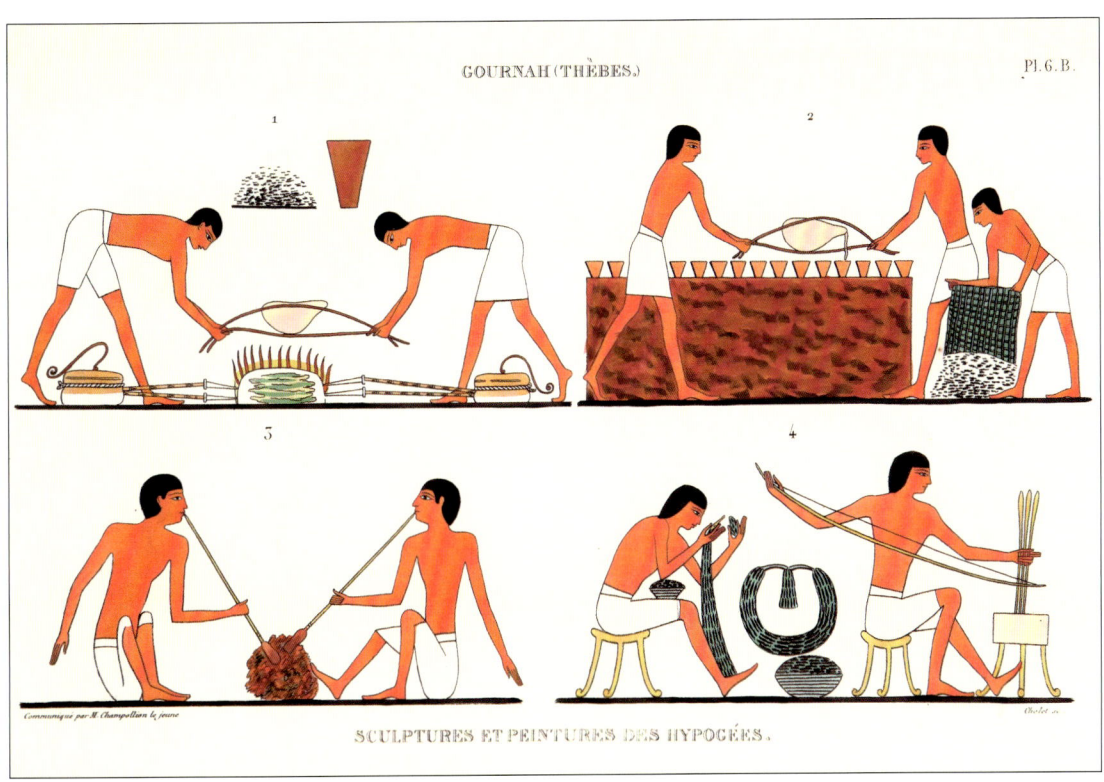

Plate 6B. Metal production. Glass and jewelry production.

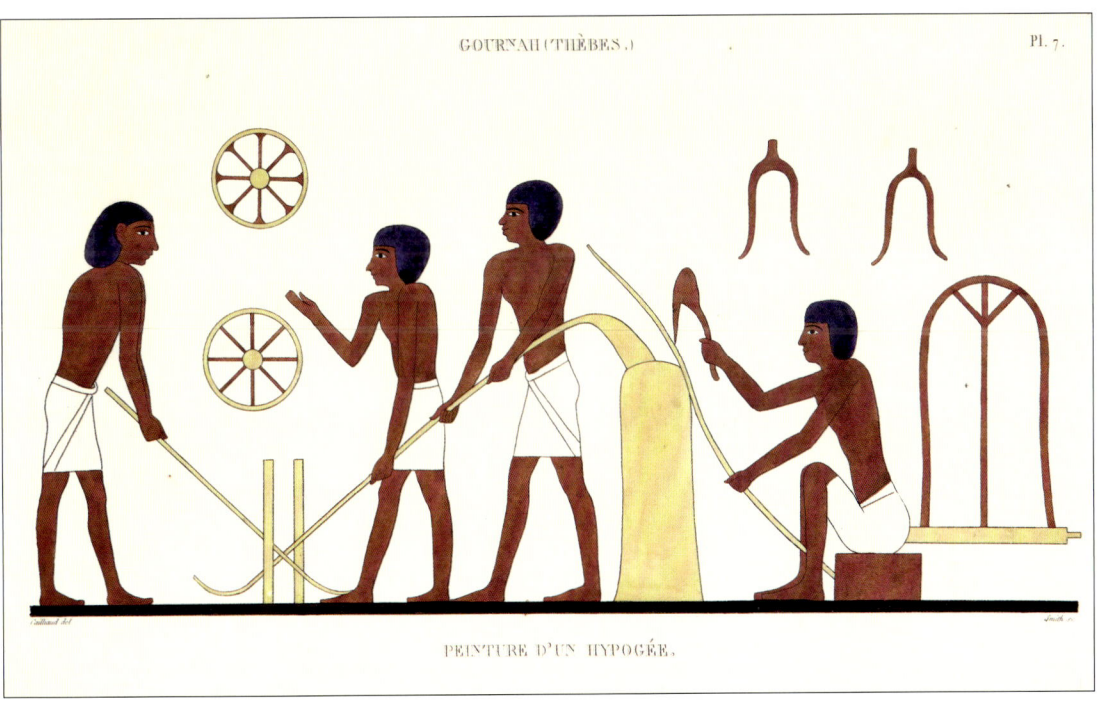

Plate 7. Wheel construction for chariots.

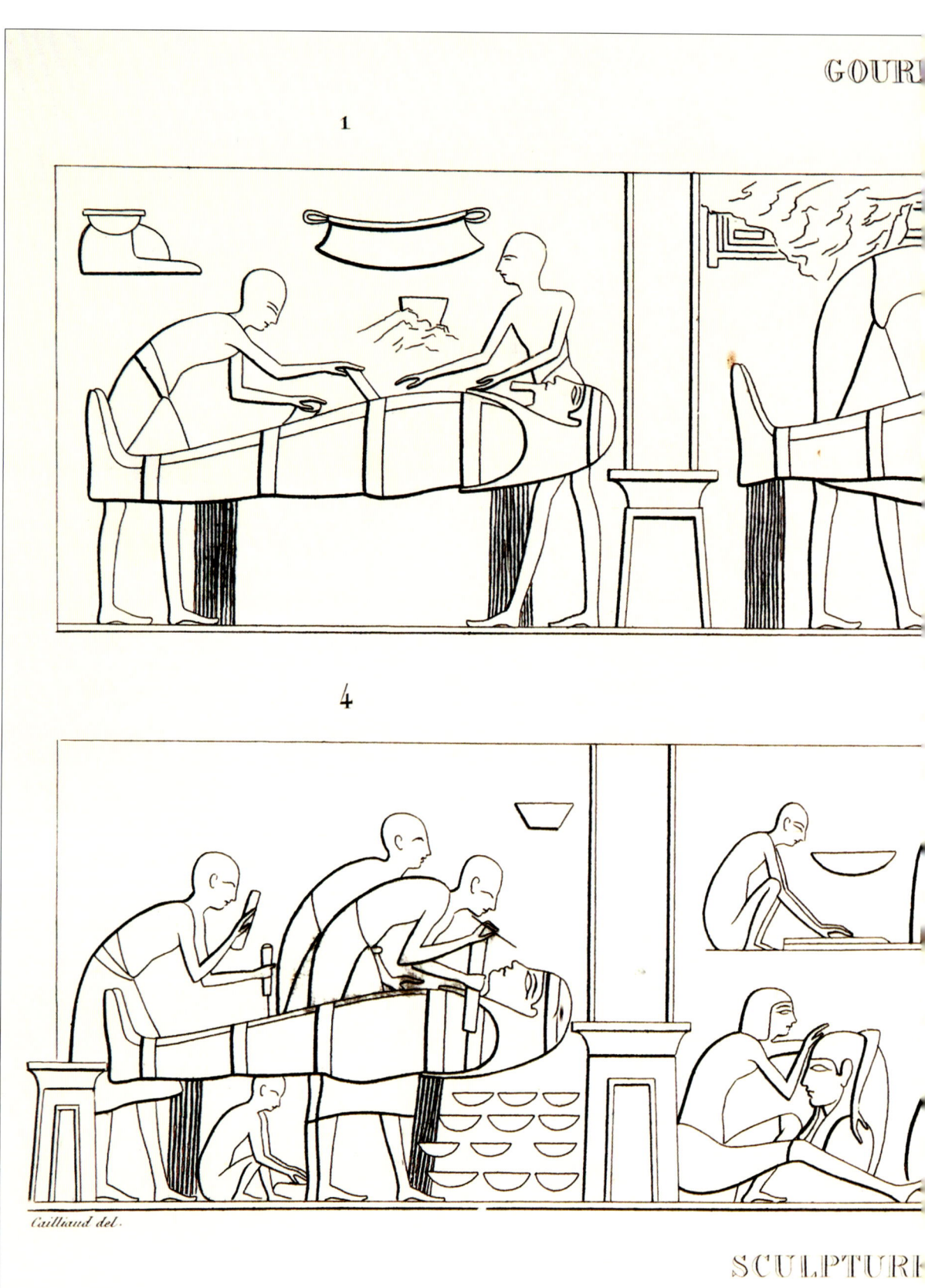

Plate 8. Making a sarcophagus and funerary equipment.

3

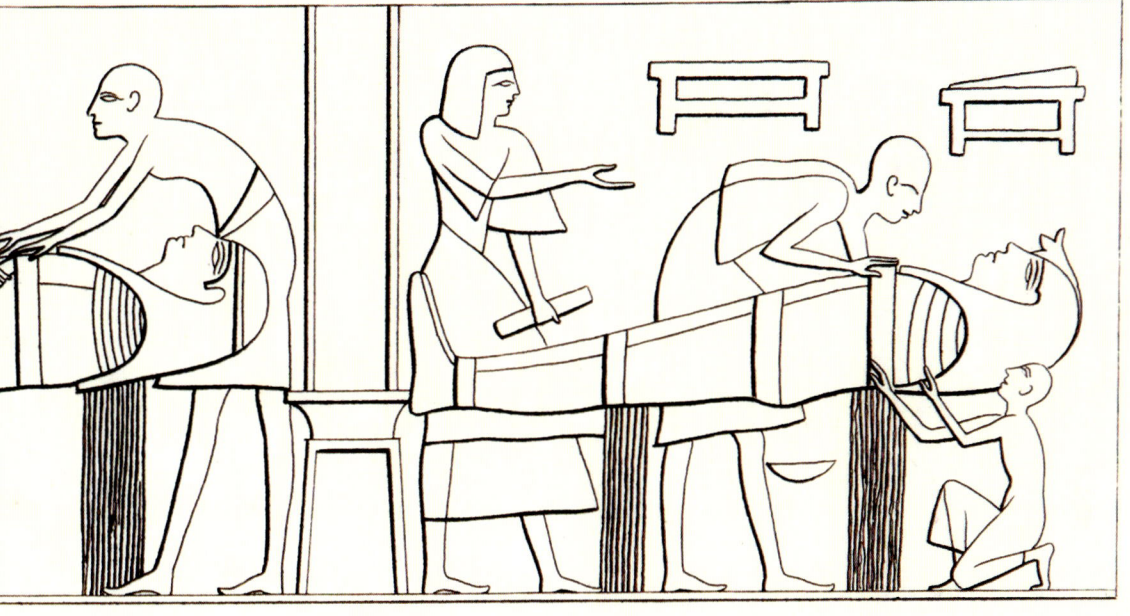

6

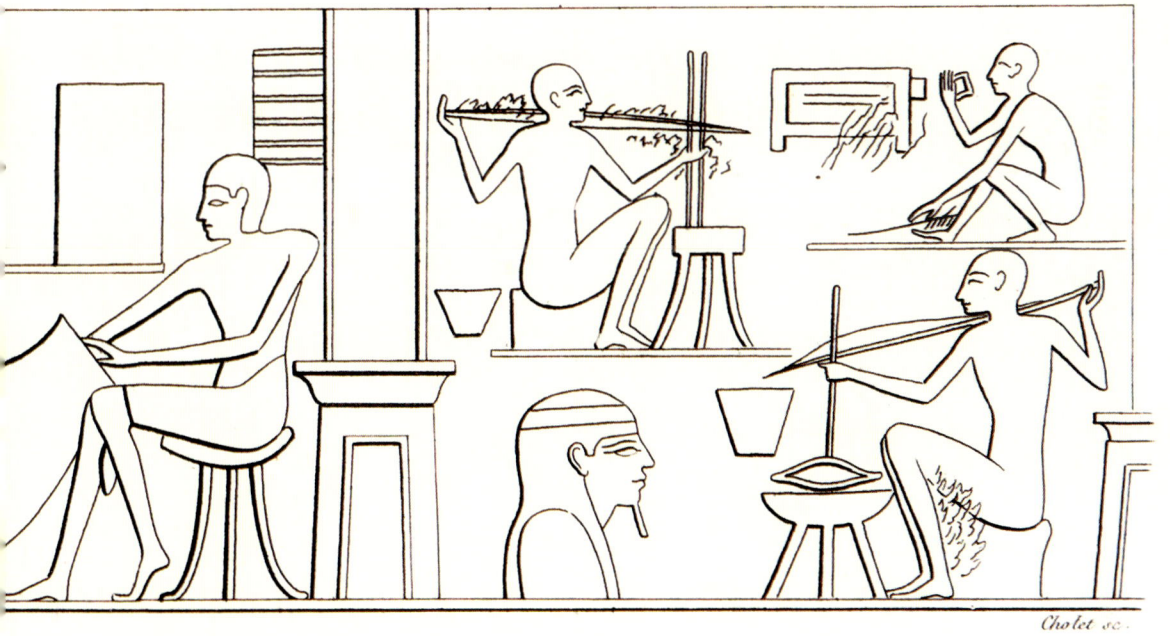

Cholet sc.

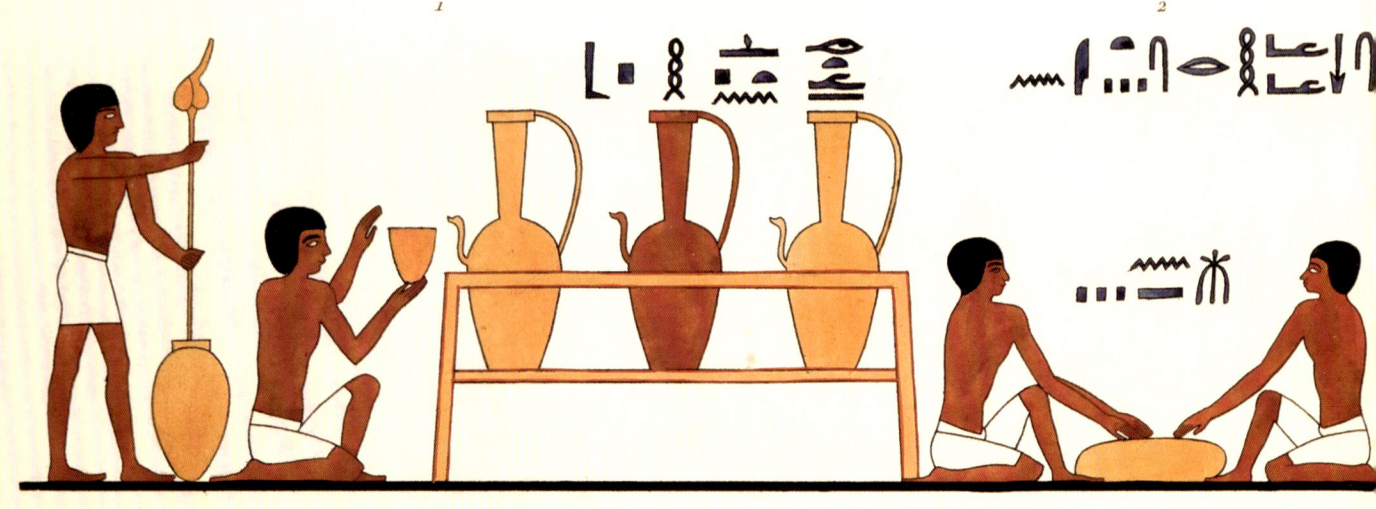

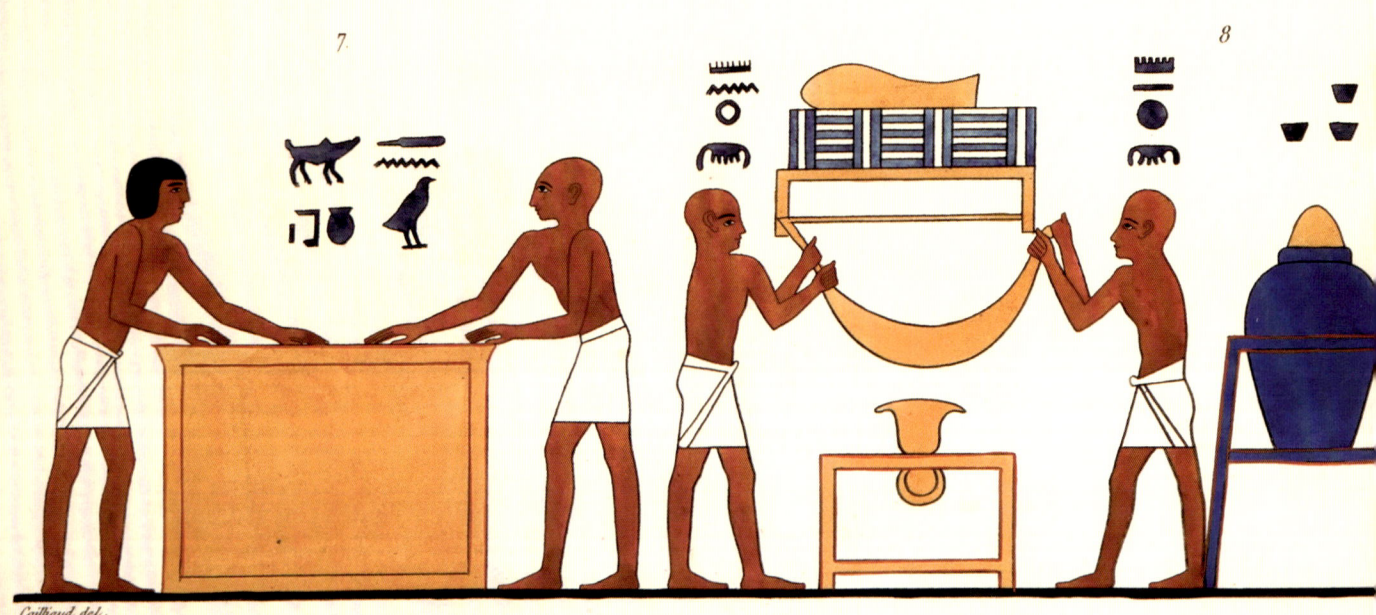

Plate 9. Woodworkers. Dyes. Perfumes.

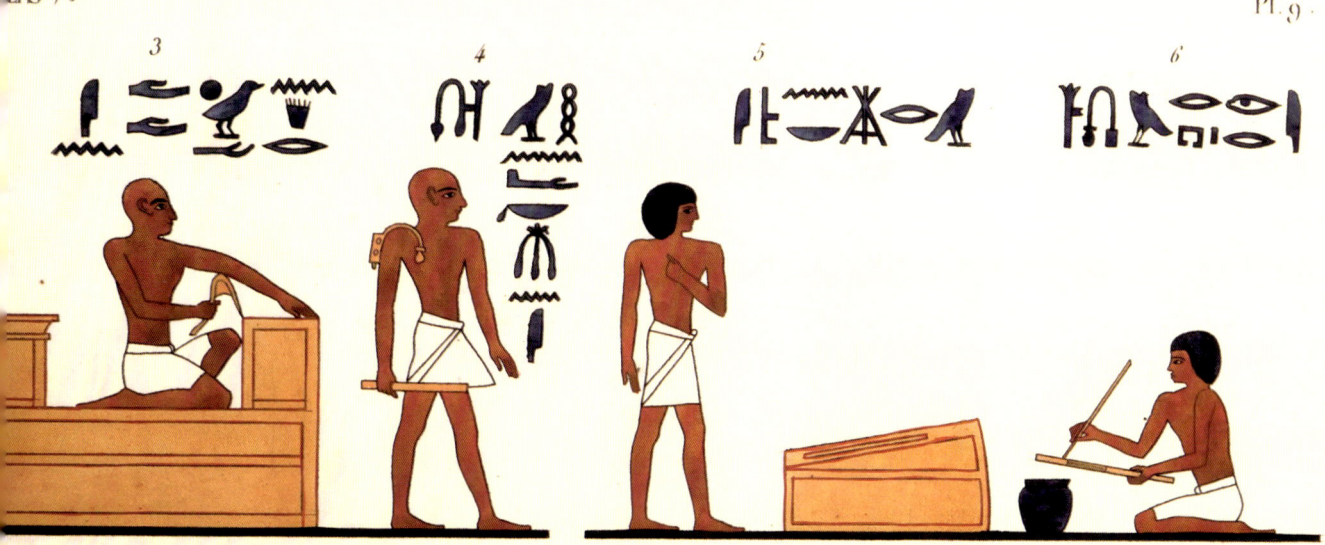

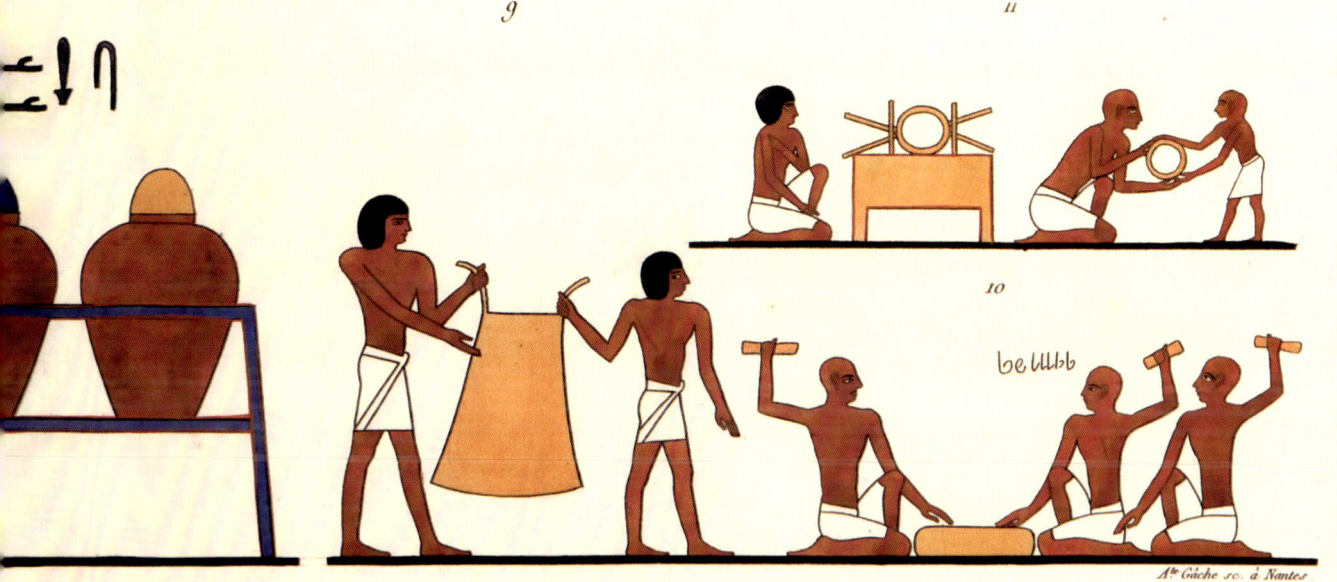

POGÉE.

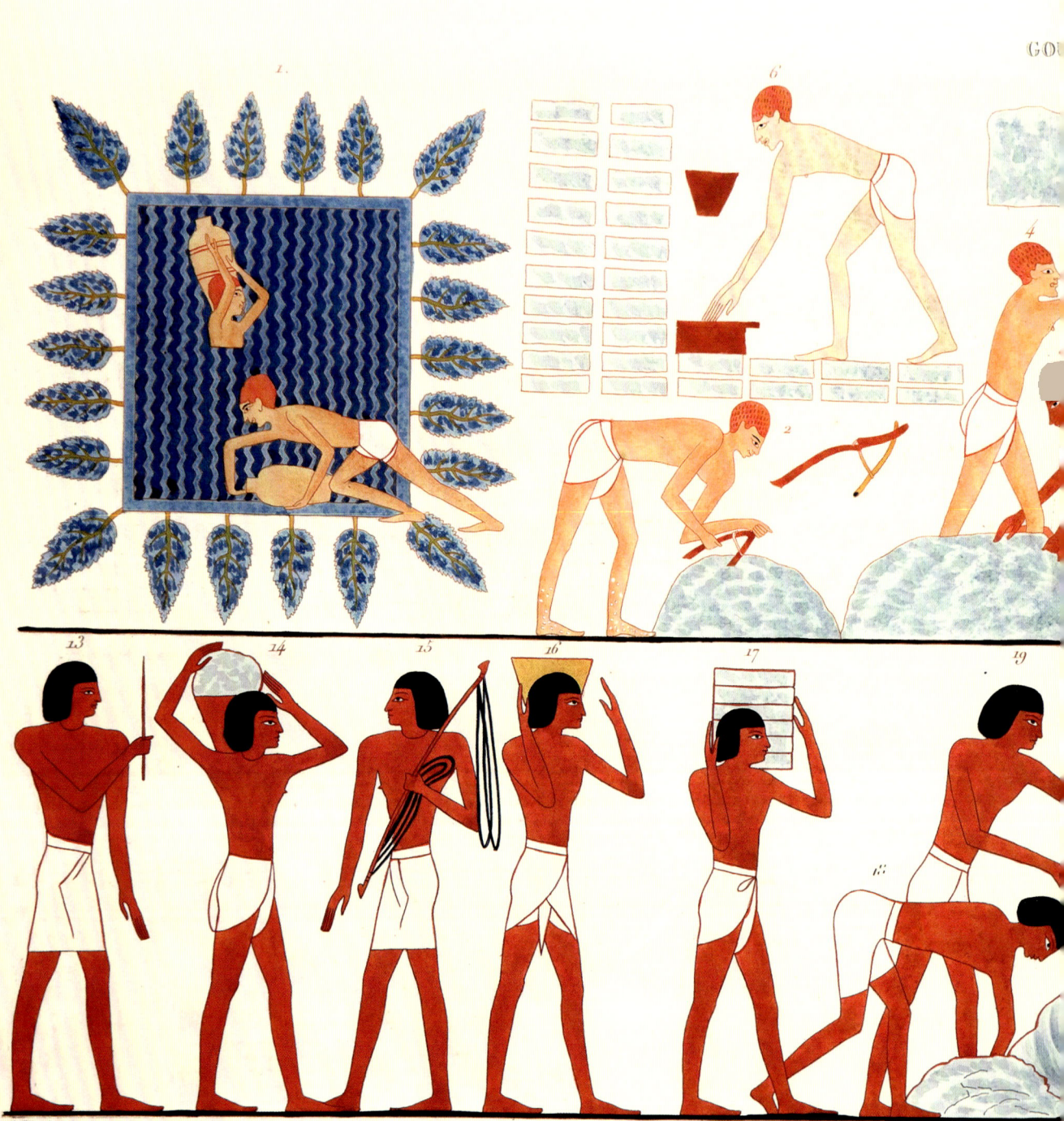

Plate 9A. Brickwork.

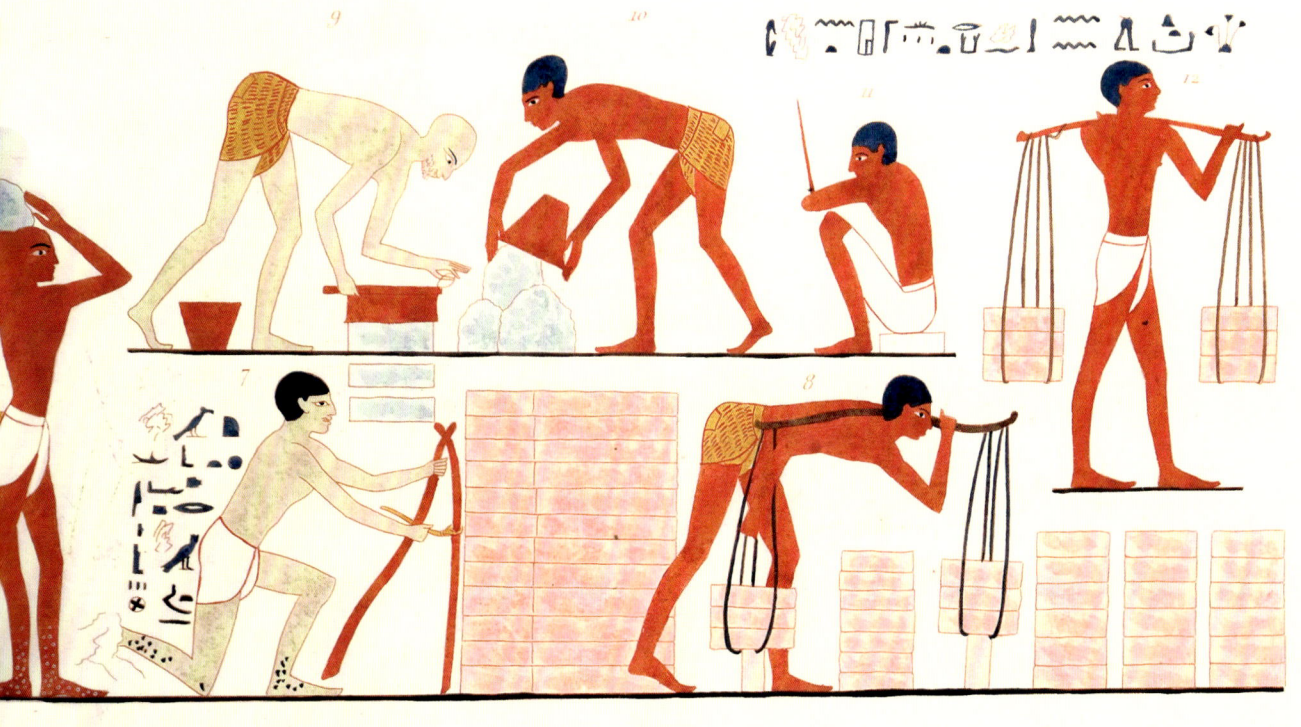

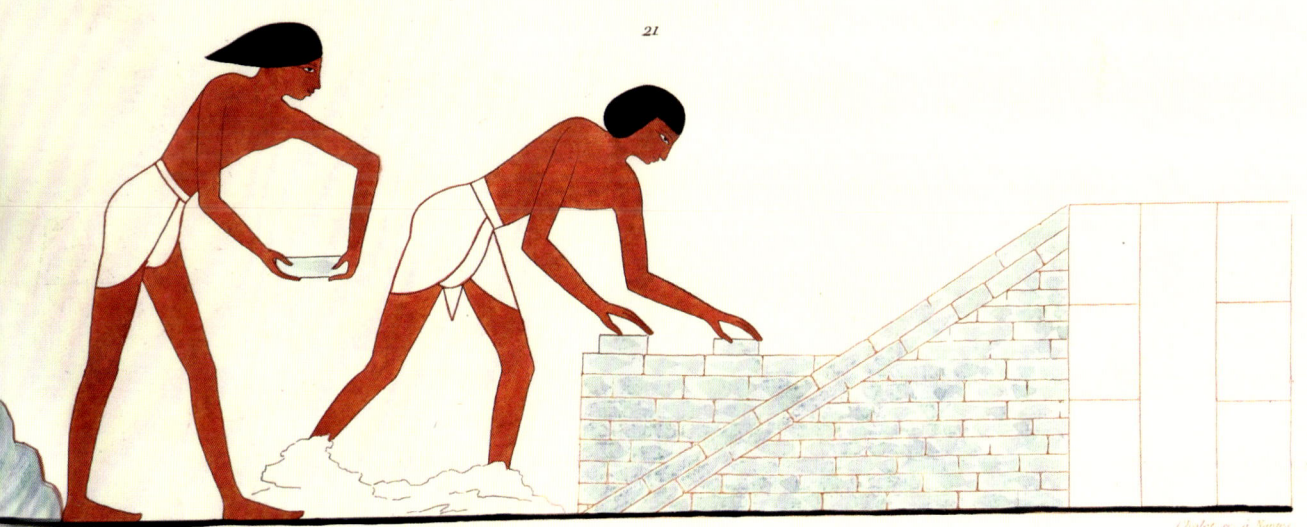

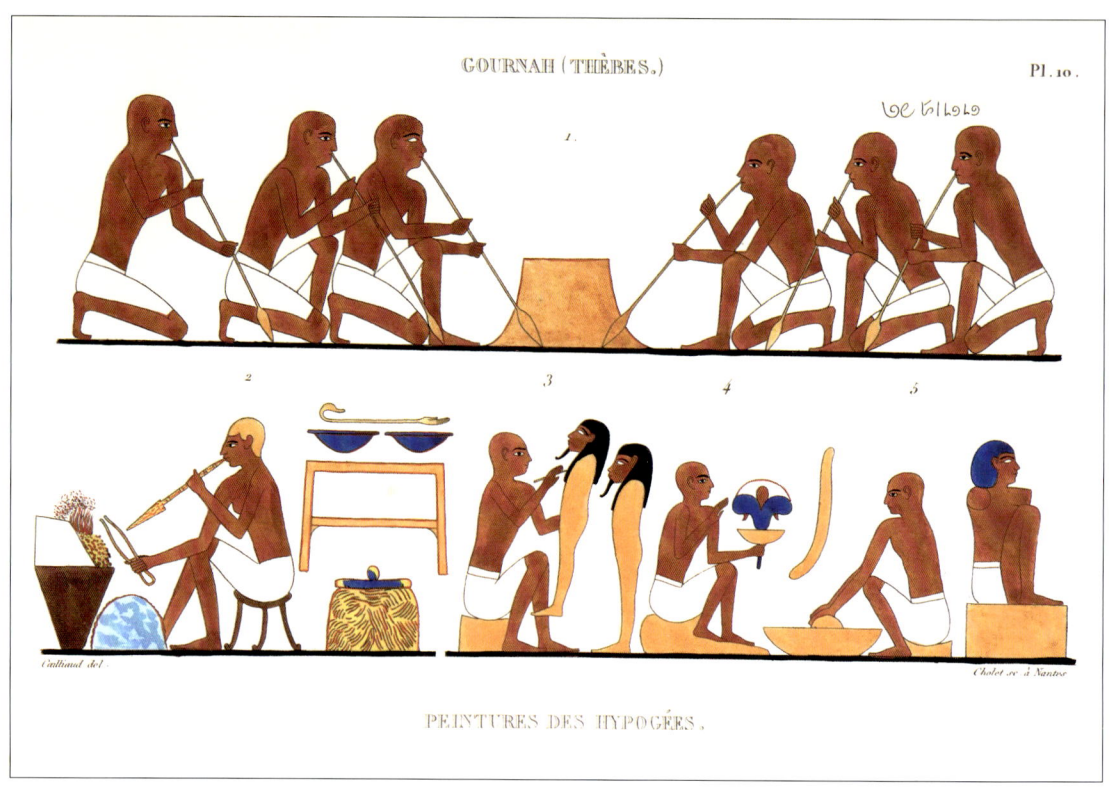

Plate 10. Glassblowing. *Shabti* sculptors. Gilders.

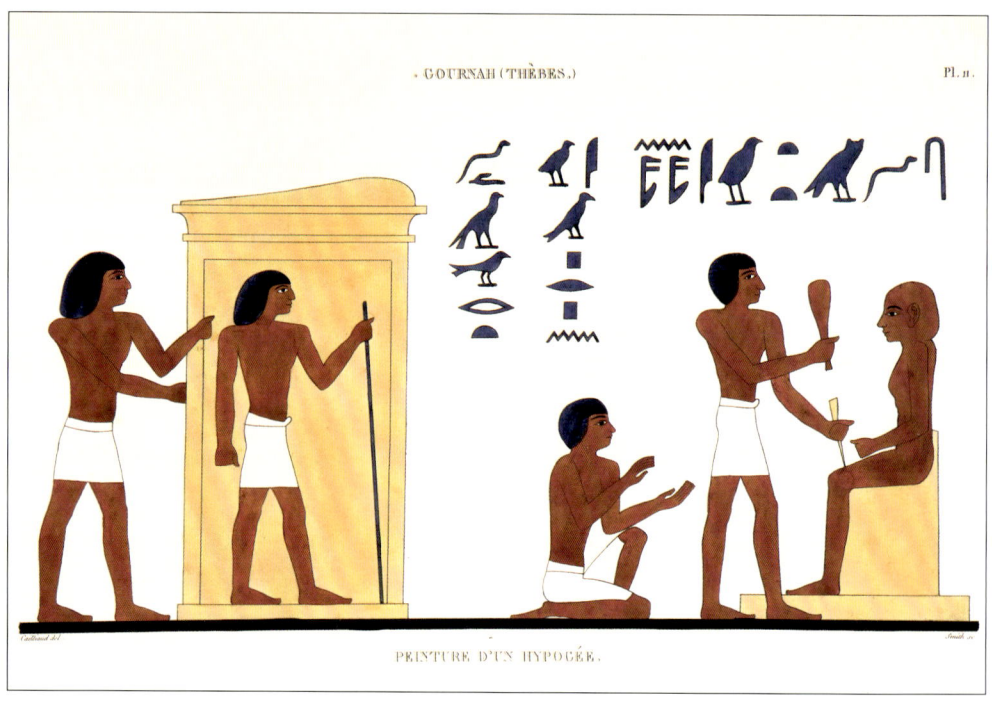

Plate 11. Sculptors.

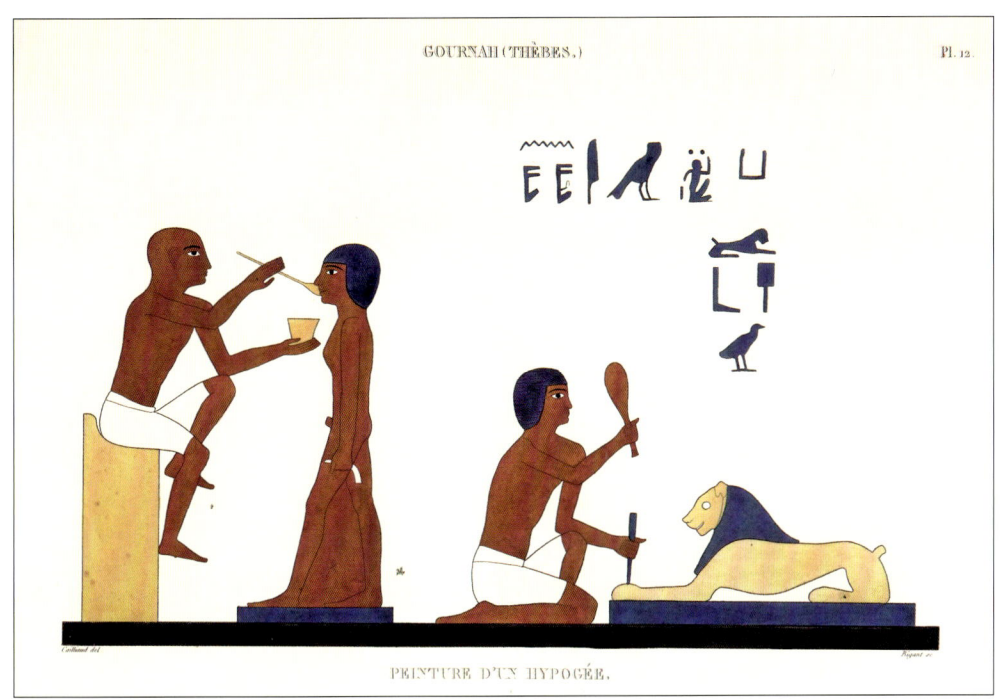

Plate 12. Painter and sculptor.

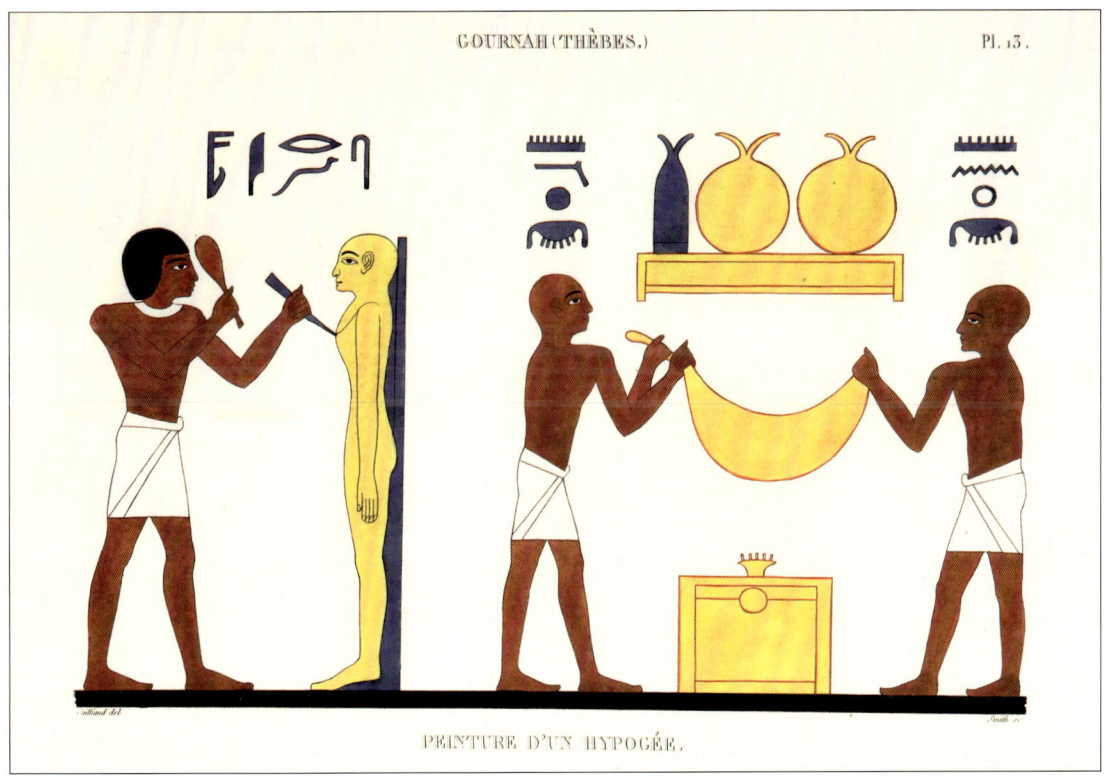

Plate 13. Sculptor and gilder.

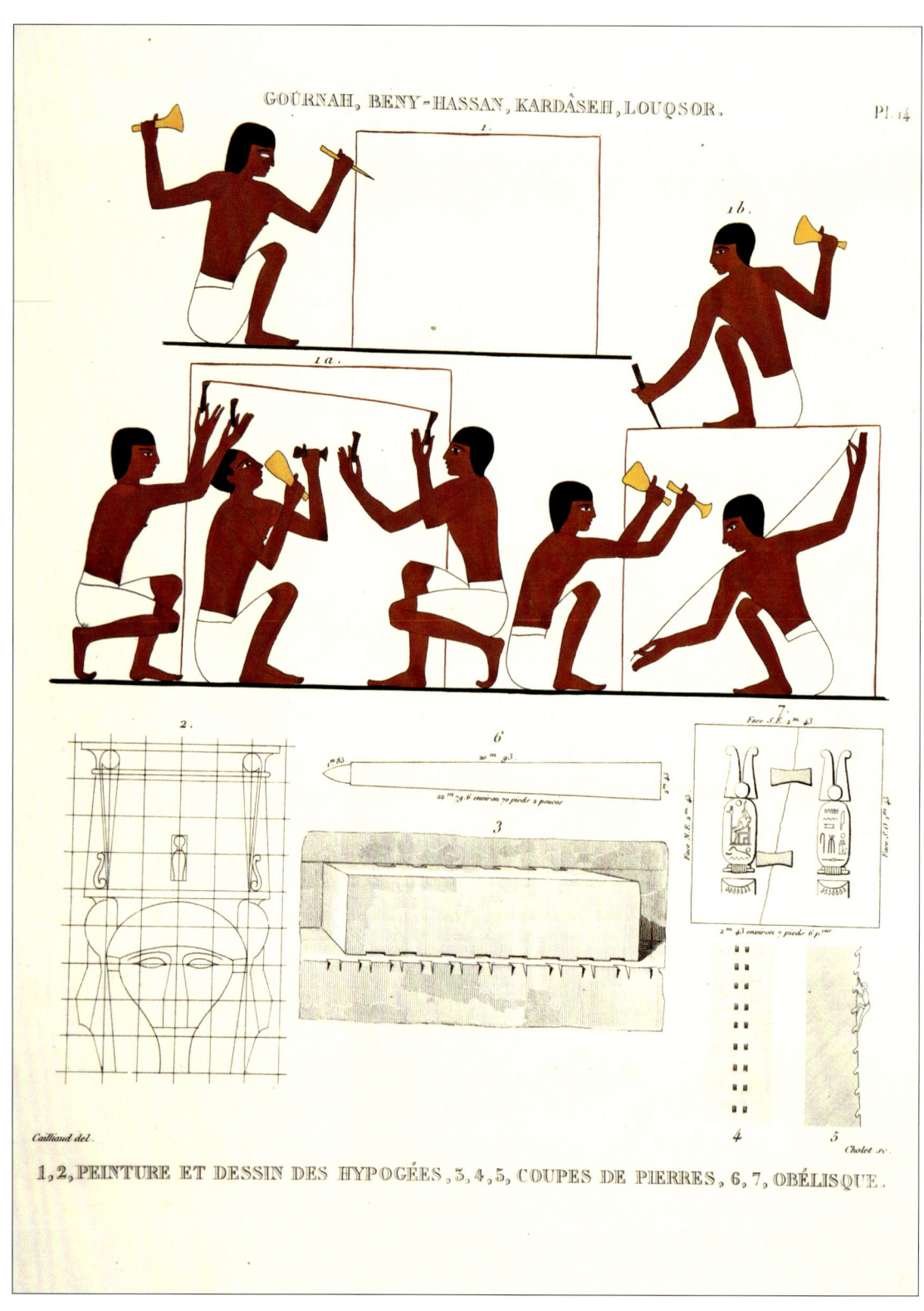

1, 2, PEINTURE ET DESSIN DES HYPOGÉES, 3, 4, 5, COUPES DE PIERRES, 6, 7, OBÉLISQUE.

Plate 14. Hewing a block of stone. Sketch of a Hathor capital. Cut stone. Obelisk and cartouche of Ramesses II.
Opposite: Plate 15. Sculpting a colossal statue.

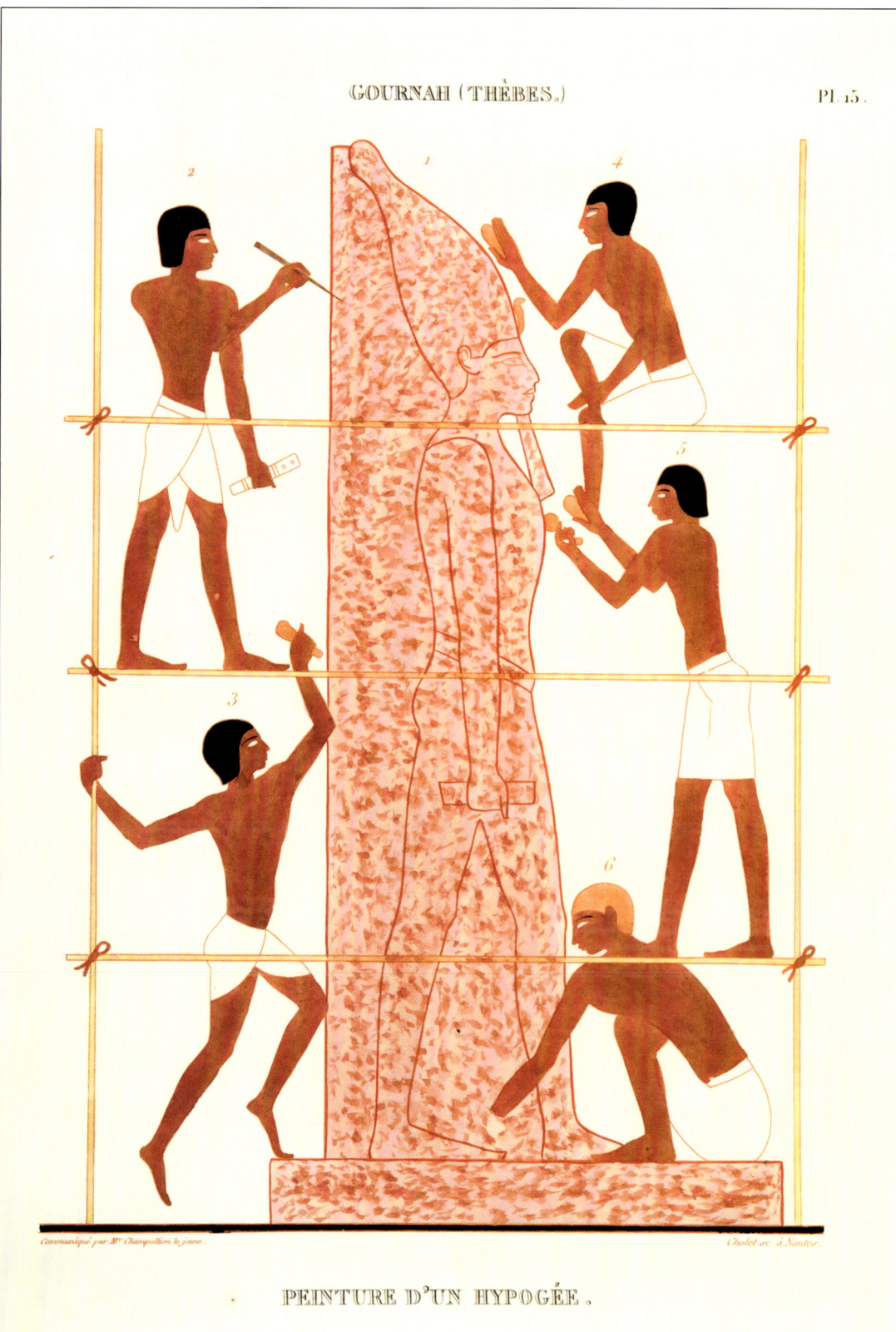

PEINTURE D'UN HYPOGÉE.

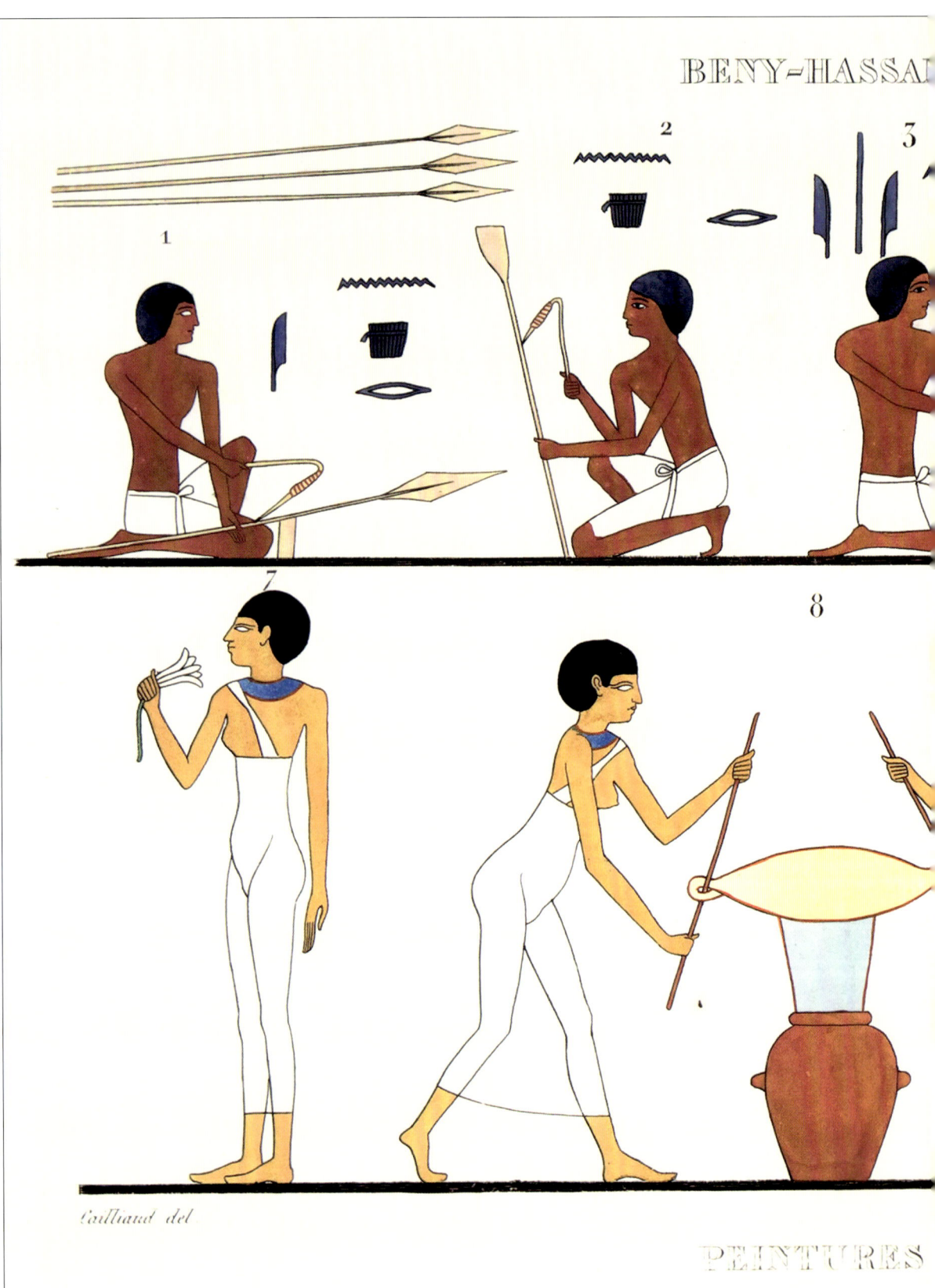

Plate 15A. Weapons (bows and arrows) and perfume making.

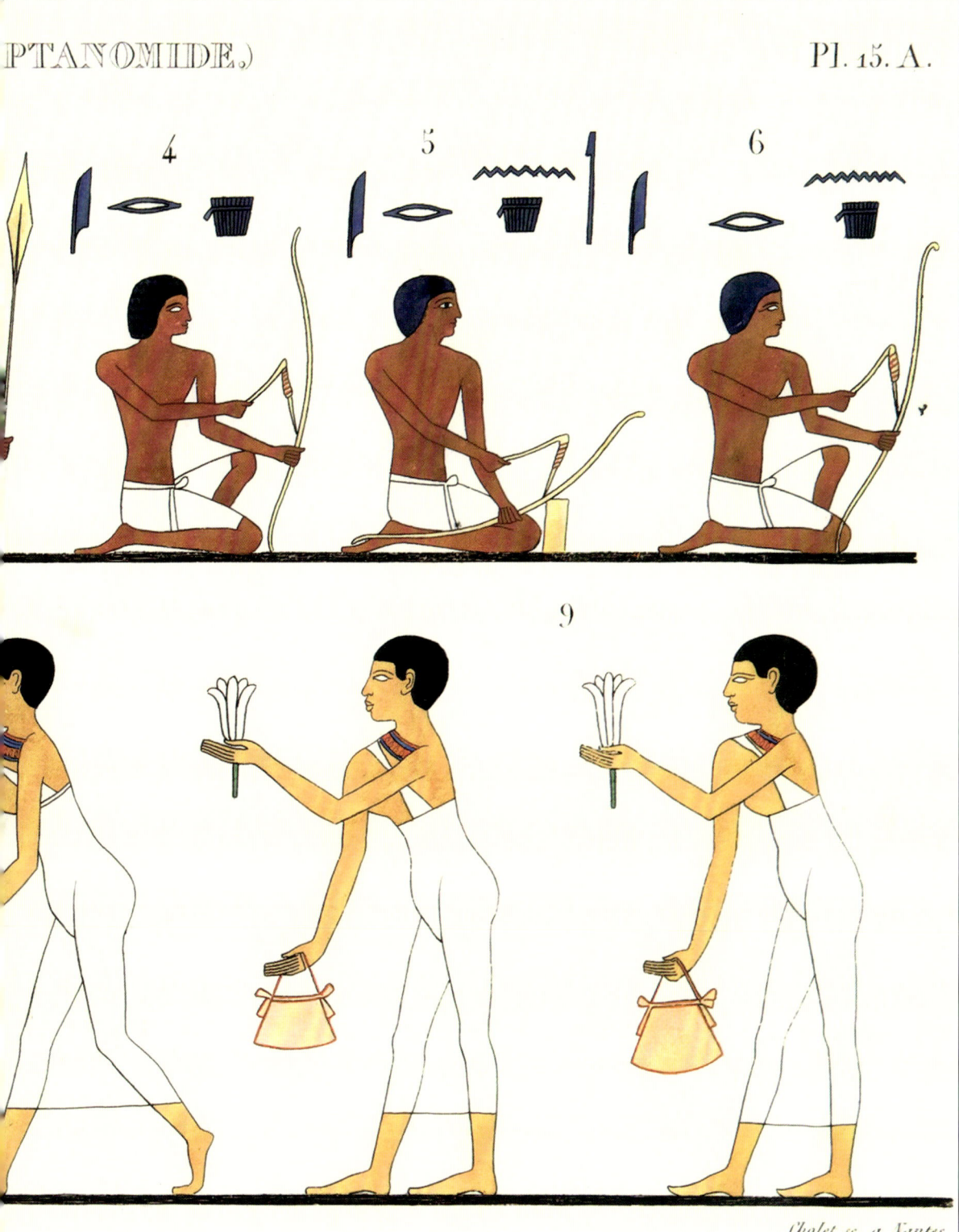

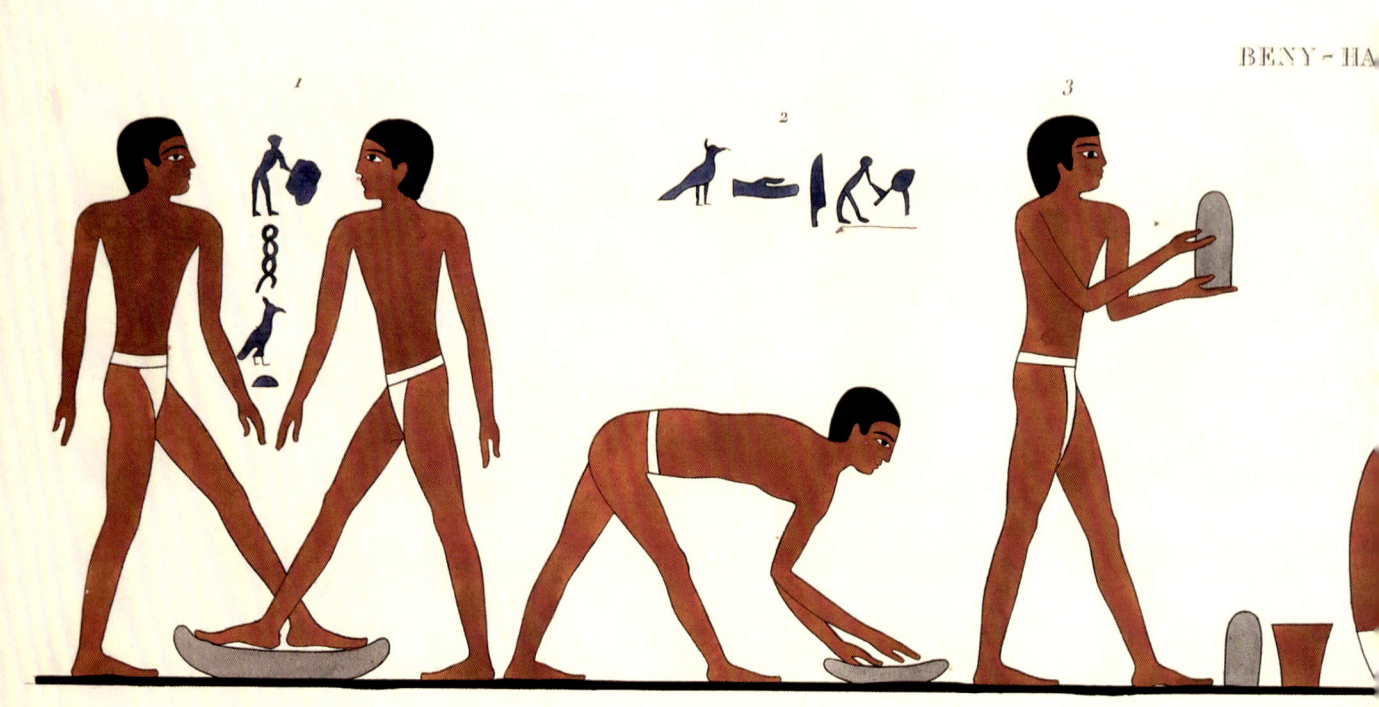

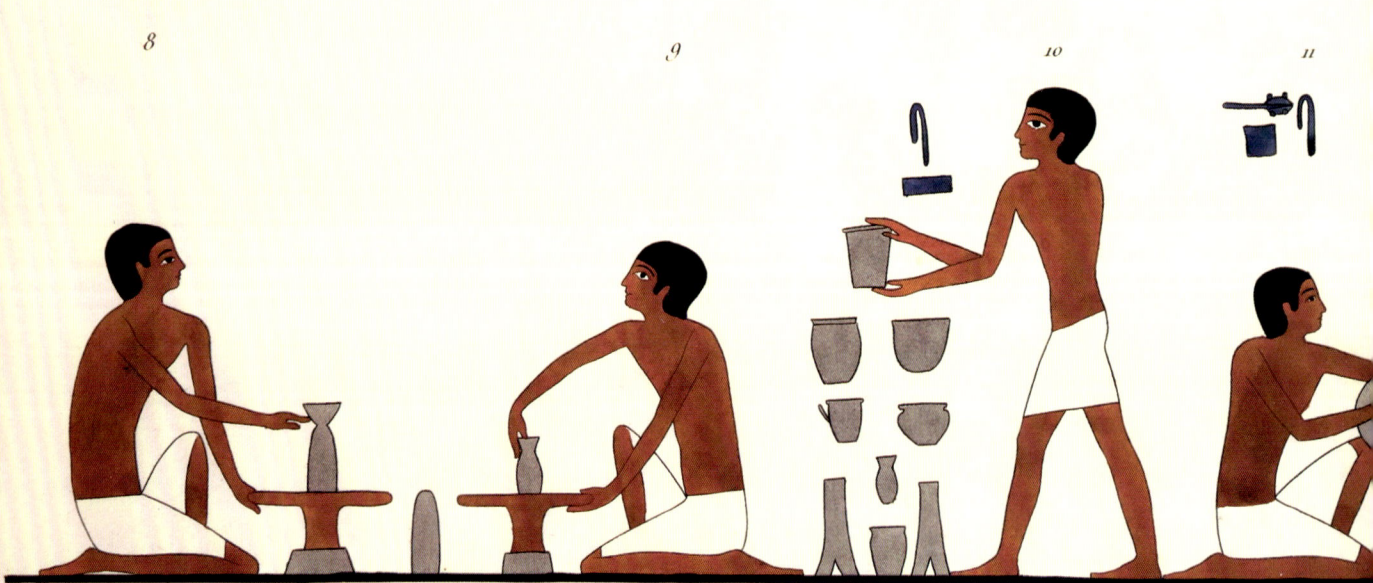

Plate 16. Pottery making.

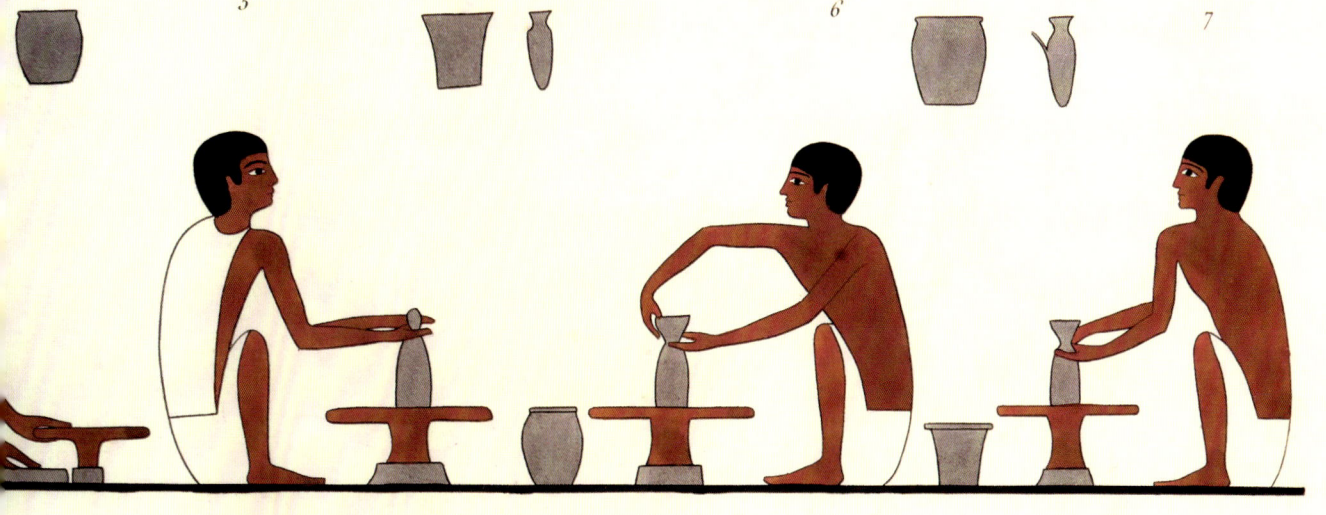

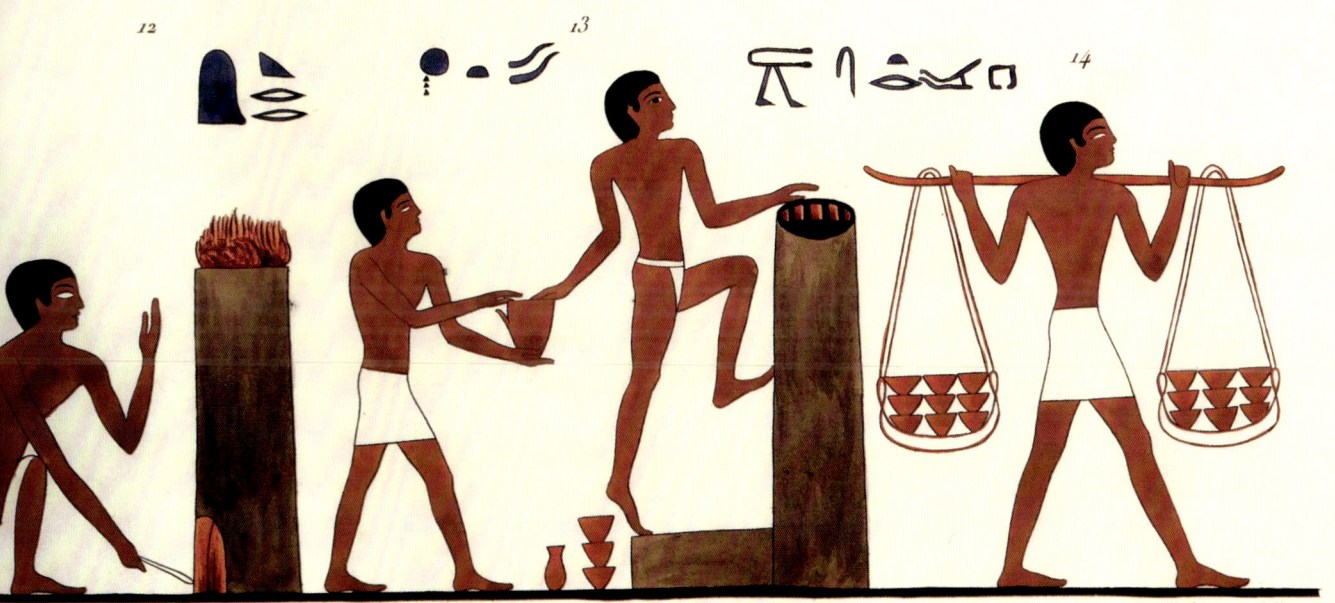

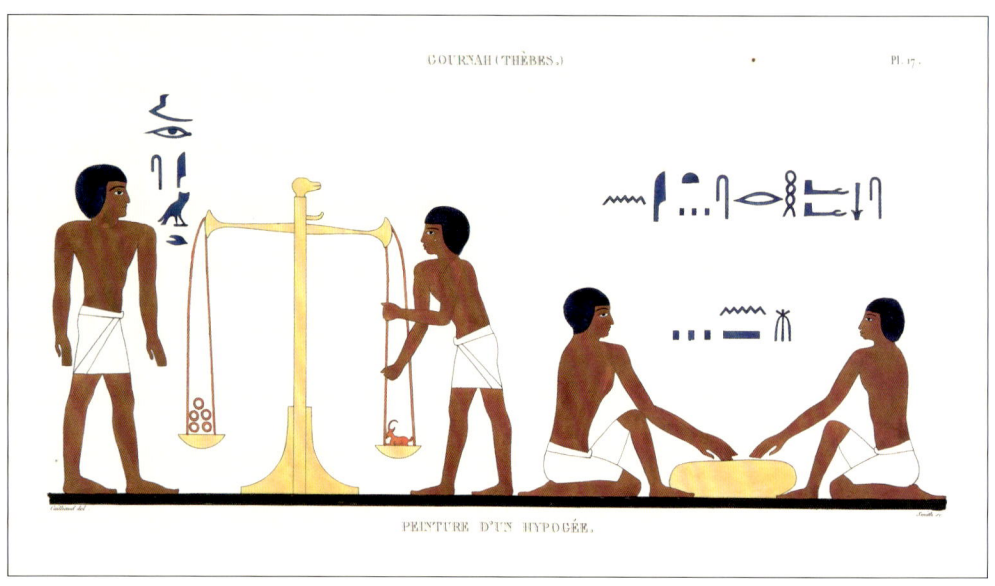

Plate 17. Weighing jewelry. Polishing.

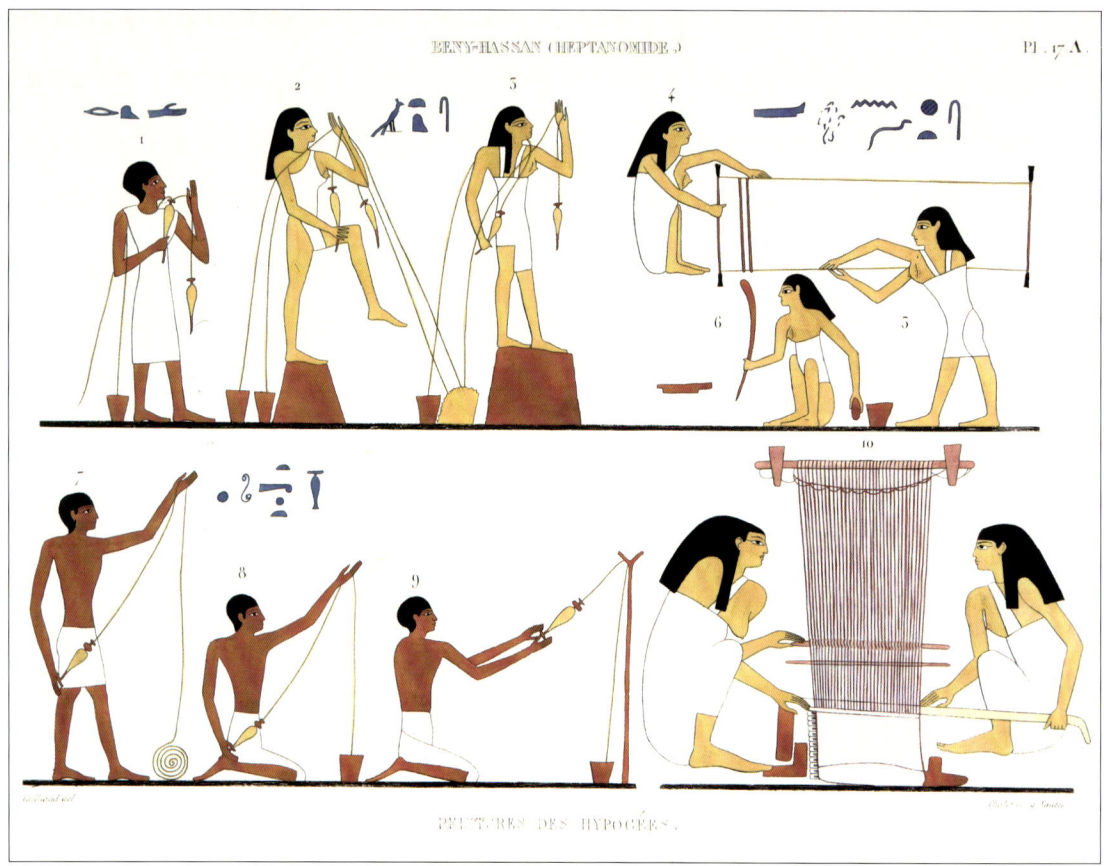

Plate 17A. Spinners and weavers.

194

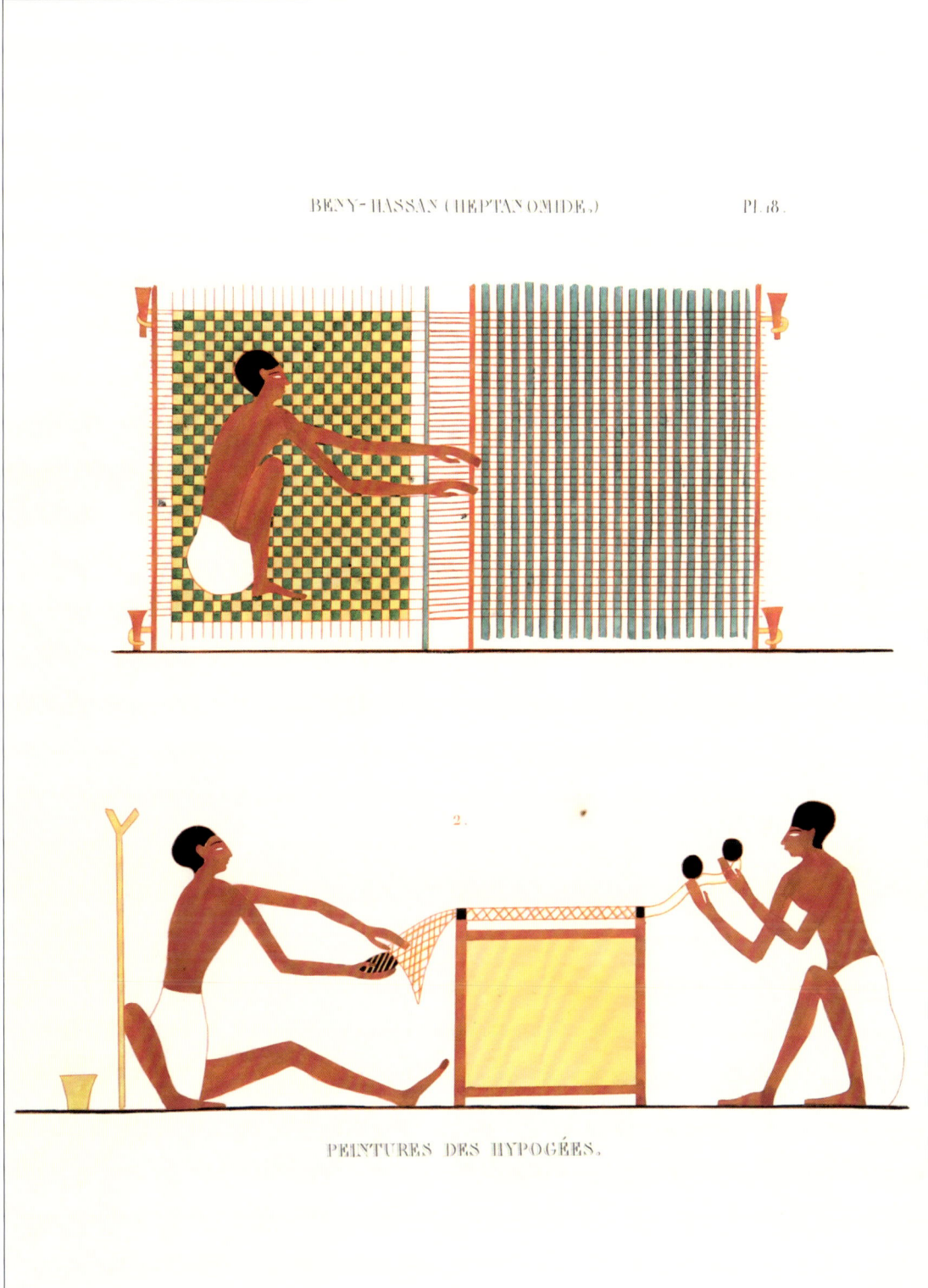

PEINTURES DES HYPOGÉES.

Plate 18. Weaving.

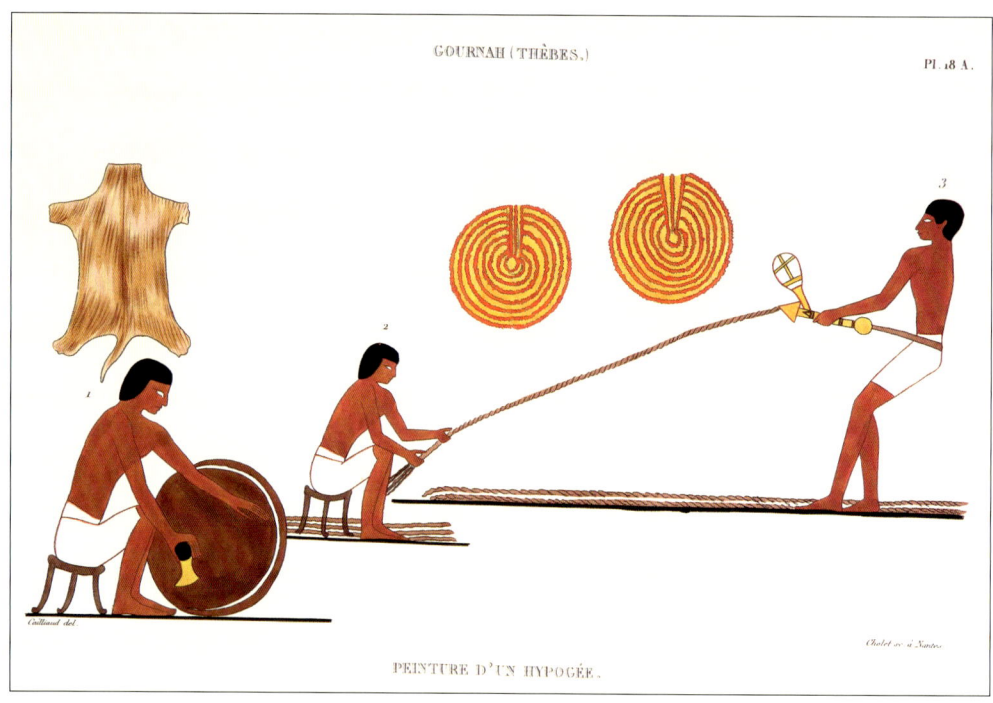

Plate 18A. Rope makers and tanners.

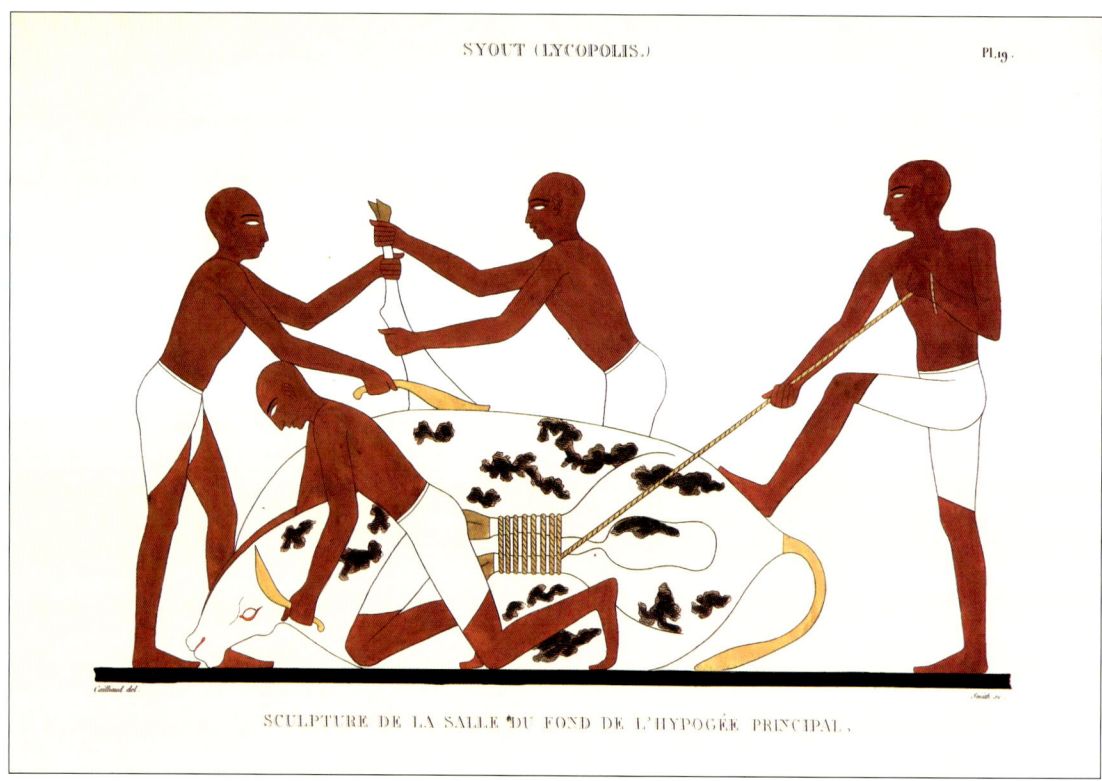

Plate 19. Quartering an ox.

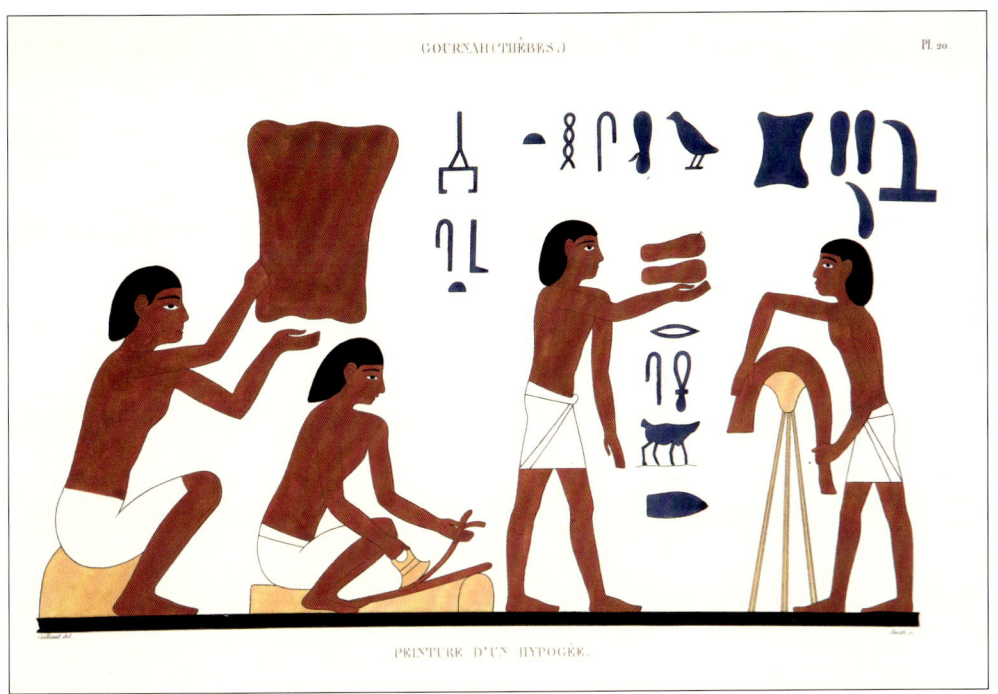

Plate 20. Leather preparation.

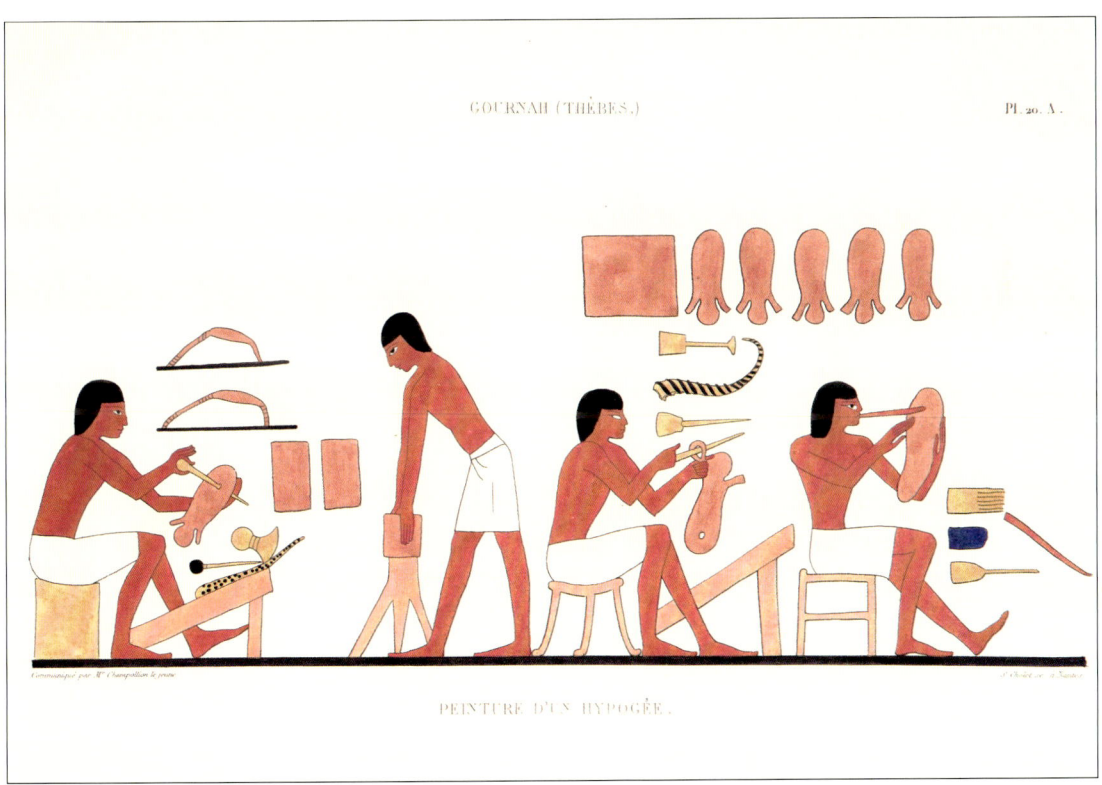

Plate 20A. Sandal making.

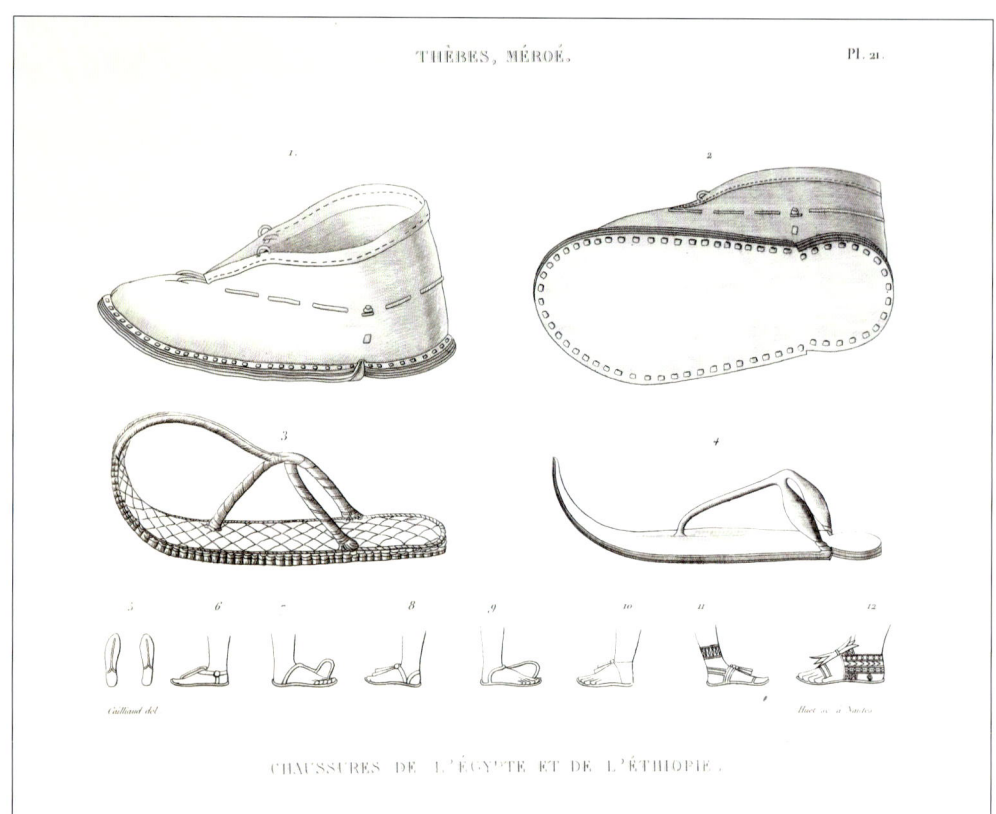

Plate 21. Examples of shoes from Egypt and Nubia.

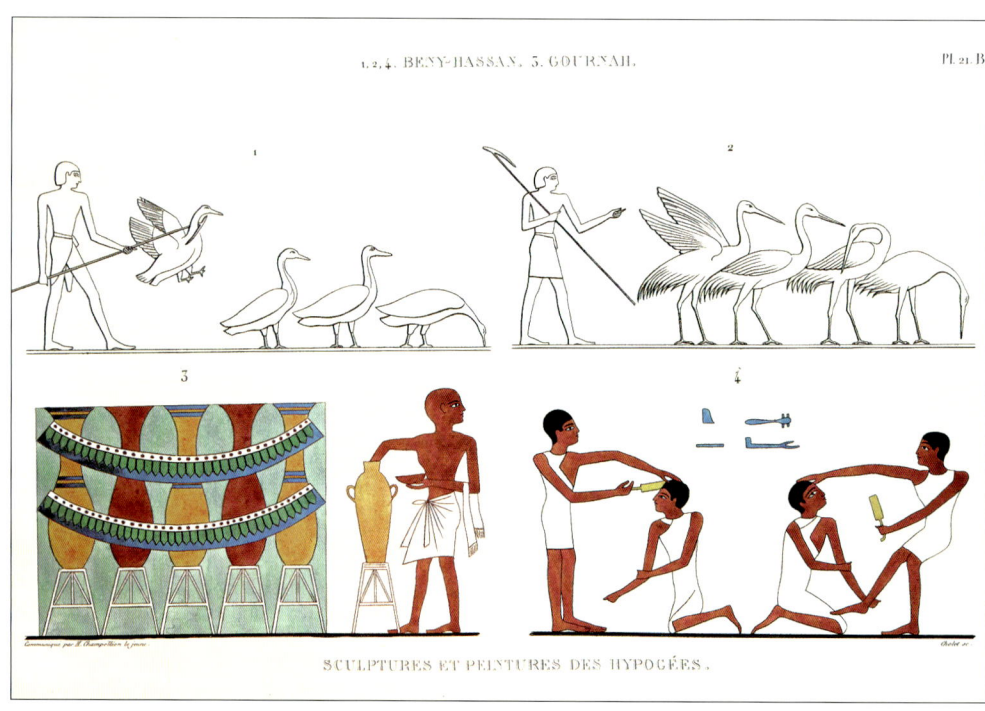

Plate 21B. Geese herders. Amphorae. Barbers.

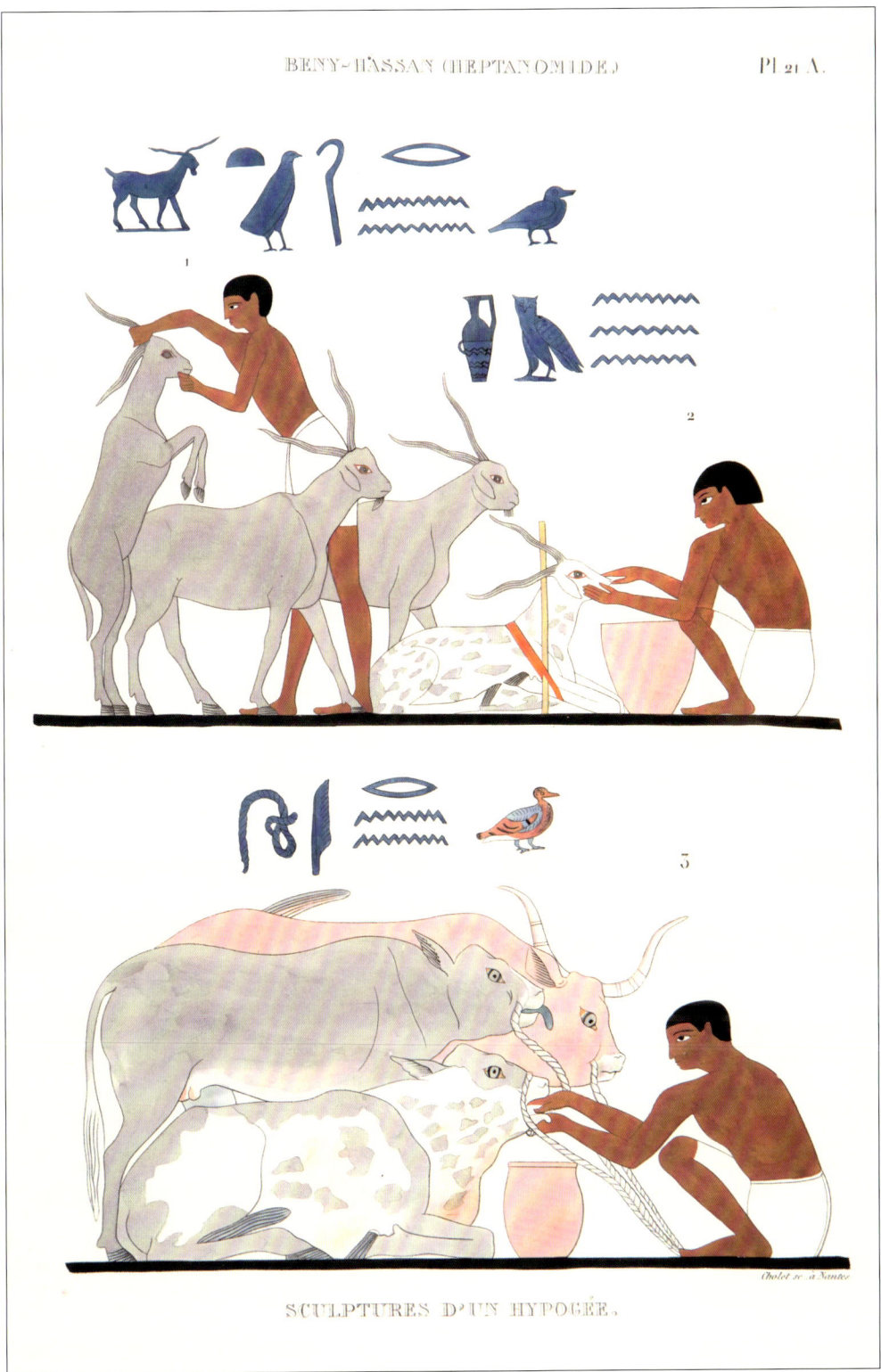

SCULPTURES D'UN HYPOGÉE.

Plate 21A. Care of antelopes and calves.

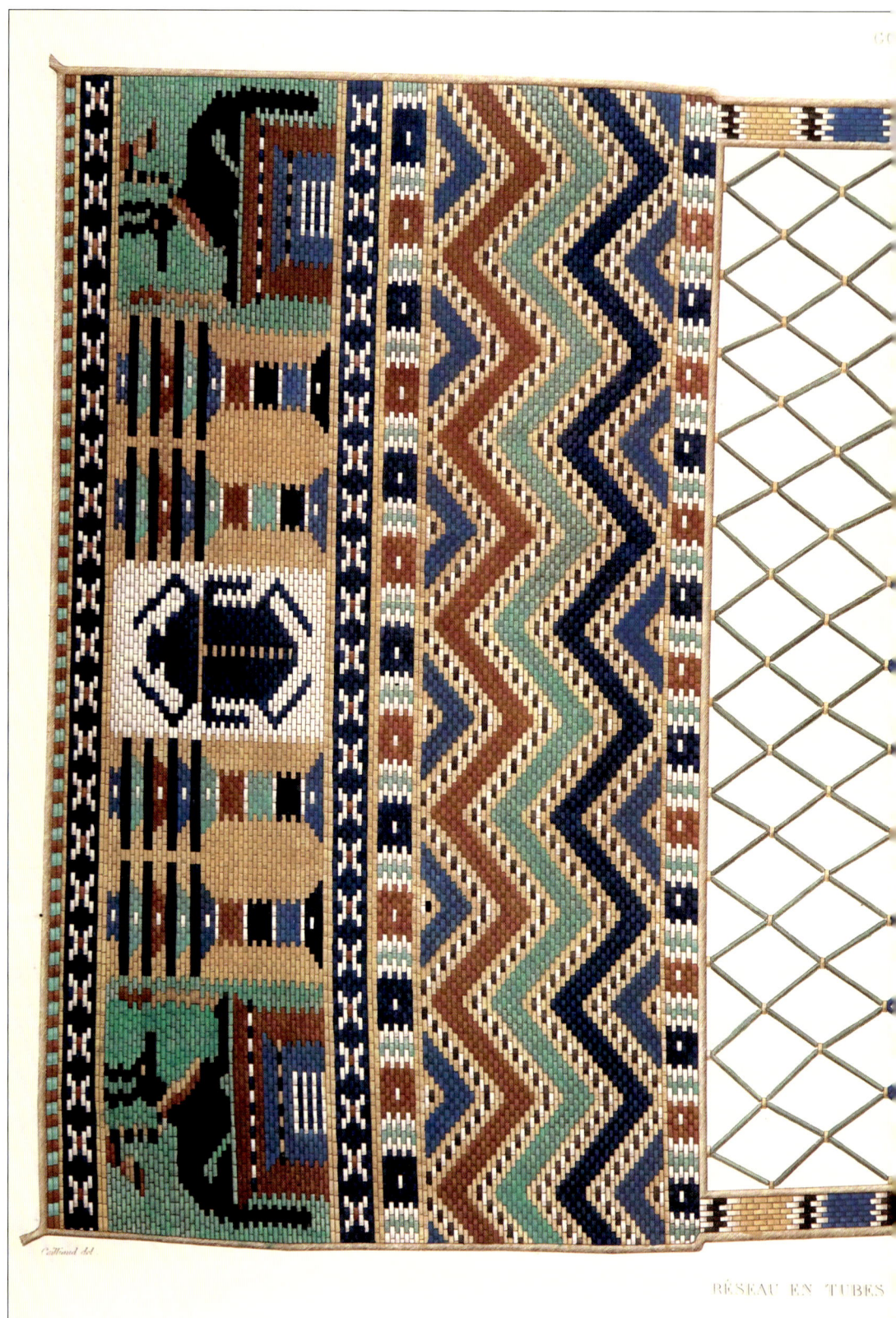

RÉSEAU EN TUBES

Plate 22. Beaded mummy cover.

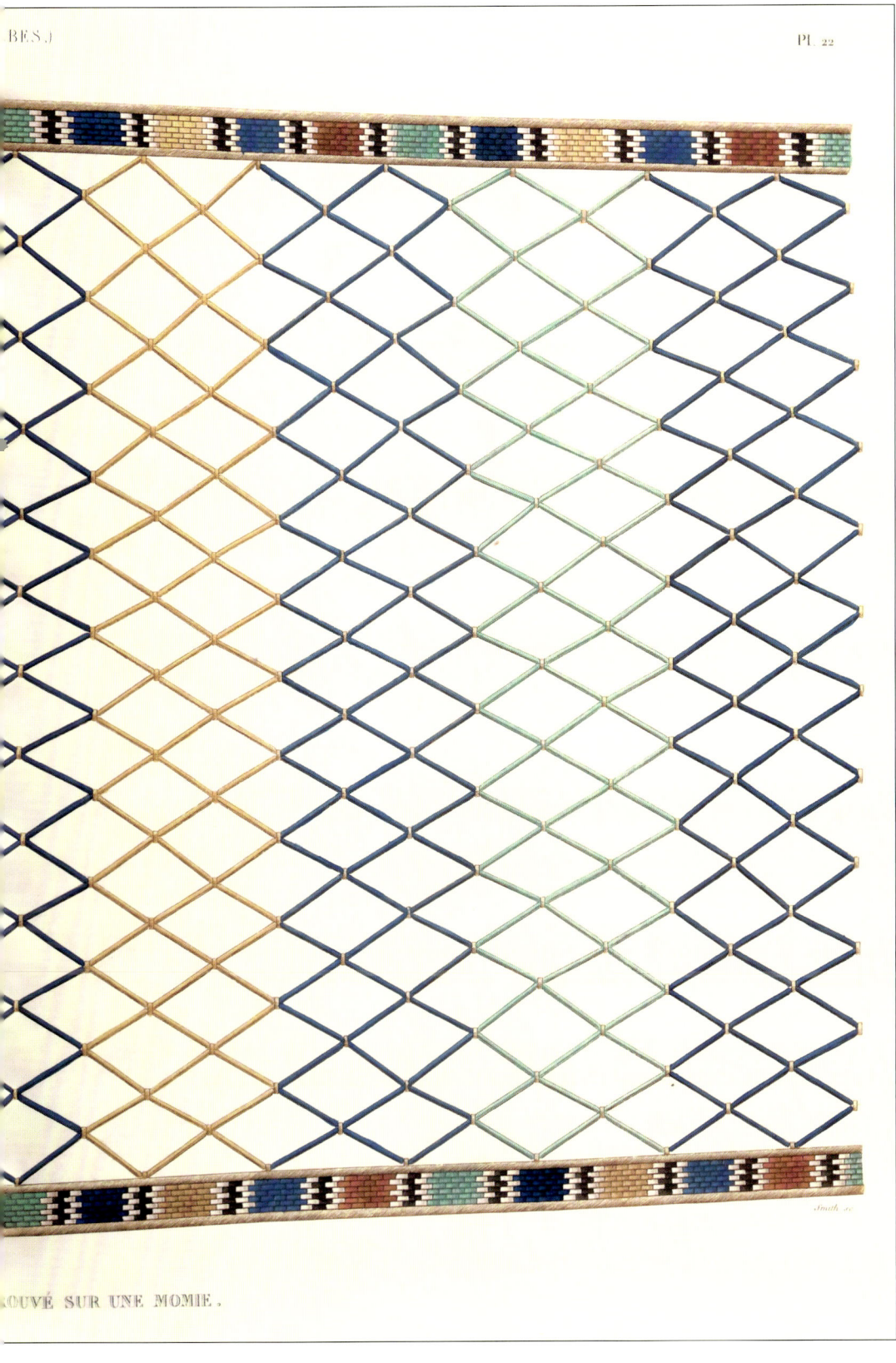

Smith sc.

OUVÉ SUR UNE MOMIE.

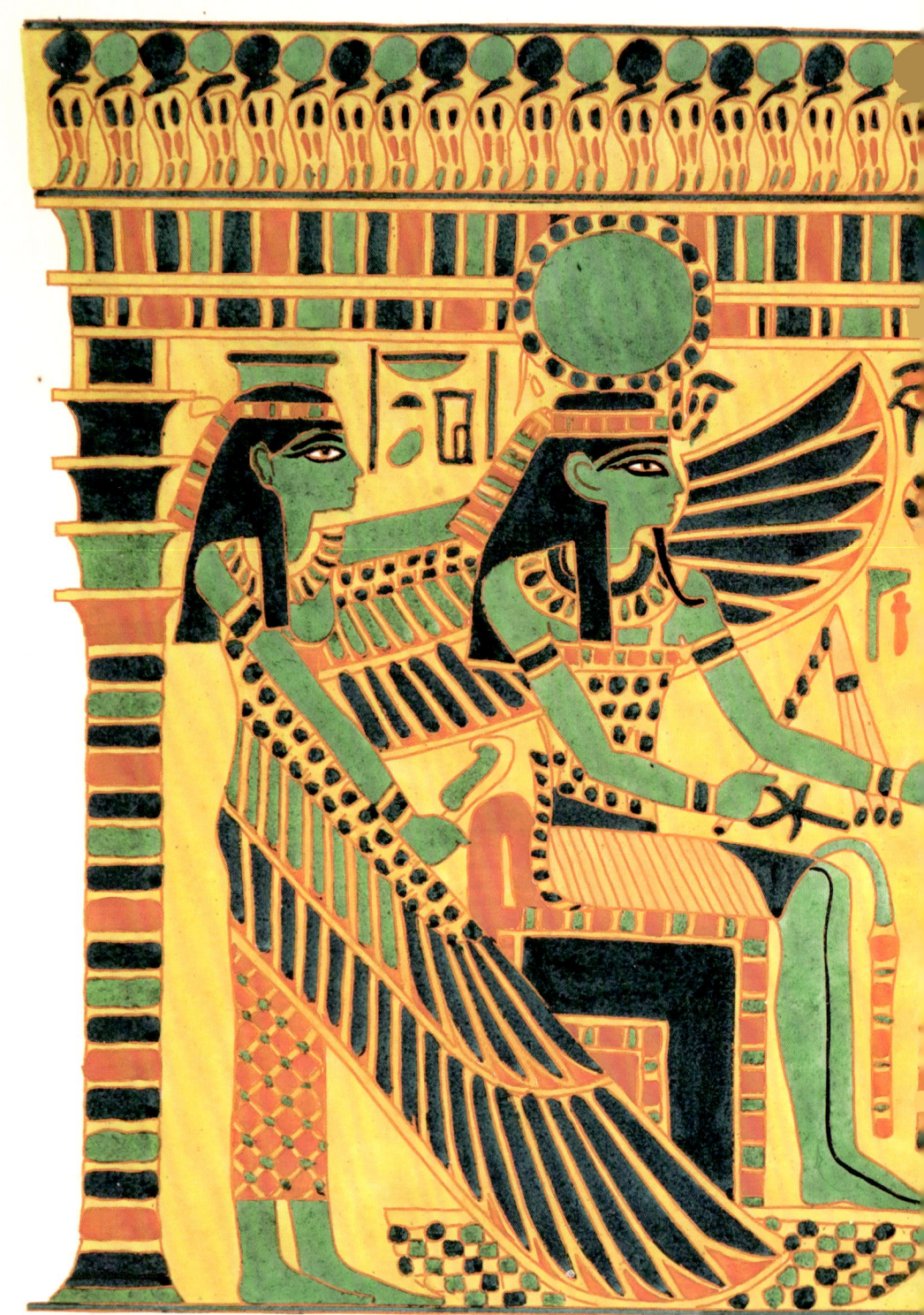

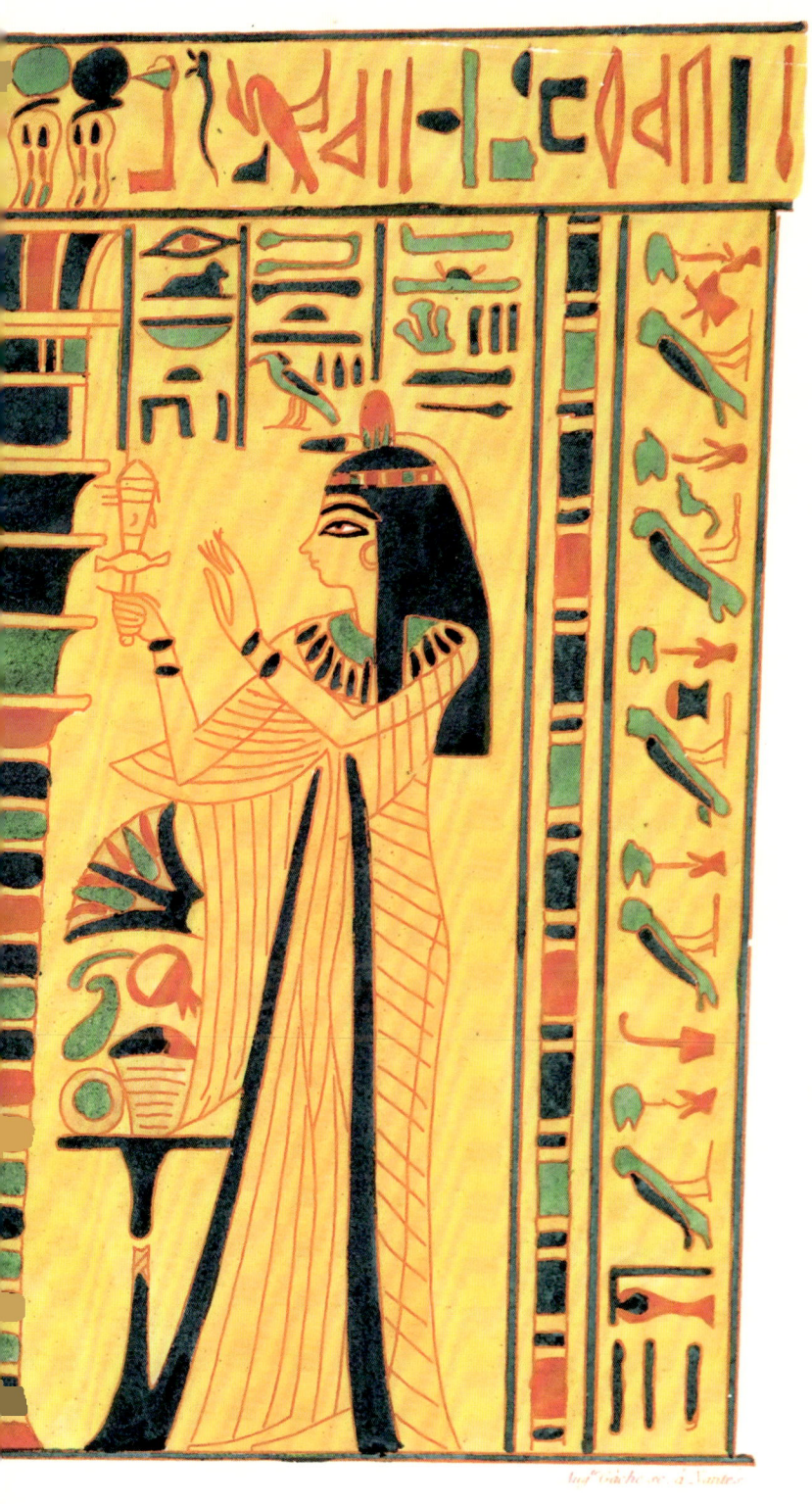

Plate 23. Figures painted on a mummy case.

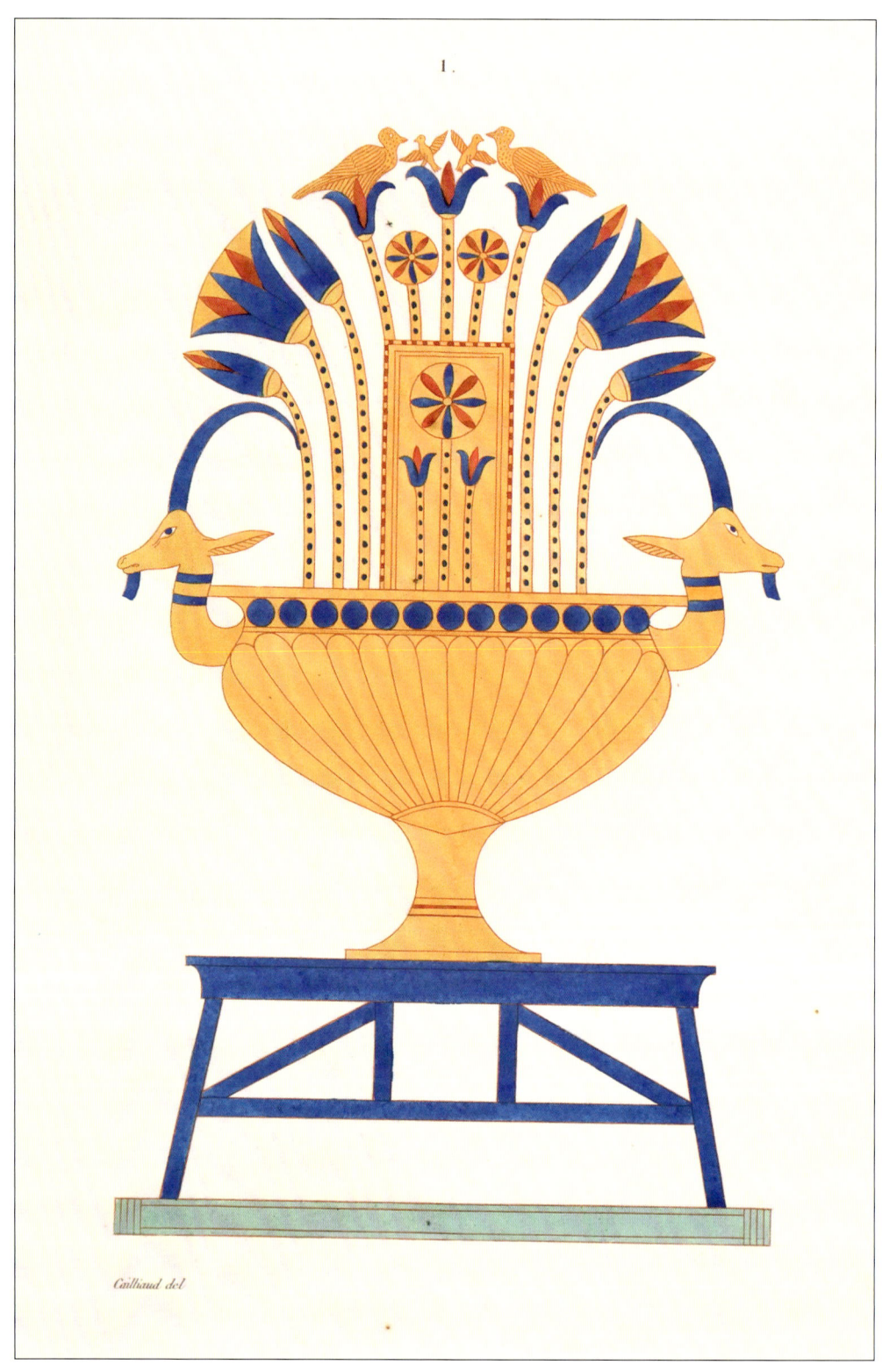

I.

Caillaud del

Plate 24. Ornate vases.

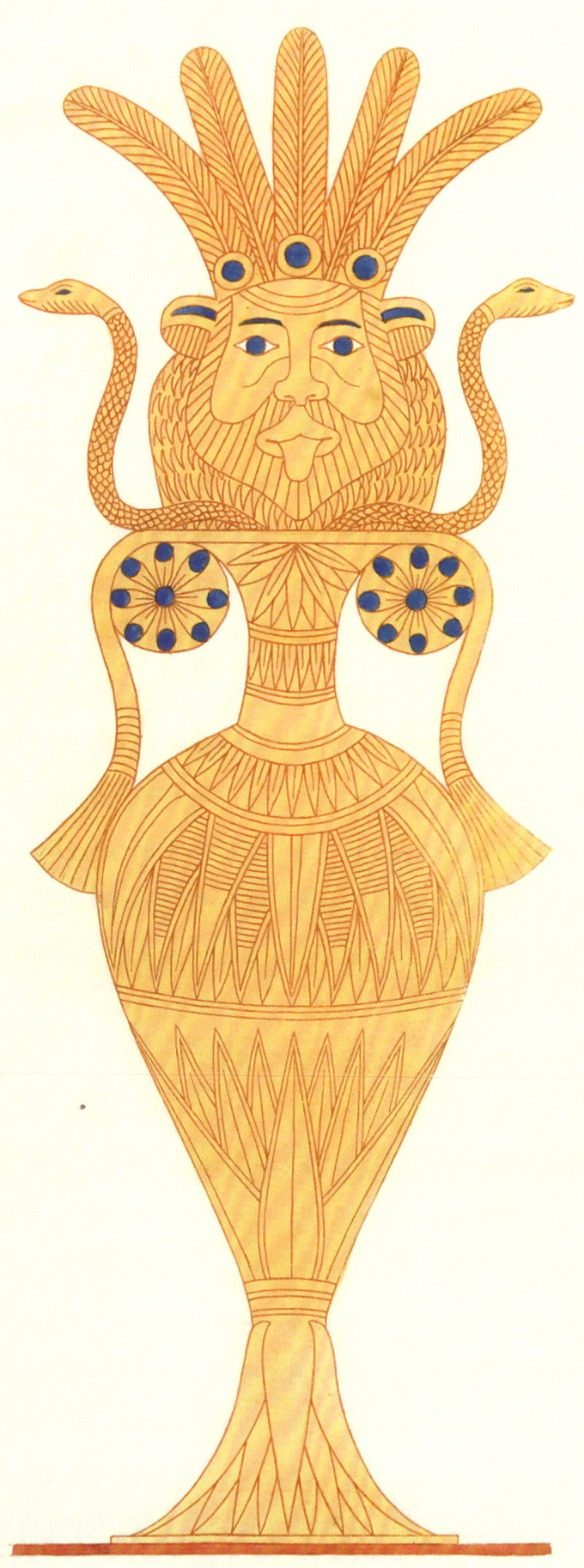

Garche sc. à Nantes.

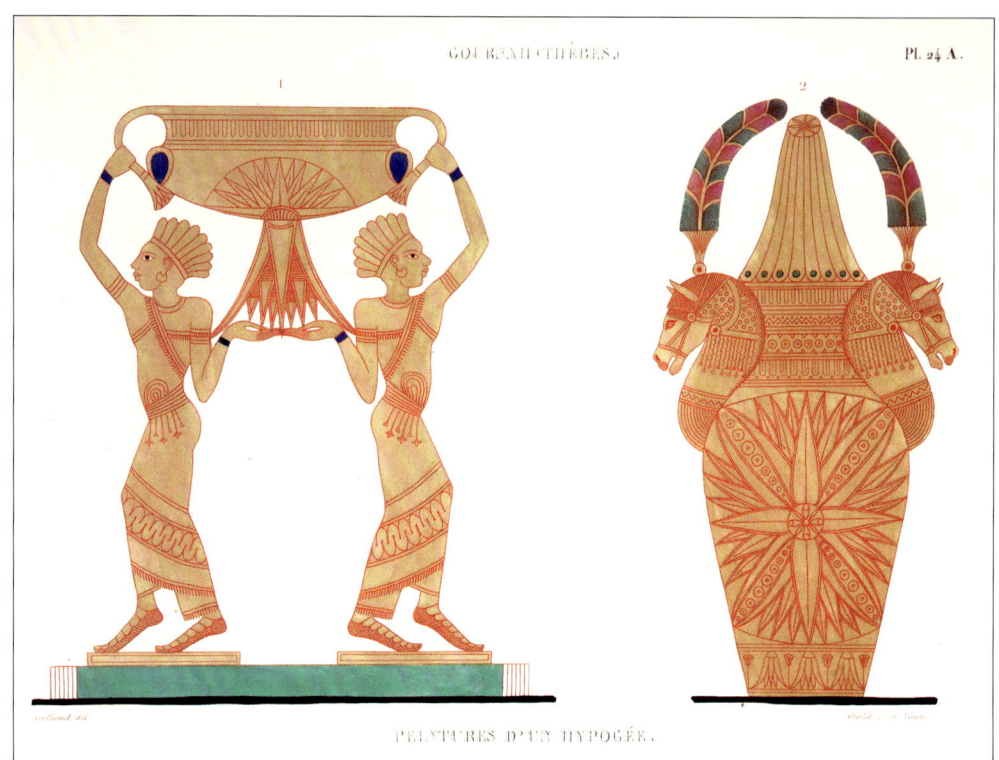

Plate 24A.
Ornate vases.

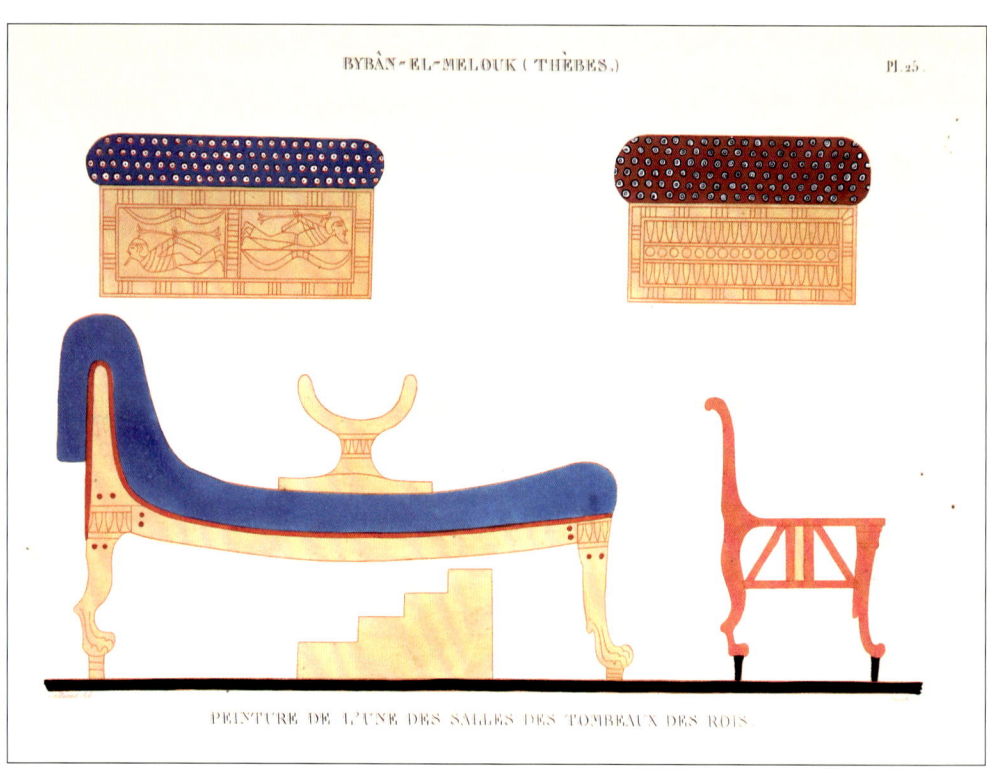

Plate 25. Seats and benches.

Opposite: Plate 25A. Seats and a bench.

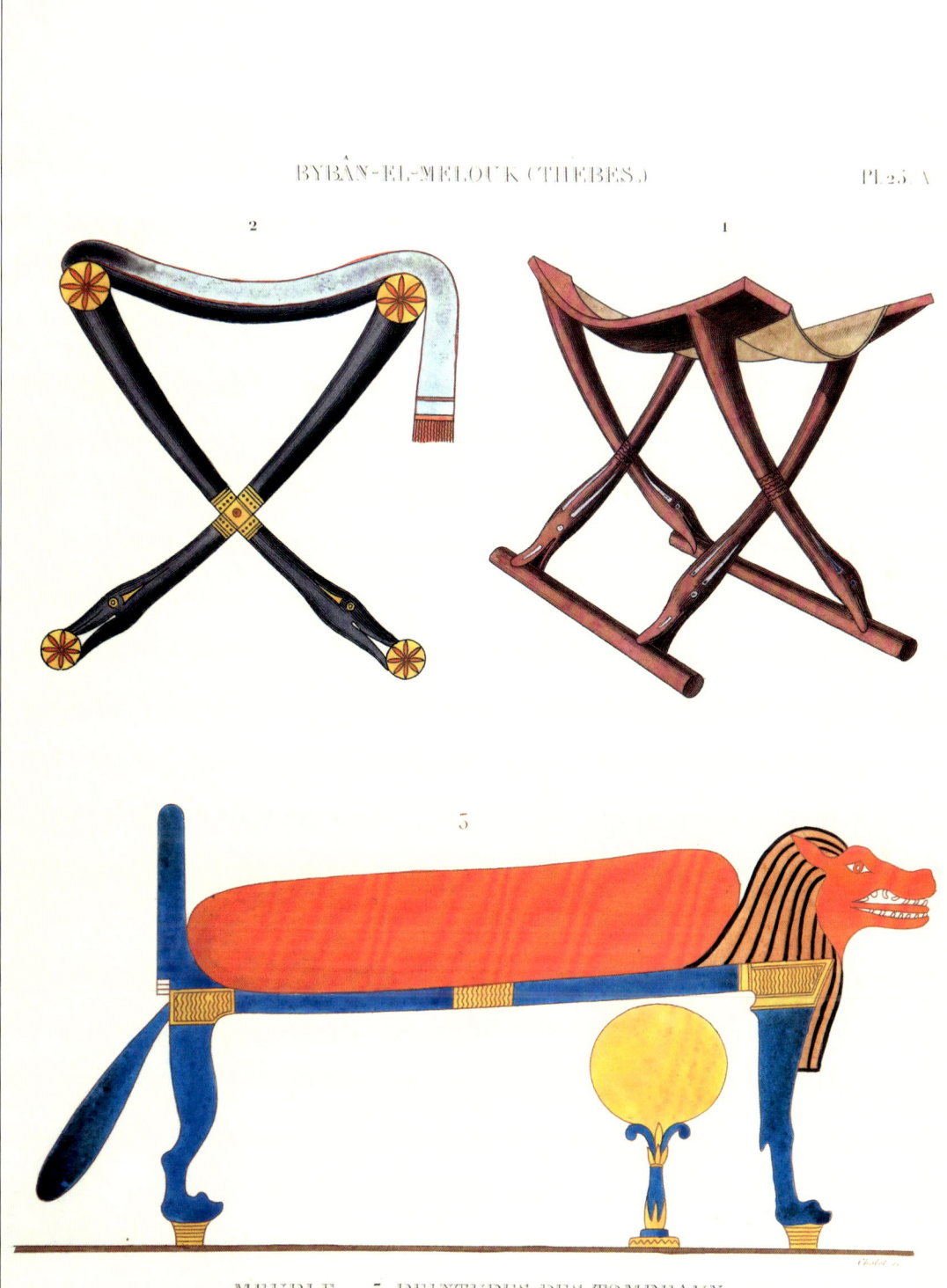

1. MEUBLE. 2,3. PEINTURES DES TOMBEAUX.

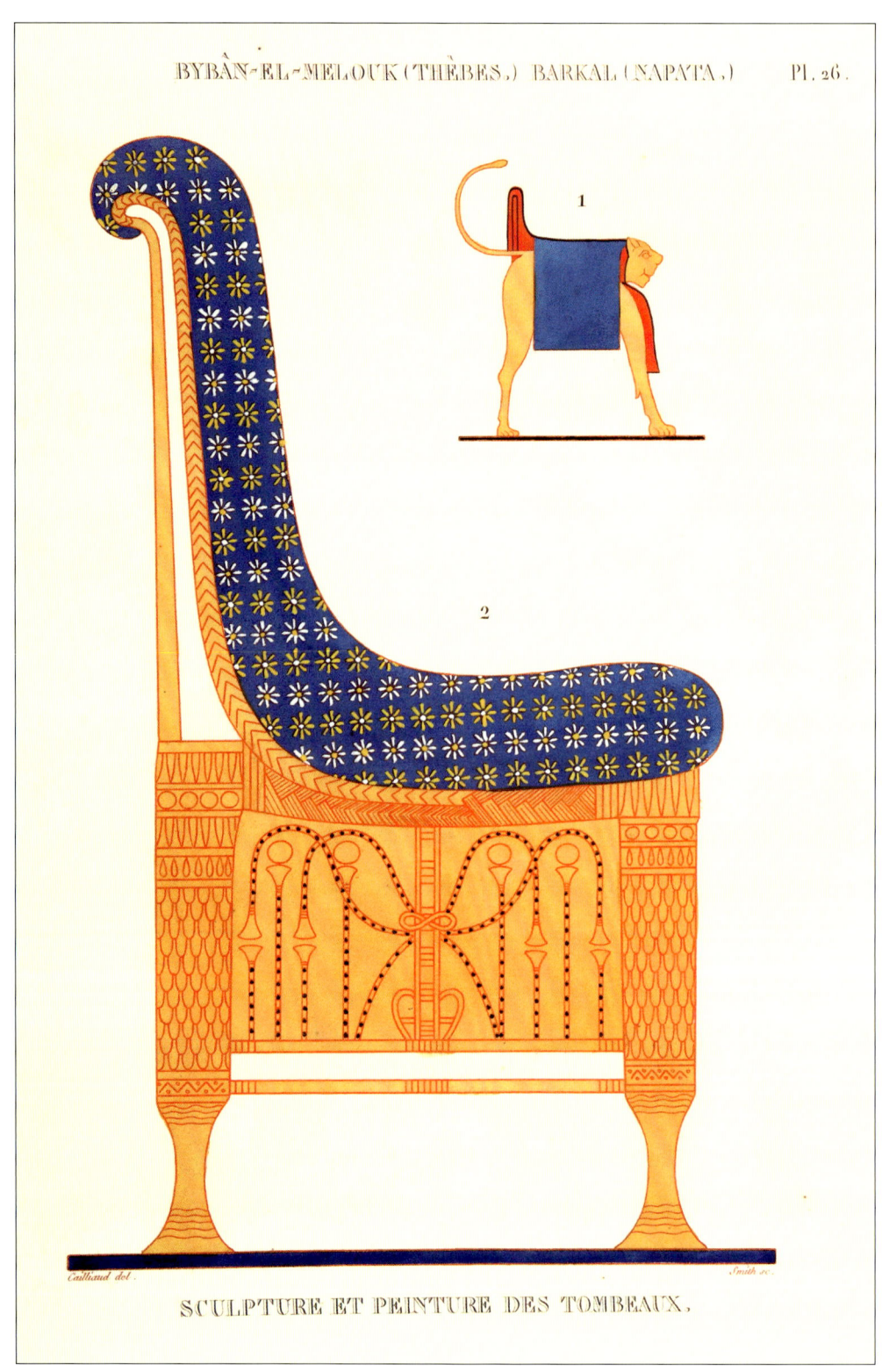

SCULPTURE ET PEINTURE DES TOMBEAUX.

Plate 26. Chair and seat.

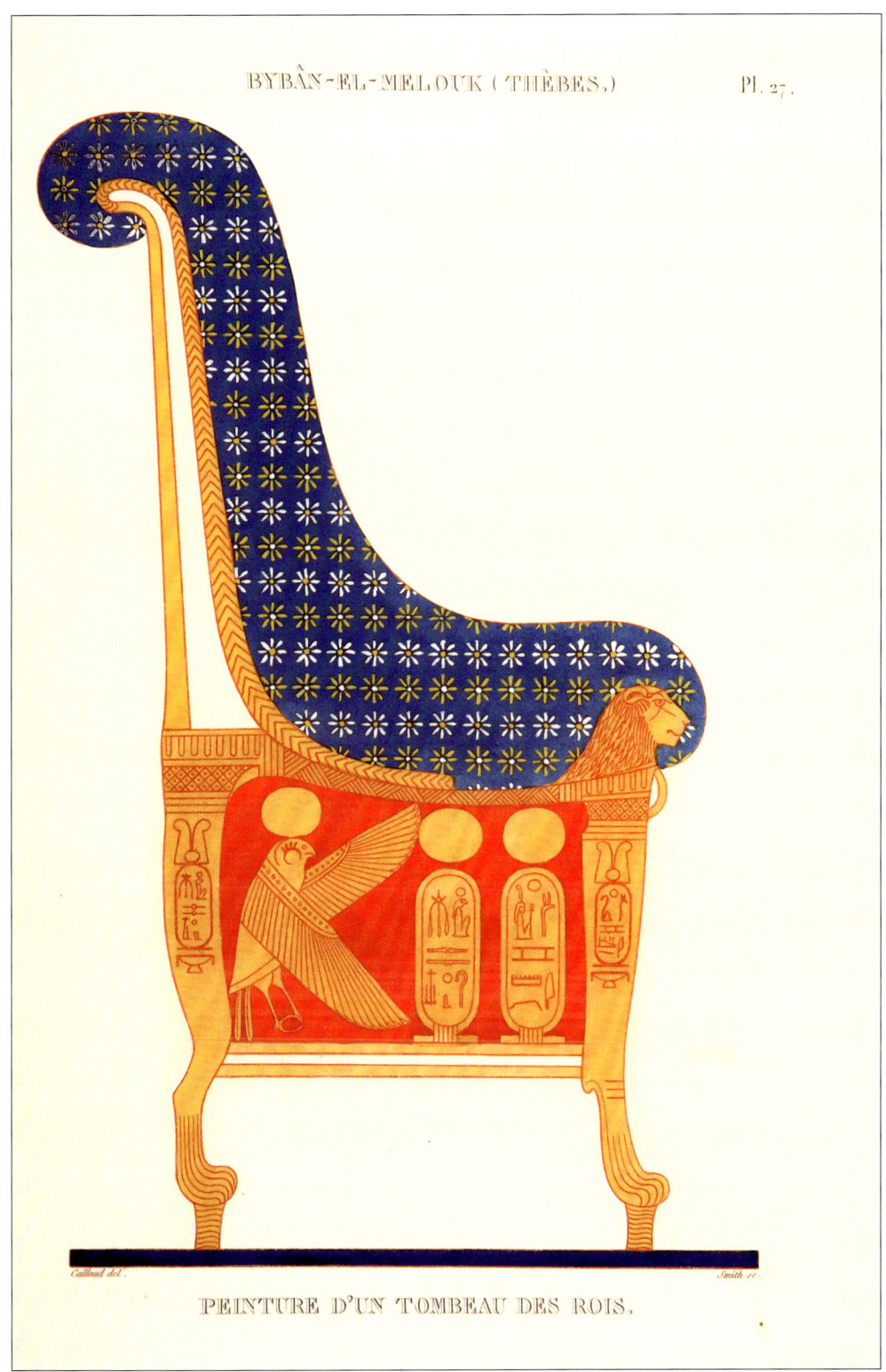

PEINTURE D'UN TOMBEAU DES ROIS.

Plate 27. Chair.

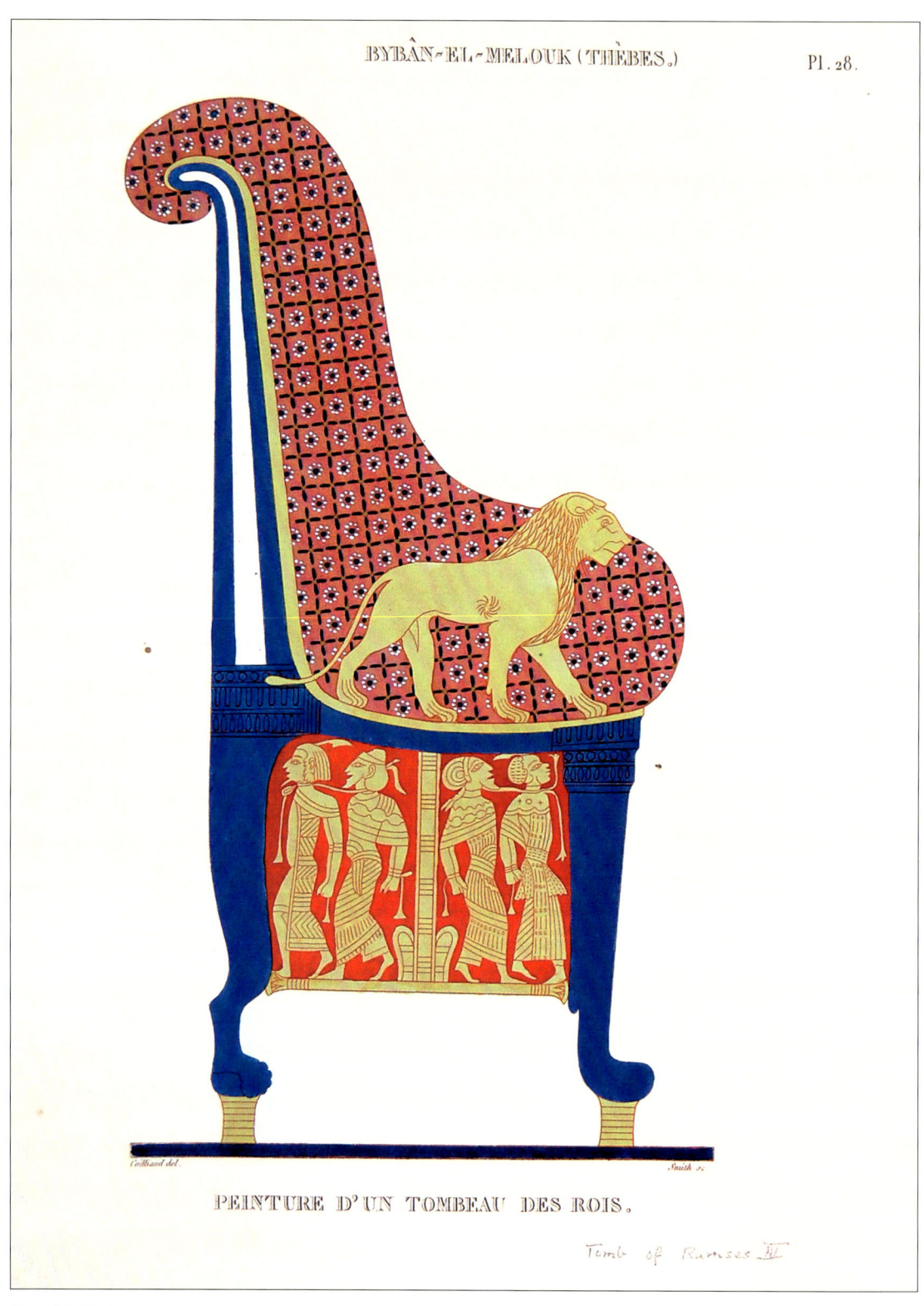

PEINTURE D'UN TOMBEAU DES ROIS.

Tomb of Ramses III

Plate 28. Chair.　　　　　　　　　　　　　　　　*Opposite:* Plate 29. Chair.

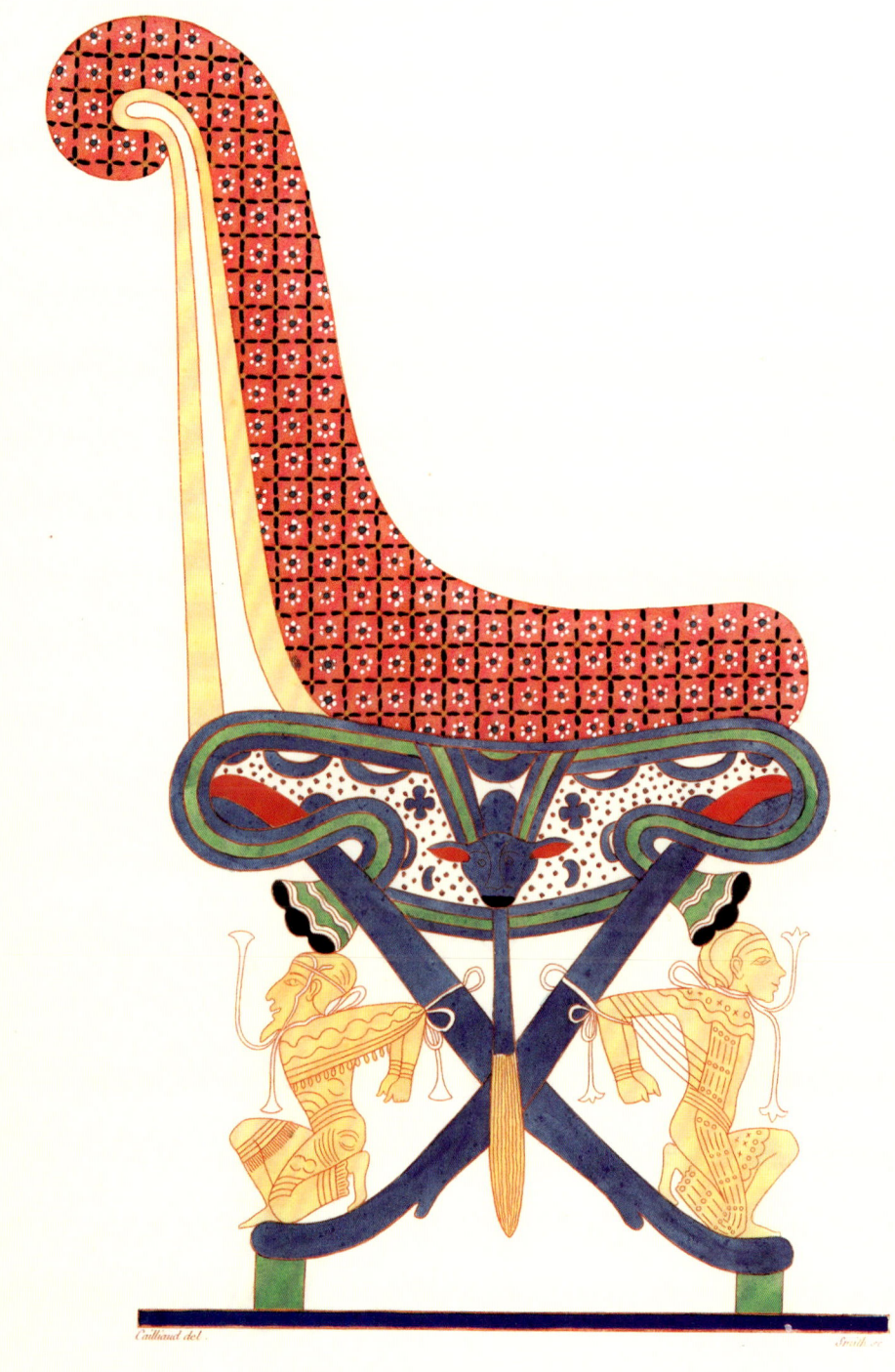

PEINTURE D'UN TOMBEAU DES ROIS.

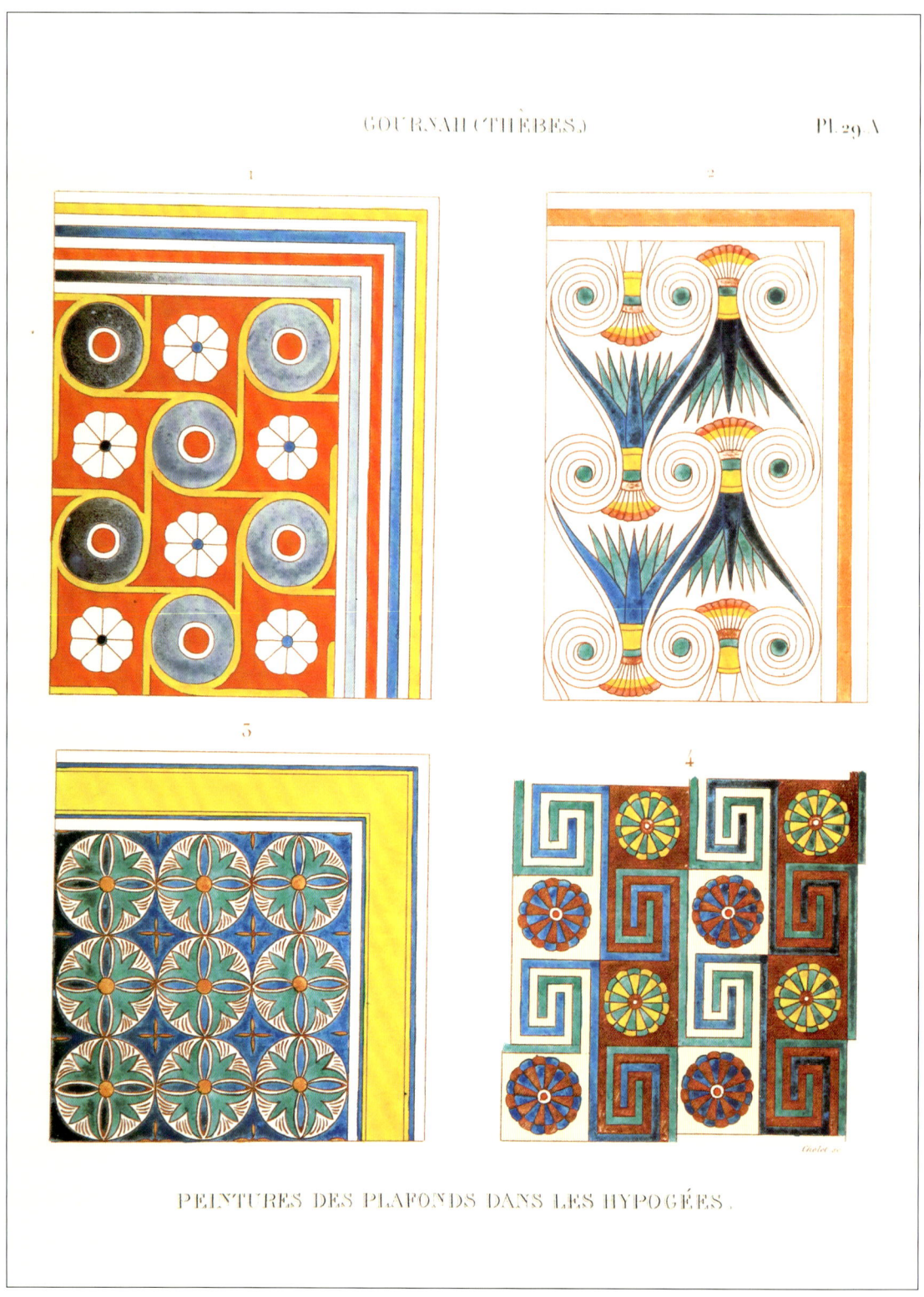

PEINTURES DES PLAFONDS DANS LES HYPOGÉES.

Plate 29A. Painted ceilings from tombs.

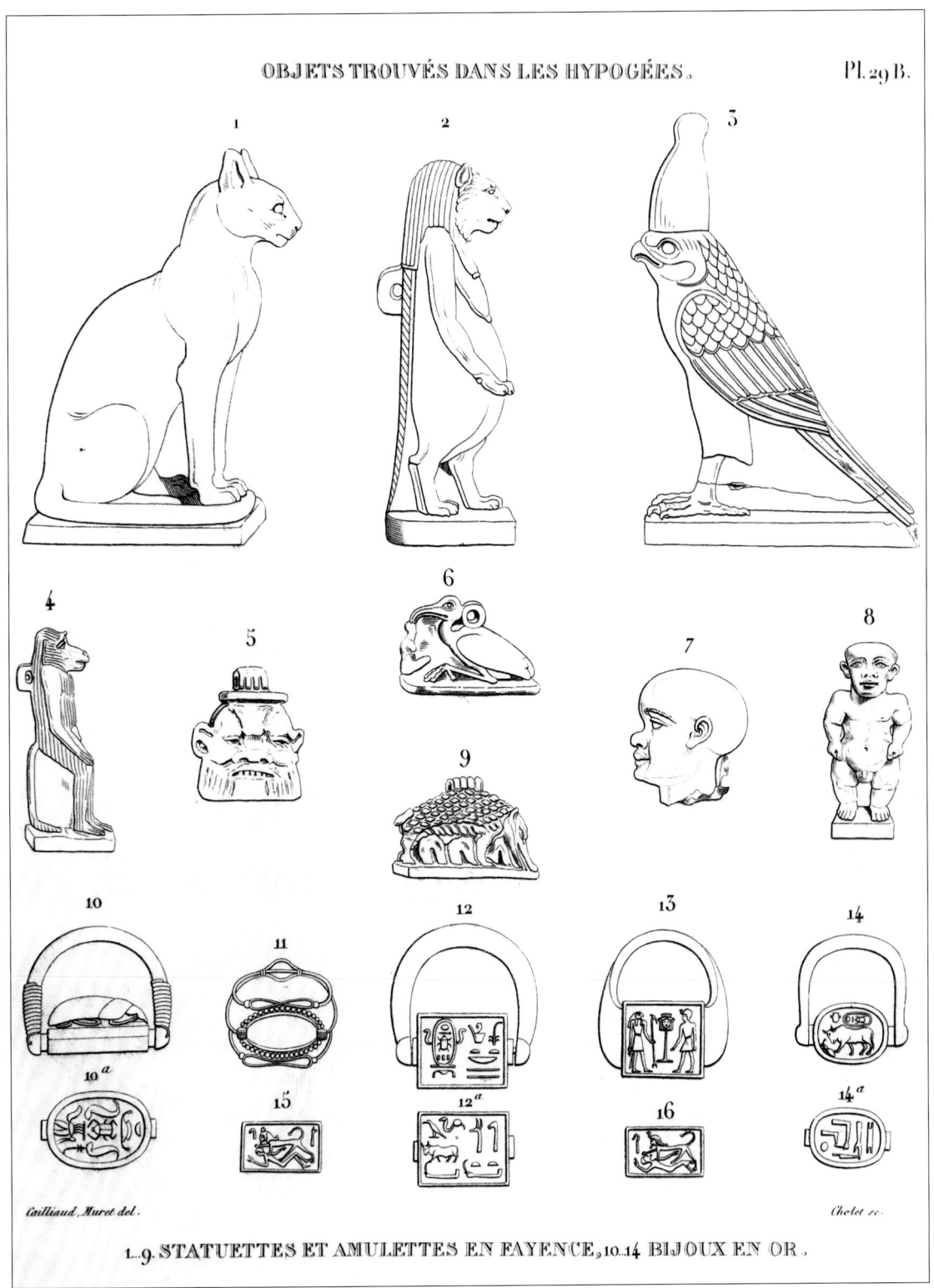

Cailliaud, Muret del.

Cholet sc.

1...9. STATUETTES ET AMULETTES EN FAYENCE, 10..14 BIJOUX EN OR.

Plate 29B. Drawings of faience statuettes and amulets. Drawings of gold jewelry.

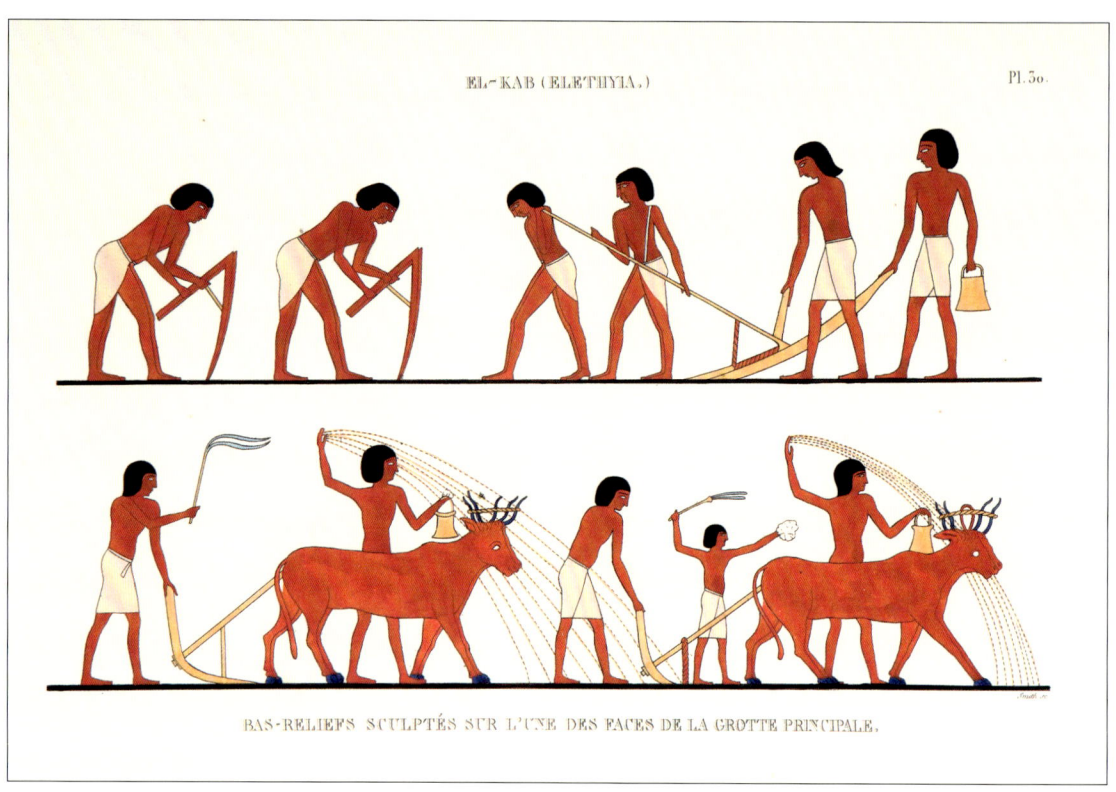

Plate 30. Tilling and sowing.

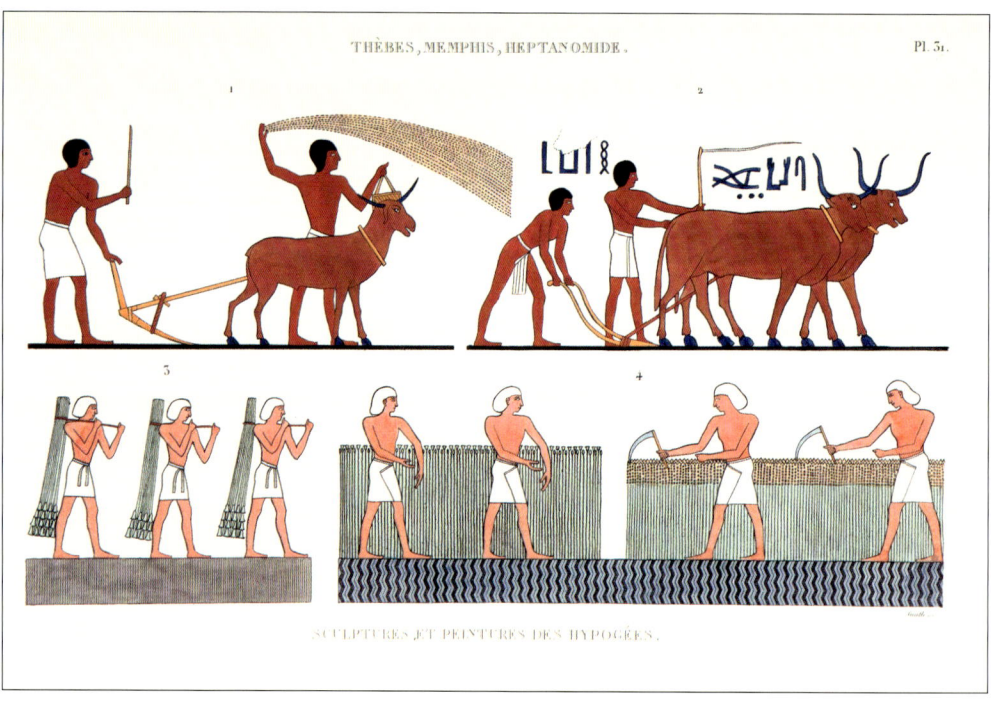

Plate 31. Sowing, plowing, and harvesting papyrus.

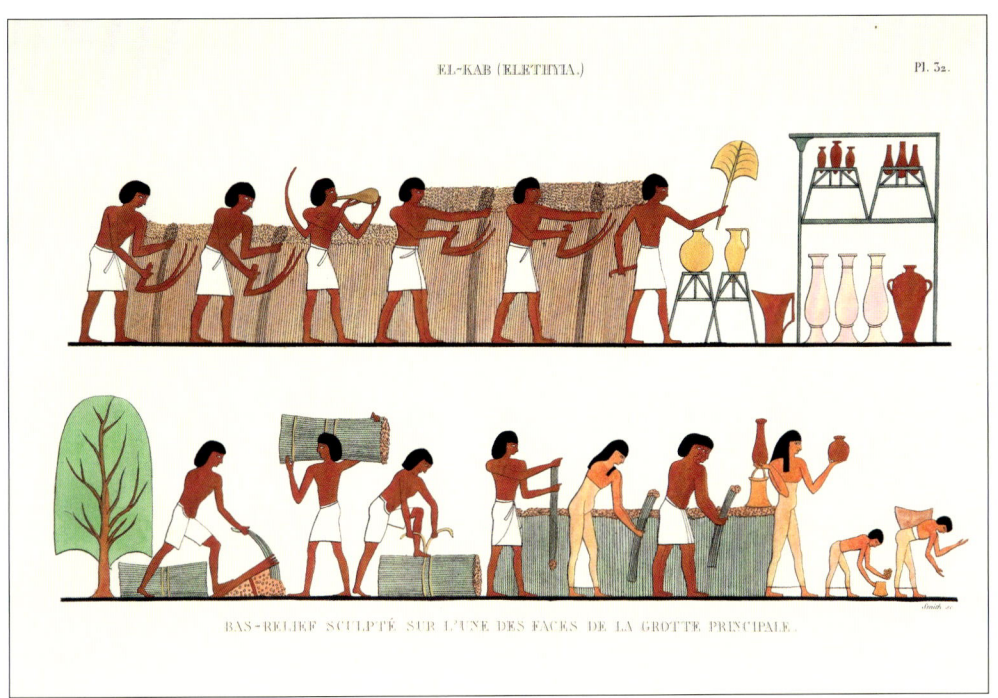

Plate 32. Harvesting for the production of oils and perfumes.

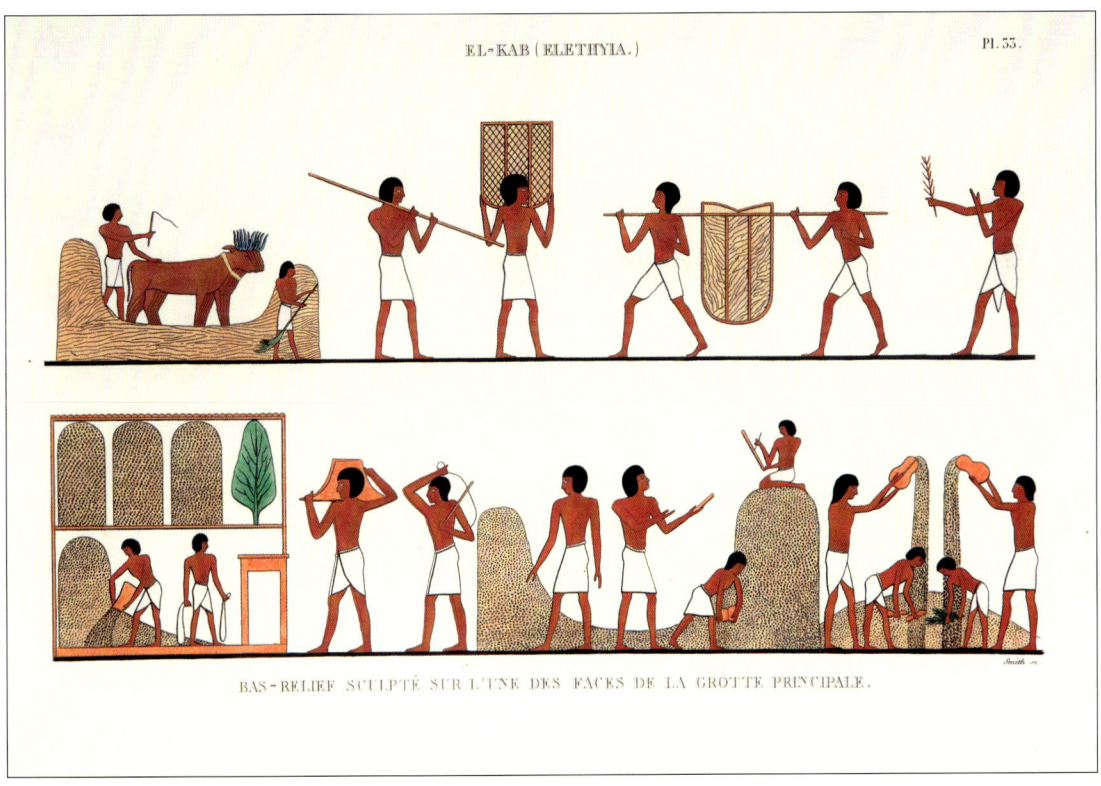

Plate 33. Threshing.

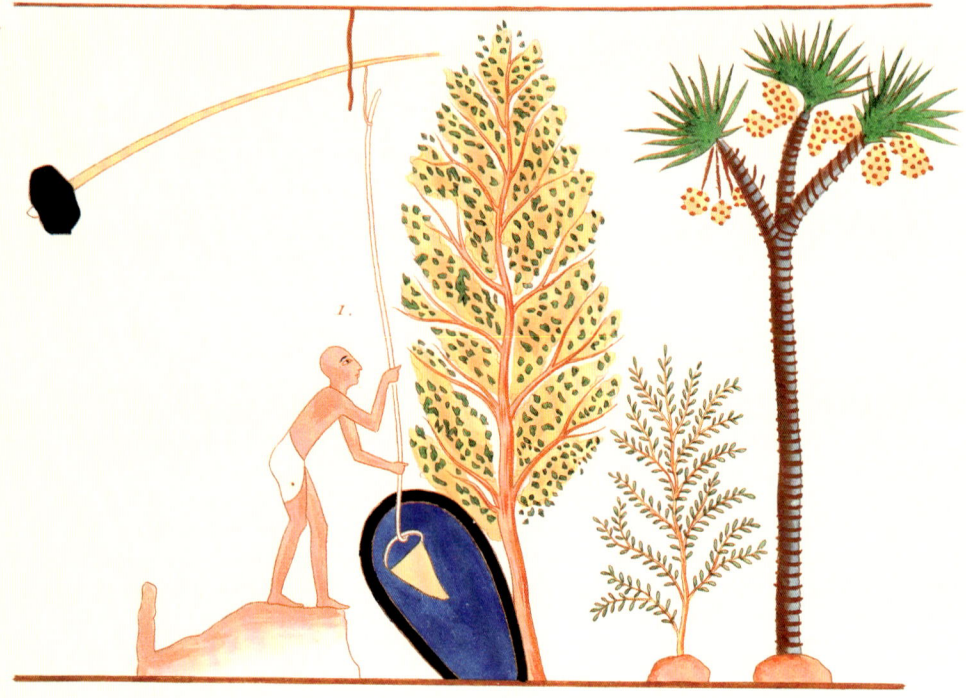

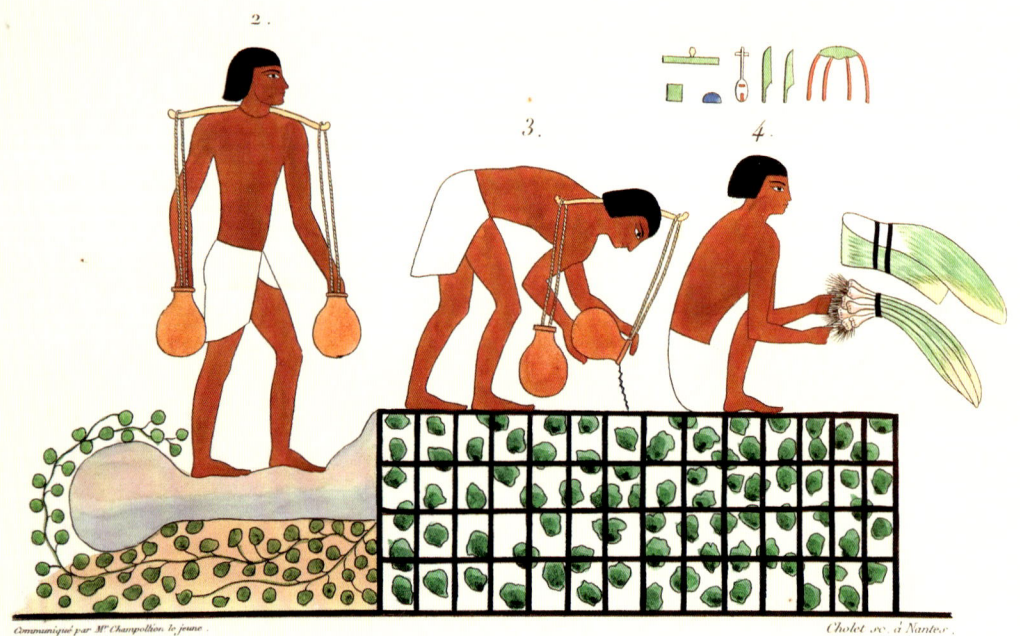

Communiqué par M. Champollion le jeune.

Cholet sc. à Nantes.

PEINTURES DES HYPOGÉES.

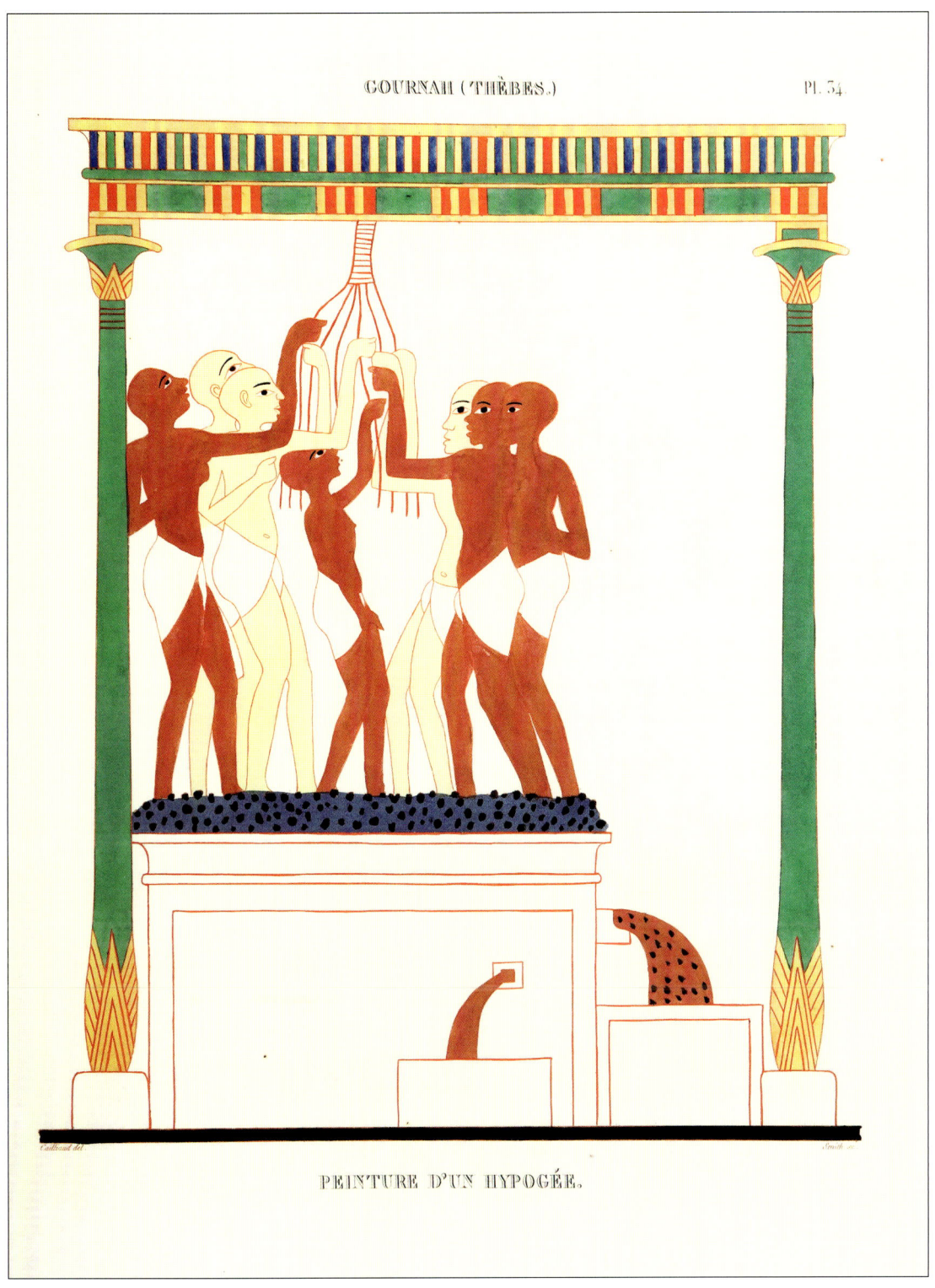

PEINTURE D'UN HYPOGÉE.

Plate 34. Trampling grapes.
Opposite: Plate 33A. The *shaduf*. Watering a garden and harvesting bulbs.

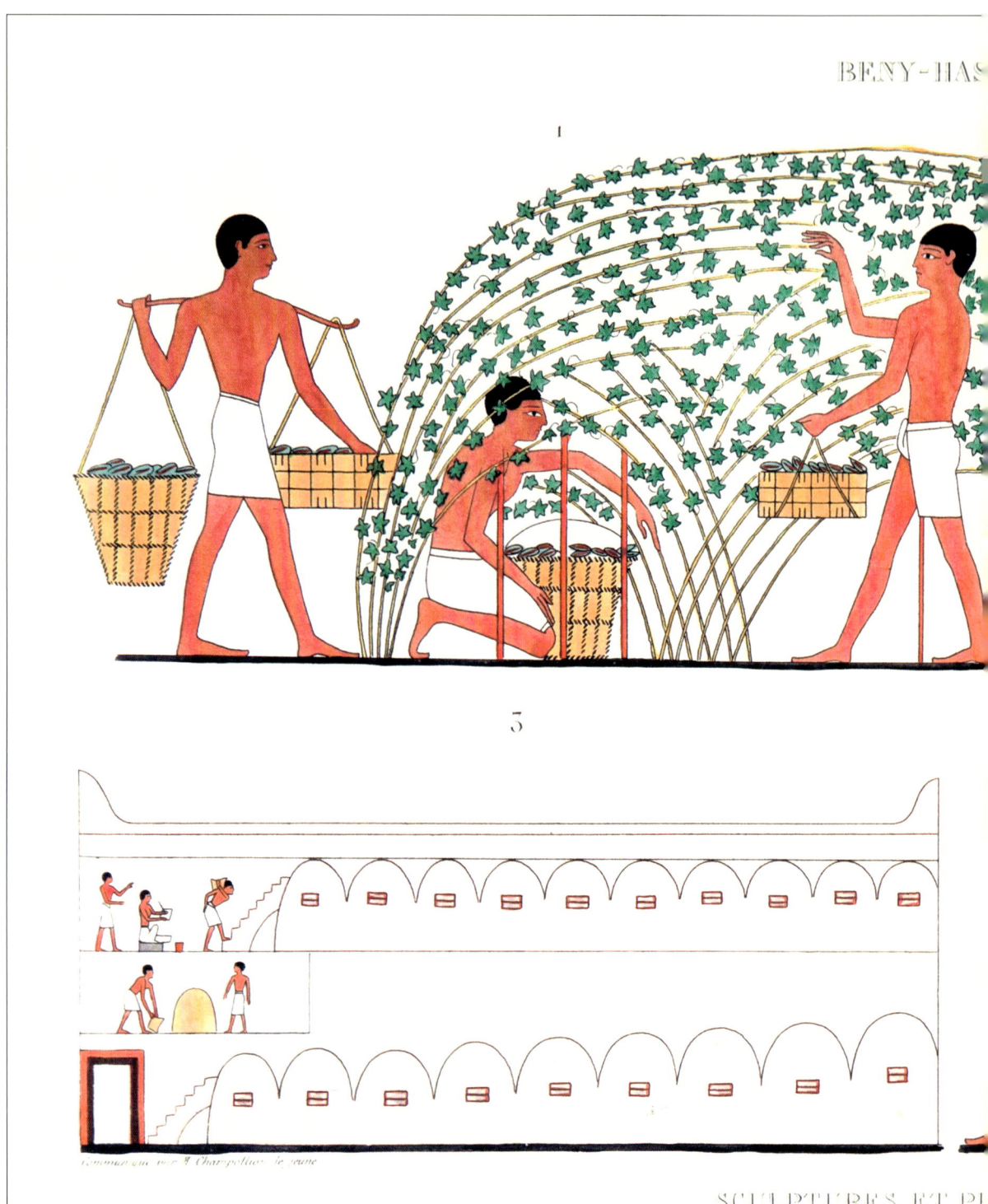

Plate 34A. Picking figs. Baboons. Granaries. Plowing.

Pl. 54. A.

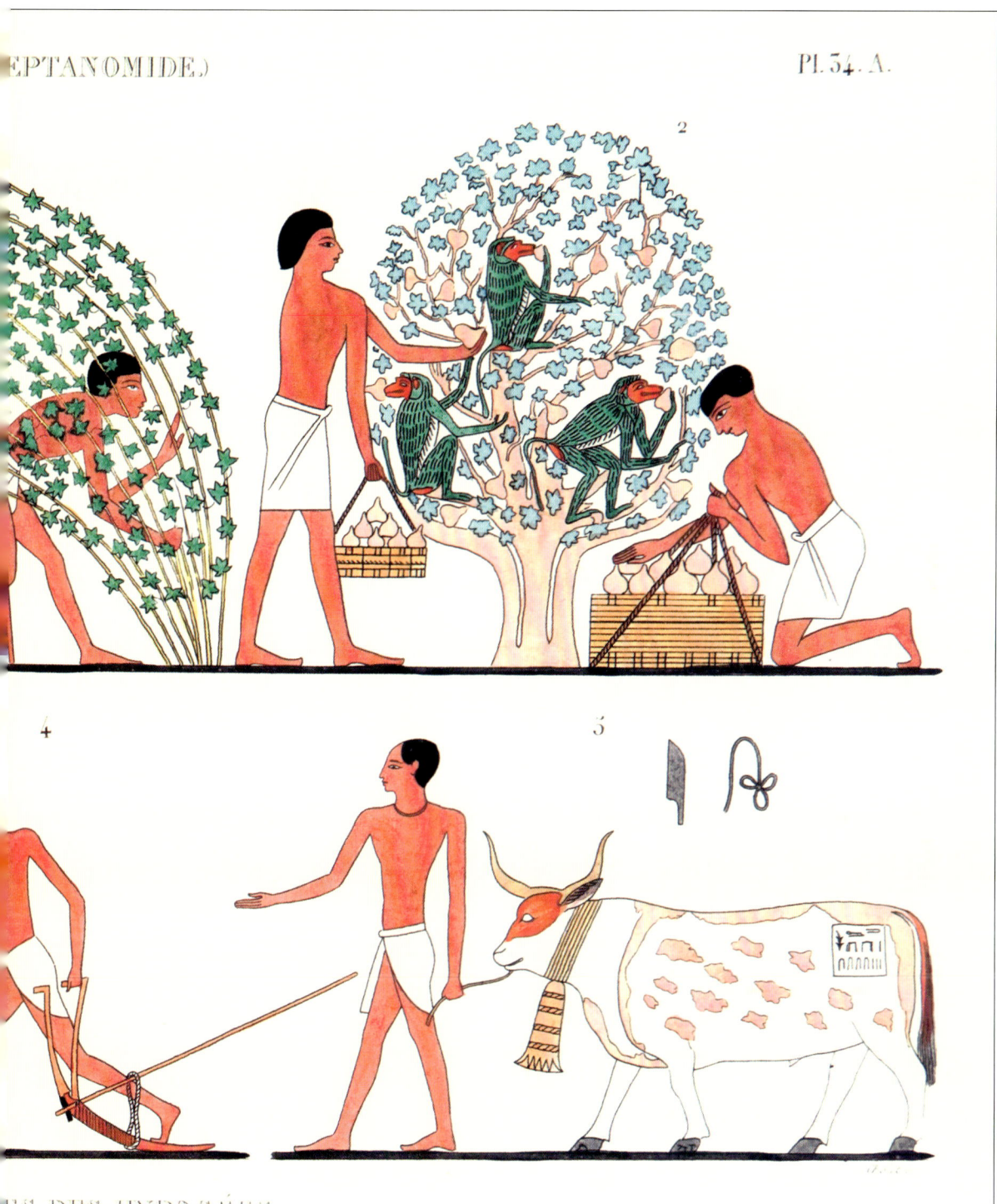

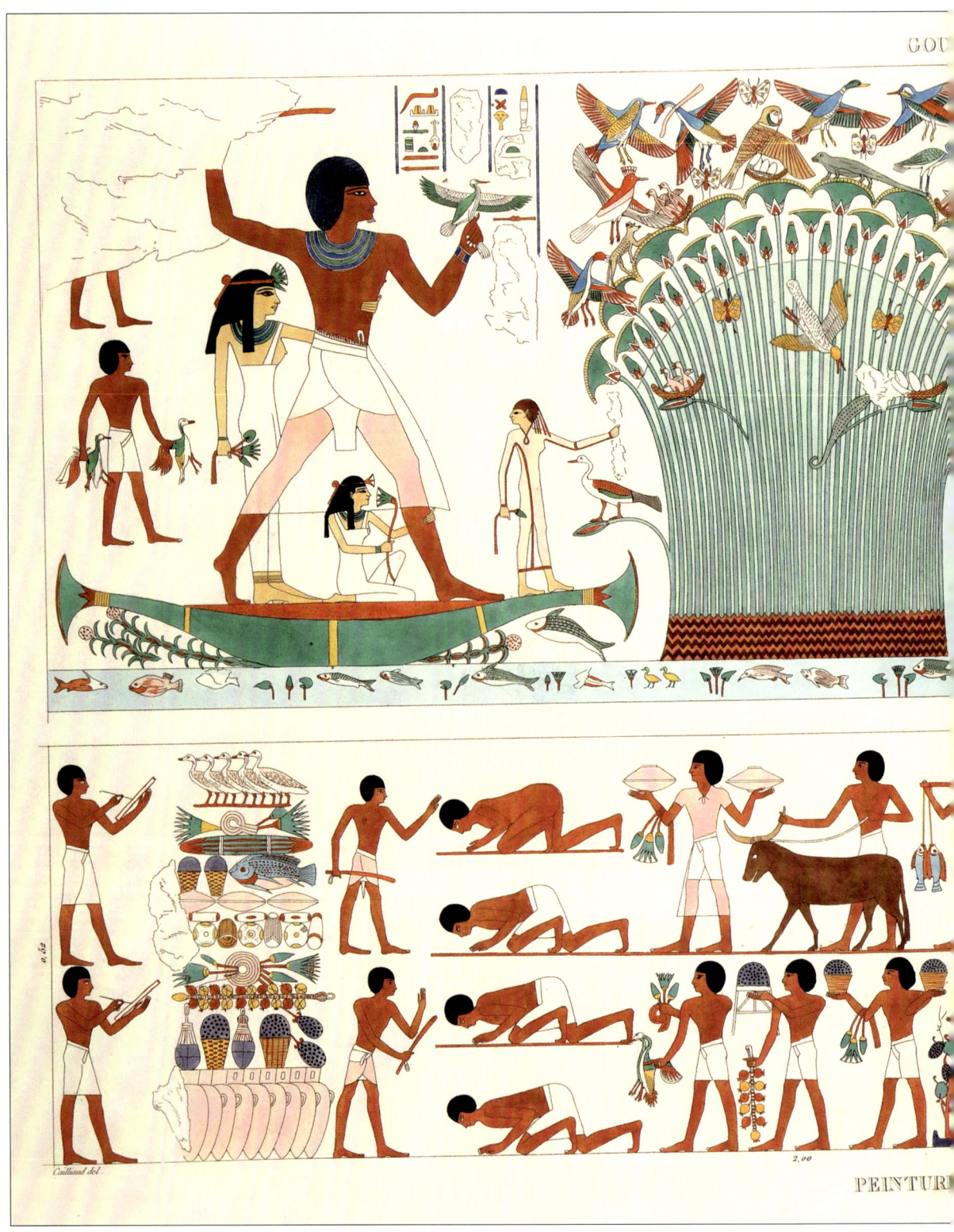

Plate 35. Scenes of fowling, fishing, crops, and revelry.

PEINTUR

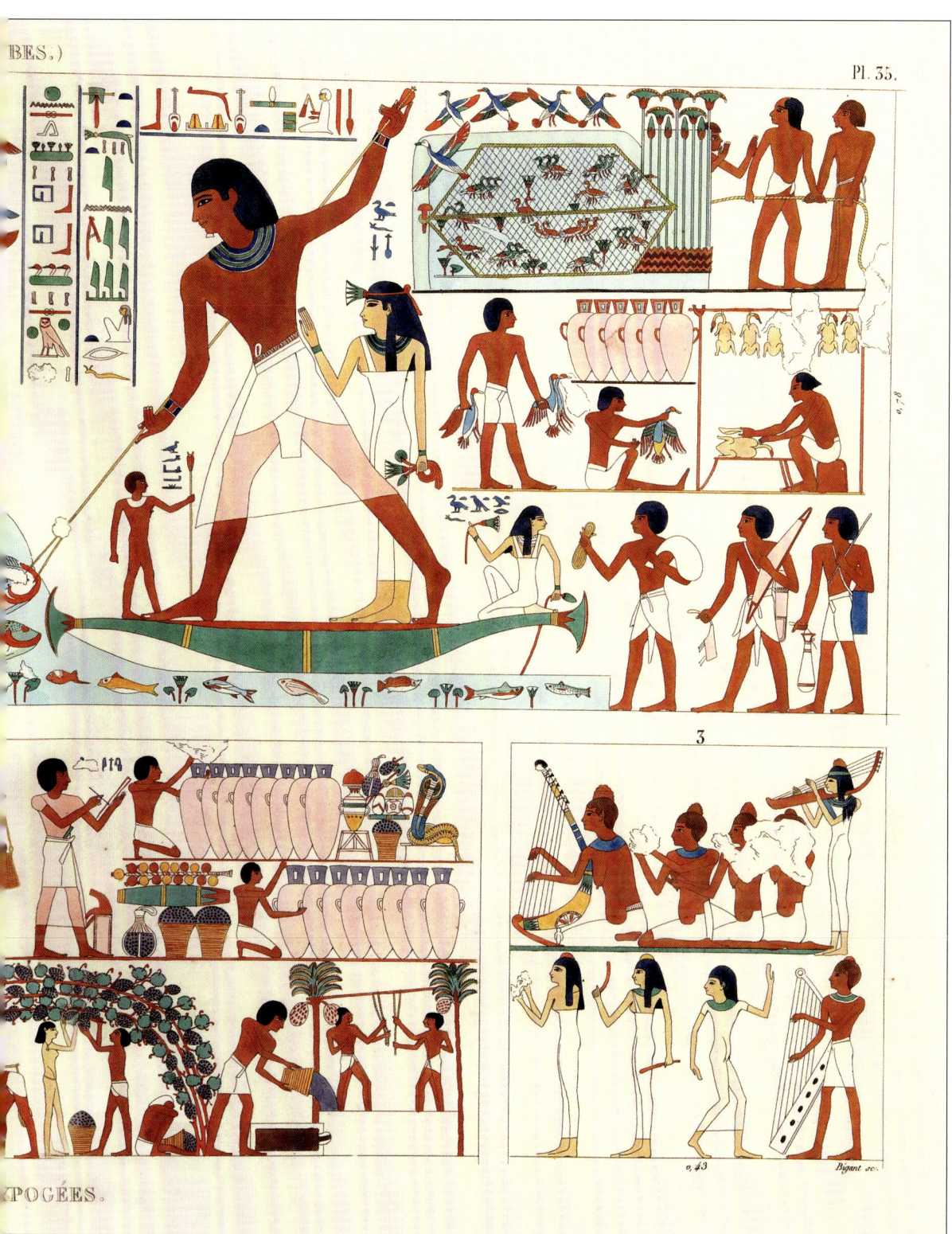

3

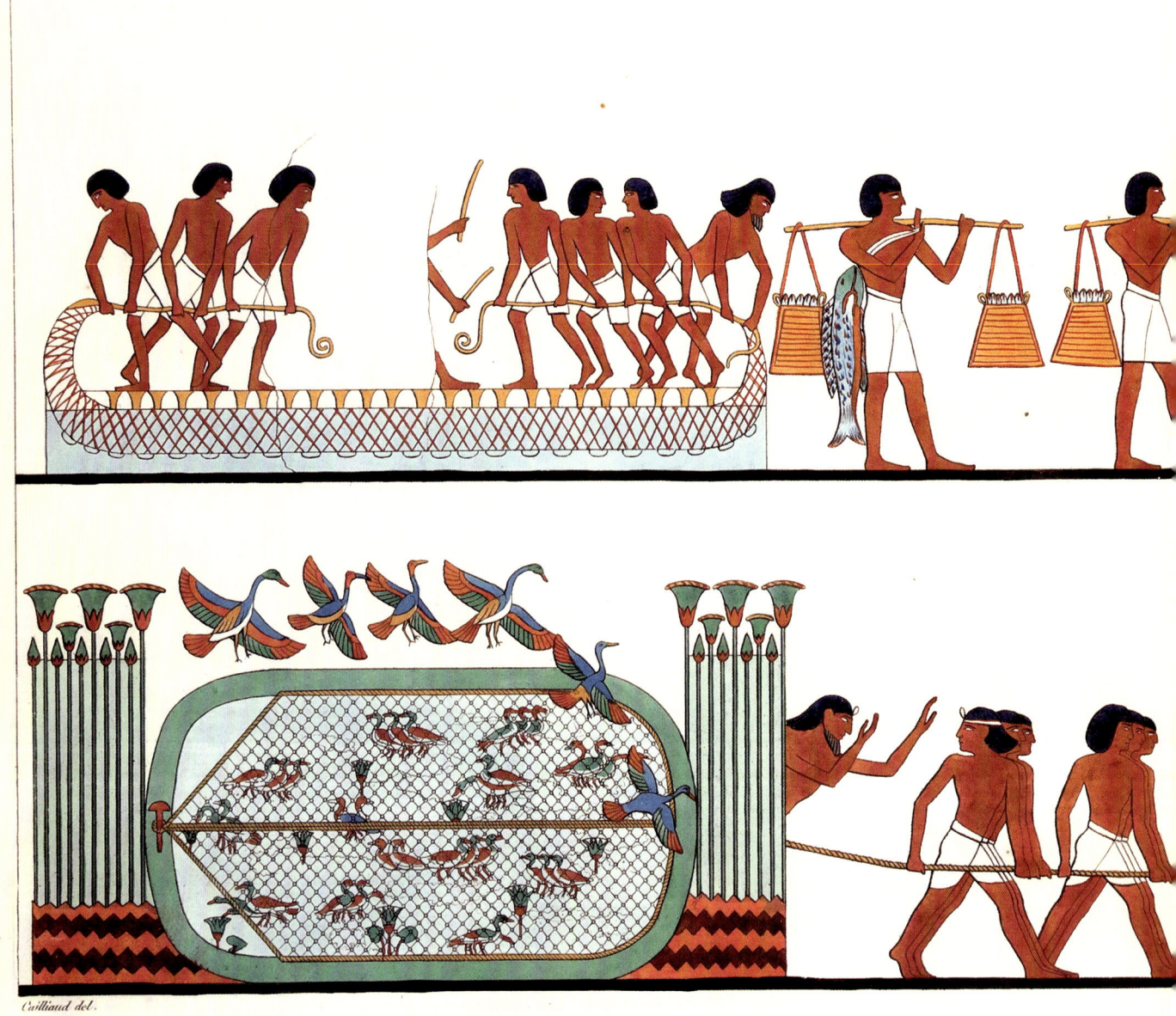

Caïlliaud del.

Plate 36. Scenes of fowling, fishing, and food preparation.

222

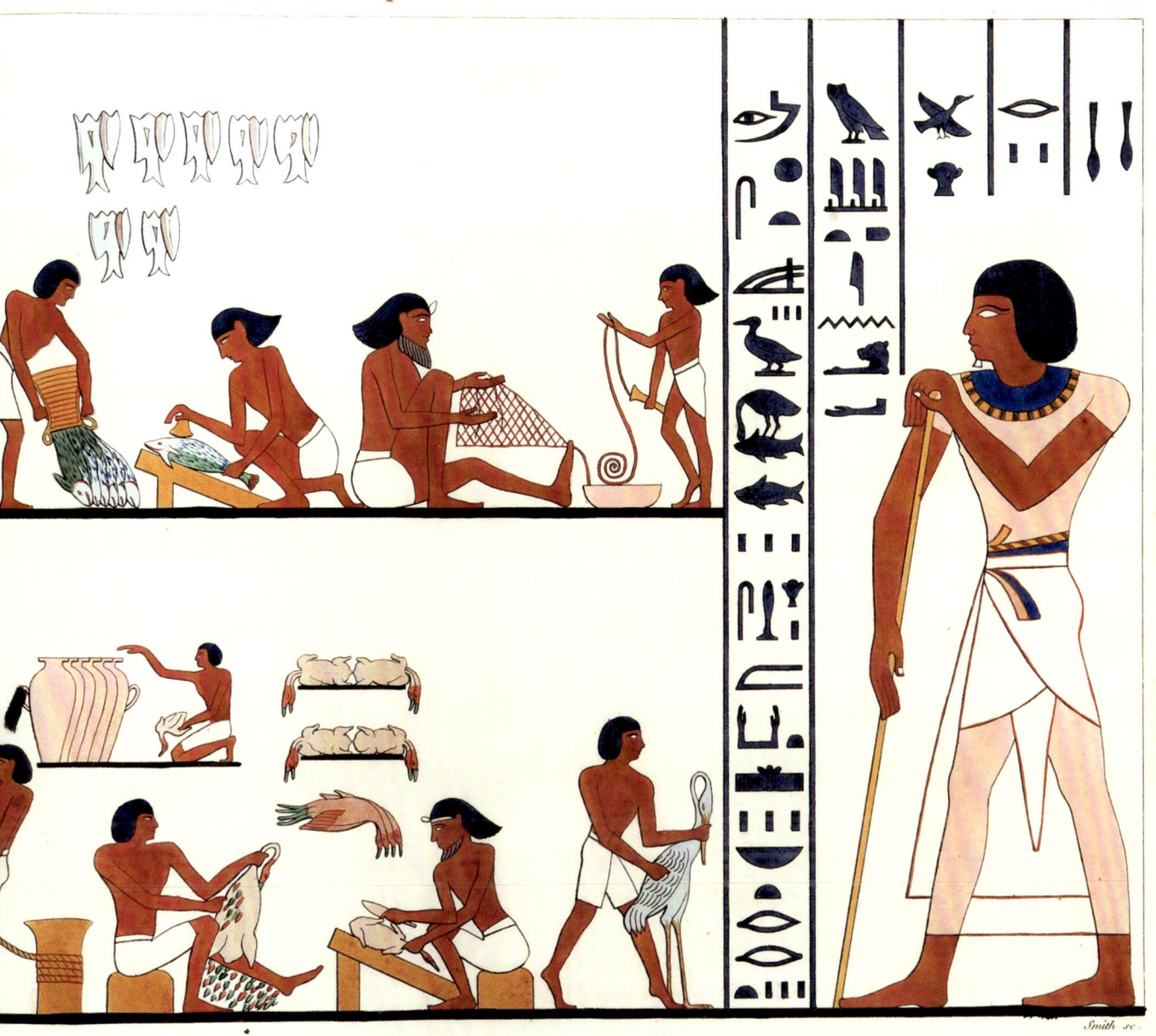

Smith sc.

Pl. 37

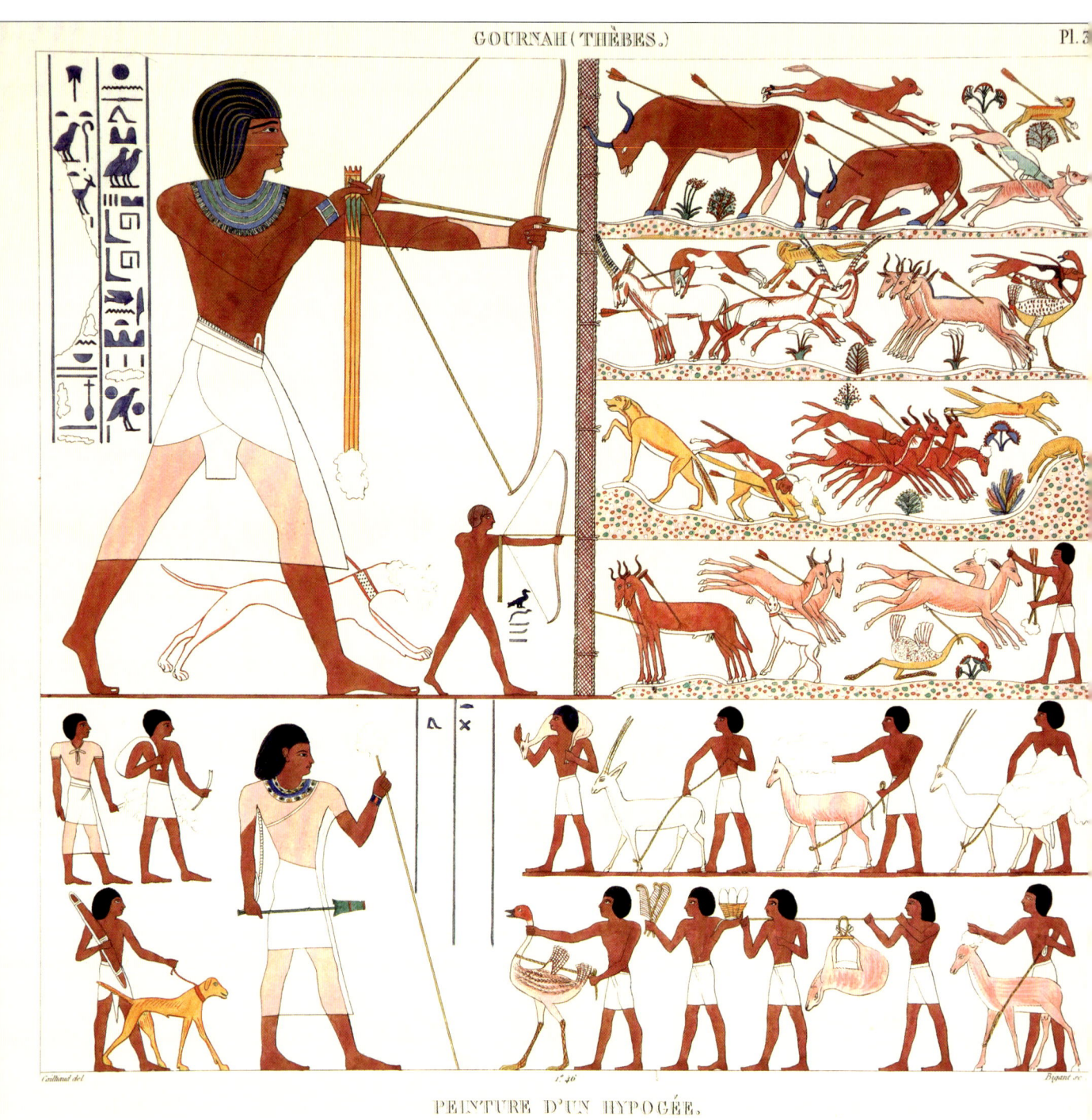

PEINTURE D'UN HYPOGÉE.

Plate 37. Scenes of hunting.

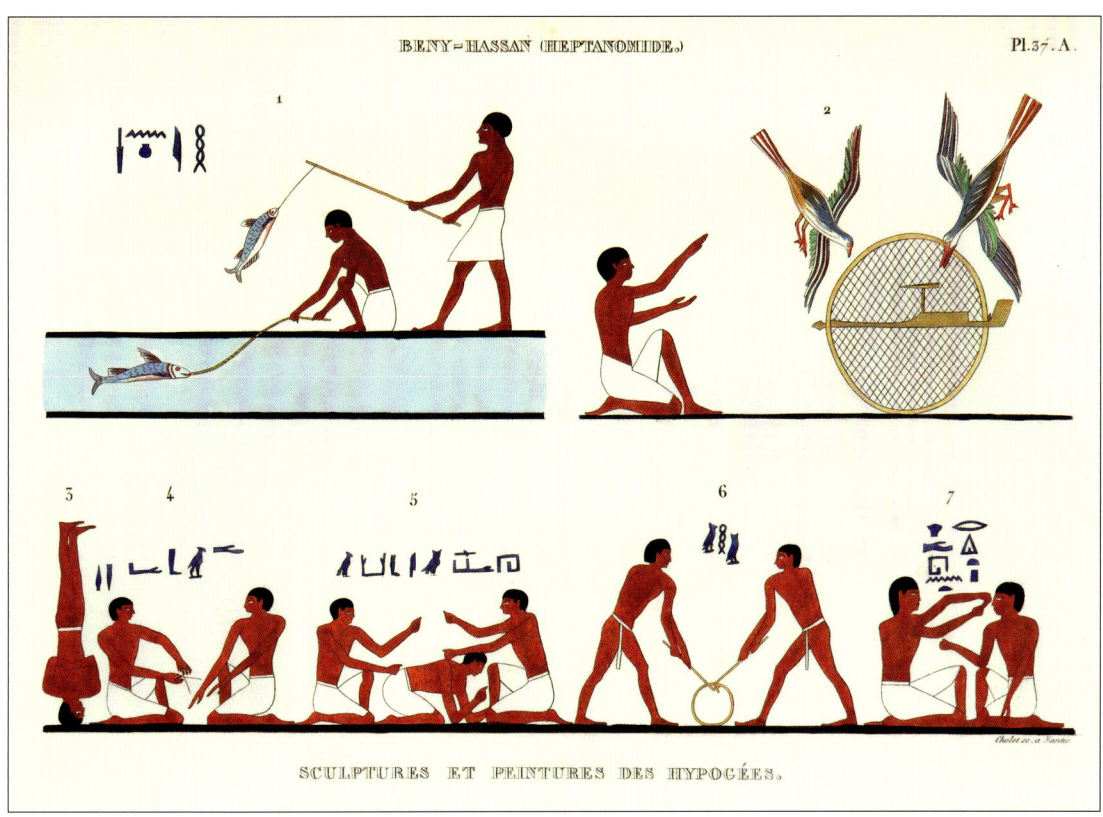

Plate 37A. Scenes of fowling and fishing, gymnastics, and games.

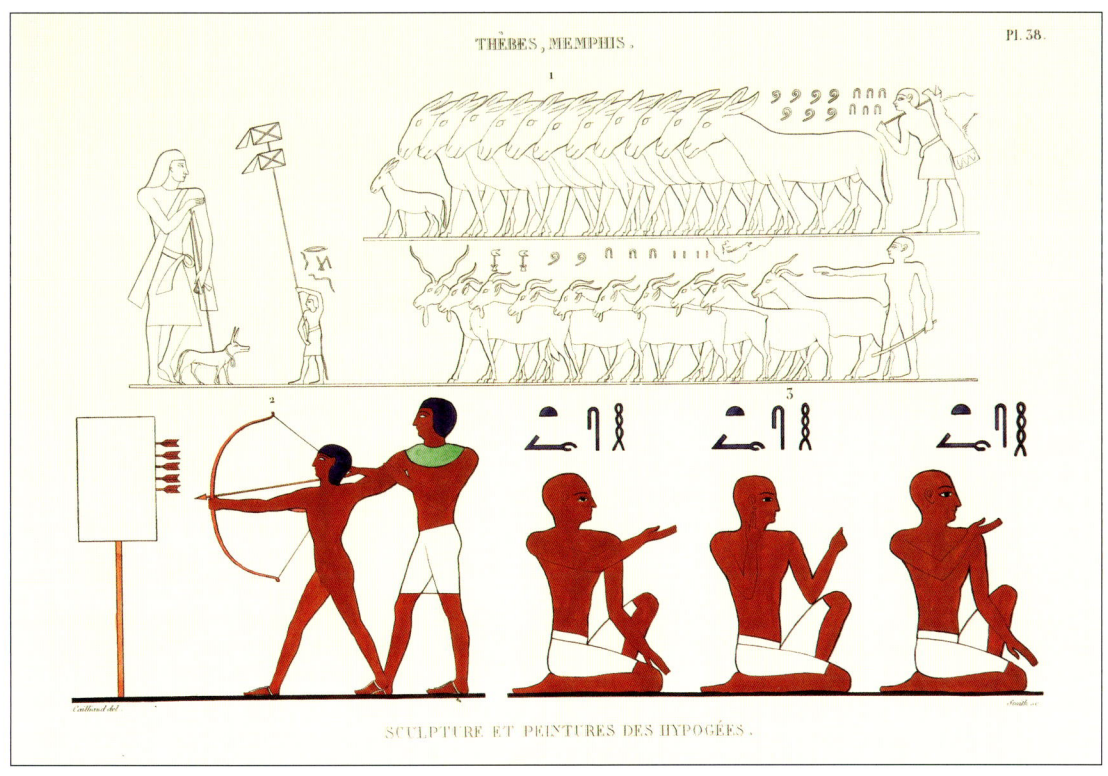

Plate 38. Herds of donkeys and goats. Archery lesson. Concentration exercises.

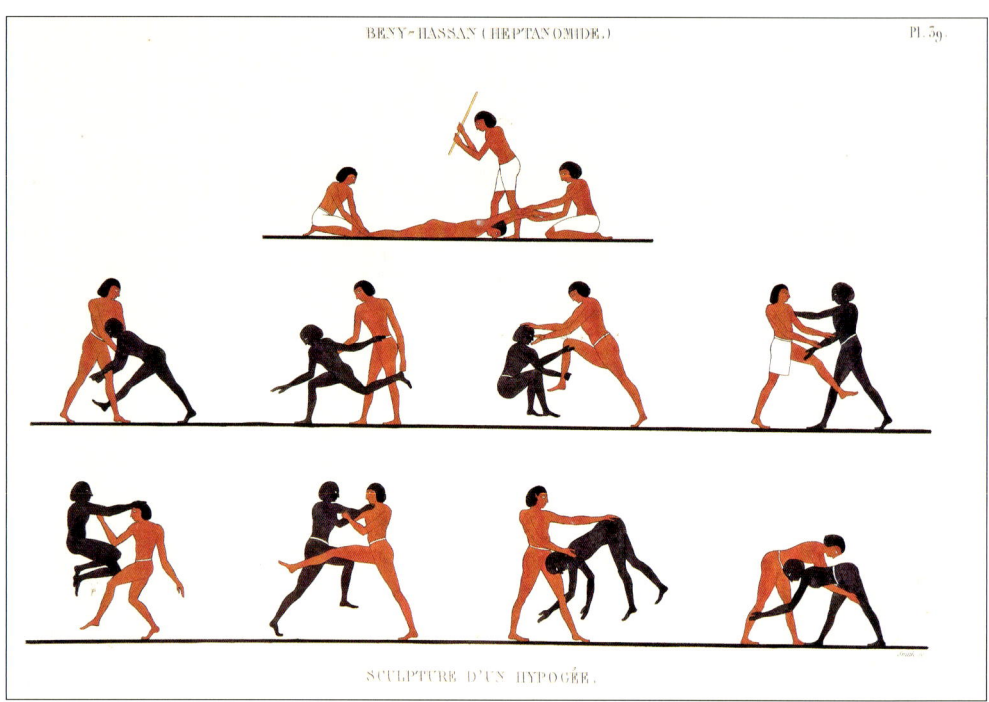

Plate 39. Scenes of warming up and wrestling.

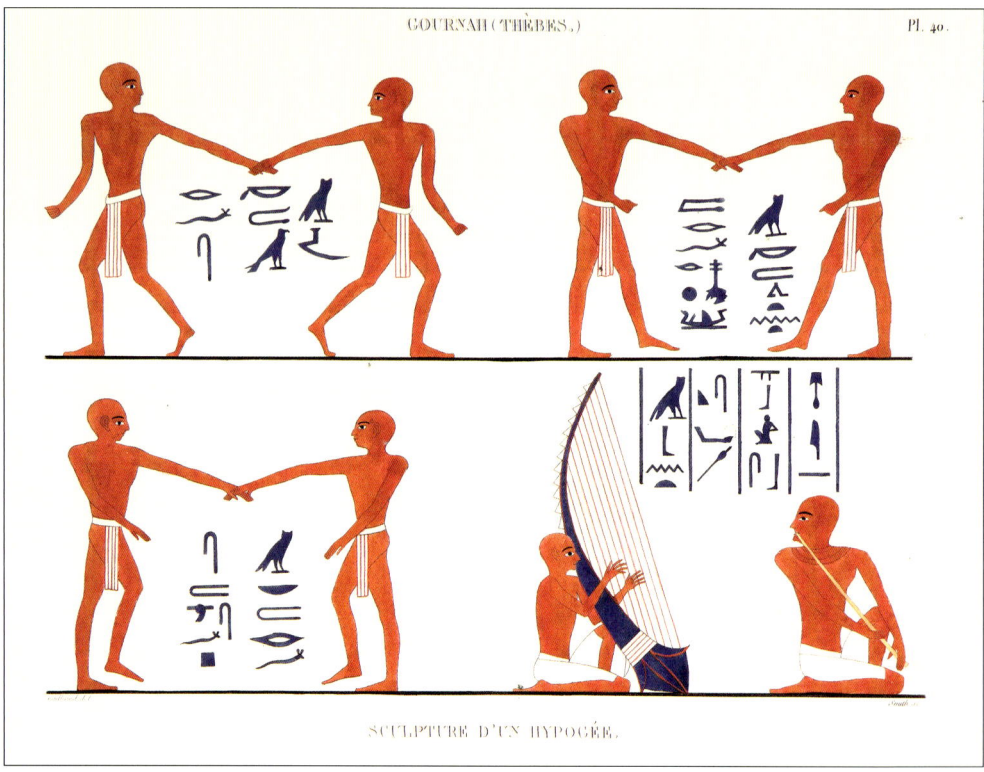

Plate 40. Dancers, harper, and flutist.

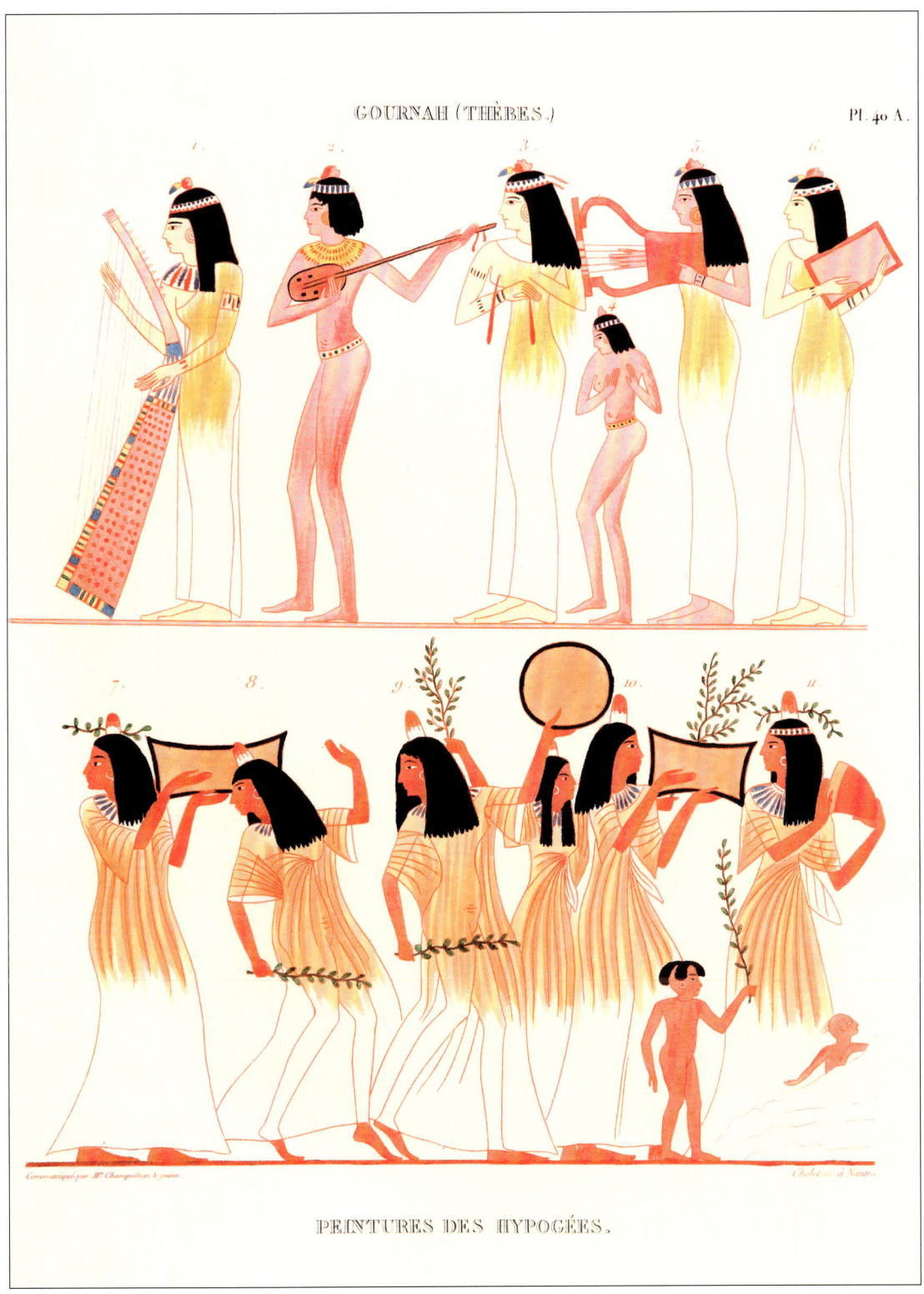

GOURNAH (THÈBES.)

PL. 40 A.

PEINTURES DES HYPOGÉES.

Plate 40A. Musicians.

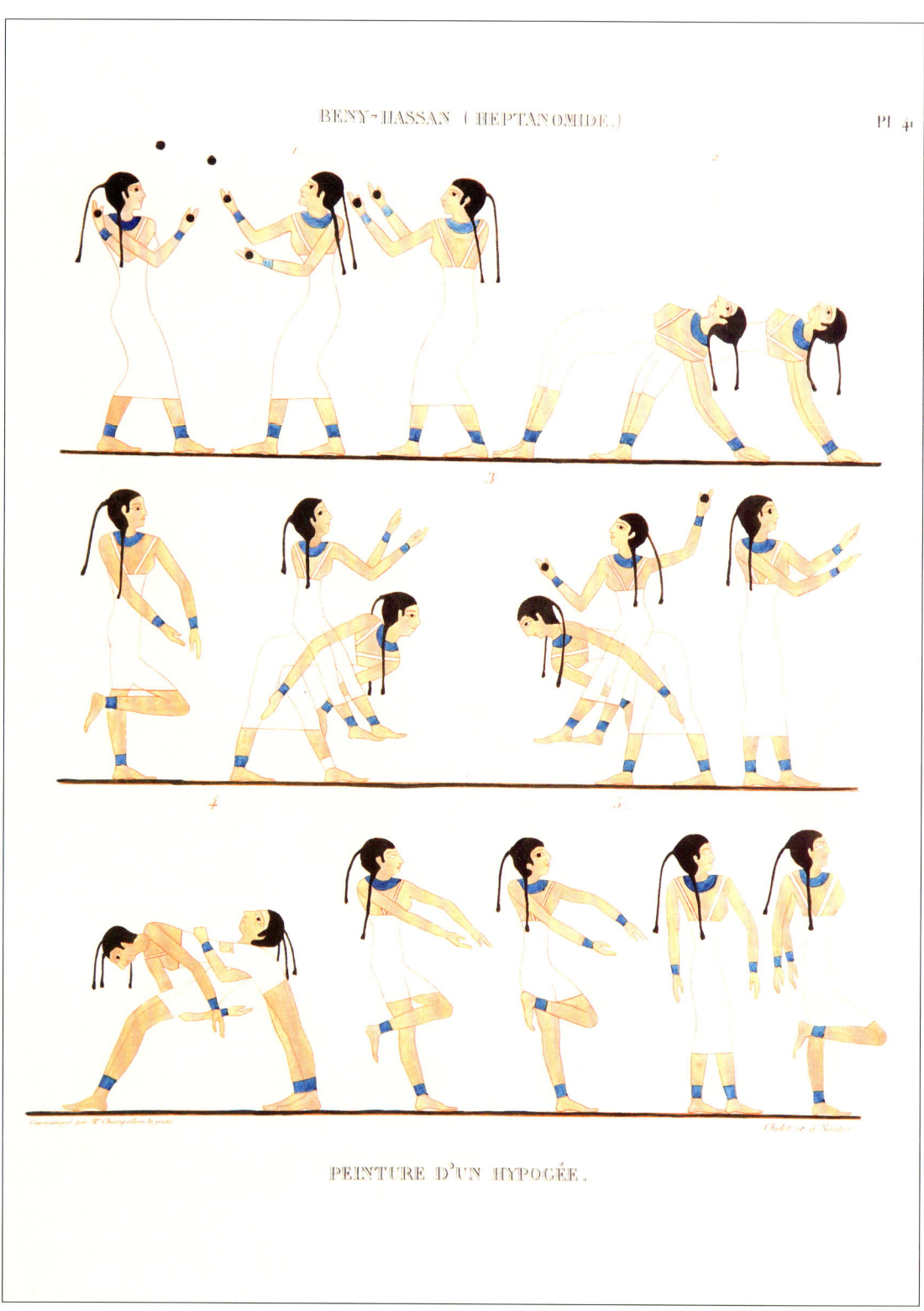

PEINTURE D'UN HYPOGÉE.

Plate 41. Ball games and acrobatics.

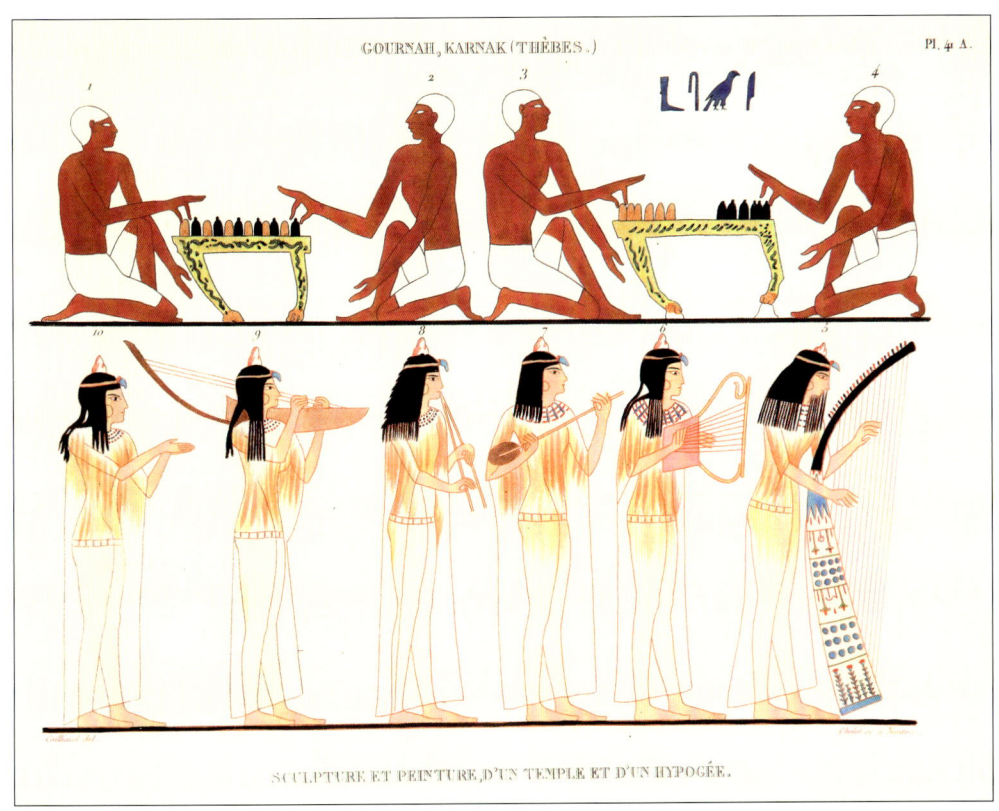

Plate 41A. Gaming and musicians.

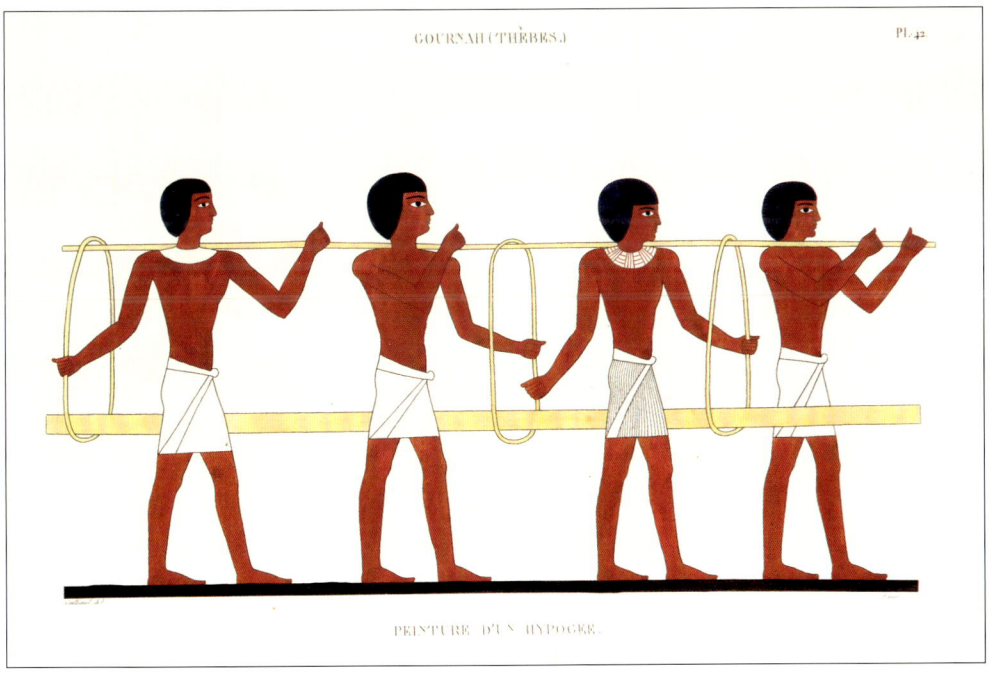

Plate 42. Carrying a beam.

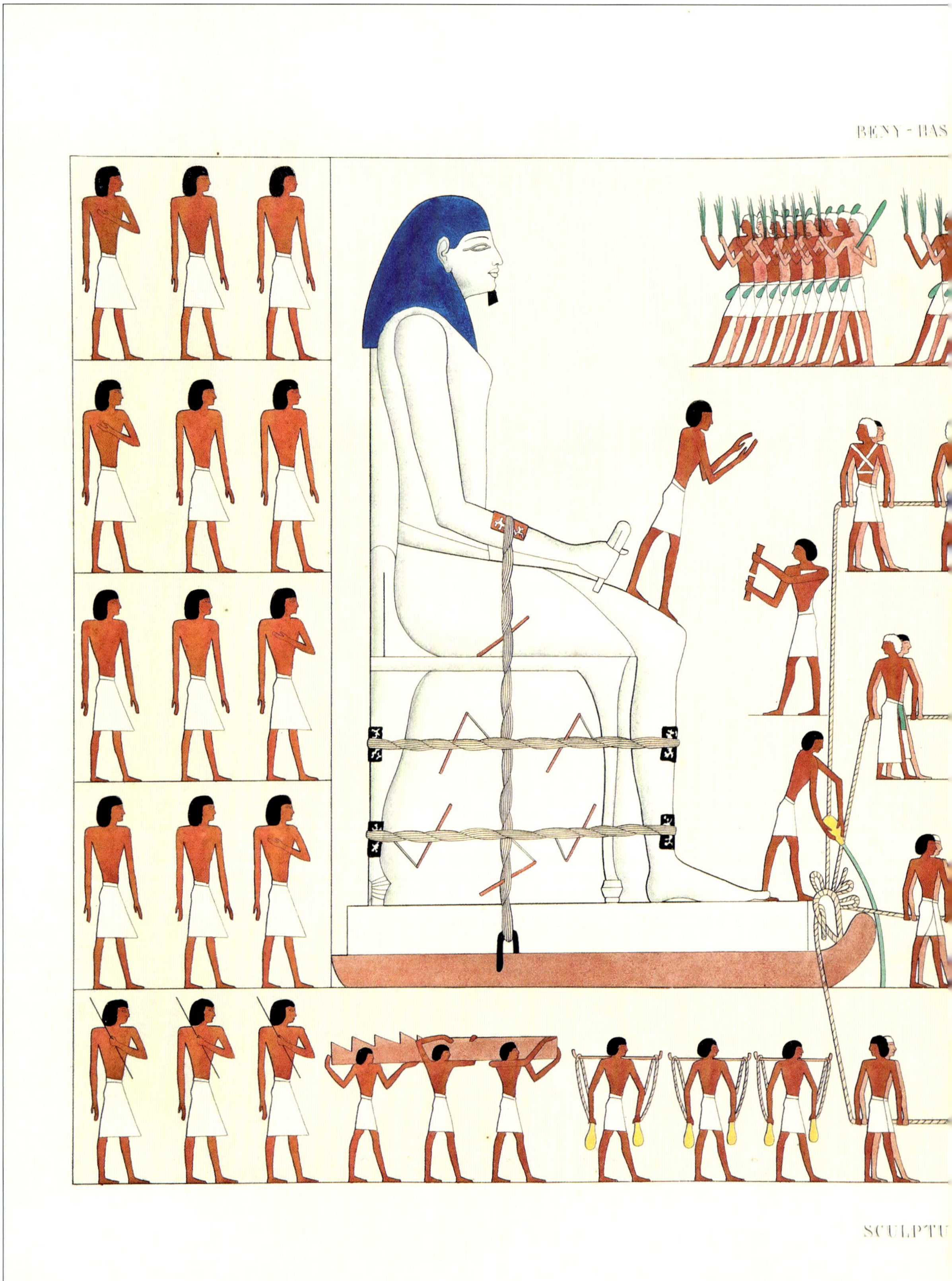

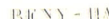

Plate 43. Moving a colossal statue.

Pl. 45.

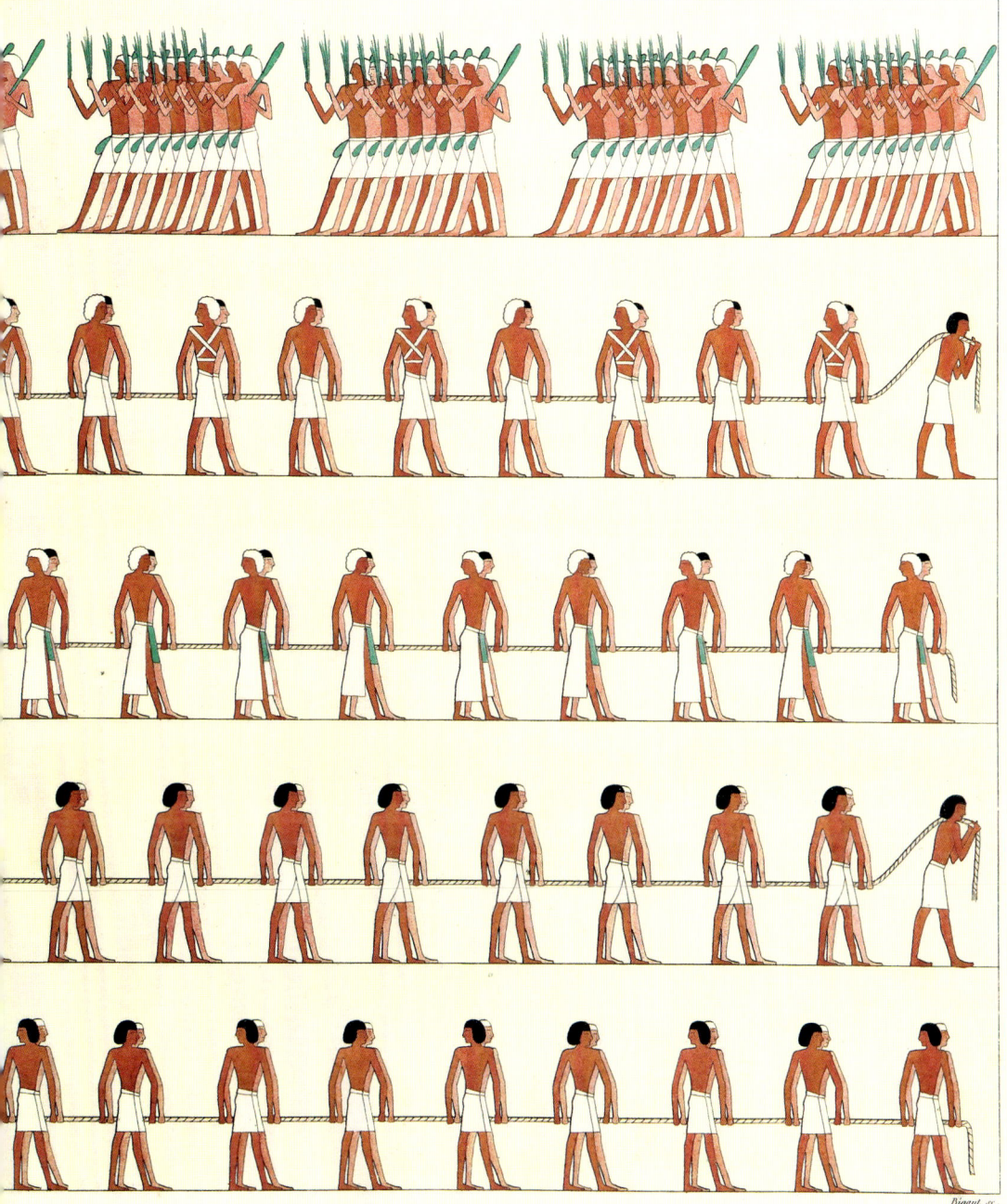

Bigaut sc.

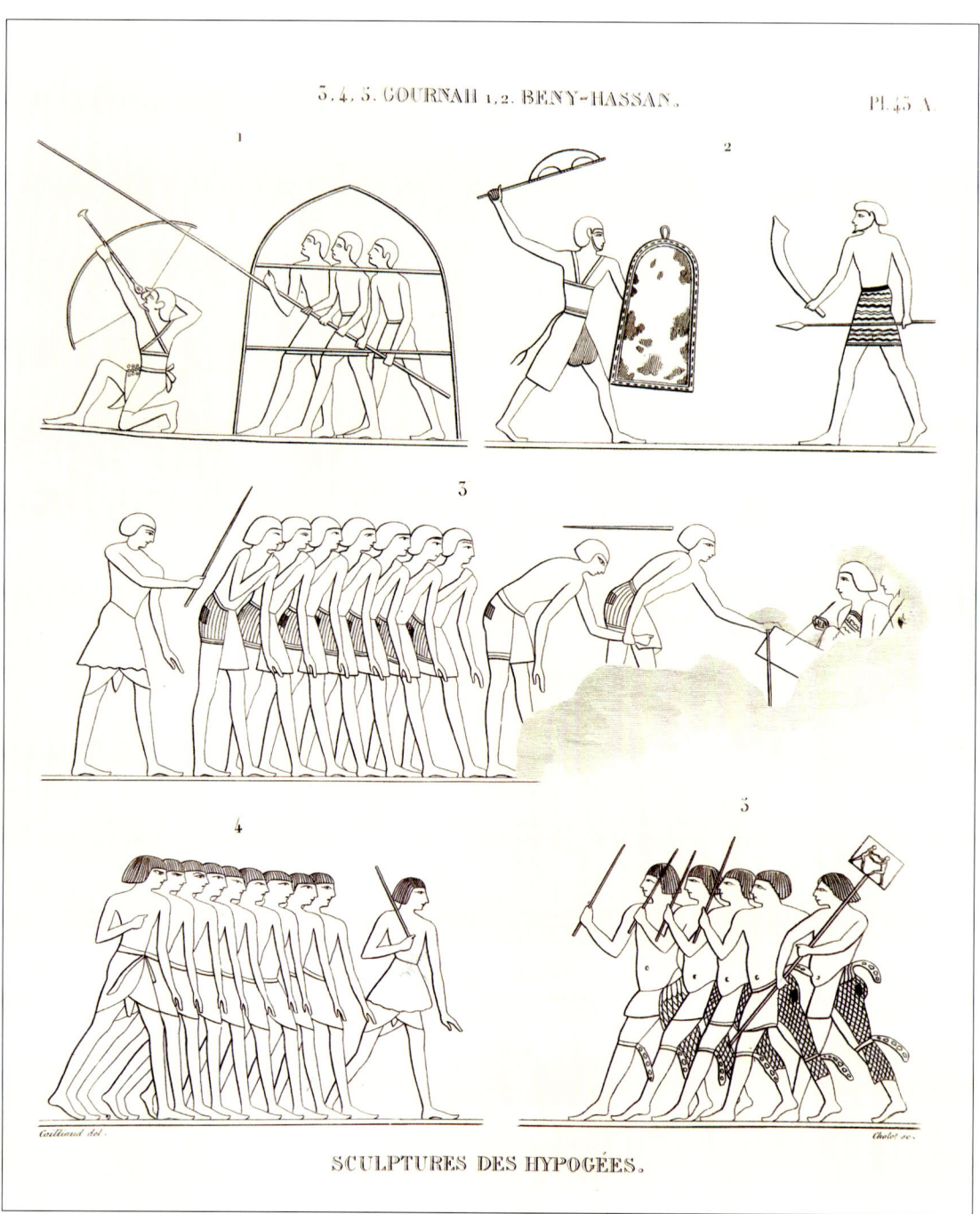

SCULPTURES DES HYPOGÉES.

Plate 43A. Soldiers training.

232

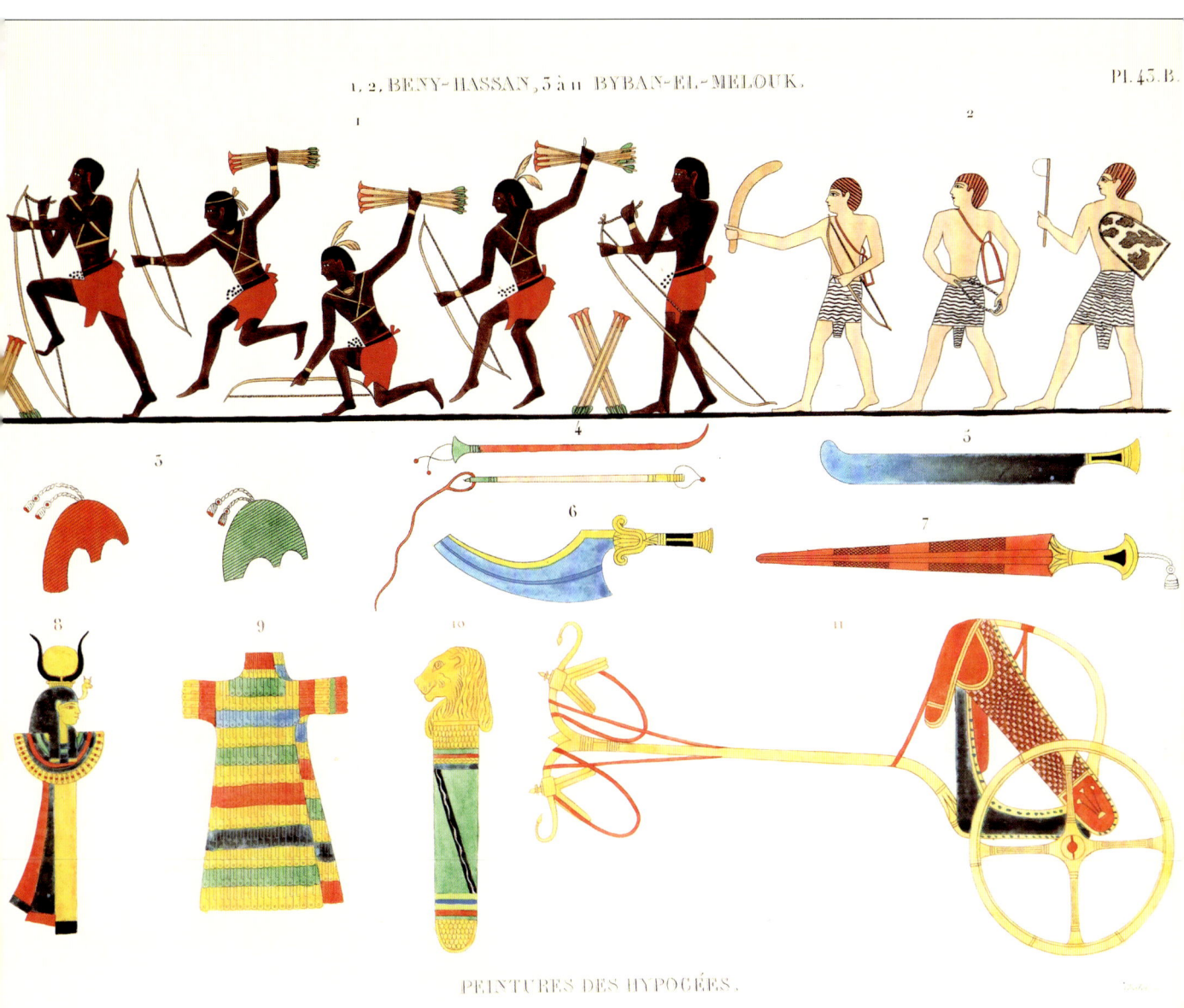

Plate 43B. Soldiers training, helmets, clothing, weapons, and chariots.

Pl. 44.

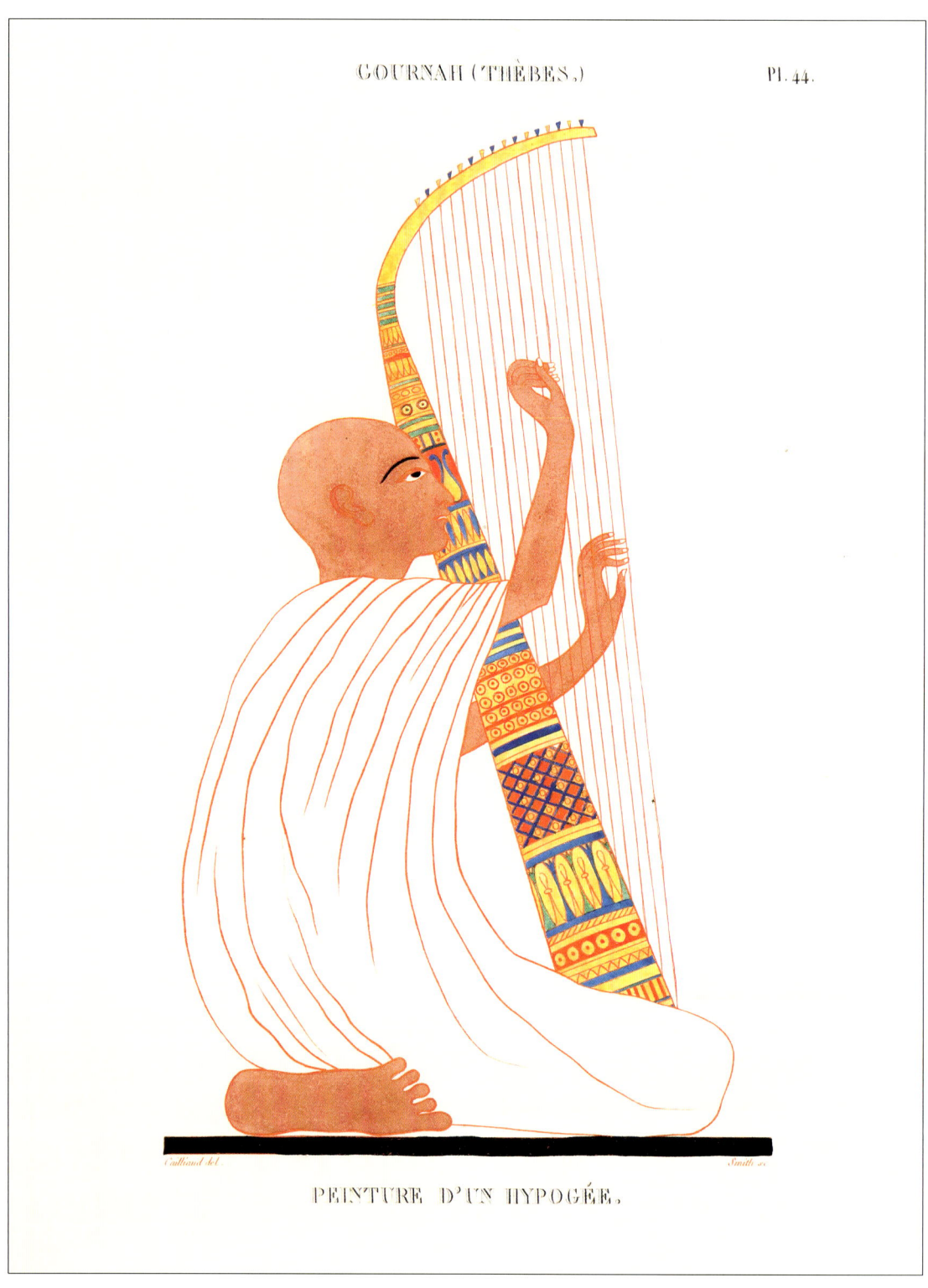

PEINTURE D'UN HYPOGÉE.

Plate 44. Harper.
Opposite: Plate 45. Harper.

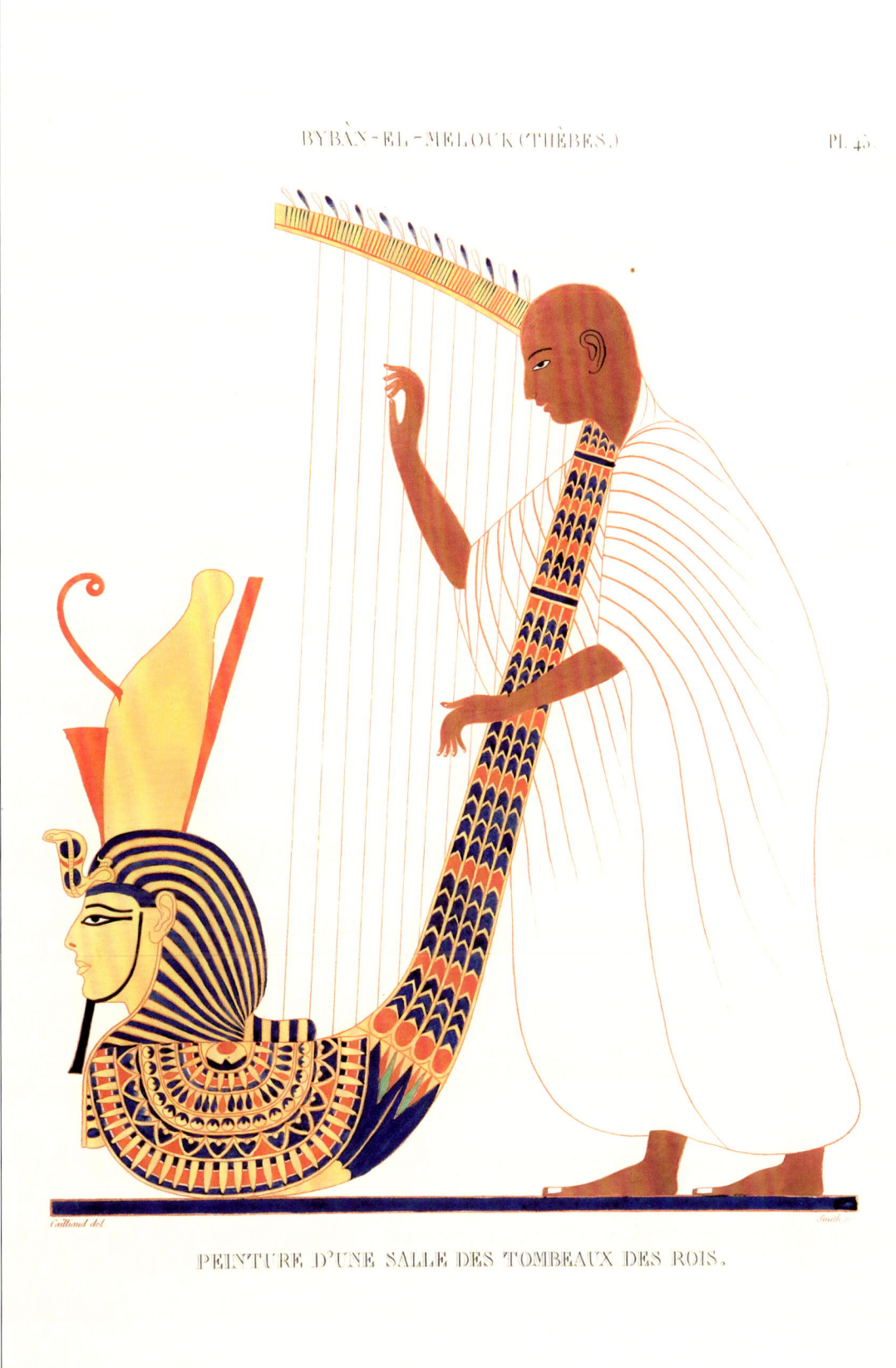

PEINTURE D'UNE SALLE DES TOMBEAUX DES ROIS.

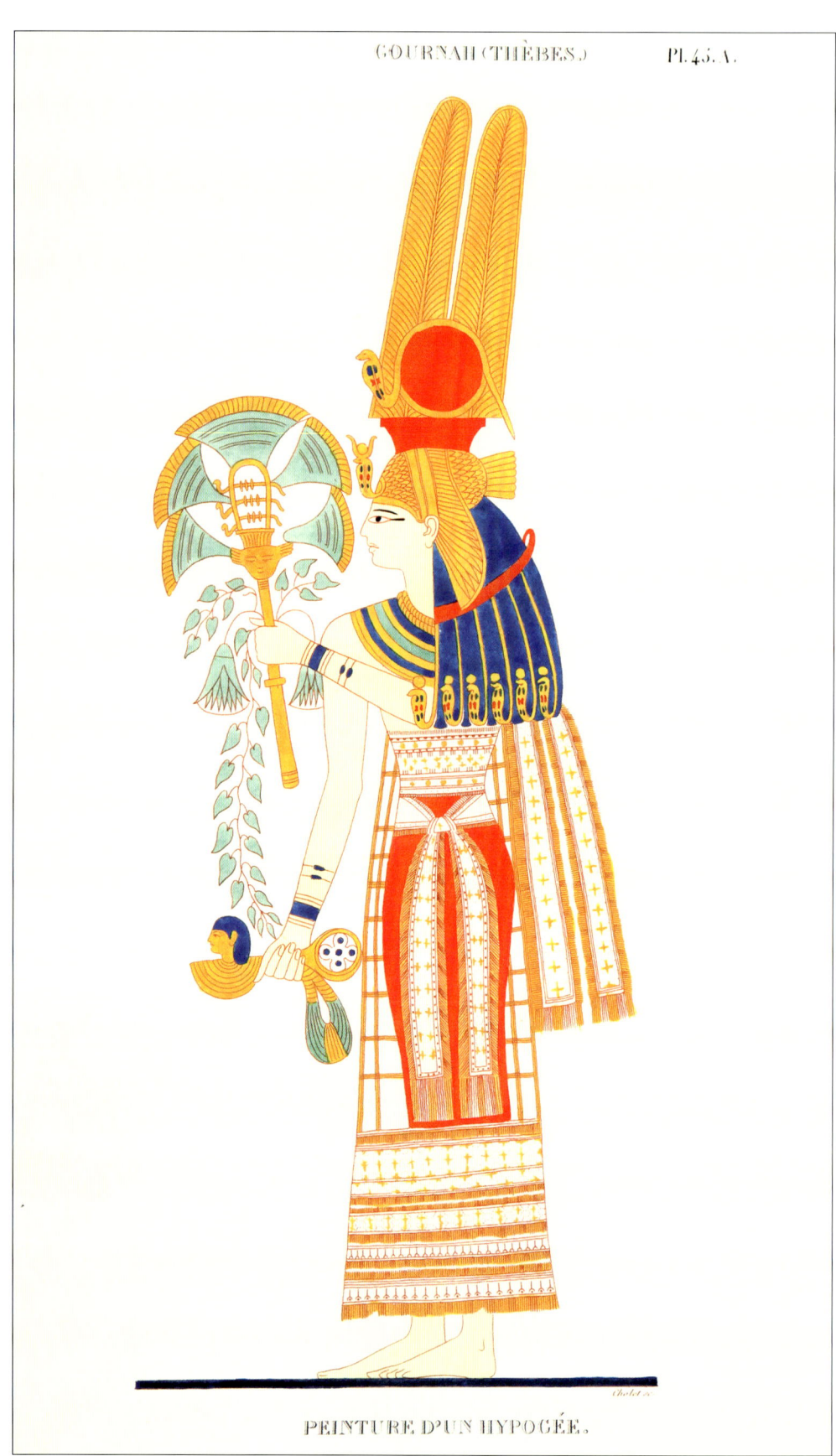

Plate 45A. Queen
holding a sistrum.
Opposite: Plate 46.
Pharaoh Horemheb.

PEINTURE D'UN HYPOGÉE.

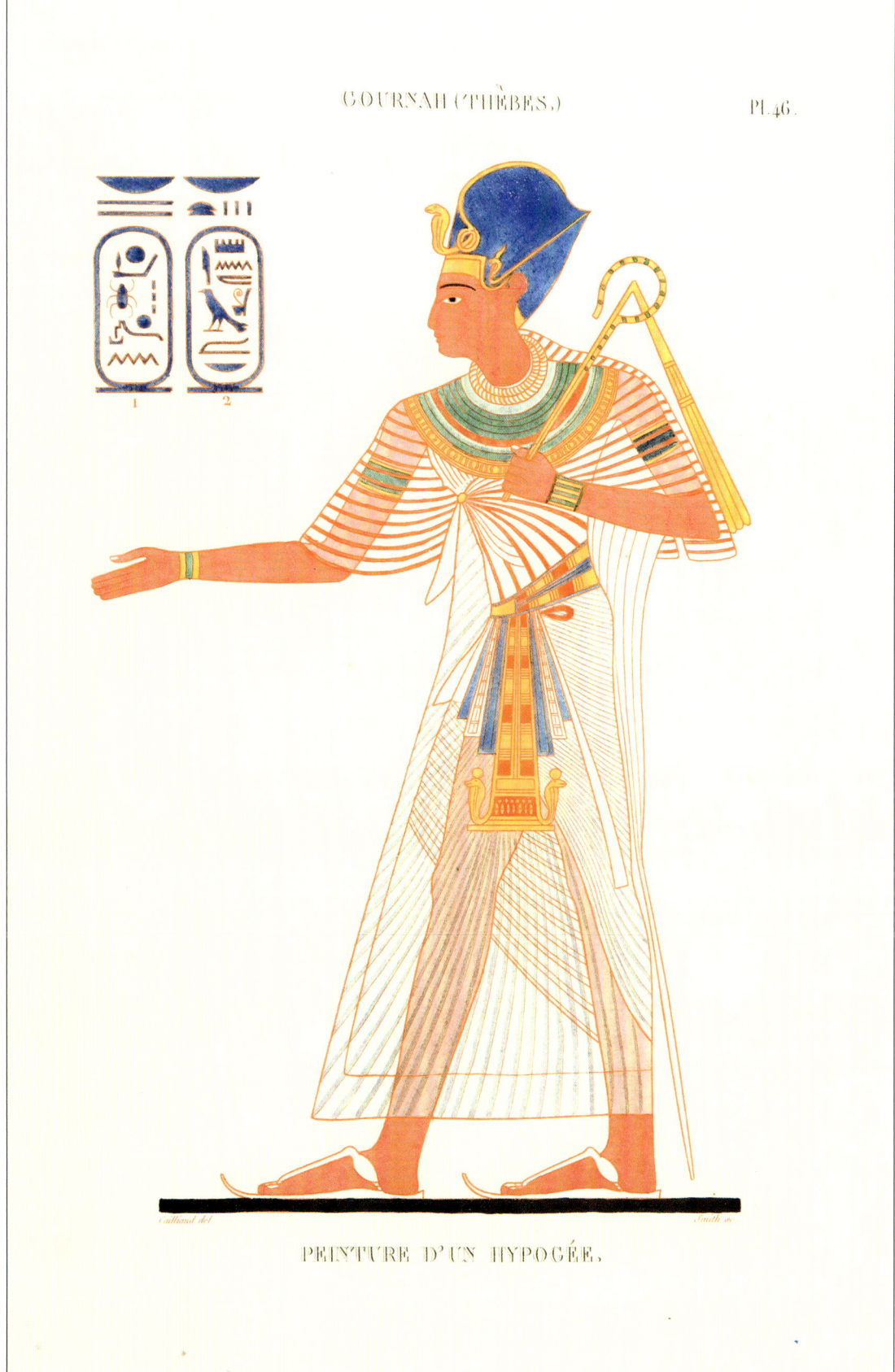

PEINTURE D'UN HYPOGÉE.

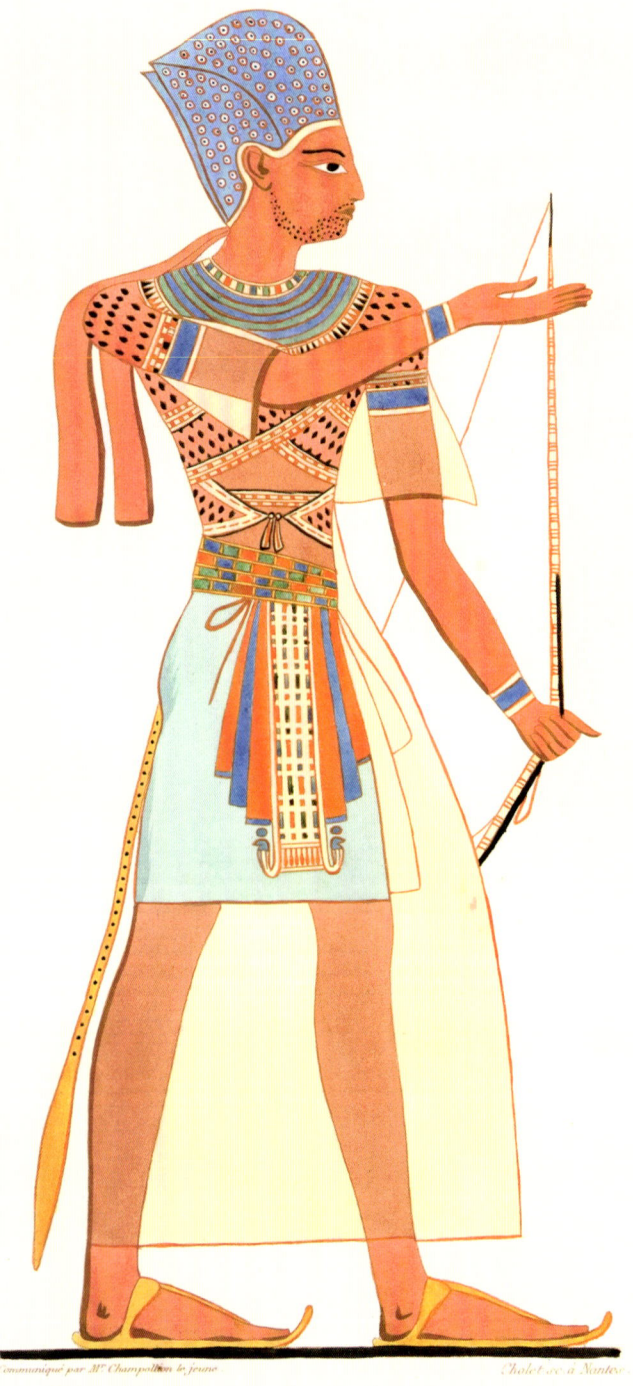

Communiqué par M.ʳ Champollion le jeune.

Chalot sc. à Nantes.

SCULPTURE D'UN TEMPLE.

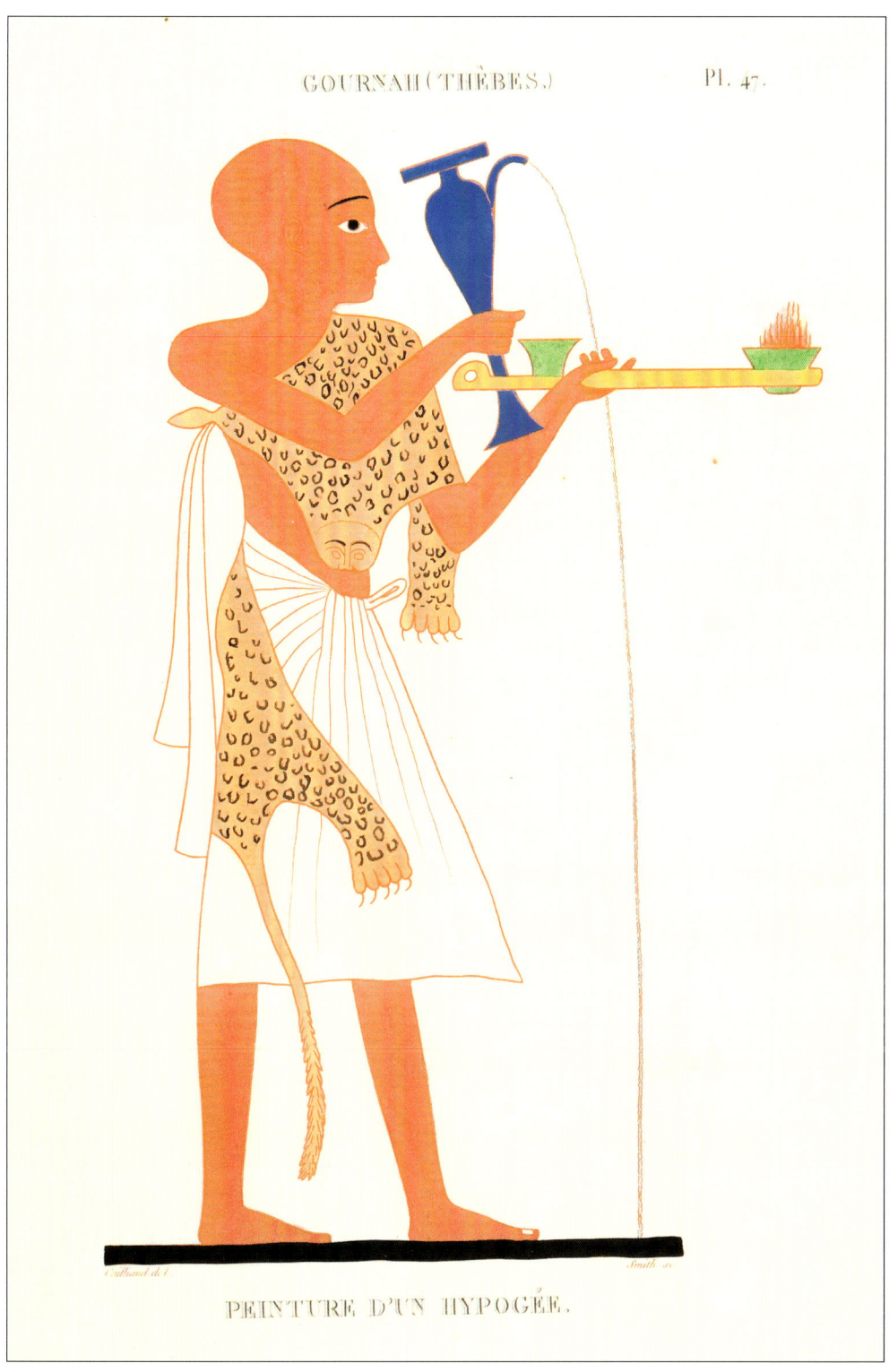

PEINTURE D'UN HYPOGÉE.

Plate 47. Priest making offerings.
Opposite: Plate 46A. Pharaoh Ramesses II holding a bow.

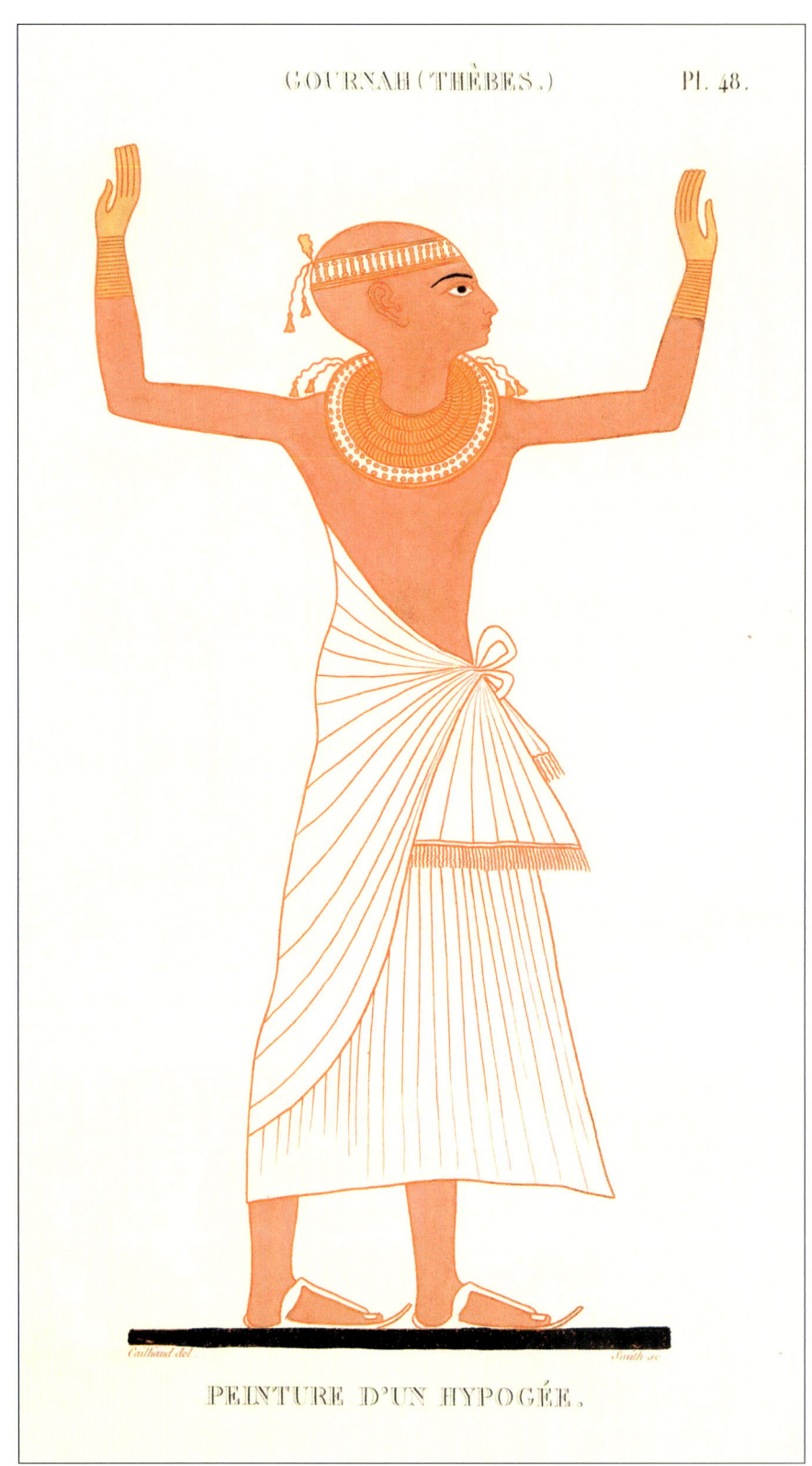

PEINTURE D'UN HYPOGÉE.

Plate 48. Priest wearing gold gloves. *Opposite:* Plate 49. Princess holding a sistrum.

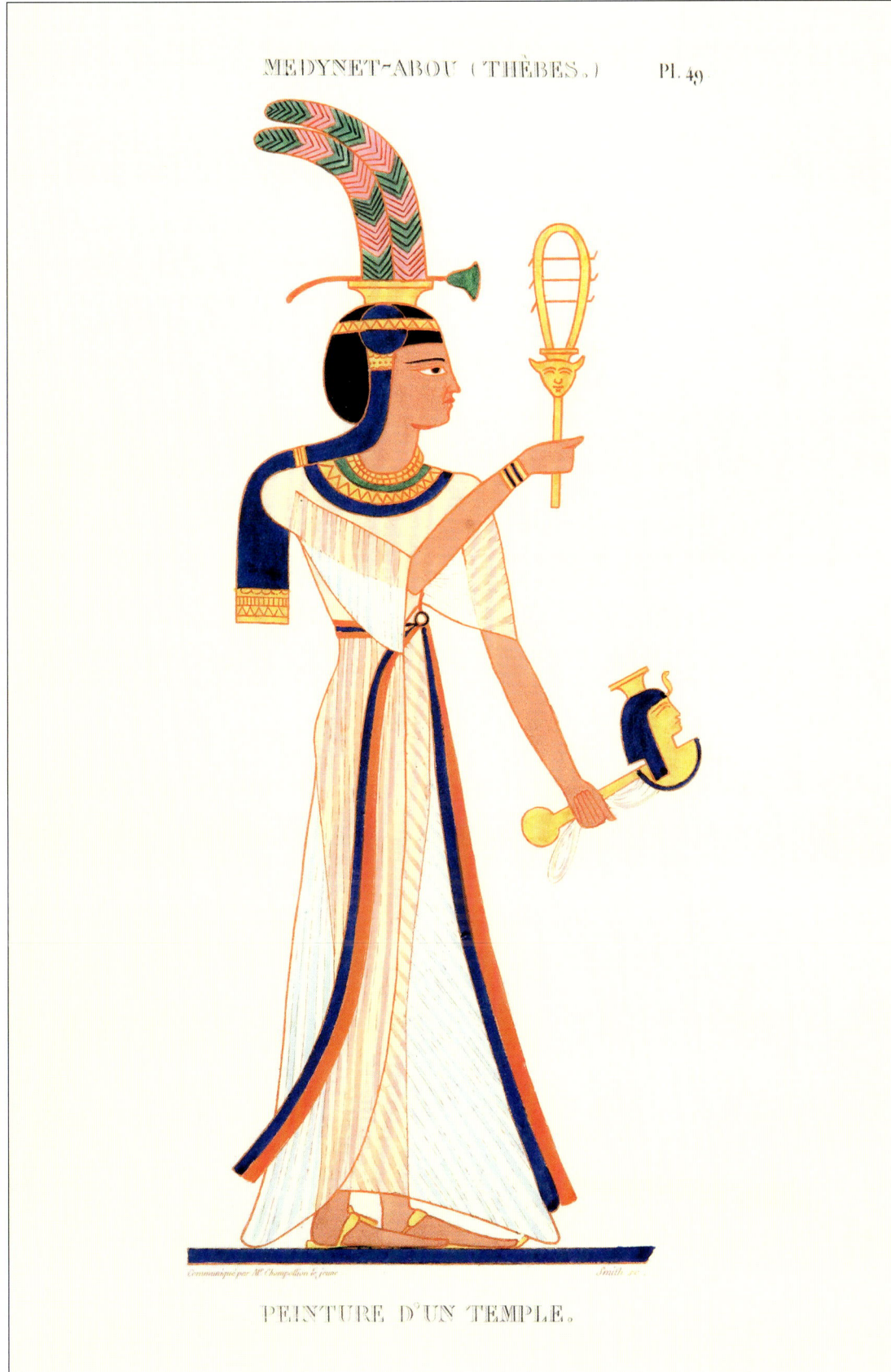

Communiqué par Mr Champollion le jeune.   Smith sc.

PEINTURE D'UN TEMPLE.

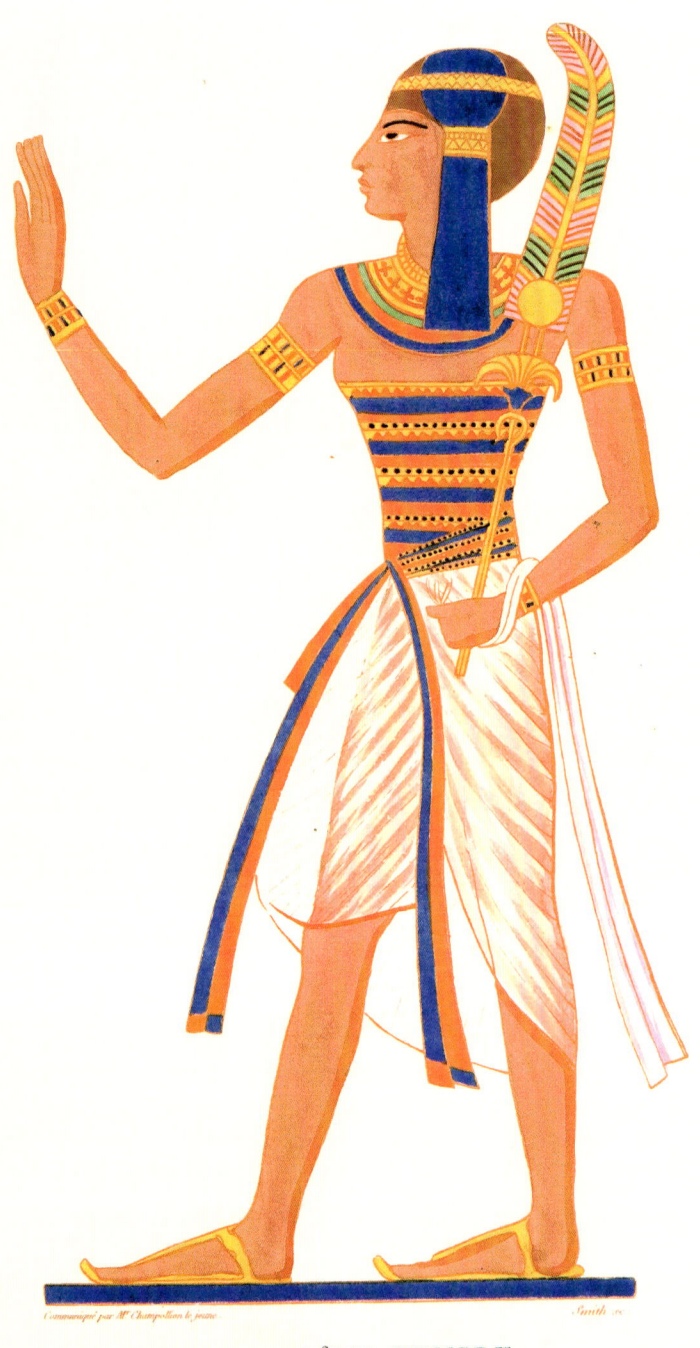

Communiqué par Mr Champollion le jeune.　　Smith sc.

PEINTURE D'UN TEMPLE.

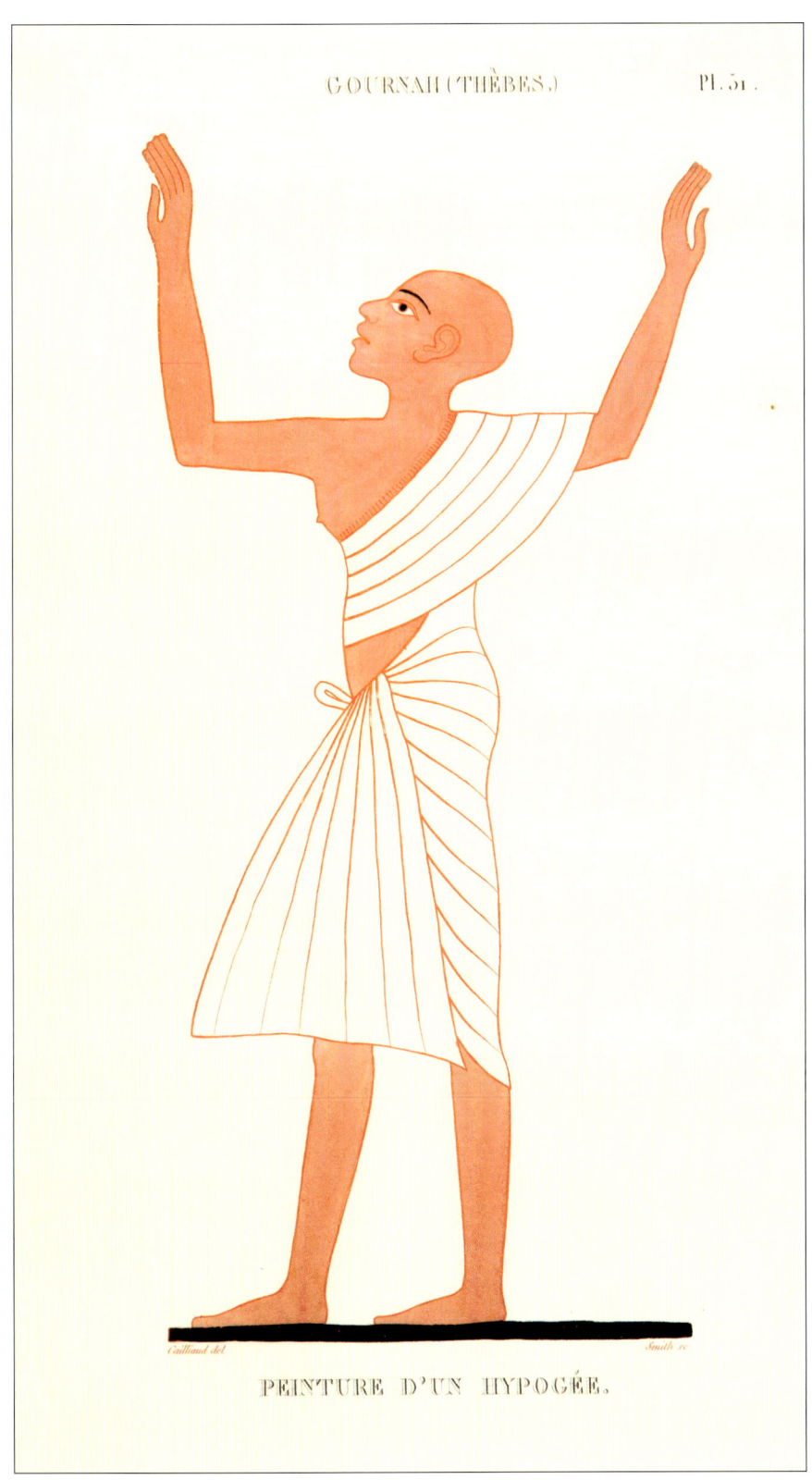

Cailliaud del.   Smith sc.

PEINTURE D'UN HYPOGÉE.

Plate 51. Priest in rapture.
Opposite: Plate 50. Prince.

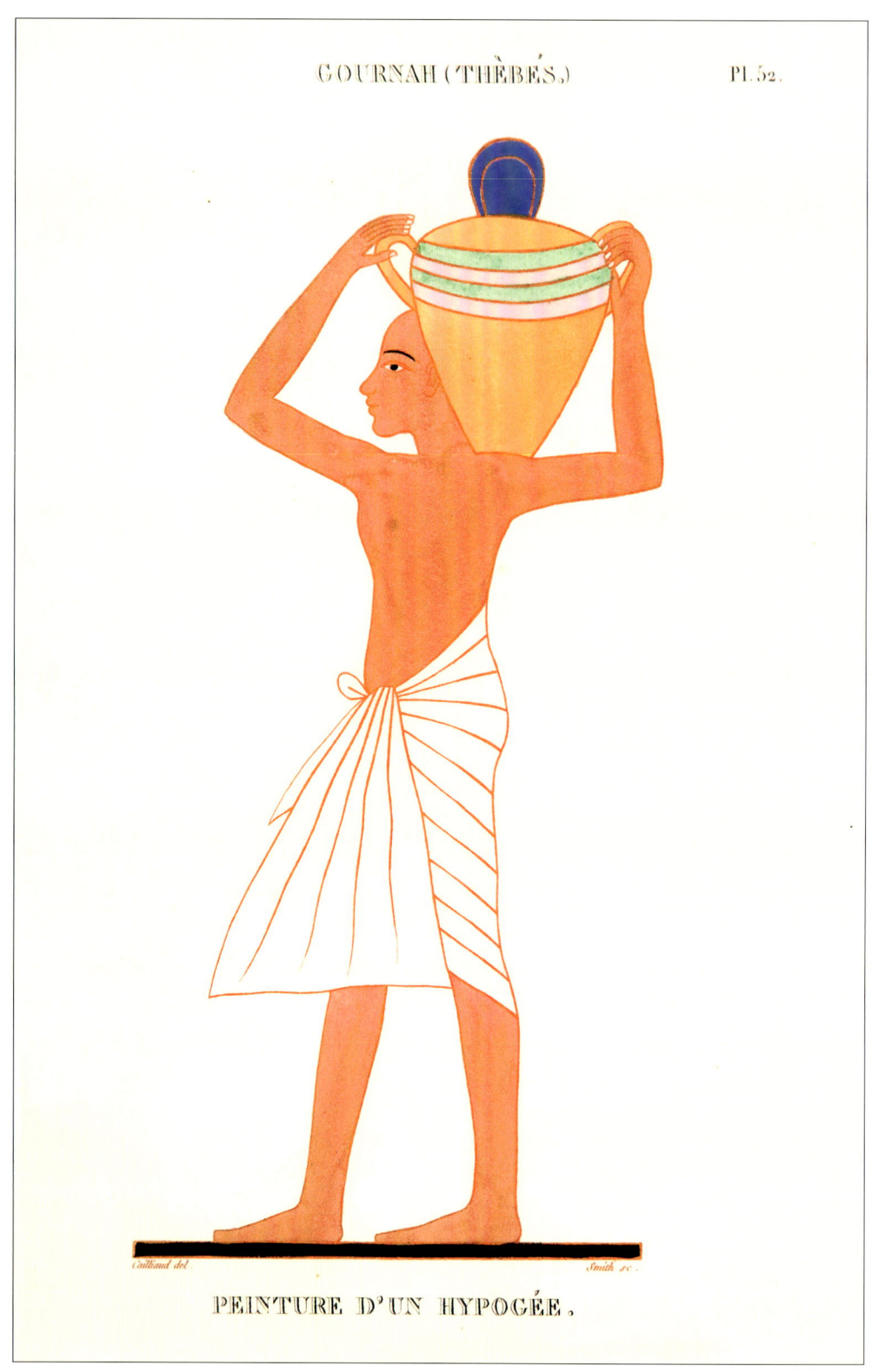

Guilliaud del　　　　Smith sc.

PEINTURE D'UN HYPOGÉE.

Plate 52. Offering bearer.

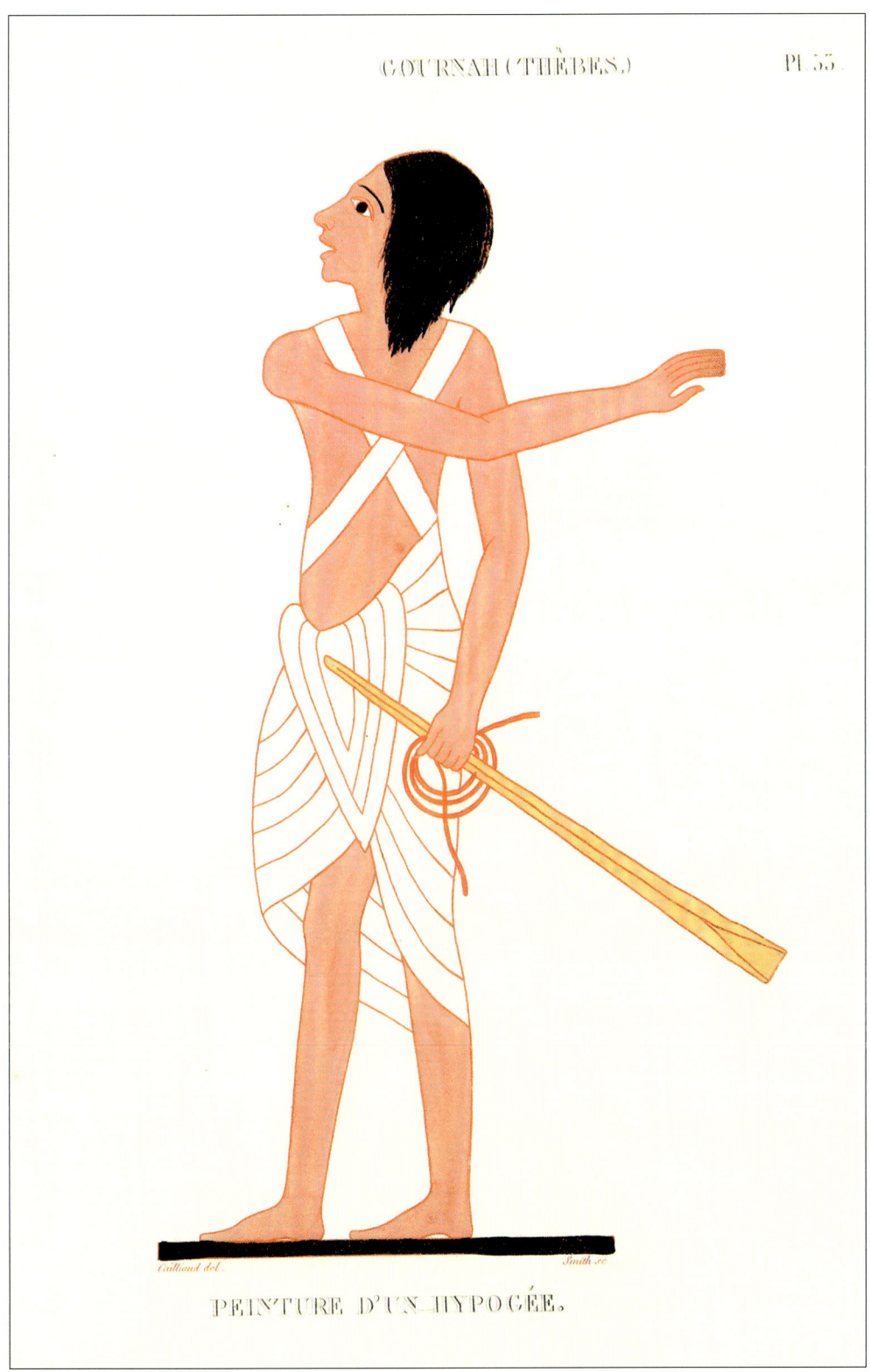

PEINTURE D'UN HYPOGÉE.

Plate 53. Officiating priest.

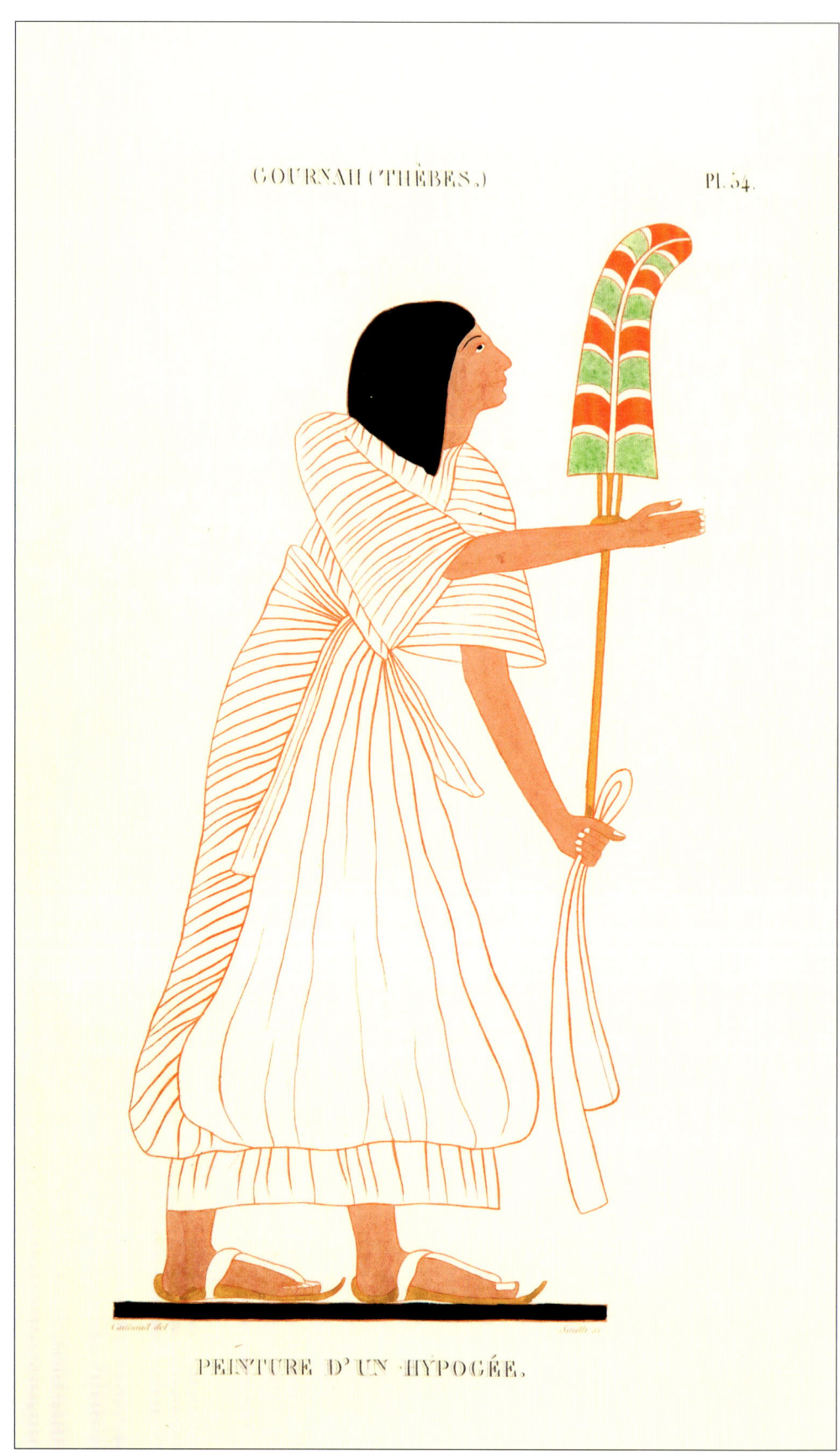

Plate 54.
Officiating priest.

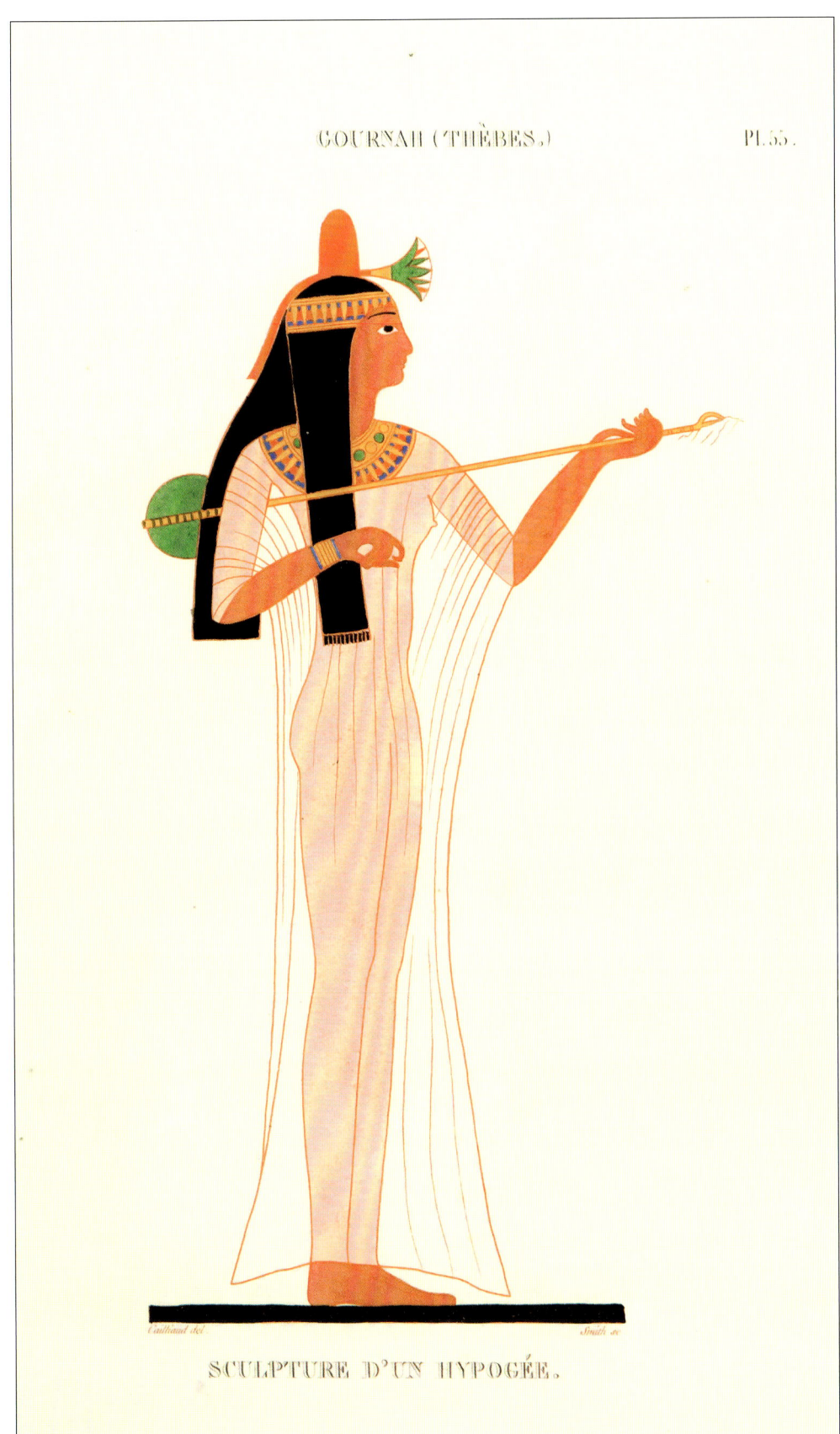

Caillaud del. Smith sc.

SCULPTURE D'UN HYPOGÉE.

Plate 55. Musician.

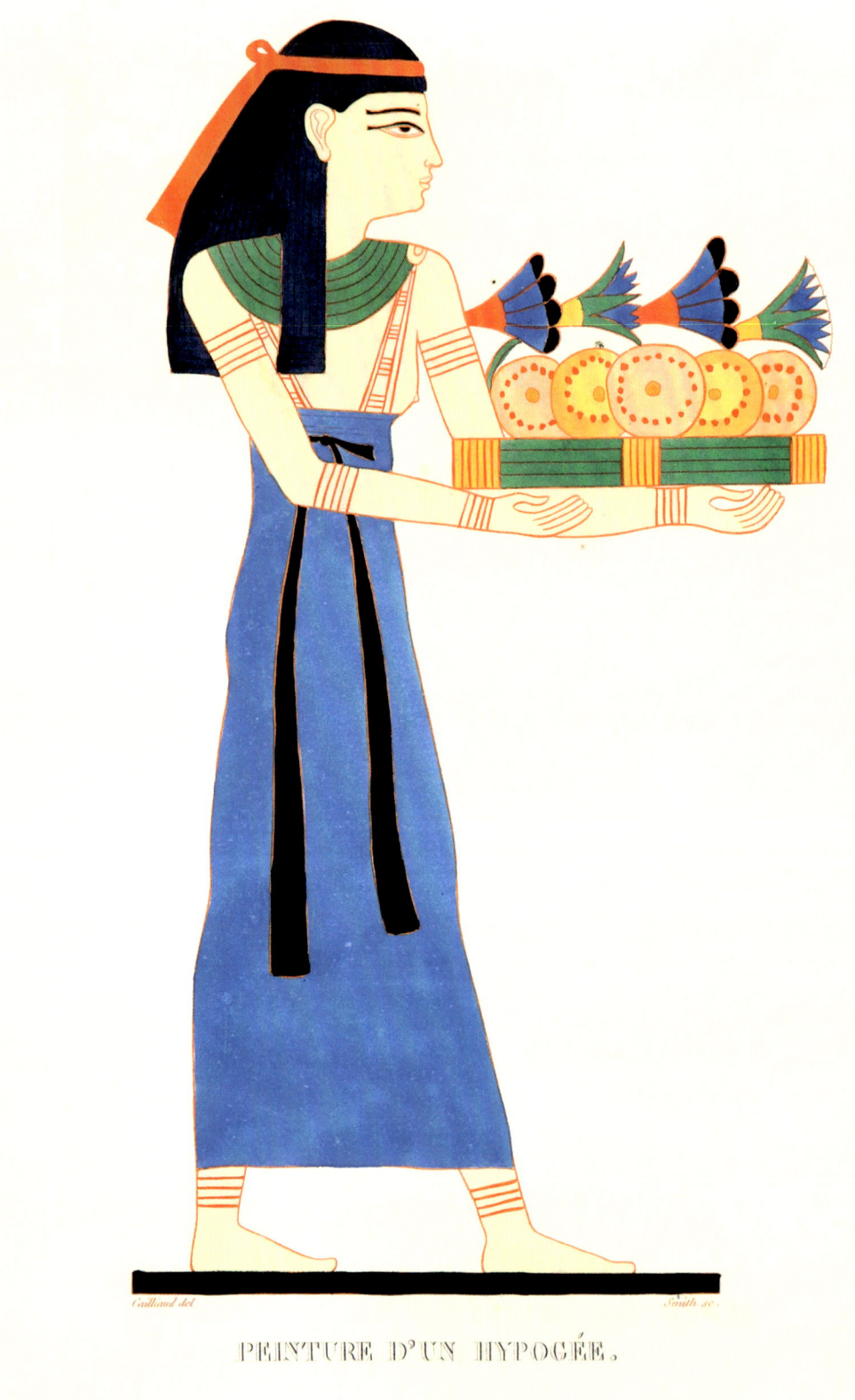

Gaillaud del

Smith sc.

PEINTURE D'UN HYPOGÉE.

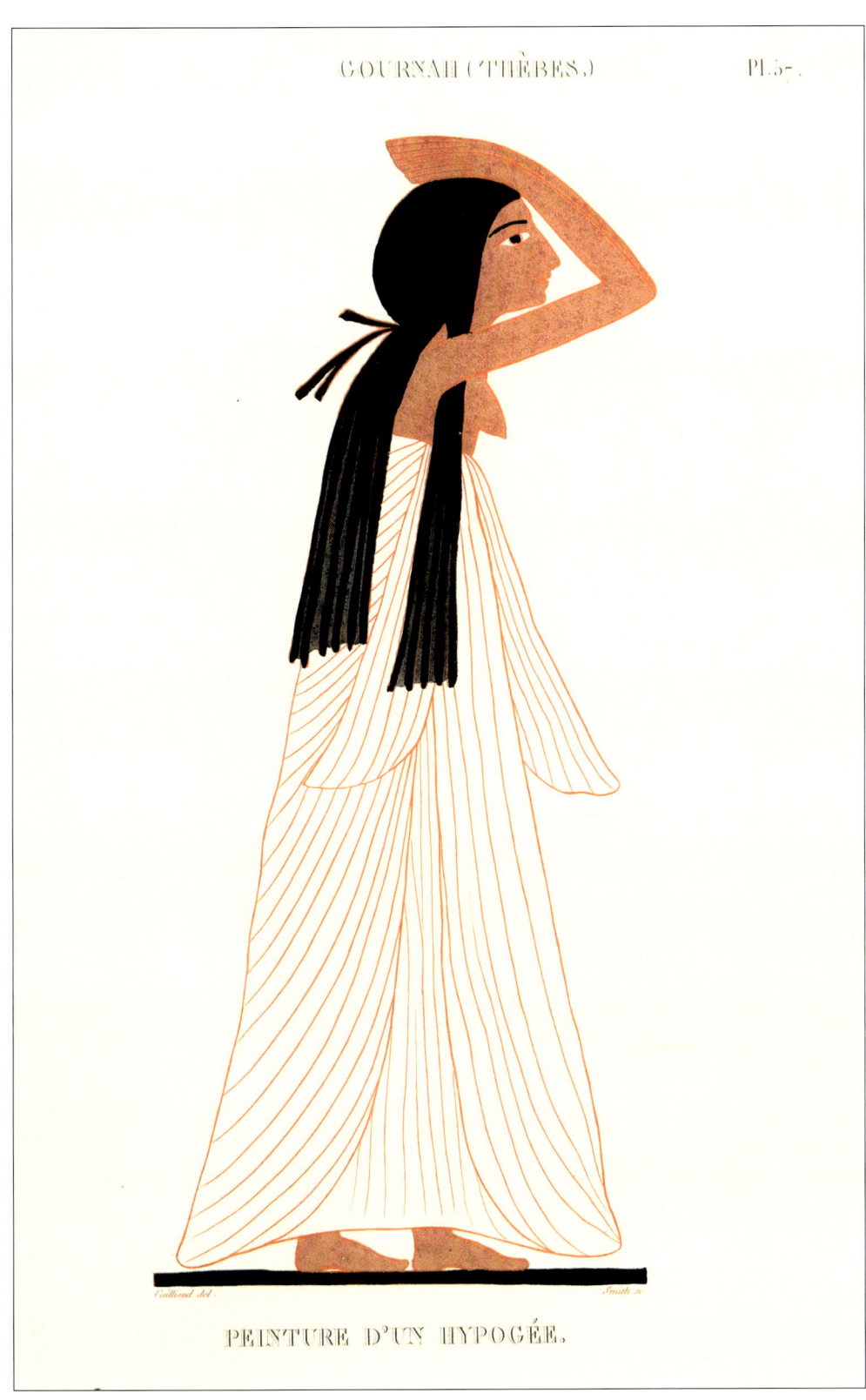

PEINTURE D'UN HYPOGÉE.

Plate 57. Mourner.
Opposite: Plate 56.
Nome goddess
bearing offerings.

249

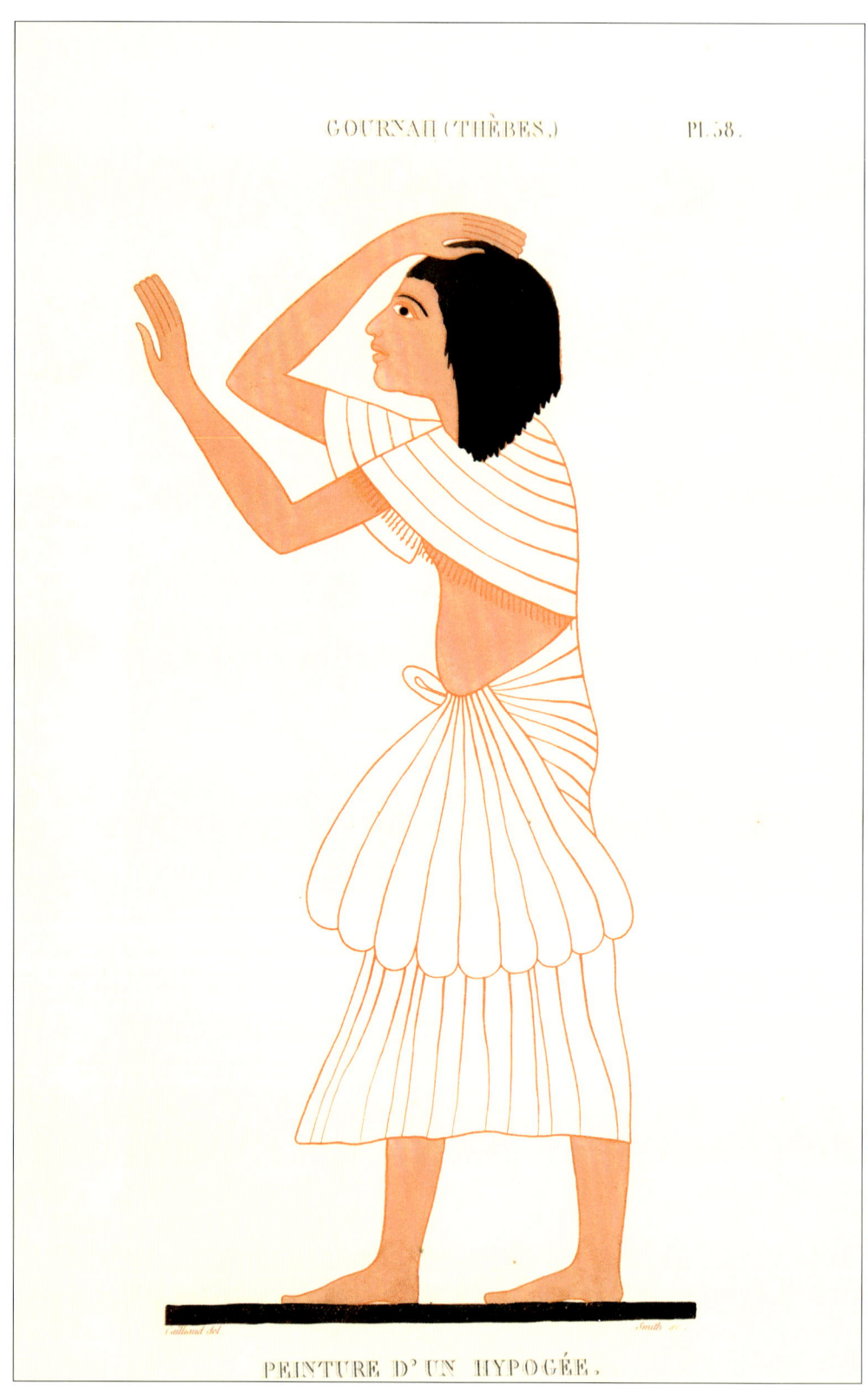

GOURNAII (THÈBES.)   PL.58.

PEINTURE D'UN HYPOGÉE.

Plate 58.
Mourning man.
Opposite: Plate 59.
Offering bearer.

250

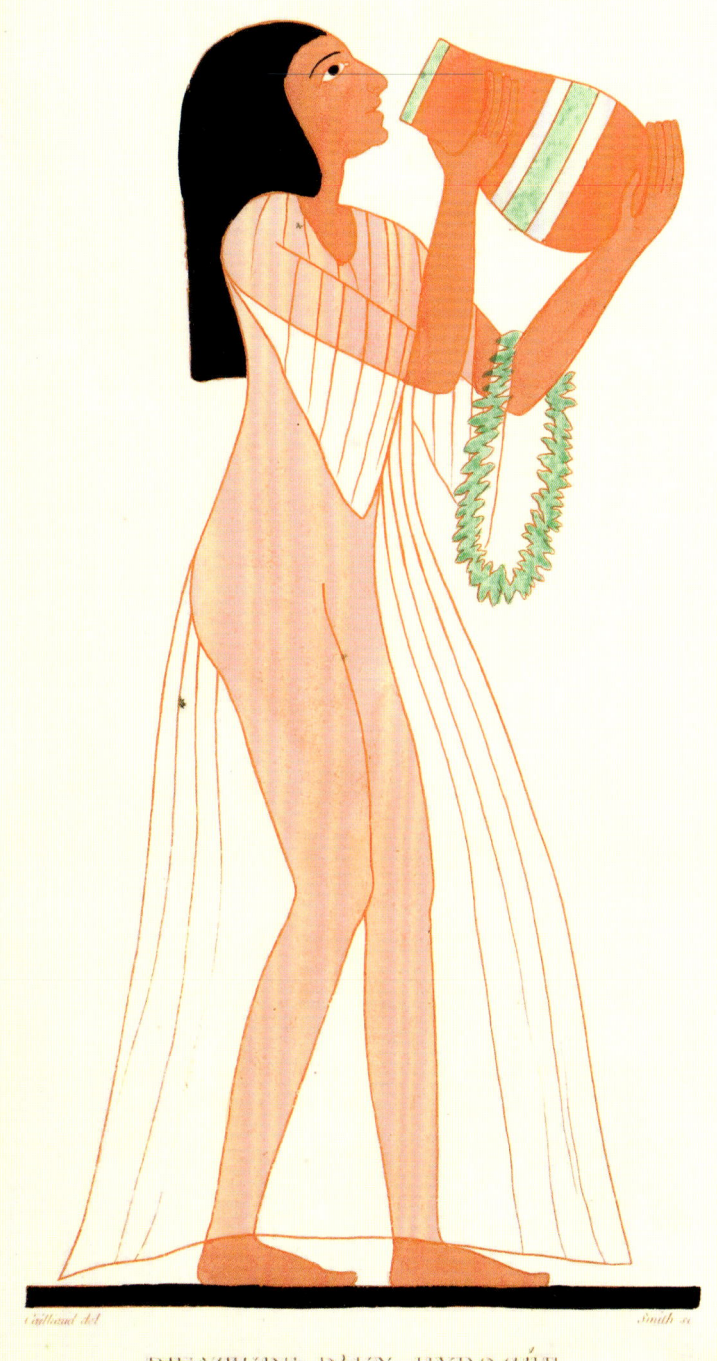

PEINTURE D'UN HYPOGÉE.

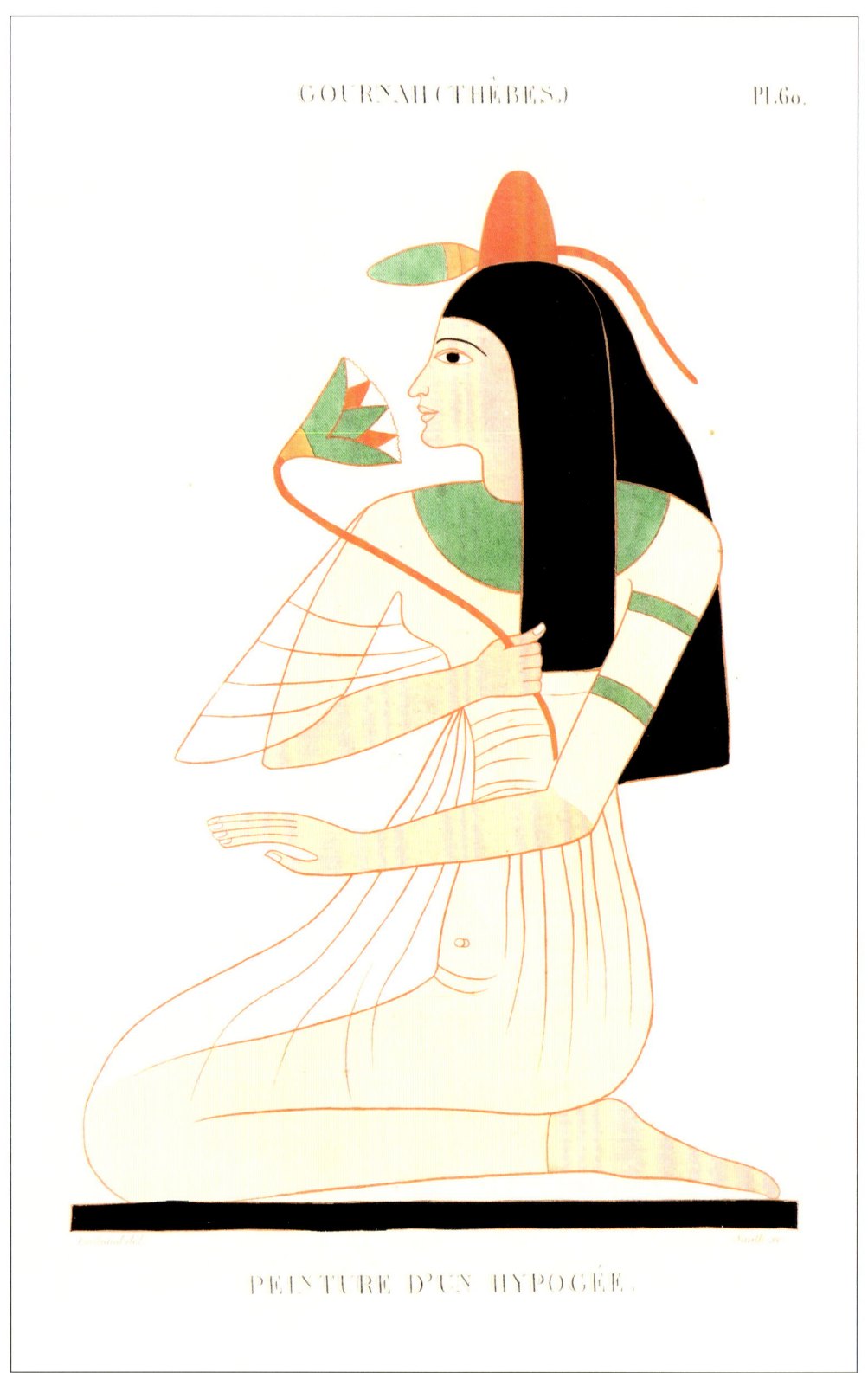

PEINTURE D'UN HYPOGÉE.

Plate 60. Woman
smelling a lotus
flower.
Opposite: Plate 61.
Head of a man
wearing a lotus
flower.

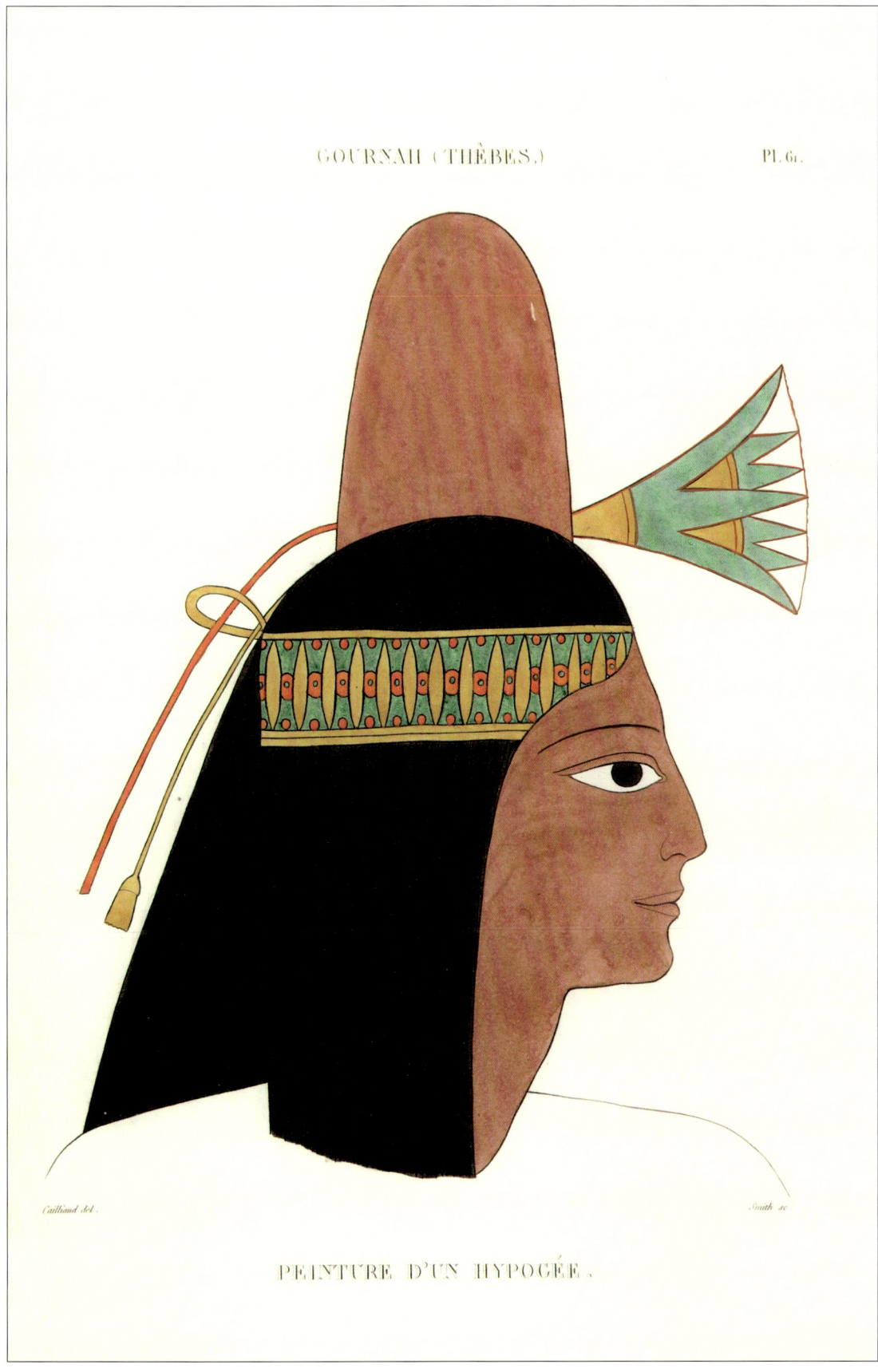

Caillaud del.　　　　　　　　　　　　　　Smith sc.

PEINTURE D'UN HYPOGÉE.

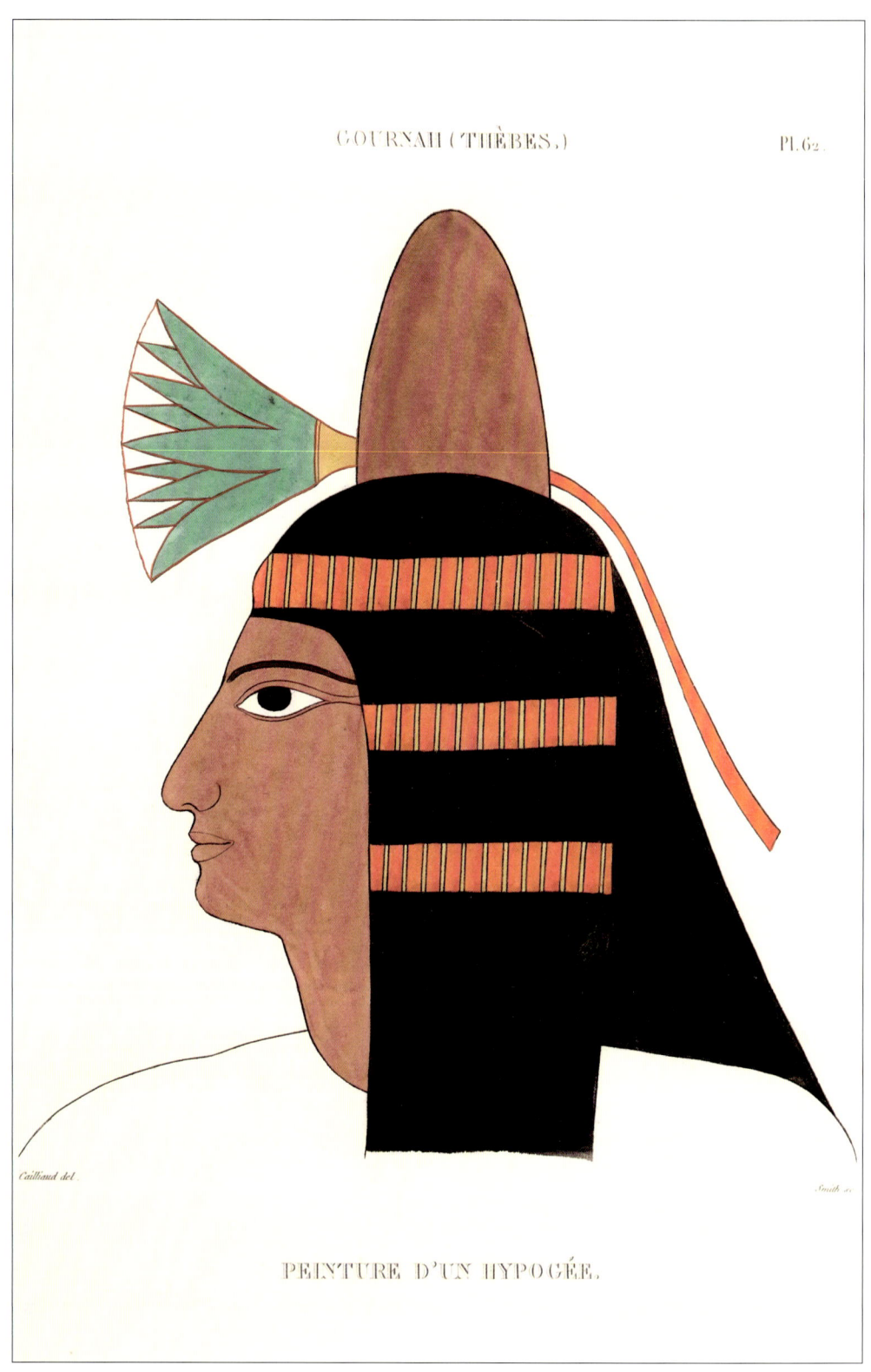

Caillaud del.

Smith sc.

PEINTURE D'UN HYPOGÉE.

Plate 62. Head of a man wearing a lotus flower.

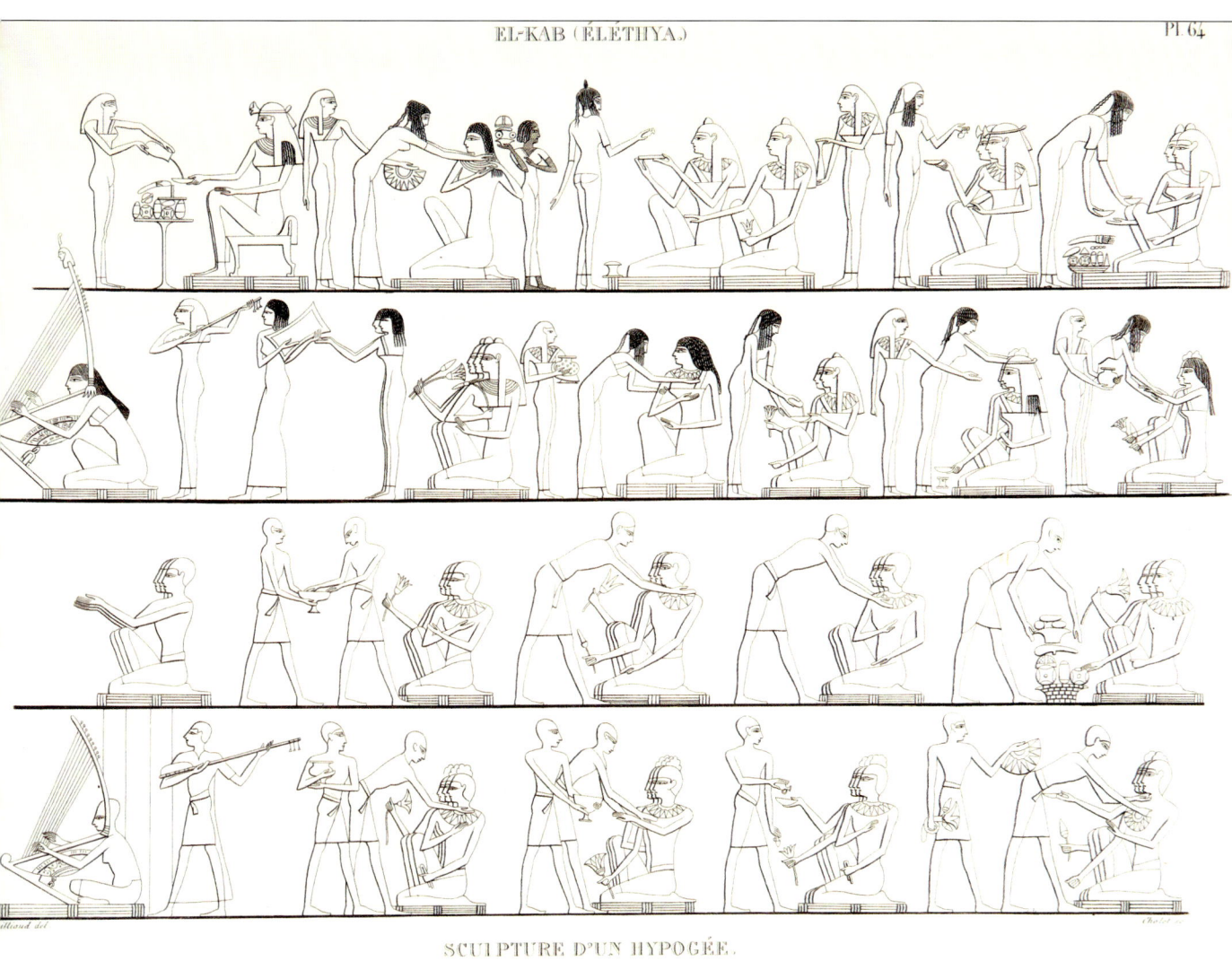

Pl. 64

SCULPTURE D'UN HYPOGÉE.

Plate 63. Figures around the Candace and Apedemak. 'Candace' was an ancient Nubian title for queens and queen mothers.

255

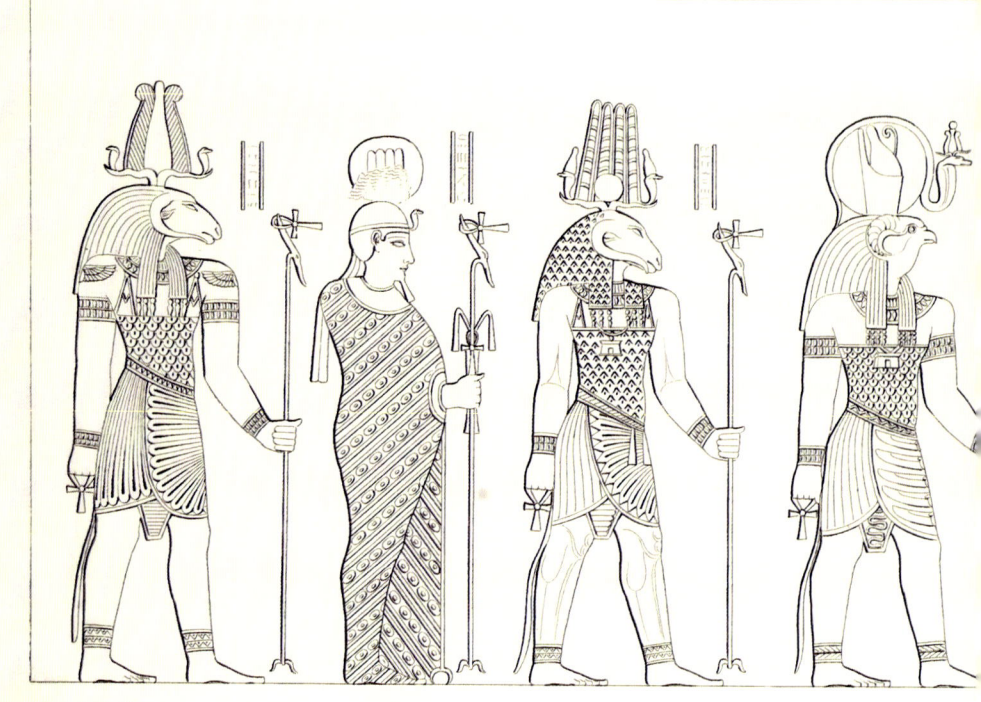

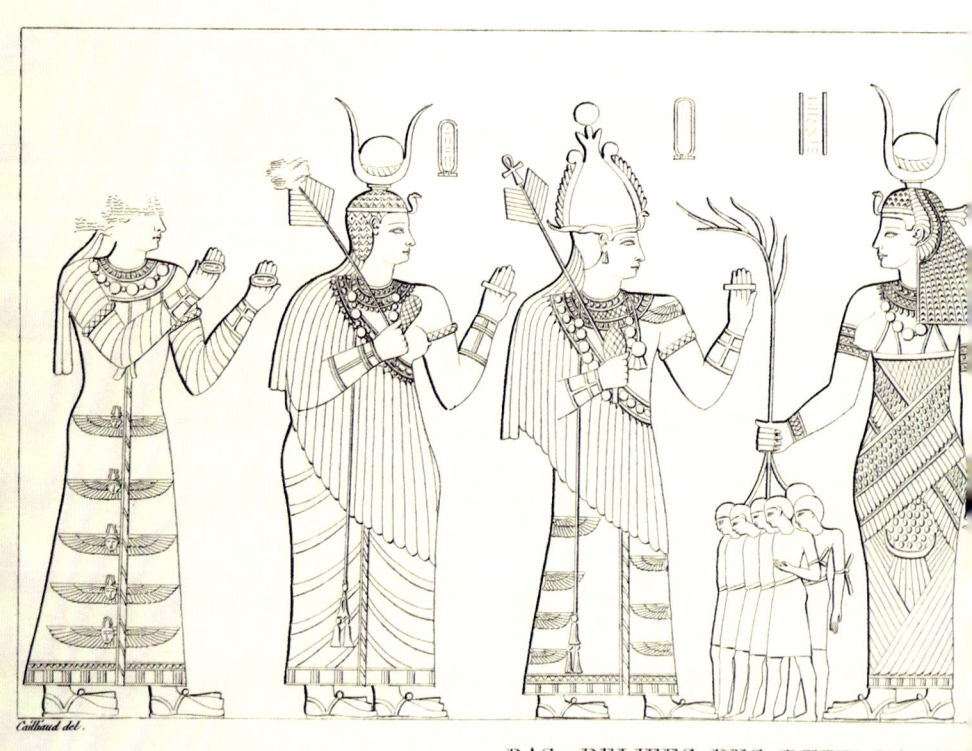

Caillaud del.

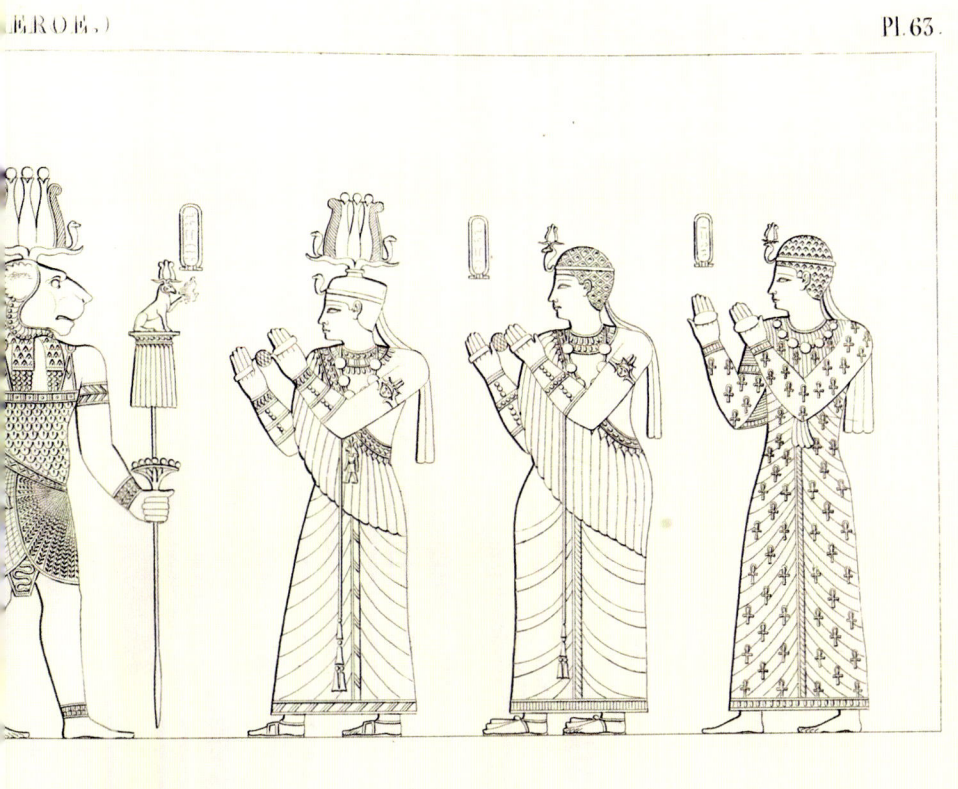

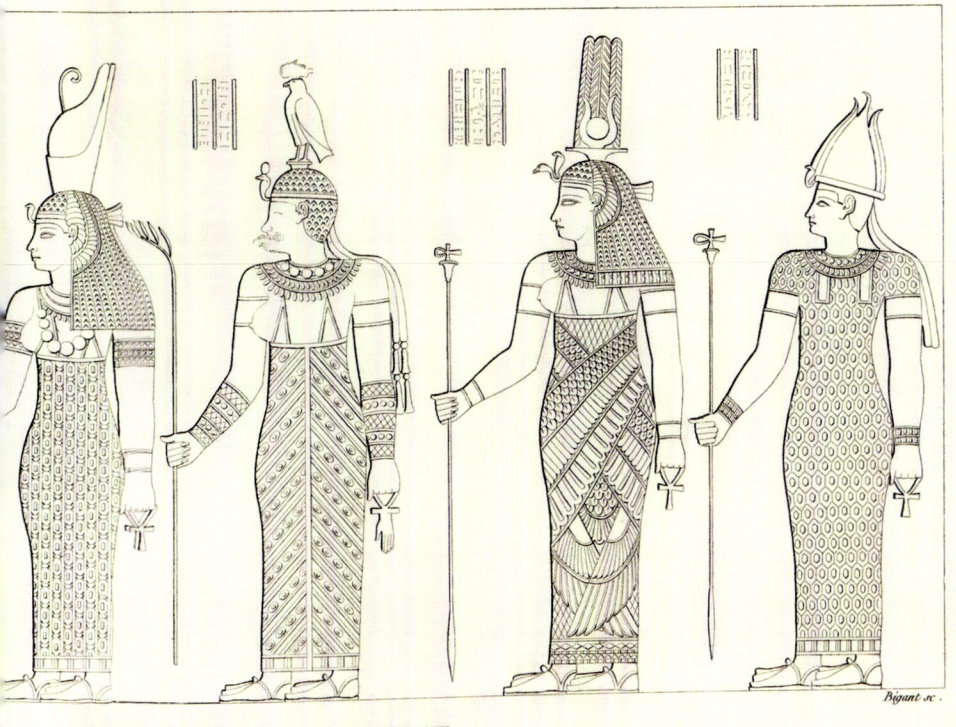

Bigant sc.

RALES DU TEMPLE DE L'OUEST.

Plate 64.
Banquet scene.

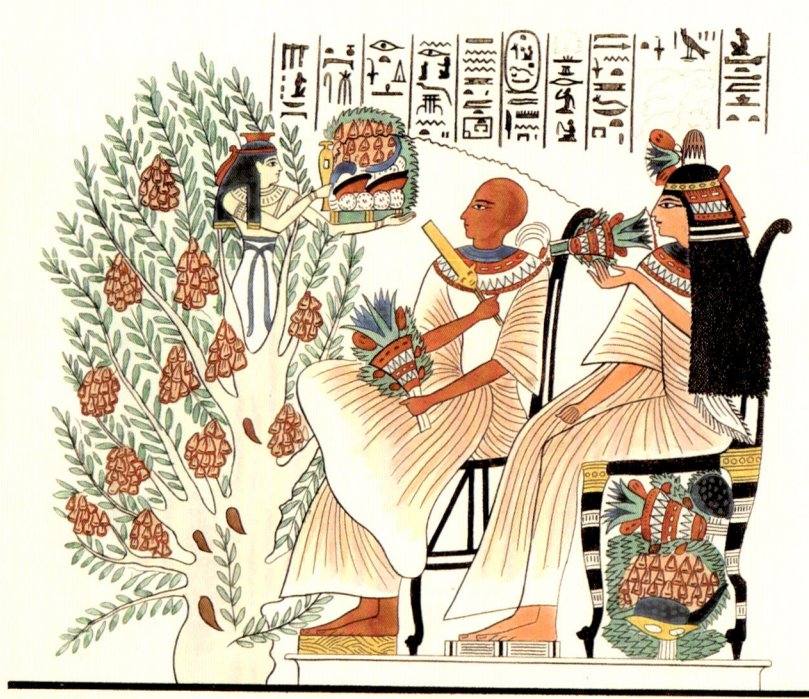

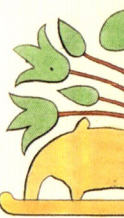

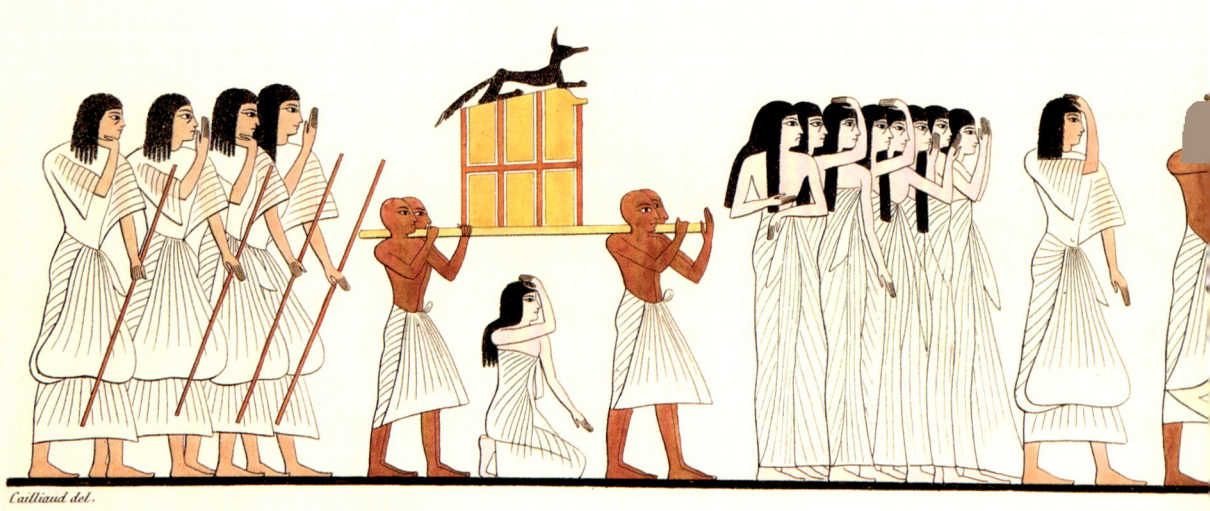

Plate 65. Offering to the tree goddess. Offering table. The *ba* visiting a mummy prepared by Anubis. The funeral procession.

2

3

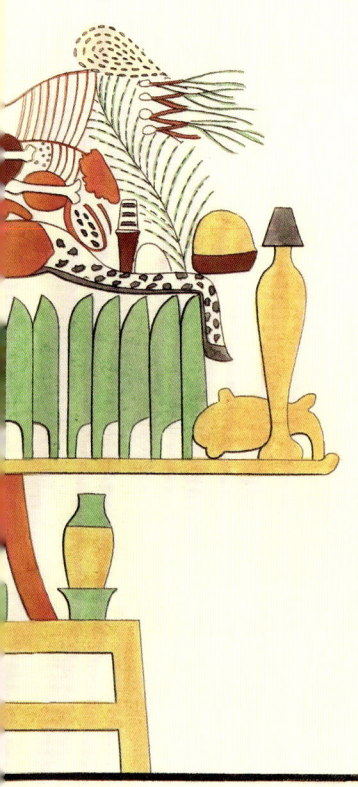

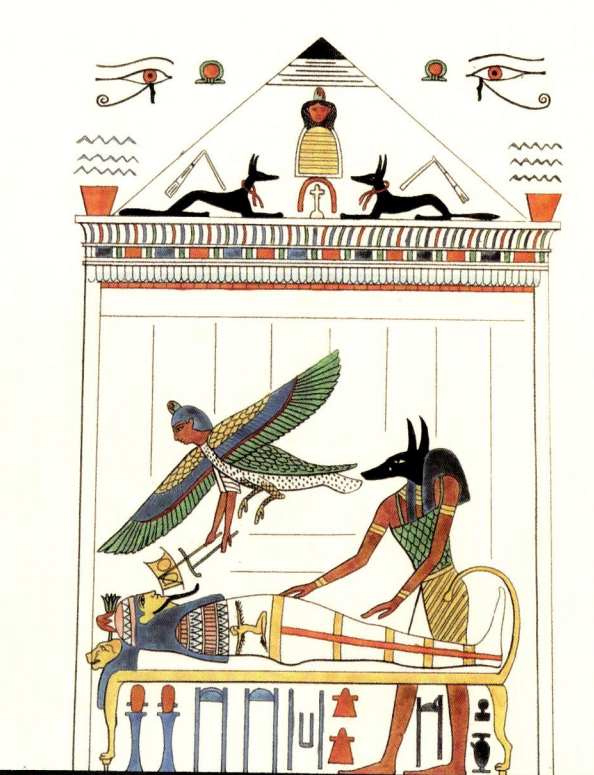

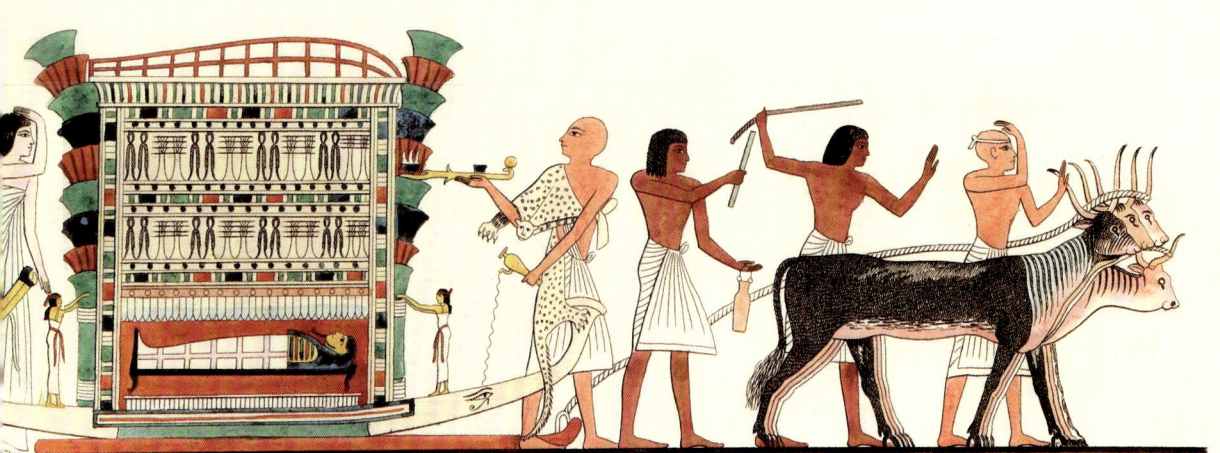

Cholet sc.

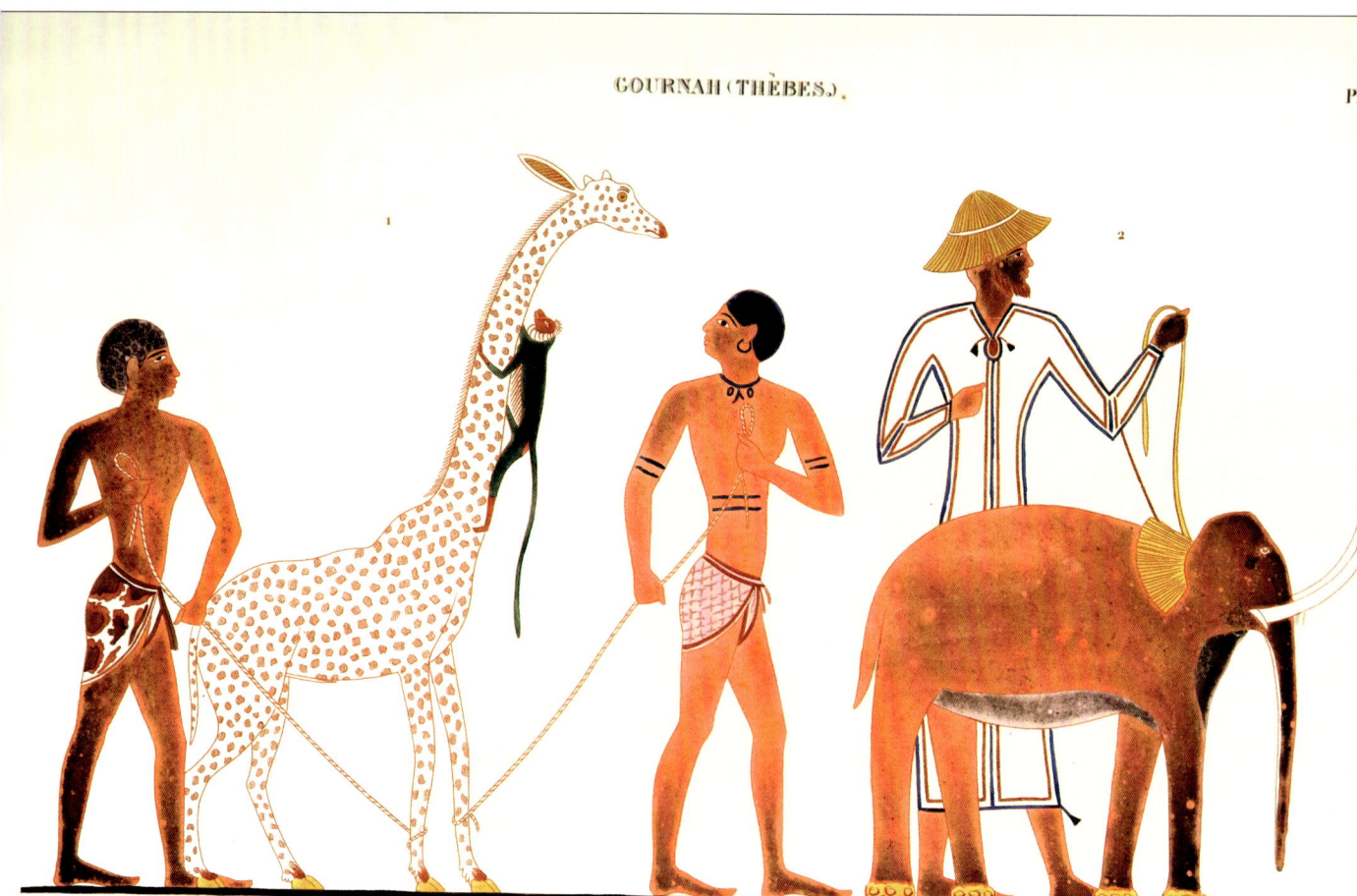

PEINTURE D'UN HYPOGÉE.

Plate 66. Offerings from people from Kush.

PLATE ATTRIBUTION

Philippe Mainterot

This appendix is meant as a guide to help readers navigate Cailliaud's artwork contained in this volume. The following table provides information on each plate, listing known artists and engravers who worked upon them, as well as the sites and monuments from which they came. In addition, Dr. Mainterot has provided references for readers interested in researching Cailliaud's work. The Porter and Moss[1] references provide further bibliographic information on the monuments from which the scenes were taken. The references to Rosellini[2] and Wilkinson[3] provide comparative material, as both men drew scenes used by Cailliaud in their own works. The final column of the table gives further information, stating definitively if we know the artist of a scene, making the best educated guess possible as to an artist if one is unknown, and identifying those images that were sent to Cailliaud by Champollion [editor's note].

---

1 Bertha Porter and Rosalind L. Moss, *Topographical Bibliography of Ancient Egyptian Hieroglyphic Texts, Reliefs, and Paintings*, vols. 1–8 (Oxford UK: Clarendon Press, 1934–95).

2 Ippolito Rosellini, *I Monumenti dell' Egitto e della Nubia: disegnati dalla spedizione scientifico-letteraria Toscana in Egitto distribuiti in ordine di materie interpretati ed illustrate* (Pisa: Presso Niccolo Capurro, c.1832–44).

3 The majority of the references to Wilkinson in this book have relied upon his *Manners and Customs*, originally published in 1837. Dr. Mainterot's comparisons, however, are based on a later edition of this work. See John Gardner Wilkinson, *The Manners and Customs of the Ancient Egyptians*, edited by Samuel Birch (London: John Murray, 1878).

TABLE 1

Plate	Scene	Artist	Engraver	Site	Monument / Location	Porter and Moss	Rosellini	Wilkinson (ed. Birch)	Notes
1	Woodworkers	Cailliaud	Bigant	Qurna	Tomb of Ibi (TT 36) ?	—	—	—	Not found in either Rosellini or Wilkinson
2	Boat building	Cailliaud	Bigant	Qurna	Tomb of Ibi (TT 36)	I.1, p. 65	Mon. Civ. XLIV, 2	II, 140	Drawn by Cailliaud
3	Boats Transportation of goods Rudders	Cailliaud	Smith	al-Kab	Tomb of Paheri (north wall)	V, p. 179	Mon. Civ. CX, 1–2	—	Drawn by Cailliaud
4	Funerary barque	Cailliaud	Smith	Qurna	Tomb of Neferhotep (TT 50)	I.1, p. 96	—	—	Drawn by Cailliaud
5	Boat with rowers	Cailliaud	Smith	Qurna	Tomb of Nedjemger (TT 138)	I.1, p. 252	—	—	Drawn by Cailliaud
5A	Woodworkers Grape pressing	Cailliaud	Cholet	Beni Hasan	Tomb of Khety [1–3], Bakt III [4–5]	IV, p. 156, 153	Mon. Civ. XLIII, 2–3 / XXXVIII, 3	I, 383	Reproduced by Cailliaud according to Rosellini
6	Chair building	Cailliaud	Gâche	Thebes	Tomb of Rekhmire (TT 100) [1]	I.1, p. 211	Mon. Civ. XLIV, 5	II, 178	Drawn by Cailliaud
6	Grape pressing			Memphis	Tomb of Iymery (Giza) [2]	III, p. 173	Mon. Civ. XXXVII, 3	II, 199	Drawn by Cailliaud
6A	Polishing a column Metal or glass manufacture	Ricci	Cholet	Qurna	Tomb of Rekhmire (TT 100) [1–2]	I.1, p. 211	Mon. Civ. XLV, 4 / L, 2	II, 188 / II, 312	Sent from Champollion to Cailliaud
6B	Metal production Glass and jewelry production	Ricci	Cholet	Thebes and Beni Hasan	Tomb of Rekhmire (TT 100) [1–2–4], of Khety [3]	I.1, p. 211 and IV, p. 156	Mon. Civ. L, 2 / LII, 4–5	II, 312	Sent from Champollion to Cailliaud
7	Wheel construction for chariots	Cailliaud	Smith	Qurna	Tomb of Ibi (TT 36)	I.1, p. 65	Mon. Civ. XLIV, 4	I, 231	Drawn by Cailliaud
8	Making a sarcophagus and funerary equipment (b/w)	Cailliaud	Cholet	Qurna	Tomb of Amenemipet (TT 41) [1–6]	I.1, p. 81	Mon. Civ. CXXVI	—	Reproduced by Cailliaud according to Rosellini
9	Woodworkers, dyes, and perfumes	Cailliaud	Gâche	Qurna	Tomb of Ibi (TT 36) [1–11]	I.1, p. 65	Mon. Civ. LI, 1	II, 235	Drawn by Cailliaud
9A	Brickwork	Cailliaud	Cholet	Qurna	Tomb of Rekhmire (TT 100)	I.1, p. 211	Mon. Civ. XLIX	I, 344	Drawn by Cailliaud
10	Glassblowing *Shabti* sculptors Gilders	Cailliaud	Cholet	Qurna	Tomb of Rekhmire (TT 100) [2], of Ibi (TT 36) [1,3–5]	I.1, p. 211, 65	Mon. Civ. LII, 3–4 / XLV, 5	II, 235	Drawn by Cailliaud

Plate	Scene	Artist	Engraver	Site	Monument / Location	Porter and Moss	Rosellini	Wilkinson (ed. Birch)	Notes
11	Sculptors	Cailliaud	Smith	Qurna	Tomb of Ibi (TT 36)	I.1, p. 65	—	—	Drawn by Cailliaud
12	Painter and sculptor	Cailliaud	Bigant	Qurna	Tomb of Ibi (TT 36)	I.1, p. 65	Mon. Civ. XLVI, 8 / XLVII, 1	—	Drawn by Cailliaud
13	Sculptor Gilder	Cailliaud	Smith	Qurna	Tomb of Ibi (TT 36)	I.1, p. 65	Mon. Civ. XLVI, 9 / LI, 2	II, 235	Drawn by Cailliaud
14	Hewing a block of stone	Cailliaud	Cholet	Qurna	Tomb of Rekhmire (TT 100) [1]	I.1, p. 212	Mon. Civ. XLVIII, 2	II, 310	Drawn by Cailliaud
	Sketch of a Hathor capital			Beni Hasan	Gebel Abu Fawda [2]	IV, p. 241	—	—	Drawn by Cailliaud
	Cut stone			Kardasa	Aswan quarry	—	—	—	Drawn by Cailliaud
	Obelisk and cartouche of Ramesses II			Luxor	Luxor Temple	—	—	—	Drawn by Cailliaud
15	Sculpting a colossal statue	Ricci	Cholet	Qurna	Tomb of Rekhmire (TT 100)	I.1, p. 212	Mon. Civ. XLVII, 3	II, 311	Sent from Champollion to Cailliaud
15A	Weapons (bows and arrows) and perfume making	Cailliaud	Cholet	Beni Hasan	Tomb of Khunes in Zawyet al-Amwat	IV, p. 135	Mon. Civ. XLIII, 5 / LXVI, 1	—	Drawn by Cailliaud
16	Pottery making	?	Gâche	Beni Hasan	Tomb of Bakt III (2)	IV, p. 154	—	II, 192	Probably drawn by Cailliaud
17	Weighing jewelry Polishing	Cailliaud	Smith	Qurna	Tomb of Ibi (TT 36)	I.1, p. 65	Mon. Civ. LI, 3	—	Drawn by Cailliaud
17A	Spinners and weavers	Cailliaud	Cholet	Beni Hasan	Tomb of Bakt III [1–6], Khety [7–9], Khnumhotep III [10]	IV, p. 155, 148	Mon. Civ. XLI	I, 317	Drawn by Cailliaud
18	Weaving	?	?	Beni Hasan	Tomb of Khety	IV, p. 155	Mon. Civ. XLI	II, 170	Probably drawn by Cailliaud
18A	Rope makers and tanners	Cailliaud	Cholet	Qurna	Tomb of Rekhmire (TT 100)	I.1, p. 211	Mon. Civ. LXV, 11	II, 178	Drawn by Cailliaud
19	Quartering an ox	Cailliaud	Smith	Asyut	Tomb of Hapydjefa I	IV, p. 262	—	—	Drawn by Cailliaud
20	Leather preparation	Cailliaud	Smith	Qurna	Tomb of Ibi (TT 36)	I.1, p. 65	Mon. Civ. LXIV, 4	—	Drawn by Cailliaud
20A	Sandal making	Ricci	Cholet	Qurna	Tomb of Rekhmire (TT 100)	I.1, p. 211	Mon. Civ. LXIV, 1	II, 188	Sent from Champollion to Cailliaud
21	Examples of shoes from Egypt and Nubia	Cailliaud	Huet	Thebes / Meroe	Egypt and Nubia	—	—	—	Drawn by Cailliaud

Plate	Scene	Artist	Engraver	Site	Monument / Location	Porter and Moss	Rosellini	Wilkinson (ed. Birch)	Notes
21A	Care of antelopes and calves	?	Cholet	Beni Hasan	Tomb of Khnumhotep III [1–3]	IV, p. 146	Mon. Civ. XXXI	—	Probably drawn by Cailliaud
21B	Geese herders	L'Hôte	Cholet	Beni Hasan	Tomb of Khety [1–2]	IV, p. 156	Mon. Civ XXX, 4	—	Sent from Champollion to Cailliaud
	Amphorae Barbers	Cherubini		Qurna	Tomb of Rekhmire (TT 100), of Khety [4]	IV, p. 155	Mon. Civ. LXXVI, 2 / LXXXVII, 5	II, 357	Sent from Champollion to Cailliaud
22	Beaded mummy cover	Cailliaud	Smith	Qurna	Louvre Museum	—	—	—	Drawn by Cailliaud
23	Figures painted on a mummy case	Cailliaud	Gâche	Qurna	Sarcophagus of Tanethereret, Louvre Museum	—	—	—	Drawn by Cailliaud
24	Ornate vases	Cailliaud	Gâche	Qurna	Tomb of Imiseba (TT 65) [1–2]	I.1, p. 129	Mon. Civ. LVII, 6-4	II, 7	Drawn by Cailliaud
24A	Ornate vases	Cailliaud	Cholet	Qurna	Tomb of Imiseba (TT 65) [1–2]	I.1, p. 129	Mon. Civ. LVII, 5-2	II, 6	Drawn by Cailliaud
25	Seats and benches	Cailliaud	Smith	Valley of the Kings	Tomb of Ramesses III (KV 11)	I.2, p. 521	Mon. Civ. XCI / XCII, 4	I, 415 / I, 416	Drawn by Cailliaud
25A	Seats and a bench	?	Cholet	Valley of the Kings	Tomb of Ramesses III (KV 11), of Seti I (KV 17) [3]	I.2, p. 522	Mon. Civ. LXXIV, 1 / XC, 4 / XCII, 2	—	Probably drawn by Cailliaud after imagery by Rosellini
26	Chair	Cailliaud	Smith	Valley of the Kings	Tomb of Ramesses III (KV 11)	I.2, p. 522	Mon. Civ. XCI	—	Drawn by Cailliaud
	Seat		Gebel Barkal		East wall, 3rd pyramid in Gebel Barkal	—	—	—	Drawn by Cailliaud
27	Chair	Cailliaud	Smith	Valley of the Kings	Tomb of Ramesses III (KV 11)	I.2, p. 522	Mon. Civ. XCI	—	Drawn by Cailliaud
28	Chair	Cailliaud	Smith	Valley of the Kings	Tomb of Ramesses III (KV 11)	I.2, p. 522	Mon. Civ. XCI	—	Drawn by Cailliaud
29	Chair	Cailliaud	Smith	Valley of the Kings	Tomb of Ramesses III (KV 11)	I.2, p. 522	Mon. Civ. XCI	—	Drawn by Cailliaud
29A	Painted ceilings from tombs	?	Cholet	Qurna	Multiple tombs in Qurna	—	Mon. Civ. LXX, 2 / LXXI, 11–12, / LXXIII, 26	I, pl. VIII	Probably drawn by Cailliaud after imagery by Rosellini

Plate	Scene	Artist	Engraver	Site	Monument / Location	Porter and Moss	Rosellini	Wilkinson (ed. Birch)	Notes
29B	Drawings of faience statuettes and amulets	Cailliaud	Cholet	?	Louvre Museum ?	—	—	—	Drawn by Cailliaud
	Drawings of gold jewelry	Muret	Cholet	?	Louvre Museum	—	—	—	Done by Muret
30	Tilling Sowing	?	Smith	al-Kab	Tomb of Paheri (north wall) [1]	V, p. 177	—	—	Probably drawn by Cailliaud
31	Sowing Plowing	?	Smith	Memphis	Tomb of Iymery (Giza) [2]	III, p. 173	—	—	Probably drawn by Cailliaud
	Harvesting papyrus			Beni Hasan	Tomb of Zawiyet al-Maiyitin [3]	—	—	—	Probably drawn by Cailliaud
	Harvesting papyrus			Thebes	Tomb of Ramesses III (KV 11) [4]	I.2, p. 521	—	—	Probably drawn by Cailliaud
32	Harvesting for the production of oils and perfumes	?	Smith	al-Kab	Tomb of Paheri (north wall)	V, p. 179	—	—	Probably drawn by Cailliaud
33	Threshing	?	Smith	al-Kab	Tomb of Paheri (north wall)	V, p. 177	Mon. Civ. XXXIII, 2 / XXXIV, 1	—	Probably drawn by Cailliaud
33A	The *shaduf*	Ricci	Cholet	Qurna	Tomb of Neferhotep (TT 49) [1]	I.1, p. 93	Mon. Civ. XL, 2	I, 281	Sent from Champollion to Cailliaud
	Watering a garden and harvesting bulbs			Beni Hasan	Tomb of Khnumhotep III [2+4]	IV, p. 145	Mon. Civ. XL, 1		Sent from Champollion to Cailliaud
34	Trampling grapes	Cailliaud	Smith	Qurna	Tomb of Neferhotep (TT 49)	I.1, p. 93	Mon. Civ. XXXVIII, 2 / XXXIX	I, 385	Drawn by Cailliaud
34A	Picking figs Baboons Granaries Plowing	Angelelli Ricci	Cholet	Beni Hasan	Tomb of Amenemhat [4], Khnumhotep III [1+2], Khety [3]	IV, p. 142, 145, 158	Mon. Civ. XXII, 5 / XXXV, 3	I, 371 / I, 380 / I, 382	Sent from Champollion to Cailliaud
35	Scenes of fowling, fishing, crops, and revelry	Cailliaud	Bigant	Qurna	Tomb of Neferhotep	I.1, p. 448	—	—	Drawn by Cailliaud
36	Scenes of fowling, fishing, and food preparation	Cailliaud	Smith	al-Kab	Tomb of Paheri (north wall)	V, p. 179	Mon. Civ. IV	—	Drawn by Cailliaud
37	Scenes of hunting	Cailliaud	Bigant	Qurna	Tomb of Neferhotep	I.1, p. 449	—	—	Drawn by Cailliaud

Plate	Scene	Artist	Engraver	Site	Monument / Location	Porter and Moss	Rosellini	Wilkinson (ed. Birch)	Notes
37A	Scenes of fowling and fishing Gymnastics and games	Cailliaud	Cholet	Beni Hasan	Tomb of Khnumhotep III [1], of Khety [2–7]	IV, p. 145, 157	Mon. Civ. VI / XXIV, 3 / CII, 5–10	I, 394 / II, 62 / II, 103 / II, 116	Probably drawn by Cailliaud
38	Herds of donkeys and goats	Cailliaud	Smith	Memphis	Tomb of Rakhaefankh (Giza) [1]	III, p. 208	—	II, 447	Drawn by Cailliaud
	Archery lesson Concentration exercises			Thebes	Tomb of Min (TT 109) [2]	I.1, p. 226	—	I, 406	Drawn by Cailliaud
39	Scenes of warming up and wrestling	?	Smith	Beni Hasan	Tombs of Amenemhat, of Bakt III	IV, p. 142, 152, 154	—	—	Probably drawn by Cailliaud
40	Dancers Harper Flutist	Cailliaud	Smith	Qurna	Tomb of Ibi (TT 36)	I.1, p. 65	—	I, 507 / I, 440	Drawn by Cailliaud
40A	Musicians	Ricci	Cholet	Qurna	Tomb of Amenhotepsaes (TT 75) [1–6], of Neferhotep (TT 49) [7–11]	I.1, p. 147, 92	Mon. Civ. XCVIII, 3 XCIX, 2	I, 439 et 443	Sent from Champollion to Cailliaud
41	Ball games Acrobatics	Ricci	Cholet	Beni Hasan	Tomb of Khety	IV, p. 155	Mon. Civ. C, 6–18	II, 54 / II, 65–66	Sent from Champollion to Cailliaud
41A	Gaming Musicians	Cailliaud	Cholet	Beni Hasan and Qurna	Tomb of Khety [1–5], of Nakht (TT 161) [5–10]	IV, p. 156 & I.1, p. 274	Mon. Civ. XCVIII, 2 / CIII	I, 32	Drawn by Cailliaud
42	Carrying a beam	Cailliaud	Bigant	Qurna	Tomb of Ibi (TT 36)	I.1, p. 65	Mon. Civ. XLVII, 5	—	Drawn by Cailliaud
43	Moving a colossal statue	Cailliaud	Bigant	Beni Hasan	Tomb of Djehutihotep II in Deir al-Bersha [1]	IV, p. 180	Mon. Civ. XLVIII, 1	II, 305	Probably drawn by Cailliaud
43A	Soldiers training (b/w)	Cailliaud	Cholet	Beni Hasan	Tomb of Bakt III [1], of Amenemhat [2]	IV, p. 153, 143	Mon. Civ. CXVI, 6–7 / CXVIII, 1	—	Reproduced by Cailliaud according to Rosellini
				Qurna	Tomb of Tjanouny (TT 74) [3–5]	I.1, p. 145	Mon. Civ. CX, 3–5	—	Reproduced by Cailliaud according to Rosellini
43B	Soldiers training	L'Hôte	Cholet	Beni Hasan	Tomb of Bakt III [1+2]	IV, p. 153	Mon. Civ. CXVII, 1–3	—	Sent from Champollion to Cailliaud
	Helmets Clothing Weapons Chariot	Rosellini		Valley of the Kings	Tomb of Ramesses III (KV 11) [3–10], of Rekhmire (TT 100) [11]	I.2, p. 522	Mon. Civ. CXXI / CXXII	I, 219	Sent from Champollion to Cailliaud

Plate	Scene	Artist	Engraver	Site	Monument / Location	Porter and Moss	Rosellini	Wilkinson (ed. Birch)	Notes
44	Harper	Cailliaud	Smith	Qurna	Tomb of Neferhotep (TT 50)	I.1, p. 95	—	—	Drawn by Cailliaud
45	Harper	Cailliaud	Smith	Valley of the Kings	Tomb of Ramesses III (KV 11)	I.2, p. 521	Mon. Civ. XCVII	I, pl. XI bis	Drawn by Cailliaud
45A	Queen holding a sistrum	Ricci	Cholet	Qurna	Tomb of Ramesses VII (KV 1)	I.2, p. 496	Mon. Stor. XIX, 22	—	Sent from Champollion to Cailliaud
46	Pharaoh Horemheb	Cailliaud	Smith	Qurna	Tomb of Neferhotep (TT 50)	I.1, p. 95	—	—	Drawn by Cailliaud
46A	Pharaoh Ramesses II holding a bow	Rosellini	Cholet	Abu Simbel	Large temple of Abu Simbel	VII, p. 104	Mon. Stor. LXXXVI	—	Sent from Champollion to Cailliaud
47	Priest making offerings	Cailliaud	Smith	Qurna	?	—	—	—	Drawn by Cailliaud
48	Priest wearing gold gloves	Cailliaud	Smith	Qurna	Tomb of Neferhotep (TT 50)	I.1, p. 95	—	—	Drawn by Cailliaud
49	Princess holding a sistrum	Rosellini	Smith	Medinet Habu	Temple of Ramesses III	II, p. 502	Mon. Stor. XVI, 5	I, 296	Sent from Champollion to Cailliaud
50	Prince	Rosellini	Smith	Medinet Habu	Temple of Ramesses III	II, p. 502	Mon. Stor. XVI, 4	I, 197	Sent from Champollion to Cailliaud
51	Priest in rapture	Cailliaud	Smith	Qurna	?	—	—	—	Drawn by Cailliaud
52	Offering bearer	Cailliaud	Smith	Qurna	Tomb of Rekhmire (TT 100)	I.1, p. 211	—	—	Drawn by Cailliaud
53	Officiating priest	Cailliaud	Smith	Qurna	?	—	—	—	Drawn by Cailliaud
54	Officiating priest	Cailliaud	Smith	Qurna	Tomb of Neferhotep (TT 50)	I.1, p. 95	—	—	Drawn by Cailliaud
55	Musician	Cailliaud	Smith	Qurna	Tomb of Neferhotep (TT 50)	I.1, p. 95	—	—	Drawn by Cailliaud
56	Nome goddess bearing offerings	Cailliaud	Smith	Valley of the Kings	Tomb of Ramesses III (KV 11)	I.2, p. 520	—	—	Drawn by Cailliaud
57	Mourner	Cailliaud	Smith	Qurna	?	—	—	—	Drawn by Cailliaud
58	Mourning man	Cailliaud	Smith	Qurna	Tomb of Neferhotep (TT 49)	I.1, p. 92	—	—	Drawn by Cailliaud
59	Offering bearer	Cailliaud	Smith	Qurna	Tomb of Neferhotep (TT 49)	I.1, p. 92	—	—	Drawn by Cailliaud
60	Woman smelling a lotus flower	Cailliaud	Smith	Qurna	Tomb of Neferhotep (TT 50)	I.1, p. 95	—	—	Drawn by Cailliaud
61	Head of a man wearing a lotus flower	Cailliaud	Smith	Qurna	Tomb of Neferhotep (TT 50)	I.1, p. 95	—	—	Drawn by Cailliaud

Plate	Scene	Artist	Engraver	Site	Monument / Location	Porter and Moss	Rosellini	Wilkinson (ed. Birch)	Notes
62	Head of a man wearing a lotus flower	Cailliaud	Smith	Qurna	Tomb of Neferhotep (TT 50)	I.1, p. 95	—	—	Drawn by Cailliaud
63	Figures around the Candace and Apedemak	Cailliaud	Bigant	Qurna	Exterior wall of the temple of Apedemak	VII, p. 269	—	—	Drawn by Cailliaud
64	Banquet scene	Cailliaud	Cholet	Qurna	Tomb of Rekhmire (TT 100)	I.1, p. 213	Mon. Civ. LXXIX	II, 38	Reproduced by Cailliaud according to Rosellini
65	Offering to the tree goddess	Cailliaud	Cholet	Qurna	Tomb of Nedjemger (TT 138) [1]	I.1, p. 252	Mon. Civ. CXXXIV, 3	—	Reproduced by Cailliaud according to Rosellini
	Offering table				?	—	Mon. Civ. CXXXIII, 4	—	Reproduced by Cailliaud according to Rosellini
	The ba visiting a mummy prepared by Anubis				Tomb of Paser (TT 106) [3]	I.1, p. 223	Mon. Civ. CXXXIV, 2	—	Reproduced by Cailliaud according to Rosellini
	The funeral procession				Tomb of Roy (TT 255) [4]	I.1, p. 339	Mon. Civ. CXXXVIII	—	Drawn by Cailliaud
66	Offerings from people from Kush	Cailliaud	Cholet	Qurna	Tomb of Rekhmire (TT 100) [1–2]	I.1, p. 209	Mon. Civ. XXII 2,3	I, pl. II B	Drawn by Cailliaud

HEADINGS WITHIN
THE HARER PAPERS' BOOKLETS

Andrew Bednarski

In addition to the eighteen chapters that form the core of this book, the Harer Papers contain a series of notes clearly meant to be reworked into chapter form. Much of this material represents the beginning of Cailliaud's thought process on a number of subjects, and warrants further investigation. As stated in the first chapter of this book, the Harer Papers also contain a series of eight booklets, distinct from the rest of the material. The titles of each of these booklets and the subject headings listed at the top the booklets' pages are as follows:

TABLE 2

Volume 1, second series, first book / Volume 1er, Seconde Série, Premier Cahier

Fertility of the soil / Fertilité du sol

Asiatic shepherd people who invaded Egypt / Peuple bergers asiatique qui envahirent l'Égypte

The Persians invaded, then other peoples / Les Perses envahire [sic] puis les autres peuples

The agricultural class / Classe d'agriculture

Encouragement to agriculture / Encouragement à l'agriculture

Various states of society / Divers états de la société

Shepherd class & & population / Classe berger & & population

Prosperity through its goods / Prospérité par ses manufactures

Agricultural prosperity / Prospérité de l'agriculture

Origin of geometry / Origine de la géométrie

Distribution of waterways / Distribution des cours d'eaux

Distribution of Nile water / Distribution des eaux du Nil

On the Nilometre / Du Nilomètre

On holidays / Des fêtes

Cutting the dam / Couper la bonde

On religious ideas related to the inundation of the Nile / Des idées religieuses attachées à l'inondation du Nil

On rain / Des pluies

The year in 12 lunar months / L'année en 12 mois lunaire

On the solar year and lunar months / De l'année solaire et mois lunaire

Egyptian months / Mois Égyptiens

On seasons / Des Saisons

On the 5 added days / Des 5 jours ajouté [sic]

The sacred year / L'année sacrée

Large herds/flocks / Des grands troupeaux

Lowered population / Population réduite

Population

Progress, erection of monolithic structures / Progrès érection des monolites [sic]

Excavations / Escavations [sic]

Egypt, a granary of abundance / L'Égypte grénier [sic] d'abondance

Eating roots / Mangeaient des racines

Measure of a cubit / Mesure coudée

On the cubit / De la coudée

Crop lands / Culture des terres

Tenant farming / Affermage des terres

Beating / Bastonade [sic]

Irrigation through canals / Irrigation par caneaux [sic]

Plowing with oxen / Labour avec des bœufs

First harvest as offering to the gods / Le premier fruit en offrande aux Dieux

Village surrounded by water / Village entouré d'eau

Plowman / Laboureur

Pigs threshing seeds / Les cochons foulant la semance [sic]

Tilling with a plow / Charue [sic] labourage

On plowing / De labourage

On the hoe / De la houe

On papyrus and without papyrus / Du jonc et sans jonc

The keepers of pigs disdained / Des gardeurs de cochons mépris

Tiresome heat for plowing, supply of water / Chaleur pénible pour le labourage, provision d'eau

Water with which to refresh oneself / Eau pour se rafraichir [sic]

Manner of sowing / Maniere [sic] d'ensemencer

Nitrate fertilizer / Engrais de nitre

The Blue Nile, the White Nile / Le fleuve bleu, fleuve blanc

Wine growing in rocky terrain / La vigne dans rocailles

Diverse harvest / Récolte diverses

On harvests / Des récoltes

Bees with beehives / Abeilles avec des ruches

Threshing / Battre le blé &

Threshing by oxen / Battre le blé par les bœufs

According to Herodotus / Comme Hérodote

The Jews threshed with oxen / Les juifs battaient avec des bœufs

Cutting wheat / Couper le blé

Agriculture

On wheat / Du blé

On dura / Du doura

Cultivation of dura / Culture du Doura

Hemp / Le chanvre

Arrival of the inundation / Arrivée de l'inondation

First inundation / Première inundation

Building of dikes / Travaux des digues

The Nile at 16 cubits / Le Nil à 16 coudées

Various heights of the Nile / Diverses hauteurs du Nil

The river rises more than in the past and overflows more / La rivière s'élève plus qu'autrefois et déborde davantage

On the level of Nile water / Du niveau des eaux du Nil

Level of the water / Niveau de l'eau

The sand covering the land / Le sable couvrant les terres

On the confines of the desert / Des confines du desert

On the holidays of peasants / Des fêtes des paysans

Volume 1, second series, second book / Volume 1er, Second Série, Seconde Cahier

On the Apis Bull / Du bœuf Apis

Superstition about the crocodile / Superstition du crocodile

Raising animals / Elévant [sic] les animaux

Herdsmen / Gardeurs de troupeaux

Education

On geese given to scribes / Des oies remises aux scribes

The Copts still hatch eggs today / Les coptes font éclosent les œufs encore aujourd'hui

Veterinary art / Art vétérinaire

Religious opinion / Opinion religieuse

Prognostication / Pronostique

Sacrifice

Oracle

Prediction / Prédiction

Sacrificial offering / Offrande en sacrifice

Ridicule of Egyptians by the Greeks / Ridicule des Egyp[tiens] par les Grecs

Religious ideas / Idés [sic] religieuses

Animals / Animaux

Egyptian priests mocking the Greeks / Prêtres Egy[ptiens] se moquant des Grecs

On the image of divinities / De l'image des divinités

Emblems of deities / Emblèmes des divinités

The Greeks gave a real existence to abstract ideas / Les Grecs donnaient une existence réelle aux idées abstract

The physical gods / Les divinités physiques

Sacred bull / Tauraut [sic] sacré

Universal belief in a creator god / Croyance universel d'une divinité créatrice

On divinity / De la divinité

On Egyptian religion / De la religion Egyp[tien]

On the sun / Du soleil

First religion / Premiere [sic] religion

On the immortality of the soul / De l'immortalité de l'âme

On the Flood / Du Déluge

Major deities / Grande [sic] divinités

On the ancient names of Ethiopia & & / Des anciens noms d'Ethiopie & &

Ancient names of peoples / Anciens noms des peoples

Holidays for Bubastis / Fêtes Bubastis

The sun, Ra / Le soleil Ré

The fame of Heliopolis / Renommée d'Héliopolis

The fame of Alexandria / Renommée d'Alexandrie

The Phoenix / Le Phénix

Emblem of the sun / Emblême [sic] du soleil

Osiris

Actions weighed / Les actions dans la balance

Transmigration of the soul / Transmigration de l'âme

Return of the soul to the god / Retour de l'âme à la divinité

Osiris mystery / Mystere [sic] d'Osiris

They recognized that Osiris was not a human being / Ils savaient bien reconnaitre qu'Osiris n'était pas un être humain

Apis and holidays in his honor / Apis et des fêtes en son honneur

On the death of Apis / De la mort d'Apis

On Osiris and Apis / D'Osiris et Apis

Wrath of Cambyses / Colère de Cambise

Wrath of Cambyses for the Apis holidays / Colère de Cambise pour les fêtes d'Apis

Ceremony / Céremonie [sic]

Volume 2, second series / Second Volume de la 2eme Série

The scepter of kings / Le sceptre des Rois [sic]

The cardinal points / Des [points] cardinaux

On a pig offered to the moon / Du cochon offert à la Lune

On the flight of pigeons / Des vols de pigeons

Division of the world / Division du monde

On the intestines of the dead / Des Intestines [sic] des morts

On the intestines of mummies / Des Intestines [sic] des momies

and the 4 gods to whom they belong / et des 4 dieux a [sic] qu'ils appartiennent

On the 4 genies of the dead / Des 4 génies des morts

Directions of temples / Directions des temples

On wishes for children / Des vœux pour les enfants

On sacred animals / Des Animaux [sic] sacré

Transmigration of the soul / Transmigration de l'âme

Dead bodies buried in a sanitary way / Les corps morts enterré par mesure sanitaire

Sacred monkeys / Singes sacrés

Cynocephalus monkeys adoring / Singes Sinocéphale [sic] en adoration

The non-sacred bat / La chauve souri non sacrée

On dogs / Des Chiens [sic]

On the wolf / Du Loup [sic]

Jackal / Chacal

On mice / Des souris

On the Labyrinth / Du Labyrinthe

The head of the lion in Ethiopia, Chandy, Naga / La tête de Lyon [sic] en Éthiopie, chandi [sic]—Naga

Hippopotamus mummy / Momie d'hippopotame

[?] bull mummy / momie de bœuf [?]

Ibis / Ibis

Stork / Cigogne

On the crocodile / Du crocodile

Ethiopian feast / Fête étiopienne [sic]

Funerals / Funérailles

Tombs / Tombeaux

Clay seals / Cachets en terre

Grief for the dead / Affliction pour les morts

Female Mourners / Pleureuses

Funerary processions / Processions funéraires

Funerary escort / Convoie funèbre

First class of priests / Première castre des Prêtres [sic]

First class of priests and queens / Castre Iere des pretres [sic] et des Reines [sic]

On priestesses / Des prêtresses

Division of land / Division des terres

On the rank of priests / Du rang des prêtres

On the power of priests / Du pouvoir des prêtres

On writing / De l'écriture

Geometry, arithmetic / Géométrie arithmétique

Prediction / Prédiction

Astronomy, prediction / Astronomie prediction

Sobriety of priests / Sobriété des prêtres

On the food reserves for priests / Des réserves pour la nourriture des prêtres

Priests' clothing / Costume des prêtres

Wooden pillow / Oreiller en bois

Priests' duty / Devoir des prêtres

Military class / Classe militaire

On the auxiliaries / Des auxiliaires

The Egyptian Army / L'armée égyptienne

The standards / Les étendars [sic]

Volume 3, first book / 3eme volume 1er cahier

Hunting animals, dogs, fowlers, hippopotamus hunters, the crocodile, Tentyris / La chasse des Animaux [sic], les chiens, les Oiseleurs [sic], les Pêcheurs [sic] d'hippopotame, le Crocodile, le Tentyris

Hunting / La chasse

On animals / Des animaux

Hatching eggs / Éclore les œufs

Use for the loss of dogs / Usage pour la perte des chiens

On birds / Des oiseaux

On fishing / De la pêche

On fish / Des Poissons [sic]

Papyrus / Papyrus

Abundance of fish / Abondance du Poisson [sic]

Yield from fishing / Produit de la Pêche [sic]

On Lake Moeris, fish yield / Du lac Mœris la pêche produit

Revenue from fishing / Revenue de la pêche

Salted fish / Poissons sale

Hippopotamus hunt / Chasse hippopotame

Animals taken from the Upper Nile / Des animaux retirés dans le haut Nil

On the sacred crocodile / Du crocodile sacré

On the arts and manufacturing / Des arts et manufactures

On the destruction of temples / De la destruction des temples

On the period of the arts / De l'époque des arts

Volume 3, second book / 3eme volume 2eme cahier

Decadence of art / Decadence [sic] de l'art

On the art of blocks / De l'art des blocs

Rule to follow in art / Regle [sic] à suivre dans les arts

Ornaments wrongly attributed to the Greeks / Les ornements à tord attribué aux grecs

On glass, porcelain, and fake stones / Du ver de la porcelaine et des pierres fausses

On soldered, mosaic glass / Du ver mosaïque soudé

Imitation emerald / Imitation d'eméraude [sic]

Cited [genie's vase?] / Citer le vase de Gêne [sic]

Emerald glass / Ver éméraude [sic]

Onyx glass / Ver en onyx

Working colored glass / Travailler le ver de couleur

Painted glass found in the oasis / Le ver peint trouvé dans l'oasis

Emerald was the best counterfeit / L'eméraude [sic] était la mieux contrefaite

Imitation stones / Imitation des pierres

Tubes of enamel for bead nets / Les tubes d'emaile pour les filets réseaux

I doubt the use of polish on granite / Je doute du verni sur le granite

Purpurin / Purpurine

Enamel / Émaille [sic]

Enamel and non-porcelain / Émaille [sic] et je dois dire non porcelaine

Cutting glass, according to Pliny / Couper le ver suivant Pline

Knowledge of chemistry for materials / Connaissance en chimie pour les étoffes

Diamond, Pliny / Diamant Pline

Stonecutting by means of an emery tool / Gravure des pierres par l'émeri tour

Chinese bottle / Bouteilles chinoise

On enamel on gold / De l'émail sur l'or

Enamel on gold and inlaying on bronze / Email sur or et incrustation sur bronze

Imitation Murrhine vases / Imitation des vases murins

On linen / Du Linge [sic]

On the exclusive use of wool for clothing against the skin / De la laine exclus pour vetement [sic] sur la peau

Quantity of cloth / Quantité de toile

Mummy cloths, especially of linen / Les toiles de momie spécialement de lin

Cotton clothing / Vêtement de cotton

Linen clothing preferred, as fresher on the body / Les vêtements de lin préféré pour être plus frais au corps

Choice of priests / Choix des prêtres

Cotton fabric for furniture, etc. / Les toiles de coton pour ameublement &

On simple and crude trades / Des métiers simples et grossiers

Craft of fine fabric, material like silk / Métiers toile très fines tissus comme la soie

Coarse mummy cloth / Toile de momie grossière

On mummy cloth / Des toiles de momies

Colored thread / Fil de couleur

Dyed thread, before being woven / Fil teint avant d'être tissue

Colored hieroglyphs in the fabric / Hiéroglyphes en couleur dans la toile

Thread dyed [?] / Le fil teint [d'avine?]

Cloth with embroidered, colored design / Etoffe avec dessin en couleur brodée

Gold thread for cloth / Fil d'or pour étoffe

On gold thread / Du fil d'or

Drawn or not drawn / Tiré ou non tire

Acids for colors / Les acide [sic] pour les couleurs

Acids on fabrics / Des acides sur les Étoffes [sic]

Hand-spun wool / La laine filée à la main

Men make fabric / Les hommes font la toile

Fabric, its production in Thebes etc. / Etoffe [sic] sa fabrication à Thèbes & &

Spindle / Fuseau à filer

Distaff / Quenouille

Room preparation / Préparation de la chambre

Fringe robe / Robe frange

Linen prepared by comb / Le lin préparé avec le peigne

Polish / Lustré calandré

Iron / Repasser

Carpet fabric / Le tissu de tapis

Rope making with leather bands / Cordier avec les bordes de cuire

On nets / Des filets

On sieves / Des cribes [sic]

On papyrus / Du Papirus [sic]

Making papyrus / Papyrus fabrique [sic]

Papyrus plant / Papyrus plante

Papyrus for boats / Papyrus pour les bateaux

Papyrus paper, their names / Papyrus papier leurs noms

On parchment / Du parchemin

Papyrus monopoly / Monopole du papyrus

Shard with writing / Tesson écrit

Limestone with writing / Pierre calcaire écrite

Lead board, bark, etc. for writing upon / Plom [sic] planche, feuille écorse [sic] & & pour écrire dessus

Waraq, the word for paper in Arabic / Warake papier en arabe

Leather currier / Corroyeurs

The preparation of skins / Préparation des peaux

Tools / Outils

Leather currier, work / Coroyeur [sic] travail

Stainer / Dégraisseur

Potters / Pottiers [sic]

Carpenter, joiner / Charpentier menuisier

Volume 3, third book / 3eme Volume, 3eme Cahier

On trees / Des arbres

On wood / Des bois

Veneering / Placage

Paint imitating wood / Peinture imitant le bois

Tools / Outils

On joiners / De menuisier

Work / Travail

Drill / Le foret

Saw / La sie [sic]

Glue / La cole [sic]

Box / Boite

Joinery / Menuiserie

Ivory veneer / Ivoire placage

Wheelwright / Charon [sic]

Carriage / Voiture

Palanquin / Palanquin

Raider / Pilleur

Cooper / Tonnelier

Mummy hunts / Les chasses de momie

Embalmers / Les ambaumeurs [sic]

Willow boats / Barque d'osier

Papyrus boats / Barque de papyrus

Boat for moving goods / Bateau de charge

On boats / Des barques

On large ships / Des grands Navires [sic]

Antiquity of ships / Antiquités des Navires [sic]

Navigation / Navigation

Boats for war / Bateaux de guerre

On boats and pulleys / Des barques et poulies

On sails / Des Voiles [sic]

On tin / De l'Étain [sic]

Trade with India / Commerce avec les Indes

Metallurgy / Métallurgie

On metals / Des métaux

Goldsmith / Travailleur en or

Gold working / Travail en or

Crucibles / Creusets

Gold objects / Objets d'or

Gold mines / Mines d'or

Work in the mines / Travail des mines

Gilding / Action de dorer

On silver / De l'argent

On coined silver / De l'argent monnayée

Weights and measures / Des poids et mesures

On the scale / De la balance

On copper, on iron / Du cuivre du fer

On bronze tools / Du bronze en outils

Gold, silver, copper, first used / L'or, l'argent, le cuivre dabord [sic] employés

On iron and on bronze / Du fer et du bronze

On iron for tools / Du fer pour les outils

Tools for cutting granite, etc. / Outils pour couper le granite &

Use of drill and emery / Usage du Dril [sic] et de l'émerie [sic]

Metal arrows / Métal aux fleches

Flint knives / Couteaux en silex

Egyptian civilization / Civilisation des Égyptiens

Period assumed for the pyramids / Époque supposée aux pyramides

On art among the Egyptians / De l'art chez les Égyptiens

On the art of drawing / De l'art du dessin

Volume 3 / 3eme Volume

Sculpture / Sculpture

Architecture /Architecture

On art in sculpture / Des arts en sculpture

On art / Des arts

On painting in sculpture / Des peintures en sculptures

On the composition of colors / Des compositions des couleurs

Sunk-relief and other sculpture / Sculpture en creux et autres

Isaiah's table / Table Isiac

Decadence of art / Décadence des arts

Capital style / Stile [sic] des chapiteaux

Painting / Peinture

The date of painting / Peinture sa date

On drawing with a grid / Du dessin avec carreau

Brushes / Pinceaux

Reed pen / Plume en roseau

Brickworks / Ouvrage en brique

Vault / Voute

Bricks and vaults / Briques voutes

Quarries / Carières [sic]

Exploitation of quarries / Carrière exploitation

Transport / Transport

Transportation of blocks / Transport des blocs

Transport of a colossus / Transport du colosse

Monolith / Monolithe

Transport of a monolith / Transport de monolithe

Obelisk / Obélisque

Obelisk, transport / Obélisque transport

Transport, inventions / Transport inventions

On the bellows of forges / Des soufflets des
forges

Siphons / Syphons [sic]

Geometry / Géométrie

Division of the days into 12 hours / Division
des jours en 12 heures

Votive objects / Objets votive

Garb / Costume

Clothing / Vetements [sic]

Clothing, priests / Vêtements les prêtres

Harpocrates' hairstyle / Coiffure d'Harpocrate

Leopard skin / La peau de léopard

Kings' clothing / Vêtement des souverains

Royal clothing / Vetement [sic] royaux

Royal crown / Couronne royale

Royal hairstyle / Coiffure royale

To shave one's beard / Se raser la barbe

With shaved head and beard / La barbe et la
tête rasée

The priests shaved their bodies / Les prêtres
se rasaient le corps

They shaved children / On rasait les enfants

The Egyptians were never bald / Les Égyptiens
jamais chauves

The head in the sun / La tête au soleil

Cap / Casquette

On wigs / Des Perruques

Depicting the beard / Figurer la barbe

Children's clothing / Vêtements des Enfants [sic]

The Evil Eye / Le mauvais œil

On sandals / Des sandales

Women's clothing / Vêtements de femme

Women's garb / Costume de femme

Hair changes colors / Les cheveux change
couleur

Jewelry / Bijoux

Women's jewelry / Bijoux de femme

Toilet / Toilette

Gold jewelry / Bijoux d'or

Seal / Cachet

Scarab / Scarabé [sic]

Ring / Bague

Gold collar / Collier d'or

Jewelry with gems / Bijoux pierreries

Ointment for the toilet / Toilette pomade [sic]

Perfume / Parfun [sic]

They degreased the body / Ils dégraissaient le
corps

On combs / Des peignes

Dyeing eyelids and eyebrows / Teindre les
paupières et les sourcils

Bottle [?] / Bouteille [à colir ?]

Mirror / Miroir

Canes, sticks / Canes bâtons

On baths / Des bains

On doctors / Des Docteurs [sic]

Illness / Maladie

Treatment / Traitement

On dreams / Des rêves

Superstition / Superstition

Physician / Médecin

Surgery / Chirurgie

PHARAONIC CHRONOLOGY

Andrew Bednarski

The following chronology of ancient Egypt is based on that presented in Ian Shaw and Paul Nicholson's *British Museum Dictionary of Ancient Egypt* (London: British Museum Press, 2002).

TABLE 3

Early Dynastic Period	**3100–2686**
First Dynasty	**3100–2890**
Narmer	c. 3100
Second Dynasty	**2890–2686**
Old Kingdom	**2686–2181**
Third Dynasty	**2686–2613**
Djoser (Netjerikhet)	2667–2648
Fourth Dynasty	**2613–2494**
Snefru	2613–2589
Khufu (Cheops)	2589–2566
Djedefra	2566–2558
Khafre (Chephren)	2558–2532
Menkaure (Mycerinus)	2532–2503
Fifth Dynasty	**2494–2345**
Sixth Dynasty	**2345–2181**

First Intermediate Period	2181–2055
Seventh and Eighth Dynasties	2181–2125
Ninth and Tenth Dynasties (Herakleopolitan)	2160–2025
Eleventh Dynasty (Thebes only)	2125–2055
Middle Kingdom	**2055–1650**
Eleventh Dynasty	**2055–1985**
Twelfth Dynasty	**1985–1795**
Senusret I (Kheperkara)	1965–1920
Senusret II (Khakheperra)	1880–1874
Senusret III (Khakaura)	1874–1855
Amenemhat III (Nimaatra)	1855–1808
Thirteenth Dynasty	**1795–after 1960**
Fourteenth Dynasty	**1750–1650**
Second Intermediate Period	**1650–1550**
Fifteenth Dynasty (Hyksos)	**1650–1550**
Sixteenth Dynasty	**1650–1550**
Seventeenth Dynasty	**1650–1550**
New Kingdom	**1550–1069**
Eighteenth Dynasty	**1550–1295**
Ahmose (Nebpehtyra)	1550–1525
Amenhotep I (Djeserkara)	1525–1504
Tuthmosis III (Menkheperra)	1479–1425
Hatshepsut (Maatkara)	1473–1458
Amenhotep II (Aakheperura)	1427–1400
Amenhotep III (Nebmaatra)	1390–1352
Amenhotep IV / Akhenaten (Neferkheperurawaenra)	1352–1336
Tutankhamun (Nebkheperura)	1336–1327
Ay (Kheperkheperura)	1327–1323
Horemheb (Djeserkheperura)	1323–1295
Nineteenth Dynasty	**1295–1186**
Seti I (Menmaatra)	1294–1279
Ramesses II (Usermaatra Setepenra)	1279–1213
Merenptah (Baenra)	1213–1203
Twentieth Dynasty	**1186–1069**
Ramesses III (Usermaatra Meryamun)	1184–1153
Ramesses IX (Neferkara Setepenra)	1126–1108

Third Intermediate Period	**1069–747**
Twenty-first Dynasty (Tanite)	**1069–945**
Twenty-second Dynasty (Bubastite / Libyan)	**945–715**
Twenty-third Dynasty (Tanite / Libyan)	**818–715**
Twenty-fourth Dynasty	**727–715**
Late Period	**747–332**
Twenty-fifth Dynasty (Kushite)	**747–646**
Twenty-sixth Dynasty (Saite)	**664–525**
Twenty-seventh Dynasty (First Persian Period)	**525–404**
Cambyses	525–522
Darius I	522–486
Xerxes I	486–465
Twenty-eighth Dynasty	**404–399**
Twenty-ninth Dynasty	**399–380**
Thirtieth Dynasty	**380–343**
Nectanebo II (Senedjemibra Setepenanhur)	360–343
Second Persian Period	**343–332**
Greek Period	**332–32**
Macedonian Dynasty	**332–305**
Alexander the Great	332–323
Ptolemaic Dynasty	**305–30**
Cleopatra VII Philopator	51–30
Ptolemy XV Caesarion	44–30
Roman Period	**30 BC–AD 395**
Augustus	30 BC–AD 14
Claudius	41–54
Nero	54–68
Domitian	81–96
Trajan	98–117
Hadrian	117–38
Division of the Roman Empire	**395**

Bibliography

Archival material

Cailliaud, Frédéric. "Journal du premier voyage en Nubie de Frédéric Cailliaud avec le chevalier Drovetti en 1816." Muséum d'histoire naturelle de Nantes.

———. "Journal du voyage au désert en Egypte supérieure (1816–1818)." Muséum d'histoire naturelle de Nantes.

———. "Journal du second voyage en Egypte à Méroé et au fleuve blanc (octobre 1819–avril 1822)." Muséum d'histoire naturelle de Nantes.

Legrain, Georges. "Inventaire méthodique de la collection d'antiquités égyptiennes conservée au Cabinet des Antiques et Médailles." Paris: Bibliothèque nationale, Rés. ms. 47007 PAR BN F°, 1894–1896: 849; D2, 284.

"Lettre de Frédéric Cailliaud à François Chabas." 12 July 1863. Paris, Bibliothèque de l'Institut de France.

Secondary sources

Allen, James P. *Middle Egyptian: An Introduction to the Language and Culture of Hieroglyphs*. Cambridge UK: Cambridge University Press, 2001.

Aristotle. *The History of Animals*. Translated by D'Arcy Wentworth Thompson. London: John Bell, 1907. http://classics.mit.edu/Aristotle/history_anim.6.vi.html

Arnold, Dorothea, and Janine Bourriau, eds. *An Introduction to Ancient Egyptian Pottery*. Mainz: Philipp von Zabern, 1993.

"Art. III—1. Voyage à l'Oasis de Thèbes et dans les Déserts situés à l'Orient et à l'Occident de la Thébaide, faits pendant les Années 1815, 1816, 1817 et 1818. Par M. Frédéric Cailliaud; et le Voyage à l'Oasis du Dakel; par M. Le Chevalier Drovetti, Consul-Général de France en

Egypte; rédigé et publié par M. Jomard, &c. Fol. Paris." *Quarterly Review* 28 (October 1822–January 1823).

"Art. III—Voyage dans le Levant en 1817 et 1818. Tome I. Large folio. Par le Comte de Forbin. Paris." *Quarterly Review* 23 (May and July 1820).

"Arts and Sciences. Egypt: The Oases." *The Literary Gazette and Journal of the Belles Lettres* no. 343 (Saturday, 16 August 1823).

Assmann, Jan. *Das Grab des Amenemope TT 41*. Mainz: Philipp von Zabern, 1991.

Aston, Barbara G., and James A. Harrell. "Stone." In *Ancient Egyptian Materials and Technology*, edited by Ian Shaw and Paul T. Nicholson, 5–77. Cambridge UK: Cambridge University Press, 2000.

Baedeker, Karl. *Egypt: Handbook for Travellers*. Leipzig: K. Baedeker, 1892.

Baud, Marcelle, and Etienne Drioton. *Tombes thébaines: Nécropole de Dirâ' Abû 'n-Nâga, Le tombeau de Roy*. Cairo: MIFAO, 1935.

Baud, Michel, ed. *Méroé, un empire sur le Nil*. Paris: Louvre, 2010.

Belzoni, Giovanni. *Narrative of the Operations and Recent Discoveries in Egypt and Nubia*. London: John Murray, 1820.

Betrò, Marilina, ed. *Ippolito Rosellini and the Dawn of Egyptology*. Translated by Anna Maria Bellizio. Cairo: Agenzia Italiana, 2010.

Bierbrier, Morris L., ed. *Who Was Who in Egyptology*. London: Egypt Exploration Society, 1995.

Bourriau, Janine, Paul T. Nicholson, and Pamela J. Rose. "Pottery." In *Ancient Egyptian Materials and Technology*, edited by Ian Shaw and Paul T. Nicholson, 121–47. Cambridge UK: Cambridge University Press, 2000.

Bovot, Jean-Luc. *Chaouabtis. Des travailleurs pharaoniques pour l'éternité*. Paris: Réunion des Musées Nationaux, 2003.

Brewer, Douglas, and Renée Friedman. *Fish and Fishing in Ancient Egypt*. Cairo: American University in Cairo Press, 1989.

Brunner, Helmut. "Trunkenheit." In *Lexicon der Ägyptologie*, vol. 6, edited by Wolfgang Helck and Eberhard Otto, 773–77. Wiesbaden: Otto Harrassowitz, 1985.

Budge, Ernest A. Wallis. *Cook's Handbook for Egypt and the Sudan*. London: Thomas Cook and Son, 1906.

Burckhardt, John L. *Travels in Nubia*. London: John Murray, 1819.

Butzer, Karl W. *Early Hydraulic Civilization in Egypt*. Chicago: University of Chicago Press, 1976.

Cailliaud, Frédéric. *Recherches sur les arts et métiers, les usages de la vie civile et domestique des anciens peuples de l'Égypte, de la Nubie et de l'Éthiopie*. Paris: Debure frères, 1831–37.

———. *Voyage à Méroé, au Fleuve Blanc, au-delà de Fazoql, dans le midi du royaume de Sennar, à Syouah et dans cinq autres oasis*. Paris: Imprimerie royale, 1826–27.

Celenko, Theodore. *Egypt in Africa*. Indianapolis IN: Indianapolis Museum of Art, 1996.

Černy, Jaroslav. "Consanguineous Marriages in Pharaonic Egypt." In *Journal of Egyptian Archaeology* 40 (1954): 23–29.

Chabas, François. "Sur un ostracon de la collection Cailliaud." *ZÄS* 5 (1867): 37–40.

Champollion, Jean-François. *Grammaire égyptienne*. Paris: Firmin Didot, 1836.

———. *Monuments de l'Égypte et de la Nubie, d'après les dessins exécutés sur les lieux sous la* direction de Champollion-le-jeune, et les descriptions autographes qu'il en a rédigées, etc. Paris: Firmin Didot, 1835–45.

———. *Monuments de l'Égypte et de la Nubie. Notices descriptives conformes aux manuscrits autographes rédigés sur les lieux par Champollion le jeune.* Paris: Firmin Didot, 1844–[74].

Champollion-Figeac, Jean-Jacques. *Égypte ancienne.* Paris: Firmin Didot, 1839.

Chauvet, Michel. *Frédéric Cailliaud, les aventures d'un naturaliste en Égypte et au Soudan 1815–1822.* Saint-Sébastien-sur-Loire: ACL, 1989.

Christophe, Louis-A. "Le ravitaillement en poissons des artisans de la nécropole thébaine à la fin du règne de Ramsès III." *Bulletin de l'Institut français d'archéologie orientale* 65 (1967): 177–99.

Clayton, Peter. *Chronicle of the Pharaohs.* London: Thames and Hudson, 1994.

d'Athanasi, Giovanni. *A Brief Account of the Researches and Discoveries in Upper Egypt.* London: John Hearne, 1836.

David, Rosalie A. "Mummification." In *Ancient Egyptian Materials and Technology*, edited by Ian Shaw and Paul T. Nicholson, 372–89. Cambridge UK: Cambridge University Press, 2000.

Davies, Nina de Garis. *The Tomb of Nefer-hotep at Thebes.* Vol. 2. New York: Metropolitan Museum of Art, 1933.

Davies, Norman de Garis. *The Rock Tombs of Deir el Gebrawi. Part I. Tomb of Aba and Smaller Tombs of the Southern Group.* London: Egypt Exploration Fund, 1902.

———. *The Tomb of Rekh-mi-Re' at Thebes.* New York: Metropolitan Museum of Art, 1943; Arno Press, 1973.

Denon, Dominique Vivant. *Voyage dans la Basse et la Haute Égypte pendant les campagnes du général Bonaparte.* Paris: P. Didot l'aîné, 1802.

Devéria, Charles Théodule. "Lettre à M. Cailliaud sur un ostracon égyptien." *Mémoires de la Société des Antiquaires de France* 25 (3rd series, vol. 5, 15 June): 129–42.

———. "L'Ostracon de la collection Cailliaud." In *Mémoires et Fragments*, edited by Gaston Maspéro, 257–63. Paris: E. Leroux, 1896–97.

Dewachter, Michel. "Introduction. Un pionnier de l'égyptologie: Mourad Effendi, alias Frédéric Cailliaud." In *Frédéric Cailliaud. Les aventures d'un naturaliste en Égypte et au Soudan*, by Michel Chauvet. Saint-Sébastien: ACL–Crocus, 1989.

Diodorus Siculus. *Library of History: Loeb Classical Library.* Translated by Charles Henry Oldfather. Cambridge MA: Harvard University Press, 1933–67.
http://penelope.uchicago.edu/Thayer/E/Roman/Texts/Diodorus_Siculus/home.html

Dodson, Aidan, and Dyan Hilton. *The Complete Royal Families of Ancient Egypt.* London: Thames and Hudson, 2004.

English, George Bethune. *A Narrative of the Expedition to Dongola and Senaar.* London: John Murray, 1822.

Fakhry, Ahmed. *Siwa Oasis.* Cairo: American University in Cairo Press, 2005.

Feucht, Erika. *Die Gräber des Nedjemger (TT 138) und des Hori (TT 259).* Mainz: Philipp von Zabern, 2006.

Fiechter, Jean-Jacques. *La moisson des dieux.* Paris: Julliard, 1994.

Finkel, Irving, ed. *Ancient Board Games in Perspective.* London: British Museum Press, 1998.

de Forbin, Louis. *Voyage dans le Levant en 1817 et 1818*. Paris: Delaunay, 1819.

"Foreign Varieties. France." *New Monthly Magazine* 13, part 1 (1 May 1820).

"Foreign Varieties. France." *The New Monthly Magazine and Universal Register* 13, part 1 (1 April 1820).

Gale, Rowena, Peter Gasson, Nigel Hepper, and Geoffrey Killen. "Wood." In *Ancient Egyptian Materials and Technology*, edited by Paul T. Nicholson and Ian Shaw, 334–71. Cambridge UK: Cambridge University Press, 2000.

Gardiner, Alan. *Egyptian Grammar, Being an Introduction to the Study of Hieroglyphs*. Oxford UK: Oxford University Press, 1950.

de Girardot, Auguste. *Frédéric Cailliaud de Nantes, voyageur, antiquaire, naturaliste*. Paris: A. Labitte, 1875.

Griffiths, John Gwyn, ed. *Plutarch's De Iside et Osiride*. Cambridge UK: University of Wales Press, 1970.

Hari, Robert. *La tombe thébaine du père divin Neferhotep (TT 50)*. Geneva: Editions de belles-lettres, 1985.

Harl, Kenneth W. *Roman Economy, 300 B.C. to A.D. 700*. Baltimore MD: Johns Hopkins University Press, 1996.

Herodotus. *The Histories, Revised*. London: Penguin Group, 2003.

Hiller, Ruth, Linda Dobbins, and Linda Jones. "The New Monthly Magazine, 1821–1854: Introduction." In *The Wellesley Index to Victorian Periodicals 1824–1900*, vol. 3, edited by Walter E. Houghton, 161–72. Toronto: University of Toronto Press, 1979.

Holy Bible containing the Old and New Testaments. New Revised Standard Version: Catholic Edition. Nashville: Catholic Bible Press, 1993.

Houghton, Esther, Priscilla Ross, and Mary Wallace. "The Quarterly Review, 1824–1900." In *The Wellesley Index to Victorian Periodicals*, edited by Walter E. Houghton, 696–702. Toronto: University of Toronto Press, 1966.

James, Thomas H.G. *Egyptian Antiquities at Kingston Lacy, Dorset: The Collection of William John Bankes*. San Francisco: KMT Communications, 1993–94.

Janssen, Jac. J. *Commodity Prices from the Ramessid Period*. Leiden: Brill, 1975.

Jomard, Edmé-François, ed. *Description de l'Égypte, ou recueil des observations et des recherches qui ont été faites en Égypte pendant l'expédition de l'armée française*. Vol. 2. Paris: Imprimerie impériale, 1812.

———. *Travels in the Oasis of Thebes, and in the Deserts Situated East and West of the Thebaid: in the years 1815, 16, 17, and 18 by M. Frederic Cailliaud*. London: Sir Richard Phillips and Co., 1822.

———. *Voyage à l'Oasis de Thèbes et dans les déserts situés à l'orient et à l'occident de la Thébaïde*. Paris: Imprimerie royale, 1821–62.

Kampp, Friederike. *Die Thebanische Nekropole. 2. Teil*. Mainz: Philipp von Zabern, 1996.

Kanawati, Naguib, and Alexandra Woods. *Beni Hassan: Art and Daily Life in an Egyptian Province*. Cairo: Supreme Council of Antiquities, 2010.

Keimer, Ludwig. "Sur un monument Égyptien du Musée du Louvre. Contribution à l'histoire de l'égyptologie." *Revue d'Egyptologie* 4 (1940): 44–65.

Kemp, Barry J. "Imperialism in New Kingdom Egypt (c.1575–1087 B.C.)." In *Imperialism in the Ancient World*, edited by Peter D.A. Garnsey and Charles Richard Whittaker, 7–57, 283–97. Cambridge UK: Cambridge University Press, 1978.

———. "Soil (including Mud-brick Architecture)." In *Ancient Egyptian Materials and Technology*, edited by Ian Shaw and Paul T. Nicholson, 78–103. Cambridge UK: Cambridge University Press, 2000.

Killen, Geoffrey. "Wood [Technology]." In *Ancient Egyptian Materials and Technology*, edited by Ian Shaw and Paul T. Nicholson, 334–71. Cambridge UK: Cambridge University Press, 2000.

Lane, Edward William. *An Account of the Manners and Customs of the Modern Egyptians: Written in Egypt during the Years 1833, –34, and –35, Partly from Notes Made during a Former Visit to That Country in the Years 1825, –26, –27, and –28*. London: Charles Knight and Co., 1836.

———. *Description of Egypt. Notes and views in Egypt and Nubia, made during the years 1825, –26, –27, –28: Chiefly consisting of a series of descriptions and delineations of the monuments, scenery, &c. of those countries; The views, with few exceptions, made with the camera-lucida*, edited by Jason Thompson. Cairo: American University in Cairo Press, 2000.

Leahy, M. Anthony. *Libya and Egypt c. 1300–750 BC*. London: School of Oriental and African Studies, Centre of Near and Middle Eastern Studies, 1990.

Leclant, Jean. "L'égyptologie avant l'expédition d'Égypte." In *L'expédition d'Égypte, une entreprise des Lumières 1798–1801*, edited by Patrice Bret. Paris: Technique et Documentation, 1999.

Ledrain, Eugène. *Monuments égyptiens de la Bibliothèque Nationale*. Paris: F. Vieweg, 1881.

Lee, Lorna, and Stephen Quirke. "Painting Materials." In *Ancient Egyptian Materials and Technology*, edited by Paul T. Nicholson and Ian Shaw, 104–20. Cambridge UK: Cambridge University Press, 2000.

Lexova, Irena. *Ancient Egyptian Dances*. Mineola NY: Dover Publications, 1999.

Mainterot, Philippe. *Aux origines de l'égyptologie. Voyages et collections de Frédéric Cailliaud (1787–1869)*. Rennes: Presses Universitaires de Rennes, 2011.

———. "Une contribution à la naissance de l'égyptologie: voyages et collections du Nantais Frédéric Cailliaud (1787–1869). Catalogue des objets." PhD diss., Université de Poitiers, 2008.

———. "Les Éthiopiens et leur cité fabuleuse dans les récits classiques." In *Méroé, un empire sur le Nil*, edited by Michel Baud, 19–21. Paris: Louvre, 2010.

Malte-Brun, Conrad. "Analyse critique du *Voyage à l'Oasis de Thèbes*." *Nouvelles Annales des Voyages*. First series, vol. 15 (1822).

———. "Analyse critique du *Voyage à l'Oasis de Thèbes*." *Nouvelles Annales des Voyages*. Second series, vol. 1 (1826).

Manley, Deborah, and Peta Rée. *Henry Salt: Artist, Traveller, Diplomat, Egyptologist*. London: Libri Publications Ltd., 2002.

Manniche, Lise. *Lost Tombs: A Study of Certain Eighteenth Dynasty Monuments in the Theban Necropolis*. London: KPI, 1988.

Marchand, Leslie A. *The Athenaeum: A Mirror of Victorian Culture*. New York: Octagon Books, 1971.

Martinez-Sève, Laurianne, Geneviève Pierrat-Bonnefois, Rémy Boucharlat, Violaine Jeammet, Valérie Matoïan, Juliette Becq, Alexandre Kaczmarczyk, and Annie Caubet. *Faïences de l'Antiquité. De l'Egypte à l'Iran*. Paris: Louvre, 2005.

Mason, Ian L. "Camels." In *Evolution of Domesticated Animals*, edited by Ian. L. Mason, 106–15. London: Longman, 1984.

Meeks, Dimitri. "Dance." In *The Oxford Encyclopedia of Ancient Egypt*, vol. 1, edited by Donald Redford, 356–60. Oxford UK: Oxford University Press, 2001.

Newberry, Percy E. *Beni Hasan. Part I and II*. London: Egypt Exploration Fund, 1893.

———. *El Bersheh. Part I*. London: The Egypt Exploration Fund, 1895.

Newman, Richard, and Margaret Serpico. "Adhesives and Binders." In *Ancient Egyptian Materials and Technology*, edited by Ian Shaw and Paul T. Nicholson, 475–94. Cambridge UK: Cambridge University Press, 2000.

Nicholson, Paul T., and Julian Henderson. "Glass." In *Ancient Egyptian Materials and Technology*, edited by Ian Shaw and Paul T. Nicholson, 195–226. Cambridge UK: Cambridge University Press, 2000.

Nicholson, Paul T., and Edward Peltenburg. "Egyptian Faience." In *Ancient Egyptian Materials and Technology*, edited by Ian Shaw and Paul T. Nicholson, 177–94. Cambridge UK: Cambridge University Press, 2000.

Niwinski, Andrzej. *The 21st Dynasty Coffins from Thebes: Chronological and Typological Studies. Theben V*. Mainz: Philipp Von Zabern, 1988.

Ogden, Jack. "Metals." In *Ancient Egyptian Materials and Technology*, edited by Ian Shaw and Paul T. Nicholson, 148–76. Cambridge UK: Cambridge University Press, 2000.

Pinch, Geraldine. *Magic in Ancient Egypt*. Austin: University of Texas Press, 1995.

Plato. *Timaeus*. Translated by Benjamin Jowett. The Internet Classics Archive, http://classics.mit.edu//Plato/timaeus.html

Pliny the Elder. *Natural History*. Translated by John Bostock. London: Taylor and Francis, 1855. http://www.perseus.tufts.edu/hopper

Pococke, Richard. *A Description of the East and Some Other Countries*. London: J. & R. Knapton, 1743.

Porter, Bertha, and Rosalind L.B. Moss. *Topographical Bibliography of Ancient Egyptian Hieroglyphic Texts, Reliefs, and Paintings. I. The Theban Necropolis. Part 1. Private Tombs*. Oxford UK: Clarendon Press, 1960.

———. *Topographical Bibliography of Ancient Egyptian Hieroglyphic Texts, Reliefs, and Paintings. I. The Theban Necropolis. Part 2. Royal Tombs and Smaller Cemeteries*. Oxford UK: Clarendon Press, 1973.

———. *Topographical Bibliography of Ancient Egyptian Texts, Reliefs, and Paintings. II. Theban Temples*. Oxford UK: Clarendon Press, 1972.

———. *Topographical Bibliography of Ancient Egyptian Hieroglyphic Texts, Reliefs, and Paintings. III. Memphis. Part I. Abu Rawash to Abusir*. Oxford UK: Clarendon Press, 1974.

———. *Topographical Bibliography of Ancient Egyptian Hieroglyphic Texts, Reliefs, and Paintings. IV. Lower and Middle Egypt*. Oxford UK: Clarendon Press, 1934.

———. *Topographical Bibliography of Ancient Egyptian Hieroglyphic Texts, Reliefs, and Paintings. V. Upper Egypt: Sites*. Oxford UK: Clarendon Press, 1937.

———. *Topographical Bibliography of Ancient Egyptian Hieroglyphic Texts, Reliefs, and Paintings VII. Nubia, the Deserts, and Outside Egypt*. Oxford UK: Oxford University Press, 1995.

Raoul-Rochette, Désiré. "Analyse critique du *Voyage à l'Oasis de Thèbes*." *Journal des Savants*, 1822.

Redford, Donald B. *Egypt, Canaan, and Israel in Ancient Times*. Princeton: Princeton University Press, 1993.

Reeves, Nicholas, and Richard H. Wilkinson. *The Complete Valley of the Kings: Tombs and Treasures of Egypt's Greatest Pharaohs*. London: Thames and Hudson, 2006.

Reisner, George A. *A History of the Giza Necropolis*. Cambridge MA: Harvard University Press, 1942.

"Reviews. Egyptian Antiquities. *Recherches sur les Arts &c. des anciens peuples de l'Egypte*, &c. Par M. F. Cailliaud. Paris, Dubure; London, Dulau & Co." *The Athenaeum. Journal of English and Foreign Literature, Science, and the Fine Arts*, no. 507 (Saturday 15 July 1837): 513–16.

"Reviews. Egyptian Antiquities. [Second Notice.]." *The Athenaeum. Journal of English and Foreign Literature, Science, and the Fine Arts*, no. 508 (Saturday 22 July 1837): 533–37.

"Reviews. Egyptian Antiquities. [Third Notice.]." *The Athenaeum. Journal of English and Foreign Literature, Science, and the Fine Arts*, no. 509 (Saturday 29 July 1837): 550–53.

Ridley, Ronald T. *Napoleon's Proconsul in Egypt: The Life and Times of Bernardino Drovetti*. London: Rubicon Press, 1998.

Rosellini, Ippolito. *I Monumenti dell' Egitto e della Nubia: disegnati dalla spedizione scientifico-letteraria Toscana in Egitto distribuiti in ordine di materie interpretati ed illustrate*. Pisa: Presso Niccolo Capurro, c. 1832–44.

Rowley-Conwy, Peter. "The Camel in the Nile Valley: New Radiocarbon Accelerator Dates from Qasr Ibrim." *Journal of Egyptian Archaeology* 74 (1988): 245–48.

de Rozière, François-Michel, and Pierre Charles Rouyer. "L'art de faire éclore les poulets en Égypte par les moyen des fours." In *Description de l'Égypte ou Recueil des observations et des recherches qui ont été faites en Égypte pendant l'expédition de l'armée française*, vol. 1, edited by Edmé-François Jomard, 203–16. Paris: Imprimerie impériale, 1809.

Russell, Terrence M. *The Discovery of Egypt: Vivant Denon's Travels with Napoleon's Army*. Stroud: Sutton Publishing Limited, 2005.

Seneca, Lucius Annaeus. *Moral Epistles: The Loeb Classical Library*, vol. 2, translated by Richard M. Gummere. Cambridge MA: Harvard University Press, 1917–25. http://www.stoics.com/seneca_epistles_book_2.html#%E2%80%98XC1

Serpico, Margaret. "Resins, Amber and Bitumen." In *Ancient Egyptian Materials and Technology*, edited by Ian Shaw and Paul T. Nicholson, 430–74. Cambridge UK: Cambridge University Press, 2000.

Seton-Williams, Veronica, and Peter Stocks. *Blue Guide. Egypt*. London: A&C Black, 1993.

Shattock, Joanne. *Politics and Reviewers: The* Edinburgh *and the* Quarterly *in the Early Victorian Age*. London: Leicester University Press, 1989.

Shaw, Ian, and Paul T. Nicholson. *British Museum Dictionary of Ancient Egypt*. London: British Museum Press, 2002.

Shaw, Ian, and Paul T. Nicholson, eds. *Ancient Egyptian Materials and Technology*. Cambridge UK: Cambridge University Press, 2000.

Silius Italicus. *Punica*. Translated by J.D. Duff. London: William Heinemann Ltd., 1961.

Stewart, Harry M. *Egyptian Shabtis*. Princes Risborough UK: Shire Publications Ltd., 1995.

Strabo. *The Geography of Strabo: Loeb Classical Library*. Translated by Horace L. Jones. Cambridge MA: Harvard University Press, 1917–32.

Strassler, Robert B. *The Landmark Herodotus: The Histories*. New York: Pantheon Books, 2007.

Sullivan, Alvin. *British Literary Magazines, the Romantic Age, 1789–1836*. Westport CT: Greenwood Press, 1983.

Thompson, Jason. *Edward William Lane, 1801–1876: The Life of the Pioneering Egyptologist and Orientalist*. London: Haus Publishing, 2010.

———. *Sir Gardner Wilkinson and His Circle*. Austin TX: University of Texas Press, 1992.

Topham, Jonathan. "'The Mirror of Literature, Amusement and Instruction' and Cheap Miscellanies in Early Nineteenth-century Britain." In *Science in the Nineteenth-Century Periodical: Reading the Magazine of Nature*, edited by Geoffrey Cantor, Gowan Dawson, Graeme Gooday, and Richard Noakes, 37–66. Cambridge UK: Cambridge University Press, 2004.

———. "Thomas Byerley, John Limbird, and the Production of Cheap Periodicals in Regency Britain." *Book History* 8 (2005): 75–106.

Trustees of the British Museum. *Jewellery through 7000 Years*. London: British Museum Publications, 1976.

Tylor, Joseph J., and Francis Ll. Griffith. *The Tomb of Paheri at El Kab*. London: Egypt Exploration Fund, 1894.

University of Chicago Oriental Institute Publications. *Medinet Habu—Volume IV. Plates 193–249. Festival Scenes of Ramses III*. Chicago: University of Chicago Press, 1940.

———. *Medinet Habu—Volume V. Plates 250–362. The Temple Proper. Part 1*. Chicago: University of Chicago Press, 1957.

———. *Medinet Habu—Volume VIII. Plates 591–60. The Eastern High Gate*. Chicago: University of Chicago Press, 1970.

Van Driel-Murray, Carol. "Leatherwork and Skin Products." In *Ancient Egyptian Materials and Technology*, edited by Ian Shaw and Paul T. Nicholson, 299–319. Cambridge UK: Cambridge University Press, 2000.

Wendrich, Willemina Z. "Basketry." In *Ancient Egyptian Materials and Technology*, edited by Ian Shaw and Paul T. Nicholson, 254–67. Cambridge UK: Cambridge University Press, 2000.

Wilkinson, John Gardner. *Manners and Customs of the Ancient Egyptians. Including their Private Life, Government, Laws, Arts, Manufactures, Religion, and Early History; derived from a comparison of the paintings, sculptures, and monuments still existing, with the accounts of ancient authors*. London: John Murray, 1837–41.

———. *Manners and Customs of the Ancient Egyptians*. Vol. 2. Edited by Samuel Birch. London: John Murray, 1878.

———. *Modern Egypt and Thebes*. London: John Murray, 1843.

———. *Topography of Thebes, and General View of Egypt. Being a Short Account of the Principal Objects Worthy of Notice in the Valley of the Nile, to the Second Cataract and Wadee Samneh, with the Fyoom, Oases, and Eastern Desert, from Sooez to Berenice; with*

Remarks on the Manners and Customs of the Ancient Egyptians and the Productions of the Country, &c. &c. London: John Murray, 1835.

Wilkinson, Richard H. *The Complete Gods and Goddesses of Ancient Egypt*. London: Thames and Hudson, 2003.

Wilson, Hilary. *Egyptian Food and Drink*. London: Shire Publications, 2008.

OTHER ONLINE SOURCES CITED

Bibliographies for tombs on Luxor's West Bank can be found on the Theban Mapping Project's homepage, http://www.tmpbibliography.com/

Bibliographies for tombs at Giza can be found on Boston's Museum of Fine Arts' Giza Archives homepage, http://www.gizapyramids.org/code/emuseum.asp

Bibliographies for tombs at Deir al-Bersha are listed on the website of the Belgian Mission to Deir al-Bersha, http://www.dayralbarsha.com/node/12

INDEX

Page numbers in **bold** indicate illustrations.
"n" following a page number indicates a footnote.

Auguste, Louis Nicolas Philippe, Comte de
    Forbin, 6, 26
Augustus 87

Bakt III 52n24, 83n179
Bankes, William John 6, 17, 26, 31, 162
banquet **220–21**, **255**
barque/boat 148, **174**, **175**; *baris* 39, 114, 132;
    boat building 148, **173**; funerary barque
    147–48, **174**; papyrus barque 48, **220**, **221**
basketry 42, 92–94, 148, **174**, **214–15**, **220–23**;
    date palm 92–93; papyrus 70; sandals 93;
    stool 93
Bellefonds, Linant de 13
Belzoni, Giovanni 6, 7, 19, 26, 31, 32, 33
Beni Hasan 49, 52, 54, 56, 75, 79, 83, 156, 159,
    162; *see also* Khety/Rotei; Khnumhotep
Berenice, *see* Ptolemaic period
Bes, *see* Panthe/Bes
Bible 41, 67n101
boat, *see* barque
Bonaparte, Napoleon 3, 4, 8, 25, 32, 151; expe-
    dition to Egypt 8, 16, 25, 32, 42
Bonomi, Joseph 29, 154, 172
Book of the Dead 27, 64n83
brickwork 81–82, 154, **155**, **184–85**
bronze 100, 102, 107, 117, 119–24, 126, 127;
    coin/medallion 120; composition 121;
    mirror 121, 122; statue 121, 123; tools 119,
    120, 122, 123, 124, 127; use of 119–21,
    123; vase 117, 119, 122, 123; weapon
    119, 122, 123, 127; *see also* metals
building/construction **178**, **229**; *see also*
    brickwork
Burckhardt, John Lewis 12, 31, 120n354
Burton, James 154, 172

Cailliaud, Auguste Damase 25, 33, 43, 168
Cailliaud, Frédéric 3–4, 7, **23**; collection 6, 9–10,
    16, 17, 18, 20, 22, 168; Egyptology 3,
    18–20, 23, 25, 171; hieroglyphs 6, 19–20,
    23, 24, 25; mineralogy 4, 22, 25, 36, 168;
    Murad Effendi 12; traveling 3, 4–9, 13–18,
    20, 25; *see also* Cailliaud *entries below*
Cailliaud's copying and drawing 6, 8, 10, 12, 13,
    16–20, 22, 151–64, 171–72; accuracy
    157–64; coherent style 154; color blocks
    164; comparison to others' work 153–57,
    162, 164; context and detail 156; mapping
    8, 12, 13, 18–19, 20; process and drafts
    164–71; truncation of figures/scenes 162,
    164; vignette 32, 156, 164

Cailliaud's work 3; criticism 31–33; English-
    language scholarship 32–33; importance
    25, 30, 42, 170–71; *Research on the Arts
    and Crafts* 20, 22, 23–24, 30–34, 35, 36,
    40, 42; *Travels in the Oasis of Thebes* 19,
    28, 30, 32–33, 39, 86n192; *Travels to
    Meroe and the White Nile* 19, 28, 30,
    36, 37, 54n27, 61; *Travels to Meroe/Arts
    and Crafts* comparison 37; *see also*
    Harer Papers
Candace 89, **256–57**
canopic jar 10, 27, 85, 86, 87, 114, 141, 142,
    181; *see also* vase
carpenter, *see* woodworking
Catherwood, Frederick 154, 172
Caviglia, Giambattista 7
Chabas, François 20, 24–25, 40, 103, 145
Champollion, Jean-François 3, 23–24, 25, 28,
    60, 61, 67, 113–15, 119, 153–54, 162;
    Egyptology 19; Franco-Tuscan expedition
    19, 23; hieroglyphic system 19, 22, 23,
    26; *Monuments of Egypt and Nubia* 23,
    24, 60
Champollion-Figeac, Jacques Joseph 19, 23–24,
    25, 28, 153–54; *Ancient Egypt* 24
Chandy 12, 94, 136
chariot 52, 60, 91, 122, 123, 129, **179**, **233**
Chauvet, Michel 33
Chnuphis/Khnum 49
clothing 47, 88, 114, 128–36; Ethiopia 88,
    138–39, **256–57**; kilt/*schenti* 75, 78, 129,
    130, 135, 147, **189**; king 128–30, 139,
    237, **238**; man 89, **243–45**; military officer
    134, **233**, **238**, **246**; mourner 145, **258**;
    priest 128, 130, 131–32, 134, 145, **239**,
    240, **243**, **245**, **246**; prince 132–33, **242**;
    princess 133, **241**; queen 133, 139, **236**;
    upper class 134, 135, **220–24**; woman 74,
    77, 134–35, 136, 138, **247**, **248**, **251**, **252**;
    working class 135, 147, **173**, **176**, **186**,
    192; *see also* headdress; jewelry; shoes
collection, *see* antiquities and collections
Constantinople 4, 25
construction, *see* building
cordage 36, 95–96, **196**, **230–31**
cosmetics 101, 139
crook 61, 129nn389–90, 143

D'Athanasi, Giovanni 7, 16
dance, *see* music and dance
dead 143nn472–73, 165–66, **167**; agricul-
    ture 64; funerary barque 147–48, **174**;

Malte-Brun, Conrad 28
Manniche, Lise 170
Mariette, August 22
Medinet Habu, *see* Ramesses III
Memphis 59, 61, 67, 75, 96, 111, 112; Serapeum 22
Meroe 10, 12, 13, 18, 27, 54, 138; gold 116, 118; pyramid 39, 116–18; woodworking 102; *see also* Kush, kingdom of
metals 36, 42, 102, 109–27, **178**, **179**; copper 122, 123; forge 124, **178**, **179**; lead 123, 126, 142; silver 118–19; steel 120, 125, 126; tin 113n312, 122, 123; *see also* bronze; gold; iron; jewelry; mining; tools
military 12, 13; clothing 134, **233**, **238**, **246**; hairstyle 138; helmet 114, 129, 138, **233**; training **232**, **233**
mining: copper 123, 126; emerald 6, 22, 31, 33, 123, 126; gold 12, 13, 109–10; iron ore 124n372, 126nn378–80; lead 126; *see also* metals
Minutoli, Heinrich Menu von, Baron 18
Moeris 63, 111
Moses 57
Moss, Rosalind L.B. 164
mourner 138, **249**, **250**, **258**
Muhammad 73
Muhammad Ali, viceroy of Egypt, 4, 6, 7, 8, 9, 13, 27, 32, 109, 126n381
mummy 86, 97, 99, **180**–**81**; bandages 91, 96, 141–42, 144; beaded mummy cover 106–107, **200**–**201**; cartonnage 144; gold 111; hypocephalic plaque 119n350, 122; iron 125; mask 111, 115; wraps 90; *see also* dead; embalming; sarcophagus
Musawwarat al-Sufra 13, 28, 82
museum: Berlin Museum 56n39; British Museum 7, 22, 26, 90, 118, 120, 121, 122, 125; cabinet of curiosities 22, 29; Leiden Museum 85, 118, 120, 125; Louvre Museum 7, 20, 22, 25, 26, 49, 85–86, 93, 101, 120, 121, 123, 124; Musée Dobrée 20; Muséum d'histoire naturelle 22, 24, 33, 34; Turin Museum 22, 78, 90, 93, 99, 101, 102, 104, 105, 111, 118, 119, 123, 124, 125
music and dance 77, **159**, **221**, **226**, **229**; harp/harper 90, 131, 154, **154**, **162**, 164, **226**, **234**, **235**; instruments 120; musician 138, **226**, **227**, **229**, **247**
Mut 85n191, 118n344, 139n458

Naga 13, 28, 89, 139nn457–58

Nantes 3; Harer Papers, Nantes booklets 34, 36, 38, 40; Musée Dobrée 20; Muséum d'histoire naturelle 22, 24, 33, 34
Napata 39, 54
Nedjemger 24, 29
Neferhotep 48, 62, **220**; tomb 6, 16–17, **17**, 24, 37, 38, 48–49, 53, 55, 61, 62, 69n114–15, 72, 135n437, 156, 164, 170; tomb, plan of 170, **171**
Neith/Seshat 49
Nero 87
Newberry, Percy E. 80n168, 159, 162
Nile River 4, 13; Blue and White Niles 13, 69; drought 67; flooding 56, 64, 67; irrigation 67–68; Nilometric scale 67
Nou/Nut 145
Nubia 10–13, 20, 27, 64, 71
Nut, *see* Nou/Nut

offering 64, 69, **221**; bearer 135, 144, **203**, **244**, **248**, **251**; for the dead 145, 146, 165, **258**–**59**; from Kush 157–58, **158**, **260**
Omdurman 13
Osiris 85, 105, 112, 113, 115, 142–43, 145n489, 146; Sons of Osiris 86
Osortasen 62
ostraca 20, 28, 57, 58

Padimenipet, funerary equipment 10, 19, 20
Panthe/Bes 121
Paphe 65, 67, **215**
papyrus **17**, 41, 48, 70, **220**; *Cyperus papyrus* 48, 70; papyrus barque 48, 70, **220**, **221**; sowing, plowing, and harvesting 71, **214**; uses 70
Passalacqua, Giuseppe 122n358, 122n361
perfume **182**, **190**–**91**, **215**
Philae 4, 7, 8, 25, 82; obelisk of Ptolemy VIII 6, 19, 25
Phra 143, 145
Phre-Sun 139
Pinedjem I 90nn219–20
Place, Victor 127
Plato 52
Pliny 50–51, 67, 70, 73, 83, 87, 110n287
Plutarch 48, 49
Pococke, Richard: *A Description of the East and Some Other Countries* 151, 152, 153, 171, 172
Porter, Bertha 164
pottery 83–86, **192**–**93**; Copts 85n190; wheel 84–85, 87; *see also* vase

85, 86, 87, **181**; glass 105, 108; gold 114–15, 119, **204**, **206**; Murrhine 87; pottery 83–86; sacred use 85, 87, 105, 119, 123; silver 119, **205**; stone 86–87; types of 85; *see also* canopic jar

vines and grape harvesting 64, 68–71, **217**, **220–21**; beer 70; grape pressing 165, **166–67**, **176**, **177**; prohibition on 68; *see also* agriculture

weapon 126n380, **233**; bow and spear 103, **190–91**; bronze 119, 122, 123, 127; dagger 122; *see also* archery

weaving **194**, **195**; rope making **196**; spinning **194**

Wilkinson, John Gardner 24, 25, 29, 41, 70, 140nn462–63, 153, 156–58, 171, 172; *General View of Egypt* 40; influence on Cailliaud's work 36, 38, 40, 41; *Manners and Customs of the Ancient Egyptians*

24, 29, 36, 38, 40, 162; *Topography of Thebes* 40

woman 168, **170**; clothing 74, 77, 134–35, 136, 138, **247**, **248**, **251**, **252**; Ethiopia 139; hairstyle 77, 135, 137, 138, **248**, **255**, **258**; widow 145, 146; *see also* games; music and dance

woodworking 41–42, 97–103, **173**, **176**, **198**; bench/reclining bed 100, **206**, **207**; boat **173**; bow and spear 103, **190–91**; box 101, **182–83**; cabinetmaker 100, 101; chair 98, 100–101, **156**, **157**, **177**, **208–11**; door 99; headrest 100, 101–102; lock 99, 100; Meroe 102; stool 100, 101, 142, **207**; table 101; wood 99–100; woodworker 24, 97, 102, 103, 147, 148, 165, **166–67**, **173**, **176**, **182–83**; *see also* sarcophagus; tools

Zubara, Mount, emerald mine 6, 22, 31, 33